Microsoft Visio 2013 Business Process Diagramming and Validation

Explore Visio Professional 2013 and improve your business information through structured diagrams and custom validation rules

David J. Parker

[PACKT] enterprise
professional expertise distilled

PUBLISHING

BIRMINGHAM - MUMBAI

Microsoft Visio 2013 Business Process Diagramming and Validation

Copyright © 2013 Packt Publishing

All rights reserved. No part of this book may be reproduced, stored in a retrieval system, or transmitted in any form or by any means, without the prior written permission of the publisher, except in the case of brief quotations embedded in critical articles or reviews.

Every effort has been made in the preparation of this book to ensure the accuracy of the information presented. However, the information contained in this book is sold without warranty, either express or implied. Neither the author, nor Packt Publishing, and its dealers and distributors will be held liable for any damages caused or alleged to be caused directly or indirectly by this book.

Packt Publishing has endeavored to provide trademark information about all of the companies and products mentioned in this book by the appropriate use of capitals. However, Packt Publishing cannot guarantee the accuracy of this information.

First published: July 2010

Second edition: November 2013

Production Reference: 1181113

Published by Packt Publishing Ltd.
Livery Place
35 Livery Street
Birmingham B3 2PB, UK.

ISBN 978-1-78217-800-2

www.packtpub.com

Cover Image by Artie Ng (artherng@yahoo.com.au)

Credits

Author
David J. Parker

Reviewers
Nikolay Belykh
JMee Hong
Alexander Meijers
Ed Richards

Acquisition Editor
Neha Nagwekar

Lead Technical Editor
Neeshma Ramakrishnan

Technical Editors
Monica John
Edwin Moses
Mrunmayee Patil

Project Coordinator
Kranti Berde

Proofreader
Stephen Copestake

Indexer
Mehreen Deshmukh

Production Coordinator
Arvindkumar Gupta

Cover Work
Arvindkumar Gupta

About the Author

David J. Parker, being frustrated as an architect in the late 80s trying to match 3D building models with spreadsheets, explored linking Unix, CAD, and SQL databases in the early 90s for facilities and cable management.

In 1996 he discovered the ease of linking data to Visio diagrams of personnel and office layouts. He immediately became one of the first Visio business partners in Europe, and was soon invited to present his applications at worldwide Visio conferences. He started his own Visio-based consultancy and development business, bVisual ltd (http://www.bvisual.net), applying analysis, synthesis, and design to various graphical information solutions.

He presents Visio solution providers and Visio Services courses for Microsoft EMEA, adding personal anecdotes and previous mistakes hoping that all can learn by them.

He wrote his first book, *Visualizing Information with Microsoft Office Visio 2007*, to spread the word about data-linked diagrams in business, and his second book, which is about creating custom rules for validating structured diagrams in Visio 2010, has now been updated and extended for Visio 2013.

He wrote WBS Modeler for Microsoft, which integrates Visio and, Project, and many other Visio solutions for various vertical markets.

David has been regularly awarded Most Valued Professional status for his Visio community work over the years, and maintains a Visio blog at http://blog.bvisual.net.

Based near to Microsoft UK in Reading, he still sees the need for Visio evangelism throughout the business and development community, and has been touring many European capitals over the last two years spreading the word of intelligent business diagramming with Visio and SharePoint.

> I would like to thank Microsoft for continuing to develop Visio, originally in Seattle, then Redmond in USA, and now in Hyderabad, India. Thank you to Dr. Stephanie Horn at Microsoft for editing the first version of this book, and my fellow Visio MVP, John Marshall, for his help and encouragement. For the second, and updated, version, I would like to thank fellow Visiophiles: Jimi Hong, Ed Richards, Alexander Meijers, and Nikolay Belykh for their comments.
>
> Most of all, I would like to thank my wife, Beena, for putting up with me as I wrote another book. Maybe that is why my kids, Kryshnan and Alyesha, have both left home!

About the Reviewers

Nikolay Belykh is a Visio specialist and an active member of Visio society. He works currently as software architect in Process4.biz, the Microsoft partner company, which received the Visio Partner Award of year 2012. The company provides the award-winning modeling tool for business processes based on Microsoft Visio.

He received his MS degree in informatics from the Novosibirks University, Russia. After his postgraduation studies, he started to work as software engineer in industrial automation, where he first got in touch with Visio.

Now he lives and works in Vienna, Austria. You can reach him on Visio forums, or on his blog site Unmanaged Visio (`http://unmanagedvisio.com`), where you can find tips and free tools for Visio developers.

JMee Hong is a Visio MVP. Her specialties include technology and applications related to data or system visualization with graphic solutions such as Visio, CAD, and so on. She runs Visio adoption center with Microsoft Korea. She as a Visio evangelist has been working with many of the commercial and public sector customers for more than 8 years.

She holds B.S in mechatronics engineering and has also studied robotics system with virtual reality software. This enables her to understand and consult any business areas' engineering or technical graphic solution, and high usability interfaces.

> I'm very honored in reviewing David J. Parker's book. He is a legend of Visio and I have always learned from him through his blog.
>
> I'm so proud of being a reviewer of his book. Thanks to all the Visio MVPs!

Alexander Meijers has been involved with Microsoft products and technologies for more than 20 years. He got introduced with SharePoint and Office since the Version 2003 came to the market, and made these products his core knowledge. With his extended knowledge of programming, he sees a lot of the opportunities the products have. Due to the fact that the SharePoint platform depends heavenly on other Microsoft products, his knowledge also extends to other products such as SQL Server, Windows, Active Directory, and Exchange Server.

He has been involved to a large extent in SharePoint implementations and a number of Office solutions. These implementations ranged from small, medium, to large business project handling and in some cases involved more than 100 thousand end users. His multidiscipline allows him to handle a large set of roles in projects such as hardcore development, lead consultant, liaison between business and IT, business advisory, project management, and lead architect. In his spare time he blogs about SharePoint and Office at http://www.sharepointinspiration.com.

www.PacktPub.com

Support files, eBooks, discount offers, and more

You might want to visit `www.PacktPub.com` for support files and downloads related to your book.

Did you know that Packt offers eBook versions of every book published, with PDF and ePub files available? You can upgrade to the eBook version at `www.PacktPub.com` and as a print book customer, you are entitled to a discount on the eBook copy. Get in touch with us at `service@packtpub.com` for more details.

At `www.PacktPub.com`, you can also read a collection of free technical articles, sign up for a range of free newsletters and receive exclusive discounts and offers on Packt books and eBooks.

PACKTLIB

`http://PacktLib.PacktPub.com`

Do you need instant solutions to your IT questions? PacktLib is Packt's online digital book library. Here, you can access, read and search across Packt's entire library of books.

Why Subscribe?

- Fully searchable across every book published by Packt
- Copy and paste, print and bookmark content
- On demand and accessible via web browser

Free Access for Packt account holders

If you have an account with Packt at `www.PacktPub.com`, you can use this to access PacktLib today and view nine entirely free books. Simply use your login credentials for immediate access.

Instant Updates on New Packt Books

Get notified! Find out when new books are published by following `@PacktEnterprise` on Twitter, or the *Packt Enterprise* Facebook page.

Table of Contents

Preface	1
Chapter 1: Overview of Process Management in Microsoft Visio 2013	7
Exploring the new process management features in Visio 2013	8
Reviewing Visio Process Management capabilities	10
Understanding the Visio BMP Maturity Model	11
Reviewing the foundations of structured diagramming	12
Reviewing the enhanced process flow templates	14
Looking at the Flowchart templates	14
Reviewing the new process flow templates	15
Understanding a BPMN Diagram	15
Understanding a Microsoft SharePoint 2013 workflow	19
Validation of process diagrams	20
Analyzing the structure of a Visio document	21
Using the Visio Process Repository	25
Publishing visual data from Visio	25
Understanding the Visio 2013 editions	27
Planning your own solutions	27
Summary	29
Chapter 2: Understanding the Microsoft Visio Object Model	31
Introducing the Visio Type libraries	31
Going beyond the object model	32
Classifying the Visio document	33
Selecting a programming language to use with Visio	35
Understanding the Drawing Explorer window	36
Understanding the Visio object model	38
Examining the Application object	38
Reviewing the ActiveDocument and ActivePage objects	39

Reviewing the Addons collection	39
Reviewing the COMAddIns collection	41
Reviewing the CurrentEdition property	42
Reviewing the DataFeaturesEnabled property	42
Reviewing the Documents collection	43
Reviewing the TypelibMinorVersion and Version properties	44
Examining the Document object	**44**
Reviewing the Advanced Properties object	45
Reviewing the DataRecordsets collection	46
Reviewing the DocumentSheet object	47
Reviewing the ID and Index properties	47
Reviewing the FullName and Name properties	47
Reviewing the Masters collection	48
Reviewing the Pages collection	48
Reviewing the ReadOnly property	49
Reviewing the Type property	49
Reviewing the Validation object	49
Examining the Master object	**50**
Reviewing the BaseID property	51
Reviewing the Hidden property	52
Reviewing the ID, Index, and IndexInStencil properties	52
Reviewing the Name and NameU properties	52
Reviewing the PageSheet object	52
Reviewing the Type property	52
Examining the Page object	**53**
Reviewing the Connects collection	53
Reviewing the ID and Index properties	55
Reviewing the Layers collection	55
Reviewing the PageSheet object	58
Reviewing the Comments and ShapeComments property	58
Reviewing the Shapes collection	61
Reviewing the Type property	62
Examining the Shape object	**62**
Reviewing the Characters and Text properties	64
Reviewing the Connects and FromConnects collections	65
Reviewing the Hyperlinks collection	65
Reviewing the ID, Index, NameID, Name, and NameU properties	65
Reviewing the IsCallout and IsDataGraphicCallout properties	65
Reviewing the LayerCount property	66
Reviewing the Master, MasterShape, and RootShape objects	66
Reviewing the OneD property	66
Reviewing the Parent object	66
Reviewing the Type property	66
Examining the Section object	**67**
Examining the Row object	**67**
Examining the Cell object	**69**
Reviewing the Column property	70
Reviewing the Error property	70

Reviewing the Formula and FormulaU properties	70
Reviewing the Name and LocalName properties	70
Reviewing the Result properties	70
Reviewing the Units property	70
Iterating through cells	71
Delving into the Connectivity API	**73**
Understanding the Shape.ConnectedShapes method	74
Understanding the Shape.GluedShapes method	76
Understanding the Shape.MemberOfContainers property	77
Understanding the Shape.CalloutsAssociated property	78
Listing the steps in a process flow	79
Summary	**83**
Chapter 3: Understanding the ShapeSheet™	**85**
Finding the ShapeSheet	**85**
Understanding sections, rows, and cells	88
Reading a cell's properties	89
Printing out the ShapeSheet settings	**93**
Understanding the functions	**95**
Important sections for rules validation	**97**
Looking at the User-defined Cells section	97
Using the category of a Shape	97
Using the structure type of a Shape	102
Checking a Container shape	103
Checking a List shape	104
Checking for attached Callout shapes	105
Looking at the Shape Data section	107
Using the String type	109
Using the Fixed List type	111
Using the Number type	112
Using the Boolean type	113
Using the Variable List type	114
Using the Date type	115
Using the Duration type	117
Using the Currency type	118
Looking at the Hyperlinks section	118
Working with Layer Membership	120
Summary	**121**
Chapter 4: Understanding the Validation API	**123**
An overview of Validation objects	**123**
Using the Validate method	126
Validating custom rules written in code	126
Working with the ValidationRuleSets collection	**127**
Adding to or updating a ruleset	129

Table of Contents

Working with the ValidationRules collection	**131**
Adding to or updating a rule	134
Verifying that a rule works	136
Working with the ValidationIssues collection	**137**
Retrieving the selected issue in the Issues window	140
Toggling the Issues window visibility	143
Listing the issues caused by a particular shape	144
Using code to clear issues	145
Retrieving an existing issue in code	145
Adding an issue in code	146
Summary	**149**
Chapter 5: Developing a Validation API Interface	**151**
Understanding the architecture of the tool	**152**
Enhancing the ThisAddin class	**154**
Listening for application events	155
Checking for the Visio Professional edition	156
Creating the ViewModel class	**157**
Creating the BaseViewModel class	159
Viewing the documents collection	159
Viewing the ValidationRuleSets collection	163
Viewing the ValidationRules collection	164
Viewing the ValidationIssues collection	166
Modifying the Visio Fluent UI	**168**
Creating the Rules Explorer window	**174**
Self-describing tree views	176
Making informative tool tips	177
Linking detail panels	179
Editing ruleset properties	179
Editing rule properties	180
Handling special key strokes	182
Adding the Explorer actions	184
Creating the Add button	186
Creating the Add Issue button	188
Creating the Paste button	190
Creating the Copy button	191
Creating the Delete button	192
Displaying the rule for a selected issue	**193**
Displaying the issues for the current selection	**196**
Summary	**201**
Chapter 6: Reviewing Validation Rules and Issues	**203**
Extensions to our ribbon	**203**
Annotating Visio diagrams with issues	**206**

Saving the current user settings	210
Displaying the issue mark-up page	210
Adding in the issue comments	214
Hiding the issue mark-up page	215
Exporting rulesets to XML	**216**
Getting the XDocument object	219
Getting the VERuleSet XElement	221
Getting the VEIssue XElement	222
Importing rulesets from XML	**223**
Creating ruleset reports	**226**
Getting the XSL stylesheet	228
Summary	**232**
Chapter 7: Creating Validation Rules	**233**
Overview of the document validation process	**234**
Validating rulesets	235
Validating rules	236
Processing a rule	236
Validation functions	**238**
Useful ShapeSheet functions	**239**
Filter and Test Expressions	**241**
Checking the type of shape	243
Checking the category of shapes	246
Checking the layer of a shape	248
Checking if the page contains relevant shapes	249
Checking for specific cell values	251
Checking that connectors are connected	254
Checking that shapes have correct connections	256
Checking whether shapes are outside containers	257
Checking whether a shape has text	258
Custom validation rules in code	259
Summary	**262**
Chapter 8: Publishing Validation Rules and Diagrams	**263**
Overview of Visio categories and templates	**263**
Creating a custom template	**267**
Adding embellishments	**268**
Adding the template description	271
The simplest method to provide a template	272
Editing the file paths for templates	273
Setting the file paths for templates	275
Creating a template preview image	277
Enhancing the quality of the preview image	282

The best method for publishing templates	285
Creating a setup project	285
Running the installation	288
Uninstalling and Repairing	291
Summary	**291**

Chapter 9: A Worked Example for Data Flow Model Diagrams – Part 1 — 293

What are Data Flow Diagrams?	**294**
Examining the standard template	**296**
Enhancing the masters	300
Editing the Data Flow master	301
Preparing for AutoConnect	302
Editing the Data Store master	305
Adding Shape Data	305
Enhancing the graphics	308
Displaying the ID value	309
Improving the group shape	310
Editing the Interface master	312
Editing the Process master	312
Adding Shape Data	312
Enhancing the graphics	313
Displaying the ID value	314
Displaying the Category value	315
Improving the group shape	316
Setting the Subprocess master	317
Enhancing the page	319
Summary	**321**

Chapter 10: A Worked Example for Data Flow Model Diagrams – Part 2 — 323

Writing the ruleset	**323**
Rule 1 – all processes must have at least one data flow in and one data flow out	325
Rule 2 – all processes should modify the incoming data, producing new forms of the outgoing data	327
Rule 3 – each data store must be involved with at least one data flow	329
Rule 4 – each external entity must be involved with at least one data flow	331
Rule 5 – a data flow must be attached to at least one process	332
Rule 6 – data flows cannot go directly from one external entity to another external entity	334
Rule 7 – do not allow a single page of a DFD to get too complex	334

Rule 8 – each component should be labeled	336
Rule 9 – each data flow should be labeled describing the data that flows through it	337
Rule 10 – each component and subcomponent should be numbered	339
Rule 11 – a data flow must be connected between two components	341
Rule 12 – a flow must not cycle back to itself	343
Summary	345

Chapter 11: A Worked Example for Data Flow Model Diagrams – Part 3 — 347

Completing the template	347
Reviewing the template	352
Creating the installer	353
Testing the Installer	357
Using a digital certificate	359
Thoughts about code in templates	361
Summary	362

Chapter 12: Integrating Validated Diagrams with SharePoint 2013 and Office365 — 363

Using SharePoint and Visio together	363
Understanding a Visio Process Repository	366
Approving and rejecting Process Diagrams	368
Creating a Visio Process Repository	369
Adding a Visio template to SharePoint	374
Adding a template as a Site Content Type	375
Adding a List and Library Content Type	376
Creating a diagram from the custom template	378
Summary	379
Index	**381**

Preface

It has been three years since the first edition of this book, and the power of Visio as a platform for visual data has been enhanced even more. Microsoft has merged the Premium edition with the far more popular Professional edition, which means that the content of this book is now accessible to literally millions more Visio users because the Professional edition is the norm in business.

Once the creators of Aldus PageMaker had successfully introduced the desktop publishing paradigm in the late eighties, some of the key personnel involved left because they decided that they could make a smarter diagramming application. Eighteen months later, they emerged with the Visio product. Now they needed to get a foothold in the market, so they targeted the leading process flow diagramming package of the day, ABC Flowcharter, as the one to outdo. They soon achieved their aim to become the number one flowcharting application, and so they went after other usage scenarios, such as network diagramming, organization charts, and building plans.

In 1999, Microsoft bought Visio Corporation and Visio gradually became Microsoft Office Visio, meaning that all add-ons had to be written in a certain manner and common Microsoft Office core libraries such as Fluent UI were ever more increasingly employed. Microsoft then dropped the Office part of the name, may be because Visio continues to be an independent profit center within Visio. The 2013 edition has seen Visio adopt the Open Packaging Convention that which had already been used by the main Office products for two versions. This potentially opens the contents of a Visio file to a mature group of developers with skills in this area.

Flowcharting still accounts for 30 percent of the typical uses that Visio is put to, but the core product did not substantially enhance its flowcharting abilities. There were some add-ons that provided rules, perhaps most notably for Data Flow Diagrams, UML, and Database Modelling (all of which have now lost their built-in rules engine), and many third parties have built whole flowcharting applications based on Visio. What all of these enhancements have in common is the imposition of a structure to the diagrams, which necessarily means the adoption of one ruleset or another. There are a lot of competing and complementary rulesets in use, but what is important is that the chosen ruleset fits the purpose it is being used for and that it can be understood by other related professionals.

It is true that a picture is worth a thousand words, but the particular thousand words understood by each individual are more likely to be the same if the picture was created with commonly available rules. The structured diagramming features and Validation API in Visio Professional 2013 enable business diagramming rules to be developed, reviewed, and deployed. The first diagramming types to have these rules applied to them are process flowcharts, reminiscent of the vertical markets attacked by the first versions of Visio itself, but these rules can and will be extended beyond this discipline.

What this book covers

Chapter 1, Overview of Process Management in Microsoft Visio 2013, introduces Microsoft Visio and the features that support process management; further, it explores the built-in templates with validation rules.

Chapter 2, Understanding the Microsoft Visio Object Model, explores the useful objects, collections, and methods in the Visio object model, in relation to validation rules.

Chapter 3, Understanding the ShapeSheet™, explores the unique ShapeSheet, and the common sections, rows, and cells, along with useful functions and formulas.

Chapter 4, Understanding the Validation API, explores the objects, collections, and methods in the Validation API.

Chapter 5, Developing a Validation API Interface, explains how to develop a tool to create and edit validation rules.

Chapter 6, Reviewing Validation Rules and Issues, extends the tool to provide an XML import/export routine of rules and issue annotation features.

Chapter 7, Creating Validation Rules, explains how to use the new tool to create validation rules, and understand common functions in rule expressions.

Chapter 8, Publishing Validation Rules and Diagrams, examines the methods for publishing validation rules for others to use.

Chapter 9, A Worked Example for Data Flow Model Diagrams – Part 1, explores customizing the Data Flow Model Diagram template in preparation for validation rules.

Chapter 10, A Worked Example for Data Flow Model Diagrams – Part 2, presents how to go through each of the twelve rules in detail, writing a validation rule for each one.

Chapter 11, A Worked Example for Data Flow Model Diagrams – Part 3, deals with preparing the new custom template for publication and creating an installation package for it.

Chapter 12, Integrating Validated Diagrams with SharePoint 2013 and Office365, explains how to understand the advantages of utilizing Visio with SharePoint with respect to validated diagrams, and how to provide a custom template via SharePoint.

What you need for this book

The following software products are used:

- Microsoft Visio 2013 Professional software.
- Free Rules Tools add-in that can be downloaded from `http://www.visiorules.com`.
- Optionally, Microsoft Visual Studio 2012 (with a little knowledge of C#)
- Optionally, Microsoft Visio 2013 SDK
- Optionally, Office365 Plus {also used in this book}.

Who this book is for

This book is primarily for Microsoft Visio users or developers who want to know how to use and extend the validation rules in Microsoft Visio 2013 Professional edition. There are some rulesets available out of the box, but the capability can be added to many sorts of diagramming, whether they are process flows, network cabling drawings, or risk dependency diagrams, for example. This is not a Visio SmartShape developer manual or a Visio automation guide, although these subjects are explored when relevant for writing validation rules, but it does shed light on the possibilities of this new powerful feature of Microsoft Visio 2013. This book will be an essential guide to understanding and creating structured diagramming rules, and will add developer tools that are not in the out-of-the-box product.

Conventions

In this book, you will find a number of styles of text that distinguish between different kinds of information. Here are some examples of these styles, and an explanation of their meaning.

Code words in text, database table names, folder names, filenames, file extensions, pathnames, dummy URLs, user input, and Twitter handles are shown as follows: "The `Documents` collection contains all of the stencils and drawings that are currently open in the Visio application."

A block of code is set as follows:

```
Public Sub EnumerateAddons()
Dim adn As Visio.Addon
    Debug.Print "EnumerateAddons : Count = " & _
        Application.Addons.Count
    Debug.Print , "Index", "Enabled", "NameU", "Name"
    For Each adn In Application.Addons
        With adn
            Debug.Print , .Index, .Enabled, .NameU, .Name
        End With
    Next
End Sub
```

New terms and **important words** are shown in bold. Words that you see on the screen, in menus or dialog boxes for example, appear in the text like this: "The **Drawing Explorer** window can be opened in the Visio UI in the **Show/Hide** group on the **DEVELOPER** tab.".

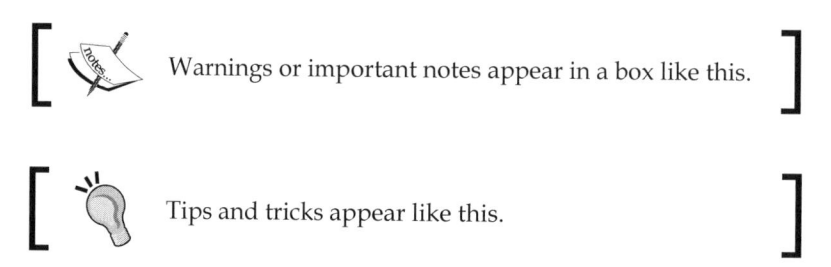

[Warnings or important notes appear in a box like this.]

[Tips and tricks appear like this.]

Reader feedback

Feedback from our readers is always welcome. Let us know what you think about this book—what you liked or may have disliked. Reader feedback is important for us to develop titles that you really get the most out of.

To send us general feedback, simply send an e-mail to feedback@packtpub.com, and mention the book title via the subject of your message.

If there is a topic that you have expertise in and you are interested in either writing or contributing to a book, see our author guide on www.packtpub.com/authors.

Customer support

Now that you are the proud owner of a Packt book, we have a number of things to help you to get the most from your purchase.

Downloading the example code

You can download the example code files for all Packt books you have purchased from your account at http://www.packtpub.com. If you purchased this book elsewhere, you can visit http://www.packtpub.com/support and register to have the files e-mailed directly to you.

Errata

Although we have taken every care to ensure the accuracy of our content, mistakes do happen. If you find a mistake in one of our books—maybe a mistake in the text or the code—we would be grateful if you would report this to us. By doing so, you can save other readers from frustration and help us improve subsequent versions of this book. If you find any errata, please report them by visiting http://www.packtpub.com/submit-errata, selecting your book, clicking on the **errata submission form** link, and entering the details of your errata. Once your errata are verified, your submission will be accepted and the errata will be uploaded on our website, or added to any list of existing errata, under the Errata section of that title. Any existing errata can be viewed by selecting your title from http://www.packtpub.com/support.

Piracy

Piracy of copyright material on the Internet is an ongoing problem across all media. At Packt, we take the protection of our copyright and licenses very seriously. If you come across any illegal copies of our works, in any form, on the Internet, please provide us with the location address or website name immediately so that we can pursue a remedy.

Please contact us at `copyright@packtpub.com` with a link to the suspected pirated material.

We appreciate your help in protecting our authors, and our ability to bring you valuable content.

Questions

You can contact us at `questions@packtpub.com` if you are having a problem with any aspect of the book, and we will do our best to address it.

1
Overview of Process Management in Microsoft Visio 2013

When Visio was first conceived of over 20 years ago, its first stated marketing aim was to outsell ABC Flowcharter, the best-selling process diagramming tool at the time. Therefore, Visio had to have all of the features from the start that are core in the creation of flowcharts, namely the ability to connect one shape to another and to have the lines route themselves around shapes. Visio soon achieved its aim, and looked for other targets to reach.

So, process flow diagrams have long been a cornerstone of Visio's popularity and appeal and, although there have been some usability improvements over the years, there have been few enhancements to turn the diagrams into models that can be managed efficiently. Microsoft Visio 2010 saw the introduction of two features, structured diagrams and validation rules, that make process management achievable and customizable, and Microsoft Visio 2013 sees these features enhanced.

In this chapter, you will be introduced to the new features that have been added to Microsoft Visio to support structured diagrams and validation. You will see where Visio fits in the **Process Management** stack, and explore the relevant out of the box content.

Overview of Process Management in Microsoft Visio 2013

Exploring the new process management features in Visio 2013

Firstly, Microsoft Visio 2010 introduced a new **Validation API** for structured diagrams and provided several examples of this in use, for example with the **BPMN (Business Process Modeling Notation) Diagram** and **Microsoft SharePoint Workflow** templates and the improvements to the **Basic Flowchart** and **Cross-Functional Flowchart** templates, all of which are found in the **Flowchart** category. Microsoft Visio 2013 has updated the version of BPMN from 1.1 to 2.0, and has introduced a new SharePoint 2013 Workflow template, in addition to the 2010 one.

Templates in Visio consist of a predefined Visio document that has one or more pages, and may have a series of docked stencils (usually positioned on the left-hand side of workspace area). The template document may have an associated list of add-ons that are active while it is in use, and, with Visio 2013 Professional edition, an associated list of structured diagram validation rulesets as well. Most of the templates that contain validation rules in Visio 2013 are in the **Flowchart** category, as seen in the following screenshot, with the exception being the **Six Sigma** template in the **Business** category.

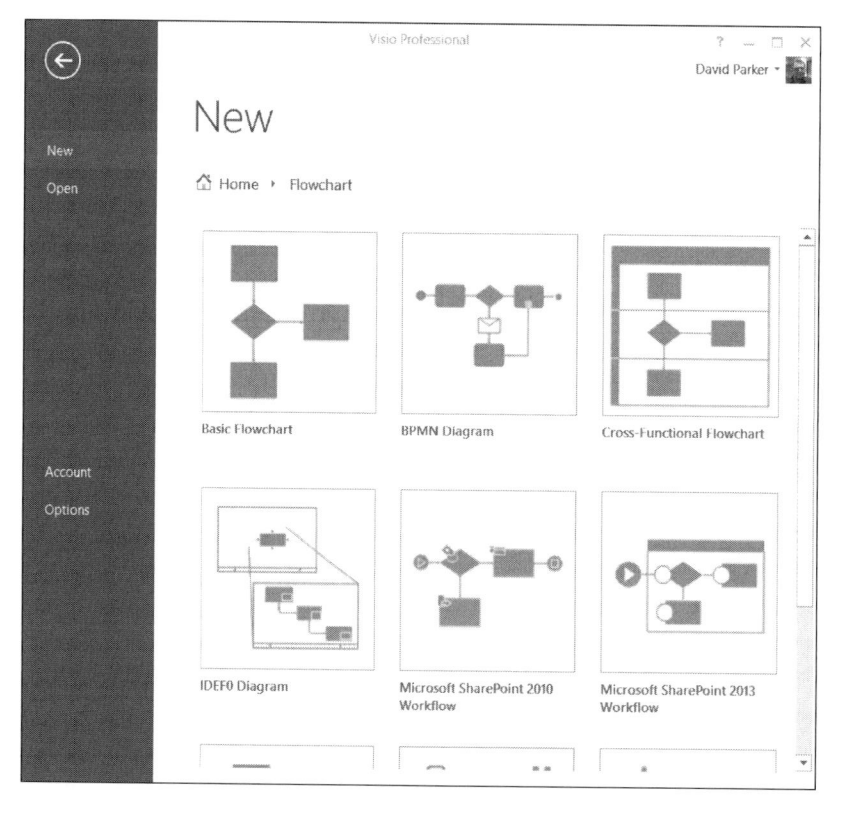

[8]

Secondly, the concept of a **Subprocess** was introduced in Visio 2010. This enables processes to hyperlink to other pages describing the subprocesses in the same document, or even across documents. This latter point is necessary if subprocesses are stored in a document library, such as Microsoft SharePoint.

The following screenshot illustrates how an existing **s**ubprocess can be associated with a shape in a larger process, selecting an existing shape in the diagram, before selecting the existing page that it links to from the drop-down menu on the **Link to Existing** button.

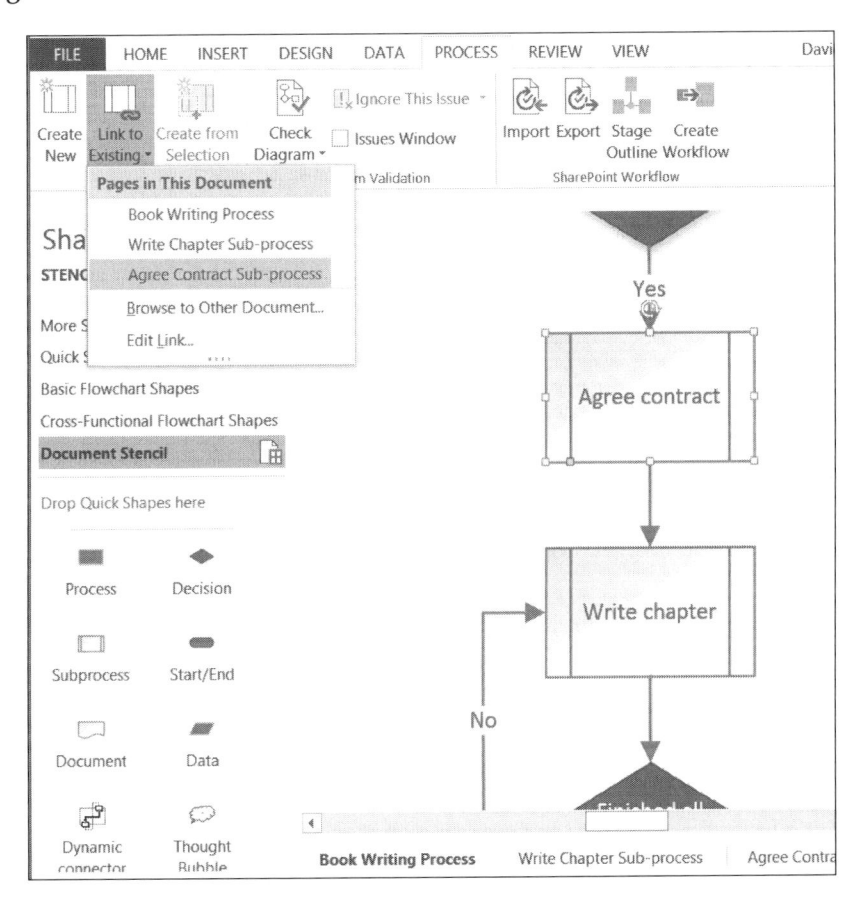

In addition, a subprocess page can be created from an existing shape, or a selection of shapes, in which case they will be moved to the newly-created page.

There were also a number of ease-of-use features introduced in Microsoft Visio 2010 to assist in the creation and revision of process flow diagrams. These include:

- Easy auto-connection of shapes
- Aligning and spacing of shapes
- Insertion and deletion of connected shapes
- Improved cross-functional flowcharts
- Subprocesses
- An infinite page option, so you need not go over the edge of the paper ever again

Microsoft Visio 2013 has added two more notable features:

- Commenting (a replacement for the old reviewer's comments)
- Co-authoring

However, this book is not about teaching the user how to use these features, since there will be many other authors willing to show you how to perform tasks that only need to be explained once. This book is about understanding the Validation API in particular, so that you can create, or amend, the rules to match the business logic that your business requires.

Reviewing Visio Process Management capabilities

Microsoft Visio now sits at the top of the **Microsoft Process Management Product Stack**, providing a **Business Process Analysis (BPA)** or **Business Process Modeling (BPM)** tool for business analysts, process owners/participants, and line of business software architects/developers.

Microsoft Process Management Product Stack

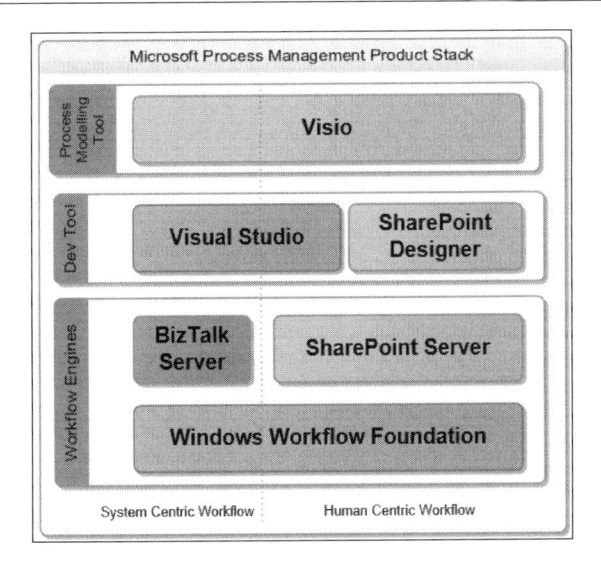

- **Process Modelling Tool**: Visio
- **Dev Tool**: Visual Studio, SharePoint Designer
- **Workflow Engines**: BizTalk Server, SharePoint Server, Windows Workflow Foundation
- System Centric Workflow | Human Centric Workflow

Of course, your particular business may not have all, or parts, of the stack, but you will see in later chapters how Visio 2013 can be used in isolation for business process management to a certain depth.

Understanding the Visio BMP Maturity Model

If we look at the **Visio BPM Maturity Model** that Microsoft has previously presented to its partners, then we can see that Visio 2013 has filled some of the gaps that were still there after Visio 2010. However, we can also see that there are plenty of opportunities for partners to provide solutions on top of the Visio platform. The maturity model shows how Visio initially provided the means to capture paper-drawn business processes into electronic format, and included the ability to encapsulate data into each shape and infer the relationship and order between elements through connectors. Visio 2007 Professional added the ability to easily link shapes, which represent processes, tasks, decisions, gateways, and so on with a data source. Along with that, data graphics were provided to enable shape data to be displayed simply as icons, data bars, text, or to be colored by value. This enriched the user experience and provided quicker visual representation of data, thus increasing the comprehension of the data in the diagrams. Generic templates for specific types of business modeling were provided.

Visio had a built-in report writer for many versions, which provided the ability to export to Excel or XML, but Visio 2010 Premium introduced the concept of validation and structured diagrams, which meant that the information could be verified before exporting. Some templates for specific types of business modeling were provided.

Overview of Process Management in Microsoft Visio 2013

Visio 2010 Premium also saw the introduction of Visio Services on SharePoint that provided the automatic (without involving the Visio client) refreshing of data graphics that were linked to specific types of data sources.

Level		Visio 2007 Professional	Visio 2010 Premium	Visio 2013 Professional	Opportunities

8	Monitor business activity by integrating BPMS and LOB applications	• Pivot Diagram
		• DataGraphics
		• Data Link
			• Visio Services
			• Excel Services
			• Mash-up API
				• HTML rendering available from any browser, any device	• Integration with other biz apps
					  • SQL AS/RS • SAP
					  • Dynamics • FileNet
					  • BizTalk • Documentum

7	Execute process models to process engine with round trip capability		• SPD Integration
			• Workflow visualization
				• Enhanced SPD integration
				• Enhanced Workflow visualization
					• Industry standard language
					  • XMI • XLANG
					  • BPEL • XPDL
					  • UML • WWF

6	Manage standardized business process within process repository		• SharePoint Repository	• Co-authoring • Commenting • BCS • SQL Azure	• Process Repository • Multi-user editing • Model merge support • Versioning / Lockout
5	Integrate business rules and validate the business models based on the rules		• Validation		• Business Rule Modeling • Business Rule Visualization • Import Rules
4	Simulate process models with analytical algorithms within Visio	• Pivot Diagram • DataGraphics • Data Link			• Static analysis • Dynamic simulation • Animation • Financial analysis • Risk analysis
3	Create Custom Shape and ShapeData set to standardize process notation	• Custom Shape • New stencil • ShapeData set		• New shapes • Enhanced graphic capabilities	• Critical path analysis • Value-chain analysis • Resource use optimization • Matrix support

2	Add process information into ShapeData and export it to Excel for process analysis	• ShapeData Reporting to Excel/XML	• Auto Layout
			• Sub process
			• BPMN 1.2
			• Six Sigma
			• Cross Functional Flowchart
				• BPMN 2.0	• Pre defined industry templates
					  • Supply Chain Management
					  • Discrete manufacturing control
					  • Mortgage approval
					  • Claims Processing
					  • Six Sigma/ISO/Quality
					  • Compliance
					  • IT Processes

1	Capture paper-based process into Visio to streamline business processes	• Templates & Stencils • Auto Connector			

Throughout this book we will be going into detail about Level 5 (**Validation**) in Visio 2013, because it is important to understand the core capabilities provided in Visio 2013. We will then be able to take the opportunity to provide custom **Business Rule Modeling** and **Visualization**.

Reviewing the foundations of structured diagramming

A **structured diagram** is a set of logical relationships between items, where these relationships provide visual organization or describe special interaction behaviors between them.

The Microsoft Visio team analyzed the requirements for adding structure to diagrams and came up with a number of features that needed to be added to the Visio product to achieve this:

- **Container Management**: The ability to add labeled boxes around shapes to visually organize them

- **Callout Management**: The ability to associate callouts with shapes to display notes
- **List Management**: To provide order to shapes within a container
- **Validation API**: The ability to test the business logic of a diagram
- **Connectivity API**: The ability to create, remove, or traverse connections easily

The following diagram demonstrates the use of **Containers** and **Callouts** in the construction of a basic flowchart, that has been validated using the **Validation API**, which in turn uses the **Connectivity API**.

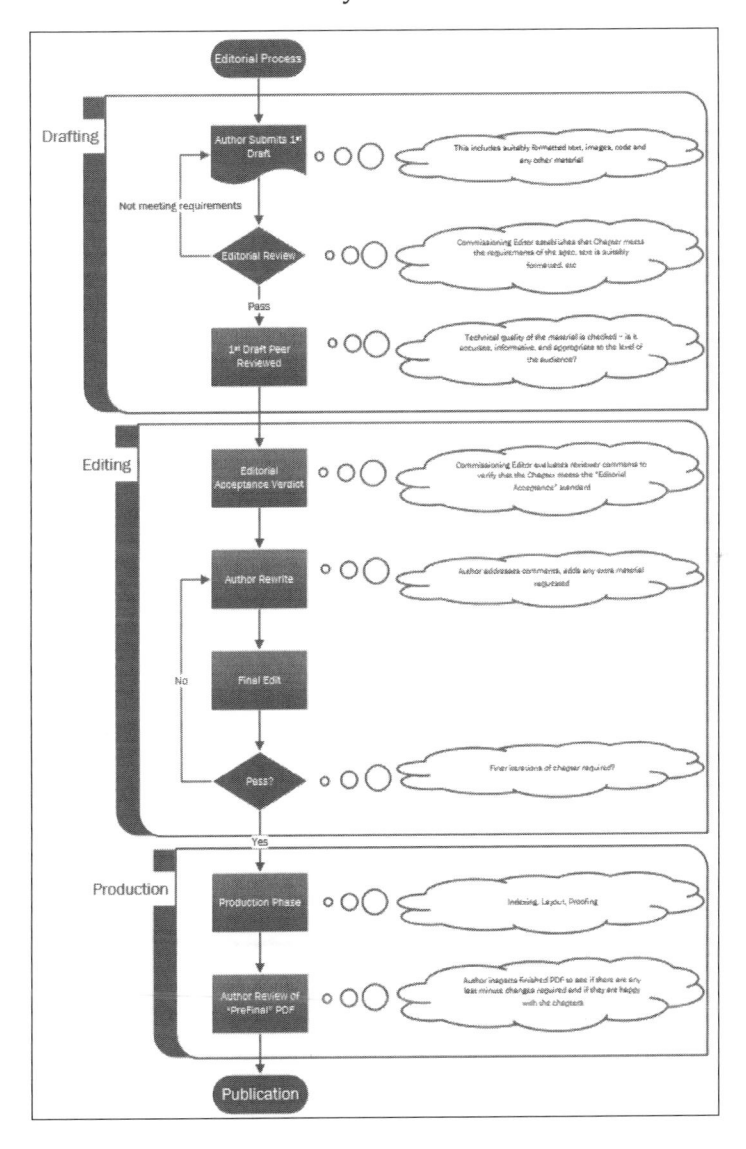

Reviewing the enhanced process flow templates

There are three process flow diagram templates: **Basic Flowchart**, **Cross-Functional Flowchart**, and **Six Sigma**, in Visio 2013 Professional edition that have been enhanced since the previous versions of Visio and include validation rules.

Looking at the Flowchart templates

There is now very little difference between the **Basic Flowchart** template and the **Cross-Functional Flowchart** template in the **Flowchart** category. In fact, they are identical apart from the latter opening with a couple of **Swimlane** shapes already placed on the page. Any **Basic Flowchart** diagram can become a **Cross-Functional Flowchart** diagram with the dragging and dropping of a **Swimlane** shape onto the page, at which point the new **CROSS-FUNCTIONAL FLOWCHART** tab will appear, as in the following screenshot:

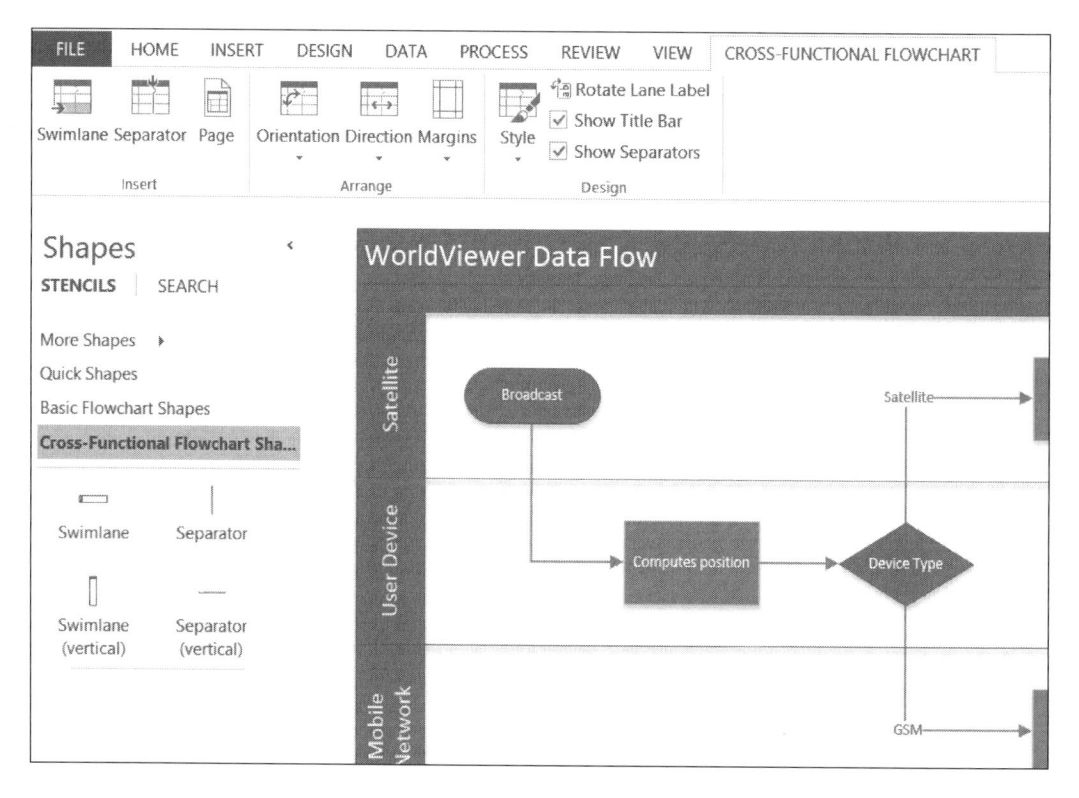

In addition, parts of the new **Six Sigma** template, in the **Business** category, use the same flowchart rules.

Reviewing the new process flow templates

There are two process flow diagram templates, in addition to the **Six Sigma Diagram** template, in the **Flowchart** category of Visio 2013 Professional Edition that include their own validation rules. The first, **BPMN Diagram**, provides native Visio support for an important and widely-used process flow notation, and the second, **Microsoft SharePoint 2013 Workflow**, enables visual development of SharePoint workflows that integrates closely with SharePoint 2013.

Understanding a BPMN Diagram

The **Object Management Group/Business Process Management Initiative** (http://bpmn.org/) promotes the **BPMN** standards. The BMPN version in Microsoft Visio 2013 is 2.0, an upgrade from Version 1.1 in Visio 2010. Although this officially added diagram types to the standard, it did not add more BPMN templates in Visio 2013. Instead, Microsoft actually simplified the number of stencils and shapes for BPMN in Visio 2013, while increasing their capability. There is no better short description of BPMN than the charter from the **OMG**'s website, which states:

> *A standard Business Process Modeling Notation (BPMN) will provide businesses with the capability of understanding their internal business procedures in a graphical notation and will give organizations the ability to communicate these procedures in a standard manner. Furthermore, the graphical notation will facilitate the understanding of the performance collaborations and business transactions between the organizations. This will ensure that businesses will understand themselves and participants in their business and will enable organizations to adjust to new internal and B2B business circumstances quickly.*

Having been involved in the creation of two other BPMN solutions based on earlier versions of Visio, I believe that the native support of BPMN is a very important development for Microsoft, because it is obviously a very popular methodology for the description of an interchange of business processes.

Overview of Process Management in Microsoft Visio 2013

The BMPN template in Visio 2010 contained five docked stencils, each of them containing a logical set of shapes, but for Visio 2013 these have been reduced to just one, **BPMN Basic Shapes**, as seen on the left of the following screenshot. The other stencils are still there, but hidden by default.

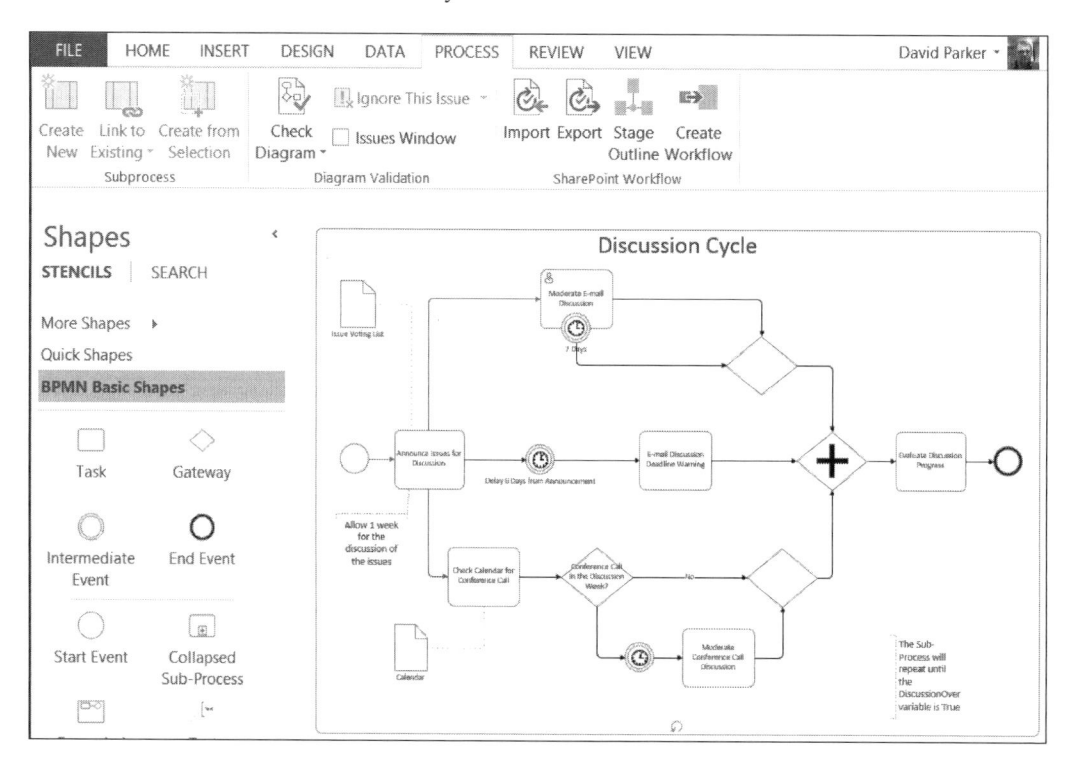

Each of the shapes has **BPMN Attributes** in the form of a set of **Shape Data**, which can be edited using the **Shape Data** window or dialog. Some shapes can also be edited using the right mouse menu.

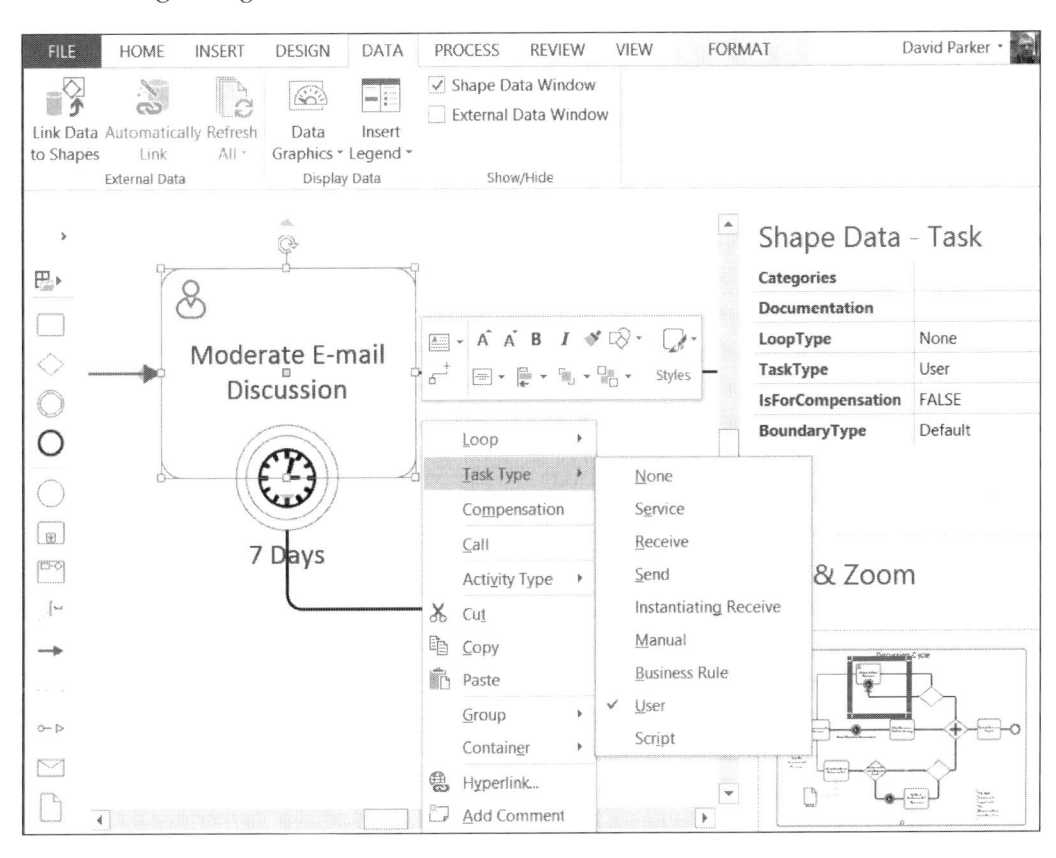

These **Shape Data** rows correspond to **BPMN Attributes**, as specified by the *OMG* specification. In the preceding screenshot, a **Task** shape is selected, revealing that there are many permutations that can be set.

The following screenshot shows all of the BPMN master shapes in the **BPMN Basic Shapes** stencil:

```
BPMN Basic Shapes

    Task                                    Gateway
    A Task is an activity that is included   Gateways control divergence and
    within a process. Drag the shape onto... convergence of Sequence Flow and of...

    Intermediate Event                      End Event
    Intermediate Events occur during the    The End Event indicates where a
    process. Drag the shape onto the dra... process will end. Drag the shape onto...

    Start Event                             Collapsed Sub-Process
    The Start Event indicates where a       A Collapsed Sub-Process is an activity
    particular process will start. Drag the s... whose details are not visible in the dia...

    Expanded Sub-Process                    Text Annotation
    An Expanded Sub-Process is an activity  Drag and drop onto the drawing page.
    whose details are visible within its bou...

    Sequence Flow                           Association
    A sequence flow shows the order in      Association is used to show a
    which activities in a process will occur... relationship between information and...

    Message Flow                            Message
    Message flow is used to show            Represents a communication between
    communication between two entities...   two participants. Drag the shape onto...

    Data Object                             Data Store
    Data Objects provide information on     Provides a mechanism for Tasks or
    the data created or used by activities i... Sub-Processes to retrieve or update st...

    Group                                   Pool / Lane
    Groups are used to make a conceptual    Drag onto the page to add a new Lane
    association between multiple elements.  or Pool. Use Lanes to organize activiti...
```

In reality, any of these Task shapes can be changed into a Collapsed SubProcess shape, and each of the Event shapes into any of the other Event shapes, by amending the **Shape Data**. Thus, the original name of the **Master** shape is really immaterial, since it is the **Shape Data** that determine how it should be understood.

Understanding a Microsoft SharePoint 2013 workflow

Microsoft Visio 2013 also includes a template and shapes for designing workflows that can be developed in tandem with **Microsoft SharePoint Designer**. With Visio 2010, you could pass the workflow back and forth between the two with no loss of data or functionality, by using a **Visio Workflow Interchange** (*.vwi) file, and the **Import** and **Export** buttons are still present on the **PROCESS** tab in the ribbon in Visio 2013, as seen in the following screenshot. However, Visio 2013 Professional and SharePoint Designer 2013 become complementary design surfaces that you can seamlessly switch between, if you have them both installed on your desktop.

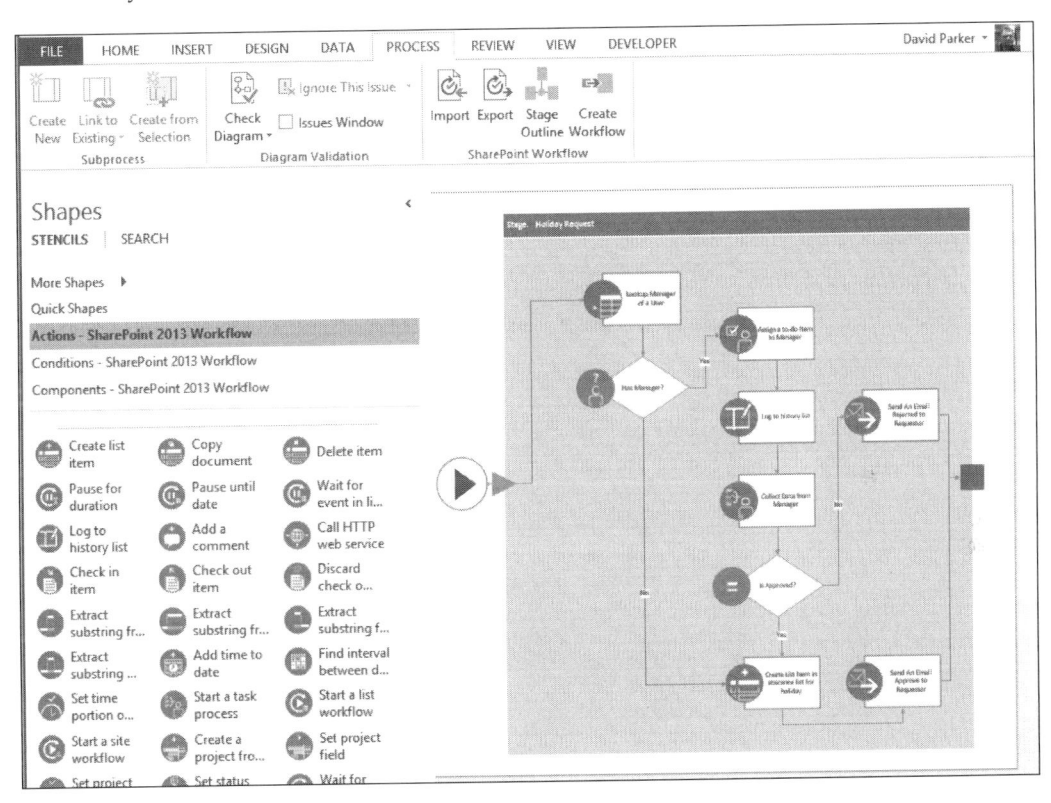

Overview of Process Management in Microsoft Visio 2013

Validation of process diagrams

Validation ensures that the diagram is compliant with the required business logic by checking that it is properly constructed. Therefore, you need to be able to verify that the ruleset being used is the one that your business requires. Visio will not provide instant feedback at the moment that you transgress a rule. However, it will check your diagram against a ruleset only when you select **Check Diagram**. It will then provide you with feedback on why any given rule has been broken.

Some of the **Validation API** can be accessed via the **PROCESS** tab on the **Diagram Validation** group; however, but there is more that is available only to developers, thus enabling you to automate some tasks if necessary. The following example of a BPMN diagram has some errors in it they would be difficult to spot if it were not for the **Issues** window that lists them, because the diagram has been validated.

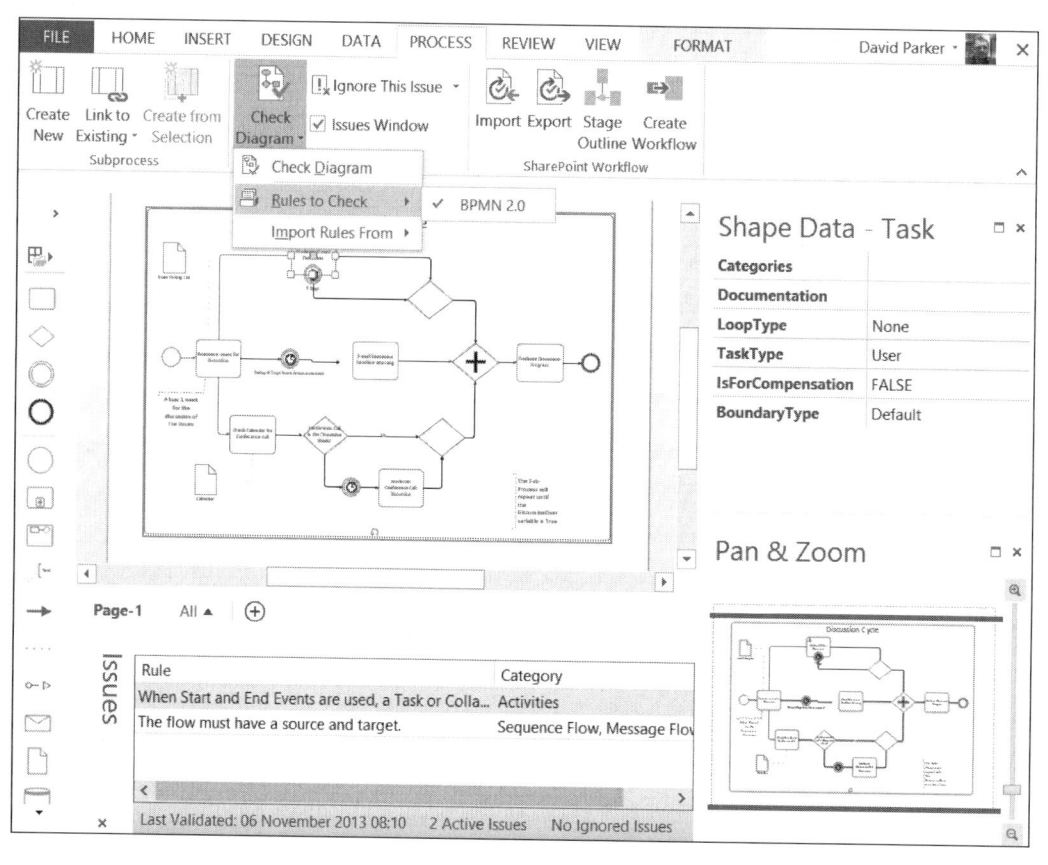

Chapter 1

The **PROCESS** tab is split into three ribbon groups. The first group on the **PROCESS** tab, **Subprocess**, is for the creation of Subprocesses, and the third group is for the **Import** and **Export** of a **SharePoint Workflow**, but it is the second group, **Diagram Validation**, that is of most interest here.

In this second group, the first button, **Check Diagram**, validates the whole document against the selected ruleset(s). You can have more than one ruleset in a document that can be enabled or disabled as required. The drop-down menu on the **Check Diagram** button (shown in the following screenshot) enables you to select which **Rules to Check**, and also to **Import Rules From** another open Visio document. It is a pity that you cannot export to/ import from XML, but we will create our own tool to do that in a later chapter.

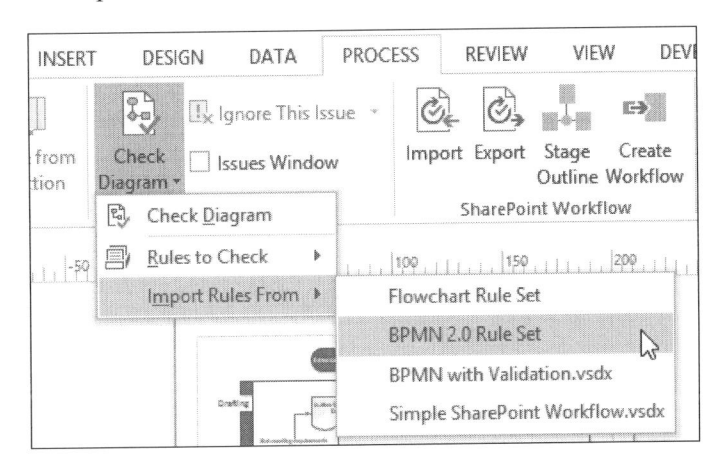

Analyzing the structure of a Visio document

At this point, we should be aware that Visio documents used to either be saved as binary (normally with a *.vsd extension) or XML format (normally with a *.vdx extension); however, in Visio 2013 they are in a new XML format that follows the Open Packaging Convention.

[21]

Visio 2013 diagram files have either a *.vsdx extension, or a *.vsdm extension if they contain macros. The easiest way to look at the contents of a Visio 2013 file is to change the extension to *.zip, and then just double-click to open it. Inside the zip file, you will find a **visio** folder, and inside that is a **validation.xml** file if there are any rules within the document, as shown in the following screenshot:

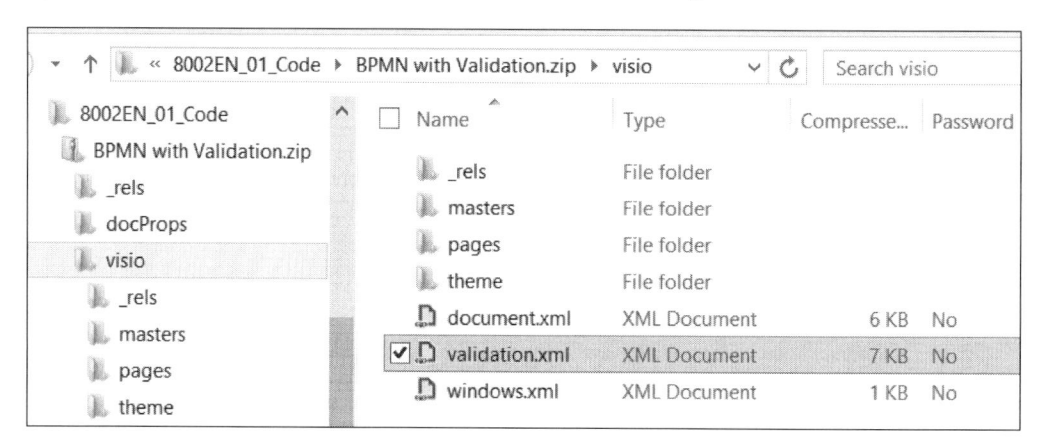

Simply double-clicking on the xml file will open it in the associated program, which in my case is Internet Explorer.

If we expand a **RuleSets** branch, and one of the **Rule** sub-branches, then we can see how a rule is defined, as shown in the following screenshot:

```
<?xml version="1.0" encoding="UTF-8"?>
<Validation xml:space="preserve"
 xmlns:r="http://schemas.openxmlformats.org/officeDocument/2006/relationships"
 xmlns="http://schemas.microsoft.com/office/visio/2012/main">
    <ValidationProperties ShowIgnored="0" LastValidated="2013-05-01T20:21:07"/>
    <RuleSets>
        <RuleSet Description="Verify a Visio BPMN diagram against the graphical aspects of the BPMN 2.0
          standard." NameU="BPMN 2.0" ID="1">
            <RuleSetFlags/>
            <Rule Description="An Association must not connect Data Objects, Data Stores or Messages."
              NameU="ImproperAssociation" ID="1" Category="Association">
                <RuleFilter>AND(HASCATEGORY("Connecting Object"),Actions.Association.Checked)
                </RuleFilter>
                <RuleTest>AGGCOUNT(FILTERSET(GLUEDSHAPES(3), "OR(HASCATEGORY(""Data
                  Object""),HASCATEGORY(""Data Store""),HASCATEGORY(""Message""))") ) <2</RuleTest>
            </Rule>
            <Rule Description="An Intermediate Cancel Event must be attached to the boundary of a
              Transaction." NameU="CancelOutsideOfTransaction" ID="2" Category="Intermediate Events">
                <RuleFilter>AND(HASCATEGORY("Event"),Actions.Cancel.Checked,
                  Actions.Intermediate.Checked)</RuleFilter>
                <RuleTest>OR(AGGCOUNT(FILTERSET(OnBoundaryOf(),"Prop.BpmnIsATransaction")) >
                  0,AGGCOUNT(FILTERSET(GLUEDSHAPES(5),"Prop.BpmnIsATransaction")) > 0)</RuleTest>
            </Rule>
```

Chapter 1

Later, we will be going into these definitions in much greater detail but, for now, notice that the **RuleFilter** and **RuleTest** elements contain formulae that precisely define what constitutes the particular rule.

The **Diagram Validation** group also has the option to show/hide the **Issues** Window, which has a right mouse menu that is identical (apart from the additional **Arrange By** menu option) to the drop-down menu on the **Ignore This Issue** button, as shown in the following screenshot:

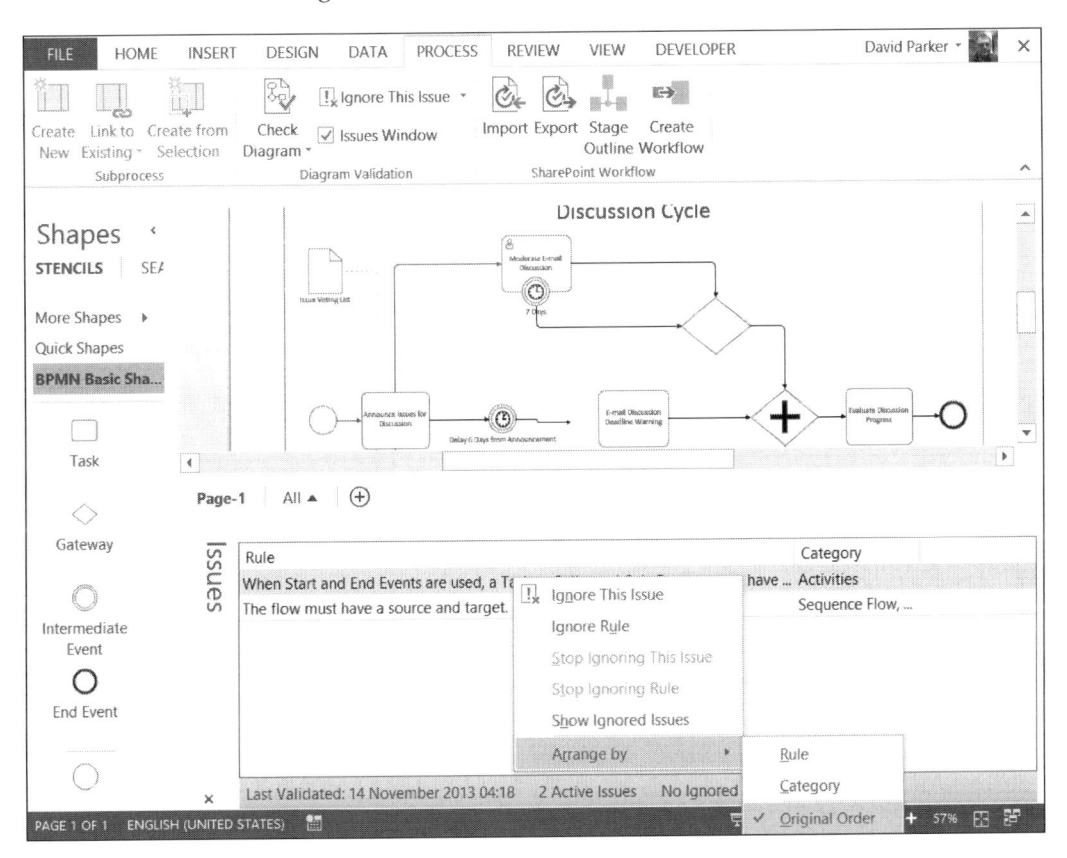

Overview of Process Management in Microsoft Visio 2013

Now that we can see that a **Rule** has an **ID**, and belongs to a **RuleSet** that also has an **ID**, we can begin to understand how an issue can be associated with a shape. So, if we expand an **Issue** element in the Visio document XML, we can see that **Issue** has **IssueTarget** and **RuleInfo** elements, as at the bottom of the following screenshot of the Validation XML.

```xml
        <Rule Description="A Non-Interrupting Start Event must be used with an Event Sub-Process."
            NameU="NoninterruptingStartEvents" ID="76" Category="Start Events">
            <RuleFilter>AND(HASCATEGORY("Event"),Actions.StartNonInterrupting.Checked)</RuleFilter>
            <RuleTest>AGGCOUNT(FILTERSET(PARENTCONTAINERS(),"AND(HASCATEGORY(""Expanded
                Sub-Process""),Actions.BoundaryEvent.Checked)"))>0</RuleTest>
        </Rule>
      </RuleSet>
    </RuleSets>
    <Issues>
      <Issue ID="1">
        <IssueTarget ShapeID="333" PageID="0"/>
        <RuleInfo RuleID="19" RuleSetID="1"/>
      </Issue>
      <Issue ID="2">
        <IssueTarget ShapeID="496" PageID="0"/>
        <RuleInfo RuleID="45" RuleSetID="1"/>
      </Issue>
    </Issues>
</Validation>
```

We can then use the **ShapeID** and the **PageID** from the preceding **Issue** to find the actual shape in the relevant page XML, by reviewing the **Shape** elements under the **Shapes** collection of **PageContents**, also identified by its **ID**, as shown in the following screenshot:

```xml
<?xml version="1.0" encoding="UTF-8"?>
<PageContents xml:space="preserve"
  xmlns:r="http://schemas.openxmlformats.org/officeDocument/2006/relationships"
  xmlns="http://schemas.microsoft.com/office/visio/2012/main">
    <Shapes>
      + <Shape Master="8" Type="Group" Name="Expanded Sub-Process" NameU="Expanded Sub-Process"
          ID="1">
      + <Shape Master="21" Type="Group" Name="Task" NameU="Task" ID="223">
      + <Shape Master="21" Type="Group" ID="246">
      + <Shape Master="22" Type="Group" Name="Start Event" NameU="Start Event" ID="269">
      + <Shape Master="23" Type="Group" Name="Data Object" NameU="Data Object" ID="282">
      + <Shape Master="21" Type="Group" ID="285">
      + <Shape Master="23" Type="Group" ID="308">
      + <Shape Master="24" Type="Shape" Name="Association" NameU="Association" ID="311">
      + <Shape Master="24" Type="Shape" ID="312">
      + <Shape Master="25" Type="Shape" Name="Sequence Flow" NameU="Sequence Flow" ID="313">
      + <Shape Master="25" Type="Shape" ID="314">
      + <Shape Master="25" Type="Shape" ID="316">
      + <Shape Master="26" Type="Group" Name="Gateway" NameU="Gateway" ID="317">
      + <Shape Master="3" Type="Shape" Name="Dynamic Connector" NameU="Dynamic Connector" ID="332">
      - <Shape Master="21" Type="Group" ID="333">
          <Cell V="5.807086614173229" N="PinX"/>
          <Cell V="4.379921259842521" N="PinY"/>
          <Cell V="0" N="LayerMember"/>
          <Cell V="0" N="Relationships" F="SUM(DEPENDSON(4,Sheet.1!SheetRef()))"/>
          <Section N="Property">
            - <Row N="BpmnName">
                <Cell V="E-mail Discussion Deadline Warning" N="Value" F="Inh" U="STR"/>
              </Row>
            </Section>
```

In fact, the **PageID** and **ShapeID** elements of an **IssueTarget** are optional because an Issue may just be associated with a page, or even with the whole document.

We will use the new Validation API to explore these **RuleSets, Rules,** and **Issues** in later chapters, and we will expose them to scrutiny so that your business can be satisfied that you have modeled the business logic correctly.

Using the Visio Process Repository

There is also a **Visio Process Repository**, which is a site template that is included with Microsoft SharePoint 2013. It provides a place to share and collaborate on process diagrams, and for reviewers to add comments. The repository has built-in file access control and version control — users can view the process diagram simultaneously and edit the diagram without corrupting the original.

This repository can therefore ensure that a user is editing the most recent version of a process diagram, and enable a user to find out about updates that have been made to processes of interest to them.

In addition, administrators can monitor whether diagrams comply with a business's internal standards, or not, or discover, for example, which processes apply to a specified department. The Validation status of the diagram is automatically updated in the Process Repository when the diagram is saved back to SharePoint.

Publishing visual data from Visio

Microsoft Visio has had, for several versions, a useful **Save As Web** feature that creates a mini-website, complete with widgets for pan and zoom, **Shape Data**, and shape reports. This has worked best using the **Vector Markup Language** (**VML**) in Microsoft Internet Explorer; or in **Scalable Vector Graphics** (**SVG**) using a web browser that supports it natively; or in older browsers that have the required plug-in. This is quite powerful, but it does require that the native Visio file is republished if any changes are made to the document. The new Open Packaging Convention XML in Visio 2013 is utilized by Visio Services in SharePoint 2013 to render the diagram in html directly, and has a JavaScript Object Model (JSOM) for developers. In addition, Microsoft has an ActiveX **Visio Viewer** control that can display native Visio files that are in the new OPC format or the older binary and XML formats.

This control is installed as default with Microsoft Outlook 2007 and later, but is also available as a separate free download from Microsoft. In fact, the Visio Viewer control has a programmable API that enables Shape Data and hyperlinks to be extracted and exposed too. While this viewer has the advantage that the native file does not need to be hosted on SharePoint with Visio Services, its reach is limited by the choice of browsers available and the willingness to make the native Visio file accessible — this is not always the best strategy.

Microsoft Visio 2013 provides Visio Services for Microsoft SharePoint. Therefore, with rendering on the server, any client that accesses the Microsoft SharePoint site will have the ability to view Visio diagrams without having to install anything locally.

The user can interact with the diagrams by clicking on shapes to view the Shape Data, navigating any embedded hyperlinks as well as pan/zoom and print capabilities. These are capabilities of the **Save As Web** and **Visio Viewer** options too. In addition, Visio 2013 introduced commenting on shapes and the ability to co-author. These features are extremely useful for collaboration.

Microsoft Visio 2007 introduced the ability to add a data recordset to a diagram and refresh that data so that the diagram could be kept up-to-date, but the **Save As Web html pages** and the **Visio Viewer ActiveX** controls are not able to automatically respond to any data changes. Therefore, the diagram can quickly become outdated, thus requiring you to refresh the diagram in Visio, and then to republish it.

Now with Visio Services, that same data recordset can be refreshed by the server, thus providing everyone who views the diagram using the new Visio web part with the latest information. This is extremely nice, but be aware that there are some limitationsfor example, no shapes will be added or deleted in this operation, but data-linked cells will have their formulas updated, which is a big advance from Visio 2010 when only linked Shape Data and Data Graphics were updated. No layer visibility changes will be respected. Still, you no longer have to republish just to refresh the data set!

> Visio has a complex layering system. Most CAD systems, for example, insist that all diagram elements belong to a single layer. This layer can either be made visible or not, or all elements on a layer can have a specified color. Drawing elements in Visio can belong to none, one, or many layers! Visio Services, however, simply ignores layers.

Understanding the Visio 2013 editions

Microsoft has merged the Professional and Premium editions from Visio 2010 into the Professional edition in Visio 2013. There is still a Standard edition, but there is a flavor of the Professional edition for 2013 that is available with certain Office365 subscriptions. The Office365 edition of Visio Professional can be used on up to 5 PCs as a Click-Once installation

You need to be aware of the relevant features that are in each of them. In the following matrix, a black dot denotes which features are in which edition:

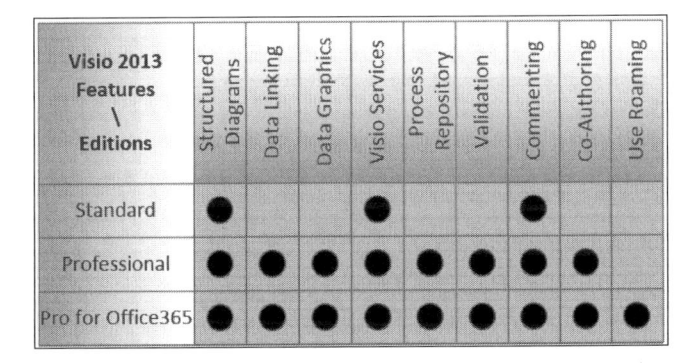

Visio 2013 Features \ Editions	Structured Diagrams	Data Linking	Data Graphics	Visio Services	Process Repository	Validation	Commenting	Co-Authoring	Use Roaming
Standard	●			●			●		
Professional	●	●	●	●	●	●	●	●	
Pro for Office365	●	●	●	●	●	●	●	●	●

Although you will need Microsoft Visio 2013 Professional Edition to use the Validation capabilities, the Standard edition will be able to review any of the diagrams created.

Planning your own solutions

By now, you should be eager to explore the out of the box structured diagram functionality, and perhaps be considering how to create validation rules for your own business. In doing so, I would advise that you always look to build upon what Visio provides—do not try to replicate it! I believe that trying to create your own Shape Data objects, or your own line routing algorithms, for example, is ultimately a waste of time as they will lead you down some dead-ends, as the routing algorithms are complex and difficult to reproduce.

The following three legacy diagram templates have had their functionality reduced because Microsoft has removed the add-ons that they were associated with. The new templates for these seem ripe for someone to create validation rules for the following:

- The **Software and Database\UML Model Diagram** solution from Visio 2010 has been removed and replaced with six UML templates, none of which have an add-on behind them to create a model in the way that it used to.

- The **Software and Database\Database Model Diagram** solution from Visio 2010 has been removed and replaced with three database modeling notation templates, none of which have an add-on behind them to create a model in the way that it used to.
- The **Software and Database\Data Flow Model Diagram** solution is one that was re-assessed for Visio 2010. We still have the template and stencil for this but the add-on has not made it through the Microsoft rationalization of Visio add-ons. Therefore, you can now construct DFD models badly without realizing it. We will attempt to remedy this omission in a later chapter by constructing a ruleset that can be used with DFD models.

The following two diagram templates in Visio have their own limitations for automation because, though they have associated add-ons, they do not have a programmers interface:

- The **Organization Chart** solution within Visio is essentially a closed add-on that has been around for many years. It has been given a facelift in Visio 2013, but experience has shown that it can only be enhanced with great care (and skill). There is no Application Programming Interface (API) to develop with.
- The **Pivot Diagram** solution is useful but also lacks an API for developers, thus making customization difficult.

One of the frequently asked questions by newbies to Visio occurs when confronted by the multiple diagram categories and types: How is a particular template supposed to be used? Often, they are directed to the Visio online help for examples of how to create certain types of diagrams but this is not always sufficient because they are really asking for automatic assistance as they create the diagram. What they usually want is in fact a guided diagramming system; they require a system that provides them with some feedback on the way that they are composing a diagram. It is easy to drag-and-drop shapes in Visio, to connect them together, to make a diagram pretty with embellishments, or to add text in a variety of ways. However, this loosely-created drawing cannot consistently convey any semantic meaning unless it follows generally accepted rules. It is the imposition of rules that turns a pretty picture into a meaningful mesh of semantic symbology. This is where Microsoft Visio 2013 Professional has made a great advance because it has provided us with the ability to create validation rules for different types of behaviors. In fact, these new features are worthy of a ribbon tab, the **PROCESS** tab, that although automatically applied to several drawing templates, is also available for use on any type of diagram.

Summary

In this chapter, we looked at an overview of the new capabilities and process diagram types in Visio 2013, especially with regard to structured and validated diagrams.

Microsoft Visio 2013 provides considerable ease-of-use features to the end user, a rich programming model for the developer, and greater capabilities for document management and sharing than ever before.

In the next chapter we will need to delve deeper into the internal structure of a Visio document and the use of its various APIs, so that you can best understand how to formulate your own rules to represent the business logic that you require.

2
Understanding the Microsoft Visio Object Model

Whatever programming language you code in, you need to understand the objects, properties, methods, relationships, and events of the application that you are working with. Without this knowledge, the development process is slow and any code you use is going to be inefficient. Visio is no different, in that it provides a programmer's interface (API) with an object model described in the **Visio Type Library**, but Visio also has a programmable **ShapeSheet** behind every shape. Therefore, the Visio Type Library can only be used efficiently if you understand the ShapeSheet, and in turn, the ShapeSheet formulae can only be used fully if you understand the Visio Type Library.

Also, if you are going to create validation rules to check the relationships and properties of structured diagrams, then you will need to understand how to traverse the Visio object model.

Therefore, this chapter is going to explain the **Microsoft Visio 15.0 Type Library** (`VisLib.dll`), and the key objects, collections, and methods in the programmer's interface of Visio; and the next chapter will reveal the ShapeSheet.

Introducing the Visio Type libraries

The publicly displayed version number of an application such as Visio can be quite different from the internal version number that is revealed to programmers. For example, Microsoft Visio 2013 is the public version number for the internal minor version number 15 (you can almost ignore the major version number because it rarely changes). Therefore, programmers need to know that the Visio Type Library version is 15, although their users will know it as Visio 2013.

Understanding the Microsoft Visio Object Model

> There was no Version 13 prior to 14 because Visio was at Version 6 (externally Visio 2000) when Microsoft bought the company in 1999. At that time, Microsoft Office was internally at Version 9, so Microsoft Visio 2002 was internally hiked up to Version 10 to be at the same version number as Microsoft Office 2002. At this point, Microsoft Visio 2003 was internally at Version 11, and Microsoft Visio 2007 was internally at Version 12. Version 13 went the same way as the thirteenth floors in high-rise buildings in the States—pandering to the superstitions of the masses.

Microsoft Visio 2013 will also install the following type libraries:

Name	File	Visio Editions
Microsoft Visio 15.0 Drawing Control Library	VisOcx.dll	All editions
Microsoft Visio 15.0 Save As Web Type Library	SaveAsWeb.dll	All editions

In addition, since Version 2007, Microsoft Outlook installs the Microsoft Visio Viewer (Vviewer.dll), which has a useful programming interface itself. It allows pages, shapes, and data to be explored, even without Visio being installed. It is also available as a separate, free download from Microsoft (see http://search.microsoft.com/en-us/DownloadResults.aspx?q=visio+viewer+2013), should you wish to use it on Windows desktops that do not have Microsoft Outlook installed.

Going beyond the object model

Some programmers think that Visio is present just to provide a graphical canvas with the symbols and lines that they need to manipulate or interrogate. Perhaps they have been used to draw items in Windows Forms applications or even XAML-based development with **WPF (Windows Presentation Foundation)**, Silverlight, or Windows 8 applications. To think like this is to misunderstand Visio, because it has a rich-diagramming engine, coupled with the ability to encapsulate data and custom behaviors in every element, not to mention the inheritance between certain types of objects. This has resulted in a fairly complex structure in parts of the object model, so that all of the desired functionality can be described fully.

Programmers who look at the Visio object model for the first time may be full of preconceptions and look in vain for the x and y coordinate of a shape on a page. They are surprised and a little frustrated that the x coordinate of a shape on a page is:

```
shape.CellsSRC(VisSectionIndices.visSectionObject,
    visRowIndices.visRowXFormOut,
    visCellIndices.visXFormPinX).ResultIU
```

The SRC part of the `CellsSRC` method is an acronym for **Section Row Column**, which will be explained later.

There is an alternative shorter form namely:

```
Shape.Cells("PinX").ResultIU
```

However, the shorter form is intrinsically more inefficient since the name has to be interpreted into the SRC indices by Visio anyway. Therefore, it is recommended that you work with the indices rather than the names, if at all possible.

The Visio object model is quite large, so I shall be selective by only discussing the parts that I think will assist in understanding and developing validation rules. There are other type libraries installed with Visio, but these are not relevant to the scope of this book. In addition, the Visio edition installed has an impact on the Visio Type Library itself. For example, the `Validation` objects and collections and the **Data Linking** features are only available if you have the **Professional** edition installed.

The other differences between the different Visio editions are the add-ons, templates, and stencils installed with it. However, as these could be moved around and copied between users (illegally), their presence (or lack of presence) cannot be relied on to ascertain the edition installed. One way to ascertain the version is to check a specific registry setting (a popular way if you are writing an installation script and are not familiar with PowerShell), or using the `CurrentEdition` property of the `Application` object.

```
HKEY_CURRENT_USER\Software\Microsoft\Office\15.0\Visio\Application\LicenseCache
```

The expected values are `STD` or `PRO`.

Classifying the Visio document

Before we get into the object model, we need to remind ourselves of the formats and types of Visio documents. Traditionally, Visio used its own binary format (which usually has an extension `*.vsd` for drawings), and then the XML format was introduced (`*.vdx` for drawings). The latter is approximately ten times larger in size than the former, although it often compresses to be smaller than the binary equivalent. The XML format is very verbose because it needs to describe the complexity of the graphics and the inheritance of elements within the document. In addition, it is not in the same zipped-up XML files in subfolders format as most of the Microsoft Office applications.

The **Visio Web Drawing** was new in Visio 2010, which, when published to SharePoint 2010, allows certain elements that are linked to data recordsets to be automatically refreshed when the underlying data is updated, without using Visio.

Microsoft Visio 2013 has a new XML format based on the Open Packaging Convention. It is a streamlined version of the old XML format, and it is broken down into many files within a zipped file.

This new Visio file format can be rendered directly by SharePoint 2013 and SharePoint Online with Office 365 if Visio Services are enabled. This feature, however, does not enable new shapes to be created or deleted or for connections to be varied during the refresh. But it can be edited by the Visio client application to make these sorts of changes. Therefore, Visio 2013 files can be rendered by a new standard web part, **VWA (Visio Web Access** control), in Microsoft SharePoint 2013, and can be set to refresh either on a timer event or manually. This means that native Visio files can be viewed, and commented upon, in any modern browser, on any modern devices such as Surface RT, iPad, or an Android Tablet.

> The VWA is able to recalculate the formulas of all the shape cells that are linked to a refreshable data recordset; however, the VWA does not support layer control.

The following diagram lists the Visio file extensions for the different classes of Visio documents. All of the file structures are the same, which means that you can just change the extension from one to another, and the Visio UI will respond to the extension to treat the file differently.

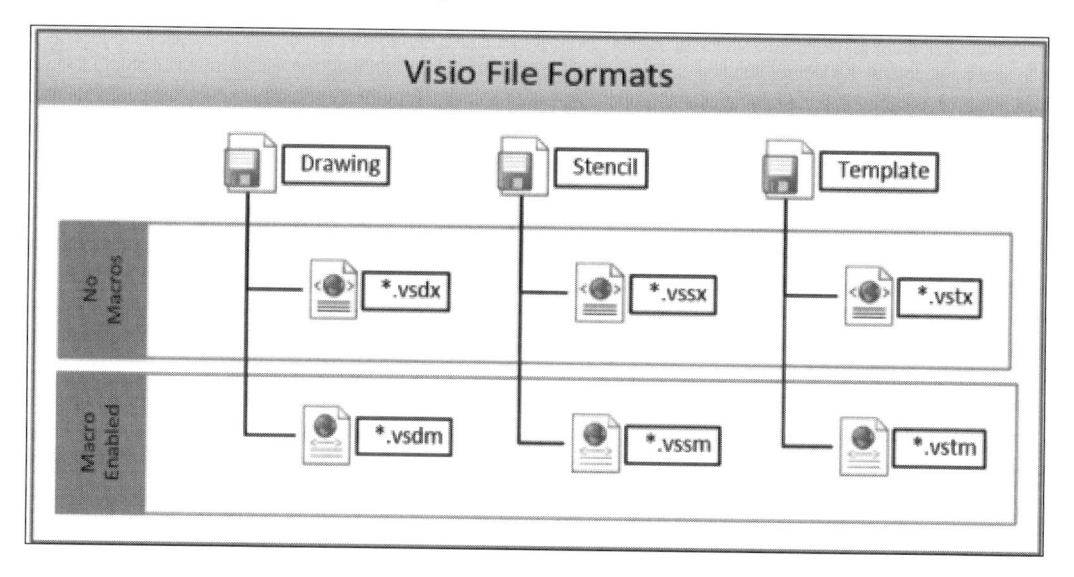

Visio File Formats

	Drawing	Stencil	Template
No Macros	*.vsdx	*.vssx	*.vstx
Macro Enabled	*.vsdm	*.vssm	*.vstm

A Visio drawing document can save its workspace along with it, which usually means that there are a collection of docked stencils that contain the shapes (properly referred to as **Masters** when they are in a stencil).

A Visio stencil is just a Visio document with the pages hidden, and is normally saved with a *.vssx extension if there are no macros present, or *.vssm if there are macros present.

A Visio template is just a Visio drawing document saved with a different extension, *.vstx if there are no macros present, and *.vstm with macros present, so that Visio knows that the default action is to open a copy of it, rather than the original document.

I mentioned that a stencil is just a Visio document with the drawing pages hidden. Well, a drawing is just a Visio document which normally has its stencil hidden. However, you can reveal this in the UI by navigating to **More Shapes | Show Document Stencil**.

> Any shape in a page in the document that is an instance of a Master must be an instance of a Master in the document stencil. It is not an instance of a Master in the stencil from which it was originally dragged and dropped.

Selecting a programming language to use with Visio

Microsoft Visio comes with **Visual Basic for Applications (VBA)** built into it, which is a very useful interface for exploring the object model and testing out ideas. In addition, Visio has a macro recorder that can provide a quick and dirty way of exploring how some of the actions are performed. However, the resultant code from the macro recorder can be very verbose in parts, and completely miss out some bits because Visio is running code inside one of the many **Add-ons** or **COM add-ins** that may be installed.

> **Downloading the example code**
> You can download the example code files for all Packt books you have purchased from your account at http://www.packtpub.com. If you purchased this book elsewhere, you can visit http://www.packtpub.com/support and register to have the files e-mailed directly to you.

Understanding the Microsoft Visio Object Model

If you want to use VBA then you will need to run Visio in Developer Mode by ticking the option available from the **Visio Options** dialog (use **File | Options** to display the following screenshot), in the **Advanced** group, as shown in the given screenshot.

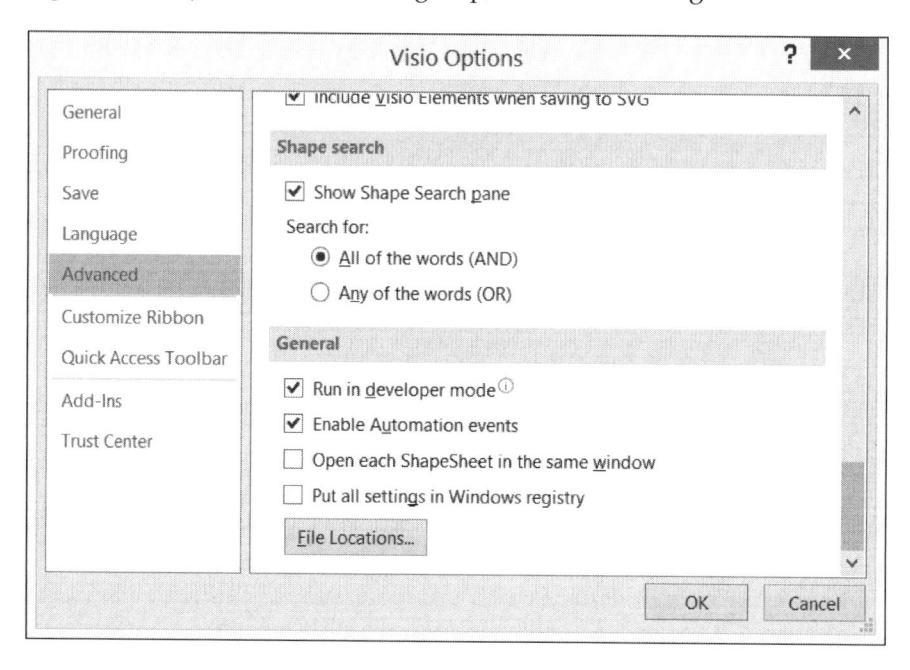

Developer Mode will also add some features to other parts of the Visio interface, such as additional options on the right mouse menu when a page and shape are selected.

Understanding the Drawing Explorer window

The **Drawing Explorer** window can be opened in the Visio UI in the **Show/Hide** group on the **DEVELOPER** tab. It is an extremely useful method for visually navigating some of the collections and objects in the Visio application. The **DEVELOPER** tab is shown in this screenshot with an additional ribbon group that was created by the Visio SDK, and a custom-extra ribbon group for some common commands that I use repeatedly.

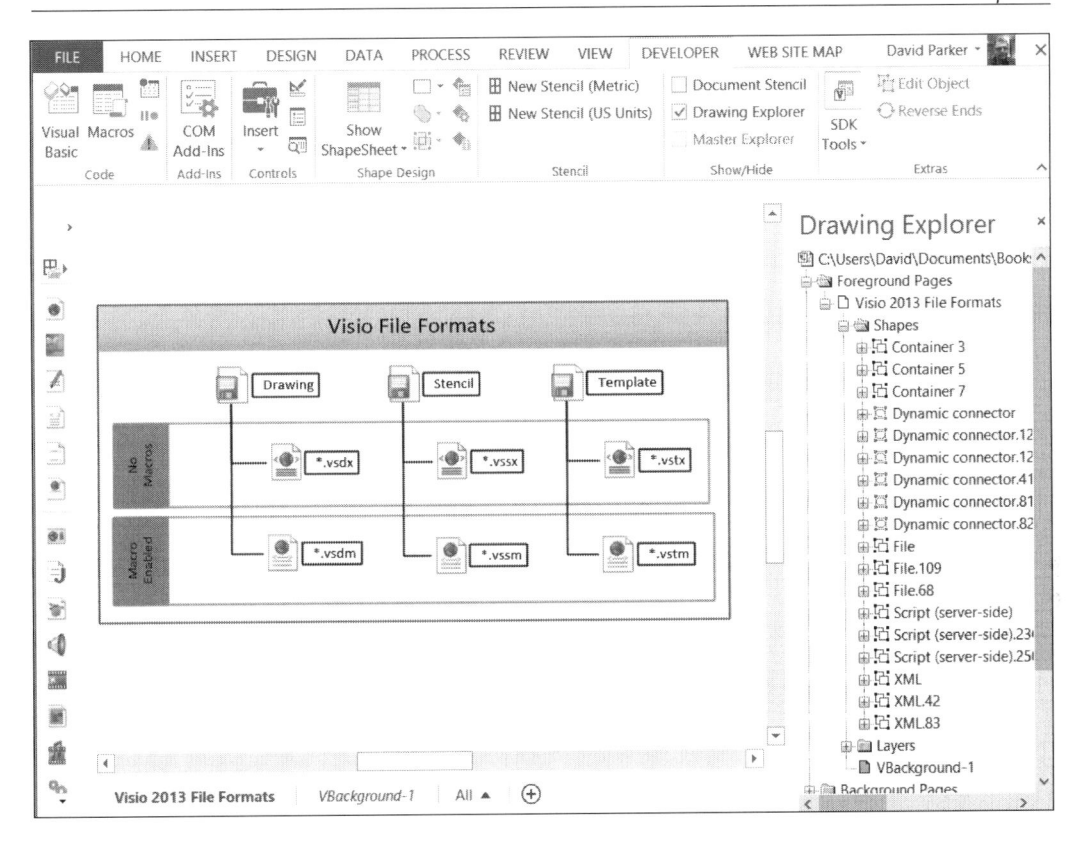

The **Drawing Explorer** window starts with the active document object as the top-level node, and displays the **Masters**, **Pages**, and **Styles** collections, among others, in subnodes.

> There are two different page collections: **Foreground Pages** and **Background Pages**. You will normally find all of the interesting shapes in the **Foreground Pages** collection, since the **Background Pages** are usually used for backgrounds and titles.

Understanding the Visio object model

We will now examine some of the key properties of the main objects in the Visio Type Library. Please note that the collections have been highlighted in the diagrams of these objects.

> The output text that is displayed within the **Immediate** window has been formatted as a table for legibility in the following code examples.

Examining the Application object

The **Application** object is the root of most collections and objects in Visio, including the Active objects, two of which are useful for traversing structured diagrams—**ActiveDocument** and **ActivePage**.

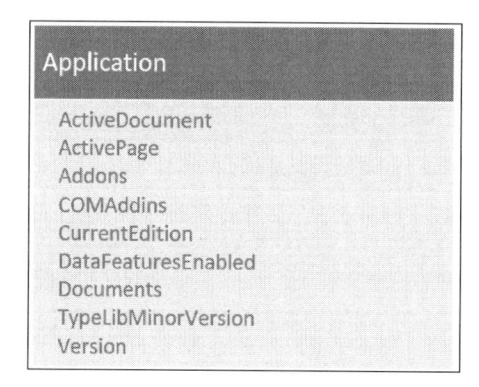

Application
- ActiveDocument
- ActivePage
- Addons
- COMAddins
- CurrentEdition
- DataFeaturesEnabled
- Documents
- TypeLibMinorVersion
- Version

The following subfunction in VBA prints out the salient information to the **Immediate** window:

```
Public Sub DebugPrintApplication()
Debug.Print "DebugPrintApplication"
    With Visio.Application
        Debug.Print , "ActiveDocument.Name", .ActiveDocument.Name
        Debug.Print , "ActivePage.Name", .ActivePage.Name
        Debug.Print , "Addons.Count", .Addons.Count
        Debug.Print , "COMAddIns.Count", .COMAddIns.Count
        Debug.Print , "CurrentEdition", .CurrentEdition
        Debug.Print , "DataFeaturesEnabled", .DataFeaturesEnabled
        Debug.Print , "Documents.Count", .Documents.Count
        Debug.Print , "TypelibMajorVersion", .TypelibMajorVersion
        Debug.Print , "TypelibMinorVersion", .TypelibMinorVersion
```

```
            Debug.Print , "Version", .Version
            Debug.Print , "Build", .Build
            Debug.Print , "FullBuild", .FullBuild
            Debug.Print , "Language", .Language
            Debug.Print , "IsVisio32", .IsVisio32
    End With
End Sub
```

An example output is:

DebugPrintApplication		
	ActiveDocument.Name	Visio Object Model.vsdm
	ActivePage.Name	Page-1
	Addons.Count	100
	COMAddIns.Count	16
	CurrentEdition	1
	DataFeaturesEnabled	True
	Documents.Count	2
	TypelibMajorVersion	4
	TypelibMinorVersion	15
	Version	15.0
	Build	4481
	FullBuild	1006702977
	Language	1033
	IsVisio32	-1

Reviewing the ActiveDocument and ActivePage objects

These objects can be referenced from the global object in VBA, but they are only available via the Application object in other languages.

Reviewing the Addons collection

Many of the Microsoft-supplied Visio templates are intended to run with some additional features that are provided as add-ons. Microsoft writes all of its additional code as C++ add-ons to Visio as Visio Solution Library files (*.vsl), which are standard DLLs with specific header information in them. Third party developers can also write Addons, but some may write them as executable files (*.exe), which are generally slower because they are not running within the Visio process thread.

You can list the Addons collections that are loaded in your Visio installation using the following code:

```
Public Sub EnumerateAddons()
Dim adn As Visio.Addon
    Debug.Print "EnumerateAddons : Count = " & _
        Application.Addons.Count
    Debug.Print , "Index", "Enabled", "NameU", "Name"
    For Each adn In Application.Addons
        With adn
            Debug.Print , .Index, .Enabled, .NameU, .Name
        End With
    Next
End Sub
```

This will output a very long list to your **Immediate** window; the first few lines are as follows:

EnumerateAddons : Count = 100

Index	Enabled	NameU	Name
1	-1	Aec	Aec
2	-1	AutoSpaceConvert	AutoSpaceConvert
3	-1	AutoSpaceDrop	AutoSpaceDrop
4	-1	AutoSpaceResize	AutoSpaceResize
5	-1	Move Shapes...	Move Shapes...
6	-1	Shape Area and Perimeter...	Shape Area and Perimeter...
7	-1	Array Shapes...	Array Shapes...
8	-1	Measure Tool	Measure Tool
9	-1	AnalystEdition.exe	AnalystEdition.exe
10	-1	BRAINSTORM	Brainstorming
11	-1	DBWiz	Database Wizard

Note that the NameU (**Universal Name**) property can be different than the Name property, although either can be used if you want to reference a particular add-on to run it. For example, if you select a shape in Visio, then type the following code into the **Immediate** window:

```
Application.Addons("Shape Area and Perimeter...").Run("")
```

This will cause the add-on to run if you have a shape selected:

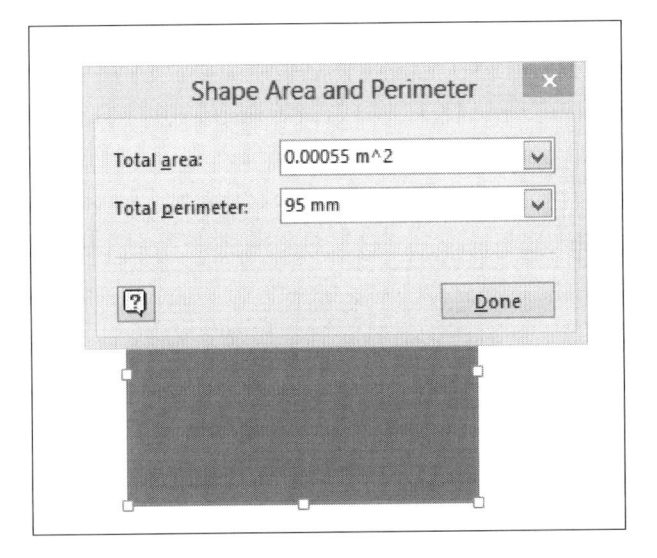

Reviewing the COMAddIns collection

Most Visio developers will use the **VSTO (Visual Studio Tools for Office)** template, installed with the Visio SDK, in Visual Studio to create a VSTO Addin. These are found in the COMAddIns collection, which is actually part of the Microsoft Office 15.0 Object Library, so you will need to set it correctly if you want **IntelliSense** to work in Visual Studio or the VB Editor.

The following code will enumerate the loaded COMAddIns in your Visio application:

```
Public Sub EnumerateCOMAddIns()
Dim adns As Office.COMAddIns
Dim adn As Office.COMAddIn
    Set adns = Application.COMAddIns
    Debug.Print "EnumerateCOMAddIns"
    Debug.Print , "Description"
    For Each adn In adns
        With adn
            Debug.Print , .Description
        End With
    Next
End Sub
```

Understanding the Microsoft Visio Object Model

The output in the **Immediate** window will be as shown in the following table (as these are custom add-ins, which I have mostly developed, you may not have most or all of the following list):

EnumerateCOMAddIns
Description
ASMLEPMTimeline
CentechDraw
DESEPMTimeline
MapPoint Office Add-In
MultiLanguageTextForVisio
multiSelect
Nexans Visio Template 3.2
NMSRoadmap
pdSelect
Mapping Edition In-Process Wrapper
RulesTools
VisioEventTestAddIn
visNet
Visual Risk Analyser
VSTOAddIn
Visio Add-In for WBS Modeler

Reviewing the CurrentEdition property

Since the `Validation` object is only in the Visio Professional edition, a further check could be included to ensure that the `CurrentEdition` value is not standard. It can be done using the following command:

```
If Application.CurrentEdition= _
    visEdition.visEditionProfessional Then
    'Insert code here
End If
```

Reviewing the DataFeaturesEnabled property

Data Linking and **Data Graphics** features are not available in Visio Standard, and they could be disabled in code in Visio Professional, so you should check that this value is `True` if you want to interact with these particular features.

Reviewing the Documents collection

The `Documents` collection contains all of the stencils and drawings that are currently open in the Visio application.

Consider this screenshot of a drawing that has been created from the **Software and Databases | UML Class** template:

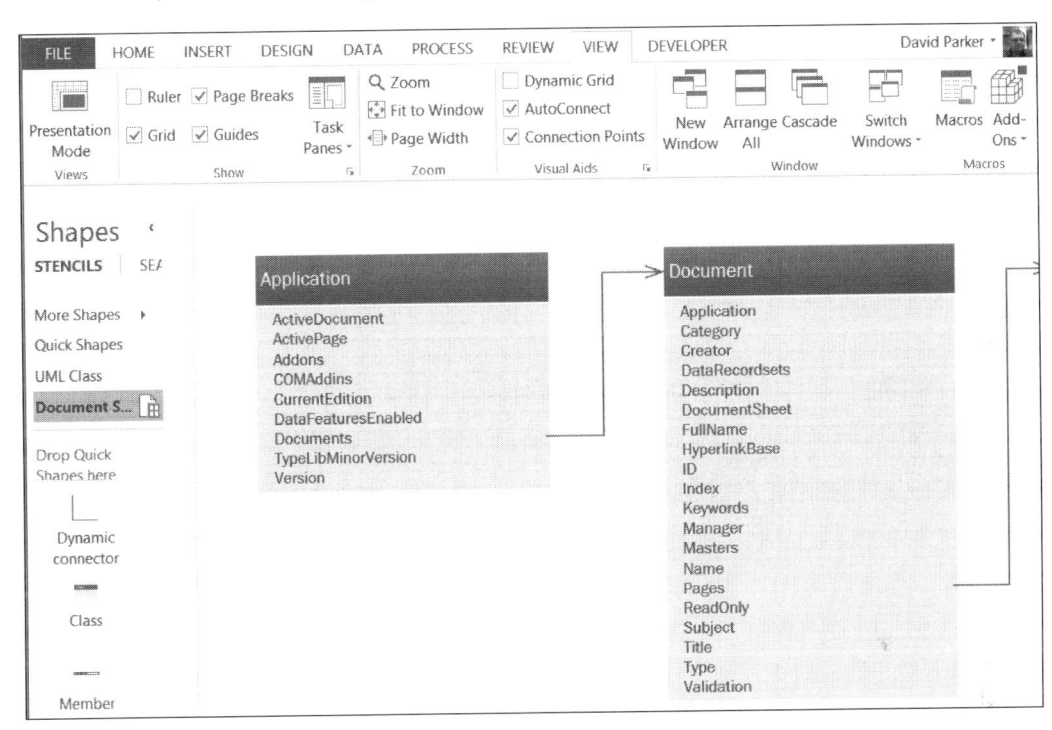

How many documents are open? Well, there is one showing, `Visio Object Model.vsd`, in the **Switch Windows** menu on the **VIEW** tab. There appear to be seven docked stencils open too.

If you were to run the following code to list the currently open documents in the Visio application:

```
Public Sub EnumerateDocuments()
Dim doc As Visio.Document
    Debug.Print "EnumerateDocuments : Count = " & _
      Application.Documents.Count
    Debug.Print , "Index", "Type", "ReadOnly", "Name", "Title"
    For Each doc In Application.Documents
        With doc
            Debug.Print , .Index, .Type, .ReadOnly, .Name, .Title
```

```
        End With
    Next
End Sub
```

Then you might get output that looks as shown in the following table:

EnumerateDocuments : Count = 2				
Index	Type	ReadOnly	Name	Title
1	1	0	Visio Object Model.vsdm	
2	2	-1	USTRME_M.VSSX	UML Class Diagram Shapes

As you can see, there are two documents, one of which is `Type = 1` (**Drawing**) and the other is `Type = 2` (**Stencil**). The **Document Stencil** is part of the drawing page, **Visio Object Model.vsd**.

Reviewing the TypelibMinorVersion and Version properties

It may also be helpful to check the version of Visio, since Validation was not available prior to Visio 2010:

```
If Application.Version = "15.0" Then
```

Or

```
If Application.TypelibMinorVersion >= 14 Then
```

Examining the Document object

The `Application.Documents` collection, seen highlighted in the following diagram, contains many `Document` objects. The `Document` object contains the collections of **DataRecordsets**, **Masters**, **Pages**, and other properties, that you may need if you are validating a document.

Application	Document
ActiveDocument	Application
ActivePage	Category
Addons	Creator
COMAddins	DataRecordsets
CurrentEdition	Description
DataFeaturesEnabled	DocumentSheet
Documents	FullName
TypeLibMinorVersion	HyperlinkBase
Version	ID
	Index
	Keywords
	Manager
	Masters
	Name
	Pages
	ReadOnly
	Subject
	Title
	Type
	Validation

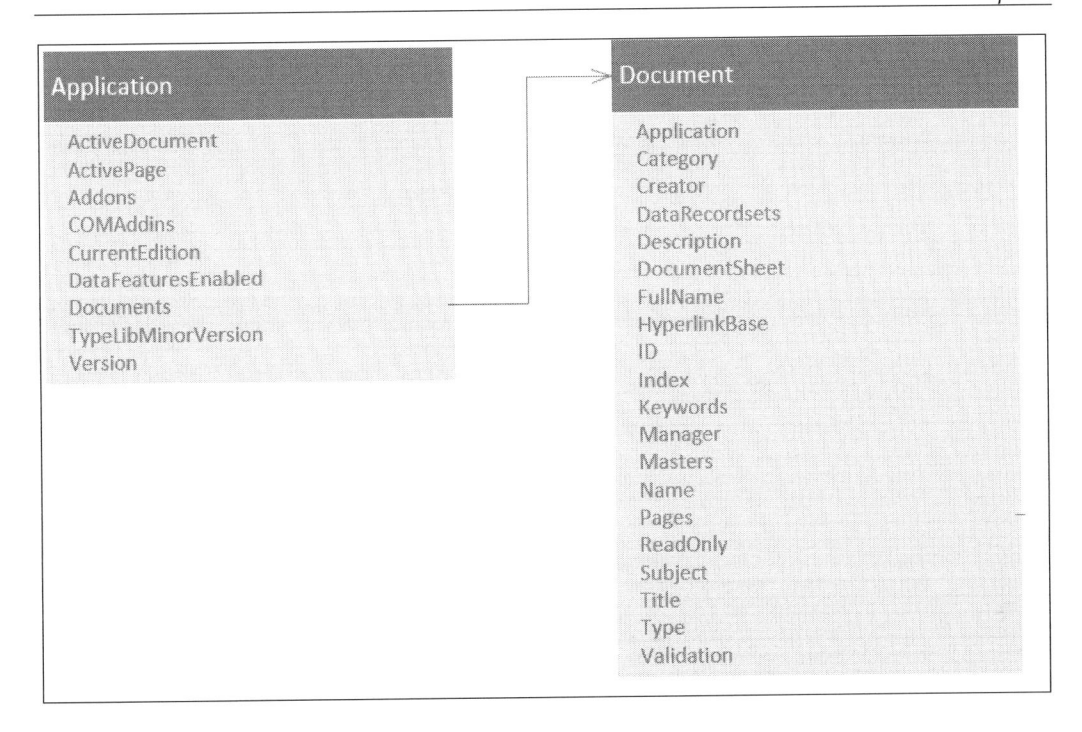

Reviewing the Advanced Properties object

The **Advanced Properties** objects, which are the document properties in the UI, could be referenced by the **Validation** expressions, as follows:

- **Category**
- **Creator** displayed as **Author** in the **Properties** dialog
- **Description** displayed as **Comments** in the **Properties** dialog
- **HyperlinkBase**
- **Keywords** displayed as **Tags** in the **Properties** dialog
- **Manager**
- **Subject**
- **Title**

Understanding the Microsoft Visio Object Model

You can view these values in the backstage panel, and in the **Advanced Properties** option on the **Properties** button. The following code will print out the document's properties:

```
Public Sub DebugPrintDocumentAdvancedProperties()
    Debug.Print "DebugPrintDocumentAdvancedProperties : " & _
        ActiveDocument.Name
    With ActiveDocument
        Debug.Print , "Title", .Title
        Debug.Print , "Subject", .Subject
        Debug.Print , "Author", .Creator
        Debug.Print , "Manager", .Manager
        Debug.Print , "Company", .Company
        Debug.Print , "Language", .Language
        Debug.Print , "Categories", .category
        Debug.Print , "Tags", .Keywords
        Debug.Print , "Comments", .Description
        Debug.Print , "HyperlinkBase", .HyperlinkBase
    End With
End Sub
```

The output will be as follows:

```
DebugPrintDocumentAdvancedProperties : Visio Object Model.vsdm
```

Title	Business Process Diagramming in Visio 2013
Subject	The Visio Object Model
Author	David Parker
Manager	Packt Publishing
Company	bVisual ltd
Language	1033
Categories	Samples
Tags	Visio,Object Model,Type Library
Comments	This document contains sample VBA code
HyperlinkBase	http://www.visiorules.com

Reviewing the DataRecordsets collection

If you are using the **Data Linking** features, then you may want to reference one or more of the `DataRecordsets` objects in the document. The following code will list the `DataRecordsets` objects in the active Visio document:

```
Public Sub EnumerateRecordsets()
Dim doc As Visio.Document
```

```
    Dim dst As Visio.DataRecordset
        Set doc = Application.ActiveDocument
        Debug.Print "EnumerateRecordsets : Count = " & _
          doc.DataRecordsets.Count
        Debug.Print , "ID", "DataConnection", "Name"
        For Each dst In doc.DataRecordsets
            With dst
                Debug.Print , .ID, .DataConnection, .Name
            End With
        Next
    End Sub
```

The output will be as follows:

```
EnumerateRecordsets : Count = 1
ID      DataConnection      Name
1       1                   Sheet1
```

> The **Pivot Diagram** feature in Visio creates multiple `DataRecordsets` that are not visible in the normal UI.

Reviewing the DocumentSheet object

The `DocumentSheet` object is the ShapeSheet of `Documents`.

If you want to ensure that a document is uniquely identifiable, since its name can be changed, then you can use the `UniqueID` property to generate a **GUID** for the `DocumentSheet` object, for example where `doc` is a `Document` object.

```
doc.DocumentSheet.UniqueID(VisUniqueIDArgs.visGetOrMakeGUID)
```

Reviewing the ID and Index properties

An `ID` property is assigned to a document when it is added to the `Documents` collection; it will be kept so long as the document exists in the collection, whereas the `Index` property may change if other documents are closed.

Reviewing the FullName and Name properties

The `Name` property is the filename without the path, while the `FullName` property is the whole path, including the filename. Note that both of these properties include the file extension.

Understanding the Microsoft Visio Object Model

Reviewing the Masters collection

The `Document` object contains the `Masters` collection as shown in the given code:

```
Public Sub EnumerateMasters()
Dim doc As Visio.Document
Dim mst As Visio.Master
    Set doc = Application.ActiveDocument
    Debug.Print "EnumerateMasters : Count = " & doc.Masters.Count
    Debug.Print , "ID", "Type", "OneD", "Hidden", "Name"
    For Each mst In doc.Masters
        With mst
            Debug.Print , .ID, .Type, .OneD, .Hidden, .Name
        End With
    Next
End Sub
```

This code will produce the output as follows:

```
EnumerateMasters : Count = 5
```

ID	Type	OneD	Hidden	Name
3	1	-1	0	Dynamic connector
5	4	0	0	Composite
8	1	0	0	Class
9	1	0	0	Member
10	1	0	0	Separator

The `Type=1` is the constant `visMasterTypes.visTypeMaster`. There are other types for fills, themes, and data graphics but they will usually be hidden to ensure that the user does not accidently drag-and-drop them off the document stencil in the UI.

Reviewing the Pages collection

The `Pages` collection of the `Document` object contains all pages in the document, regardless of the type; thus you may need to filter by type when you are traversing them.

The following code provides a simple enumeration of the pages:

```
Public Sub EnumeratePages()
Dim doc As Visio.Document
Dim pag As Visio.Page
    Set doc = Application.ActiveDocument
    Debug.Print "EnumeratePages : Count = " & doc.Pages.Count
```

[48]

```
        Debug.Print , "Index", "ID", "Type", "Name"
        For Each pag In doc.Pages
            With pag
                Debug.Print , .Index, .ID, .Type, .Name
            End With
        Next
    End Sub
```

The output will be as follows:

EnumeratePages	:	Count	= 3
Index	ID	Type	Name
1	0	1	Page-1
2	5	1	Page-2
3	6	1	Page-3

> The value of the ID property does not need to be contiguous

Reviewing the ReadOnly property

This is a Boolean (True/False) property. Usually, docked stencils are read-only, and Visio-supplied ones cannot normally be edited. If you need to save a document in code, then it is useful to check that it can be saved first.

Reviewing the Type property

You can test for the type of document in code to ensure that it is the type that you want:

```
If doc.Type=VisDocumentTypes.visTypeDrawing Then
...
```

The other types are visTypeStencil and visTypeTemplate.

Reviewing the Validation object

The Validation object provides access to the **Validation API** and will be discussed at length in *Chapter 4, Understanding the Validation API*.

Examining the Master object

When a Master shape is dragged and dropped from a stencil onto a page (or by using any of the `PageDrop` methods), then Visio checks the local document stencil to see if the master already exists.

If a master name exists already and it has not been edited locally, or even if it has and the `MatchByName` property is `true`, then the shape becomes an instance of the local master. If it does not exist, then the master is copied from the docked stencil to the local stencil, so that the shape can become an instance of it.

> The `MatchByName` property can be set by editing a master's properties in the user interface, and changing the **Match Master By Name on Drop** checkbox in the **Master Properties** dialog.

If you open a master on your local document stencil via **Edit Master | Edit Master Shape**, then you can open the **Master Explorer** window. You can then see that it is usually composed of a single shape which often has a **Shapes** collection within it.

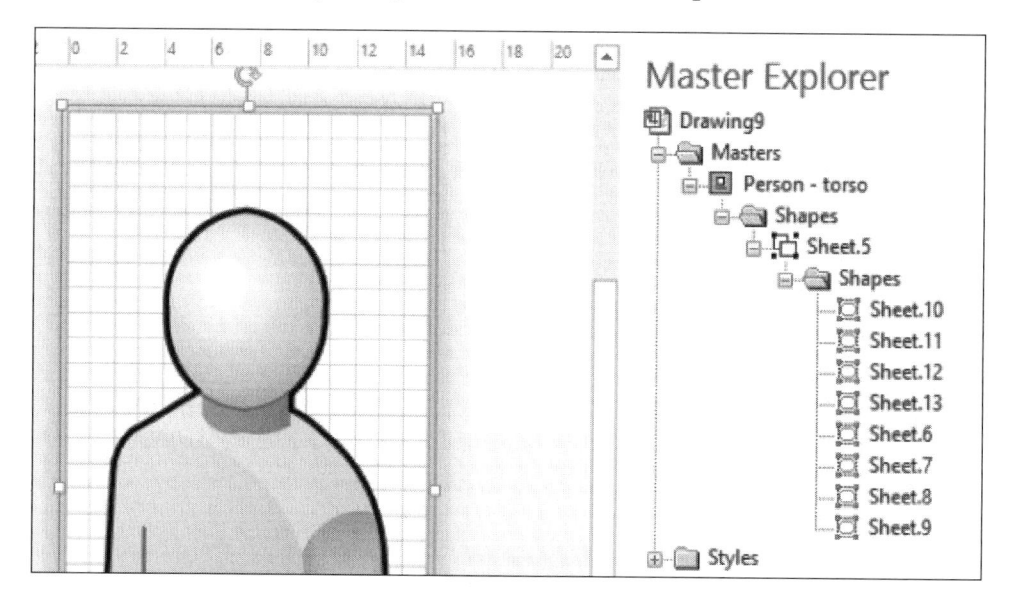

You can do a certain amount of editing to the shape in a local master, and have these changes propagated to all instances within the document. However, many users make the assumption that you can simply replace the master in a document to update the instances. This is not so, although some third-parties have attempted to make tools that can perform this task.

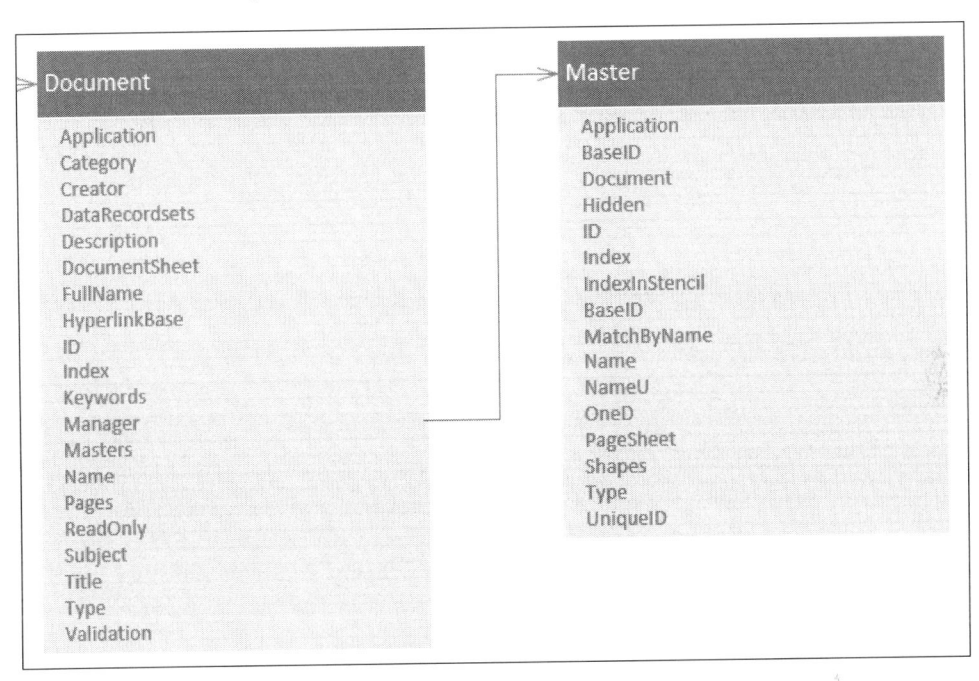

Document	Master
Application	Application
Category	BaseID
Creator	Document
DataRecordsets	Hidden
Description	ID
DocumentSheet	Index
FullName	IndexInStencil
HyperlinkBase	BaseID
ID	MatchByName
Index	Name
Keywords	NameU
Manager	OneD
Masters	PageSheet
Name	Shapes
Pages	Type
ReadOnly	UniqueID
Subject	
Title	
Type	
Validation	

Reviewing the BaseID property

It is possible that many Masters have been derived from the same root Masters, in which case they would all have the same `BaseID`.

Reviewing the Hidden property

If this value is `true`, then the `Master` object is hidden in the UI, but it still can have shape instances. This is merely the display position of the `Master` object in the stencil.

Reviewing the ID, Index, and IndexInStencil properties

An `ID` property is assigned to a master when it is added to the Masters collection, and it will be kept so long as the document exists. The `Index` property is the read-only ordinal position in the stencil, but the `IndexInStencil` property controls the display position in the stencil, and can be modified.

Reviewing the Name and NameU properties

The `Name` property is the displayed name, which could be different to the universal `NameU` property.

Reviewing the PageSheet object

The `PageSheet` object is the ShapeSheet of the `Master` object (or a `Page` object).

If you wanted to ensure that a page is uniquely identifiable, since its name can be changed, then you can use the `UniqueID` property to generate a GUID for the `PageSheet` object, for example, where `pag` is a `Page` object.

```
pag.PageSheet.UniqueID(VisUniqueIDArgs.visGetOrMakeGUID)
```

Reviewing the Type property

There are many different types of Master, since they are used to define data graphics, fills, lines, and themes; so it can be useful to check first.

```
If master.Type = Visio,visMasterTypes.visTypeMaster Then
...
```

Examining the Page object

The `Page` object contains the `Connects`, `Layers`, and most importantly, the `Shapes` collections.

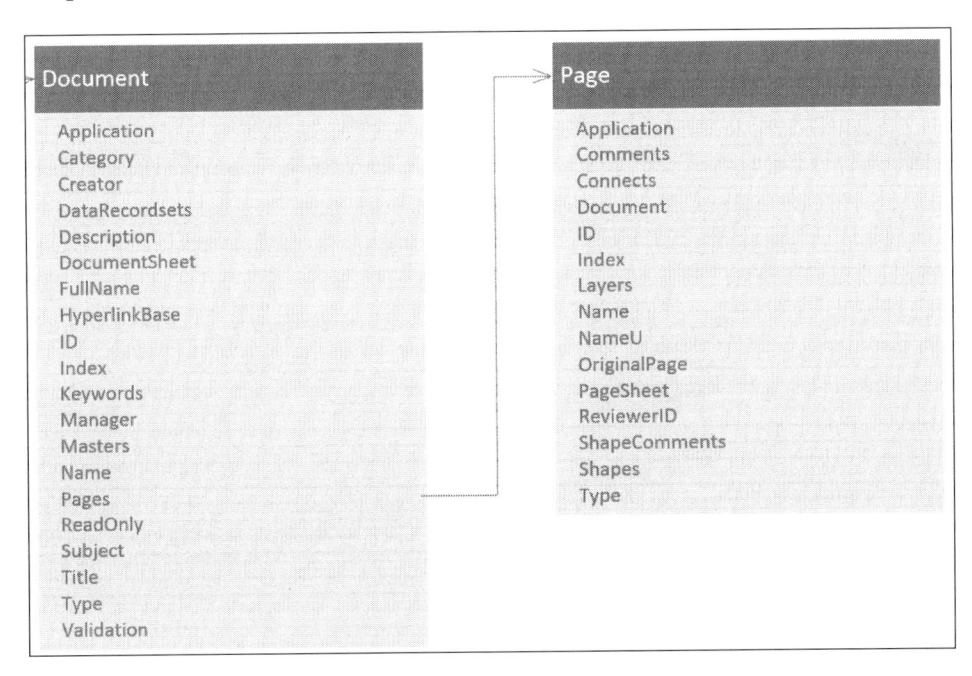

Document	Page
Application	Application
Category	Comments
Creator	Connects
DataRecordsets	Document
Description	ID
DocumentSheet	Index
FullName	Layers
HyperlinkBase	Name
ID	NameU
Index	OriginalPage
Keywords	PageSheet
Manager	ReviewerID
Masters	ShapeComments
Name	Shapes
Pages	Type
ReadOnly	
Subject	
Title	
Type	
Validation	

The `ReviewerID` property is not intended to be used anymore, because Visio 2013 has introduced the `Comments` and `ShapeComments` collections.

Reviewing the Connects collection

The page has a `Connects` collection that contains all of the shape connections in it. A developer can now use the simpler `ConnectedShapes` and `GluedShapes` methods, described later in this chapter, but it is worth understanding this collection.

Understanding the Microsoft Visio Object Model

In a process diagram, most flowchart shapes are connected to each other via a **Dynamic Connector** shape. So, each Dynamic Connector (which is `OneD`) shape is usually connected to a flowchart shape at each end of it. The cell at the start of the line is called `BeginX`, and the cell at the end is called `EndX`.

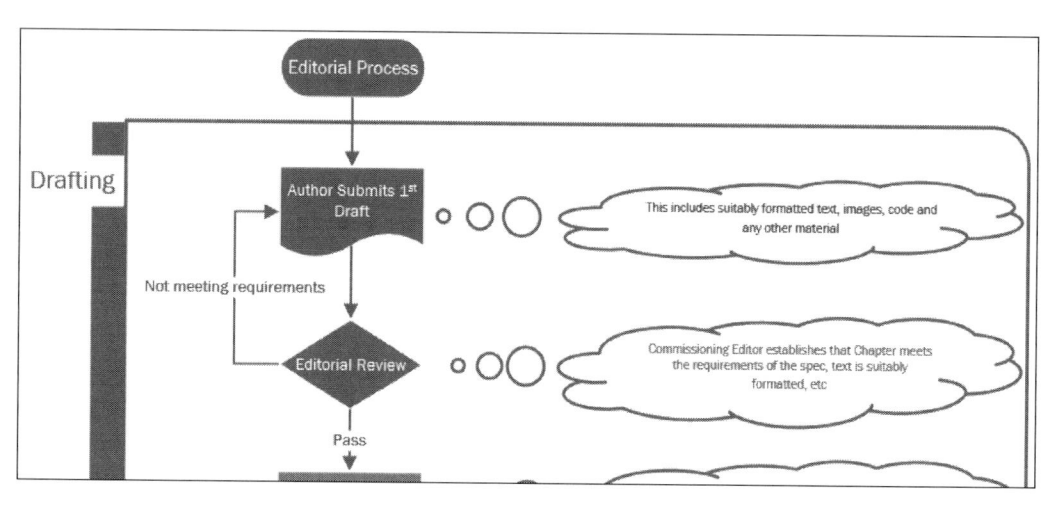

There may be times that you may need to check the particular connection point that a connector is glued to. For example, you may have named the connection point rows because they represent a network port or something specific. Therefore, it is useful to know that you can iterate the `Connects` collection with the following code:

```
Public Sub EnumeratePageConnects()
Dim pag As Visio.Page
Dim con As Visio.Connect
    Set pag = Application.ActivePage
    Debug.Print "EnumeratePageConnects : Count = " & _
      pag.Connects.Count
    Debug.Print , "Index", "FromSheet.Name", "FromCell.Name", _
      "FromSheet.Text ", _
        "ToSheet.Name", "ToCell.Name", "ToSheet.Text"
    For Each con In pag.Connects
        With con
            Debug.Print , .Index, .FromSheet.Name, .FromCell.Name, _
              .FromSheet.Text, _
                .ToSheet.Name, .ToCell.Name, .ToSheet.Text
        End With
    Next
End Sub
```

The following are the first few rows of the example output:

```
EnumeratePageConnects : Count = 24
```

Index	FromSheet. Name	FromCell. Name	FromSheet. Text	ToSheet. Name	ToCell. Name	ToSheet. Text
1	Dynamic connector	BeginX		Start/End	PinX	Editorial Process
2	Dynamic connector	EndX		Document	PinX	Author Submits 1st Draft
3	Dynamic connector.5	BeginX		Document	PinX	Author Submits 1st Draft
4	Dynamic connector.5	EndX		Decision	PinX	Editorial Review
5	Dynamic connector.7	BeginX	Pass	Decision	PinX	Editorial Review

The text on each shape is displayed in the output to make it easier to understand, but it is more likely that you will need to read the Shape Data on each shape in more complex diagrams.

Reviewing the ID and Index properties

An `ID` property is assigned to a page when it is added to the `Pages` collection; it will be kept, whereas the `Index` property will change if the page order is modified.

Reviewing the Layers collection

A page can contain many layers, which can have their `Visible` and `Print` setting toggled among other options. However, changing the display of layers by updating the `Visible` property is not supported in the Visio Web Access—you will see the layers in the state they were when the Visio document was saved to SharePoint. This is probably because a Visio shape can belong to none or many layers, making the correlation to XAML very difficult.

Users often confuse layers with the display order in the Z-order or index. The Z-index is controlled by the index of the shape within the page. The `Move Forwards`, `Move to Front`, `Move Backwards`, and `Move to Back` commands merely change the index of the affected shapes. However, Visio 2010 introduced a new way to control the display level, which will be discussed in the next chapter. The Visio user can access the layer settings from the **Layer Properties** dialog.

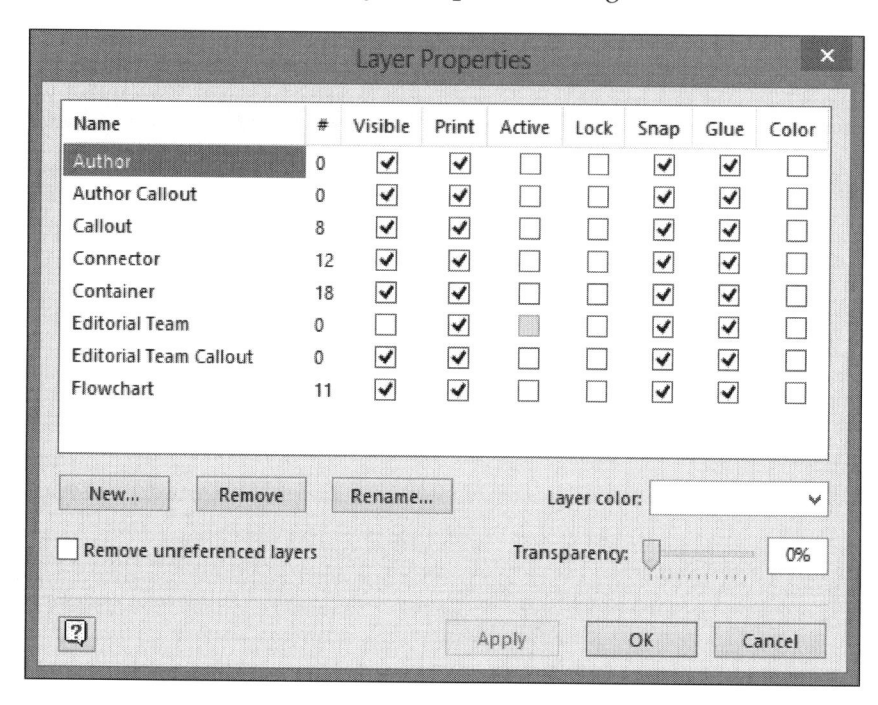

Name	#	Visible	Print	Active	Lock	Snap	Glue	Color
Author	0	✔	✔	☐	☐	✔	✔	☐
Author Callout	0	✔	✔	☐	☐	✔	✔	☐
Callout	8	✔	✔	☐	☐	✔	✔	☐
Connector	12	✔	✔	☐	☐	✔	✔	☐
Container	18	✔	✔	☐	☐	✔	✔	☐
Editorial Team	0	☐	✔	▨	☐	✔	✔	☐
Editorial Team Callout	0	✔	✔	☐	☐	✔	✔	☐
Flowchart	11	✔	✔	☐	☐	✔	✔	☐

The sum of the number of shapes on each layer can be less or greater than the total number of shapes on a page, because a shape can belong to none or multiple layers, and shapes with subshapes can have different layer membership.

The **Drawing Explorer** window provides an easy way of viewing the list of shapes assigned to each layer.

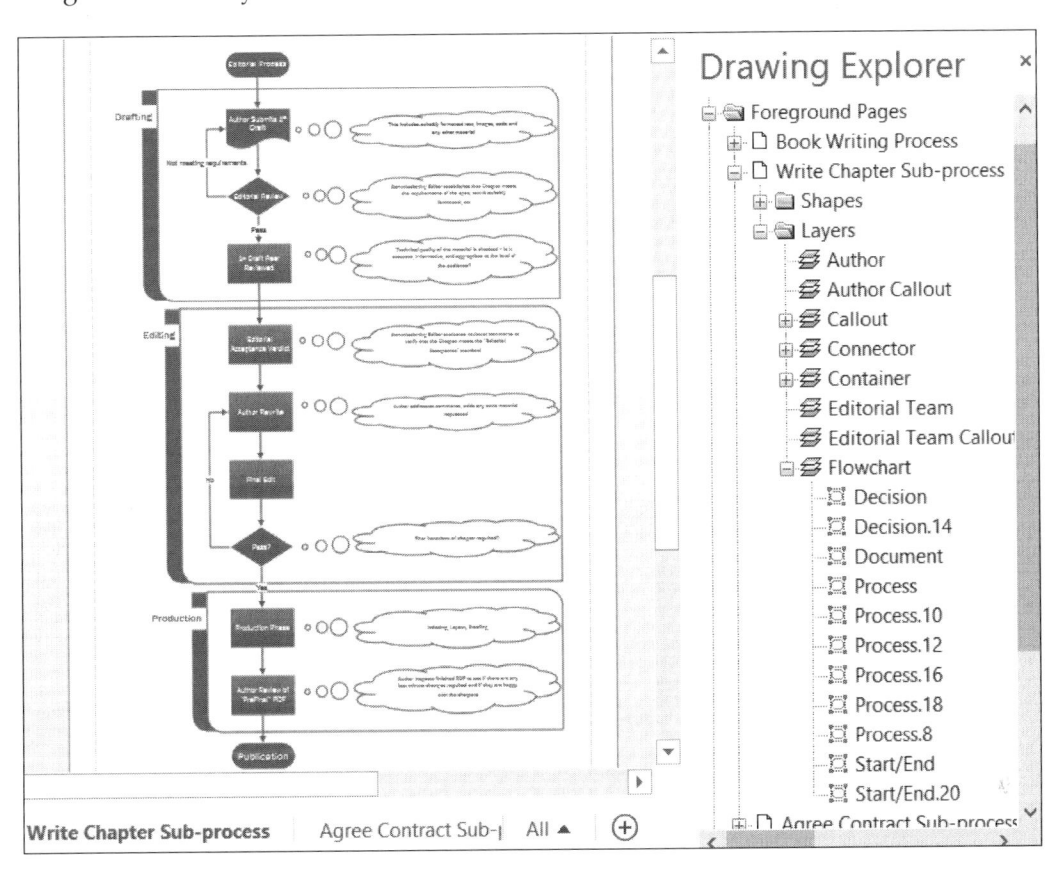

It is important to understand that there is no guarantee that a similar named layer will have the same index on different pages in the same document. Also, layer control is generally done at a page level, rather than a document level. Therefore, it is useful to understand how you can iterate the layers on a page in code, as in the following example:

```
Public Sub EnumeratePageLayers()
Dim pag As Visio.Page
Dim lyr As Visio.Layer
    Set pag = Application.ActivePage
    Debug.Print "EnumeratePageLayers : Count = " & _
      pag.Layers.Count
    Debug.Print , "Index", "Row", "Visible", "Print", "Name"
    For Each lyr In pag.Layers
        With lyr
```

```
                Debug.Print , .Index, .Row,
                    .CellsC(VisCellIndices.visLayerVisible),
                    .CellsC(VisCellIndices.visLayerPrint), .Name
            End With
        Next
    End Sub
```

The output will be as follows:

```
EnumeratePageLayers : Count = 8
    Index    Row      Visible    Print    Name
    1        0        1          1        Flowchart
    2        1        1          1        Connector
    3        2        1          1        Callout
    4        3        1          1        Author Callout
    5        4        0          1        Editorial Team
    6        5        1          1        Editorial Team Callout
    7        6        1          1        Author
    8        7        1          1        Container
```

Layers are useful for controlling visibility of shapes assigned to them, and they provide a way of retrieving a selection of shapes. They can also be part of a validation expression.

Reviewing the PageSheet object

The `PageSheet` object is the ShapeSheet of the `Master` or a `Page` object. (See the *Examining the Master object* section covered previously).

Reviewing the Comments and ShapeComments property

The **REVIEW** tab in Visio 2013 has been revised because a new method of commenting on pages and shapes has been introduced and is intended to replace the reviewers' markup in the previous versions. Comments can now be added by Visio or SharePoint 2013 users via the Visio Web Access control. The latter method means that even those users who do not have Visio installed can add comments to Visio documents.

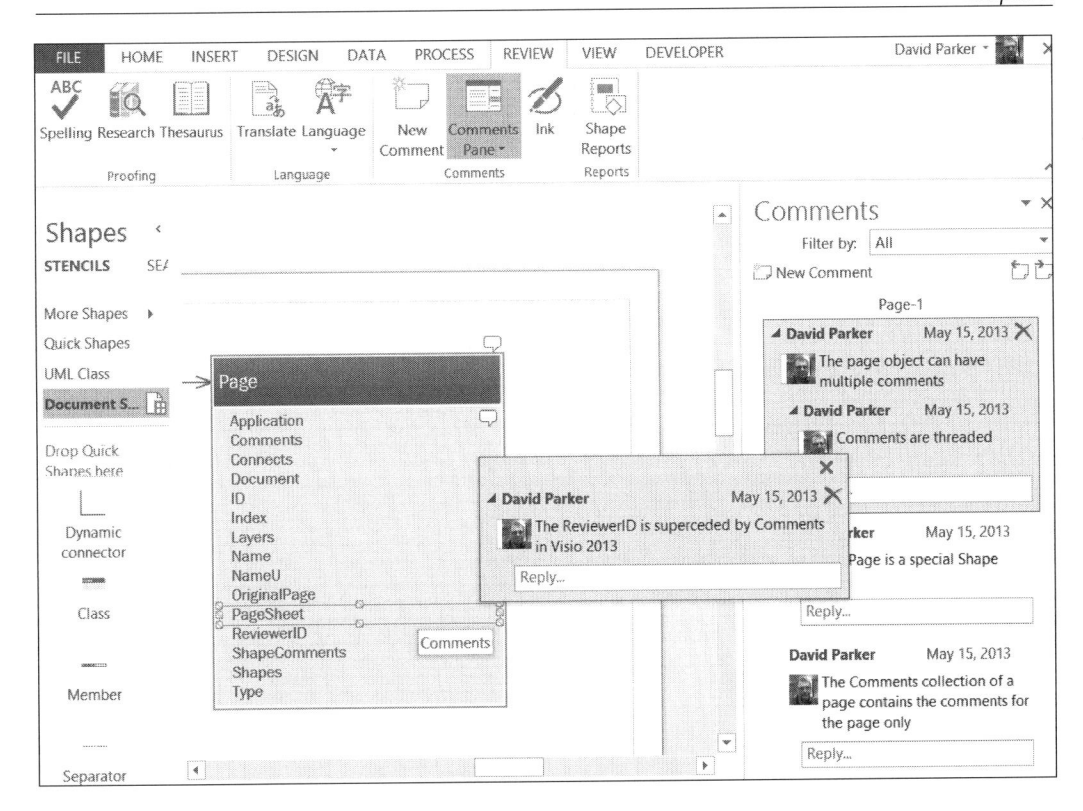

The following code can be run to list the active page comments and all of the comments of the shapes on the page:

```
Public Sub EnumerateComments()
Dim pag As Visio.Page
    Set pag = Application.ActivePage
    Debug.Print "UserName : " & pag.Application.Settings.UserName
    Debug.Print "UserInitials : " & _
      pag.Application.Settings.UserInitials
    Debug.Print "EnumerateComments for " & pag.Name
    Debug.Print , "Source", "Date", "Initials", "Name", "Text"
    Dim cmnt As Visio.Comment
    For Each cmnt In pag.Comments
         Debug.Print , cmnt.CreateDate, cmnt.AuthorInitials, _
             cmnt.AuthorName, cmnt.AssociatedObject, cmnt.Text
    Next
End Sub
```

Understanding the Microsoft Visio Object Model

The output will be as follows:

```
UserName : David Parker

UserInitials : DP

EnumerateComments for Page-1
```

Date	Initials	Name	Associated Object	Text
15/05/2013 10:18:45	DP	David Parker	Member.158	The Comments collection is new in Visio 2013
15/05/2013 10:45:59	DP	David Parker	Member.93	The ShapeComments collection of a page contains all of the comments on each of the shapes in the page
15/05/2013 10:46:50	DP	David Parker	Member.81	The Comments collection of a page contains the comments for the page only
15/05/2013 10:48:22	DP	David Parker	Page-1	The page object can have multiple comments
15/05/2013 10:49:19	DP	David Parker	Page-1	Comments are threaded
15/05/2013 10:50:09	DP	David Parker	Member.103	The ReviewerID is superceded by Comments in Visio 2013
15/05/2013 11:05:02	DP	David Parker	Class.75	The Page is a special Shape

The `ShapeComments` collection does not work at the time of writing, but it has been reported to Microsoft. However, you can use the `AssociatedObject` property to figure out the target page or shape.

> Comments are not displayed in the Microsoft SharePoint 2010 Web Part, which displays the Visio document for the web format (`*.vdw`).

Reviewing the Shapes collection

Each Page, Master, or Shape object can have a Shapes collection. The Shapes collections contain all of the shapes, whether they are instances of a Master, or simple drawn lines, rectangles, text, and so on.

In the following example, I have shown simply how to iterate through the shapes on a page:

```
Public Sub EnumeratePageShapes()
Dim pag As Visio.Page
Dim shp As Visio.Shape
    Set pag = Application.ActivePage
    Debug.Print "EnumeratePageShapes : Count = " &
      pag.Shapes.Count
    Debug.Print , "Index", "ID", "Type", "OneD", "Is Instance",
      "Name", "Text"
    For Each shp In pag.Shapes
        With shp
            Debug.Print , .Index, .ID, .Type, .OneD, Not .Master
              Is Nothing, .Name, .Text
        End With
    Next
End Sub
```

A few lines from the output are as follows:

EnumeratePageShapes : Count = 34

Index	ID	Type	OneD	Is Instance	Name	Text
1	63	2	0	True	Notch	Production
2	69	2	0	True	Notch.69	Editing
3	75	2	0	True	Notch.75	Drafting
4	1	3	0	True	Start/End	Editorial Process
5	3	3	-1	True	Dynamic connector	
6	2	3	0	True	Document	Author Submits 1st Draft
7	5	3	-1	True	Dynamic connector.5	
8	4	3	0	True	Decision	Editorial Review

Understanding the Microsoft Visio Object Model

It may be necessary to test that specific shapes exist on a page during the validation process. For example, it may be a requirement that there is a Start/End flowchart shape.

Reviewing the Type property

There are several types of pages in Visio, namely **Foreground**, **Background**, and **Markup**. Any page in Visio can have an associated **Background** page and any number of associated **Markup** pages used by reviewers. Therefore, it is usual to check the page type in code before continuing with any operations on it.

```
If pag.Type = visPageTypes.visTypeForeground Then
...
```

The **Markup** page type is still present in Visio 2013, but you are encouraged to use the new method of adding comments to the page and shapes.

Examining the Shape object

The `Shape` object is the most important object in the Visio application, and it needs to be seen as a whole with its member `Sections`, `Rows`, and `Cells` to understand its complexity.

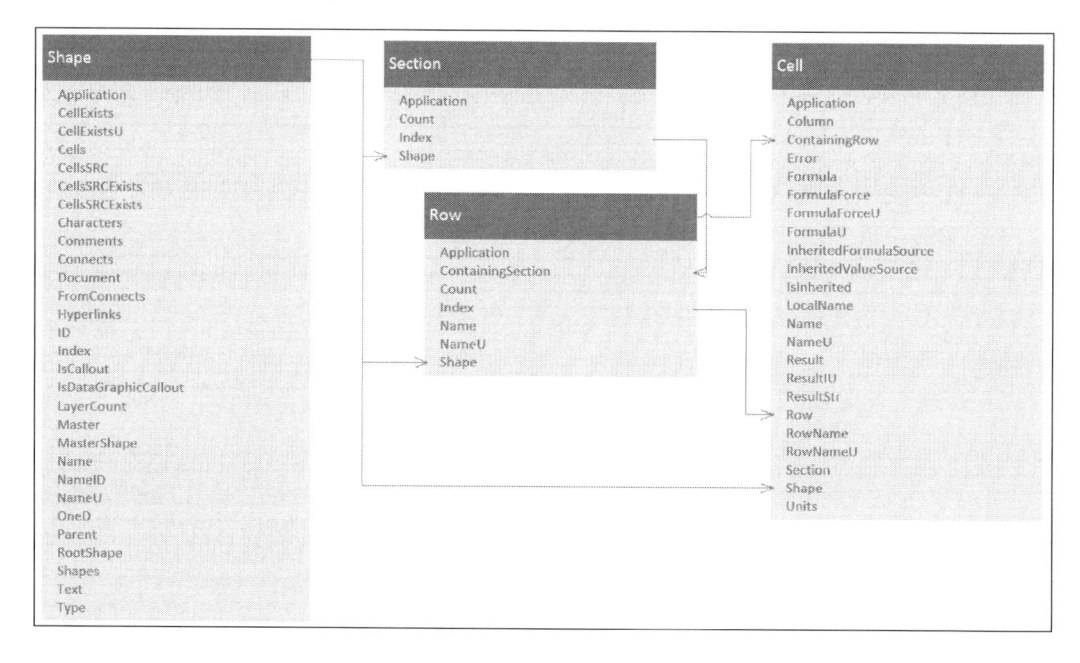

Shape
- Application
- CellExists
- CellExistsU
- Cells
- CellsSRC
- CellsSRCExists
- CellsSRCExists
- Characters
- Comments
- Connects
- Document
- FromConnects
- Hyperlinks
- ID
- Index
- IsCallout
- IsDataGraphicCallout
- LayerCount
- Master
- MasterShape
- Name
- NameID
- NameU
- OneD
- Parent
- RootShape
- Shapes
- Text
- Type

Section
- Application
- Count
- Index
- Shape

Row
- Application
- ContainingSection
- Count
- Index
- Name
- NameU
- Shape

Cell
- Application
- Column
- ContainingRow
- Error
- Formula
- FormulaForce
- FormulaForceU
- FormulaU
- InheritedFormulaSource
- InheritedValueSource
- IsInherited
- LocalName
- Name
- NameU
- Result
- ResultIU
- ResultStr
- Row
- RowName
- RowNameU
- Section
- Shape
- Units

[62]

I have not shown all the properties or relationships of the objects in the preceding screenshot, but have hopefully shown how they relate to each other.

Here is a function that prints out basic information about a selected shape into the **Immediate** window in VBA:

```
Public Sub DebugPrintShape()
If Application.ActiveWindow.Selection.Count = 0 Then
    Exit Sub
End If
Dim shp As Visio.Shape
    Set shp = Application.ActiveWindow.Selection.PrimaryItem
    Debug.Print "DebugPrintShape : " & shp.Name
    With shp
        Debug.Print , "Characters.CharCount", _
            .Characters.CharCount
        Debug.Print , "Connects.Count", .Connects.Count
        Debug.Print , "FromConnects.Count", .FromConnects.Count
        Debug.Print , "Hyperlinks.Count", .Hyperlinks.Count
        Debug.Print , "ID", .ID
        Debug.Print , "Index", .Index
        Debug.Print , "IsCallout", .IsCallout
        Debug.Print , "IsDataGraphicCallout", _
            .IsDataGraphicCallout
        Debug.Print , "LayerCount", .LayerCount
        Debug.Print , "Has Master", Not .Master Is Nothing
        Debug.Print , "Has MasterShape", _
        Not .MasterShape Is Nothing
        Debug.Print , "Name", .Name
        Debug.Print , "NameID", .NameID
        Debug.Print , "NameU", .NameU
        Debug.Print , "OneD", .OneD
        Debug.Print , "Parent.Name", .Parent.Name
        Debug.Print , "Has RootShape", Not .RootShape Is Nothing
        Debug.Print , "Text", .Text
        Debug.Print , "Type", .Type
    End With
End Sub
```

Understanding the Microsoft Visio Object Model

The preceding code produces the following output in my sample workflow, as shown in the given table, when the **Document** shape with the text `Author Submits 1st Draft` is selected before the code is run:

DebugPrintShape : Document	
Characters.CharCount	24
Connects.Count	0
FromConnects.Count	3
Hyperlinks.Count	0
ID	2
Index	6
IsCallout	False
IsDataGraphicCallout	False
LayerCount	1
Has Master	True
Has MasterShape	True
Name	Document
NameID	Sheet.2
NameU	Document
OneD	0
Parent.Name	Write Chapter Sub-process
Has RootShape	True
Text	Author Submits 1st Draft
Type	3

Reviewing the Characters and Text properties

Every shape in Visio has a text block, regardless of whether there are any characters in it. This text block can be multiple lines, contain different fonts and formats, and can even contain references to other cell values. Indeed, if a text block does contain references to other cells, then the `shape.Text` property in code will display special characters instead of the actual value. However, `shape.Characters.Text` will return the referenced cell's values. Therefore, it is usually better to use the `shape.Characters.Text` property.

Reviewing the Connects and FromConnects collections

The `Connects` collection contains the connections that the source shape is connected to, whereas the `FromConnects` collection contains the connections that are connected to the source shape.

Sounds easy, but it isn't. Traversing a structured diagram using these collections gets terribly messy, so use the newly added `ConnectedShapes` and `GluedShapes` methods, as described in the *Delving into the Connectivity API* section covered later in this chapter.

Reviewing the Hyperlinks collection

Hyperlinks can be created in the UI, in code, or even automatically by using **Data Linking**. Hyperlinks can contain `http:`, `https:`, and even `mailto:` URLs. Therefore, you may need to be aware of them, and even report on them.

Reviewing the ID, Index, NameID, Name, and NameU properties

The `Index` property is controlled by the Z-index or Z-order in the user interface (by using **Send to Back**, **Bring to Front**, and so on), whereas the `ID` property is a sequential number that is assigned when the shape is created. The `NameID` property is a concatenation of `Sheet` and `ID`.

The `Name` and `NameU` properties are automatically created, usually as a concatenation of the `Master.Name` and `ID` properties, and are originally identical. These properties can be modified (even independently of each other), but they must be unique for the `Shapes` collection of the parent. The `NameU` property is the `Shapes` collection's locale-independent name, but `Name` can be locale-specific.

Reviewing the IsCallout and IsDataGraphicCallout properties

The `IsCallout` property was a new property for Visio 2010, implemented so that you can spot more easily whether a shape is one of the new callout shapes. `IsDataGraphicCallout` was introduced in Visio 2007 so that you can identify if the parent shape is a Data Graphic shape.

Reviewing the LayerCount property

A shape can be a member of none, one, or multiple layers, which can lead to great complexity. You may wish to have a rule that a shape must only belong to a single layer.

Reviewing the Master, MasterShape, and RootShape objects

A shape in Visio can either be an instance of a `Master` object, that is one that has been dragged and dropped from a stencil, or it is one that is just drawn, like a line, rectangle, ellipse, or text. You can test this by checking if the `shape.Master` or `shape.MasterShape` object exists (`Is Nothing`) or not.

If the shape is part of a `Master` instance, then the `RootShape` object is the top-level shape of the instance.

Reviewing the OneD property

The `OneD` property is `true` if the shape is set to behave like a line.

Reviewing the Parent object

The `Parent` property is never `Nothing`, but it can be either a `Page`, `Master`, or `Shape` property.

Note that the `Parent` object may also be one of the following `Containing` properties:

- A shape in the `Page.Shapes` collection always has values for the `ContainingPage` and `ContainingPageID` properties
- A shape in the `Master.Shapes` collection always has values for the `ContainingMaster` and `Containing MasterID` properties
- A shape in the `Shape.Shapes` collection always has values for the `ContainingShape` and `ContainingShapeID` properties

Reviewing the Type property

A shape can be a group of other shapes, in which case the `shape.Type` property will be equal to `VisShapeTypes.visTypeGroup`, and the `shape.Shapes` collection will probably contain other shapes.

There are other shape types too, such as **Guide** and **Ink**, but most will be `VisShapeTypes.visTypeShape` or `VisShapeTypes.visTypeGroup`.

Examining the Section object

Visio ShapeSheets have two types of Section objects—fixed and variable. You can always rely upon a fixed `Section` object being present; thus, you do not need to test for its existence before referencing it.

However, some sections are optional (and, in the case of Geometry, there may be multiple occurrences). Therefore, you may need to test for their existence before referencing them. The most common variable `Section` objects that you will need to be aware of are for **Shape Data**, **User-defined Cells**, and less often, **Hyperlinks**. You will learn more about these in *Chapter 3, Understanding the ShapeSheet™*.

Use the enum `VisSectionIndices` in the Visio Type Library to get the right integer value for the `Section.Index` property. For example, you could test for the presence of a Shape Data section object in a shape as follows (where `shp` is a `Shape` object):

```
If shp.SectionExists(VisSectionIndices.visSectionProp,
   VisExistsFlags.visExistsAnywhere) Then...
```

You can get the number of `Rows` (the collection of `Rows`) in a `Section` object using the `RowCount` method as follows:

```
For i = 0 to shp.RowCount(VisSectionIndices.visSectionProp) -1...
```

Examining the Row object

Sections contain `Row` objects, just like a worksheet in Excel, and each `Row` contains cells. All of the interesting information is at the `Cell` object level.

Take this example where a **Document** shape is selected.

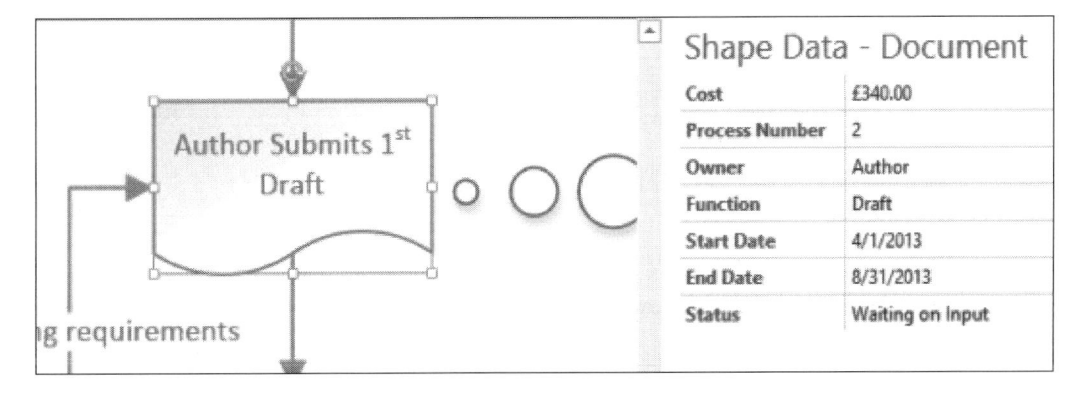

Shape Data - Document	
Cost	£340.00
Process Number	2
Owner	Author
Function	Draft
Start Date	4/1/2013
End Date	8/31/2013
Status	Waiting on Input

[67]

Understanding the Microsoft Visio Object Model

You can enumerate through the cells of the **Shape Data** section using the following code:

```
Public Sub EnumerateShapePropRows()
If Application.ActiveWindow.Selection.Count = 0 Then
    Exit Sub
End If
Dim shp As Visio.Shape
Dim iRow As Integer
Dim cel As Visio.Cell
    Set shp = Application.ActiveWindow.Selection.PrimaryItem
    Debug.Print "EnumerateShapePropRows : " & shp.Name
    If Not shp.SectionExists(VisSectionIndices.visSectionProp, _
      VisExistsFlags.visExistsAnywhere) Then
        Debug.Print , "Does not contain any Shape Data rows"
        Exit Sub
    End If
    With shp
        Debug.Print , "Shape Data row count : ", _
          .RowCount (VisSectionIndices.visSectionProp)
        Debug.Print , "Row", "RowName", "Label"
      For iRow = 0 To .RowCount(VisSectionIndices.visSectionProp) _
          - 1
            Set cel = .CellsSRC(VisSectionIndices.visSectionProp, _
              iRow, 0)
            Debug.Print , cel.Row, cel.RowName, _
              .CellsSRC(VisSectionIndices.visSectionProp, iRow, _
              VisCellIndices.visCustPropsLabel).ResultStr ("")
        Next iRow
    End With
End Sub
```

The output will be as follows:

EnumerateShapePropRows	: Document	
Shape Data row count	7	
Row	RowName	Label
0	Cost	Cost
1	ProcessNumber	Process Number
2	Owner	Owner
3	Function	Function
4	StartDate	Start Date
5	EndDate	End Date
6	Status	Status

> I had to use the `CellsSRC()` method to iterate through the Row object, and that I had to understand what values to use for the third parameter.

Moreover, I know that the `RowName` object is safe to use on the **Shape Data** section, but some `Section` objects do not have names for their `Row` objects.

I have also displayed the difference between the `RowName` and the `Label` object of a Shape Data row. Note that the `RowName` object cannot contain any special characters or spaces, whereas `Label` can.

Examining the Cell object

We must look a little more closely at the `Cell` object because this is where the important ShapeSheet formulae are written and the resultant values are returned. Although it is more efficient to retrieve a `Cell` object by using the `CellsSRC()` property of the `Shape` object, it will not always be readily available because the `Cell` object belongs to an optional Section. In this case, it may be necessary to use the `Cells()` and `CellsU()` properties. It is usually prudent to employ the `CellsExists()` or `CellsExistsU()` properties first. The following screenshot lists the cell properties:

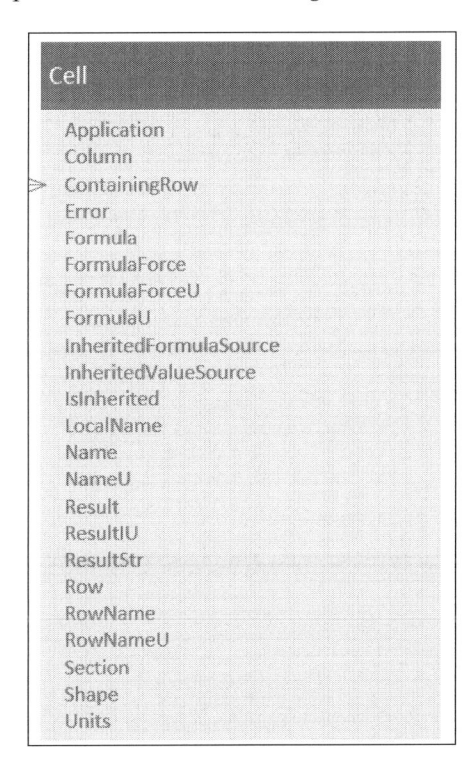

```
Cell
    Application
    Column
  > ContainingRow
    Error
    Formula
    FormulaForce
    FormulaForceU
    FormulaU
    InheritedFormulaSource
    InheritedValueSource
    IsInherited
    LocalName
    Name
    NameU
    Result
    ResultIU
    ResultStr
    Row
    RowName
    RowNameU
    Section
    Shape
    Units
```

Reviewing the Column property

There are different numbers of columns in different Sections of ShapeSheet. Therefore, you should use the `Section` specific values of the `VisCellIndices` enum to refer to a specific cell column. For example, the **User-defined Cells** section column indices begin with `visCellIndices.visUser`. However, all of the **Shape Data** section column indices begin with `visCellIndices.visCustProps` because Shape Data used to be called **Custom Properties**.

Reviewing the Error property

If a `Cell` formula is unable to evaluate, then the `Error` value is one of the `VisCellError` enum values. This value is generated along with the result.

Reviewing the Formula and FormulaU properties

Every `Cell` in Visio can contain a formula. This formula can contain references to other cells; because Visio works with multiple languages, the `Formula` string is the localized version of the `FormulaU` string, which is in English.

Reviewing the Name and LocalName properties

For some languages, the `LocalName` property may be different from the English `Name` property.

Reviewing the Result properties

There are quite a few different cell properties that begin with `.Result` because the data type is agnostic. Generally, you can retrieve text values using the `.ResultStr("")` property, and numeric values using the `.ResultIU` property. **IU** stands for **Internal Units** in this case (inches), but you could also use the `.Result("m")` property to return a numeric property formatted in the units of your choice.

Also, be aware that there is a powerful `Application.ConvertResult` method that you can use to convert values between units.

Reviewing the Units property

This is an integer value from the `VisUnitCodes` enum.

Iterating through cells

Now that we understand a bit more about the `Cell` object, we can iterate through some cells in the **Shape Data** rows of a selected shape. The following code utilizes the `CellsSRC()` property of the `Shape` object to print out the name, formula, and resultant values of all the **Shape Data** rows in each of the selected shapes in Visio:

```
Public Sub EnumerateShapePropCells()
If Application.ActiveWindow.Selection.Count = 0 Then
    Exit Sub
End If
Dim shp As Visio.Shape
Dim iRow As Integer
Dim iCol As Integer
Dim cel As Visio.Cell
    Set shp = Application.ActiveWindow.Selection.PrimaryItem
    Debug.Print "EnumerateShapePropRows : " & shp.Name
    If Not shp.SectionExists(VisSectionIndices.visSectionProp, _
      VisExistsFlags.visExistsAnywhere) Then
        Debug.Print , "Does not contain any Shape Data rows"
        Exit Sub
    End If
    With shp
        Debug.Print , "Shape Data row count : ", _
          .RowCount(VisSectionIndices.visSectionProp)
        Debug.Print , "Row", "RowName"
        Debug.Print , , "Column", "Cell.Name", "Cell.Formula", _
          "Cell.ResultIU", "Cell.ResultStr("""")"
        For iRow = 0 To
          .RowCount(VisSectionIndices.visSectionProp) - 1
        For iCol = 0 To
          .RowsCellCount(VisSectionIndices.visSectionProp, iRow)
            - 1
                Set cel = 
                  .CellsSRC(VisSectionIndices.visSectionProp, _
                    iRow, iCol)
                Debug.Print , , iCol, cel.Name, cel.Formula, _
                  cel.ResultIU, cel.ResultStr("")
            Next iCol
        Next iRow
    End With
End Sub
```

On my selected **Document** shape, the top of the output looks like this:

EnumerateShapePropRows	: Document			
Shape Data row count :			7	
Column	Cell.Name	Cell.Formula	Cell.ResultIU	Cell.ResultStr("")
0	Prop.Cost	CY(340,"GBP")	340	£340.00
1	Prop.Cost.Prompt	""	0	
2	Prop.Cost.Label	"Cost"	0	Cost
3	Prop.Cost.Format	"@"	0	@
4	Prop.Cost.SortKey	""	0	
5	Prop.Cost.Type	7	7	7
6	Prop.Cost.Invisible	FALSE	0	FALSE
7	Prop.Cost.Verify	FALSE	0	FALSE
8	Prop.Cost.DataLinked		0	FALSE
9	Prop.CostH27		0	FALSE
10	Prop.CostI27		0	FALSE
11	Prop.CostJ27		0	FALSE
12	Prop.CostK27		0	FALSE
13	Prop.CostL27		0	FALSE
14	Prop.Cost.LangID	1033	1033	1033
15	Prop.Cost.Calendar	0	0	0

The cells numbered 9 to 13 stick out because they do not appear in the UI at all. In fact, these are reserved for internal use or future use by Microsoft, so use them at your peril!

Chapter 2

Delving into the Connectivity API

All of the preceding sections were to get you used to the object model a bit, so that you can understand how to traverse a structured diagram and retrieve the information that you want. The **Connectivity API** also provides easy methods for creating and deleting connections, but we are simply interested in traversing connections in order to check or export the process steps to another application.

Here is the top part of the **Write Chapter Sub-process** page that demonstrates some of the key features of the Connectivity API. They are done in the following sequence:

1. The flow shapes are connected together, creating a logical sequence of steps.
2. Some steps have an associated callout with extra notes.
3. Some steps are within a Container shape to define the phase.

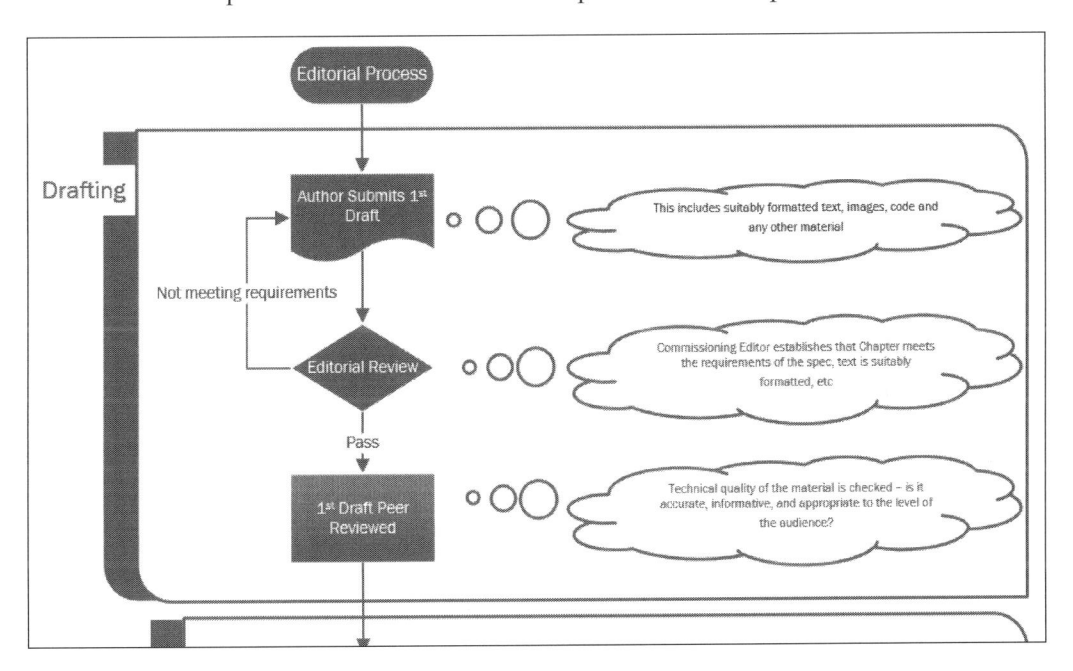

Now we will traverse the diagram in code, and list out the steps in their phases with any associated notes, but first we need to understand a few of the new methods in the Connectivity API.

Understanding the Shape.ConnectedShapes method

The `Shape.ConnectedShapes` method returns an array of **identifiers** (**IDs**) of shapes that are one degree of separation away from the given shape (that is, separated by a 1-D connector).

The method has two arguments: `Flags` and `CategoryFilter`.

- `Flags`: This filters the list of returned shape IDs by the directionality of the connectors, using the `VisConnectedShapesFlags` enum for All, Incoming, or Outgoing nodes.
- `CategoryFilter`: This filters the list of the returned shape IDs by limiting it to IDs of shapes that match the specified category. A shape's categories can be found in the `User.msvShapeCategories` cell of its ShapeSheet.

So, we can use the new `ConnectedShapes` method to list all of the significant connections in my **Write Chapter Sub-process** page. I have used the existence of the `Prop.Cost` cell as a test for shape significance.

```
Public Sub ListNextConnections()
Dim shp As Visio.Shape
Dim connectorShape As Visio.Shape
Dim sourceShape As Visio.Shape
Dim targetShape As Visio.Shape
Dim aryTargetIDs() As Long
Dim arySourceIDs() As Long
Dim targetID As Long
Dim sourceID As Long
Dim i As Integer
Const CheckProp As String = "Prop.Cost"
For Each shp In Visio.ActivePage.Shapes
    If Not shp.OneD Then
        If shp.CellExists(CheckProp, Visio.visExistsAnywhere) Then
            Debug.Print "Shape", shp.Name, shp.Text
            arySourceIDs = _
              shp.ConnectedShapes(visConnectedShapesOutgoingNodes, _
                "")
            For i = 0 To UBound(arySourceIDs)
                Set sourceShape = _
                  Visio.ActivePage.Shapes.ItemFromID(arySourceIDs(i))
                If sourceShape.CellExists(CheckProp, _
                  Visio.visExistsAnywhere) Then
                    Debug.Print , "<", sourceShape.Name, _
```

```
                        sourceShape.Text
                    End If
                Next
                aryTargetIDs = _
                  shp.ConnectedShapes(visConnectedShapesIncomingNodes, _
                    "")
                For i = 0 To UBound(aryTargetIDs)
                    Set targetShape = _
      Visio.ActivePage.Shapes.ItemFromID(aryTargetIDs(i))
                    If targetShape.CellExists(CheckProp, _
                        Visio.visExistsAnywhere) Then
                        Debug.Print , ">", targetShape.Name, _
                            targetShape.Text
                    End If
                Next
            End If
        End If
    Next
End Sub
```

The top of the output from the preceding function will appear as follows:

Shape	Start/End	Editorial Process	
	<	Document	Author Submits 1st Draft
Shape	Document	Author Submits 1st Draft	
	<	Decision	Editorial Review
	>	Start/End	Editorial Process
	>	Decision	Editorial Review
Shape	Decision	Editorial Review	
	<	Document	Author Submits 1st Draft
	<	Process	1st Draft Peer Reviewed
	>	Document	Author Submits 1st Draft
Shape	Process	1st Draft Peer Reviewed	
	<	Process.8	Editorial Acceptance Verdict
	>	Decision	Editorial Review

Understanding the Microsoft Visio Object Model

Shape	Start/End	Editorial Process	
Shape	Process.8	Editorial Acceptance Verdict	
	<	Process.10	Author Rewrite
	>	Process	1st Draft Peer Reviewed
Shape	Process.10	Author Rewrite	
	<	Process.12	Final Edit
	>	Process.8	Editorial Acceptance Verdict
	>	Decision.14	Pass?
Shape	Process.12	Final Edit	
	<	Decision.14	Pass?
	>	Process.10	Author Rewrite
Shape	Decision.14	Pass?	
	<	Process.10	Author Rewrite
	<	Process.16	Production Phase
	>	Process.12	Final Edit
Shape	Process.16	Production Phase	
	<	Process.18	Author Review of "PreFinal" PDF
	>	Decision.14	Pass?
Shape	Process.18	Author Review of "PreFinal" PDF	
	<	Start/End.20	Publication
	>	Process.16	Production Phase
Shape	Start/End.20	Publication	
	>	Process.18	Author Review of "PreFinal" PDF

Understanding the Shape.GluedShapes method

The `Shape.GluedShapes` method returns an array of identifiers for the shapes that are glued to a shape. For instance, if the given shape is a 2-D shape that has multiple connectors attached to it, this method would return the IDs of those connectors. If the given shape is a connector, this method would return the IDs of the shapes to which its ends are glued.

The method has three arguments: `Flags`, `CategoryFilter`, and `OtherConnectedShape`:

- `Flags`: This filters the list of returned shape IDs by the directionality of the connectors, using the `VisGluedShapesFlags` enum for `All1D`, `All2D`, `Incoming1D`, `Incoming2D`, `Outgoing1D`, or `Outgoing2D` nodes.
- `CategoryFilter`: This filters the list of returned shape IDs by limiting it to IDs of shapes that match the specified category. A shape's categories can be found in the `User.msvShapeCategories` cell of its ShapeSheet.
- `OtherConnectedShape`: This is an optional, additional shape to which returned shapes must also be glued

The method is used as follows:

```
arIDs = Shape.GluedShapes(Flags, CategoryFilter,
  pOtherConnectedShape)
```

Understanding the Shape.MemberOfContainers property

We can return an array of IDs of the Containers that have a shape within.

You can use the `ID` property to return the Container shape, get its `ContainerProperties` object, and, in this case, return the text from the shape.

Here is a private function that I will use in the `main` function in the following code:

```
Private Function getContainerText(ByVal shp As Visio.Shape) As
  String
'Return text of any containers,
'or an empty string if there are none
Dim aryTargetIDs() As Long
Dim targetShape As Visio.Shape
Dim returnText As String
Dim i As Integer
    returnText = ""
    aryTargetIDs = shp.MemberOfContainers
    On Error GoTo exitHere
    For i = 0 To UBound(aryTargetIDs)
        Set targetShape = _
          shp.ContainingPage.Shapes.ItemFromID(aryTargetIDs(i))
        If Len(returnText) = 0 Then
            returnText =
              targetShape.ContainerProperties.Shape.Text
```

```
        Else
            returnText = returnText & vbCrLf & _
                targetShape.ContainerProperties.Shape.Text
        End If
    Next
exitHere:
    getContainerText = returnText
End Function
```

Understanding the Shape.CalloutsAssociated property

The `Shape.CalloutsAssociated` property will return an array of shape IDs of any associated callouts.

You can use the ID to return the callout shape and, in this case, return the text from within that shape.

Here is a private function that I will use in the `main` function:

```
Private Function getCalloutText(ByVal shp As Visio.Shape) As
  String
'Return text of any connected callouts,
'or an empty string if there are none
Dim aryTargetIDs() As Long
Dim targetShape As Visio.Shape
Dim returnText As String
Dim i As Integer
    returnText = ""
    aryTargetIDs = shp.CalloutsAssociated
    On Error GoTo exitHere
    For i = 0 To UBound(aryTargetIDs)
        Set targetShape = _
          shp.ContainingPage.Shapes.ItemFromID(aryTargetIDs(i))
        If Len(returnText) = 0 Then
            returnText = targetShape.Characters.Text
        Else
            returnText = returnText & vbCrLf & _
```

```
            targetShape.Characters.Text
        End If
    Next
exitHere:
    getCalloutText = returnText
End Function
```

Listing the steps in a process flow

In order to create a sequential listing of the steps in the page, we need to create a function that will call itself to iterate through the connections out from the source shape. Accordingly, the following `getNextConnected()` method will recursively build a collection of connected shapes by employing the `ConnectedShapes()` method of the Shape object:

```
Private Function getNextConnected(ByVal shp As Visio.Shape, ByVal
  dicFlowShapes As Dictionary, ByVal colSteps As Collection) As
  Collection
'Return a collection of the next connected steps
Dim aryTargetIDs() As Long
Dim targetShape As Visio.Shape
Dim returnCollection As Collection
Dim i As Integer
    dicFlowShapes.Add shp.NameID, shp
    aryTargetIDs = _
      shp.ConnectedShapes(visConnectedShapesOutgoingNodes, "")
    For i = 0 To UBound(aryTargetIDs)
        Set targetShape = _
          shp.ContainingPage.Shapes.ItemFromID(aryTargetIDs(i))
        If Not targetShape.Master Is Nothing And _
          dicFlowShapes.Exists(targetShape.NameID) = False Then
            colSteps.Add targetShape
            getNextConnected targetShape, dicFlowShapes, colSteps
        End If
    Next
    Set getNextConnected = colSteps
End Function
```

Finally, we can create the public function that will list the steps. For simplicity, we are only following the direct route and we are not displaying the text on the connector lines.

Understanding the Microsoft Visio Object Model

We have introduced the `Visio.Selection` object because it contains a collection of shapes returned by the `Page.CreateSelection()` method, which is extremely useful for getting a filtered collection of shapes by **Layer**, **Master**, **Type**, and so on.

> The **Dictionary** object is used in the preceding and following code, so you will need to ensure that the **Microsoft Scripting Runtime** library (`C:\Windows\system32\scrun.dll`) is ticked in the **References** dialog opened from the **Tools** menu in the Visual Basic user interface.

```
Public Sub ListProcessSteps()
Dim sel As Visio.Selection
Dim pag As Visio.Page
Dim shp As Visio.Shape
Dim shpStart As Visio.Shape
Dim shpEnd As Visio.Shape
Dim iStep As Integer
Dim dicFlowShapes As Dictionary
    Set dicFlowShapes = New Dictionary
    Set pag = Visio.ActivePage
    'Find the Start and End shapes on the Page
    'Assume that they are the instances of the Master "Start/End"
    'Assume that the Start has no incoming connections
    'and the End shape has no outgoing connections
    Set sel = pag.CreateSelection(visSelTypeByMaster, 0, _
        pag.Document.Masters("Start/End"))
    If Not sel.Count = 2 Then
        MsgBox "There must be one Start shape and one End shape
          only", _
            vbExclamation, "ListProcessSteps"
        Exit Sub
    End If
    For Each shp In sel
        If shpStart Is Nothing Then
            Set shpStart = shp
            Set shpEnd = shp
        ElseIf UBound(shp.ConnectedShapes
          (visConnectedShapesOutgoingNodes, "")) > -1 _
            And UBound(shp.ConnectedShapes
              (visConnectedShapesIncomingNodes, "")) = -1 Then
                Set shpStart = shp
        ElseIf UBound(shp.ConnectedShapes
          (visConnectedShapesIncomingNodes, "")) > -1 _
            And UBound(shp.ConnectedShapes
              (visConnectedShapesOutgoingNodes, "")) = -1 Then
```

```
                Set shpEnd = shp
            End If
        Next
        iStep = 1
    Dim nextSteps As Collection
    Dim nextShp As Visio.Shape
    Dim iNext As Integer
        Set nextSteps = New Collection
        Set nextSteps = getNextConnected(shpStart, dicFlowShapes, _
            nextSteps)
        Debug.Print "Step", "Master.Name", "Phase", "Text", "Notes"
        Debug.Print iStep, shpStart.Master.Name, _
            getContainerText (shpStart), shpStart.Text, _
            getCalloutText(shpStart)
        For iNext = 1 To nextSteps.Count
            iStep = iNext + 1
            Set nextShp = nextSteps.Item(iNext)
            Debug.Print iStep, nextShp.Master.Name, _
                getContainerText(nextShp), nextShp.Characters.Text,
                getCalloutText (nextShp)
        Next
        If Not nextShp Is shpEnd Then
            MsgBox "Theprocess did not finish on the End shape", _
                vbExclamation, "ListProcessSteps"
        End If
    End Sub
```

With a fanfare of trumpets, we get a simple listing of each step in the following order:

Step	Master.Name	Phase	Text	Notes
1	Start/End		Editorial Process	
2	Document	Drafting	Author Submits 1st Draft	This includes suitably formatted text, images, code and any other material
3	Decision	Drafting	Editorial Review	Commissioning Editor establishes that Chapter meets the requirements of the spec, text is suitably formatted, etc

Step	Master.Name	Phase	Text	Notes
4	Process	Drafting	1st Draft Peer Reviewed	Technical quality of the material is checked - is it accurate, informative, and appropriate to the level of the audience?
5	Process	Editing	Editorial Acceptance Verdict	Commissioning Editor evaluates reviewer comments to verify that the Chapter meets the "Editorial Acceptance" standard
6	Process	Editing	Author Rewrite	Author addresses comments, adds any extra material requested
7	Process	Editing	Final Edit	
8	Decision	Editing	Pass?	Finer iterations of chapter required?
9	Process	Production	Production Phase	Indexing, Layout, Proofing
10	Process	Production	Author Review of "PreFinal" PDF	Author inspects finished PDF to see if there are any last minute changes required and if they are happy with the chapters
11	Start/End		Publication	

Summary

In this chapter, we delved into the Visio object model, and looked at the hierarchy of the objects and collections.

We looked at the analytical parts of the Connectivity API, which enabled us to navigate connections and to retrieve surrounding containers and associated callouts.

We also used this knowledge to build a function that does some rudimentary checks of a diagram structure, and to list the steps in a process flow.

In the next chapter, we will look into the ShapeSheet and how to use the functions within it.

3
Understanding the ShapeSheet™

Microsoft Visio is a unique data diagramming system, and most of that uniqueness is due to the power of the **ShapeSheet,** which is a window on the Visio object model. It is the ShapeSheet that enables you to encapsulate complex behavior into apparently simple shapes by adding formulae to the cells using functions. The ShapeSheet was modeled on a spreadsheet, and formulae are entered in a similar manner to cells in an Excel worksheet.

Validation rules are written as quasi-ShapeSheet formulae so you will need to understand how they are written. Validation rules can check the contents of ShapeSheet cells, in addition to verifying the structure of a diagram. Therefore, in this chapter you will learn about the structure of the ShapeSheet and how to write formulae.

Finding the ShapeSheet

There is a ShapeSheet behind every single Document, Page and Shape, and the easiest way to access the ShapeSheet window is to run Visio in Developer mode.

> You can tick **Run in developer mode** in the **General** section of the **Advanced** tab in the **Visio Options** dialog that is opened by navigating to **File | Options**.

Understanding the ShapeSheet™

This mode adds the **DEVELOPER** tab to the Fluent UI, which has a **Show ShapeSheet** button. The drop-down list on the button allows you to choose which ShapeSheet window to open, as in the following screenshot:

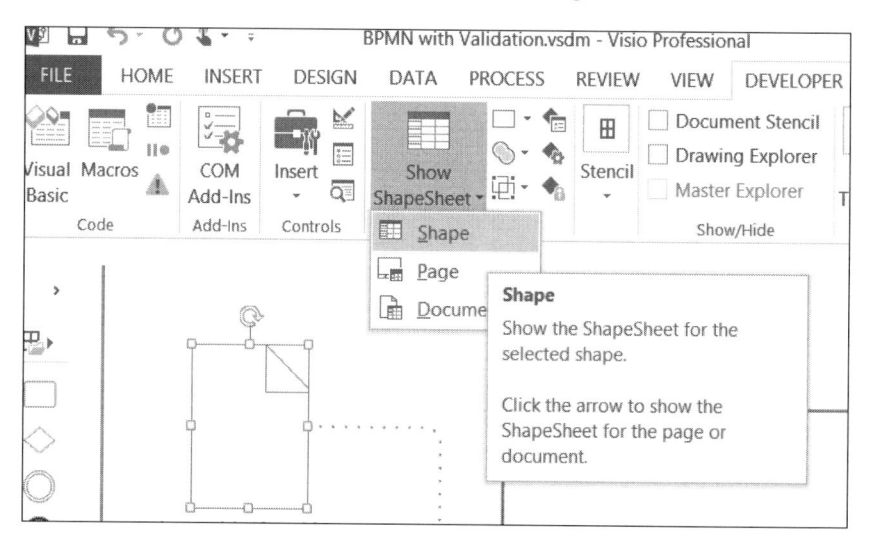

Alternatively, you can use the right-mouse menu of a shape or page, or on the relevant level within the **Drawing Explorer** window, as shown in the following screenshot:

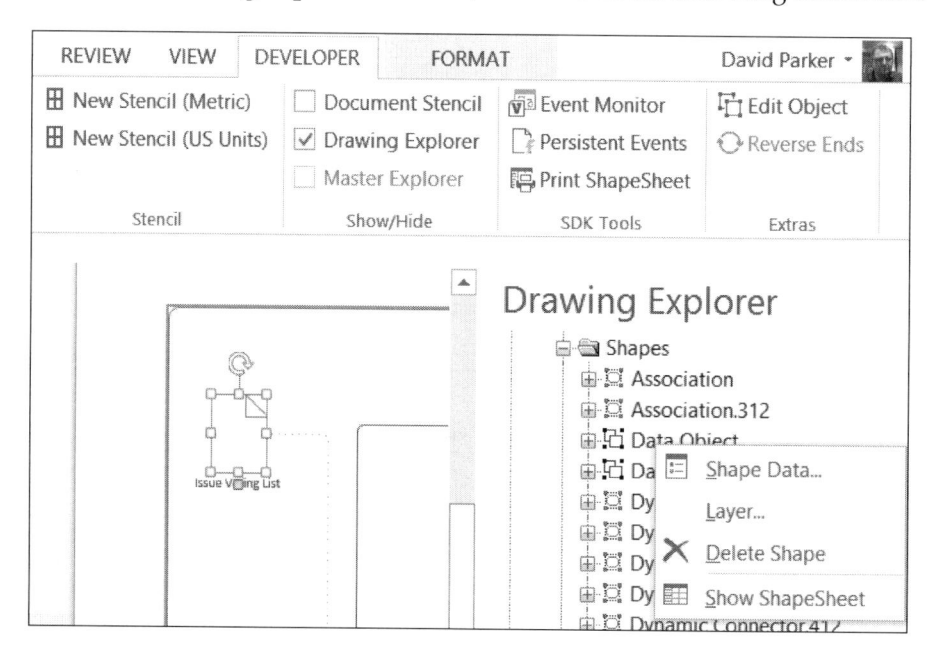

The **ShapeSheet** window, opened by clicking on the **Show ShapeSheet** menu option, displays the requested sections, rows, and cells of the item selected when the window was opened. It does not automatically change to display the contents of any subsequently selected shape in the Visio drawing page—you must open the ShapeSheet window again to do that. The **SHAPESHEET TOOLS** ribbon, which is displayed when the ShapeSheet window is active, has a **Sections** button on the **View** group of the **DESIGN** tab to allow you to vary the requested sections on display.

You can also open the **View Sections** dialog from the right mouse menu within the ShapeSheet window, as shown in the next screenshot:

You cannot alter the display order of sections in the ShapeSheet window, but you can expand/collapse them by clicking on the section header.

The syntax for referencing the shape, page, and document objects in ShapeSheet formula is listed in the following table:

Object	ShapeSheet formula	Comment
Shape	`Sheet.n!`	Where n is the ID of the shape.
		Can be omitted when referring to cells in the same shape.

Object	ShapeSheet formula	Comment
Page.PageSheet	ThePage!	Used in the ShapeSheet formula of shapes within the page.
Page	Pages[page name]!	Used in the ShapeSheet formula of shapes in other pages.
Document.DocumentSheet	TheDoc!	Used in the ShapeSheet formula in pages or shapes of the document.

Understanding sections, rows, and cells

There are a finite number of sections in a ShapeSheet; some sections are mandatory for the type of element they are, while others are optional. For example, the **Shape Transform** section, which specifies the shape's size, angle, and position, exists for all types of shapes and is therefore mandatory. The **1-D Endpoints** section, which specifies the co-ordinates of either end of the line, is only relevant, and thus displayed, for **OneD** shapes (such as connectors; it is also mandatory but is not seen in for **non-OneD** shapes. Neither of these sections is optional, because they are required for the specific type of OneDshape. Sections such as **User-defined Cells** and **Shape Data** are optional and they may be added to the ShapeSheet if they do not exist already. If you click on the **Insert** button on the **SHAPESHEET TOOLS** ribbon, under the **Sections** group of the **DESIGN** tab, then you can see a list of the sections that you may insert into the selected ShapeSheet.

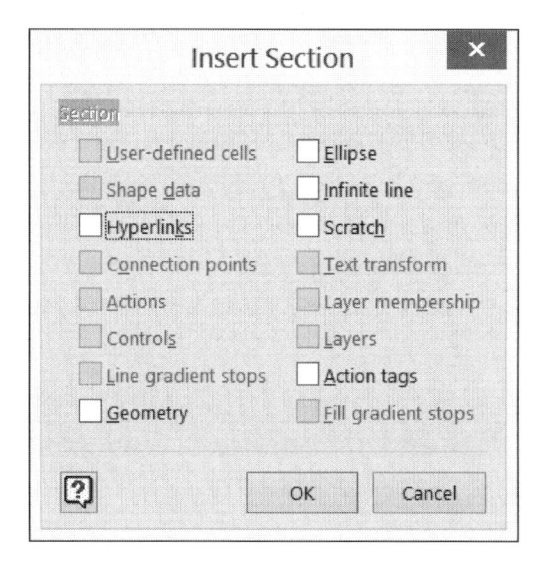

In the preceding screenshot, the **User-defined cells** option is grayed out because this optional section already exists.

It is possible for a shape to have multiple **Geometry**, **Ellipse**, or **Infinite** line sections. In fact, a shape can have a total of 139 of them.

Reading a cell's properties

If you select a cell in the **ShapeSheet**, then you will see the formula in the formula edit bar immediately below the ribbon as follows:

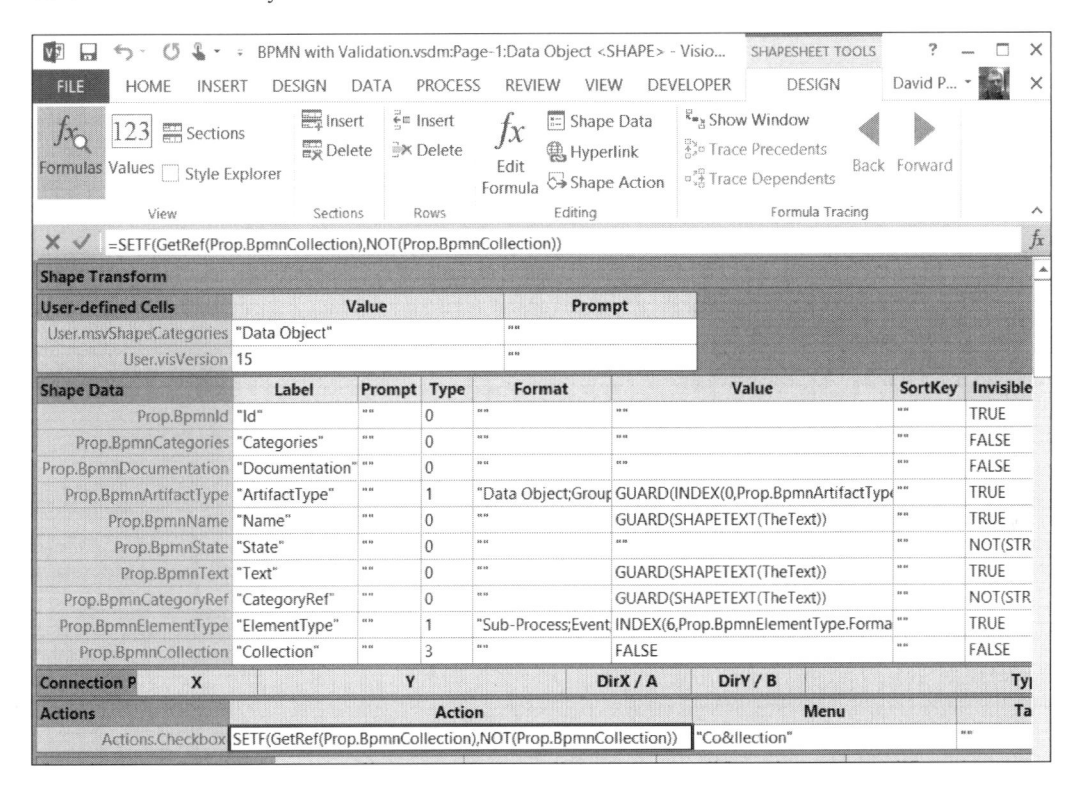

You can view the ShapeSheet **Formulas** (and I thought the plural was formulae!) or **Values** by clicking on the relevant button in the **View** group on the **ShapeSheet Tools** ribbon.

Notice that Visio provides **IntelliSense** when editing formulae. This was new in Visio 2010, and is a great help to all ShapeSheet developers.

Understanding the ShapeSheet™

Also notice that the contents of cells are shown in blue text sometimes, while others are black. This is because the blue text denotes that the values are stored locally with this shape instance, while the black text refers to values that are stored in the Master shape. Usually, the more black text you see, the more memory-efficient the shape is, since less is needed to be stored with the shape instance. Of course, there are times when you cannot avoid storing values locally, such as the **PinX** and **PinY** values in the preceding screenshot, since these define where the shape instance is in the page. The following VBA code returns 0 (`False`):

```
ActivePage.Shapes("Task").Cells("PinX").IsInherited
```

But the following code returns -1 (`True`):

```
ActivePage.Shapes("Task").Cells("Width").IsInherited
```

The **Edit Formula** button opens a dialog to enable you to edit multiple lines, since the edit formula bar only displays a single line and some formulae can be quite large.

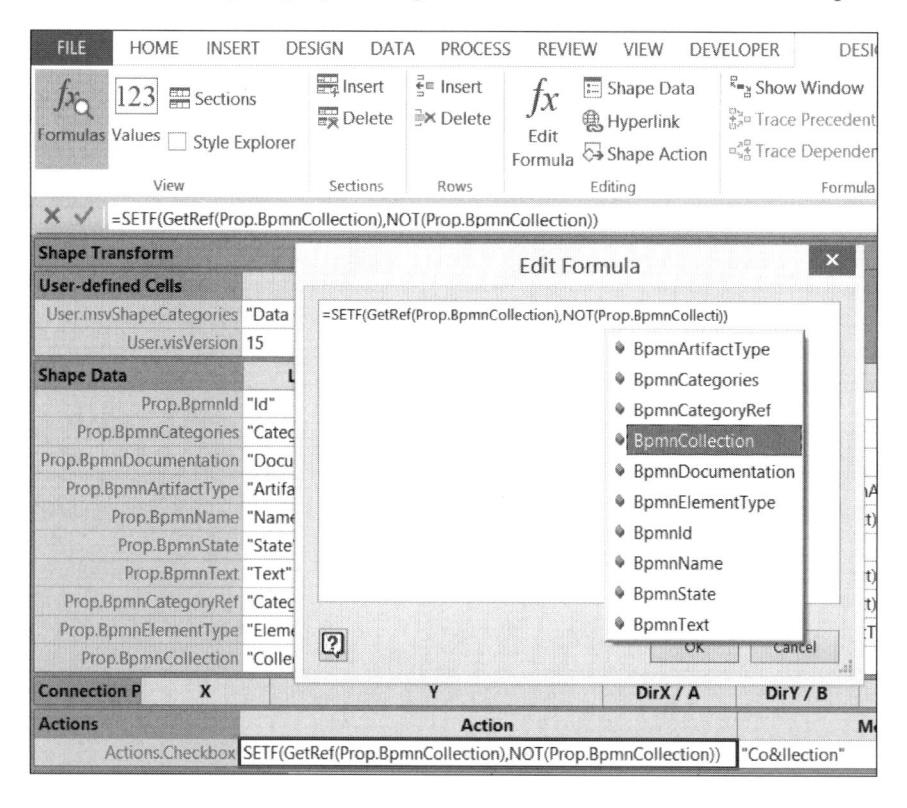

You can display the **Formula Tracing** window using the **Show Window** button in the **Formula Tracing** group on the **SHAPESHEET TOOLS** ribbon in the **DESIGN** tab. You can decide whether to **Trace Dependents**, which displays other cells that have a formula that refers to the selected cell, or **Trace Precedents**, which displays other cells that the formula in this cell refers to.

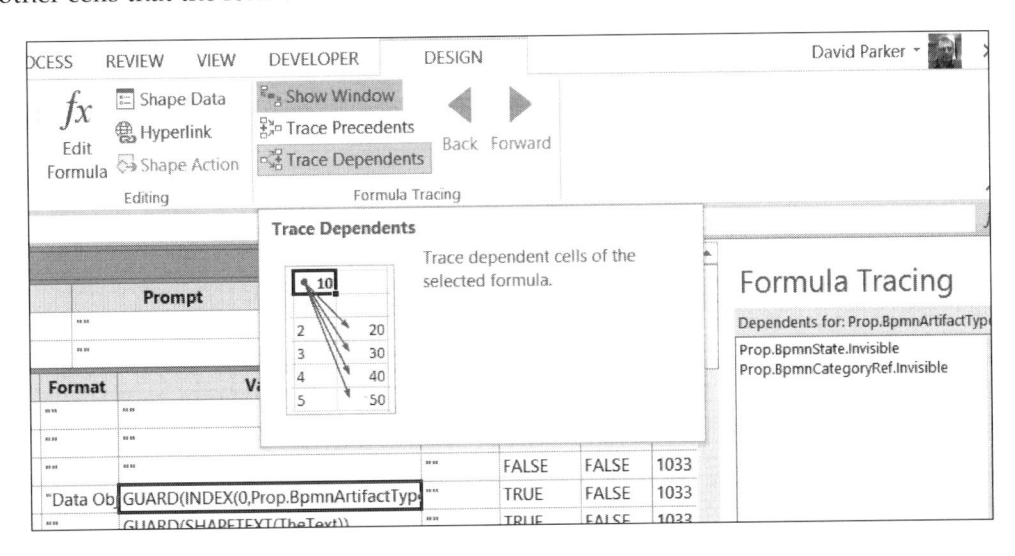

Of course, this can be done in code too. For example, the following VBA code will print out the selected cell in a ShapeSheet into **Immediate Window**:

```
Public Sub DebugPrintCellProperties()
'Abort if ShapeSheet not selected in the Visio UI
    If Not Visio.ActiveWindow.Type = Visio.VisWinTypes.visSheet Then
        Exit Sub
    End If
Dim cel As Visio.Cell
    Set cel = Visio.ActiveWindow.SelectedCell
'Print out some of the cell properties
    Debug.Print "Section", cel.Section
    Debug.Print "Row", cel.Row
    Debug.Print "Column", cel.Column
    Debug.Print "Name", cel.Name
    Debug.Print "FormulaU", cel.FormulaU
    Debug.Print "ResultIU", cel.ResultIU
    Debug.Print "ResultStr("""")", cel.ResultStr("")
    Debug.Print "Dependents", UBound(cel.Dependents)
'cel.Precedents may cause an error
On Error Resume Next
    Debug.Print "Precedents", UBound(cel.Precedents)

End Sub
```

Understanding the ShapeSheet™

> *Alt+F11* is a quick way to get into the Visual Basic Editor, and *Ctrl+G* is a quick way to open the Immediate Window.

In an earlier screenshot, where the `Actions.Checkbox.Action` cell is selected in the **Data Object** shape from the **BPMN Basic Shapes** stencil, the `DebugPrintCellProperties` macro outputs the following:

Section	240
Row	0
Column	3
Name	Actions.Checkbox.Action
FormulaU	SETF(GetRef(Prop.BpmnCollection),NOT(Prop.BpmnCollection))
ResultIU	0
ResultStr("")	0.0000
Dependents	0
Precedents	1

> I have tried to be selective about the properties displayed to illustrate some points.

Firstly, any cell can be referred to by either its name or section/row/column indices, commonly referred to as **SRC**.

Secondly, the **FormulaU** should produce a **ResultIU** of 0, if the formula is correctly formed and there is no numerical output from it.

Thirdly, the **Precedents** and **Dependents** are actually an array of referenced cells.

Printing out the ShapeSheet settings

You can download and install the Microsoft Visio SDK from the **Visio Developer Center** (visit `http://msdn.microsoft.com/en-us/office/aa905478.aspx`). This will install an extra group, **Visio SDK**, on the **Developer** ribbon and three extra buttons, with one of them being **Print ShapeSheet**.

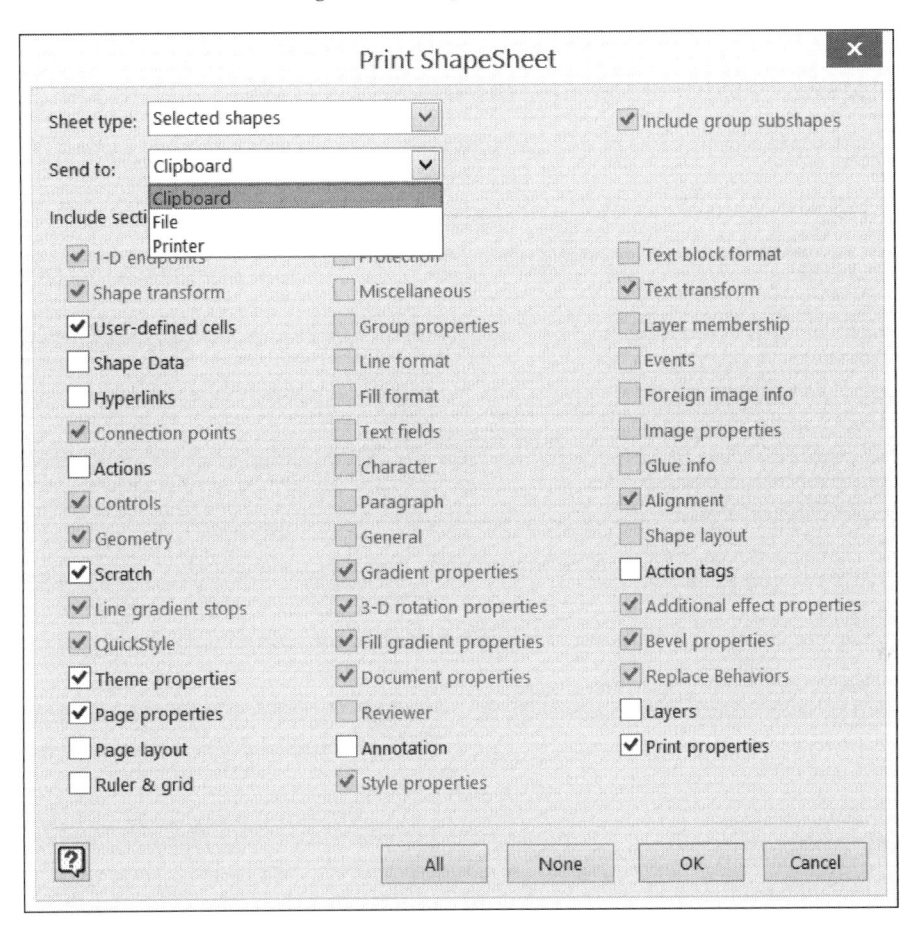

[93]

Understanding the ShapeSheet™

I have chosen the **Clipboard** option and pasted the report into an Excel worksheet, as in the following screenshot:

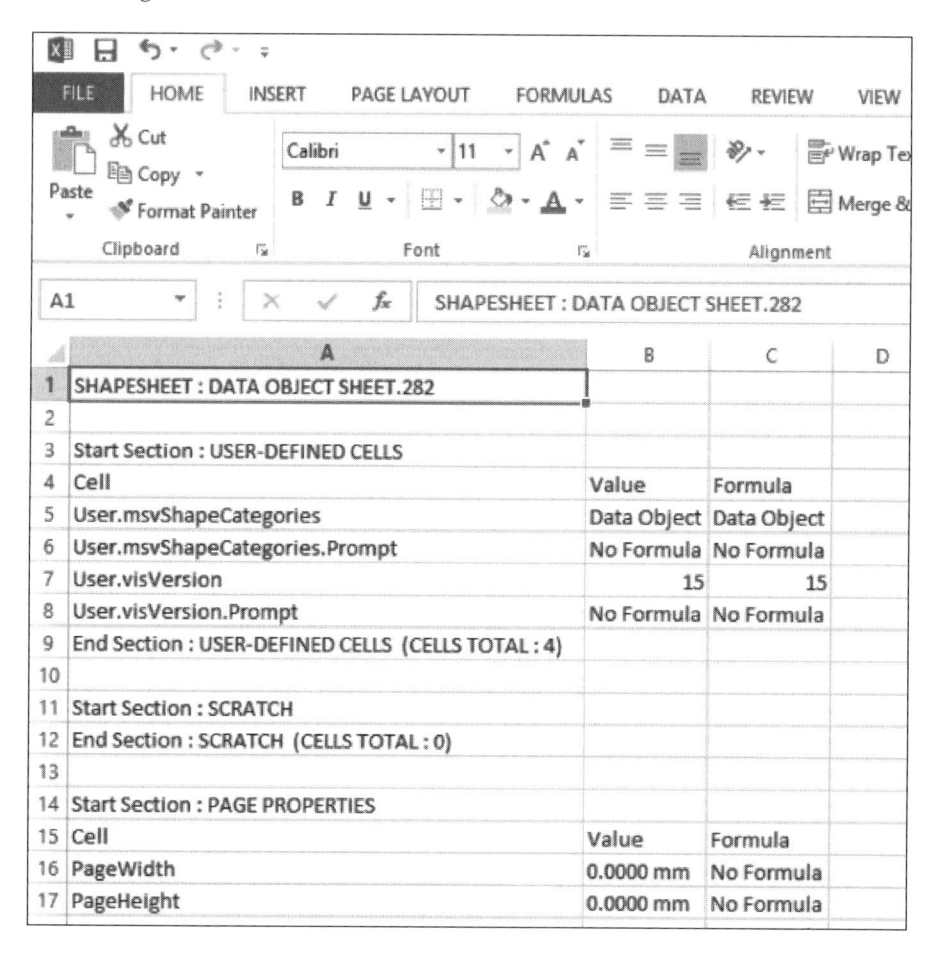

	A	B	C	D
1	SHAPESHEET : DATA OBJECT SHEET.282			
2				
3	Start Section : USER-DEFINED CELLS			
4	Cell	Value	Formula	
5	User.msvShapeCategories	Data Object	Data Object	
6	User.msvShapeCategories.Prompt	No Formula	No Formula	
7	User.visVersion	15	15	
8	User.visVersion.Prompt	No Formula	No Formula	
9	End Section : USER-DEFINED CELLS (CELLS TOTAL : 4)			
10				
11	Start Section : SCRATCH			
12	End Section : SCRATCH (CELLS TOTAL : 0)			
13				
14	Start Section : PAGE PROPERTIES			
15	Cell	Value	Formula	
16	PageWidth	0.0000 mm	No Formula	
17	PageHeight	0.0000 mm	No Formula	

The output displays the cell name, value, and formulae in each section, in an extremely verbose manner. This makes for many rows in the worksheet, and a varying number of columns in each section.

Understanding the functions

A function defines a discrete action, and most functions take a number of arguments as input. Some functions produce an output as a value in the cell that contains the formula, while others redirect the output to another cell; some do not produce a useful output at all.

The **Developer ShapeSheet Reference** in the Visio SDK contains a description of each of the 210 functions available in Visio 2013, and there are some more that are reserved for use by Visio itself. There have been 13 new functions introduced since Visio 2010.

Formulae can be entered into any cell, but some cells will be updated by the Visio engine or by specific add-ons, thus overwriting any formula that may be within the cell. Formulae are entered starting with the = (equals) sign, just as in Excel cells, so that Visio can understand that a formula is being entered rather than just text. Some cells have been primed to expect text (strings) and will automatically prefix what you type with =" (equals double-quote) and close with "(double-quote) if you do not start typing with an equal sign.

For example, the NOW() function returns the current date time value, which you can modify by applying a format, say, =FORMAT(NOW(),"dd/MM/YYYY"). In fact, the NOW() function will evaluate every minute, so be careful about how you use it because it can slow down Visio itself, if you use it in too many shapes.

The user-defined section is often used for formulas that perform calculations but they will only evaluate if they contain a reference to cells that undergo a value change, unless you specify that it only updates at a specific event. You could, for example, cause a formula to be evaluated when the shape is moved, by adding the DEPENDSON() function, in the following example:

```
=DEPENDSON(PinX,PinY)+SETF(GetRef(Prop.ShapeMoved),"="""&
FORMAT(NOW(),"dd/MM/YYYY HH:mm")&"""")
```

However, the same DEPENDSON() function would be unnecessary in the following formula because the **PinX** and **PinY** cells are already referenced, and a change in their values would automatically cause the formula to be evaluated:

```
=SETF(GetRef(Prop.Coordinate),"="""&FORMAT(PinX,"0.000")&","&FORMAT(PinY,"0.000")&"""")
```

Understanding the ShapeSheet™

The normal user will not see the result of any values unless there is something changing in the UI. This could be a value in the **Shape Data** that could cause linked **Data Graphics** to change. Or there could be something more subtle, such as the display of some geometry within the shape, such as the **Compensation** symbol in the **BPMN Task** shape, as shown in the following screenshot:

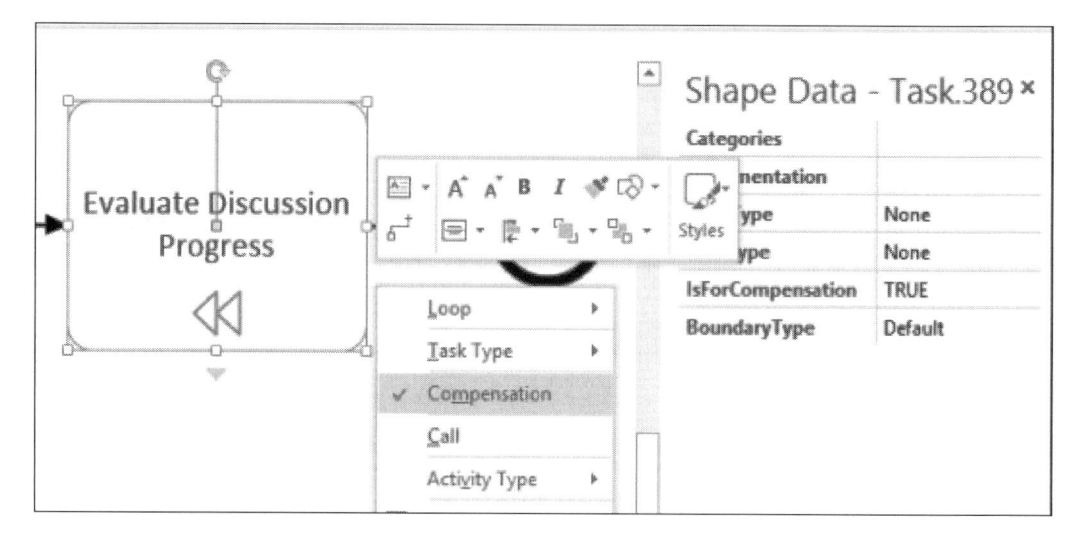

In the preceding example, you can see that the **Compensation** right-mouse menu option is checked, and the **IsForCompensation Shape Data** value is **TRUE**. These values are linked, and the **Task** shape itself displays the two triangles at the bottom edge.

The custom right mouse menu options are defined in the **Actions** section of the shape's **ShapeSheet**, and one of the cells, **Checked**, holds a formula to determine if a tick should be displayed or not. In this case, the `Actions.Compensation.Checked` cell contains the following formula, which is merely a cell reference:

```
=Prop.BpmnIsForCompensation
```

`Prop` is the prefix used for all cells in the **Shape Data** section because this section used to be known as **Custom Properties**. The `Prop.BpmnIsForCompensation` row is defined as a **Boolean** (True/False) **Type**, so the returned value is going to be `1` or `0` (`True` or `False`).

Thus, if you were to build a validation rule that required a **Task** to be for **Compensation**, then you would have to check this value.

You will often need to branch expressions using the following:

```
IF(logical_expression, value_if_true, value_if_false).
```

[96]

You can nest expressions inside each other.

You will often need to use the logical expression evaluators like the following:

- `AND(logical_expression1, logical_expression2 [, opt_logical_expression3][,...] [, opt_logical_expressionN])`
- `OR(logical_expression1, logical_expression2 [, opt_logical_expression3][,...] [, opt_logical_expressionN])`

You may also need to reverse a Boolean value using `NOT(logical_expression)`.

These are the main evaluators and there are no looping functions available. Now let's look at each relevant ShapeSheet section.

Important sections for rules validation

When validating documents, there are some sections that are more important and more regularly used than others. Therefore, we will look at just a few of the sections in detail.

Looking at the User-defined Cells section

The **User-defined Cells** section is used to store hidden variables (because they are never displayed in the UI unless you open the ShapeSheet) and perform calculations. There are just two columns in this section. The first, **Value**, is normally where the real work is done, and the second, **Prompt**, is often used as a description of the row.

> You can make **Shape Data** rows invisible too (by setting the **Invisible** cell to `True`), usually, though, you do not need the overhead of all the other cells in the row, so a **User-defined Cell** is more efficient.

Microsoft will often use specially named **User-defined Cell** rows to hold specific information. For example, the **Task** shape has a named row, `User.msvShapeCategories`, which is used to specify the category or categories that it belongs to. The **Task** shape belongs, not surprisingly, to the `Task` category, but it could have belonged to multiple categories by having them expressed as a semi-colon separated list.

Using the category of a Shape

Visio 2010 introduced the new function `HASCATEGORY(category)` in order to support structured diagrams.

[97]

Understanding the ShapeSheet™

In the BPMN diagrams, the **Task** shape has the `Task` category, so the following formula will return `TRUE` for the **Task** shape:

```
=HASCATEGORY("Task")
```

But the following will return `FALSE` because the string is case-sensitive:

```
=HASCATEGORY("task")
```

Therefore, it is important to know what the exact spelling and case are for the values in the `User.msvShapeCategories` cells.

Consequently, the following VBA macro, `ListStencilShapeCategories`, will list all of the categories used in the docked stencils, and then it will optionally list the stencil title, master name, and a count of the number of categories that the master belongs to.

> We are using the `Dictionary` object in the following code, so you will need to ensure that the **Microsoft Scripting Runtime** library (`C:\Windows\system32\scrrun.dll` or `C:\Windows\SysWOW64\scrrun.dll`) is ticked in the **References** dialog opened from the **Tools** menu in the Visual Basic user interface.

The sub-function calls a sub-routine to collect the categories in each master, and then passes the data to another sub-routine for optional display.

```
Public Sub ListStencilShapeCategories()
'List the categories used in the docked stencils
    If Not Visio.ActiveWindow.Type = _
        Visio.VisWinTypes.visDrawing Then
        Exit Sub
    End If
Dim aryStencils() As String
    Visio.ActiveWindow.DockedStencils aryStencils
Dim stenCounter As Integer
Dim sten As Visio.Document
Dim mst As Visio.Master
Dim shp As Visio.Shape
Dim category As String
Dim colMasters As Collection
Dim dicCategories As Dictionary
    Set dicCategories = New Dictionary
    'Loop thru the stencils
    For stenCounter = 0 To UBound(aryStencils)
        'Do not read the document stencil
        If Len(aryStencils(stenCounter)) > 0 Then
```

```
                Set sten = _
                    Visio.Documents(aryStencils(stenCounter))
                'Loop thru each master in the stencil
                For Each mst In sten.Masters
                    Set shp = mst.Shapes.Item(1)
                    'Check that the Category cell exists
                    If shp.CellExists("User.msvShapeCategories", _
                        VisExistsFlags.visExistsAnywhere) Then
                        CollectShapeCategories _
                            shp, dicCategories, colMasters
                    End If
                Next
            End If
        Next

        OutputStencilShapeCategories _
            dicCategories, aryStencils, colMasters

    End Sub
```

The preceding sub-function calls a sub-routine to collect the shape categories.

```
    Private Sub CollectShapeCategories( _
        ByVal shp As Visio.Shape, _
        ByRef dicCategories As Dictionary, _
        ByRef colMasters As Collection)
    Dim categories() As String
    Dim catCounter As Integer
        'The default List Separator is ;
        categories = _
            Split(shp.Cells("User.msvShapeCategories").ResultStrU(""), _
";")
        For catCounter = 0 To UBound(categories)
            If dicCategories.Exists(categories(catCounter)) Then
                Set colMasters = dicCategories.
Item(categories(catCounter))
                colMasters.Add shp.Document.Title & " - " & shp.Parent.
Name & _
                    " (" & UBound(categories) + 1 & ")"
                Set dicCategories.Item(categories(catCounter)) = _
                    colMasters
            Else
                Set colMasters = New Collection
                colMasters.Add shp.Document.Title & " - " & shp.Parent.
Name & _
```

Understanding the ShapeSheet™

```
                " (" & UBound(categories) + 1 & ")"
            dicCategories.Add _
                categories(catCounter), colMasters
        End If
    Next catCounter
End Sub
```

The second sub-routine takes the collected data and offers to display it in message boxes:

```
    Private Sub OutputStencilShapeCategories( _
        ByVal dicCategories As Dictionary, _
        ByVal aryStencils As Variant, _
        ByVal colMasters As Collection)
Dim msg As String
Dim catCounter As Integer
    msg = "There are " & UBound(dicCategories.Keys) + 1 & _
        " categories in the " & _
        UBound(aryStencils) + 1 & " docked stencils:" & vbCrLf
    For catCounter = 0 To UBound(dicCategories.Keys)
        Set colMasters = _
            dicCategories.Item(dicCategories.Keys(catCounter))
        msg = msg & vbCrLf & dicCategories.Keys(catCounter) & _
            " - " & colMasters.Count & " masters"
    Next catCounter
    msg = msg & vbCrLf & vbCrLf & "Do you want to view the details?"
Dim ret As Integer
Dim mstCounter As Integer
    ret = MsgBox(msg, vbInformation + vbYesNo, _
        "ListStencilShapeCategories")
    If Not ret = vbYes Then
        Exit Sub
    End If

    'Display the masters for each category
    For catCounter = 0 To UBound(dicCategories.Keys)
        Set colMasters = _
            dicCategories.Item(dicCategories.Keys(catCounter))
        msg = colMasters.Count & _
            " masters that have the Category : " & _
            dicCategories.Keys(catCounter) & vbCrLf
        For mstCounter = 1 To colMasters.Count
            msg = msg & vbCrLf & colMasters.Item(mstCounter)
        Next mstCounter
        msg = msg & vbCrLf & vbCrLf & _
```

```
            "Do you want to continue to view the next category?"
        ret = MsgBox(msg, vbInformation + vbYesNo, _
            "ListStencilShapeCategories")
        If Not ret = vbYes Then
            Exit For
        End If
    Next catCounter
End Sub
```

If you run this macro with, say, a blank document created from the **BPMN Diagram (Metric)** template, then you will be presented with a list of all of the categories found in the docked stencils, as shown in the following screenshot:

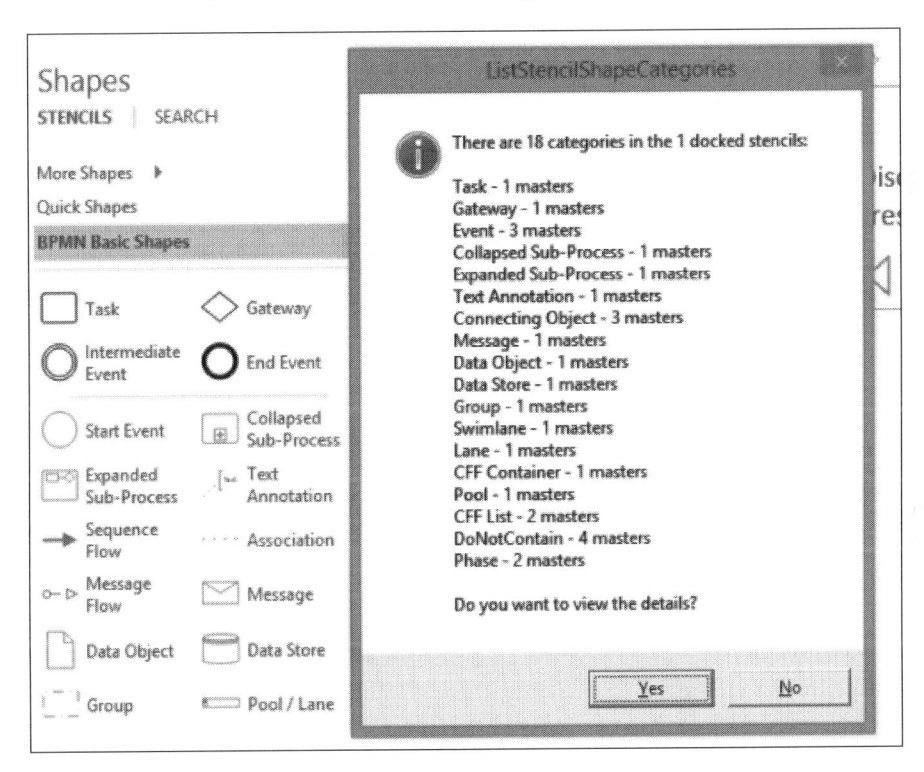

Understanding the ShapeSheet™

If you continue to view the details of the listed categories, you will be presented with a dialog listing the stencil, master, and category count in brackets:

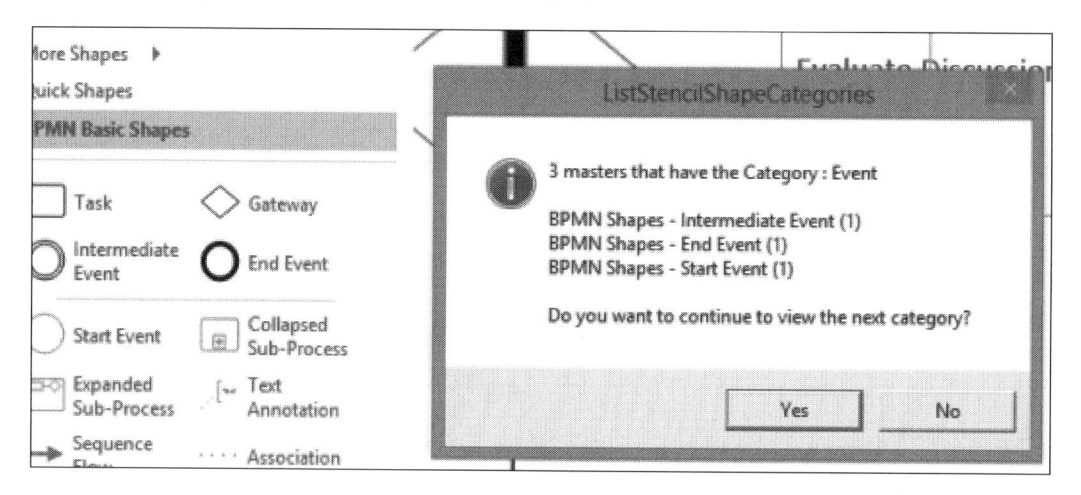

This is essential information for building validation rules that use the category.

> The category can also be used to prevent shapes from being contained by container shapes. Simply include the special category `DoNotContain` in the `User.msvShapeCategories` formula.

Using the structure type of a Shape

Visio 2013's structured diagrams use another specifically named **User-defined Cell**, `User.msvStructureType`, to define the **Structure Type** of the shape.

You are spared the VBA code for the `ListStencilStructureTypes` method in this text because it is very similar to the preceding `ListStencilShapeCategories` method, but we can discover that there are three different Structure Types in the BPMN stencils. They are:

Container: There are 12 masters in all, including Expanded Sub-Process, Pool/Lane, and Group

Callout: There is only one master, Text Annotation

List: There are two masters, Swimlane List, and Phase List

Chapter 3

Checking a Container shape

The formula, `=CONTAINERCOUNT()`, returns 1 in the examples because the **Document** shape is inside the container shape labeled **Drafting**. If there are nested containers, then the function will return the total number of containers that the shape is within.

If the shape is inside a container, then you can use the new `=CONTAINERSHEETREF(index[, category])` function to get a reference to the container shape, and thus to any of the cells inside it. As there can be multiple containers, `index`, which is one-based (the first index number is 1, not 0), specifies which one to return. The `category` argument is optional.

Perhaps surprisingly, the `CONTAINERMEMBERCOUNT()` returns 9 in this example, because it includes the three flowchart shapes, the three callouts, and the three connectors between the flowchart shapes, even though the last three are 1-D shapes. If either end of a connector is outside the container, then it would not be counted. Also, note that the lines between the callouts and the flowchart shapes are part of the callout shape and thus do not count either, as can be seen in the following screenshot:

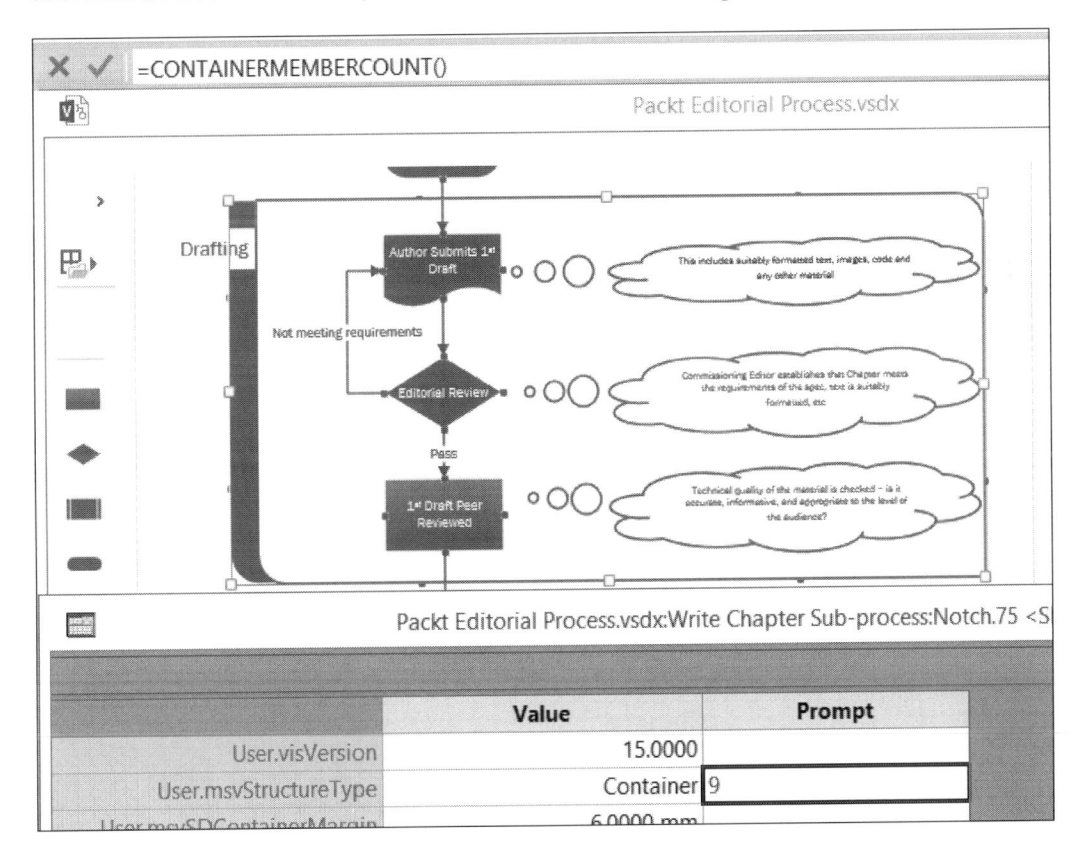

[103]

Checking a List shape

In this example, we have used the **Class** and **Member** shapes from **UML Class** stencil in the **UML Class** template to construct a partial **Visio Type Library** object model. We have added two **User-defined Cells** to the **ShapeSheet** of the **Member** master shape so that the item contains index of its position in the **Class** and the text of the **Class** shape. The **User.ListOrder** and **User.ListHeaderText** in the following screenshot are the extra rows:

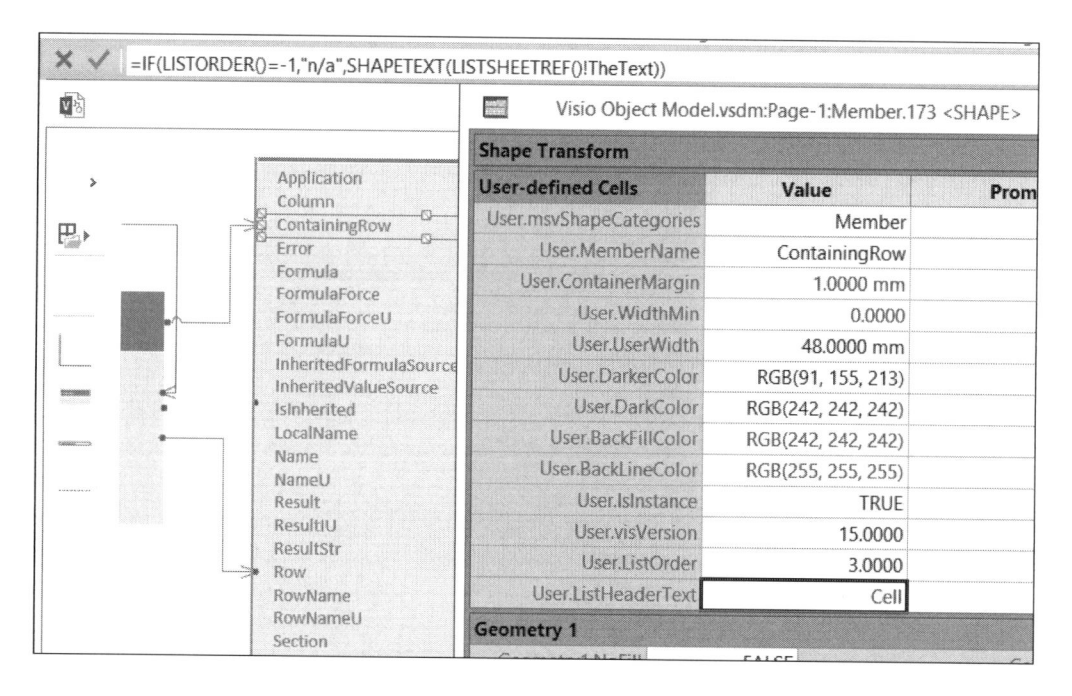

This is achieved by using the following formula in the User.ListOrder.Value cell:

   =LISTORDER()

The ListSheetRef() function will return the containing list box shape (if there is one), and then its cells and properties can be referenced by following this with an exclamation mark. Therefore, the formula to return the text of the container list box in the User.ListHeaderText.Value cell is:

   =SHAPETEXT(LISTSHEETREF()!TheText)

However, this formula will display =#REF! if the list item is not within a list box, so a more complete formula is:

   =IF(LISTORDER()=-1,"n/a",SHAPETEXT(LISTSHEETREF()!TheText))

Alternatively, these values could be surfaced to the UI as Shape Data rows, in which case you would protect them from being overwritten by using the GUARD() function.

=GUARD(IF(LISTORDER()=-1,"n/a",SHAPETEXT(LISTSHEETREF()!TheText)))

The GUARD() function can be put around the formula in any cell to protect its contents from accidental updating via the UI. It can even prevent a user from changing the position, size, or rotation. In code, you would have to use the FORMULAFORCE property to update guarded contents because using the normal FORMULA property would cause an error.

In either case, having these values available on the **List box item** makes reports and rule validation much easier.

A **List** shape can contain the function LISTMEMBERCOUNT() in order to get the number of list item shapes within it.

Checking for attached Callout shapes

In the following examples, we have added a new row to the **User-defined Cells** section, named CalloutShapes, of the first **Document** shape in my example **Packt Editorial Process** diagram. We have entered the function CALLOUTCOUNT() into the **Value** cell of this row, and you can see that the result is displayed as 1.0000 in the following screenshot:

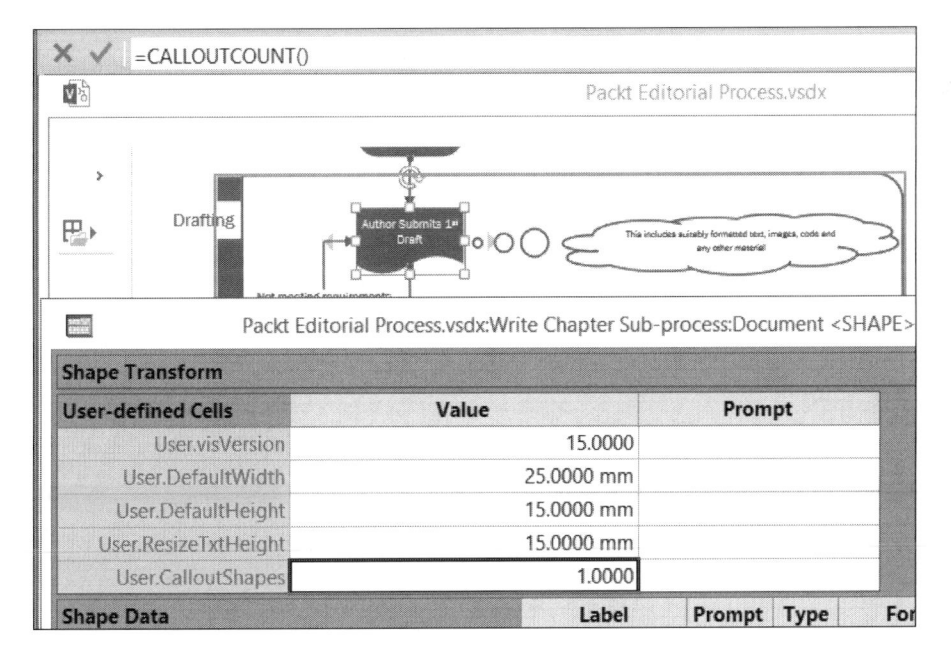

Understanding the ShapeSheet™

This is because there is a single Callout shape connected to this shape.

When a **Callout** shape is connected to another shape you can get at any of the cells in that target shape by use of the `CALLOUTTARGETREF()` function.

In the following example, as shown in the following screenshot, we have used a formula to return the text of the target shape. The following formula uses the `ShapeText()` function to return the text of the associated **Callout** shape:

```
=SHAPETEXT(CALLOUTTARGETREF()!TheText)
```

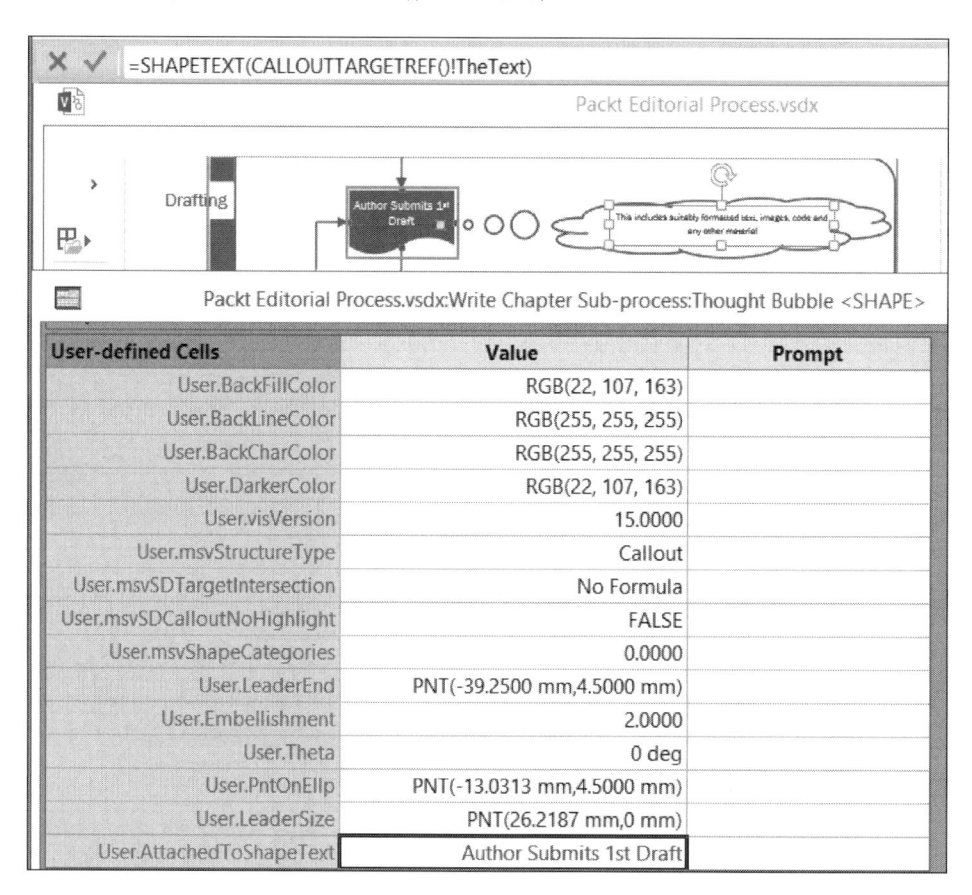

User-defined Cells	Value	Prompt
User.BackFillColor	RGB(22, 107, 163)	
User.BackLineColor	RGB(255, 255, 255)	
User.BackCharColor	RGB(255, 255, 255)	
User.DarkerColor	RGB(22, 107, 163)	
User.visVersion	15.0000	
User.msvStructureType	Callout	
User.msvSDTargetIntersection	No Formula	
User.msvSDCalloutNoHighlight	FALSE	
User.msvShapeCategories	0.0000	
User.LeaderEnd	PNT(-39.2500 mm,4.5000 mm)	
User.Embellishment	2.0000	
User.Theta	0 deg	
User.PntOnEllp	PNT(-13.0313 mm,4.5000 mm)	
User.LeaderSize	PNT(26.2187 mm,0 mm)	
User.AttachedToShapeText	Author Submits 1st Draft	

For example, this could be surfaced in the UI as a **Shape Data** row, thus making reporting easier.

Looking at the Shape Data section

The **Value** cell stores the actual values; because it is the default cell in the row, it can be retrieved in a ShapeSheet formula as `Prop.Cost`, for example, rather than `Prop.Cost.Value`. Other cells have to be referenced explicitly, as say, `Prop.Cost.Invisible`, for example.

The ShapeSheet developer cannot move **Shape Data** rows up or down, but the display order can be modified by entering text into the `SortKey` cells. The Visio UI will sort the **Shape Data** rows according to the text sort order of the values in these cells.

The visibility of a **Shape Data** row is controlled by the Boolean result of the formula in the **Invisible** cell.

There are eight different types in **Shape Data** rows, almost all of which are data types. So, it is important to understand how to handle their values in any rule validation. The following screenshot shows the drop-down list for the **Type** cell in the ShapeSheet displaying the eight available types:

Each type is defined by an enumerator `visPropTypes`, which has the following values:

- String
- Fixed list
- Number
- Boolean
- Variable list
- Date or time
- Duration
- Currency

Understanding the ShapeSheet™

The default **Type** is 0, so if the **Type** has not been set then it is assumed to be String.

Each row in the **Shape Data** section can be named and has a **Label** that is displayed in the UI. If a row is not specifically named, then it will be automatically named Row_1, Row_2, and so on.

If your Visio diagrams have been used with **Data | Link Data to Shapes**, then you need to know that this feature will attempt to link the data by matching the text in the **Shape Data** row's **Label** cell with the column header, or the field name of the external data first, and it is case-sensitive. If the target shape does not already have a **Shape Data** row, then Visio will automatically create a row named after the **Label** text, but with a _VisDM_ prefix, and any spaces or special characters removed. Note that the last four Shape Data rows in the following screenshot were automatically created by the Link Data to Shapes action, while the other **Shape Data** rows exist in the master shape, and that **CPU (MHz)** and **Memory (MB)** are unnecessary duplicate rows, since rows labeled **CPU** and **Memory** already existed.

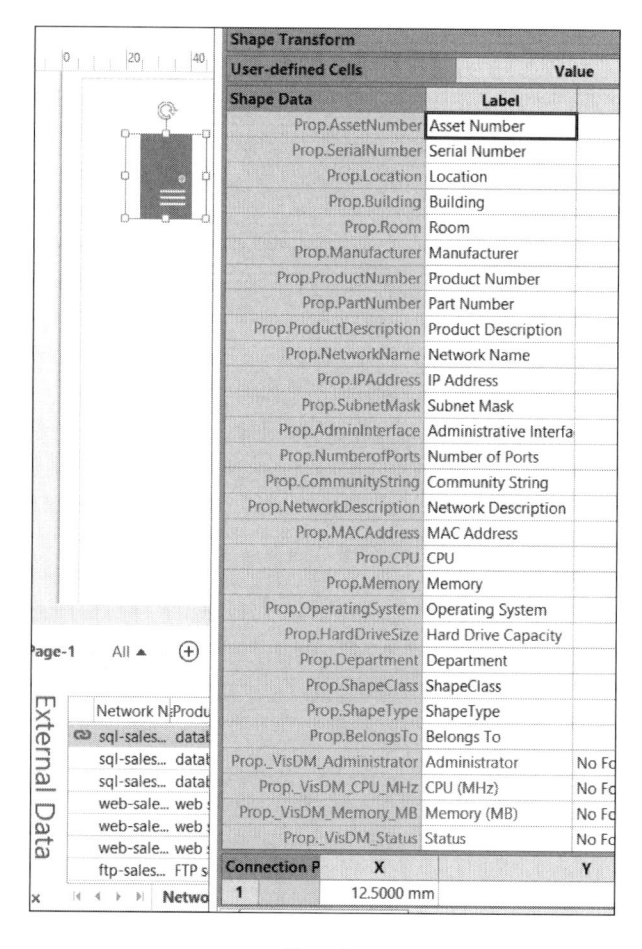

Shape Data	Label	
Prop.AssetNumber	Asset Number	
Prop.SerialNumber	Serial Number	
Prop.Location	Location	
Prop.Building	Building	
Prop.Room	Room	
Prop.Manufacturer	Manufacturer	
Prop.ProductNumber	Product Number	
Prop.PartNumber	Part Number	
Prop.ProductDescription	Product Description	
Prop.NetworkName	Network Name	
Prop.IPAddress	IP Address	
Prop.SubnetMask	Subnet Mask	
Prop.AdminInterface	Administrative Interface	
Prop.NumberofPorts	Number of Ports	
Prop.CommunityString	Community String	
Prop.NetworkDescription	Network Description	
Prop.MACAddress	MAC Address	
Prop.CPU	CPU	
Prop.Memory	Memory	
Prop.OperatingSystem	Operating System	
Prop.HardDriveSize	Hard Drive Capacity	
Prop.Department	Department	
Prop.ShapeClass	ShapeClass	
Prop.ShapeType	ShapeType	
Prop.BelongsTo	Belongs To	
Prop._VisDM_Administrator	Administrator	No Fo
Prop._VisDM_CPU_MHz	CPU (MHz)	No Fo
Prop._VisDM_Memory_MB	Memory (MB)	No Fo
Prop._VisDM_Status	Status	No Fo

Therefore, you may need to match values based on **Label** rather than the **Name** row, if your solution uses **Link Data to Shapes**.

> The older **Database Wizard** feature does use the row **Name** to perform its matching.

Using the String type

String data is just text that has been entered into a Shape Data row. It may have been imported from elsewhere, for example using the **Link Data to Shapes** feature, or it may just have been entered manually. In either case, if your validation rules are using text values to match, then you may be wise to ensure that the case is consistent by using the LOWER() or UPPER() functions, which will force the text to be in lowercase or uppercase respectively. Alternatively, use case sensitivity on the following string matching functions.

The **Format** cell may contain a pattern that modifies the display of the string to be in lowercase or uppercase, but that does not mean that the **Value** is in these cases.

You can use the STRSAME(string1,string2[,opt_ignore_case]) and STRSAMEEX (string1,string2,localeID,flag) functions to compare two strings, though you may need to use TRIM(string) to remove any accidental spaces at the beginning and end of the string.

Visio also provides a few functions to get specific parts of a string. The LEFT(string[,num_of_chars]) and RIGHT(string[,num_of_chars]) functions will return the specified number of characters (the default is 1) from the start or end of a string. The MID(string,start_num,num_of_chars) function will extract characters from within a string.

You can get the starting position of a string within another by using the FIND(find_text,within_text[,opt_start_num][,opt_ignore_case]) function. You may also need to use LEN(string) to get the number of characters in a text string.

Be aware that there are some solutions that will automatically enter the string values, and there are others that may contain special formulae to retrieve a value. For example, the **Cross Functional Flowchart** template in Visio 2013 gets the value of the Prop.Function **Shape Data** row of a shape from the text that has been entered into the **Swimlane** that it is within.

Understanding the ShapeSheet™

> The display of the **Value** cell can be toggled between **Formulas** and **Values** from the first two buttons on the **View** group of the **DESIGN** tab of the **SHAPESHEET TOOLS** ribbon, or by using the right mouse menu of the ShapeSheet window.

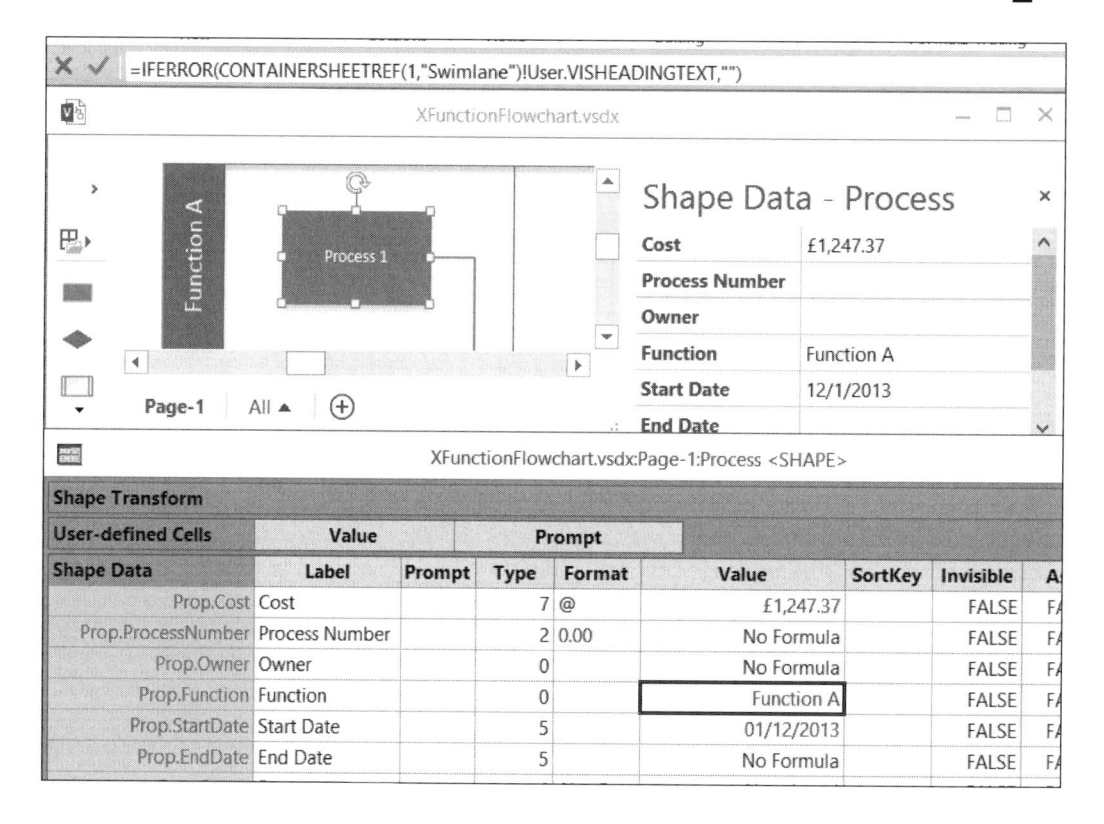

This is done with the following formula in the **Value** cell:

```
=IFERROR(CONTAINERSHEETREF(1,"Swimlane")!User.VISHEADINGTEXT,"")
```

What this means is that, if the shape is surrounded by a container with the category **Swimlane**, return the value in the `User.visHeadingText` cell; otherwise, just return an empty string.

Therefore, the `Prop.Function.Value` will be `""` if the **Process** shape is not inside a Swimlane shape; otherwise, it will be the value of the text in the container Swimlane shape.

Using the Fixed List type

If a **Shape Data** row is set to a `Fixed List` type, then the value must exist in the drop-down list.

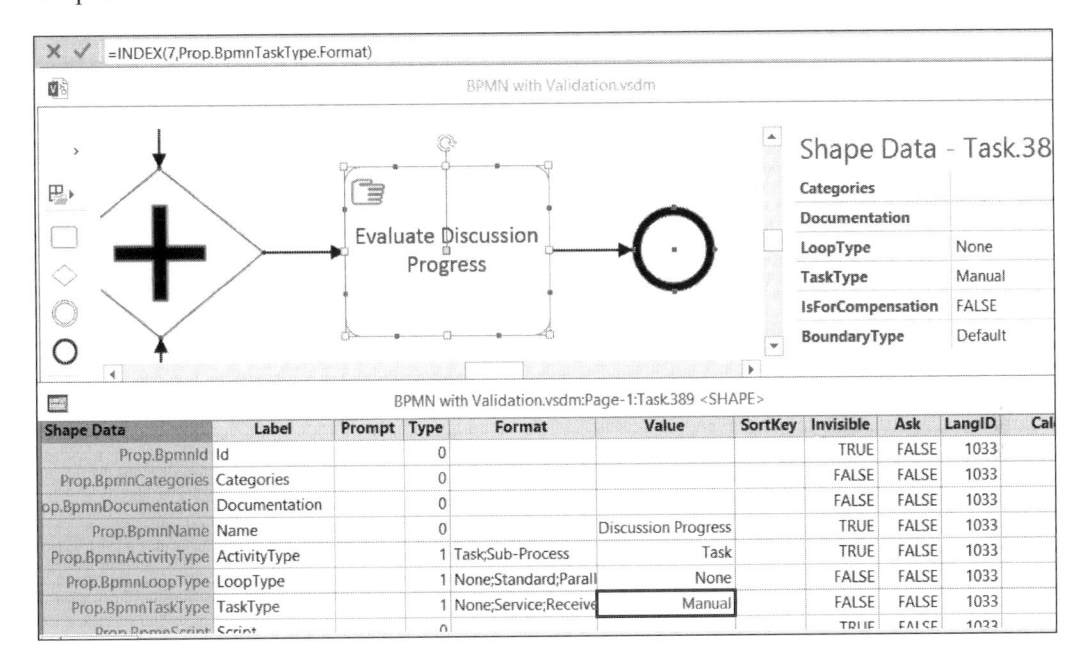

[Screenshot of Visio showing a BPMN diagram with Shape Data panel and Shape Data table for Task.389, including columns: Shape Data, Label, Prompt, Type, Format, Value, SortKey, Invisible, Ask, LangID. Formula bar shows `=INDEX(7,Prop.BpmnTaskType.Format)`. Rows include Prop.BpmnId, Prop.BpmnCategories, Prop.BpmnDocumentation, Prop.BpmnName (Discussion Progress), Prop.BpmnActivityType (Task;Sub-Process / Task), Prop.BpmnLoopType (None;Standard;Parall / None), Prop.BpmnTaskType (None;Service;Receive / Manual), Prop.BpmnScript.]

Recent versions of Visio will automatically create a formula in the **Value** cell that returns the string value at a specific zero-based index in this list. For example look at the following value:

    =INDEX(2,Prop.BpmnStatus.Format)

It will return the third item from the semi-colon separated list in the `Prop.BpmnStatus.Format` cell, which contains the formula:

    ="None;Ready;Active;Cancelled;Aborting;Aborted;Completing;Completed"

Thus, the value is `Active`.

If you were using rules based on a Fixed List value, it might be better to use the index rather than the string value, since this could be mistyped or even translated into a different language. Therefore, you could get the index position using the `LOOKUP()` function as follows:

    =LOOKUP(Prop.BpmnStatus,Prop.BpmnStatus.Format)

Understanding the ShapeSheet™

Using the Number type

Visio stores numbers as double precision numerals, but the **Format** cell may be used to modify the display in the UI. The following screenshot shows that the Define Shape Data dialog provides a drop-down list of the most popular formats for numbers, and the formula is stored in the **Format** cell:

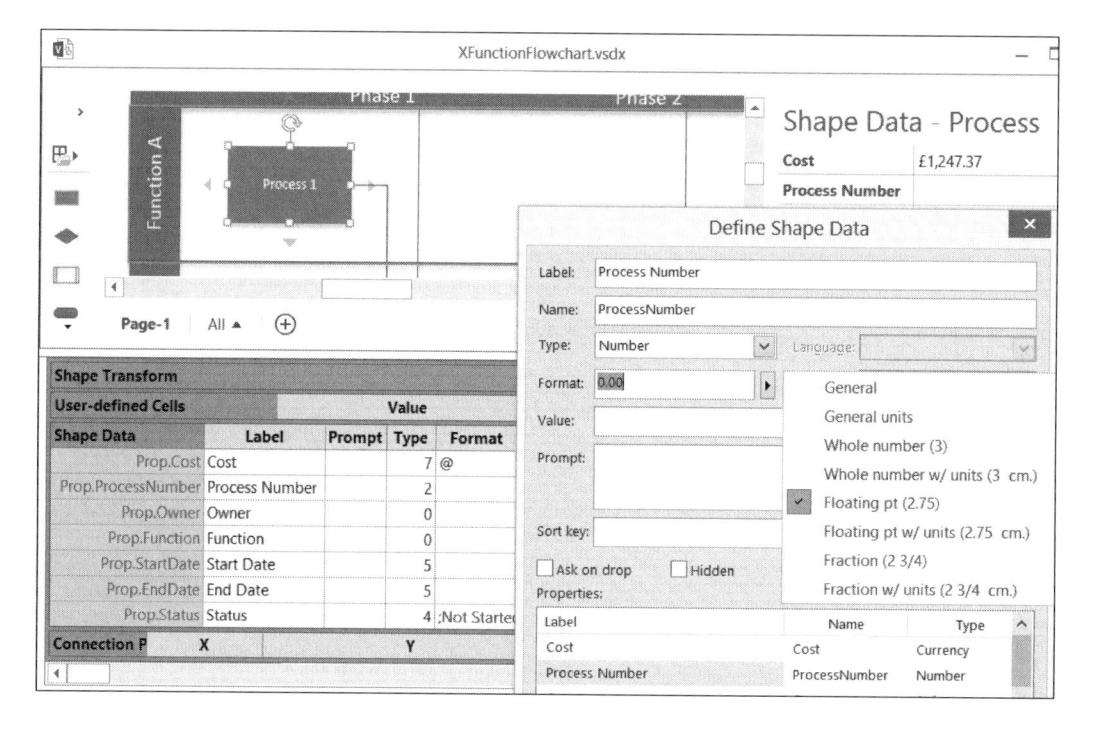

However, Visio also provides some functions to enable rounding and calculations. Commonly used functions are as follows:

- `ROUND(number,numberofdigit)` to round a number to a given precision
- `INT(number)` to round down to the previous integer
- `INTUP(number)` to round a number up to the next integer
- `FLOOR(number[, opt_multiple])`, which rounds a number towards zero, to the next integer, or the next instance of the optional multiple
- `CEILING(number[, opt_multiple])`, which rounds a zero away from zero

The `MODULUS(number, divisor)` function can also be useful if you need to formulate a rule that requires specific values to be entered, for example.

`ABS(number)` function returns the absolute value, and `SIGN(number[, opt_fuzz])` returns a value that represents the sign of a number.

Since Visio is a graphics system, there are a large number of functions for dealing with points, lines, and angles, that are not really relevant for rules validation.

You can simply compare number values using the equals sign (=), and you can add values using `number1+number2`, or `SUM(number1[, opt_number2] [, opt_number3] [, ...] [, opt_number14])`. Multiplication and division of values is simple, using `number1*number2` and `number1/number2` respectively.

You can get the maximum or minimum value of a series of values with `MAX(number1,number2,...,numberN)` or `MIN(number1,number2,...,numberN)`.

Using the Boolean type

The Boolean type is often referred to as the True/False or Yes/No type, so this type returns FALSE (zero) or TRUE (non-zero). Visio actually stores TRUE as 1 internally but some other programming languages use -1, so you may need to use the ABS() function to get the absolute value, depending on your circumstances. The following screenshot also shows that the Shape Data window automatically provides a drop-down list for Boolean types:

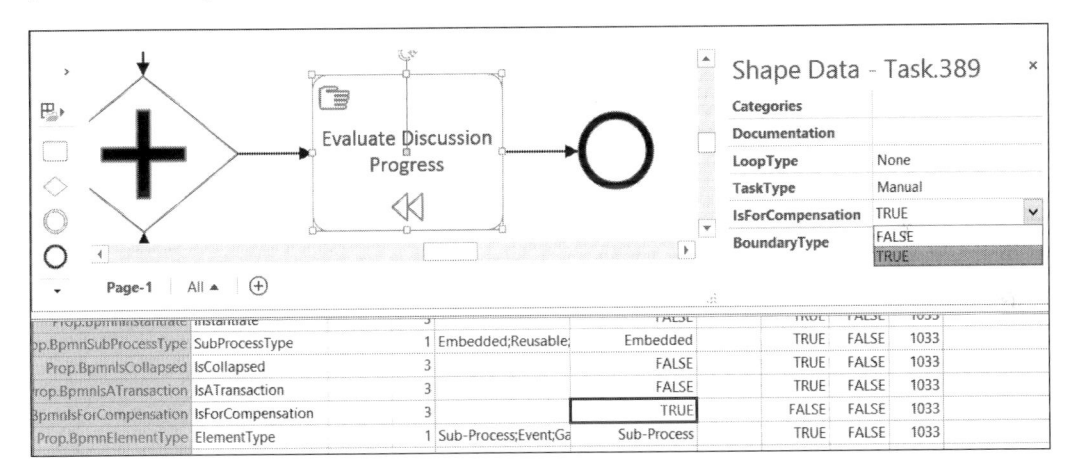

[113]

Using the Variable List type

A **Variable List** type is similar to the **Fixed List** mentioned earlier, but it is usually not appropriate to retrieve the index position of the selected value because Visio will automatically add values to the list if the user enters a value that is not present already. As can be seen in the following example, this even means that the same word can be repeated in the list if the case is different.

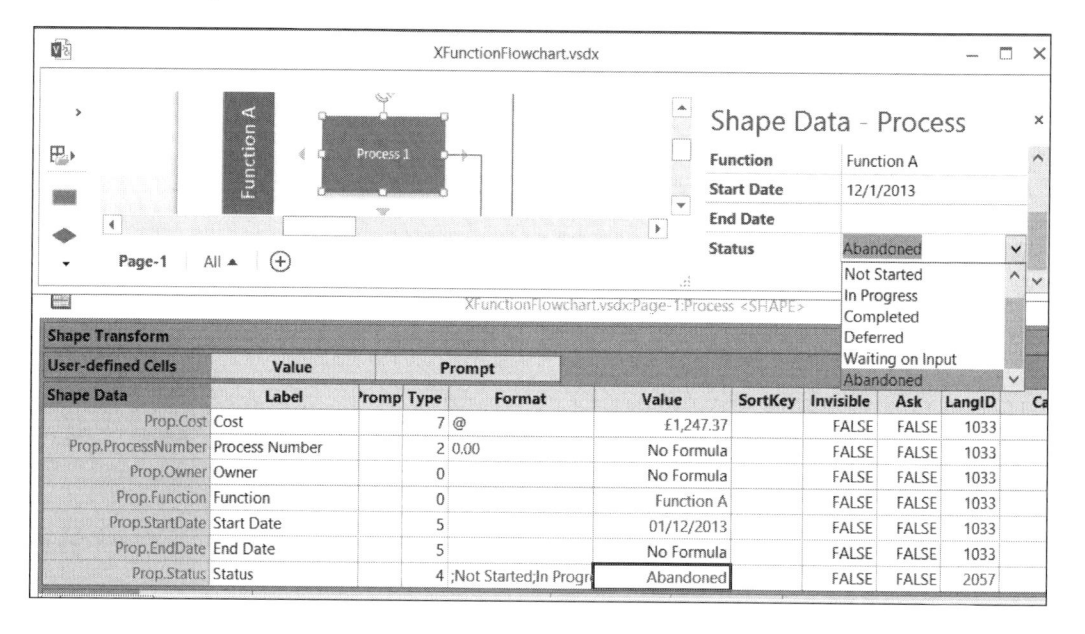

Also, the list is only extended for this particular shape instance; other process shapes in the diagram Variable List type will have their own variable list.

So, a variable list may seem like a flexible feature for the user, but it is a nightmare for data validation; the resultant text value should be treated just like the `String` type.

Using the Date type

Visio provides a date picker for the user if the **Type** is set as Date for a **Shape Data** row. However, a custom solution may use either a date or a time picker, since a DATETIME(double) value is actually stored. It is a Standard OLE automation date time data type, which means that you will need to use FromOADate and TOOADate in .Net languages.

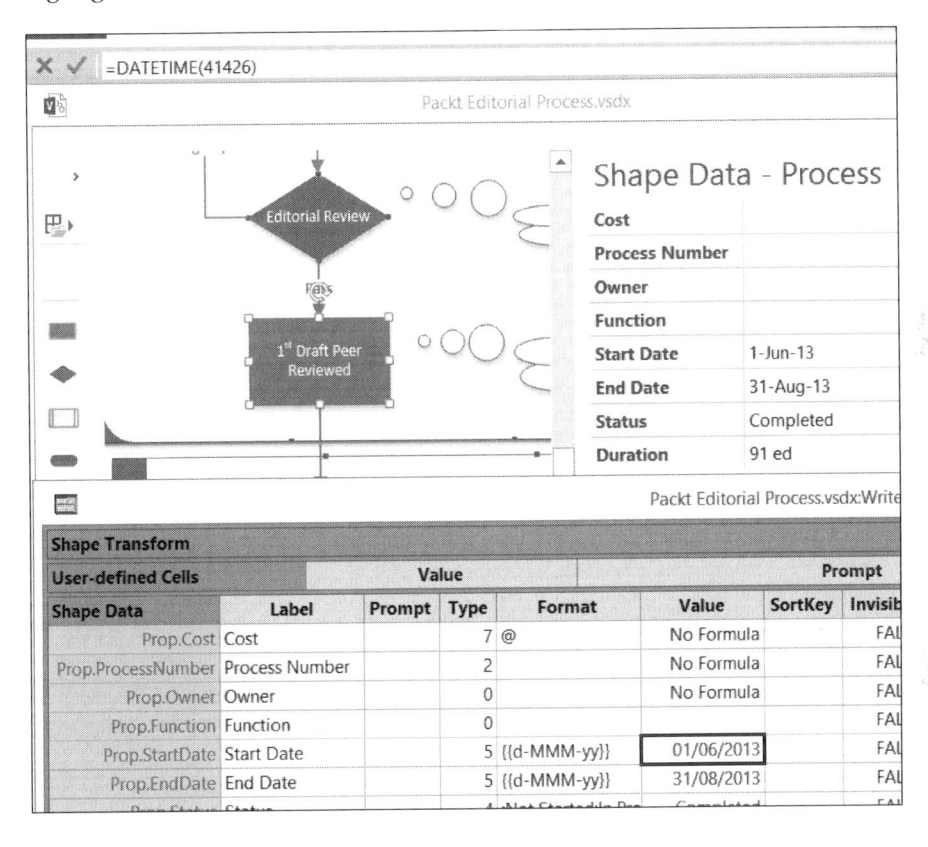

Understanding the ShapeSheet™

The display format of the date time value can be modified using the **Format** cell, but any rules validation should use the double precision number value. This will avoid any problems with the optional positioning of day and months in a date string. The UK, for example, always uses DD/MM/YY, but the US uses MM/DD/YY.

There are a number of functions that enable you to get to specific integer parts of a date time value. They are:

- `DAY(datetime[, opt_lcid])`
- `MONTH(datetime[, opt_lcid])`
- `YEAR(datetime[, opt_lcid])`
- `HOUR(datetime[, opt_lcid])`
- `MINUTE (datetime[, opt_lcid])`
- `SECOND(datetime[, opt_lcid])`

There are also a couple of functions to return the integer value of the day in the week or in the year, namely, `WEEKDAY (datetime[, opt_lcid])` and `DAYOFYEAR(datetime[, opt_lcid])`.

If you need to convert text to dates or times then you can use the `DATETIME(datetime|expression[, opt_lcid])`, `DATEVALUE(datetime|expression[, opt_lcid])` or `TIMEVALUE(datetime|expression[, opt_lcid])` functions.

However, if you have the integer parts of a date or time, then use the `DATE(year,month,day)` or `TIME(hour,minute,second)` functions.

> Visio uses the System date; therefore the earliest date that can be stored is 30th December 1899.

Since date and time are stored as double precision numbers internally, with the date being the part before the decimal point and the time being the part after the decimal point, you can check if they are equal (=), before (<), or after (>) easily enough, but you may wish to check one date time against another within a duration range. For example, you may want to verify that `Prop.EndDate` is greater than the `Prop.StartDate` plus the `Prop.Duration`. This could be expressed as:

```
= Prop.EndDate<(Prop.StartDate+Prop.Duration)
```

This will return `True` or `False`.

Similarly, you could test if `Prop.EndDate` is within the next 12 weeks by using the following:

```
=Prop.EndDate<(Now()+12 ew.)
```

You can use any of the duration units in such formulae.

Using the Duration type

Visio can store duration values expressed as elapsed day (`ed.`), hour (`eh.`), minute (`em.`), second (`es.`), or week (`ew.`). They are all stored internally as days and fractions of days. The following screenshot demonstrates calculating the duration between the `Prop.StartDate` and `Prop.EndDate` values:

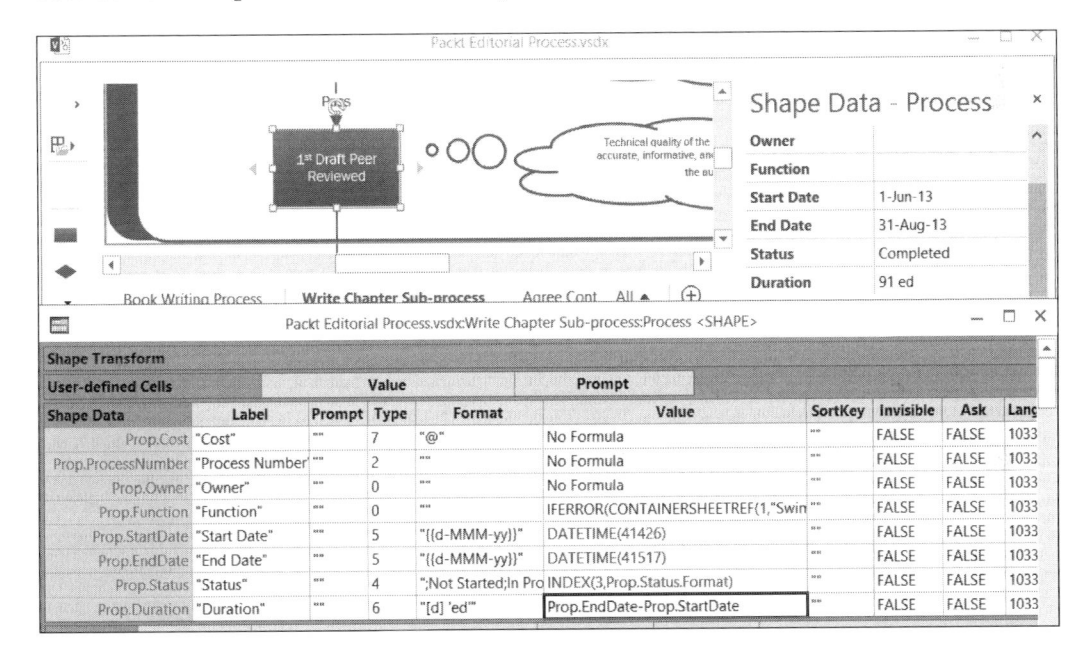

> The **Format** cell may have been used to modify the presentation in the UI. The **Visio Developer SDK** contains a page called **About Format Pictures** in the documentation, where you can review all of the different format pictures.

[117]

Using the Currency type

The last type is **Currency**, the display of which defaults to the system settings, although it is stored as a double precision number. The following screenshot shows the **Prop.Cost.Value** cell formula stored as **CY(340,"GBP")**, but the value is displayed as **£340.00**. The CY function will format the value according to the style in the system's *Region and Language* settings.

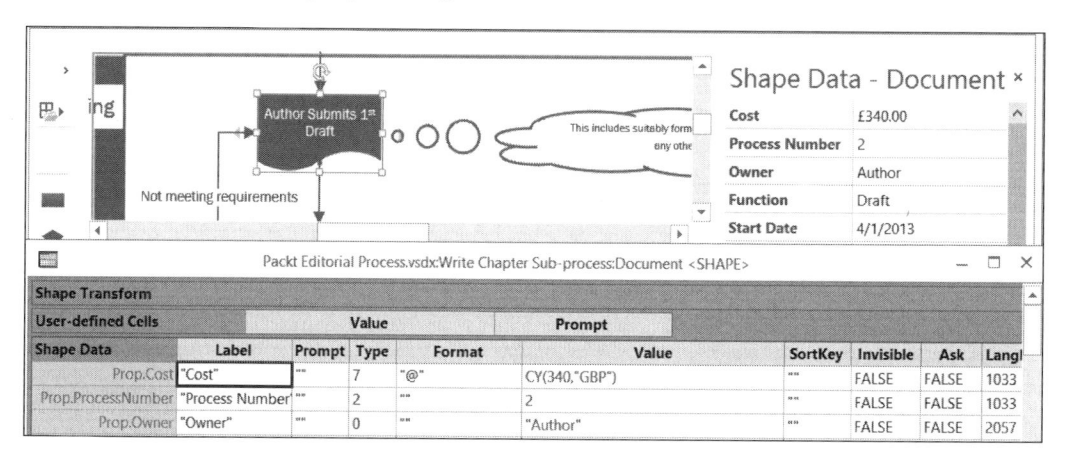

Generally, you would treat Currency in a similar manner to the Number type described earlier.

Looking at the Hyperlinks section

A shape in Visio can have multiple hyperlinks but one row has a reserved name, `Hyperlink.msvSubprocess`, to provide a link to a sub-process page. The following screenshot shows that a row in the **Hyperlinks** section, which has a value in either the **Address** or **SubAddresss** column, will be a menu item on the right mouse click menu, provided the **Invisible** column value is **FALSE**.

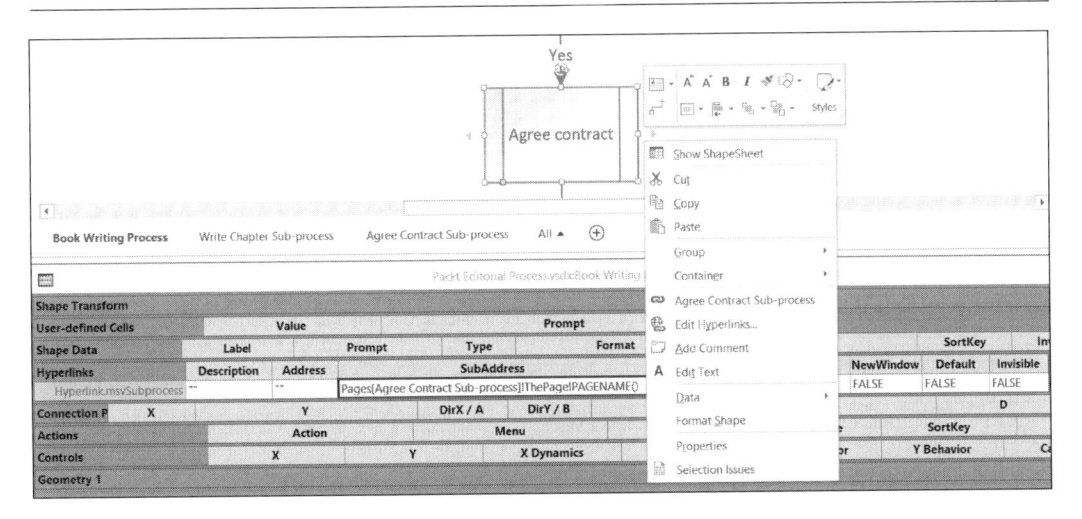

So, you can test if a shape has a sub-process reference with the following formula:

```
=NOT(ISERR(INT(INDEX(0,"Hyperlink.msvSubprocess.NewWindow"))))
```

This is checking for the existence of the named Hyperlink row that is created by the **Subprocess** commands on the **PROCESS** tab. There is no function to check directly for the existence of a row; moreover, since the **Hyperlinks** section is optional, there is no guarantee that the `Hyperlink.msvSubProcess` cell exists at all. The INDEX function is used to get the value in a list, and you can pass the name of cells as a string to this function. Normally when you enter the name of a cell as an argument to a function, it is immediately converted into an object reference, or will return an error if the cell does not exist. This prevents you from entering formulas with references to non-existent cells. However, the name of a non-existent cell can be entered by name as part of a list as an argument to the INDEX function, which will then try to resolve the name of the cell to obtain the value in that cell. Of course it will fail to find a value if the cell does not exist and by choosing a cell that can only contain a Boolean value, the ISERR function will return the error result of the attempted conversion to an integer by using the INT function. All that remains is to reverse the error result with the NOT function to change the meaning to verify the existence of a cell.

Understanding the ShapeSheet™

> Zero converts to FALSE in a cell that is used to store Boolean values in Visio, and any non-zero number converts to TRUE.

You cannot easily test a page to check if it is a sub-process, or where it is used in a main process, because a sub-process may be part of many parent processes.

Working with Layer Membership

Shape **Layer Membership** is more complicated than you might think. The ShapeSheet of the page stores the **Layers** for that page and, as you can see from the following screenshot, an individual shape's ShapeSheet merely stores a list of indexes of the page's **Layers**.

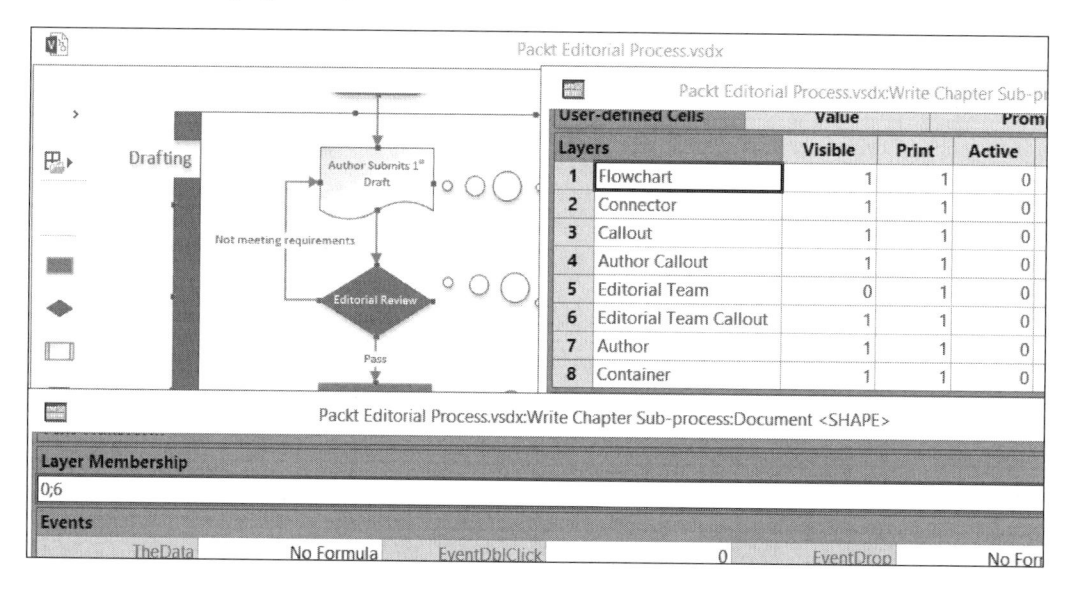

Layers with the same name may have a different index number on different pages within the same document. Therefore, you cannot create a rule that tests for a layer by index.

The layer settings in the page control whether a layer is visible or printable.

You could have a rule that insists that all relevant shapes must be assigned to a layer, which is given as:

```
=NOT(STRSAME(LayerMember,""))
```

Or a rule that states that it must be on one layer only:

```
=NOT(AND(STRSAME(LayerMember,""),FIND(";",LayerMember,1)))
```

You can then check if the assigned layer is currently visible:

```
=INT(INDEX(0,"ThePage!Layers.Visible["&INDEX(0,LayerMember)+1&"]"))
```

Notice how you can refer to the ShapeSheet of the page using the `ThePage!` syntax. You can similarly refer to the ShapeSheet of the document using the `TheDoc!` syntax.

Summary

In this chapter, we have explored a lot of the ShapeSheet functions that can be used in validation tests, and we have focused on the ShapeSheet sections that are probably most relevant for creating validation rules.

You may have noticed that there are no functions for checking connectivity in this chapter. Well, they are part of the new quasi-ShapeSheet functions that can only be used with the Validation API, so we will examine those later.

In the next chapter, we will examine the new **Validation Rules API** and you will understand why it is important to understand both the Visio object model and **ShapeSheet** functions, if you want to be able to analyze existing rules or create your own.

4
Understanding the Validation API

The **Validation API** was new in Visio 2010 Premium edition but is now part of Visio 2013 Professional; it provides the opportunity for creating diagramming rules. These rules can help eliminate common errors and enables companies to enforce diagramming standards. A well-structured drawing could then be used to export the encapsulated data and drawn relationships between elements to some external application, if desired.

In the first chapter, we had an overview of the user interface of the **Diagram Validation** group on the **PROCESS** tab, and a quick look at the elements in the XML format. In this chapter we will explore the objects, collections, and methods in the Validation API.

An overview of Validation objects

The Validation object model is accessed from the Visio **Document** object. The **Validation** object is only available if the code is running in Visio 2013 Professional edition, so you should check the edition, as described previously in *Chapter 2, Understanding the Microsoft Visio Object Model*.

Understanding the Validation API

[Diagram showing Document → Validation object hierarchy with ValidationIssues, ValidationIssue, ValidationRuleSets, ValidationRuleSet, ValidationRules, and ValidationRule classes and their properties]

Document
- Validation

Validation
- Application
- Document
- Issues
- LastValidatedDate
- ObjectType
- RuleSets
- ShowIgnoredIssues
- Stat
- *Validate*

ValidationIssues
- Item
- ItemFromID

ValidationIssue
- Rule

ValidationRuleSets
- Item
- ItemFromID

ValidationRuleSet
- Rules

ValidationRules
- Item

ValidationRule
- RuleSet

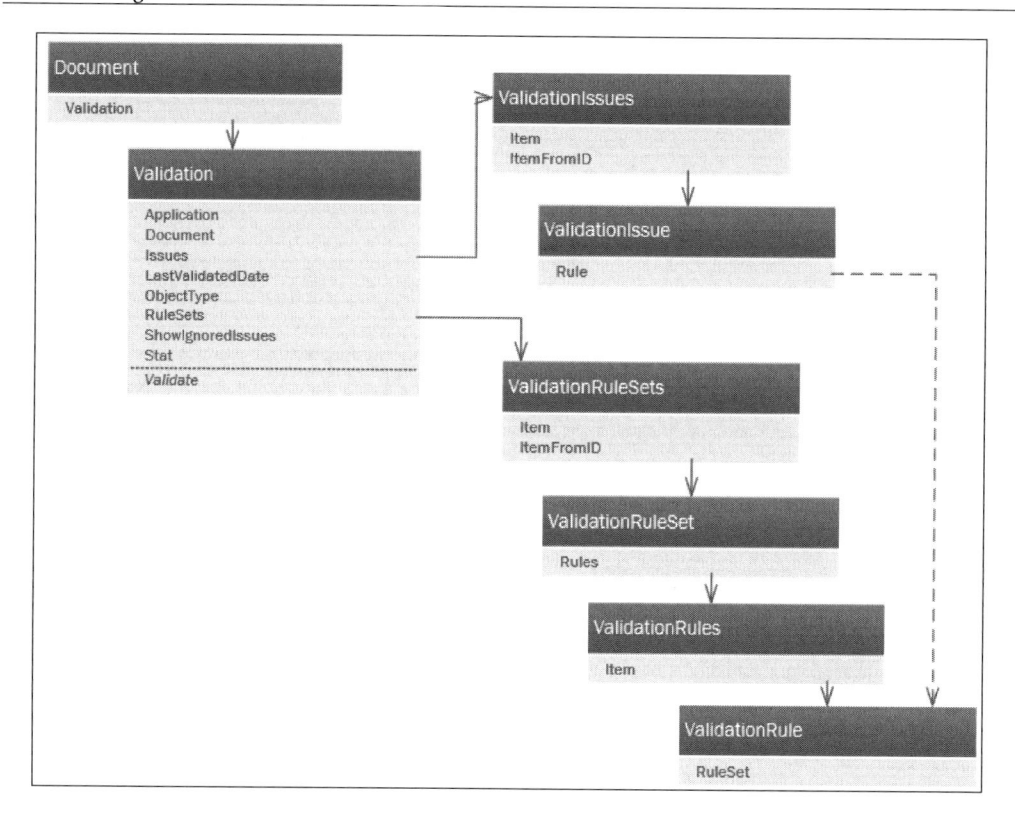

The **Validation** object contains two collections, **Issues** and **RuleSets**, that lead you to the main areas of the API.

The **ShowIgnoredIssues** property merely dictates whether or not the **Issues** window displays ignored issues. If the user selects to show ignored issues, they are shown as grayed out, as seen in the following screenshot:

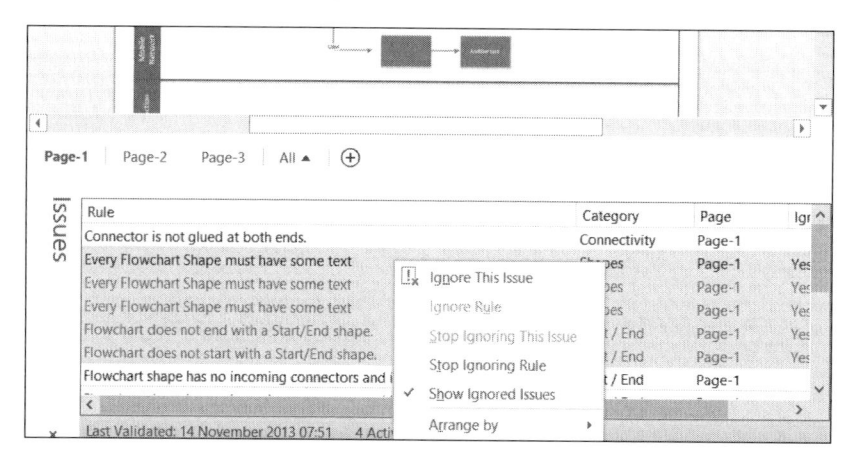

[Screenshot of Issues window showing rules list with context menu containing: Ignore This Issue, Ignore Rule, Stop Ignoring This Issue, Stop Ignoring Rule, Show Ignored Issues (checked), Arrange by]

[124]

The following `DebugPrintValidation` macro will display the detail of the validation object but notice that you have to delve into the `Issues`, `Issue`, and `Rule` objects to retrieve the count of ignored issues, as displayed in the UI. In fact, an issue can be ignored individually, or by virtue of its rule being marked as ignored.

```
Public Sub DebugPrintValidation()
Debug.Print "DebugPrintValidation"
Dim ignoredIssues As Integer
    With Visio.ActiveDocument.Validation
        ignoredIssues = getIgnoredIssueCount(.issues)
        Debug.Print , "ActiveDocument.Name", .Document.Name
        Debug.Print , "Total issues", .issues.Count
        Debug.Print , "Active issues", _
            .issues.Count - ignoredIssues
        Debug.Print , "Ignored issues", ignoredIssues
        Debug.Print , "LastValidatedDate", .LastValidatedDate
        Debug.Print , "RuleSets.Count", .RuleSets.Count
        Debug.Print , "ShowIgnoredIssues", .ShowIgnoredIssues
        Debug.Print , "Stat", .Stat
    End With
End Sub


Private Function getIgnoredIssueCount(ByVal issues As
ValidationIssues) As Integer
Dim i As Integer
Dim issue As ValidationIssue
    For Each issue In issues
        i = i + (Abs(issue.Ignored = True) Or Abs(issue.Rule.Ignored =
            True))
    Next
    getIgnoredIssueCount = i
End Function
```

The preceding code will give an output like this:

DebugPrintValidation	
ActiveDocument.Name	WorldViewer Data Flow.vsdx
Total issues	5
Active issues	3
Ignored issues	2
LastValidatedDate	09/06/2013 08:37:59
RuleSets.Count	1

Understanding the Validation API

DebugPrintValidation	
ShowIgnoredIssues	True
Stat	0

Using the Validate method

You cannot "Validate" a document unless you have at least one ruleset in it. The `Validate([ruleSet as RuleSet][, flags as visValidationFlags])` method has two optional parameters—`RuleSet` to use, and `flags` to indicate whether the **Issues** window should be opened.

Validate will check the ruleset, if specified (or all enabled rulesets if none are specified), and clear any existing issues before creating any new issues found. The `LastValidatedDate` will be set so that you can check when a document was validated.

Validating custom rules written in code

You do not have to add all rules within a ruleset. You can have custom validation code for difficult tasks such as checking cyclic routes in process flows, and then run your code whenever the `Validate()` method is called.

The `Document` object has a `RuleSetValidated` event that will fire for every ruleset after validation. It is done as follows:

```
Private Sub Document_RuleSetValidated(ByVal RuleSet As
  IVValidationRuleSet)
    Debug.Print "Document_RuleSetValidated for" & RuleSet.Name,
  Now()
End Sub
```

It is not worth checking the `Validation` object for the number of issues until after all rulesets have been processed, because it does not get updated incrementally during `Validate()`.

> The preceding code is in Visual Basic for Applications, which provides a `Document` object `WithEvents` in the `ThisDocument` class. In general, it is not considered a good coding practice to use `WithEvents` because it can unintentionally create a very chatty application that wastes processing time raising unnecessary events. It is far better to use the `AddAdvise (EventCode As Integer, SinkIUnkOrIDisp, IIDSink As String, TargetArgs As String)` method to create events as required (see the Visio SDK Documentation for more information).

[126]

You can now add whatever code you want to for a ruleset, and then run the code after the ruleset has been validated. You can then add any issues to the `Validation.Issues` collection using the `ValidationRule.AddIssue([TargetPage As Page] [,TargetShape As Shape])` method.

Working with the ValidationRuleSets collection

Validation Rules are grouped within `ValidationRuleSets`. The UI provides the ability to import a built-in ruleset (Flowchart or BPMN 2.0) or a ruleset from another open Visio document, but the programmer can use the `Add(NameU as String)` or `AddCopy(RuleSet as ValidationRuleSet[, NameU])` methods to create a new one.

The following code could be run from the **Immediate** window in VBA:

```
Visio.ActiveDocument.Validation.RuleSets.Add "bVisual"
```

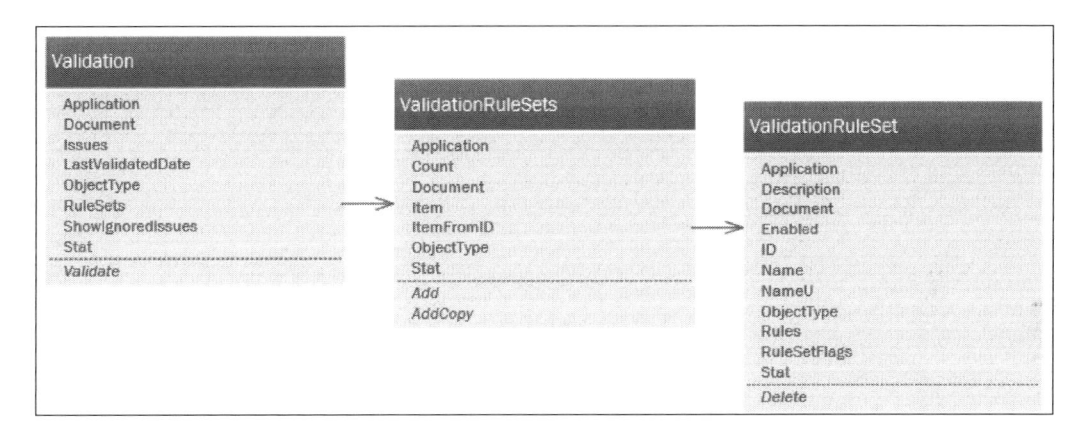

You can retrieve a ruleset by its `index` position in the collection, using `ValidationRuleSets.Item(index)`, or by its **ID** using `ValidationRuleSets.ItemFromID(ID)`. Once you have retrieved a ruleset, you can read its **Name** (this can be edited to be a localized version), **NameU**, **Description** (displayed as the tool tip in the UI), or check if the `RuleSets` is enabled for validation.

Understanding the Validation API

The `RuleSetFlags` value determines if the ruleset is visible in the **Rules to Check** dropdown in the UI, shown as follows:

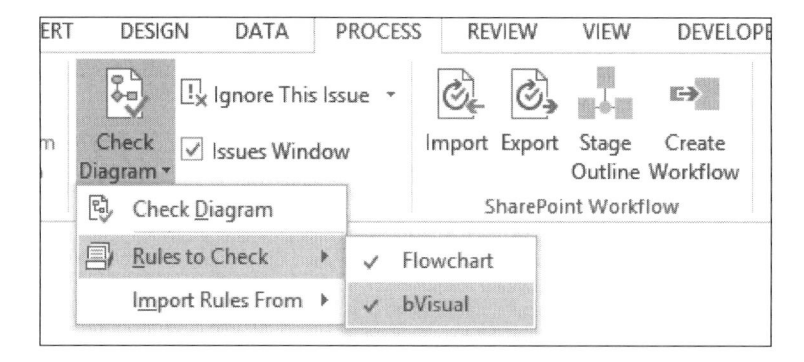

The default value is 0 (`VisRuleSetFlags.visRuleSetDefault`), but you can change it to 1 (`VisRuleSetFlags.visRuleSetHidden`) if you do not want it to appear in the **Rules to Check** menu.

The following macro, `EnumerateRuleSets`, displays a list of the rulesets in the active document:

```
Public Sub EnumerateRuleSets()
Dim doc As Visio.Document
Dim ruleSet As Visio.ValidationRuleSet
    Set doc = Visio.ActiveDocument
    Debug.Print "EnumerateRuleSets : Count =", _
      doc.Validation.RuleSets.Count
    Debug.Print , "ID", "Enabled", "RuleSetFlags", _
      "Count of Rules", "Name", "Description"
    For Each ruleSet In doc.Validation.RuleSets
        With ruleSet
            Debug.Print , .ID, .Enabled, _
                .RuleSetFlags, .Rules.Count, _
                .NameU, .Description
        End With
    Next
End Sub
```

This will produce an output shown as follows:

EnumerateRuleSets : Count = 2					
ID	Enabled	RuleSetFlags	Count of Rules	Name	Description
1	True	0	11	Flowchart	Verify that Flowchart shapes are connected properly.
4	True	0	0	bVisual	

Adding to or updating a ruleset

Well, you can always copy a ruleset from another document in the UI, but you can also create a new one in code or update an existing one. This can be done as follows:

```
Public Sub AddOrUpdateRuleSet()
Dim ruleSet As Visio.ValidationRuleSet
Dim ruleSetNameU As String
Dim doc As Visio.Document
    Set doc = Visio.ActiveDocument
    ruleSetNameU = "bVisual"
    'Check if the rule set exists already
    Set ruleSet = _
        getRuleSet(doc, ruleSetNameU)
    If ruleSet Is Nothing Then
        'Create the new rule set
        Set ruleSet = _
            doc.Validation.RuleSets.Add(ruleSetNameU)
    End If
    ruleSet.Name = "Be Visual"
    ruleSet.Description = "Example Rule Set"
    ruleSet.Enabled = True
    ruleSet.RuleSetFlags = visRuleSetDefault

End Sub

Private Function getRuleSet(ByVal doc As Visio.Document, _
    ByVal nameU As String) As Visio.ValidationRuleSet
Dim retVal As Visio.ValidationRuleSet
Dim ruleSet As Visio.ValidationRuleSet
    Set retVal = Nothing
```

Understanding the Validation API

```
            For Each ruleSet In doc.Validation.RuleSets
                If UCase(ruleSet.nameU) = UCase(nameU) Then
                    Set retVal = ruleSet
                    Exit For
                End If
            Next
            Set getRuleSet = retVal
    End Function
```

Notice how the tool tip and displayed name are updated in the UI:

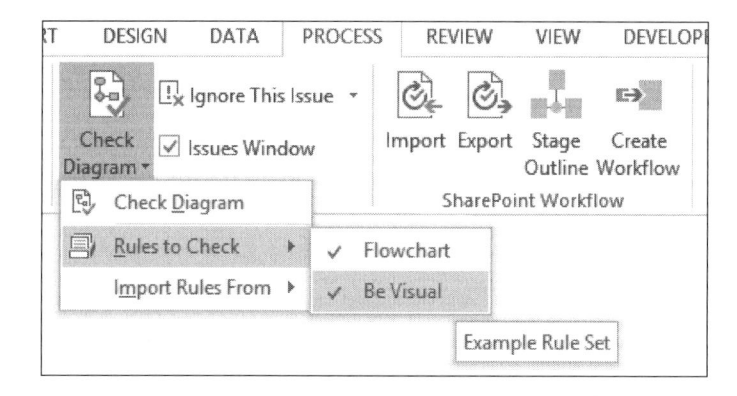

Of course, you can also delete a ruleset as follows:

```
    Public Sub DeleteRuleSet()
    Dim ruleSetNameU As String
    Dim doc As Visio.Document
        Set doc = Visio.ActiveDocument
        ruleSetNameU = "bVisual"
        'Check if the rule set exists already
        If Not getRuleSet(doc, ruleSetNameU) Is Nothing Then
            'Delete the rule set
            doc.Validation.RuleSets(ruleSetNameU).Delete
        End If
    End Sub
    End Sub
```

> You can use the NameU or Index of a ruleset to retrieve it from the Validation.RuleSets collection.

[130]

Working with the ValidationRules collection

Once you have a ruleset, you can review, amend, or add to the rules within it. You can add a rule using the `ValidationRules.AddRule(NameU as string)` method. Note that `NameU` is really for use in code, since it is the **Description** property that is displayed in the `UI`. `NameU` that must be unique within the `Rules` collection of the parent `ValidationRuleSet`.

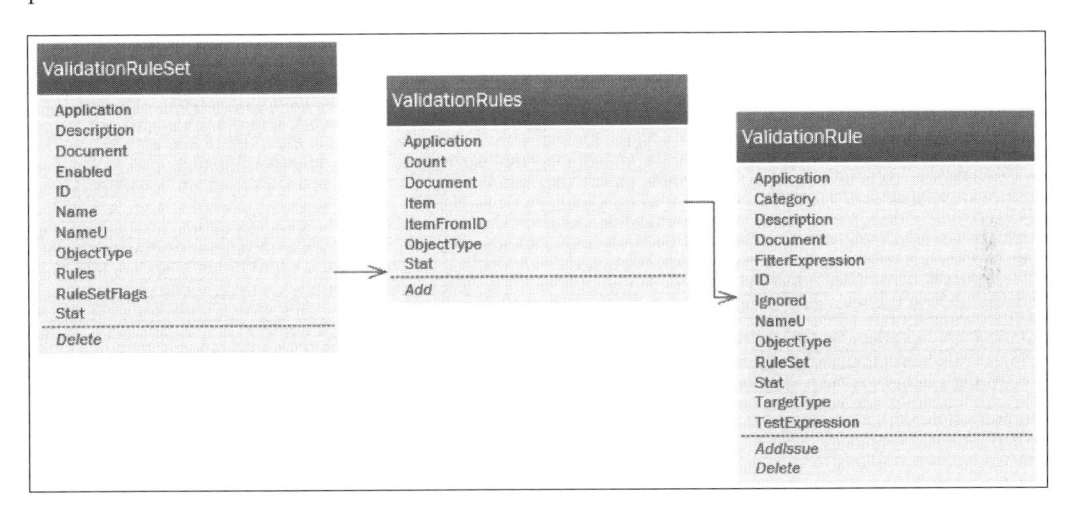

```
ValidationRuleSet
    Application
    Description
    Document
    Enabled
    ID
    Name
    NameU
    ObjectType
    Rules
    RuleSetFlags
    Stat
    Delete

ValidationRules
    Application
    Count
    Document
    Item
    ItemFromID
    ObjectType
    Stat
    Add

ValidationRule
    Application
    Category
    Description
    Document
    FilterExpression
    ID
    Ignored
    NameU
    ObjectType
    RuleSet
    Stat
    TargetType
    TestExpression
    AddIssue
    Delete
```

You can retrieve a rule by its `index` position in the collection, using `ValidationRules.Item(index)`, or by its `ID` using `ValidationRules.ItemFromID(ID)`. Once you have retrieved `ValidationRule` you can read its `NameU` and `Description` or check whether the ruleset is ignored for validation:

```
Public Sub EnumerateRules()
Dim doc As Visio.Document
Dim ruleSet As Visio.ValidationRuleSet
Dim rule As Visio.ValidationRule
    Set doc = Visio.ActiveDocument

    For Each ruleSet In doc.Validation.RuleSets
        If ruleSet.Enabled Then
            Debug.Print "EnumerateRules for RuleSet : " & _
                ruleSet.nameU & " : Count = " & _
                ruleSet.Rules.Count
            Debug.Print "ID", "Ignored", "Category", _
                "NameU", "Description", _
                "T" & vbCrLf, _
```

Understanding the Validation API

```
                "FilterExpression",, "TestExpression"
            For Each rule In ruleSet.Rules
                With rule
                    Debug.Print .ID, .Ignored, .Category, _
                        .nameU, .Description, _
                        .TargetType & vbCrLf, _
                        .FilterExpression,, _
                        .TestExpression
                End With
            Next
        End If
    Next
End Sub
```

The output from this looks as follows (note that the lines are wrapped line columns for clarity):

\multicolumn{6}{l}{EnumerateRules for RuleSet : Flowchart : Count = 11}
ID	Ignored	Category	NameU	Description	T
	FilterExpression		TestExpression		
1	False	Connectivity	UngluedConnector	Connector is not glued at both ends.	0
	ROLE()=1		AND(AGGCOUNT(GLUEDSHAPES(4)) = 1, AGGCOUNT(GLUEDSHAPES(5)) = 1)		
2	False	Start / End	StartWithout Terminator	Flowchart shape has no incoming connectors and is not a Start/End shape.	0
	AND(OR(HASCATEGORY("Flowchart"),ONLAYER("Flowchart")),NOT(OR(HASCATEGORY("Start/End"),STRSAME(LEFT(MASTERNAME(750),9),"Start/End"),STRSAME(LEFT(MASTERNAME(750),10),"Terminator"))))		AGGCOUNT(GLUEDSHAPES(1)) > 0		

Chapter 4

ID	Ignored	Category	NameU	Description	T
	FilterExpression		TestExpression		
3	False	Start / End	EndWithout Terminator	Flowchart shape has no outgoing connectors and is not a Start/End shape.	0
	AND(OR(HASCATEGORY("Flowchart"),ONLAYER("Flowchart")),NOT(OR(HASCATEGORY("Start/End"),STRSAME(LEFT(MASTERNAME(750),9),"Start/End"),STRSAME(LEFT(MASTERNAME(750),10),"Terminator"))))		AGGCOUNT(GLUEDSHAPES(2)) > 0		

```
EnumerateRules for RuleSet : Flowchart : Count = 11
```

At last, we are starting to see how the validation logic of each rule works and you can see why the last chapter was about understanding the **ShapeSheet** functionality.

You should always set a value for the `Category` of a rule because the UI can optionally group by `Category`, which helps the user fix any issues arising.

`TargetType` can be one of three values of the `VisRuleTargets` enumerator, which defines the scope of the rule. They are:

- `VisRuleTargets.visRuleTargetShape` (0)
- `VisRuleTargets.visRuleTargetPage` (1)
- `VisRuleTargets.visRuleTargetDocument` (2)

You can create an issue for a rule using the `AddIssue([TargetPage as Page] [,TargetShape as Shape])` method, but you should ensure that the relevant optional arguments are set. `TargetType` of the rule determines which optional arguments should be set. For example, if the `TargetType = 0` then you should include both the `TargetPage` and `TargetShape` parameters. If the `TargetType = 1` then you should only set the `TargetPage` parameter; if the `TargetType = 2` then do not set any parameter. This is important as it controls the behavior when you select an issue in the **Issues** window.

The **Ignored** flag can be set in the UI or by the developer in code.

Understanding the Validation API

The `FilterExpression` property is evaluated against each of the potential targets, as defined by the `TargetType` property. If the `FilterExpression` property returns `True` then the `TestExpression` is evaluated, but if it returns `False` (or if there is invalid syntax), then the target is skipped. The `TestExpression` property is then evaluated and, if it returns `True`, then the target is deemed to comply with the rule. If it returns `False` (or if there is invalid syntax), then `ValidationIssue` is added to the `Validation.Issues` collection.

Lastly, you can remove a rule from a ruleset with the `Rule.Delete()` method.

Adding to or updating a rule

Later, we will go into the `FilterExpression` property and the `TestExpression` property in great detail but, for now, we are going to create a simple rule that checks that there are no blank pages in our document. To do this, we have added a rule called `NoShapesInPage` to the `bVisual` ruleset in the following code:

```
Public Sub AddOrUpdateRule()
Dim ruleSet As Visio.ValidationRuleSet
Dim rule As Visio.ValidationRule
Dim ruleNameU As String
Dim doc As Visio.Document
    Set doc = Visio.ActiveDocument
    ruleNameU = "NoShapesInPage"
    Set ruleSet = getRuleSet(doc, "bVisual")
    If ruleSet Is Nothing Then
        Exit Sub
    End If
    Set rule = getRule(ruleSet, ruleNameU)
    If rule Is Nothing Then
        Set rule = ruleSet.Rules.Add(ruleNameU)
    End If
    rule.Category = "Shapes"
    rule.Description = _
        "A page must contain at least one shape"
    rule.TargetType = visRuleTargetPage
    rule.FilterExpression = ""
    rule.TestExpression = "AggCount(ShapesOnPage())>0"

End Sub

Private Function getRule(ByVal ruleSet As Visio.ValidationRuleSet, _
    ByVal nameU As String) As Visio.ValidationRule
Dim retVal As Visio.ValidationRule
```

```
    Dim rule As Visio.ValidationRule
        Set retVal = Nothing
        For Each rule In ruleSet.Rules
            If UCase(rule.nameU) = UCase(nameU) Then
                Set retVal = rule
                Exit For
            End If
        Next
        Set getRule = retVal
    End Function
```

Notice that we have set the target to the page, and `TestExpression` is `AggCount(ShapesOnPage())>0`, which will evaluate to `True` if there are any shapes on the page:

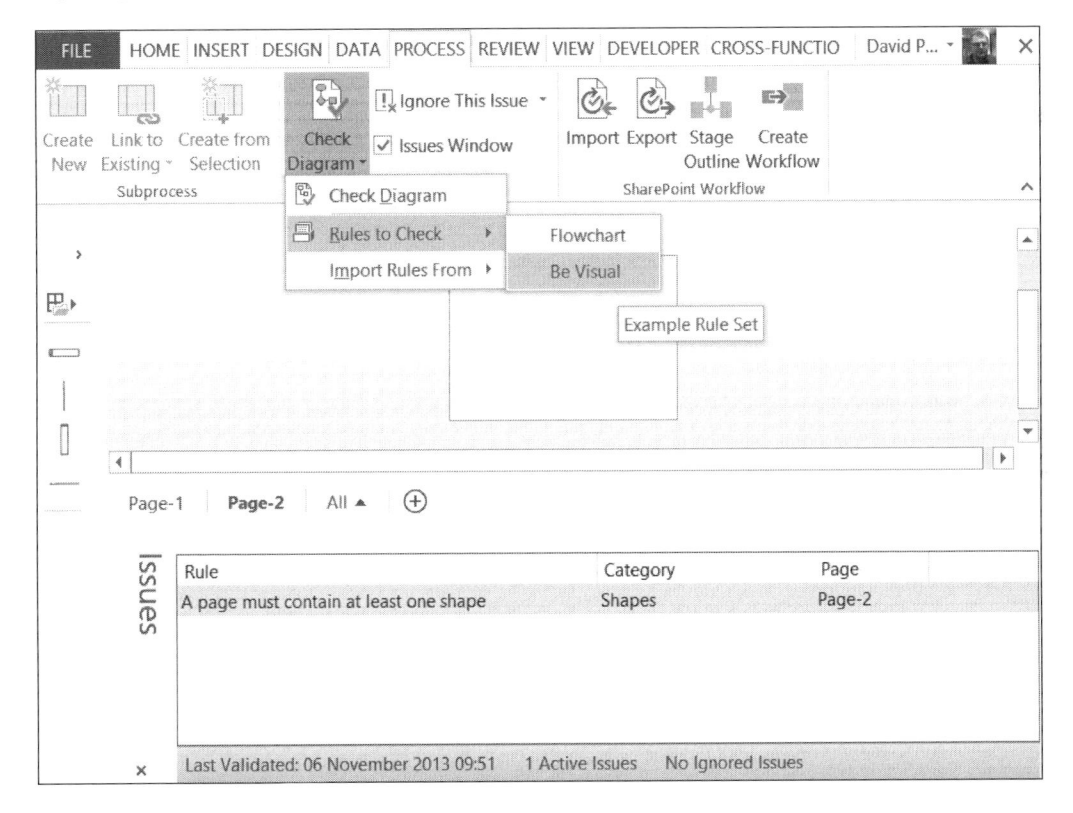

> Since a document must usually have at least one page, this rule would also ensure that there are shapes in the document. The only exception would be if a document only contains background pages, because rules are not validated for background pages.

Understanding the Validation API

Another example might be a rule that every flowchart shape should have some text. If we assume that every flowchart shape is on the `Flowchart` layer, then we could construct a `FilterExpression` that tests for this. This will ensure that only relevant shapes are processed with `TestExpression` that checks for the existence of text:

```
Public Sub AddOrUpdateRuleA()
Dim ruleSet As Visio.ValidationRuleSet
Dim rule As Visio.ValidationRule
Dim ruleNameU As String
Dim doc As Visio.Document
    Set doc = Visio.ActiveDocument
    ruleNameU = "FlowchartShapesMustHaveText"
    Set ruleSet = getRuleSet(doc, "bVisual")
    If ruleSet Is Nothing Then
        Exit Sub
    End If
    Set rule = getRule(ruleSet, ruleNameU)
    If rule Is Nothing Then
        Set rule = ruleSet.Rules.Add(ruleNameU)
    End If
    rule.Category = "Shapes"
    rule.Description = _
        "Every Flowchart Shapes must have some text"
    rule.TargetType = visRuleTargetShape
    rule.FilterExpression = "ONLAYER(""Flowchart"")"
    rule.TestExpression = _
        "NOT(STRSAME(SHAPETEXT(TheText), """"))"
End Sub
```

This rule uses the ShapeSheet function `SHAPETEXT(shapename!TheText[,flag])` combined with the `STRSAME("string1", "string2"[, ignoreCase])` function to check for an empty text string.

Verifying that a rule works

This is not a simple question because you do not get any error syntax checking when you are writing the Filter and Test Expressions for rules. The `FilterExpression` has to return `True` if the page or shape is to be checked against the `TestExpression`. Therefore, simply toggle the formula in `TestExpression` between `True` and `False` (or 1 and 0), while observing if the expected page or shapes raise an issue or not by validating the document.

Chapter 4

Once you are satisfied that `FilterExpression` is working, you can move on to verifying `TestExpression`. This should also return a Boolean value, and should return `False` in order to raise an issue. Therefore, reverse the logic by wrapping the formula with `NOT(...)`. This should result in the raising of an issue where there is a match. As we did earlier, reverse the logic, and observe if this causes the expected issues to be alternately raised or not.

If there is no change in the issues raised, at either stage when the logic is toggled, then there must be a syntax error in `FilterExpression` or `TestExpression`.

You will learn more about writing these expressions in *Chapter 7, Creating Validation Rules*.

> Validation rules that target the document are only re-evaluated when the entire document changes. Since this occurs infrequently, there may be cases where an issue that targets the document remains in the document after it has been fixed by the user—a user may fix an issue and still see it in the **Issues** window after a validation is run. For this reason, Microsoft recommends that you only use validation rules that target the document when you are using a custom solution to manage validation issues. When you manage validation issues in code, you will be able to re-evaluate the validation rule at your discretion.

Working with the ValidationIssues collection

The `ValidationIssues` collection stores the issues created by the `Validation.Validate([RuleSet as ValidationRuleSet] [, Flags as ValidationFlags])` method and by the `RuleSet.AddIssue([TargetPage as Page] [,TargetShape as Shape])` method. It can be reset using the `Clear()` method, which will also zero `LastValidatedDate` of the parent `Validation` object.

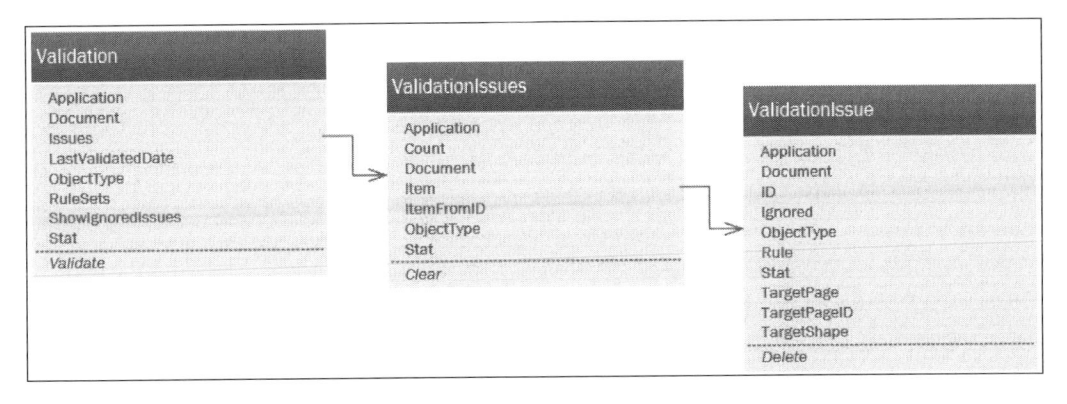

Validation	ValidationIssues	ValidationIssue
Application	Application	Application
Document	Count	Document
Issues	Document	ID
LastValidatedDate	Item	Ignored
ObjectType	ItemFromID	ObjectType
RuleSets	ObjectType	Rule
ShowIgnoredIssues	Stat	Stat
Stat	Clear	TargetPage
Validate		TargetPageID
		TargetShape
		Delete

[137]

Understanding the Validation API

Most issues are automatically created by the `Validate()` method but you can write code to add issues whenever the user clicks on **Check Diagram** against a particular ruleset. You would do this by listening to the `RuleSetValidated(RuleSet as ValidationRuleSet)` event of the `Application`, `Documents`, or `Document` object. This technique is used by the **Microsoft SharePoint 2013 Workflow** template in Visio 2013.

You can enumerate the current issues in a document, and check which rule has been transgressed, using the following code:

```
Public Sub EnumerateIssues()
Dim issue As Visio.ValidationIssue
Dim shpName As String
Dim doc As Visio.Document
    Set doc = Visio.ActiveDocument

    Debug.Print "EnumerateIssues : Count = " & _
      doc.Validation.issues.Count
    Debug.Print , "ID", "Ignored", "Rule.NameU", _
      TargetPage.Name", "TargetShape.Name"
    For Each issue In doc.Validation.issues
        If issue.targetShape Is Nothing Then
            shpName = ""
        Else
            shpName = issue.targetShape.Name
        End If
        Debug.Print , issue.ID, issue.Ignored, _
          issue.rule.nameU, _
          issue.TargetPage.Name, shpName
    Next
End Sub
```

The `EnumerateIssues()` macro will produce an output similar to this:

EnumerateIssues : Count = 6

ID	Ignored	Rule.NameU	TargetPage.Name	TargetShape.Name
121	False	NoEndTerminator	Page-1	
122	False	EndWithoutTerminator	Page-1	Process.32
123	False	NoShapeText	Page-1	Process.32
124	False	FlowchartShapes MustHaveText Page-1	Process.32	
125	False	EndWithoutTerminator	Page-1	Process.34
126	False	NoShapesInPage	Page-2	

Chapter 4

> Three entries do not have a target shape because the rule applies to a page.

Compare the previous listings in the table with that seen in the following screenshot:

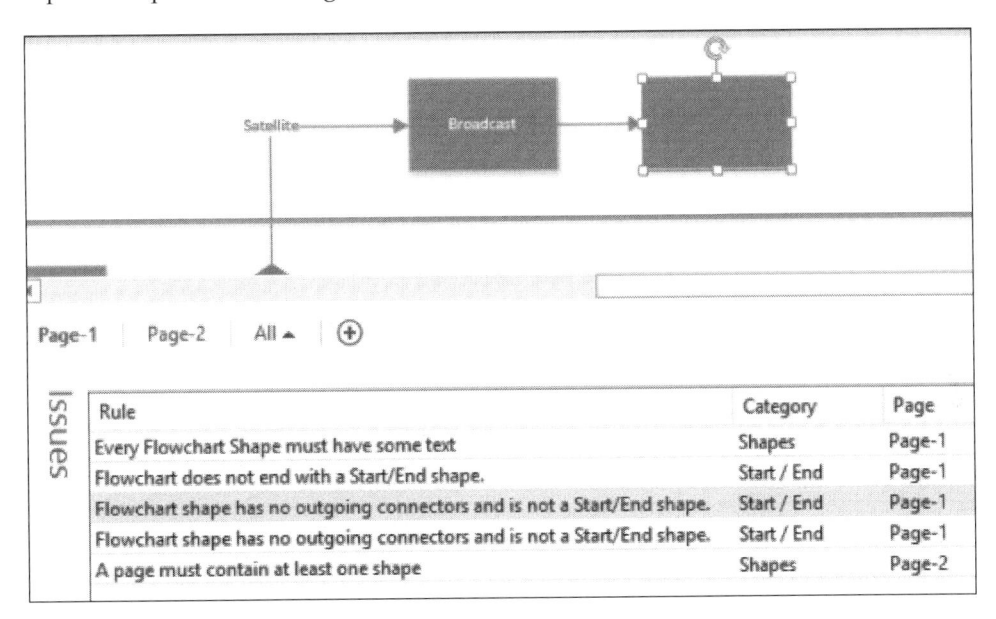

Rule	Category	Page
Every Flowchart Shape must have some text	Shapes	Page-1
Flowchart does not end with a Start/End shape.	Start / End	Page-1
Flowchart shape has no outgoing connectors and is not a Start/End shape.	Start / End	Page-1
Flowchart shape has no outgoing connectors and is not a Start/End shape.	Start / End	Page-1
A page must contain at least one shape	Shapes	Page-2

Firstly, you can tell that this is a multi-page document because the **Page** column is not displayed if there is only one foreground page.

Secondly, you cannot see which shape (if any) is the target of the issue. The user can see the shape in the page when an issue is selected because Visio automatically selects it. However, it is impossible to see how many issues a particular shape has.

You can retrieve an issue by its `index` position in the collection, using `ValidationIssues.Item(index)`, or by its ID using `ValidationIssues.ItemFromID(ID)`. Once you have retrieved an issue, you can access the rule that was broken and, if applicable, the page and shape involved.

Retrieving the selected issue in the Issues window

The **Issues** window is a built-in subwindow of the active window in Visio. If you were to write some code to enumerate through the subwindows of the active window, then you can see that there are a number of built-in windows that may or may not be visible:

```
Public Sub EnumerateWindows()
Dim win As Visio.Window
    Debug.Print "EnumerateWindows : Count =" _
        & Application.ActiveWindow.Windows.Count
    Debug.Print , "ID", "Type", "Visible", "Caption"
    For Each win In Application.ActiveWindow.Windows
        Debug.Print , win.ID, win.Type, _
            win.Visible, win.Caption
    Next win
End Sub
```

The `EnumerateWindows()` macro will produce a listing similar to the following table:

EnumerateWindows : Count =9

ID	Type	Visible	Caption
8650	7	True	Basic Flowchart Shapes
2263	10	True	Issues
1670	10	False	Size & Position
2044	10	False	
1721	10	False	
1653	10	False	Pan & Zoom
8654	7	True	Cross-Functional Flowchart Shapes
1658	10	False	Shape Data
1669	10	True	Shapes

Here you can see that there are different types of windows, and they all have a unique ID. In fact, the Type = 10 is the constant `visWinTypes.visAnchorBarAddon`, and the ID = 2263 is the constant `visWinTypes.visWinIDValidationIssues`.

Knowing this, you can write some code to get more information about the selected issue by using the following code:

```
Public Sub DebugPrintIssue()
Dim issue As Visio.ValidationIssue
    Set issue = GetSelectedIssue
    If issue Is Nothing Then
        Exit Sub
    End If
    Debug.Print "DebugPrintIssue : " & issue.ID
    With issue
        Debug.Print , "Ignored", .Ignored
        Debug.Print , "RuleSet.Name", .rule.ruleSet.Name
        Debug.Print , "Rule.ID", .rule.ID
        Debug.Print , "Rule.NameU", .rule.nameU
        Debug.Print , "Rule.Description", .rule.Description
        Debug.Print , "Rule.Category", .rule.Category
        Debug.Print , "Rule.FilterExpression", _
            .rule.FilterExpression
        Debug.Print , "Rule.TestExpression", .rule.TestExpression
        Debug.Print , "TargetPageID", .TargetPageID
        If Not .TargetPage Is Nothing Then
            Debug.Print , "TargetPage.Name", .TargetPage.Name
        End If
        If Not .targetShape Is Nothing Then
            Debug.Print , "TargetShape.ID", .targetShape.ID
            Debug.Print , "TargetShape.Name", _
                .targetShape.Name
        End If
    End With
End Sub

Private Function GetSelectedIssue() As ValidationIssue
Dim issue As Visio.ValidationIssue
Dim win As Visio.Window
    Set win = _
        Application.ActiveWindow.Windows.ItemFromID( _
        VisWinTypes.visWinIDValidationIssues)
    If win.Visible = False Then
        Set issue = Nothing
    Else
        Set issue = win.SelectedValidationIssue
    End If
    Set GetSelectedIssue = issue
End Function
```

Understanding the Validation API

So, with the fourth issue selected in the preceding listing, the **Immediate** window displayed is the following:

DebugPrintIssue : 125	
Ignored	False
RuleSet.Name	Flowchart
Rule.ID	3
Rule.NameU	EndWithoutTerminator
Rule.Description	Flowchart shape has no outgoing connectors and is not a Start/End shape.
Rule.Category	Start / End
Rule.FilterExpression	AND(OR(HASCATEGORY("Flowchart"),ONLAYER("Flowchart")),NOT(OR(HASCATEGORY("Start/End"),STRSAME(LEFT(MASTERNAME(750),9),"Start/End"),STRSAME(LEFT(MASTERNAME(750),10),"Terminator"))))
Rule.TestExpression	AGGCOUNT(GLUEDSHAPES(2)) > 0
TargetPageID	0
TargetPage.Name	Page-1
TargetShape.ID	34
TargetShape.Name	Process.34

There are times when you need to react to the user selecting an issue in the UI. In this case, you can listen to the `SelectionChanged` event of the `ActiveWindow` in the Visio Application.

Notice that the **Issues** window itself, as with all of the add-on windows, does not have a selection changed event. Instead, you must listen to the `SelectionChanged` event of the parent window, which fires whenever the shape selection changes. When a user clicks an issue in the **Issues** window, then all shapes in the drawing window are deselected. If the issue is not a document issue, then the target page is activated in the drawing window; if there is a target shape, then this is selected in the drawing window.

The following code snippet, from the `ThisDocument` class, is not perfect because it has to listen for the `SelectionChanged` event of the drawing window object in order to retrieve the selected item in the **Issues** window, if it is open. This event only fires if the user selects an issue for a different shape or page in the **Issues** window. It does not detect a change of selection if the user subsequently selects another item in the **Issues** window that belongs to the same shape or page as the previously selected item.

Chapter 4

In the following code, the `RuleSetValidated` event for the `Document` object will be enabled because VBA automatically creates the `Document` object `WithEvents` in the `ThisDocument` class; however, the `StartListening()` method is required to initialize the `WithEvents` `Window` object for the drawing window itself.

```
Option Explicit

Private WithEvents mWin As Visio.Window

Public Sub StartListening()
    Set mWin = Application.ActiveWindow
End Sub

Private Sub Document_RuleSetValidated( _
    ByVal RuleSet As IVValidationRuleSet)
    Debug.Print "Document_RuleSetValidated for " & _
        RuleSet.Name, Now()
End Sub

Private Sub mWin_SelectionChanged(ByVal Window As IVWindow)
    Dim winIssues As Window
    Set winIssues = _
        Window.Windows.ItemFromID( _
        VisWinTypes.visWinIDValidationIssues)

    If Not winIssues.SelectedValidationIssue Is Nothing Then
        Debug.Print "mWin_SelectionChanged", _
            "Issue = " & _
            winIssues.SelectedValidationIssue.Rule.Description
    Else
        Debug.Print "mWin_SelectionChanged", "No Issue"
    End If

End Sub
```

Toggling the Issues window visibility

In the last section, you listed all of the current windows using the `EnumerateWindows()` method, and you could see that the ID of the **Issues** window is 2263. This is, in fact, the value of the constant `Visio.VisWinTypes.visWinIDValidationIssues`. You can use this constant to toggle the visibility of the **Issues** window in the UI with the following method:

```
Public Sub ToggleIssuesWindowVisibility()
Dim win As Visio.Window
    Set win = ActiveWindow.Windows.ItemFromID( _
        Visio.VisWinTypes.visWinIDValidationIssues)
    win.Visible = Not win.Visible
End Sub
```

Note that the **Issues** window is automatically made visible whenever the document is validated.

Listing the issues caused by a particular shape

A shape does not have a collection of issues directly associated with it. You will need to retrieve the relevant issues from the `Document.Validation.ValidationIssues` collection as follows:

```
Public Sub EnumerateShapeIssues()
If Application.ActiveWindow.Selection.Count = 0 Then
    Exit Sub
End If
Dim shp As Visio.Shape
Dim issue As Visio.ValidationIssue
    Set shp = Application.ActiveWindow.Selection.PrimaryItem
    Debug.Print "EnumerateShapeIssues : " & shp.Name
    Debug.Print , "ID", "Ignored", "Rule.NameU"
    For Each issue In shp.Document.Validation.issues
        If issue.targetShape Is shp Then
            Debug.Print , issue.ID, _
                issue.Ignored, issue.rule.nameU
        End If
    Next
End Sub
```

This will produce an output similar to this table:

EnumerateShapeIssues : Process.32		
ID	Ignored	Rule.NameU
122	False	EndWithoutTerminator
123	False	NoShapeText
124	False	FlowchartShapesMustHaveText

Using code to clear issues

When you are writing rules and then validating them in code, you will soon realize that Visio does not automatically clear all of the issues which were previously created, nor does Visio necessarily revalidate the same rule on an existing shape. It assumes that, by default, the rules have not changed. Therefore, if the diagram has not been changed, then it is not necessary to revalidate the shapes against the rules. So, it may be necessary to force Visio to revalidate by removing all existing issues. Fortunately, this can be done simply as follows:

```
Public Sub ClearAllIssues()
    Visio.ActiveDocument.Validation.issues.Clear
End Sub
```

Retrieving an existing issue in code

There will be times when you will need to test whether a particular document, page, or shape has already raised an issue for a specific rule. The following `getIssue()` method will retrieve an existing issue, if there is one; otherwise it will return `Nothing`. You should pass in the rule object, and then the `targetPage` object (or `Nothing`), and `targetShape` (or `Nothing`), as appropriate for the `TargetType` of the rule:

```
Private Function getIssue( _
  ByVal rule As Visio.ValidationRule, _
  ByVal targetPage As Visio.Page, _
  ByVal targetShape As Visio.Shape) As Visio.ValidationIssue
Dim retVal As Visio.ValidationIssue
Dim issue As Visio.ValidationIssue
    Set retVal = Nothing
    For Each issue In Visio.ActiveDocument.Validation.issues
        If issue.rule Is rule Then
            If rule.TargetType = visRuleTargetShape And _
              Not targetShape Is Nothing Then
                If targetShape Is issue.targetShape Then
                    Set retVal = issue
                    Exit For
                End If
            ElseIf rule.TargetType = visRuleTargetPage And _
              Not targetPage Is Nothing Then
                If targetPage Is issue.targetPage Then
                    Set retVal = issue
                    Exit For
                End If
            ElseIf rule.TargetType = _
```

Understanding the Validation API

```
            visRuleTargetDocument Then
                Set retVal = issue
                Exit For
            End If

        End If
    Next
    Set getIssue = retVal
End Function
```

Adding an issue in code

There are times when `FilterExpression` and `TestExpression` cannot adequately define the rule you want to check; then it is easier to write a bit of code. One such example could be ensuring that every page in the document is of portrait orientation. This involves iterating through all of the foreground pages in the document to check if the height is greater than the width. In a real solution, we should probably check that the ratio is correct, too. To do this, we'll first have to add an empty rule with a macro that utilizes the `getRuleSet()` and `getRule()` methods created earlier. This is done as follows:

```
Public Sub AddOrUpdateRuleB()
Dim ruleSet As Visio.ValidationRuleSet
Dim rule As Visio.ValidationRule
Dim ruleNameU As String
    ruleNameU = "PagesMustBePortraitOrientation"
    Set ruleSet = getRuleSet(Visio.ActiveDocument, "bVisual")
    If ruleSet Is Nothing Then
        Exit Sub
    End If
    Set rule = getRule(ruleSet, ruleNameU)
    If rule Is Nothing Then
        Set rule = ruleSet.Rules.Add(ruleNameU)
    End If
    rule.Category = "Pages"
    rule.Description = _
        "Every page must be portrait orientation"
    rule.TargetType = visRuleTargetDocument
    rule.FilterExpression = ""
    rule.TestExpression = ""
End Sub
```

Now that we have a rule, we need to create some custom validation code, and utilize the getIssue() method from earlier. So, if getIssue() does indeed return something, then it is first deleted using the ValidationIssue.Delete() method, in order to ensure that a new ID is generated when the ValidationRule.AddIssue() method is called:

```
Public Sub CheckAllPagesArePortrait( _
    ByVal ruleSet As Visio.ValidationRuleSet)
Dim isPortrait As Boolean
Dim pageHeight As Double
Dim pageWidth As Double
Dim pag As Visio.Page
Dim issue As Visio.ValidationIssue
Dim rule As Visio.ValidationRule
    Set rule = _
        getRule(ruleSet, "PagesMustBePortraitOrientation")
    If rule Is Nothing Then
        Exit Sub
    End If
    For Each pag In ruleSet.Document.Pages
        If pag.Type = visTypeForeground Then
            pageHeight = pag.PageSheet.CellsSRC( _
                Visio.VisSectionIndices.visSectionObject, _
                Visio.VisRowIndices.visRowPage, _
                Visio.VisCellIndices.visPageHeight).ResultIU
            pageWidth = pag.PageSheet.CellsSRC( _
                Visio.VisSectionIndices.visSectionObject, _
                Visio.VisRowIndices.visRowPage, _
                Visio.VisCellIndices.visPageWidth).ResultIU
            isPortrait = pageHeight > pageWidth
            If isPortrait = False Then
                Set issue = getIssue(rule, pag, Nothing)
                If Not issue Is Nothing Then
                    issue.Delete
                End If
                Set issue = rule.AddIssue(pag)
            End If
        End If
    Next
End Sub
```

So, all we need now is to call the `CheckAllPagesArePortrait()` method when the ruleset is validated, as we saw earlier using the `Document_RuleSetValidated` event:

```
Private Sub Document_RuleSetValidated( _
    ByVal ruleSet As IVValidationRuleSet)
        If ruleSet.NameU = "bVisual" Then
            CheckAllPagesArePortrait ruleSet
        End If
End Sub
```

This will ensure that our custom validation code is run and any pages that are not portrait orientation create an issue for that rule. These issues will then appear in the **Issues** window in the UI.

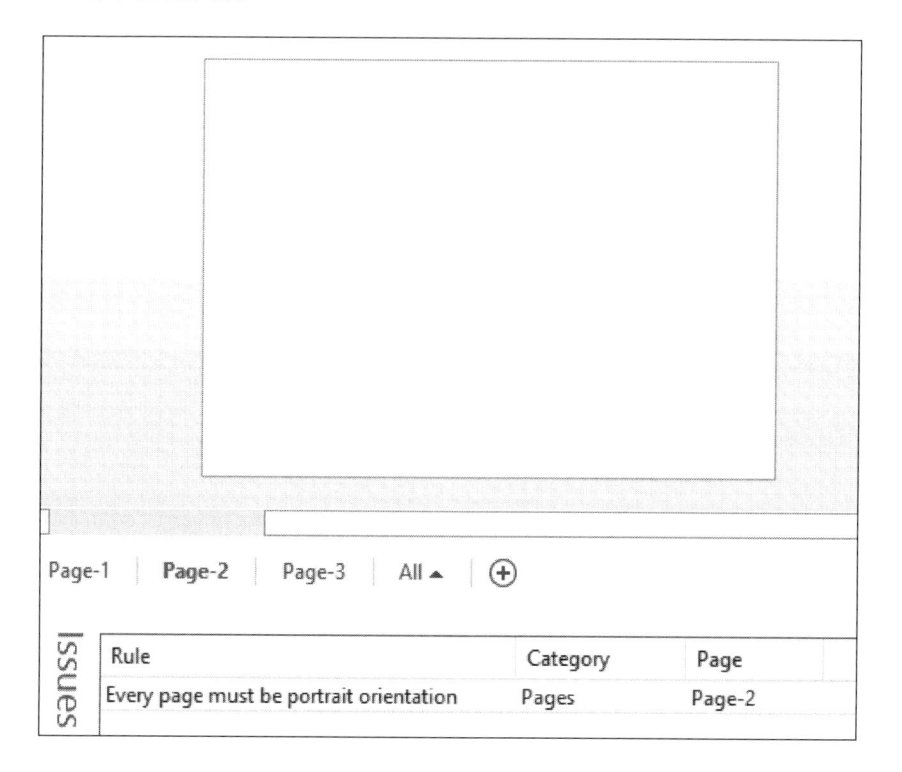

Rule	Category	Page
Every page must be portrait orientation	Pages	Page-2

Although we have seen how to add issues in code using a custom validation rule, it would be more auditable to write your own rules using the `FilterExpression` and `TestExpression` formulae as often as possible. This is because you can expose these rules to public scrutiny more easily, and they can be copied from one ruleset to another, either by copying-and-pasting between the unzipped versions of your Visio documents, before zipping them back up again, or by using the utility introduced in the next chapter.

Summary

In this chapter, we have examined the **Validation API** and seen how we can review or create rulesets and rules. We have also seen how rules can be validated to create issues automatically and how issues can be created in code as the result of custom validation code.

In the next chapter, we are going to start building a Visio VSTO 2012 add-in that we can use to analyze existing rules, or create new ones more easily. You are also going to switch from VBA to using C# in Visual Studio 2012, so that you can have a proper development tool to use.

5
Developing a Validation API Interface

Microsoft Visio 2013 does not provide a user interface to the **Validation API** that rules developers can use, so this chapter is devoted to building a useful tool to enable the tasks to be performed easily. The tool will enable you to review and amend existing rules, to create new rules, and to even perform tests on rules. We will create an explorer panel that displays a selectable tree view of the open rulesets, and an editable panel to display the detail of the ruleset or rule selected in the tree view.

Don't worry if you are not a C# coder, because the completed tool is available from the companion website http://www.visiorules.com. However, we will go through the development of this tool in this chapter because it introduces you to using C#, rather than VBA that we used in the previous chapters.

This chapter will also describe how to use this tool, so it should be worth reading through, even if you are not a C# coder. It will cover the following topics:

- The architecture of the tool – a VSTO (Visual Studio Tools for Office) add-in with a WPF (Windows Presentation Foundation) UI
- The `ThisAddin` class – listening for Visio application events and checking the Visio edition
- Creating the `ViewModel` – wrapping the Validation API objects to enable automatic updating of the UI of the new tool
- Modifying the Fluent UI – using callbacks in the ribbon
- Creating the **Rules Explorer** window – the tree view and detail panels, and the new ribbon buttons
- Displaying the rule for a selected issue
- Displaying the issues for the current selection

Understanding the architecture of the tool

This tool is developed in Microsoft Visual Studio Ultimate 2012, using C# and .NET Framework 4.5. This means that it can be developed as a Visio 2013 Add-in using VSTO 2013, as in the following screenshot. This will make deployment simple using **ClickOnce**, because once it has been installed it will periodically check to see if there is an updated version available.

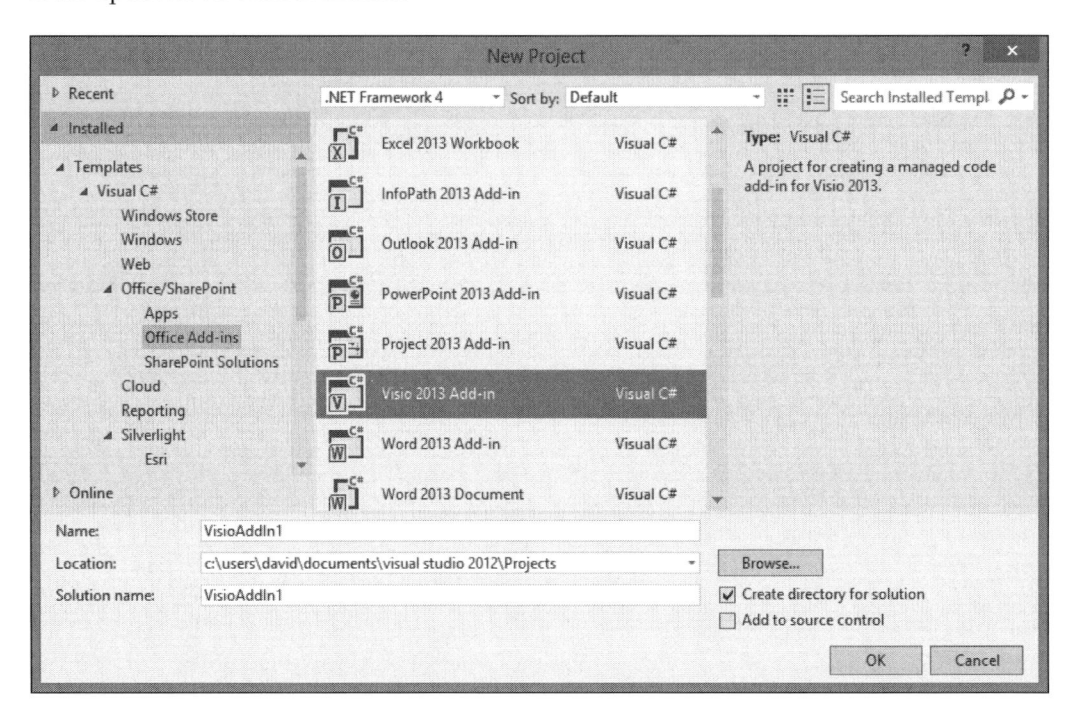

We have called the project `ValidationExplorer2`; it will be extended in later chapters to provide enhanced capabilities.

We are using **Windows Presentation Foundation (WPF)** to create the UI elements wherever possible because it has become a popular preference over the last few years. Visio is a COM application; therefore the WPF elements have to be hosted within a WinForm control. The effort is worth it, though, because of the superior data-binding and UI element flexibility.

Programming in WPF promotes the adoption of a data-driven model, rather than the event-driven model more common in WinForm applications. A programming guide pattern called **Model View View Model (MVVM)** has evolved over the last few years for working with WPF and Silverlight; this should be followed where possible. However, as this is only a small application and it is hosted inside a COM application, we have not adopted all of its patterns, but we have tried to follow the spirit. The most important part of this model for m is the binding of the UI elements to views of the data. This is particularly important for XAML-based coding, because XAML can be so verbose that trying to follow programming logic within it is a thankless and almost impossible task. It is far easier to separate the design of the UI, which is described in XAML, from the current state of the interface. For example, we have added `IsSelected` and `IsExpanded` properties to the classes bound to the main tree view. These properties are merely bound (both ways) to the state of the interface. This means that the code can set the values of the object properties, and the UI will respond automatically. There is no need to iterate through the tree view nodes in the UI, or indeed to find the tree view node by its key to select it. The magic of data binding *just does it*.

> The XAML binding capability is reminiscent of the Visio ShapeSheet formula capability. Perhaps that is why I like it so much!

The Visio add-in template will create the `ThisAddin` class automatically because this is the main hook into your project when the host application starts. The Solution window shows the top-level structure of the solution files and folders:

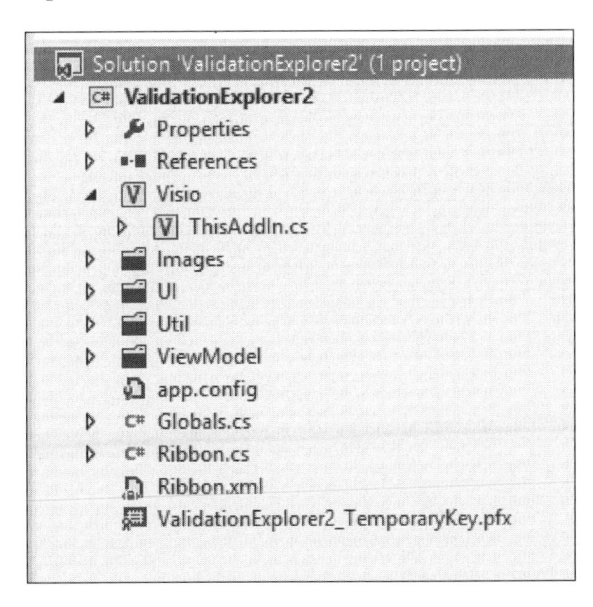

The **data layer** is provided by the Visio objects and, in particular, by the new **Validation** objects described in the earlier chapters.

The **UI layer** comprises WinForms controls as hosts for XAML User Controls, or just XAML Windows, and are created in the UI folder.

The business logic or **view model layer** consists of classes and collections that can be bound to the UI, and are created in the ViewModel folder.

Enhancing the ThisAddin class

The ThisAddIn_Startup() event is a good place to test for the correct Visio version and edition, along with checking that the Visio application events are indeed enabled; otherwise this add-in will not work properly anyway.

```
private void ThisAddIn_Startup(object sender, System.EventArgs e)
{
  try
  {
    veApplication.VisioApplication = this.Application;
    /* check prereq's */
    // check for Visio >= 2013 and Edition = PRO
    if (!this.IsVisio15ProfessionalInstalled)
    {
      MessageBox.Show(
          "This add-in requires the Professional edition of Visio",
          "Visio Professional edition required", MessageBoxButton.OK,
          MessageBoxImage.Exclamation
          );
      return;
    }
    // events must be enabled
    // -1 is TRUE, 0 is FALSE, typically anything other than 0 is TRUE
    if (!Convert.ToBoolean(Globals.ThisAddIn.Application.EventsEnabled))
    {
      if (MessageBox.Show(
            "Event are currently disabled, this add-in requires events to be enabled. " +
            "Would you like to enable events now?",
            "Rules Tools",
            MessageBoxButton.OKCancel,
```

```
                MessageBoxImage.Information,
                MessageBoxResult.OK) == MessageBoxResult.OK)
      {
        // convert to short from TRUE which ends up being 1
        Globals.ThisAddIn.Application.EventsEnabled = Convert.
ToInt16(true);
      }
    }
    // init locals
    this.documents = new Dictionary<int, VEDocument>();
    // connect to events
    VisioEvents_Connect();
  }
  catch (COMException ex)
  {
    throw ex;
  }
  catch (Exception ex)
  {
    throw ex;
  }
}
```

Listening for application events

We need to listen for the creation, opening, or closing of any documents so that our VEDocuments collection can be maintained.

> Refer to http://msdn.microsoft.com/en-us/library/office/ff768620.aspx for more information.

Therefore, the following VisioEvents_Connect() method is called by the ThisAddIn_Startup event.

```
    private void VisioEvents_Connect()
    {
      Globals.ThisAddIn.Application.DocumentOpened +=
          new Visio.EApplication_DocumentOpenedEventHandler(
              VisioApplication_DocumentOpened);
      Globals.ThisAddIn.Application.DocumentCreated +=
          new Visio.EApplication_DocumentCreatedEventHandler(
              VisioApplication_DocumentCreated);
      Globals.ThisAddIn.Application.BeforeDocumentClose +=
```

Developing a Validation API Interface

```
            new Visio.EApplication_BeforeDocumentCloseEventHandler(
                VisioApplication_BeforeDocumentClose);
            //Listen for selection changes
            Globals.ThisAddIn.Application.SelectionChanged +=
                new Visio.EApplication_SelectionChangedEventHandler(
                    Window_SelectionChanged);
            //Listen for key strokes for addon
            Globals.ThisAddIn.Application.OnKeystrokeMessageForAddon +=
                new Visio.EApplication_OnKeystrokeMessageForAddonEventHandle
    r(VisioApplication_MessageForAddon);
            //Listen for import of rulesets
            Globals.ThisAddIn.Application.ExitScope +=
                new Visio.EApplication_ExitScopeEventHandler(VisioApplicati
    on_ExitScopeEvent);
        }
```

The last event listens to the `SelectionChanged` event, because this is required later to ascertain the currently selected issue in the **Issues** window.

> The `SelectionChanged` event will only fire when an issue pertaining to a different shape or page from the previous one is selected. Unfortunately, there is no selection changed event for the **Issues** window.

There is also a `VisioEvents_Disconnect()` method called by the `ThisAddIn_Shutdown()` event.

> If you want an even more efficient method for handling events in Visio, then check out the `AddAvise` method. Never use the `WithEvents` keyword that is available in VB.net because it is far too chatty.

Checking for the Visio Professional edition

In an earlier chapter, we saw how to test for the Visio edition in VBA; here is the equivalent as a C# method:

```
        internal bool IsVisio15ProfessionalInstalled
        {
          get
          {
            bool retVal = false;

            // the installed version of Visio has to be 14 or > and the
    edition has to be PRO or >
```

[156]

```
        if (this.Application.TypelibMinorVersion > 14)
        {
           // CurrentEdition tells us that their Editions is
Professional
           if (this.Application.CurrentEdition == Visio.VisEdition.
visEditionProfessional)
           {
              retVal = true;
           }
        }
        return retVal;
     }
  }
```

Creating the ViewModel class

We created new classes to mirror the relevant parts of the **Visio Type Library** objects, and all of the **Validation API** objects and collections. We prefixed these wrapper classes with VE for ValidationExplorer, which is the project name. The next screenshot shows the files in the ViewModel folder in the Solution window:

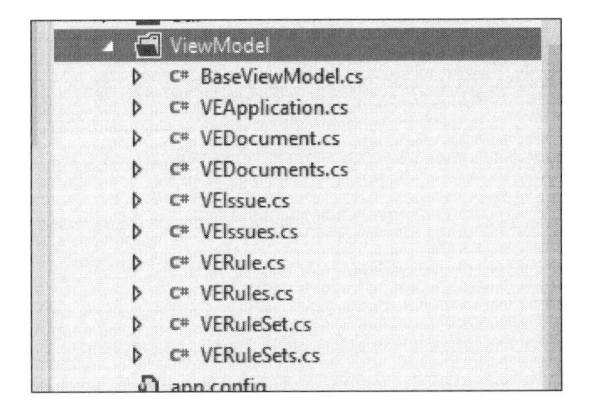

> When you select a folder in the **Solution Explorer**, then select **Project**, **Add Class** and so on, Visual Studio will automatically insert the folder name to the namespace of the class.

As the Visio objects are COM objects, you cannot bind directly to them successfully because XAML really needs to bind to dependency objects that can notify the UI of any changes that take place.

Developing a Validation API Interface

Therefore, we created a `BaseViewModel` abstract class that implements the `System.ComponentModel.INotifyPropertyChanged` interface; this will notify the client when property values are changed.

All of my wrapper object classes implement this base class. The wrapper collections implement the `System.Collections.ObjectModel.ObservableCollection<T>` class because this will provide notifications when items are added, removed, or when the whole list is refreshed. The class diagram from Visual Studio 2012 shows how all of the view model classes are related:

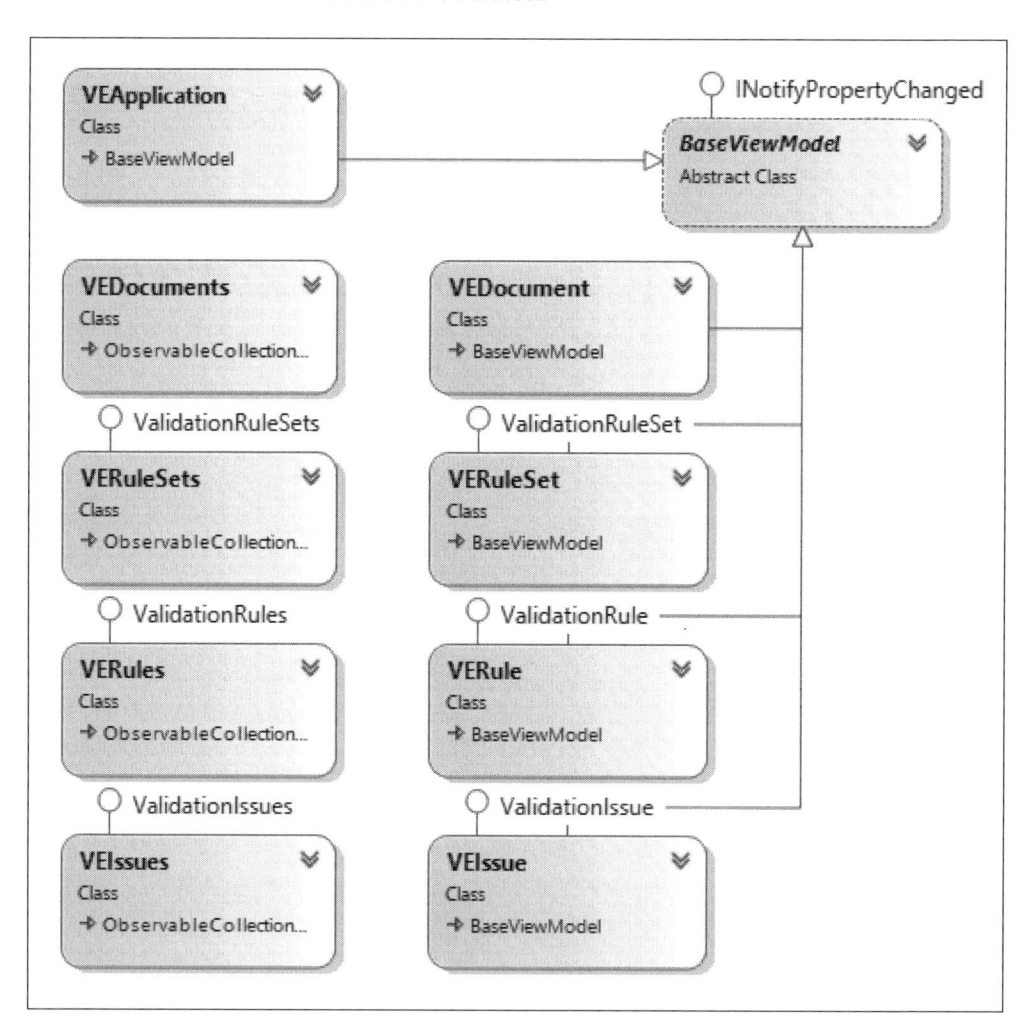

Chapter 5

Each of the classes also implements the corresponding Visio class, and the Validation objects are explicitly implemented so that individual properties can be enhanced, if required.

Creating the BaseViewModel class

The `BaseViewModel` class merely implements the `INotifyPropertyChanged` interface explicitly, as shown in the next screenshot:

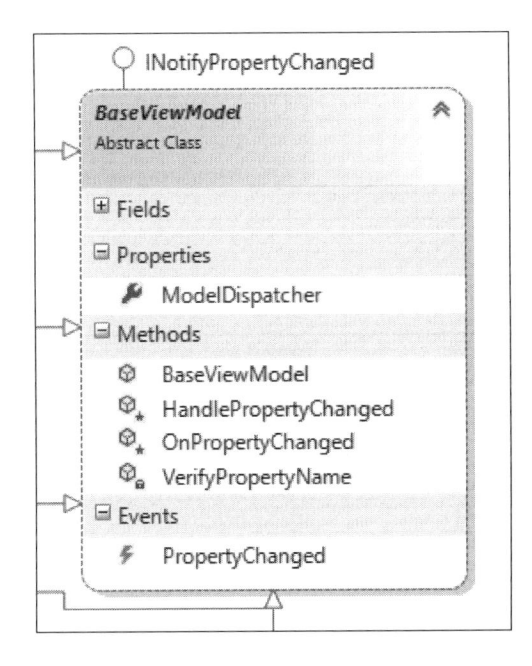

```
INotifyPropertyChanged

BaseViewModel
Abstract Class

⊞ Fields
⊟ Properties
    ModelDispatcher
⊟ Methods
    BaseViewModel
    HandlePropertyChanged
    OnPropertyChanged
    VerifyPropertyName
⊟ Events
    PropertyChanged
```

Each of the classes that implement this base class will have the important `OnPropertyChanged` method available. It is this that ensures that the data-bound UI is kept automatically synchronized.

Viewing the documents collection

We created the `VEApplication` class to be the top level of our mirror hierarchy. This contains the `ObservableCollection` called `VEDocuments`, which in turn provides access to each `VEDocument`.

Developing a Validation API Interface

The following class diagram displays the properties and methods of the `VEApplication`, `VEDocuments`, and `VEDocument` classes:

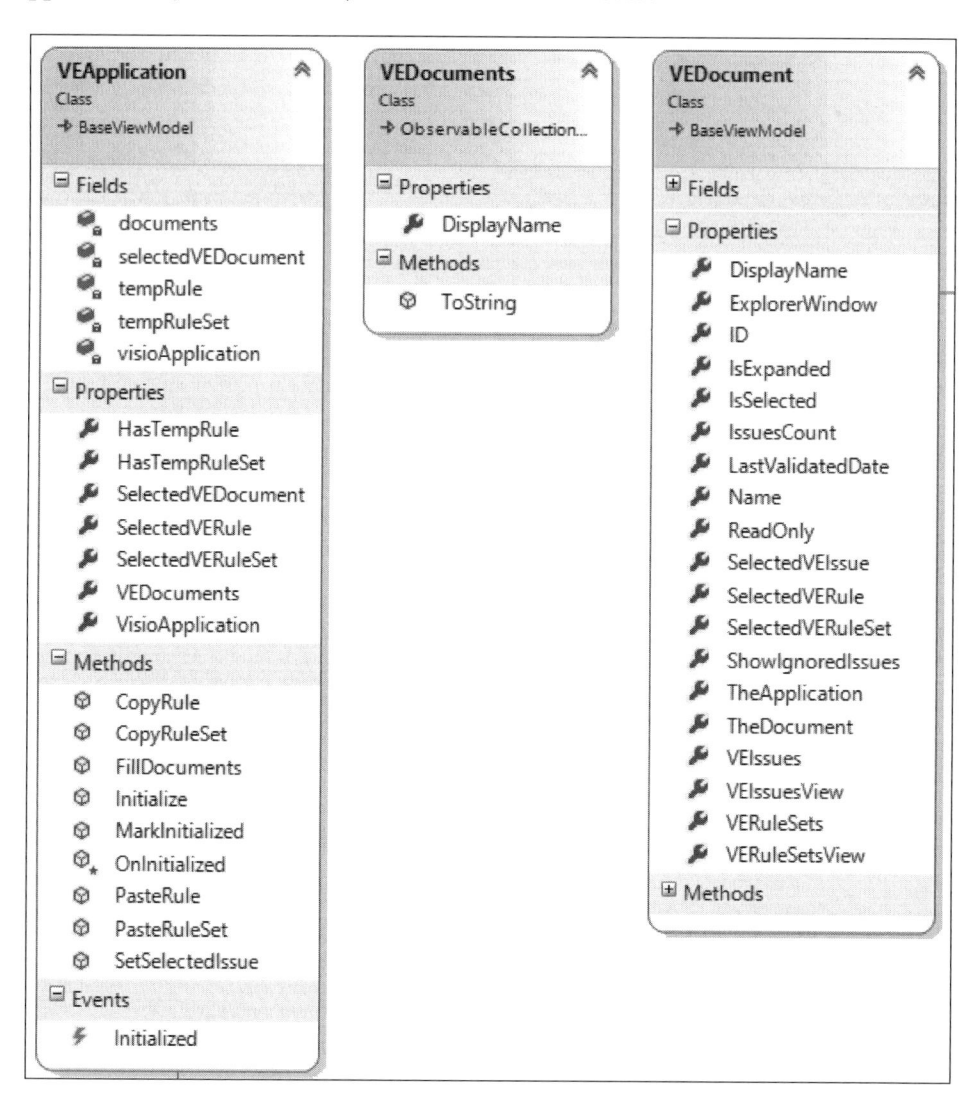

VEApplication
Class
→ BaseViewModel

Fields
- documents
- selectedVEDocument
- tempRule
- tempRuleSet
- visioApplication

Properties
- HasTempRule
- HasTempRuleSet
- SelectedVEDocument
- SelectedVERule
- SelectedVERuleSet
- VEDocuments
- VisioApplication

Methods
- CopyRule
- CopyRuleSet
- FillDocuments
- Initialize
- MarkInitialized
- OnInitialized
- PasteRule
- PasteRuleSet
- SetSelectedIssue

Events
- Initialized

VEDocuments
Class
→ ObservableCollection...

Properties
- DisplayName

Methods
- ToString

VEDocument
Class
→ BaseViewModel

Fields

Properties
- DisplayName
- ExplorerWindow
- ID
- IsExpanded
- IsSelected
- IssuesCount
- LastValidatedDate
- Name
- ReadOnly
- SelectedVEIssue
- SelectedVERule
- SelectedVERuleSet
- ShowIgnoredIssues
- TheApplication
- TheDocument
- VEIssues
- VEIssuesView
- VERuleSets
- VERuleSetsView

Methods

The `FillDocuments` method in the `VEApplication` class creates the collection of `VEDocuments` from the open list of Visio documents. This is only used on initialization because, once created, documents will be added or removed from the collection in response to the relevant events (`VisioApplication_DocumentCreated`, `VisioApplication_DocumentOpened`, and `VisioApplication_BeforeDocumentClose`).

The following method thus iterates through the open Visio documents and creates a new `VEDocument` object for each relevant Visio Document:

```
public void FillDocuments()
{
  this.VEDocuments.Clear();
  if (visioApplication == null) return;
  foreach (Visio.Document doc in visioApplication.Documents)
  {
    //Only add drawings and templates to the collection
    if (doc.Type == Visio.VisDocumentTypes.visTypeDrawing
        || doc.Type == Visio.VisDocumentTypes.visTypeTemplate)
    {
      this.VEDocuments.Add(new VEDocument(this, doc));
      VEDocument ved = this.VEDocuments.Single(dc => dc.ID == doc.ID);
      ved.IsExpanded = true;
      //Set the Selected Document
      if (visioApplication.ActiveDocument.ID == doc.ID)
      {
        this.SelectedVEDocument = ved;
      }
    }
  }
  OnPropertyChanged("VEDocuments");
}
```

> The stencil documents are filtered out by testing the type of the document.

One of the coolest bits of C# is the terseness of the **Lambda** expressions in **LINQ** statements. For example, the preceding code contains the following line:

```
VEDocument ved = this.VEDocuments.Single(dc => dc.ID == doc.ID);
```

This is such a simple way to select a specific element from a collection.

The `VEDocument` class contains the properties and methods for controlling the extra forms in the add-in, and we have surfaced the methods for adding, copying, pasting, and deleting rulesets, rules, and issues because this is the entry point to these collections.

Developing a Validation API Interface

The following class diagram displays the methods of the `VEDocuments` class:

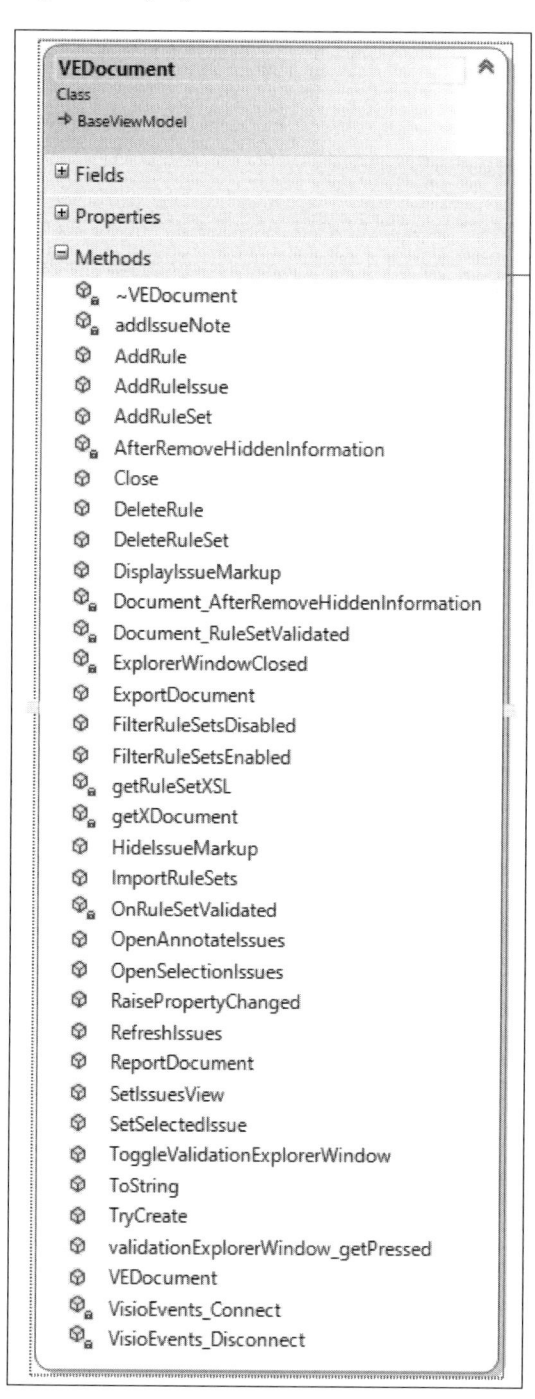

VEDocument
Class
→ BaseViewModel

⊞ Fields
⊞ Properties
⊟ Methods
- ~VEDocument
- addIssueNote
- AddRule
- AddRuleIssue
- AddRuleSet
- AfterRemoveHiddenInformation
- Close
- DeleteRule
- DeleteRuleSet
- DisplayIssueMarkup
- Document_AfterRemoveHiddenInformation
- Document_RuleSetValidated
- ExplorerWindowClosed
- ExportDocument
- FilterRuleSetsDisabled
- FilterRuleSetsEnabled
- getRuleSetXSL
- getXDocument
- HideIssueMarkup
- ImportRuleSets
- OnRuleSetValidated
- OpenAnnotateIssues
- OpenSelectionIssues
- RaisePropertyChanged
- RefreshIssues
- ReportDocument
- SetIssuesView
- SetSelectedIssue
- ToggleValidationExplorerWindow
- ToString
- TryCreate
- validationExplorerWindow_getPressed
- VEDocument
- VisioEvents_Connect
- VisioEvents_Disconnect

Viewing the ValidationRuleSets collection

Each `VEDocument` object contains an `ObservableCollection` called `VERuleSets`, which in turn provides access to each `VERuleSet` object.

The `VERuleSets` and `VERuleSet` classes implement `Visio.ValidationRuleSets` and `Visio.ValidationRuleSet` respectively, which means that all of the properties and methods for them are available to the developer. However, special attention must be paid to ensuring that the notifiable properties are updated whenever the underlying properties are changed. Similarly, it is necessary to create custom methods to add and delete objects from the collections so that the observable collections are kept synchronized.

The following class diagram displays the properties and methods of the `VERuleSets` and `VERuleSet` classes:

ValidationRuleSets

VERuleSets
Class
→ ObservableCollection<VERuleSe...>

Fields

Properties
- Application
- DisplayName
- Document
- GetCount
- ObjectType
- Stat
- this
- VEDocument

Methods
- Add
- AddCopy
- AddRuleSet
- DeleteRuleSet (+ 1 overl...)
- fillRuleSets
- get_ItemFromID
- GetEnumerator
- GetRuleSet
- PasteRuleSet
- SuggestRuleSetName
- ToString
- UnSelect
- VERuleSets

ValidationRuleSet

VERuleSet
Class
→ BaseViewModel

Fields

Properties
- Application
- Description
- DisplayName
- Document
- Enabled
- ID
- IsExpanded
- IsSelected
- Name
- NameU
- ObjectType
- Rules
- RuleSetFlags
- SelectedVERule
- Stat
- VEDocument
- VERules

Methods
- Delete
- GetXElement
- RaisePropertyChanged
- ToString
- UnSelect
- VERuleSet (+ 1 overload)

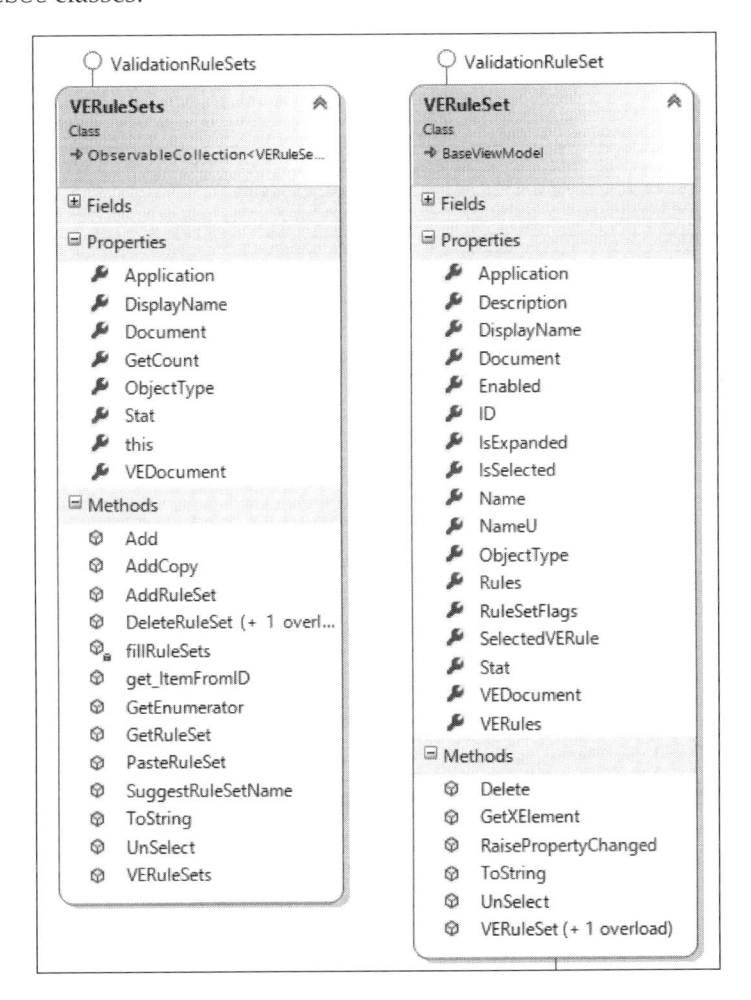

Viewing the ValidationRules collection

Each `VERuleSet` object contains an `ObservableCollection` called `VERules`, which in turn provides access to each `VEule`.

The `VERules` and `VERule` classes implement `Visio.ValidationRules` and `Visio.ValidationRule` respectively, which means that all of their properties and methods are available to the developer.

The following class diagram displays the properties and methods of the `VERules` and `VERule` classes:

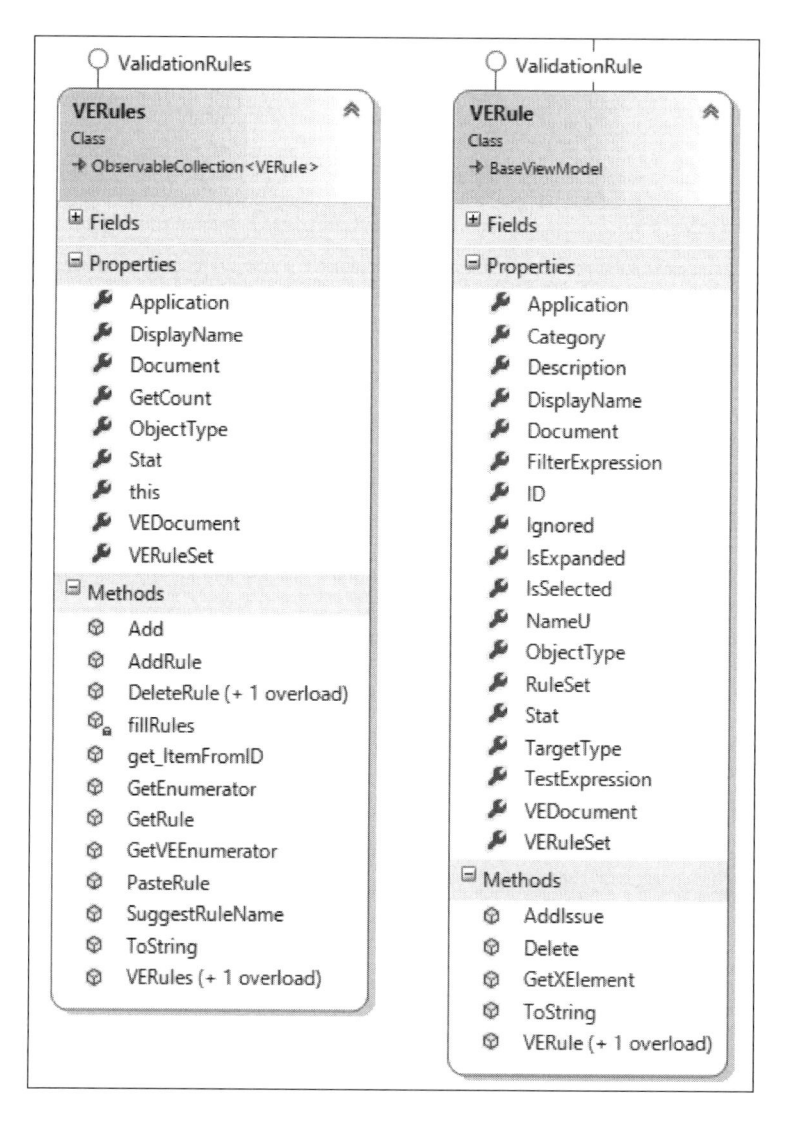

ValidationRules

VERules
Class
→ ObservableCollection<VERule>

Fields

Properties
- Application
- DisplayName
- Document
- GetCount
- ObjectType
- Stat
- this
- VEDocument
- VERuleSet

Methods
- Add
- AddRule
- DeleteRule (+ 1 overload)
- fillRules
- get_ItemFromID
- GetEnumerator
- GetRule
- GetVEEnumerator
- PasteRule
- SuggestRuleName
- ToString
- VERules (+ 1 overload)

ValidationRule

VERule
Class
→ BaseViewModel

Fields

Properties
- Application
- Category
- Description
- DisplayName
- Document
- FilterExpression
- ID
- Ignored
- IsExpanded
- IsSelected
- NameU
- ObjectType
- RuleSet
- Stat
- TargetType
- TestExpression
- VEDocument
- VERuleSet

Methods
- AddIssue
- Delete
- GetXElement
- ToString
- VERule (+ 1 overload)

Chapter 5

The constructor for the VERules class takes the Visio.ValidationRules and the VERuleSet object to create the collection of VERule objects:

```
public class VERules : ObservableCollection<VERule>, Visio.
ValidationRules
  {
    #region Fields
    public ICollectionView VERulesView;
    #endregion

    #region Properties

    private VEDocument veDocument;
    public VEDocument VEDocument
    {
      get { return veDocument; }
    }

    private VERuleSet veRuleSet;
    public VERuleSet VERuleSet
    {
      get { return veRuleSet; }
    }

    public string DisplayName
    {
      get
      {
        return "Rules [Count=" + this.GetCount.ToString() +
          "] for " + Document.Name;
      }
    }

    #endregion

    #region Methods

    private Visio.ValidationRules rules;
    public VERules(Visio.ValidationRules rles, VERuleSet verset)
    {
      rules = rles;
      veRuleSet = verset;
      veDocument = verset.VEDocument;
      fillRules();

      //Set the default views
      this.VERulesView = CollectionViewSource.GetDefaultView(this);
```

[165]

```
        //Group by Category, sort by Description
        this.VERulesView.GroupDescriptions.Add(new PropertyGroupDescript
ion("Category"));
        this.VERulesView.SortDescriptions.Add(new
SortDescription("Description", ListSortDirection.Ascending));

        OnPropertyChanged(new PropertyChangedEventArgs("GetCount"));
        this.VERuleSet.RaisePropertyChanged("DisplayName");
      }
```

Viewing the ValidationIssues collection

We wanted to be able to view the issues for a page, or a selection of shapes, grouped by each shape. Therefore, we decided to create the `VEIssues` collection of `VEIssue` objects.

These objects need to be created when the document is first opened and then re-created whenever the document is validated. Similar to the `VEApplication` class, there is a call to the `VisioEvents_Connect()` method in the constructor, and a call to the `VisioEvents_Disconnect()` method in the destructor.

```
        private void VisioEvents_Connect()
        {
          if (this.document != null)
          {
            this.document.RuleSetValidated +=
                new Visio.EDocument_RuleSetValidatedEventHandler(Docume
nt_RuleSetValidated);
          }
        }

        private void VisioEvents_Disconnect()
        {
          this.document.RuleSetValidated -=
              new Visio.EDocument_RuleSetValidatedEventHandler(Document_
RuleSetValidated);
        }

        private void Document_RuleSetValidated(Visio.ValidationRuleSet
rset)
        {
          OnRuleSetValidated(rset);
        }

        private void OnRuleSetValidated(Visio.ValidationRuleSet rset)
        {
          //Refresh the issues
```

```
    this.RefreshIssues();
}

public void RefreshIssues()
{
    this.LastValidatedDate = document.Validation.LastValidatedDate;
    OnPropertyChanged("LastValidatedDate");
    this.ShowIgnoredIssues = document.Validation.ShowIgnoredIssues;
    OnPropertyChanged("ShowIgnoredIssues");
    this.VEIssues.FillIssues();
}
```

The following class diagram displays the properties and methods of the `VEIssues` and `VEIssue` classes:

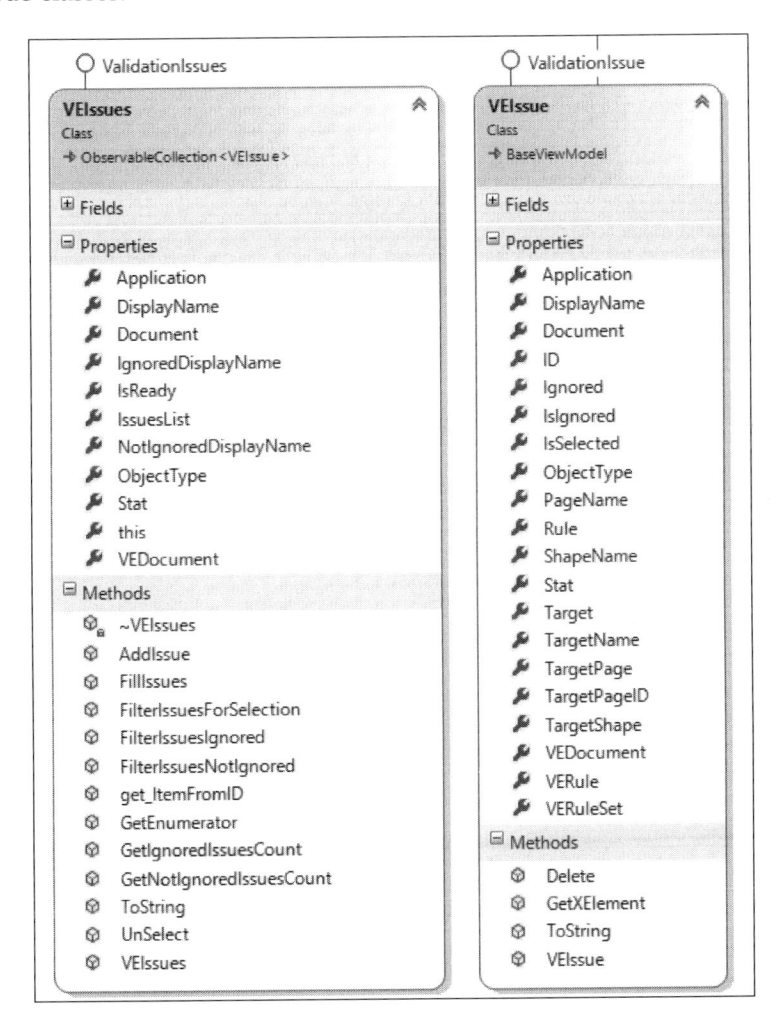

VEIssues
Class
→ ObservableCollection<VEIssue>

Fields

Properties
- Application
- DisplayName
- Document
- IgnoredDisplayName
- IsReady
- IssuesList
- NotIgnoredDisplayName
- ObjectType
- Stat
- this
- VEDocument

Methods
- ~VEIssues
- AddIssue
- FillIssues
- FilterIssuesForSelection
- FilterIssuesIgnored
- FilterIssuesNotIgnored
- get_ItemFromID
- GetEnumerator
- GetIgnoredIssuesCount
- GetNotIgnoredIssuesCount
- ToString
- UnSelect
- VEIssues

VEIssue
Class
→ BaseViewModel

Fields

Properties
- Application
- DisplayName
- Document
- ID
- Ignored
- IsIgnored
- IsSelected
- ObjectType
- PageName
- Rule
- ShapeName
- Stat
- Target
- TargetName
- TargetPage
- TargetPageID
- TargetShape
- VEDocument
- VERule
- VERuleSet

Methods
- Delete
- GetXElement
- ToString
- VEIssue

Fortunately, for this add-in, we can listen to the `Visio.EDocument_RuleSetValidatedEventHandler(Document_RuleSetValidated)` event because the validation objects are all created at this time. We will describe how this is used later in this chapter.

Modifying the Visio Fluent UI

The Fluent UI was new in Visio 2010, bringing it in line with the big three in Office (Word, Excel, and PowerPoint). This means that there are a lot more relevant resources available on the Web for developers to refer to. Before Microsoft bought Visio in 1999, the Visio application had its own **UIObject API** that provided a programming model for menus, toolbars, the status bar, and accelerator keys. One of the first changes to be made, after the Microsoft acquisition, was the adoption of the Microsoft Office **CommandBars API** in Visio. This meant that developers could start using the same UI objects as other Office developers. But then the big three Office applications got the new Ribbon in the 2007 version. This is now improved and commonly called the Fluent UI; thus, even though the legacy UI objects may still be available in the Visio type library, it is recommended that developers get to grips with the Ribbon object.

One of the good things about the Fluent UI is the ability to describe the modifications that you want in an XML file. You can even modify built-in ribbon tabs in this XML file, which is fortunate because the new **PROCESS** tab has plenty of unused space at the right-hand side. So, we created a `Ribbon.xml` file that described a new group, labeled **Rules Tools**, with a large button to open the main **Rules Explorer** window. The next five smaller buttons are only usable when the **Rules Explorer** window is open, so they are disabled until then. The last button can be pressed any time because it displays the issues for the selection or page (if nothing is selected). We have also reproduced the **Selection Issues** button on the right mouse menu of a shape or page, as seen in the following screenshot:

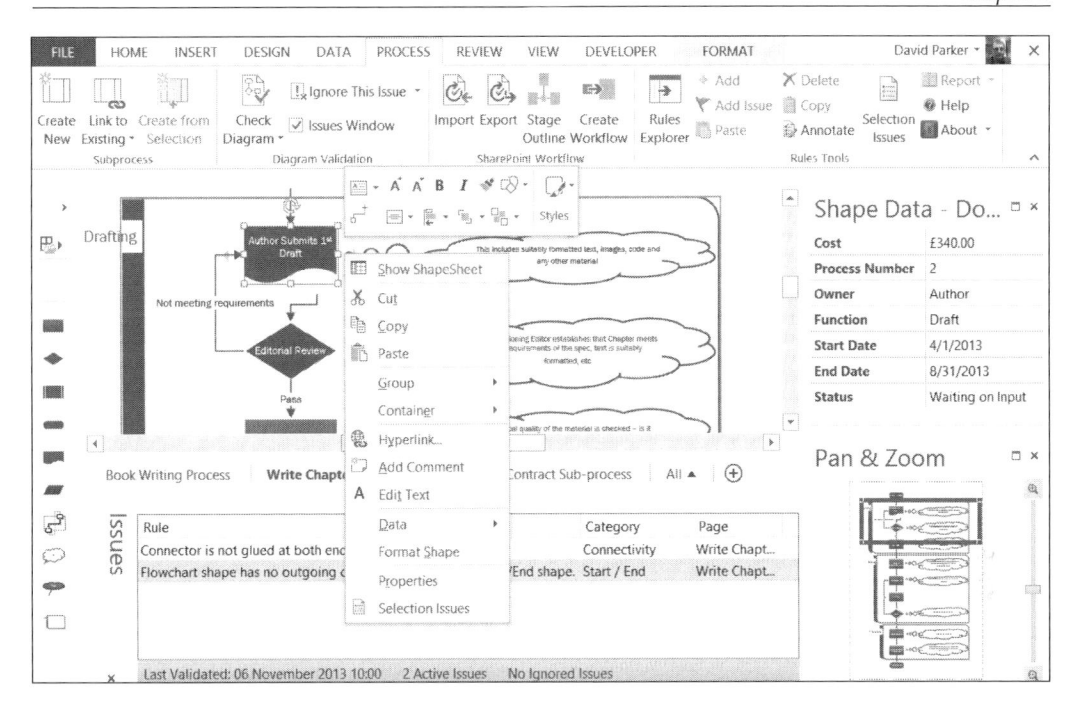

I cannot pretend that I took the months of usability research that Microsoft would have done for the optimum size and appearance of the buttons in the **Rules Tools** group, but I have tried to put an order to them. Also, I should thank Chris Hopkins of Microsoft for his excellent article about extending the Visio Ribbon at: `http://blogs.msdn.com/chhopkin/archive/2009/11/20/ribbon-extensibility-for-visio-solutions-in-visio-2010.aspx`.

Developing a Validation API Interface

This is an abbreviation of the `Ribbon.xml` file that creates this modification to the UI:

```xml
<?xml version="1.0" encoding="UTF-8"?>
<customUI xmlns="http://schemas.microsoft.com/office/2009/07/customui"
        onLoad="Ribbon_Load">
  <ribbon>
    <tabs>
      <tab idMso="TabProcess" >
        <group id="RulesTools"
            imageMso="ReviewReviewingPaneVertical"
                    label="Rules Tools" autoScale="true">
          <button id="buttonValidationExplorerWindow"
            imageMso="ReviewReviewingPaneVertical"
                                    size="large"
                                    onAction="OnAction"
                                    getEnabled="GetEnabled"
                                    getLabel="GetLabel"
                                    getSupertip="GetSupertip"
                                    getVisible="GetVisible"
                />
          <separator/>

          <button id="buttonRuleAdd"
                                    getImage="GetImage"
                                    onAction="OnAction"
                                    getEnabled="GetEnabled"
                                    getLabel="GetLabel"
                                    getSupertip="GetSupertip"
                                    getVisible="GetVisible"
                />

          <button id="buttonIssues"
                                        size="large"
                                    getImage="GetImage"
                                    onAction="OnAction"
                                    getEnabled="GetEnabled"
                                    getLabel="GetLabel"
                                    getSupertip="GetSupertip"
                                    getVisible="GetVisible"
                />
        </group>
      </tab>
    </tabs>
  </ribbon>
```

```xml
<contextMenus>
  <contextMenu idMso="ContextMenuShape1D"  >
    <button id="buttonIssues1D"
                        getImage="GetImage"
                        onAction="OnAction"
                        getEnabled="GetEnabled"
                        getLabel="GetLabel"
                        getSupertip="GetSupertip"
                        getVisible="GetVisible"
                            />
    <button id="buttonReverse1D"
                        getImage="GetImage"
                        onAction="OnAction"
                        getEnabled="GetEnabled"
                        getLabel="GetLabel"
                        getSupertip="GetSupertip"
                        getVisible="GetVisible"
                            />
  </contextMenu>
  <contextMenu idMso="ContextMenuShape" >
    <button id="buttonIssues2D"
                        getImage="GetImage"
                        onAction="OnAction"
                        getEnabled="GetEnabled"
                        getLabel="GetLabel"
                        getSupertip="GetSupertip"
                        getVisible="GetVisible"
                            />
  </contextMenu>
  <contextMenu idMso="ContextMenuDrawingPage" >
    <button id="buttonIssuesPage"
                        getImage="GetImage"
                        onAction="OnAction"
                        getEnabled="GetEnabled"
                        getLabel="GetLabel"
                        getSupertip="GetSupertip"
                        getVisible="GetVisible"
                            />
  </contextMenu>
 </contextMenus>
</customUI>
```

Developing a Validation API Interface

The `idMso="TabProcess"` attribute is the important bit to know, because `TabProcess` is `control.id` of the **PROCESS** tab in Visio 2013. If you do not use the `idMso` attribute, then you need to use the `id` attribute to create your own unique identifier.

The `Ribbon.xml` file has effectively got code behind in a class called `Ribbon.cs`, and this class contains the callbacks specified in the `getImage`, `onAction`, `getEnabled`, `getLabel`, `getSupertip`, and `getVisibile` methods. These neat methods enable you to centralize the custom images, text, and actions, in addition to defining when each control is enabled.

For example, the following snippet is an extract from the `Ribbon` class that returns the label for each of the buttons:

```
public string GetLabel(Microsoft.Office.Core.IRibbonControl control)
{
  switch (control.Id)
  {
    case "buttonValidationExplorerWindow":
      {
        return "Rules Explorer";
      }
    case "buttonRuleAdd":
      {
        return "Add...";
      }
    case "buttonIssues":
      {
        return "Selection Issues";
      }
    case "buttonReportRules":
      {
        return "Report";
      }
  }
  return "";
}
```
Similar calls return the image for each button.

```
public System.Drawing.Bitmap GetImage(
```

```
            Microsoft.Office.Core.IRibbonControl control)
    {
        switch (control.Id)
        {
          case "buttonRuleAdd":
            {
                return GetResourceImage("base_plus_sign_32.png");
            }
          case "buttonIssues":
            {
                return GetResourceImage("bulleted_list_options.png");
            }
        }
        return null;
    }
```

The preceding function calls the GetResourceImage() method to extract Resource images from the Images folder.

```
        private System.Drawing.Bitmap GetResourceImage(string image)
    {
        // build up a relative path to the image.
        System.Uri imageLocation = new
            System.Uri("/RulesTools;component/Images/" + image,
            System.UriKind.Relative);
        // Use the helper methods on WPF's application
        // class to create an image.
        using (Stream resourceStream = System.Windows.Application.GetRes
ourceStream(imageLocation).Stream)
        {
            return new System.Drawing.Bitmap(resourceStream);
        }
    }
```

Developing a Validation API Interface

The overall effect is a pleasing extension to the built-in **PROCESS** tab, which can be seen in the following screenshot:

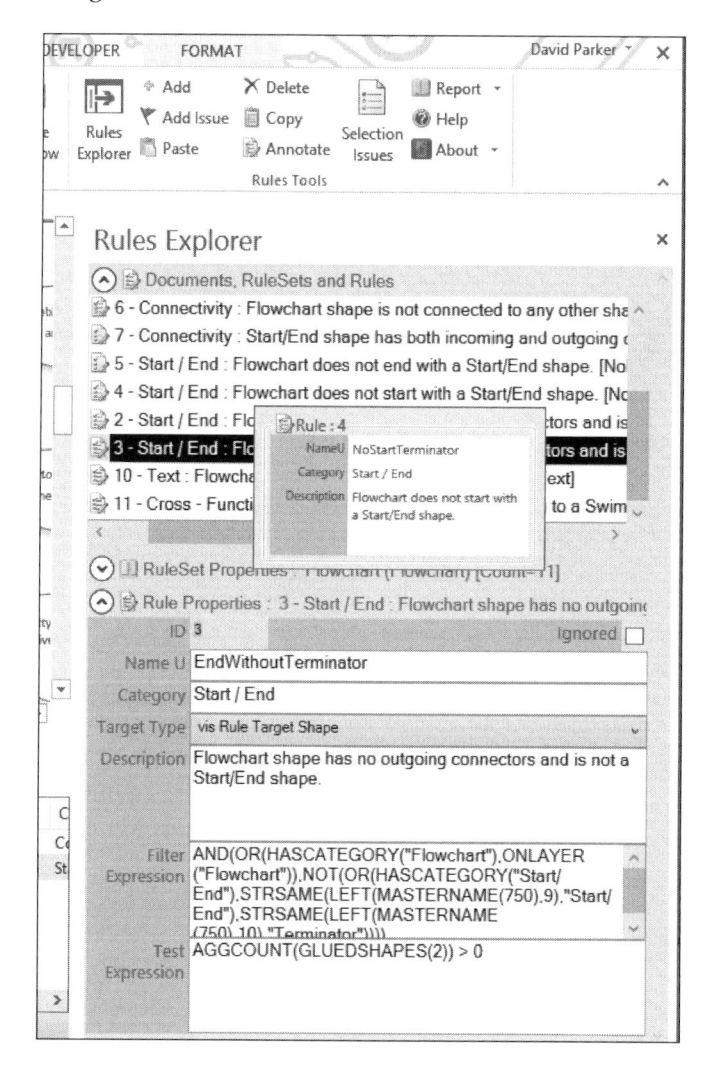

Creating the Rules Explorer window

The **Rules Explorer** Window is a Visio anchor window, of which there are many examples available, including some in the Microsoft Visio 2013 SDK. The resultant window is a sub-window of the document window, just as with a number of other built-in windows such as the **Drawing Explorer**, **Shape Data** window and, of course, the new **Issues** window. These windows can float free, anchored to an edge of the drawing window or merged with other sub-windows.

The following screenshot of Visual Studio 2012 shows that the `FormExplorer` class merely acts as a host for the `UserControlExplorer` control:

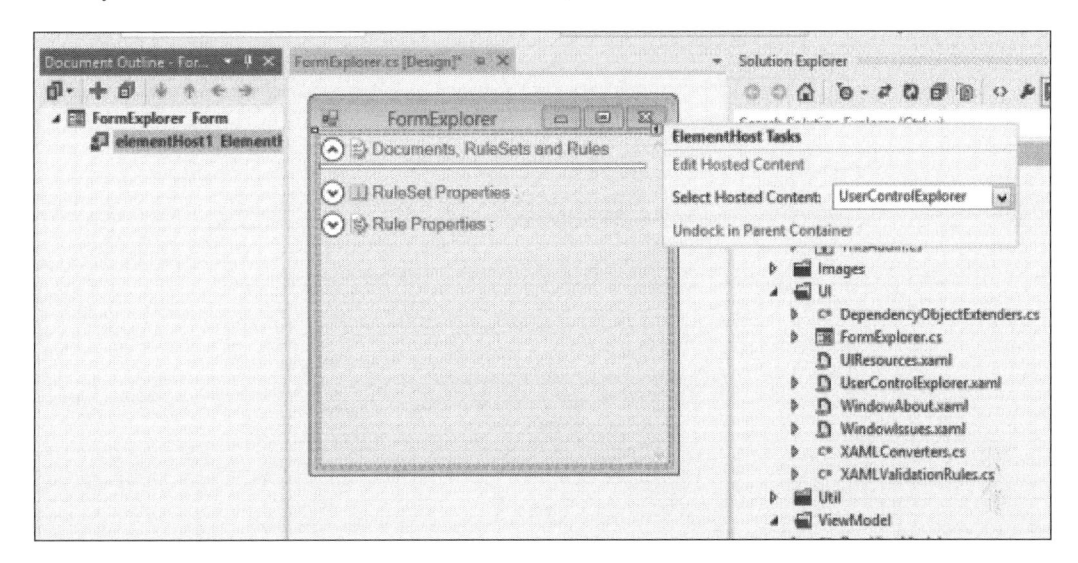

The `UserControlExplorer` control is the WPF control that contains all of the goodies and some code behind. The next image of the Visual Studio 2012 UI shows the `UserControlExplorer.xaml` file:

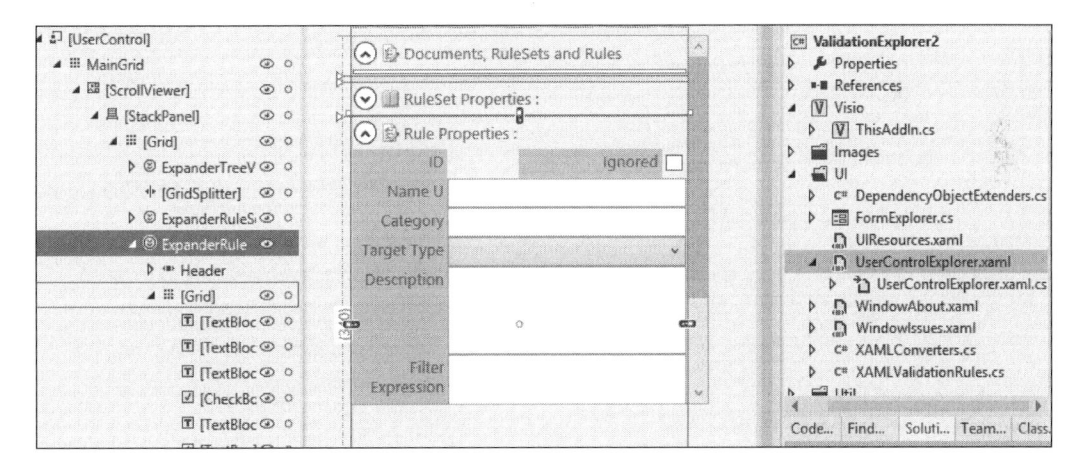

The **Document Outline** shows that very little is defined directly within the `TreeViewMain` element because it calls on templates defined in `Resources`.

Self-describing tree views

We wanted the tree view to display the open documents, their rulesets, and the rules within them. This is achieved by creating three `HierarchicalDataTemplate` definitions—`DocumentTemplate`, `RuleSetTemplate`, and `RuleTemplate`.

```xml
<TreeView Grid.Row="0" Name="TreeViewMain"
    Background="White"
    ItemsSource="{Binding Path=VEDocuments}"
    ItemTemplate="{StaticResource ResourceKey=DocumentTemplate}"
    SelectedItemChanged="TreeViewMain_SelectedItemChanged"
    OverridesDefaultStyle="False"
    />
```

The `ResourceKey` property of the `ItemTemplate` attribute specifies `HierarchicalDataTemplate` that is defined in the `ResourceDictionary` of `UserControl`.

```xml
<HierarchicalDataTemplate x:Key="DocumentTemplate"
                          DataType="{x:Type localVM:VEDocument}"
                          ItemsSource="{Binding Path=VERuleSetsView}"
                          ItemTemplate="{StaticResource ResourceKey=RuleSetTemplate}"
                          >
    <StackPanel Orientation="Horizontal"
            ToolTip="{StaticResource ResourceKey=DocumentToolTip}">
        <Image Source="..\Images\Page.png"
                Style="{StaticResource ResourceKey=ImageStyle}"/>
        <TextBlock Text="{Binding Path=DisplayName}"
                Style="{StaticResource ResourceKey=TreeItemStyle}" />
    </StackPanel>
</HierarchicalDataTemplate>
```

Thus, the `HierarchicalDataTemplate` for each `DataType` specifies the template for its child items.

Making informative tool tips

WPF enables a developer to create larger and more interesting tool tips than those usually created with WinForms applications.

Each of the tree view items has a tool tip defined in XAML in order to display the most important details for it, as shown in the following screenshot:

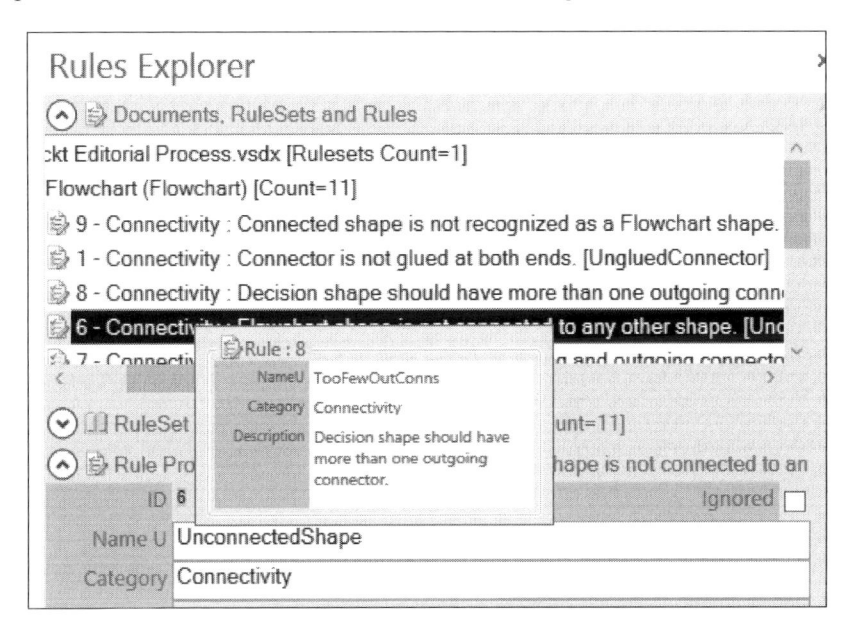

The `RuleToolTip` is defined in the `UserControlExplorer.xaml` file:

```
<ToolTip x:Key="RuleToolTip">
    <Border Style="{StaticResource ResourceKey=ToolTipBorderStyle}">
        <GroupBox >
            <GroupBox.Header>
                <StackPanel Orientation="Horizontal">
                    <Image Source="..\Images\IssueTracking_32x32.png"
                           Style="{StaticResource ResourceKey=ImageStyle}" />
                    <TextBlock Text="Rule : " />
                    <TextBlock Text="{Binding Path=ID}" />
                </StackPanel>
            </GroupBox.Header>
            <Grid Style="{DynamicResource ResourceKey=ToolTipGridStyle}">
```

```xml
            <Grid.ColumnDefinitions>
                <ColumnDefinition Width="60" />
                <ColumnDefinition Width="140" />
            </Grid.ColumnDefinitions>
            <Grid.RowDefinitions>
                <RowDefinition Height="18" />
                <RowDefinition Height="18" />
                <RowDefinition Height="54" />
            </Grid.RowDefinitions>

            <TextBlock Text="NameU"
                    Style="{StaticResource ResourceKey=ToolTipLabelStyle}"
                    Grid.Row="0" Grid.Column="0" />
            <TextBlock Text="{Binding Path=NameU}"
                        Style="{StaticResource ResourceKey=ToolTipTextBlockStyle}"
                    Grid.Row="0" Grid.Column="1" />

            <TextBlock Text="Category"
                    Style="{StaticResource ResourceKey=ToolTipLabelStyle}"
                    Grid.Row="1" Grid.Column="0" />
            <TextBlock Text="{Binding Path=Category}"
                        Style="{StaticResource ResourceKey=ToolTipTextBlockStyle}"
                    Grid.Row="1" Grid.Column="1" />

            <TextBlock Text="Description"
                    Style="{DynamicResource ResourceKey=ToolTipLabelStyle}"
                    Grid.Row="2" Grid.Column="0" />
            <TextBlock Text="{Binding Path=Description}"
                        Style="{StaticResource ResourceKey=ToolTipTextBlockStyle}"
                    Grid.Row="2" Grid.Column="1"
                    TextWrapping="Wrap"/>
        </Grid>
      </GroupBox>
    </Border>
  </ToolTip>
```

Linking detail panels

We want the relevant detail panel to be displayed whenever a ruleset or a rule is selected in the tree view, in a master-detail relationship. This detail panel will enable the editing of a ruleset or a rule.

Editing ruleset properties

You can edit a ruleset by selecting the ruleset tree view item. This enables and expands the **RuleSet Properties** panel, thus providing access to the **Enabled**, **NameU**, **Name**, **Flags**, and **Description** properties. Remember that the **NameU** is the internal unique identifier, while the **Name** can be localized, if desired. The following screenshot shows the editable panel for the selected ruleset:

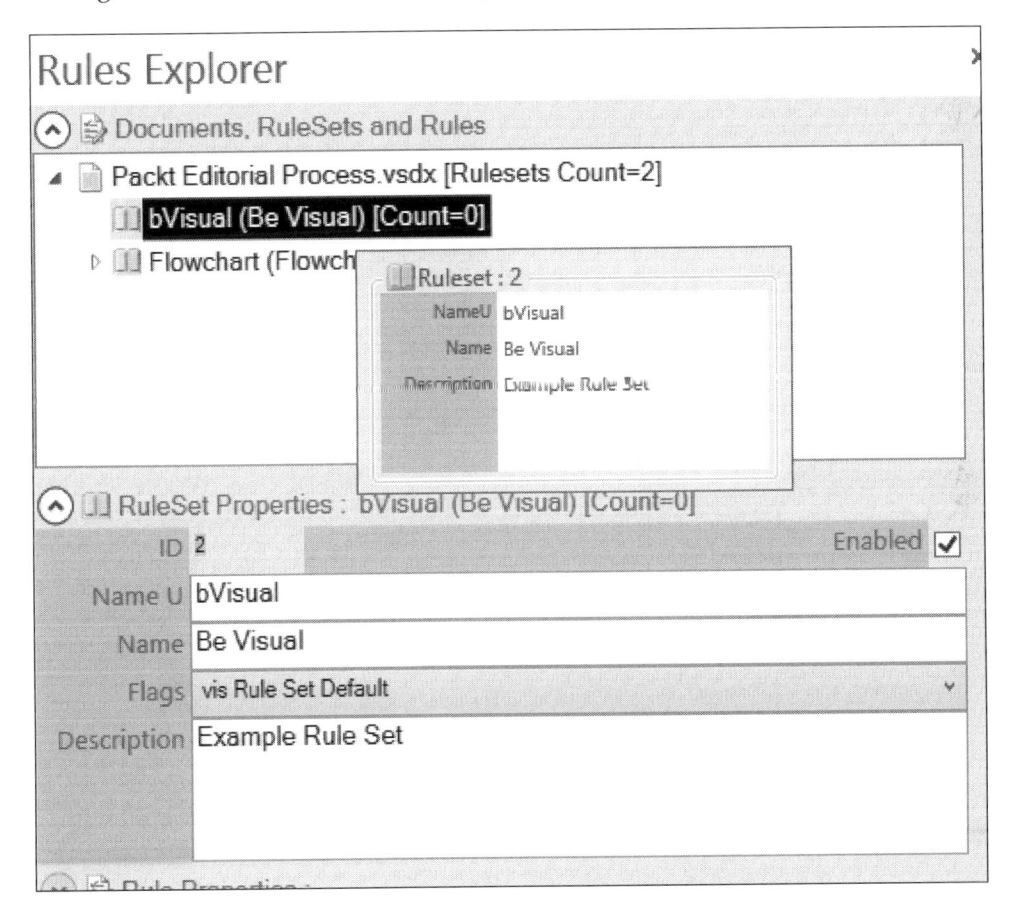

Developing a Validation API Interface

The **Flags** property is selected from a combo box that contains the humanized version of the `Visio.VisRuleSetFlags` enumerator, as shown in the following screenshot:

> I borrowed the code for this from Tom F Wright's CodeProject article: http://www.codeproject.com/KB/WPF/enumlistconverter.aspx.

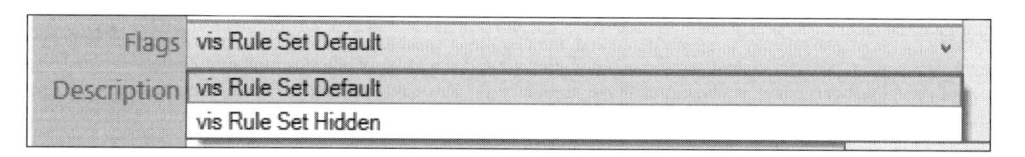

Flags	vis Rule Set Default
Description	vis Rule Set Default
	vis Rule Set Hidden

This technique requires a `Resources` reference in the XAML:

```
<localUI:VisRuleSetFlagsListConverter x:Key="VisRuleSetFlagsListConverter"/>
```

This `Converter` is then specified in the `ItemSource` and `SelectedIndex` of the `ComboBox` element:

```
<ComboBox ItemsSource="{Binding
    Source={StaticResource ResourceKey=VisRuleSetFlagsListConverter}}"
    SelectedIndex="{Binding Path=Flags, Mode=TwoWay,
    Converter={StaticResource ResourceKey=VisRuleSetFlagsListConverter}}"
    Grid.Row="3" Grid.Column="1" Grid.ColumnSpan="3" />
```

Editing rule properties

Whenever the user selects a rule in the tree view of the **Rules Explorer** window, the **Rule Properties** expander is automatically expanded, thus providing easy access to the properties for viewing or editing. The next screenshot shows the editable panel for the selected rule:

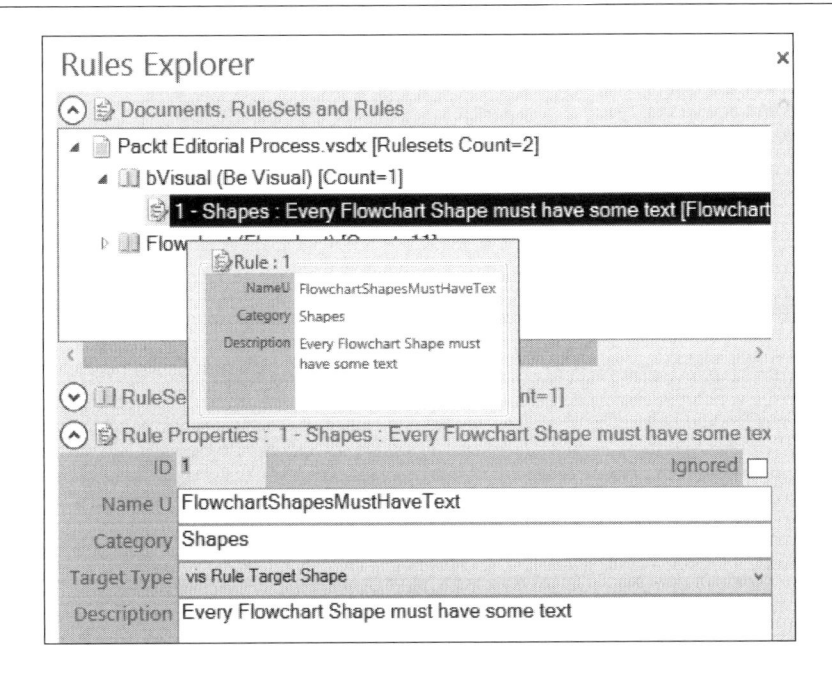

The expander for the **Documents, Rulesets and Rules** tree view (and **RuleSet Properties**) can be collapsed, and the vertical scrollbar positioned, to allow full access to the **Rule Properties** panel, as shown in the following screenshot:

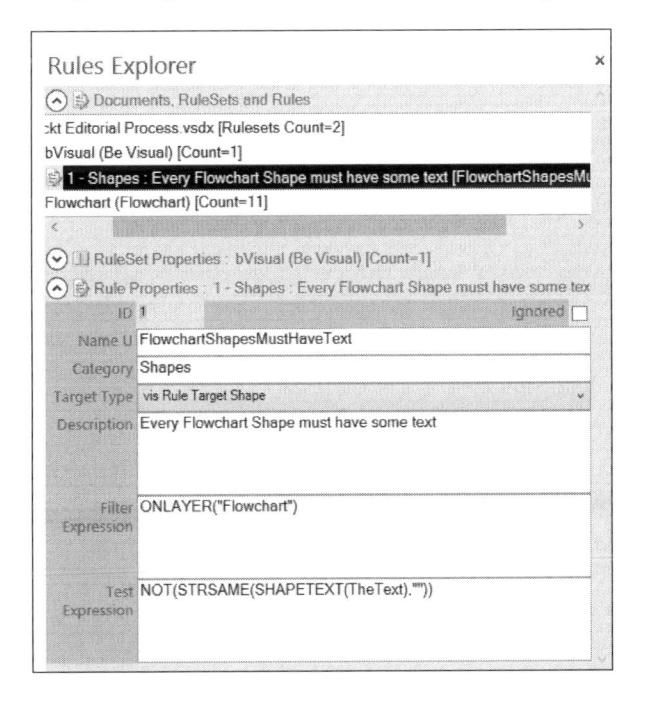

[181]

Developing a Validation API Interface

The XAML data binding and the underlying `VERule` object ensure that the `Visio.ValidationRule` object is automatically updated but, of course, the Visio document must be saved eventually to preserve these changes.

Handling special key strokes

The user can type normal characters into the text boxes in the detail panels but there are some special key combinations that will act upon the drawing page rather than the **add-in** window, unless they are handled. In particular, a rules developer will want to use *Delete*, *Ctrl+C*, *Ctrl+X*, and *Ctrl+V* to delete, copy, cut, and paste. Other useful keys are *Ctrl+A*, *Ctrl+Z*, and *Ctrl+Y* to select all, undo, and redo.

> See the following MSDN article for more information about the `OnMessageKeystrokeForAddon` event: `http://msdn.microsoft.com/en-us/library/ms427669.aspx`.

Firstly, the `ThisAddin.VisioEvents_Connect()` method was enhanced to add the `OnKeystrokeMessageForAddon` event, which is as follows:

```
Globals.ThisAddIn.Application.OnKeystrokeMessageForAddon +=
    new Visio.EApplication_
OnKeystrokeMessageForAddonEventHandler(
        VisioApplication_MessageForAddon);
```

The `VisioApplication_MessageForAddon()` event was written to handle each of the anticipated keystrokes in order to action upon the currently active text box.

```
public System.Windows.Controls.TextBox
    CurrrentTextBox = null;
private bool VisioApplication_MessageForAddon(
    Microsoft.Office.Interop.Visio.MSGWrap msg)
{
    if (CurrrentTextBox == null) return false;
    if ((int)msg.wParam == (int)System.Windows.Forms.Keys.Delete)
    {
        if (CurrrentTextBox.SelectionLength > 0)
        {
            CurrrentTextBox.Text.Remove(
                CurrrentTextBox.SelectionStart,
                CurrrentTextBox.SelectionLength);
            CurrrentTextBox.SelectedText = "";
        }
        return true;
    }
```

```csharp
        else if (System.Windows.Input.Keyboard.IsKeyDown(
            System.Windows.Input.Key.LeftCtrl) == true ||
            System.Windows.Input.Keyboard.IsKeyDown(
              System.Windows.Input.Key.RightCtrl) == true)
    {
      if ((int)msg.wParam == (int)System.Windows.Forms.Keys.A)
      {
        CurrrentTextBox.SelectionStart = 0;
        CurrrentTextBox.SelectionLength = CurrrentTextBox.Text.
Length;
        CurrrentTextBox.SelectedText = CurrrentTextBox.Text;
        return true;
      }
      else if ((int)msg.wParam == (int)System.Windows.Forms.Keys.C)
      {
        Clipboard.SetText(CurrrentTextBox.SelectedText);
        return true;
      }
      else if ((int)msg.wParam == (int)System.Windows.Forms.Keys.X)
      {
        Clipboard.SetText(CurrrentTextBox.SelectedText);
        if (CurrrentTextBox.SelectionLength > 0)
        {
          CurrrentTextBox.Text =
            CurrrentTextBox.Text.Remove(
            CurrrentTextBox.SelectionStart,
            CurrrentTextBox.SelectionLength);
          CurrrentTextBox.SelectedText = "";
        }
        return true;
      }
      else if ((int)msg.wParam == (int)System.Windows.Forms.Keys.V)
      {
        if (Clipboard.ContainsText() == false) return false;
        CurrrentTextBox.SelectedText = Clipboard.GetText();
        return true;
      }
      else if ((int)msg.wParam == (int)System.Windows.Forms.Keys.Z)
      {
        CurrrentTextBox.Undo();
        return true;
      }
      else if ((int)msg.wParam == (int)System.Windows.Forms.Keys.Y)
      {
```

```
            CurrrentTextBox.Redo();
            return true;
        }
          else return false;
    }
      return false;
}
```

The GotFocus event was then added to the textbox controls in the UserControlExplorer.xaml file that is used for editing text, as in the following example:

```
<TextBox Text="{Binding Path=NameU, Mode=TwoWay}"
         GotFocus="TextBox_GotFocus"
         Style="{DynamicResource ResourceKey=TBStyle}"
         Grid.Row="1"
         Grid.Column="1" Grid.ColumnSpan="3" />
```

The TextBox_GotFocus() event handler was added to the code in the UserControlExplorer.xaml.cs class as follows:

```
private void TextBox_GotFocus(object sender,
   RoutedEventArgs e)
{
   if (sender is System.Windows.Controls.TextBox)
   {
     Globals.ThisAddIn.CurrrentTextBox =
        (System.Windows.Controls.TextBox)sender;
   }
   else
   {
     Globals.ThisAddIn.CurrrentTextBox = null;
   }
}
```

Adding the Explorer actions

The smaller action buttons are available when the **Rules Explorer** window is open.

The Ribbon class contains a method to test if this **Explorer Window** is open for the active document:

```
public static bool IsExplorerWindowOpen(Visio.Document document)
{
   //Check if the explorer window is open
   if (document != null)
```

```
      {
        foreach (Visio.Window win in document.Application.Windows)
        {
          if (win.Document == document)
          {
            foreach (Visio.Window subWin in win.Windows)
            {
              if (subWin.Caption == Globals.AnchorBarTitle)
              {
                return subWin.Visible;
              }
            }
          }
        }
      }
      return false;
    }
```

The particular actions that the buttons perform depend upon the type of item selected in the tree view. Therefore, we added a couple of methods to the `Ribbon` class that test if `VERuleSet` or `VERule` is selected in the tree view.

```
    public static bool IsRuleSetSelected(Visio.Document document)
    {
      //Check if the explorer window is open
      if (document != null)
      {
        //Get the VEDocument
        ViewModel.VEDocument ved = Globals.ThisAddIn.VEApp.
 VEDocuments.Single(doc => doc.ID == document.ID);
        //Test if SelectedRuleSet is null
        return ved.SelectedVERuleSet != null;
      }
      return false;
    }

    public static bool IsRuleSelected(Visio.Document document)
    {
      //Check if the explorer window is open
      if (document != null)
      {
        //Get the VEDocument
        ViewModel.VEDocument ved = Globals.ThisAddIn.VEApp.
 VEDocuments.Single(doc => doc.ID == document.ID);
        //Test if SelectedRule is null
```

Developing a Validation API Interface

```
        return ved.SelectedVERule != null;
    }
    return false;
}
```

Of course, something needs to set the `SelectedVERuleSet` and `SelectedVERule` properties of the active VEDocument instance. This is done in the `TreeViewMain_SelectedItemChanged()` event in the code in the `UserControlExplorer.xaml` file. This event is also used to set the DataContext of the expanders for the RuleSet and Rule Properties panels.

Creating the Add button

The **Add** button action will add a ruleset if a document is selected in the tree view, but it will add a rule if a ruleset is selected in the tree view. Then, the new item itself is automatically selected in the tree view, as shown in the following screenshot:

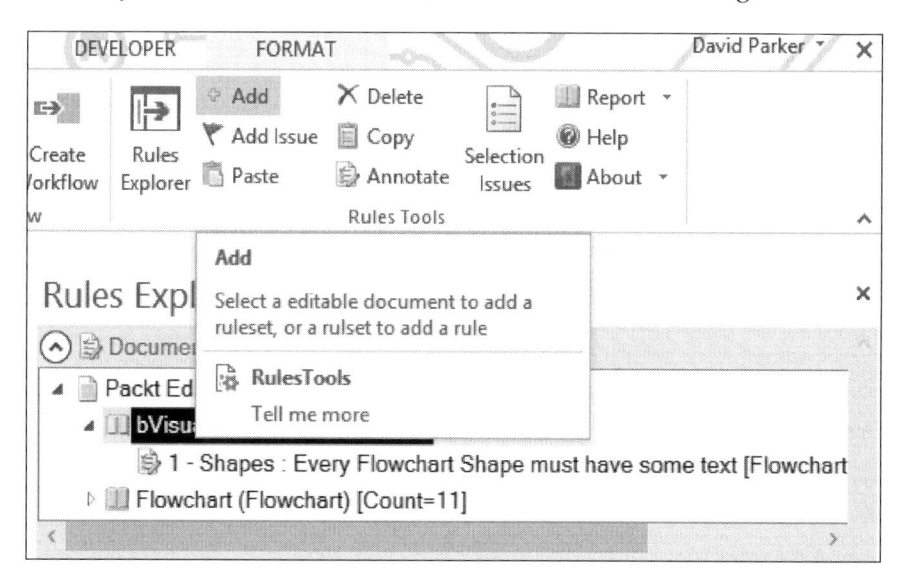

The `OnAction(Office.IRibbonControl control)` callback defines the case for the `buttonRuleAdd` button. It tests whether a `VEDocument` or `VERuleSet` is selected, and then calls the relevant method in the `VEDocument` object.

```
case "buttonRuleAdd":
{
    //Only enable if a ruleset or rule is selected
    bool isWinOpen = Ribbon.IsExplorerWindowOpen(
      Globals.ThisAddIn.Application.ActiveDocument);
    if (isWinOpen)
```

[186]

```
    {
      if (Ribbon.IsRuleSetSelected(
        Globals.ThisAddIn.Application.ActiveDocument))
      {
        Globals.ThisAddIn.VEApp.SelectedVEDocument.AddRule();
      }
      else if (!Ribbon.IsRuleSelected(
        Globals.ThisAddIn.Application.ActiveDocument))
      {
        Globals.ThisAddIn.VEApp.SelectedVEDocument.AddRuleSet();
      }
      else
      {
        System.Windows.MessageBox.Show(this.GetSupertip(control),
            this.GetLabel(control),
            System.Windows.MessageBoxButton.OK,
            System.Windows.MessageBoxImage.Information);
      }
    }
    else
    {
      System.Windows.MessageBox.Show(this.GetSupertip(control),
          this.GetLabel(control),
          System.Windows.MessageBoxButton.OK,
          System.Windows.MessageBoxImage.Information);
    }
    break;
}
```

For example, the `AddRule()` method ensures that a unique new name is proposed, and then passed through to the `AddRule()` method of the `VERuleSet` object:

```
public void AddRule()
{
  try
  {
    if (this.SelectedVERuleSet != null)
    {
      //Add a rule
      string newName =
        this.SelectedVERuleSet.VERules.SuggestRuleName();
      VERule ver =
        this.selectedVERuleSet.VERules.AddRule(newName);
      this.selectedVERuleSet.SelectedVERule = ver;
      this.SelectedVERule =
```

```
          this.selectedVERuleSet.SelectedVERule;
    }
  }
  catch (Exception)
  {
    throw;
  }
}

public VERule AddRule(string NameU)
{
  Visio.ValidationRule rul = rules.Add(NameU);
  this.Add(new VERule(rul, veRuleSet));
  OnPropertyChanged(new
    PropertyChangedEventArgs("GetCount"));
  this.VERuleSet.RaisePropertyChanged("DisplayName");
  return this.Single(ver => ver.NameU == NameU);
}
```

Notice that this method creates a new `Visio.ValidationRule` first, then adds this to the `VERules ObservableCollection`. It then calls the `OnPropertyChanged()` method to ensure that the UI display of the `VERules` is updated.

The `AddRuleSet()` method is similar to the `AddRule()` method.

Creating the Add Issue button

The **Add Issue** button action will simply add an issue to a rule, as shown in the following screenshot:

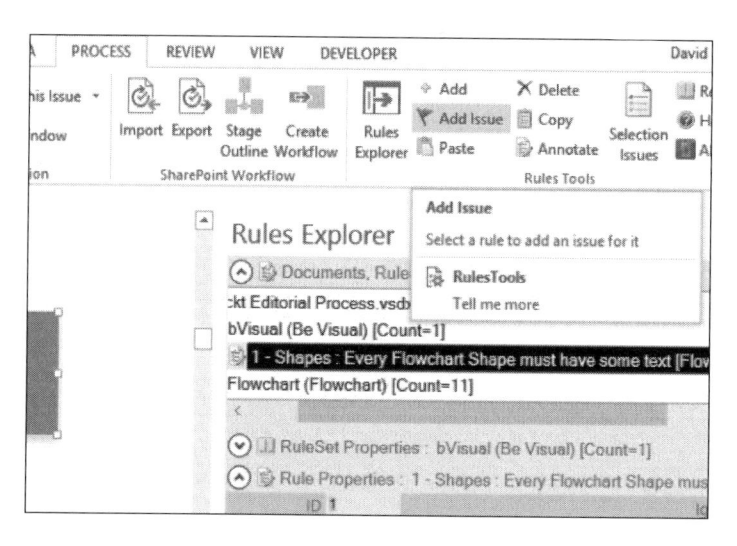

The `AddRuleIssue()` method in the `VEDocument` class establishes the `TargetType` of the rule, then adds the issue to the relevant item or items.

```
public void AddRuleIssue()
{
  try
  {
    if (this.SelectedVERule != null)
    {
      //Add an issue for the rule
      if (this.selectedVERule.TargetType ==
        Visio.VisRuleTargets.visRuleTargetDocument)
      {
        Visio.ValidationIssue iss =
          this.selectedVERule.AddIssue();
        this.VEIssues.AddIssue(iss);
      }
      else if (this.selectedVERule.TargetType ==
        Visio.VisRuleTargets.visRuleTargetDocument)
      {
        Visio.ValidationIssue iss =
          this.selectedVERule.AddIssue(
          document.Application.ActivePage);
        this.VEIssues.AddIssue(iss);
      }
      else
      {
        foreach (Visio.Shape shp in
          document.Application.ActiveWindow.Selection)
        {
          Visio.ValidationIssue iss =
              this.selectedVERule.AddIssue(
              document.Application.ActivePage, shp);
          this.VEIssues.AddIssue(iss);
        }
      }
    }
  }
  catch (Exception)
  {
    throw;
  }
}
```

Creating the Paste button

The **Paste** button action will paste a previously copied ruleset or rule to the selected document or ruleset respectively, as in the next screenshot:

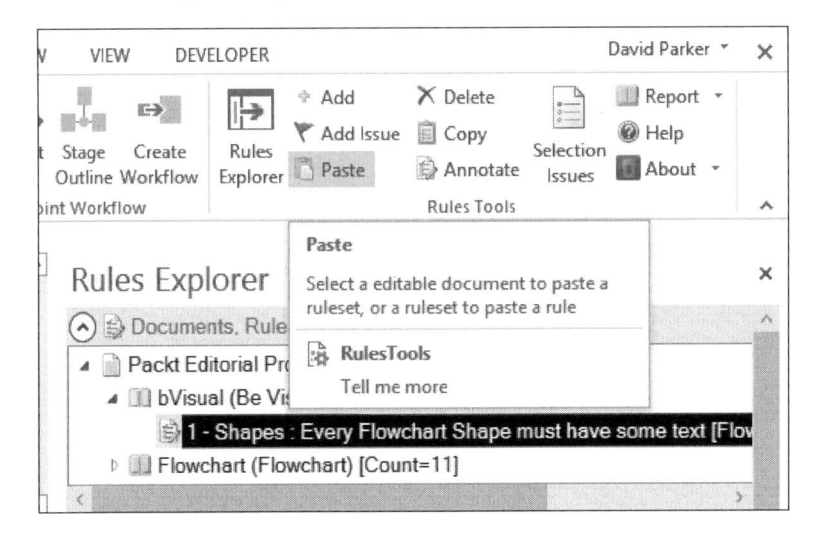

The `VEApplication.PasteRule()` method establishes that a `VERuleSet` item is selected, and that there is a temporary `VERule` object copied. It then calls the `VERules.PasteRule()` method.

```
public void PasteRule()
{
  if (this.SelectedVERuleSet != null
    && tempRule != null)
  {
    VERule newVer =
      this.SelectedVERuleSet.VERules.PasteRule(tempRule);
    this.SelectedVEDocument.SelectedVERule = newVer;
  }
}
```

The `VERules.PasteRule()` method checks if a new unique name is required before creating a new rule and cloning the properties:

```
public VERule PasteRule(VERule sourceRule)
{
  VERule newVer = null;
  if (this.Count(ver => ver.NameU ==
    sourceRule.NameU) == 0)
  {
```

```csharp
      //Use same name
      newVer = this.AddRule(sourceRule.NameU);
    }
    else
    {
      //Get a new name
      string newName = this.SuggestRuleName();
      newVer = this.AddRule(newName);
    }
    //Set all of the Visio Validation properties
    newVer.Ignored = sourceRule.Ignored;
    newVer.Category = sourceRule.Category;
    newVer.Description = sourceRule.Description;
    newVer.FilterExpression = sourceRule.FilterExpression;
    newVer.TestExpression = sourceRule.TestExpression;
    newVer.TargetType = sourceRule.TargetType;
    OnPropertyChanged(new
      PropertyChangedEventArgs("GetCount"));
    this.VERuleSet.RaisePropertyChanged("DisplayName");
    return newVer;
  }
```

Creating the Copy button

The **Copy** action will take a copy of the selected ruleset or rule, so that it is available for the **Paste** action, as shown in the following screenshot:

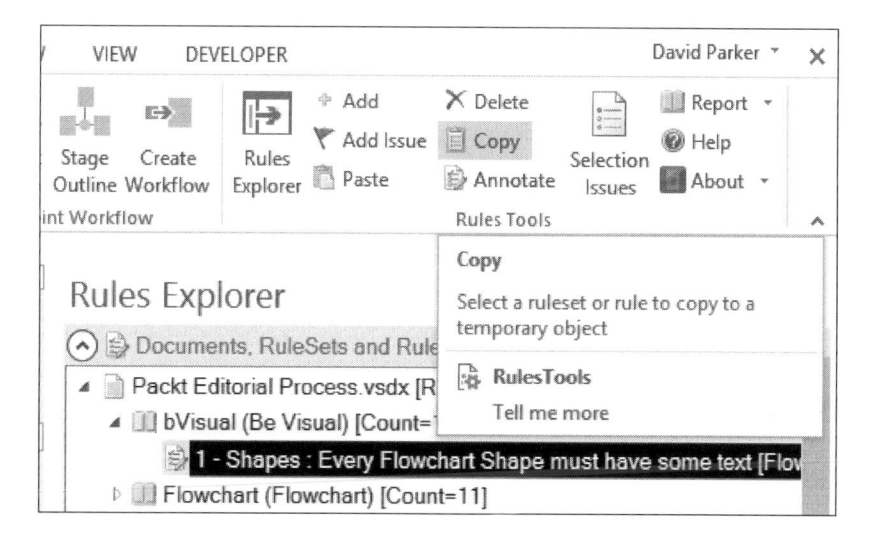

Developing a Validation API Interface

The `VEApplication.CopyRule()` method simply copies the `SelectedVERule` object to a temporary object and then ensures that the `HasTempRule` property is notified.

```
public void CopyRule()
{
  tempRule = this.SelectedVERule;
  OnPropertyChanged("HasTempRule");
}
```

There is a similar `VEApplication.CopyRuleSet()` method that is called if the user has a `VERuleSet` object selected in the **Validation Explorer** tree view, rather than a `VERule` object.

Creating the Delete button

The **Delete** action enables the user to delete the selected ruleset or rule, as in the next screenshot:

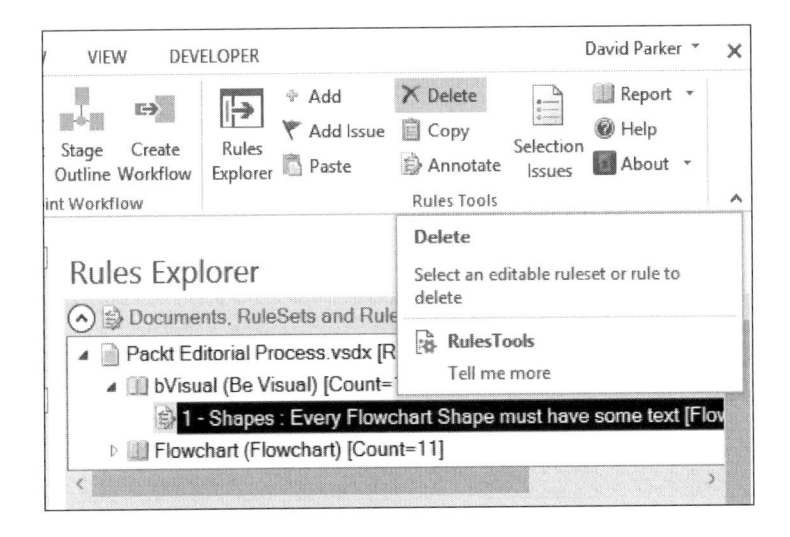

The `VERules.DeleteRule()` method ensures that the `Visio.ValidationRules` collection and the `VERules ObservableCollection` are kept synchronized:

```
public void DeleteRule(VERule ver)
{
  Visio.ValidationRule rul = this.rules[ver.NameU];
  this.Remove(ver);
  rul.Delete();
  OnPropertyChanged(new
    PropertyChangedEventArgs("GetCount"));
  this.VERuleSet.RaisePropertyChanged("DisplayName");
}
```

Chapter 5

There is a similar `VERuleSets.DeleteRuleSet()` method that is called if the user has a `VERuleSet` object selected in the **Validation Explorer** tree view, rather than a `VERule` object.

Displaying the rule for a selected issue

The built-in Issues Window, which is opened from the **Diagram Validation** group on the **PROCESS** tab, provides an existing method for a user to select an issue. Therefore we can synchronize the selected rule in the **Rules Explorer** whenever an issue is selected. This enables the rules developer to analyze the expressions used.

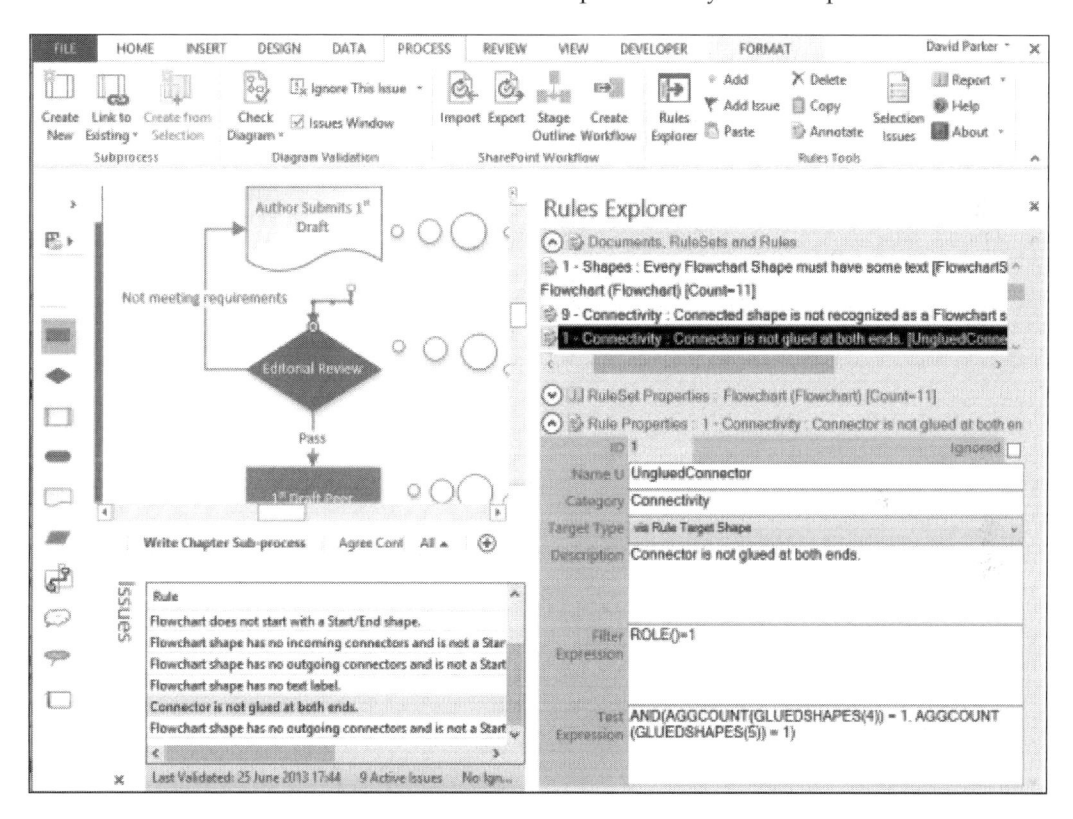

Actually, the **Issues** window does not cause any events at all but it does select the target shape or page whenever an issue is selected in the window.

Developing a Validation API Interface

Thus, we can use the `Application.Window_SelectionChanged()` event to test if the **Issues** window is open. If it is, then the selected issue ID is sent into the `veApplication.SetSelectedIssue()` method:

```
public void SetSelectedIssue(int? docid, int? issue)
{
  if (docid.HasValue && this.VEDocuments.Count() > 0)
  {
    selectedVEDocument =
      this.VEDocuments.Single(doc => doc.ID == docid);
    selectedVEDocument.SetSelectedIssue(issue);
  }
  else
  {
    selectedVEDocument = null;
  }
}
```

The `VEApplication.SetSelectedIssue()` method then gets the correct `VEDocument` object and passes the `issue` ID through to it via the `selectedVEDocument.SetSelectedIssue(issue)` method.

```
public void SetSelectedIssue(int? iss)
{
  if (iss.HasValue)
  {
    if (this.VEIssues.Count(issu => issu.ID == iss.Value) == 0)
return;
    this.SelectedVEIssue = this.VEIssues.Single(issu => issu.ID ==
iss.Value);

    var resultIssues = from isu in this.VEIssues select isu;
    foreach (VEIssue issu in resultIssues)
    {
      if (issu.ID != selectedVEIssue.ID) issu.IsSelected = false;
    }
    selectedVEIssue.IsSelected = true;

    var results = from rls in this.VERuleSets select rls;
    foreach (VERuleSet rls in results)
    {
      rls.IsSelected = false;
      rls.UnSelect();
    }
    if (this.VERuleSets.Count > 0)
```

[194]

```
            {
                this.SelectedVERuleSet = this.VERuleSets.Single(rs => rs.ID
        == selectedVEIssue.Rule.RuleSet.ID);
                selectedVERuleSet.IsSelected = true;
                selectedVERuleSet.IsExpanded = true;
                this.SelectedVERule = selectedVERuleSet.VERules.Single(rl =>
        rl.ID == selectedVEIssue.Rule.ID);
                selectedVERule.IsSelected = true;
            }
            else
            {
                this.SelectedVEIssue = null;
                this.SelectedVERuleSet = null;
                this.SelectedVERule = null;
            }
        }
        else
        {
            this.SelectedVEIssue = null;
            this.SelectedVERuleSet = null;
            this.SelectedVERule = null;
        }
    }
```

Now, because the `IsSelected` property of the tree view items is bound to the `IsSelected` property of the underlying objects, the UI instantly reacts and displays the details of the rule for the selected issue in the **Issues** window.

For example, the `UserControlExplorer.xaml` file contains the `HierarchicalDataTemplate` for the rule. This definition does not contain any binding for the `TreeViewItem` because it merely describes the UI elements for the item. In order to set the binding for the item, and to vary the colors when it is selected, you can define a `Style` with the `TargetType="{x:Type TreeViewItem}"` attribute. This style will automatically be applied to each `TreeViewItem` as follows:

```
        <Style TargetType="{x:Type TreeViewItem}">
            <Setter Property="Background"
                    Value="Transparent" />
            <Setter Property="Foreground"
                    Value="Black" />
            <Setter Property="IsExpanded"
                    Value="{Binding Path=IsExpanded}" />
            <Setter Property="IsSelected"
                    Value="{Binding Path=IsSelected}" />
            <Style.Triggers>
```

```xml
        <DataTrigger
          Binding="{Binding Path=IsSelected}" Value="True">
          <Setter Property="Background"
                  Value="Black" />
          <Setter Property="Foreground"
                  Value="White" />
        </DataTrigger>
      </Style.Triggers>
    </Style>
```

Displaying the issues for the current selection

The **Selection Issues** button opens a dialog that contains just the issues for the selected page or shapes. If there are multiple issues on the page, or on a shape, then they are grouped together for clarity.

We have already expressed a preference for using WPF where possible. However, the VSTO template, which is a Windows Forms project, hides the WPF window item type from selection if you try to add one. You are only offered the **User Control (WPF)** to add in the WPF category of installed templates. Fortunately, you can select this option and then make some simple changes to the code to turn a **User Control (WPF)** into a **Window (WPF)**. In this case, we added a new **UserControl (WPF)** named WindowIssues. We then edited the XAML of the WindowIssues.xaml file.

From:

```
<UserControl x:Class="ValidationExplorer2.UI.WindowIssues"
```

To:

```
<Window x:Class="ValidationExplorer2.UI.WindowIssues"
```

Similarly, we edited the WindowIssues.xaml.cs file and changed the following line:

From:

```
    public partial class WindowIssues : UserControl
```

To:

```
    public partial class WindowIssues : Window
```

Chapter 5

The `WindowIssues` class is now a true WPF window that can be edited to display the issues for the selection, grouped by each shape, as in the next screenshot:

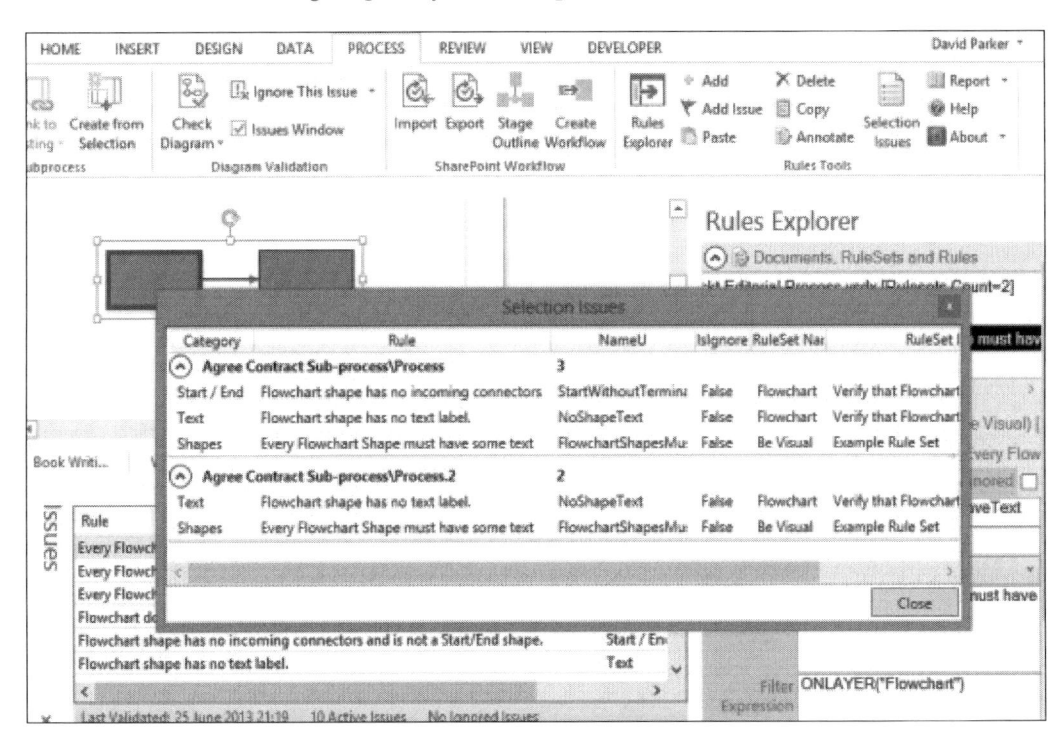

The `ThisAddin` class has a method to open the selected issues dialog.

```
public void OnActionOpenSelectionIssues()
{
   VEDocument document = this.documents[Globals.ThisAddIn.
Application.ActiveDocument.ID];
   if (document != null)
   {
      // this is our document so call open window
      document.OpenSelectionIssues();
   }
}
```

[197]

Developing a Validation API Interface

The `OpenSelectionIssues()` method is quite simple, because the list view in the `WindowIIssues.xaml` file is based on a filtered view of the current document `VEIssues` observable collection:

```
public void OpenSelectionIssues()
{
  Globals.ThisAddIn.VEApp.SelectedVEDocument = this;
  UI.WindowIssues frm = new UI.WindowIssues();
  frm.ShowDialog();
}
```

The `WindowIssues.xaml` file defines the list view, complete with its grouping.

First, you need to include an extra namespace:

```
xmlns:dat="clr-namespace:System.Windows.Data;assembly=PresentationFramework"
```

Next, you can use this namespaces to define the `CollectionViewSource` grouping, as follows:

```
<CollectionViewSource Source="{Binding Path=VEIssues}"
x:Key="listingDataView"
                                        Filter="CollectionViewSource_
Filter">
     <CollectionViewSource.GroupDescriptions>
       <dat:PropertyGroupDescription PropertyName="TargetName" />
     </CollectionViewSource.GroupDescriptions>
   </CollectionViewSource>
```

You can then reference this collection view source in `ListView`:

```
<ListView Name="ListViewMain"
          SelectionChanged="ListViewMain_SelectionChanged"
          ItemsSource="{Binding Source={StaticResource
             ResourceKey=listingDataView}}" IsEnabled="False">
```

Next, you can define the `ListView.GroupStyle` binding to the name of the group:

```
<ListView.GroupStyle>
  <GroupStyle>
    <GroupStyle.ContainerStyle>
      <Style TargetType="{x:Type GroupItem}">
        <Setter Property="Margin" Value="0,0,0,5"/>
        <Setter Property="Template">
          <Setter.Value>
            <ControlTemplate TargetType="{x:Type GroupItem}">
```

```xml
            <Expander IsExpanded="True" BorderBrush="#FFA4B97F"
BorderThickness="0,0,0,1">
                <Expander.Header>
                    <DockPanel>
                        <TextBlock FontWeight="Bold" Text="{Binding
Path=Name}"
Margin="5,0,0,0" Width="300"/>
                        <TextBlock FontWeight="Bold"
Text="{Binding Path=ItemCount}"/>
                    </DockPanel>
                </Expander.Header>
                <Expander.Content>
                    <ItemsPresenter />
                </Expander.Content>
            </Expander>
        </ControlTemplate>
    </Setter.Value>
  </Setter>
</Style>
</GroupStyle.ContainerStyle>
</GroupStyle>
</ListView.GroupStyle>
```

Lastly, `ListView.View` can be defined binding to the properties of the `VEIssue` objects:

```xml
<ListView.View>
  <GridView >
    <GridViewColumn Width="120" Header="Category"
      DisplayMemberBinding="{Binding Path=Rule.Category}"/>
    <GridViewColumn Width="240" Header="Rule"
      DisplayMemberBinding="{Binding Path=Rule.Description}"/>
    <GridViewColumn Width="120" Header="NameU"
      DisplayMemberBinding="{Binding Path=Rule.NameU}"/>
    <GridViewColumn Width="60" Header="IsIgnored"
      DisplayMemberBinding="{Binding Path=IsIgnored}"/>
    <GridViewColumn Width="120" Header="RuleSet Name"
      DisplayMemberBinding="{Binding Path=Rule.RuleSet.Name}"/>
    <GridViewColumn Width="240" Header="RuleSet Description"
      DisplayMemberBinding="{Binding Path=Rule.RuleSet.
Description}"/>
  </GridView>
</ListView.View>
```

Developing a Validation API Interface

The constructor in the code sets the `DataContext` for `UserControlIssues`:

```
public WindowIssues()
{
  InitializeComponent();
  if (Globals.ThisAddIn.VEApp.SelectedVEDocument != null)
  {
    this.DataContext = Globals.ThisAddIn.VEApp.SelectedVEDocument;
  }
}
```

The `CollectionViewSource_Filter()` method is called in the XAML definition of the `CollectionViewSource` and is defined as follows:

```
    private void CollectionViewSource_Filter(object sender,
FilterEventArgs e)
    {

      ViewModel.VEIssue issue = e.Item as ViewModel.VEIssue;
      bool ignore = (issue.IsIgnored == true
          && Globals.ThisAddIn.Application.ActiveDocument.Validation.
ShowIgnoredIssues == false);
      if (ignore == true) { e.Accepted = false; return; }

      if (Globals.ThisAddIn.Application.ActiveWindow.Selection.Count
== 0)
      {
        //Check for the active page
        if (issue.TargetPage == Globals.ThisAddIn.Application.
ActivePage
            && issue.TargetShape == null)
          e.Accepted = true;
        else e.Accepted = false;
      }
      else
      {
        //Check for the Target Shape in the active selection
        foreach (Visio.Shape shp in Globals.ThisAddIn.Application.
ActiveWindow.Selection)
        {
          if (issue.TargetPage == Globals.ThisAddIn.Application.
ActivePage
              && issue.TargetShape != null)
          {
            if (shp == issue.TargetShape)
            {
```

```
                e.Accepted = true;
                break;
            }
            else { e.Accepted = false; }
        }
        else e.Accepted = false;
    }
  }
}
```

Summary

In this chapter we started to develop a Visio 2013 Add-In that enables the rules developer to analyze which rules have been transgressed to cause any particular issue. We have provided an interface that allows the rules developer to add, copy, paste, modify, and delete rulesets and rules.

In the next chapter, we are going to extend the add-in to provide an export of rules to XML, and to a report so that the rules can be reviewed. We will provide an import of rulesets from the XML files that we created. Finally, we will also create annotations for issues in Visio so that the diagrams can be viewed with corresponding issues to assist the rules developer in analyzing the reason for failing validation.

6
Reviewing Validation Rules and Issues

In the previous chapter, we created a tool to allow us to review and edit rules in Microsoft Visio 2013 Professional. In this chapter, we will extend this tool to provide an import/export routine of rules to an XML file, or to an HTML report, and enable you to add issues as annotations in Visio diagrams. These features will allow rules to be stored, restored, printed out, and pondered over, along with the issues that they may create in a diagram. This should provide confidence in their fitness for purpose.

As before, I will not be offended if you do not follow all of the coding, but please read the bits about using the extra features.

Extensions to our ribbon

Our **Rules Tools** group in the **PROCESS** tab of the Visio ribbon needs to be extended to include our new features:

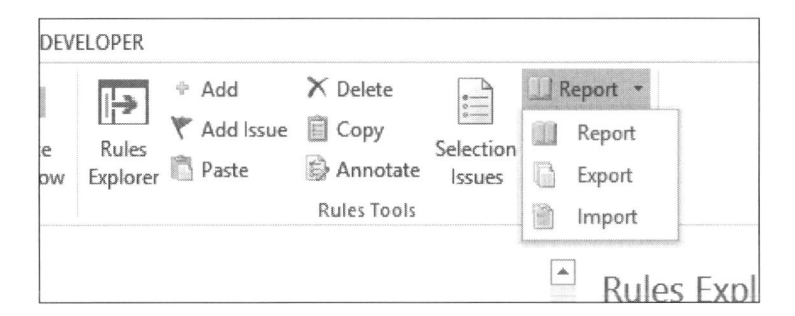

Reviewing Validation Rules and Issues

There are four new buttons required:

- Annotate
- Report
- Export
- Import

These are added to the `Ribbon.xml` file and the relevant call-backs are added to the `Ribbon` class.

The **Annotate** button is enabled for all diagrams but the other buttons are only enabled when the **Rules Explorer** window is open, and I have arranged them on the drop-down menu of a split button.

The `OnAction` event of the **Annotate** button checks whether the active page type is a `visTypeForeground`. This is because a user may inadvertently be on a reviewer (`visTypeMarkup`) or background (`visTypeBackground`) page when the button is pressed. This is explained further in the next section. Initially, the `Ribbon` class gets the call-back from the clicked button, and then re-directs it to the `ThisAddin` class:

```
            case "buttonAnnotate":
                Globals.ThisAddIn.OnActionAnnotateIssues();
                break;
So, the ThisAddin class has the following method:
    public void OnActionAnnotateIssues()
    {
      VEDocument document = this.documents[
        Globals.ThisAddIn.Application.ActiveDocument.ID];
      if (document != null)
      {
        // this is our document so call open window
        document.OpenAnnotateIssues();
      }
    }
```

The `VEDocument` class has the `OpenAnnotateIssues()` method that checks the page type and whether the user is in markup mode or not (this is done by checking the value of a specific cell in the document's ShapeSheet):

```
    public void OpenAnnotateIssues()
    {
      Globals.ThisAddIn.VEApp.SelectedVEDocument = this;
      //Toggle the issues annotation
      if (Globals.ThisAddIn.VEApp.VisioApplication.ActivePage.Type ==
        Visio.VisPageTypes.visTypeForeground)
```

```
            if (this.document.DocumentSheet.get_CellsSRC(
                (short)Visio.VisSectionIndices.visSectionObject,
                (short)Visio.VisRowIndices.visRowDoc,
                (short)Visio.VisCellIndices.visDocViewMarkup).ResultIU ==
  0)
            { this.DisplayIssueMarkup(); }
            else
            { this.HideIssueMarkup(); }
         else
            this.HideIssueMarkup();
      }
```

Both the **Export RuleSets** and **RuleSets Report** buttons will output a single ruleset if a rule or ruleset item is selected in the **Rules Explorer** window, or all of the rulesets if a document item is selected. Then, the export method is as follows:

```
Globals.ThisAddIn.VEApp.SelectedVEDocument.ExportDocument(
true, true);
```

And the report method is called as follows:

```
Globals.ThisAddIn.VEApp.SelectedVEDocument.ReportDocument(
true, false);
```

The two arguments passed through are whether to include rulesets and issues in the action. Actually, while I have provided exporting rules sets and issues to XML, I have not included a report for issues currently. Therefore, the second argument for `ReportDocument` is `false`. Perhaps, you would like to create a XSL report for issues.

The action for the **Import RuleSets** button simply checks that a document has been selected in the **Rules Explorer** before importing the rulesets in the selected XML document.

```
            if (Globals.ThisAddIn.VEApp.SelectedVEDocument != null)
            {
                Globals.ThisAddIn.VEApp.SelectedVEDocument.
  ImportRuleSets();
            }
            else
            {
                System.Windows.MessageBox.Show(this.
  GetSupertip(control),
                    this.GetLabel(control),
                    System.Windows.MessageBoxButton.OK,
                    System.Windows.MessageBoxImage.Information);
            }
```

Reviewing Validation Rules and Issues

Annotating Visio diagrams with issues

One useful feature of Visio is the ability to add reviewers' comments and scribbles via the **REVIEW** tab.

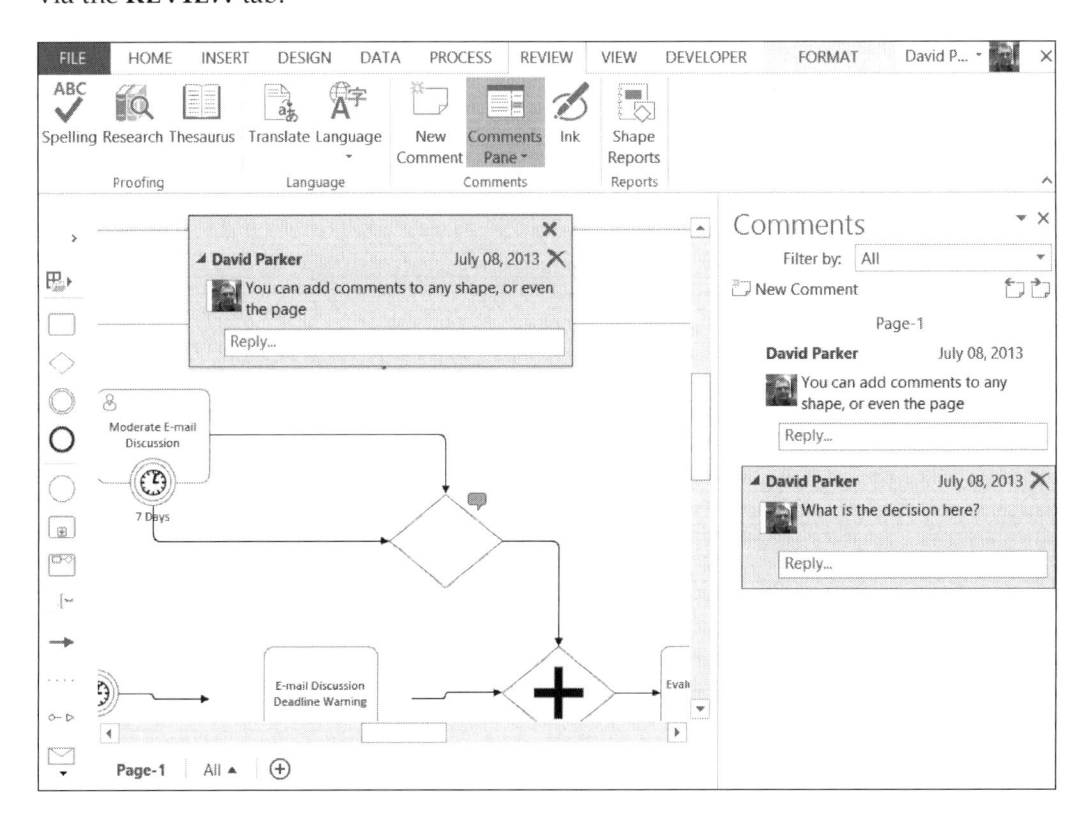

In fact, this feature has been changed for Visio 2013 and is a replacement for the old mark-up feature that was present in the previous versions of Visio. However, the old feature is still present, and accessible via code, but hidden from normal users (unless they are added back in again with the **Customize the Ribbon** feature). There were some good reasons for Microsoft providing a different way of adding page and shape comments. For example, the new comments are also editable via Visio Services on SharePoint 2013, and the comments are actually associated directly with shapes. I have utilized the old mark-up feature to display issues, so that they do not become confused with other shape comments.

Normally, comments are assigned to the currently signed-in user or you can create them for the local user, which you can set by navigating to **File | Options** manually.

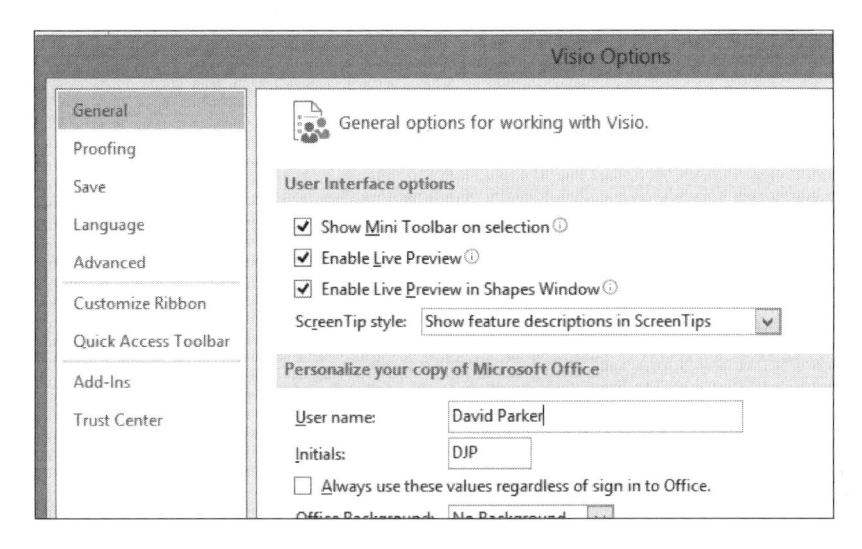

The **Always use these values regardless of sign in to Office** checkbox is a new setting in Visio 2013 that allows the local user to be used rather than the Microsoft identity (Settings.UseLocalUserInfo).

In fact, these old-style mark-up comments are actually stored as annotation rows in the ShapeSheet of the page, and are not printable. When you switch on mark-up tracking, a new special page is created as an overlay over the existing page. This new page is of type *Visio.VisPageTypes.visTypeMarkup*, and it is named after the foreground page that it is associated with, but with a suffix of the user's initials.

Reviewing Validation Rules and Issues

The idea is that a drawing can be passed from user to user, with each adding their own distinct mark-up page, without affecting the original drawing. These mark-up pages appear as **Background Pages** in the **Drawing Explorer** panel.

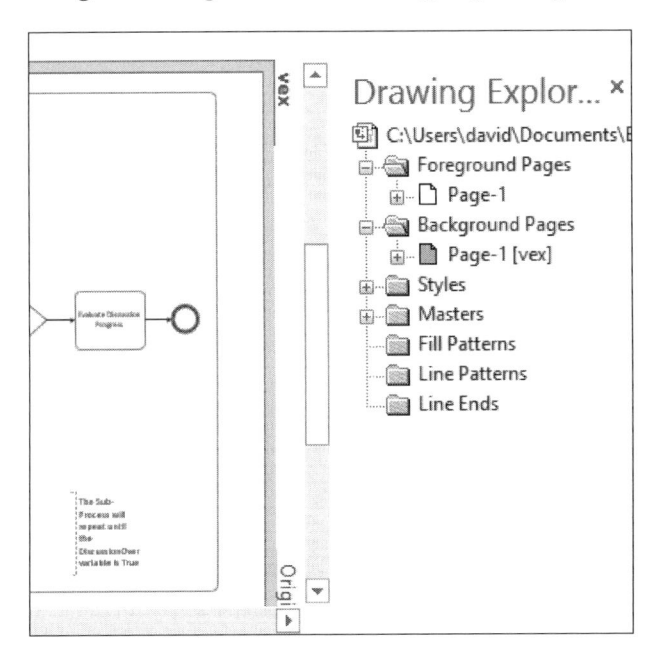

When you add a comment using the **Annotate** button in the **RulesTools** add-in, it gets added as a row in the **Annotation** section of the ShapeSheet of the page:

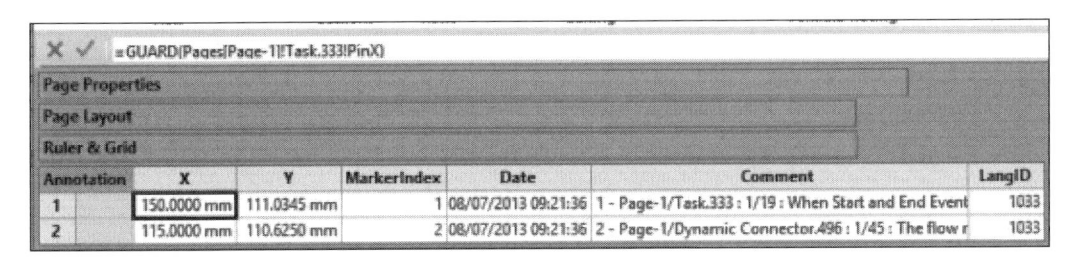

You can see that each comment has an **X** and **Y** value for its location in the page, an index, and a datetime stamp.

The **Annotate** button automatically reveals the old **Reviewing** pane to the right of the diagram.

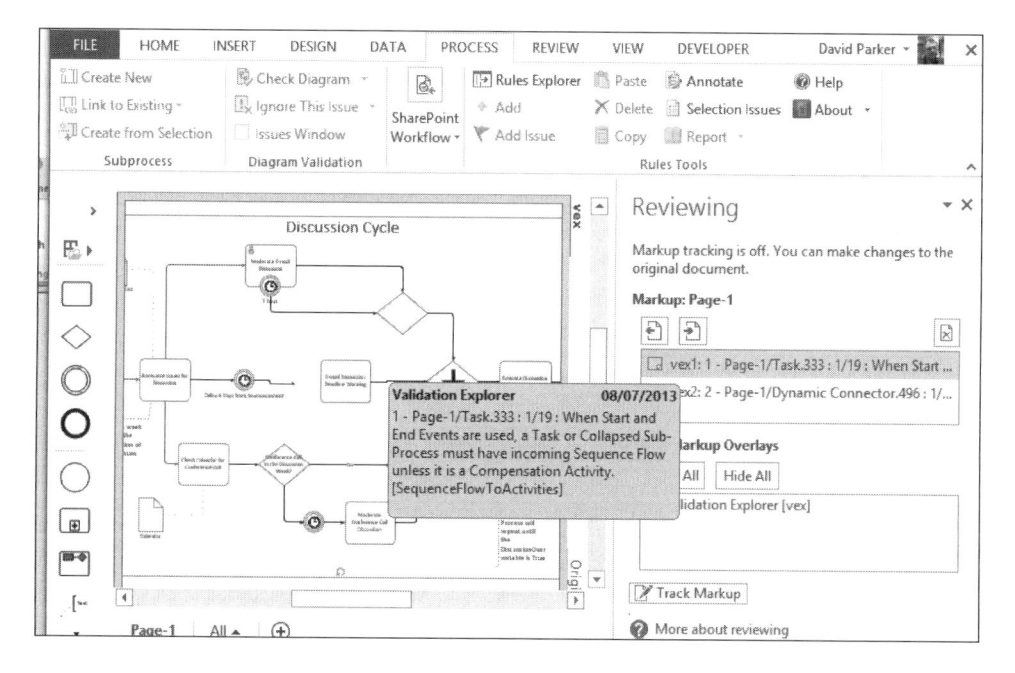

You can click on a comment in the **Reviewing** pane to display the details of the comment.

I did not want these issue notes to be confused with any notes that the current user may wish to create, so I decided to create a dummy user, `Validation Explorer`, with the initials `vex`, in order to keep them clearly distinct. Of course, I do not expect anyone to manually add this dummy user; it will be added automatically. The only trace that it exists will be an entry in the **Reviewer** section of the ShapeSheet of the document, because this is where Visio automatically creates an entry when mark-up is switched on:

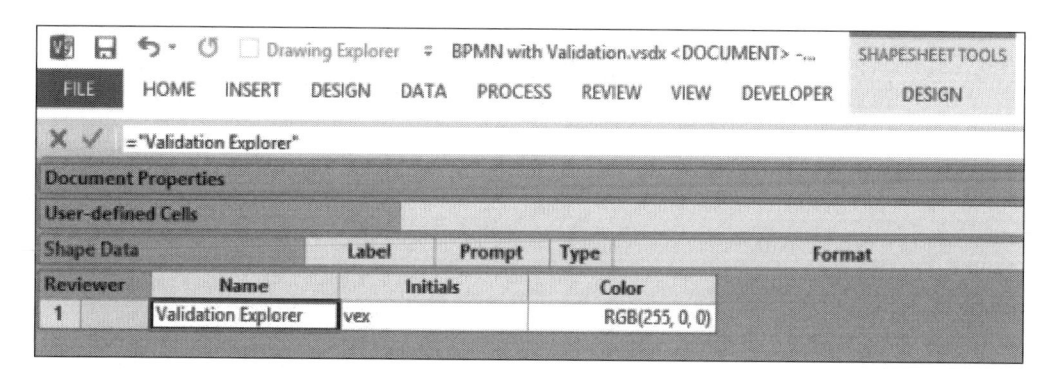

Saving the current user settings

There are two `Application Settings` to provide the strings for the dummy user, which can be opened from the **Settings** tab on the panel opened from the **Project | ValidationExplorer2 Properties...** menu option:

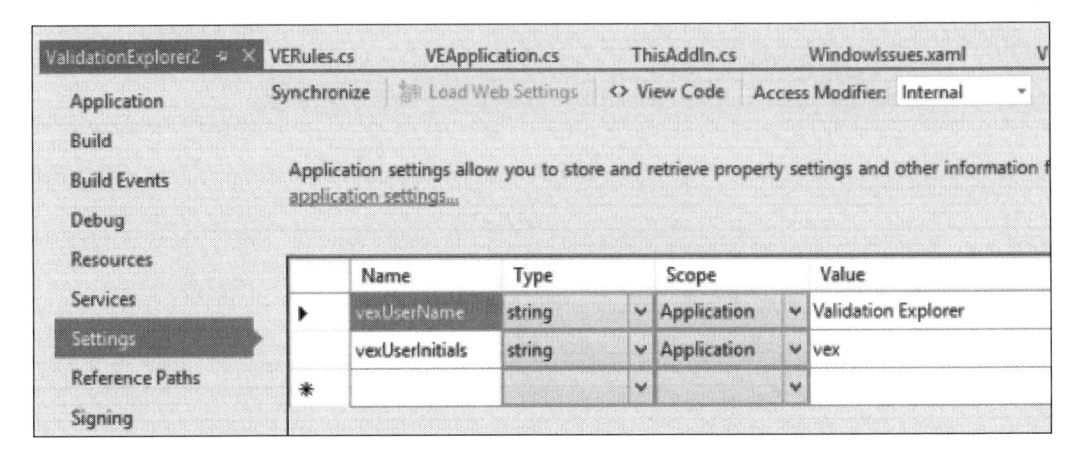

I then added private strings to store the current user's settings.

```
private string theUserName = "";
private string theUserInitials = "";
private bool useLocalUserInfo = false;
```

These variables are set during the constructor of the VEDocument class:

```
this.theUserName =
    veApplication.VisioApplication.Settings.UserName;
this.theUserInitials =
    veApplication.VisioApplication.Settings.UserInitials;
this.useLocalUserInfo =
veApplication.VisioApplication.Settings.UseLocalUserInfo;
```

They will be required in order to set the user details back again.

Displaying the issue mark-up page

The **Annotate** button adds the issues to the Reviewer Comments automatically for the page and each shape that has issues. This allows the user to easily see all of the issues for a selected shape.

Chapter 6

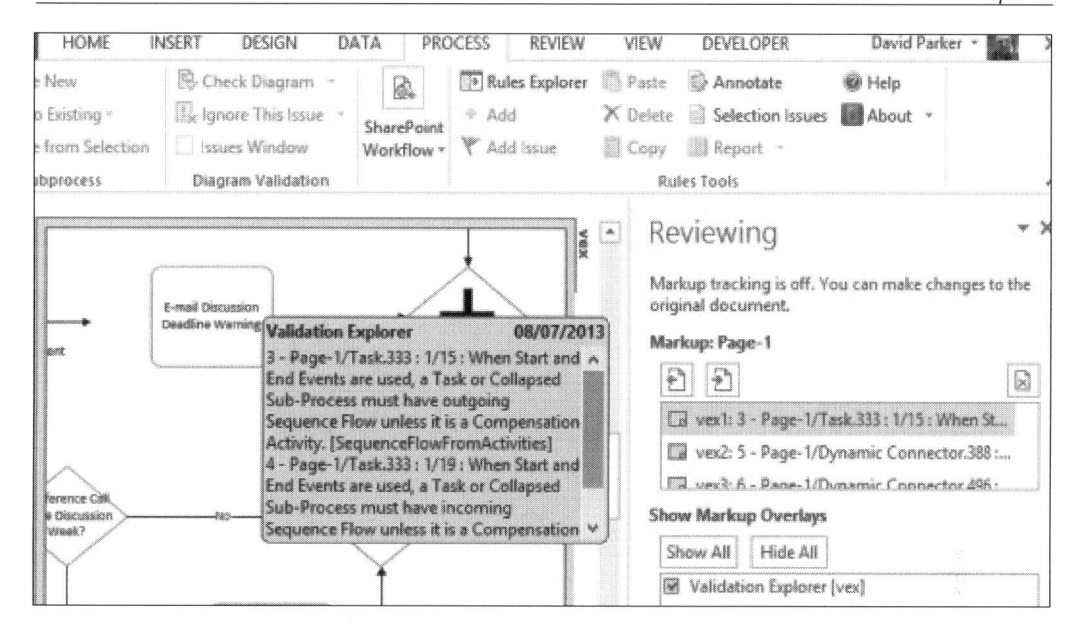

After checking that the active page is not already a mark-up page, this method collects all of the issues that are not ignored in the current page and groups them by the page or shape, using the power and simplicity of `Linq`. It then transfers these objects into a `Dictionary` because experimentation found that the `pagIssues` collection is emptied as soon as the active page is changed. This happens because I have elsewhere set up `ViewCollection` on the `VEIssues` collection that automatically filters by the active page.

The Visio application settings are then changed to the dummy user before mark-up tracking and viewing are switched on. This automatically changes the active page to the mark-up page.

The comments are then added to the mark-up page and finally mark-up tracking is switched off; however, mark-up viewing is left on so that the user can see the comments.

```
public void DisplayIssueMarkup()
{
  try
  {
    //Check the page type
    Visio.Page pag =
        (Visio.Page)veApplication.VisioApplication.ActiveWindow.Page;
    if (pag.Type == Visio.VisPageTypes.visTypeMarkup) return;

    //Group the issues for this page by target
```

Reviewing Validation Rules and Issues

```
          var pagIssues = from issu in this.VEIssues
                    where issu.IsIgnored == false
                    && issu.TargetPageID == pag.ID
                    group issu by issu.Target into g
                    select new { Target = g.Key, Issues = g };

      //Transfer into a dictionary
      //otherwise it will be empty when the page changes
      var dicIssues =
        new Dictionary<object, List<VEIssue>>();
      foreach (var v in pagIssues)
      {
        List<VEIssue> lst = new List<VEIssue>();
        foreach (var i in v.Issues)
        {
          lst.Add(i);
        }
        dicIssues.Add(v.Target, lst);
      }
      //Set the dummy user settings
      veApplication.VisioApplication.Settings.UseLocalUserInfo =
true;
      veApplication.VisioApplication.Settings.UserName =
        Properties.Settings.Default.vexUserName;
      veApplication.VisioApplication.Settings.UserInitials =
        Properties.Settings.Default.vexUserInitials;
      //Turn on Track Markup
      //this will use the User settings to
      //either create a new markup page
      //or go to a previously created one
      this.document.DocumentSheet.get_CellsSRC(
        (short)Visio.VisSectionIndices.visSectionObject,
        (short)Visio.VisRowIndices.visRowDoc,
        (short)Visio.VisCellIndices.visDocAddMarkup).FormulaU =
          true.ToString();
      //Turn on View Markup
      this.document.DocumentcSheet.get_CellsSRC(
        (short)Visio.VisSectionIndices.visSectionObject,
        (short)Visio.VisRowIndices.visRowDoc,
        (short)Visio.VisCellIndices.visDocViewMarkup).FormulaU =
          true.ToString();

      //Get the markup page
      pag = (Visio.Page)veApplication.VisioApplication.ActiveWindow.
Page;
      if (pag.Type == Visio.VisPageTypes.visTypeMarkup)
      {
```

```csharp
          int rvwrID = pag.ReviewerID;
          //Clear any existing annotations
          if (pag.PageSheet.get_SectionExists(
             (short)Visio.VisSectionIndices.visSectionAnnotation,
             (short)Visio.VisExistsFlags.visExistsAnywhere) != 0)
          {
            pag.PageSheet.DeleteSection(
               (short)Visio.VisSectionIndices.visSectionAnnotation);
          }

          //Add notes to the markup page
          foreach (var k in dicIssues.Keys)
          {
            string note = @"";
            List<VEIssue> lst = (List<VEIssue>)dicIssues[k];
            foreach (VEIssue i in lst)
            {
              note += i.DisplayName + "\n";
            }
            if (k is Visio.Page)
            { addIssueNote(pag, null, rvwrID, note); }
            else if (k is Visio.Shape)
            { addIssueNote(pag, (Visio.Shape)k, rvwrID, note); }
          }
          //Turn off track markup
          this.document.DocumentSheet.get_CellsSRC(
             (short)Visio.VisSectionIndices.visSectionObject,
             (short)Visio.VisRowIndices.visRowDoc,
             (short)Visio.VisCellIndices.visDocAddMarkup).FormulaU =
                false.ToString();
        }
      }
      catch (Exception)
      {
        throw;
      }
      //Set the Settings back to the current user
      veApplication.VisioApplication.Settings.UserName =
         this.theUserName;
      veApplication.VisioApplication.Settings.UserInitials =
         this.theUserInitials;
      veApplication.VisioApplication.Settings.UseLocalUserInfo =
         this.useLocalUserInfo ;
    }
```

Reviewing Validation Rules and Issues

Adding in the issue comments

The issue comments are added to the mark-up page with the following method:

```
private void addIssueNote(
  Visio.Page pag, Visio.Shape shp, int rvwrID, string msg)
{
  //Get the last row number in the
  //Annotations section of the ShapeSheet of the page
  int intAnnotationRow = pag.PageSheet.AddRow(
    (short)Visio.VisSectionIndices.visSectionAnnotation,
    (short)Visio.VisRowIndices.visRowLast, 0);
  if (shp != null)
  {
    //Add the comment
    pag.PageSheet.get_CellsSRC(
      (short)Visio.VisSectionIndices.visSectionAnnotation,
      (short)intAnnotationRow,
      (short)Visio.VisCellIndices.visAnnotationX).FormulaU =
        "=GUARD(Pages[" + shp.ContainingPage.Name + "]!" +
        shp.NameID + "!PinX)";
    pag.PageSheet.get_CellsSRC(
      (short)Visio.VisSectionIndices.visSectionAnnotation,
      (short)intAnnotationRow,
      (short)Visio.VisCellIndices.visAnnotationY).FormulaU =
        "=GUARD(Pages[" + shp.ContainingPage.Name + "]!" +
        shp.NameID + "!PinY)";
  }
  else
  {
    //Add the comment at the centre of the page,
    //but allow it to be re-positioned, if required
    pag.PageSheet.get_CellsSRC(
      (short)Visio.VisSectionIndices.visSectionAnnotation,
      (short)intAnnotationRow,
      (short)Visio.VisCellIndices.visAnnotationX).FormulaU =
        "=PageWidth*0.5";
    pag.PageSheet.get_CellsSRC(
      (short)Visio.VisSectionIndices.visSectionAnnotation,
      (short)intAnnotationRow,
      (short)Visio.VisCellIndices.visAnnotationY).FormulaU =
        "=PageHeight*0.5";
  }
  //Add the reviewer ID
  pag.PageSheet.get_CellsSRC(
```

```csharp
      (short)Visio.VisSectionIndices.visSectionAnnotation,
      (short)intAnnotationRow,
      (short)Visio.VisCellIndices.visAnnotationReviewerID).FormulaU
=
        rvwrID.ToString();
    //Add the index
    pag.PageSheet.get_CellsSRC(
      (short)Visio.VisSectionIndices.visSectionAnnotation,
      (short)intAnnotationRow,
      (short)Visio.VisCellIndices.visAnnotationMarkerIndex).FormulaU
=
        (intAnnotationRow + 1).ToString();
    //Add timestamp
    pag.PageSheet.get_CellsSRC(
      (short)Visio.VisSectionIndices.visSectionAnnotation,
      (short)intAnnotationRow,
      (short)Visio.VisCellIndices.visAnnotationDate).FormulaU =
        "DATETIME(" + DateTime.Now.ToOADate() + ")";
    //Add the concatenated issues
    pag.PageSheet.get_CellsSRC(
      (short)Visio.VisSectionIndices.visSectionAnnotation,
      (short)intAnnotationRow,
      (short)Visio.VisCellIndices.visAnnotationComment).FormulaU =
      "\"" + msg + "\"";
}
```

Hiding the issue mark-up page

This is only called if the active page type is not a foreground page. It ensures that the active page is returned to the foreground page by ensuring that tracking and viewing of mark-up is switched off. Finally, an attempt is made to hide the **Reviewing** pane by using the DoCmd() method on the Visio application object. This will only toggle the visibility, though, but it is most probable that it is visible, so this will hide it most of the time.

```csharp
public void HideIssueMarkup()
{
  try
  {
    //Ensure that the user Settings are correct
    veApplication.VisioApplication.Settings.UserName =
      this.theUserName;
    veApplication.VisioApplication.Settings.UserInitials =
      this.theUserInitials;
```

```
            veApplication.VisioApplication.Settings.UseLocalUserInfo =
              this.useLocalUserInfo;

            //Turn off Add Markup
            this.document.DocumentSheet.get_CellsSRC(
              (short)Visio.VisSectionIndices.visSectionObject,
              (short)Visio.VisRowIndices.visRowDoc,
              (short)Visio.VisCellIndices.visDocAddMarkup).FormulaU =
                false.ToString();
            //Turn off View Markup
            this.document.DocumentSheet.get_CellsSRC(
              (short)Visio.VisSectionIndices.visSectionObject,
              (short)Visio.VisRowIndices.visRowDoc,
              (short)Visio.VisCellIndices.visDocViewMarkup).FormulaU =
                false.ToString();
            //Hide the Reviewer pane (probably)
            this.TheApplication.VisioApplication.DoCmd(
              (short)Visio.VisUICmds.visCmdTaskPaneReviewer);
         }
         catch (Exception)
         {
           throw;
         }
      }
```

Exporting rulesets to XML

Even though there is an option to import a ruleset from another Visio document, I know that some rules developers would like to export and import rulesets to XML. This allows rulesets to be stored, restored, and analysed more easily.

I decided that the XML structure exported should be the same as the Visio 2013 XML format, and thus use a part of the Visio XML schema. This means using the same namespaces, but it would mean that any XSL stylesheets developed for our export would also work for the validation.xml files found within the zip files that are standard Visio 2013 XML format (*.vsdx and *.vstx files).

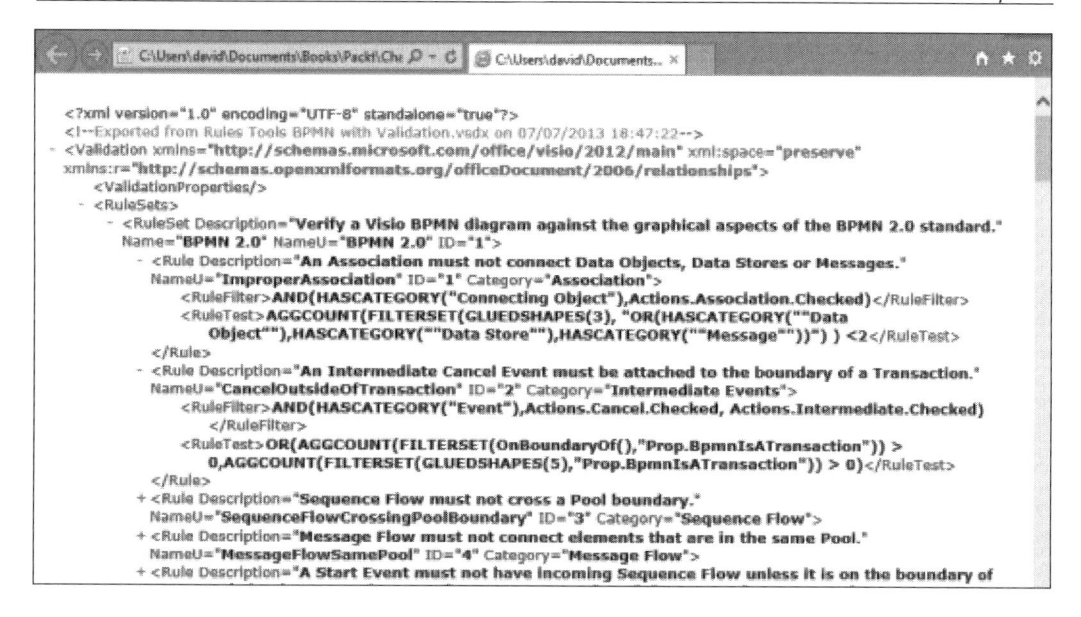

```
<?xml version="1.0" encoding="UTF-8" standalone="true"?>
<!--Exported from Rules Tools BPMN with Validation.vsdx on 07/07/2013 18:47:22-->
<Validation xmlns="http://schemas.microsoft.com/office/visio/2012/main" xml:space="preserve"
 xmlns:r="http://schemas.openxmlformats.org/officeDocument/2006/relationships">
    <ValidationProperties/>
    <RuleSets>
        <RuleSet Description="Verify a Visio BPMN diagram against the graphical aspects of the BPMN 2.0 standard."
            Name="BPMN 2.0" NameU="BPMN 2.0" ID="1">
            <Rule Description="An Association must not connect Data Objects, Data Stores or Messages."
                NameU="ImproperAssociation" ID="1" Category="Association">
                <RuleFilter>AND(HASCATEGORY("Connecting Object"),Actions.Association.Checked)</RuleFilter>
                <RuleTest>AGGCOUNT(FILTERSET(GLUEDSHAPES(3), "OR(HASCATEGORY(""Data
                    Object""),HASCATEGORY(""Data Store""),HASCATEGORY(""Message""))") ) <2</RuleTest>
            </Rule>
            <Rule Description="An Intermediate Cancel Event must be attached to the boundary of a Transaction."
                NameU="CancelOutsideOfTransaction" ID="2" Category="Intermediate Events">
                <RuleFilter>AND(HASCATEGORY("Event"),Actions.Cancel.Checked, Actions.Intermediate.Checked)
                </RuleFilter>
                <RuleTest>OR(AGGCOUNT(FILTERSET(OnBoundaryOf(),"Prop.BpmnIsATransaction")) >
                    0,AGGCOUNT(FILTERSET(GLUEDSHAPES(5),"Prop.BpmnIsATransaction")) > 0)</RuleTest>
            </Rule>
            + <Rule Description="Sequence Flow must not cross a Pool boundary."
                NameU="SequenceFlowCrossingPoolBoundary" ID="3" Category="Sequence Flow">
            + <Rule Description="Message Flow must not connect elements that are in the same Pool."
                NameU="MessageFlowSamePool" ID="4" Category="Message Flow">
            + <Rule Description="A Start Event must not have incoming Sequence Flow unless it is on the boundary of
```

I decided to include the option to export the issues in a document, too, because someone may have the need to use them in an external program. Having the issues available in XML format means that they could be displayed as a table, for example, so that they can be reviewed independently.

```
<?xml version="1.0" encoding="UTF-8" standalone="true"?>
<!--Exported from Rules Tools BPMN with Validation.vsdx on 07/07/2013 18:47:22-->
<Validation xmlns="http://schemas.microsoft.com/office/visio/2012/main" xml:space="preserve"
 xmlns:r="http://schemas.openxmlformats.org/officeDocument/2006/relationships">
    <ValidationProperties/>
    + <RuleSets>
    - <Issues>
        - <Issue ID="1">
            <RuleInfo Rule="19" RuleSet="1"/>
            <IssueTarget ShapeID="333" PageID="0"/>
        </Issue>
        - <Issue ID="2">
            <RuleInfo Rule="45" RuleSet="1"/>
            <IssueTarget ShapeID="496" PageID="0"/>
        </Issue>
    </Issues>
</Validation>
```

The `ExportDocument()` method first constructs a title for `SaveFile` dialog, depending upon the `include` options provided. The default name proffered for the XML file uses the drawing file name as a base.

Reviewing Validation Rules and Issues

> Alternatively, you can manually change the extension of a Visio 2013 file to ZIP and then open the ZIP file to extract the `Validation.xml` file; or, indeed, you can reverse the process to import a ruleset.

Once a file name has been obtained, the `System.XMl.Linq.XDocument` object is created, saved, and opened in the associated application.

```
public void ExportDocument(
  bool includeRulesets, bool includeIssues)
{
  try
  {
    //Set the title for the SaveFile dialog
    string title = "";
    if (includeRulesets) title += "RuleSets";
    if (includeRulesets && includeIssues) title += " and ";
    if (includeIssues) title += "Issues";
    string shortName =
       System.IO.Path.GetFileNameWithoutExtension(this.document.FullName);
    string fileName =
       System.IO.Path.Combine(this.document.Path, shortName + ".xml");
    Microsoft.Win32.SaveFileDialog dlg =
       new Microsoft.Win32.SaveFileDialog();
    dlg.Title = "Save " + title;
    dlg.InitialDirectory =
       System.Environment.GetFolderPath(
          System.Environment.SpecialFolder.MyDocuments);
    dlg.FileName = shortName + " " + title + ".xml";
    dlg.OverwritePrompt = true;
    dlg.DefaultExt = ".xml";
    dlg.Filter = "XML documents (.xml)|*.xml";
    if (dlg.ShowDialog() == true)
    {
      fileName = dlg.FileName;
    }
    else return;
    XDocument xDoc = getXDocument(includeRulesets, includeIssues);
    if (xDoc != null)
    {
      //Save the file
      xDoc.Save(fileName);
      //Open the file with the associated program
```

```
      System.Diagnostics.ProcessStartInfo startInfo =
        new System.Diagnostics.ProcessStartInfo(fileName);
      startInfo.WindowStyle =
        System.Diagnostics.ProcessWindowStyle.Normal;
      System.Diagnostics.Process.Start(startInfo);
    }
  }
  catch (Exception)
  {
    throw;
  }
}
```

Getting the XDocument object

First, this method creates the required `XNamespace` objects then it creates a new `XDocument` object and retrieves the `XElement` objects for `VERules` and/or `VEIssues` of `VEDocument`.

```
private XDocument getXDocument(
  bool includeRulesets, bool includeIssues)
{
  try
  {
    //Validation
    //   ValidationPoperties
    //      LastValidated
    //      ShowIgnored
    //   RuleSets
    //      RuleSet
    //         ID
    //         NameU
    //         Description
    //         Rule
    //            ID
    //            NameU
    //            Category
    //            Description
    //            RuleFilter
    //            RuleTest
    //   Issues
    //      Issue
    //         ID
    //         IssueTarget
```

Reviewing Validation Rules and Issues

```
//      PageID
//      ShapeID
//   RuleInfo
//      RuleSetID
//      RuleID

XNamespace xns =
   "http://schemas.microsoft.com/office/visio/2012/main";
XNamespace xnsr =
   "http://schemas.openxmlformats.org/officeDocument/2006/relationships";
XDocument xdoc =
   new XDocument(new XDeclaration("1.0", "utf-8", "yes"),
   new XComment("Exported from Rules Tools " + this.document.Name +
      " on " + System.DateTime.Now.ToUniversalTime().ToString()),
      new XElement(xns + "Validation",
         new XAttribute(XNamespace.Xmlns + "r", xnsr.NamespaceName),
         new XElement(xns + "ValidationProperties")
         )
      );

XElement validNode = xdoc.Element(xns + "Validation");
if (includeRulesets)
{
  if (this.SelectedVERuleSet == null)
  {
    validNode.Add(new XElement(xns + "RuleSets",
    from el in this.VERuleSets
    select el.GetXElement(xns)
    ));
  }
  else
  {
    validNode.Add(new XElement(xns + "RuleSets",
    from el in this.VERuleSets
    where (el.ID == this.selectedVERuleSet.ID)
    select el.GetXElement(xns)
    ));
  }
}
if (includeIssues)
{
```

```
            validNode.Add(new XElement(xns + "Issues",
            from el in this.VEIssues
            select el.GetXElement(xns)
            ));
      }

      return xdoc;
    }
    catch (Exception)
    {

    }
    return null;
}
```

Getting the VERuleSet XElement

This method creates an XElement for the VERuleSet object, and then adds an XElement for each VERule in the VERules collection.

```
      public XElement GetXElement(XNamespace xns)
      {
        XElement retNode;
        try
        {
          retNode = new XElement(xns + "RuleSet",
              new XAttribute("ID", this.ID),
              new XAttribute("NameU", this.NameU),
              new XAttribute("Name", this.Name),
              new XAttribute("Description", this.Description));
          retNode.Add(from ver in this.VERules
                      select ver.GetXElement(xns));
        }
        catch (Exception)
        {
          throw;
        }
        return retNode;
      }
```

Getting the VEIssue XElement

This method creates an `XElement` for the `VEIssue` object, and then adds an `XElement` for the `RuleInfo` and `IssueTarget`.

```
public XElement GetXElement(XNamespace xns)
{
  XElement retNode;
  try
  {
    retNode = new XElement(xns + "Issue",
        new XAttribute("ID", this.ID),
        new XElement(xns + "RuleInfo",
            new XAttribute("RuleSet",
              this.Rule.RuleSet.ID),
            new XAttribute("Rule",
              this.Rule.ID)
            )
        );
    if (this.Ignored)
    {
      retNode.Add(
        new XAttribute("Ignored", this.Ignored));
    }
    if (this.TargetPage != null ||
      this.TargetShape != null)
    {
      XElement targetNode =
        new XElement(xns + "IssueTarget");
      if (this.TargetPage != null)
        targetNode.Add(
          new XAttribute("PageID",
            this.TargetPage.ID));
      if (this.TargetShape != null)
        targetNode.Add(
          new XAttribute("ShapeID",
            this.TargetShape.ID));
      retNode.Add(targetNode);
    }
  }
  catch (Exception)
  {
    throw;
  }
  return retNode;
}
```

Importing rulesets from XML

This method first requests the user to select the XML file (this can be in the standard Visio XML file format too) which contains the ruleset or rulesets to import from. It then iterates through the ruleset and rule elements to add them to the selected `VEDocument`.

If it encounters a ruleset with the same name as an existing ruleset in the selected `VEDocument`, then the user is prompted to overwrite or not.

Imported rulesets are immediately added to the **Rules Explorer** tree view.

```
public void ImportRuleSets()
{
  try
  {
    string title = "RuleSets";
    string fileName = "";
    Microsoft.Win32.OpenFileDialog dlg =
      new Microsoft.Win32.OpenFileDialog();
    dlg.Title = "Import " + title;
    dlg.InitialDirectory =
      System.Environment.GetFolderPath(
        System.Environment.SpecialFolder.MyDocuments);
    dlg.DefaultExt = ".xml";
    dlg.Filter =
      "XML documents (.xml)|*.xml";
    if (dlg.ShowDialog() == true)
    {
      fileName = dlg.FileName;
    }
    else return;

    XDocument xdoc = XDocument.Load(fileName);
    XNamespace xns =
      "http://schemas.microsoft.com/office/visio/2012/main";
    XNamespace xnsr =
      "http://schemas.openxmlformats.org/officeDocument/2006/relationships";

    //Get the Validation element (abort if none found)
    XElement validNode = xdoc.Element(xns + "Validation");
    if (validNode == null) return;
    //Get the RuleSets element (abort if none found)
    XElement ruleSetsNode = validNode.Element(xns + "RuleSets");
    if (ruleSetsNode == null) return;
    foreach (XElement ruleSetNode in
```

```csharp
              ruleSetsNode.Elements(xns + "RuleSet"))
    {
      //Get the NameU attribute
      string rsName = ruleSetNode.Attribute("NameU").Value;
      //Set the default response
      System.Windows.MessageBoxResult process =
        System.Windows.MessageBoxResult.Yes;
      //Check if the rule set exists already
      if (this.VERuleSets.Count(ver => ver.NameU == rsName) > 0)
      {
        //Ask to replace an existing ruleset (or skip if declined)
        process = System.Windows.MessageBox.Show(
            "The rule set, " + rsName +
              ", exists already.\nDo you wish to replace it?",
            "Import Ruleset",
            System.Windows.MessageBoxButton.YesNo,
            System.Windows.MessageBoxImage.Question,
            System.Windows.MessageBoxResult.Yes);
         if (process == System.Windows.MessageBoxResult.No) break;
         this.VERuleSets.DeleteRuleSet(rsName);
      }
      else process = System.Windows.MessageBoxResult.Yes;
      //Add a new VERuleSet object to this VEDocument
      VERuleSet vrset = this.VERuleSets.AddRuleSet(rsName);
      //Set the properties of the VERuleSet from the attributes
      foreach (XAttribute xat in ruleSetNode.Attributes())
      {
        switch (xat.Name.LocalName)
        {
          case "Name":
            vrset.Name = xat.Value;
            break;
          case "Description":
            vrset.Description = xat.Value;
            break;
          case "RuleSetFlags":
            vrset.RuleSetFlags =
                (Visio.VisRuleSetFlags)Convert.ToInt32(xat.Value);
            break;
        }
      }
      //Set the remaining properties of the VERuleSet from the
elements
      foreach (XElement xelm in ruleSetNode.Elements())
      {
        switch (xelm.Name.LocalName)
        {
```

```csharp
                    case "Rule":
                        string rName = xelm.Attribute("NameU").Value;
                        VERule vrle = vrset.VERules.AddRule(rName);
                        //Set the properties of the VERule from the attributes
                        foreach (XAttribute xat in xelm.Attributes())
                        {
                          switch (xat.Name.LocalName)
                          {
                            case "Category":
                              vrle.Category = xat.Value;
                              break;
                            case "Description":
                              vrle.Description = xat.Value;
                              break;
                            case "TargetType":
                              vrle.TargetType =
                                (Visio.VisRuleTargets)Convert.ToInt32(xat.Value);
                              break;
                          }
                        }
                        //Set the remaining properties of the VERule from the elements
                        foreach (XElement xelmR in xelm.Elements())
                        {
                          switch (xelmR.Name.LocalName)
                          {
                            case "RuleFilter":
                              vrle.FilterExpression = xelmR.Value;
                              break;
                            case "RuleTest":
                              vrle.TestExpression = xelmR.Value;
                              break;
                          }
                        }
                        break;
                  }
                }
              }
            }
      catch (Exception)
      {
        throw;
      }
    }
```

[225]

Reviewing Validation Rules and Issues

Creating ruleset reports

It is a relatively simple operation to use `System.Xml.Xsl` and `System.Xml.XPath` to iterate through the elements in the `XDocument` created by the `getXDocument()` method. The result is an HTML page that can be displayed in any browser:

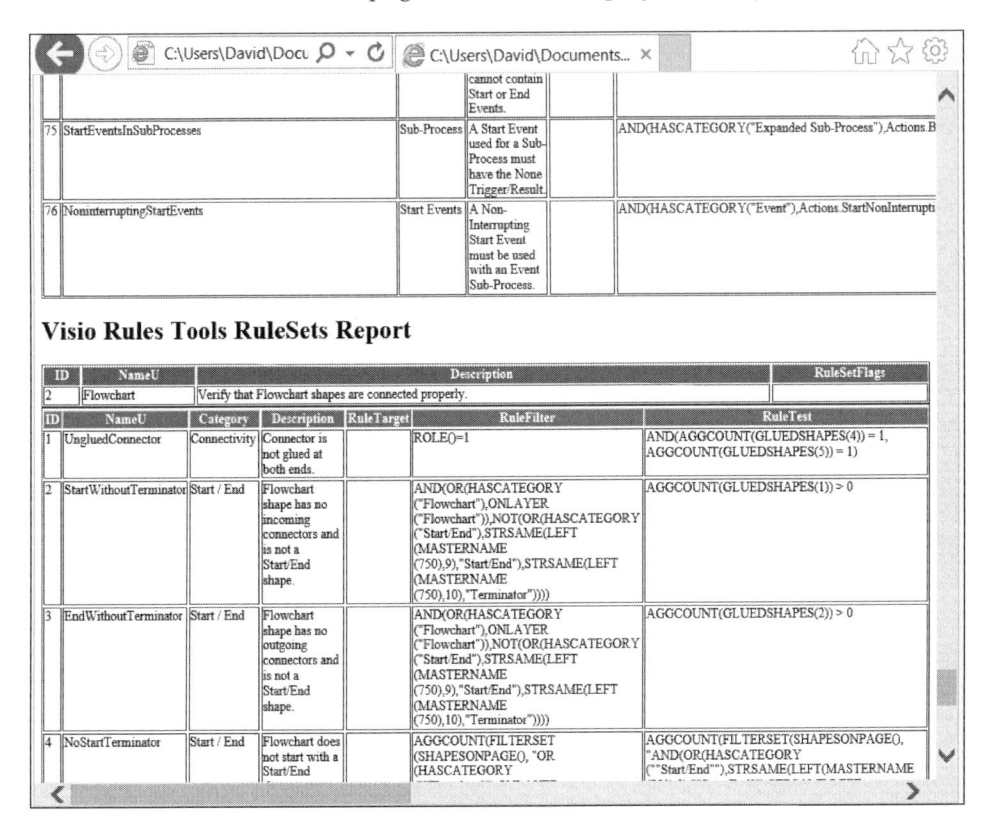

> This is a very utilitarian display. I will let you format the report to your own requirements!

The `ReportDocument()` method prompts for the name of an HTML document to output to.

```
public void ReportDocument(
  bool includeRulesets, bool includeIssues)
{
  try
  {
    string title = "";
    if (includeRulesets)
```

[226]

```csharp
          title += "RuleSets";
        if (includeRulesets && includeIssues)
          title += " and ";
        if (includeIssues)
          title += "Issues";
        string shortName =
          System.IO.Path.GetFileNameWithoutExtension(
            this.document.FullName);
        string fileName = System.IO.Path.Combine(
          this.document.Path, shortName + ".html");
        Microsoft.Win32.SaveFileDialog dlg =
          new Microsoft.Win32.SaveFileDialog();
        dlg.Title = "Save " + title;
        dlg.InitialDirectory =
          System.Environment.GetFolderPath(
            System.Environment.SpecialFolder.MyDocuments);
        dlg.FileName = shortName + " " + title + ".html";
        dlg.OverwritePrompt = true;
        dlg.DefaultExt = ".html";
        dlg.Filter = "HTML documents (.html)|*.html";
        if (dlg.ShowDialog() == true)
        {
          fileName = dlg.FileName;
        }
        else return;
        XDocument xDoc = getXDocument(
          includeRulesets, includeIssues);
        if (xDoc == null)
        {
          return;
        }
        //Get the XSL Stylesheet
        string xslMarkup = getRuleSetXSL();
        // Load the style sheet.
        XslCompiledTransform xslt =
          new XslCompiledTransform();
        xslt.Load(
          System.Xml.XmlReader.Create(
            new StringReader(xslMarkup)));
        //Save the XDocument to a temporary file
        string tempFile =
          System.IO.Path.GetTempFileName();
        xDoc.Save(tempFile);
        //Execute the transform and output to html.
```

```
        xslt.Transform(tempFile, fileName);
        //Delete the temporary file
        System.IO.File.Delete(tempFile);

        //Open in web browser (associated programme)
        System.Diagnostics.ProcessStartInfo startInfo =
          new System.Diagnostics.ProcessStartInfo(fileName);
        startInfo.WindowStyle =
          System.Diagnostics.ProcessWindowStyle.Normal;
        System.Diagnostics.Process.Start(startInfo);
    }
    catch (Exception)
    {
      throw;
    }
}
```

Getting the XSL stylesheet

The XSL template returned by this method can be saved as a file, say `RuleSets.xslt`, and can be used to transform the `validation.xml` file contained in any Visio 2013 document that contains rulesets.

> XSL (XML Style Language) describes how to display an XML file of a given type. See http://www.w3.org/Style/XSL/WhatIsXSL.html for more information.

The output will be a ruleset report in HTML.

```
<?xml version='1.0' encoding='UTF-8' ?>
<xsl:stylesheet version='1.0'
    xmlns:xsl='http://www.w3.org/1999/XSL/Transform'
    xmlns:r='http://schemas.openxmlformats.org/officeDocument/2006/relationships'
    xmlns:v='http://schemas.microsoft.com/office/visio/2012/main'>
<xsl:output method="html"/>

<xsl:template match="//v:Validation/v:RuleSets/v:RuleSet">
<html>
  <body>
  <h1>Visio Rules Tools RuleSets Report</h1>
   <table border="1" width='100%'>
     <tr style='background-color:teal;color:white;font-weight:bold'>
      <th>ID</th>
```

```xml
            <th>NameU</th>
            <th>Description</th>
            <th>RuleSetFlags</th>
          </tr>
          <tr>
            <td><xsl:value-of select="@ID"/></td>
            <td><xsl:value-of select="@NameU"/></td>
            <td><xsl:value-of select="@Description"/></td>
            <td><xsl:value-of select="RuleSetFlags"/></td>
          </tr>
        </table>
        <table border="1" width='100%'>
          <tr style='background-color:gray;color:white;font-weight:bold'>
            <th>ID</th>
            <th>NameU</th>
            <th>Category</th>
            <th>Description</th>
            <th>RuleTarget</th>
            <th>RuleFilter</th>
            <th>RuleTest</th>
          </tr>
<xsl:for-each select='v:Rule'>
   <tr style='vertical-align:top'>
     <td>
       <xsl:value-of select='@ID'/>
     </td>
     <td>
       <xsl:value-of select='@NameU'/>
     </td>
     <td>
       <xsl:value-of select='@Category'/>
     </td>
     <td>
       <xsl:value-of select='@Description'/>
     </td>
     <td>
       <xsl:value-of select='@RuleTarget'/>
     </td>
     <td>
       <xsl:value-of select='v:RuleFilter'/>
     </td>
     <td>
       <xsl:value-of select='v:RuleTest'/>
     </td>
```

Reviewing Validation Rules and Issues

```
    </tr>
</xsl:for-each>
    </table>
   </body>
</html>
</xsl:template>

</xsl:stylesheet>
```

Save the main body of the `getRuleSetXSL()` into a `RuleSets.xslt` file, then use a tool such as **XML Notepad** to open a Visio XML format document. You can use Visual Studio to process an XML file with a selected XSLT file too, but I like the **Tree View** display in **XML Notepad**.

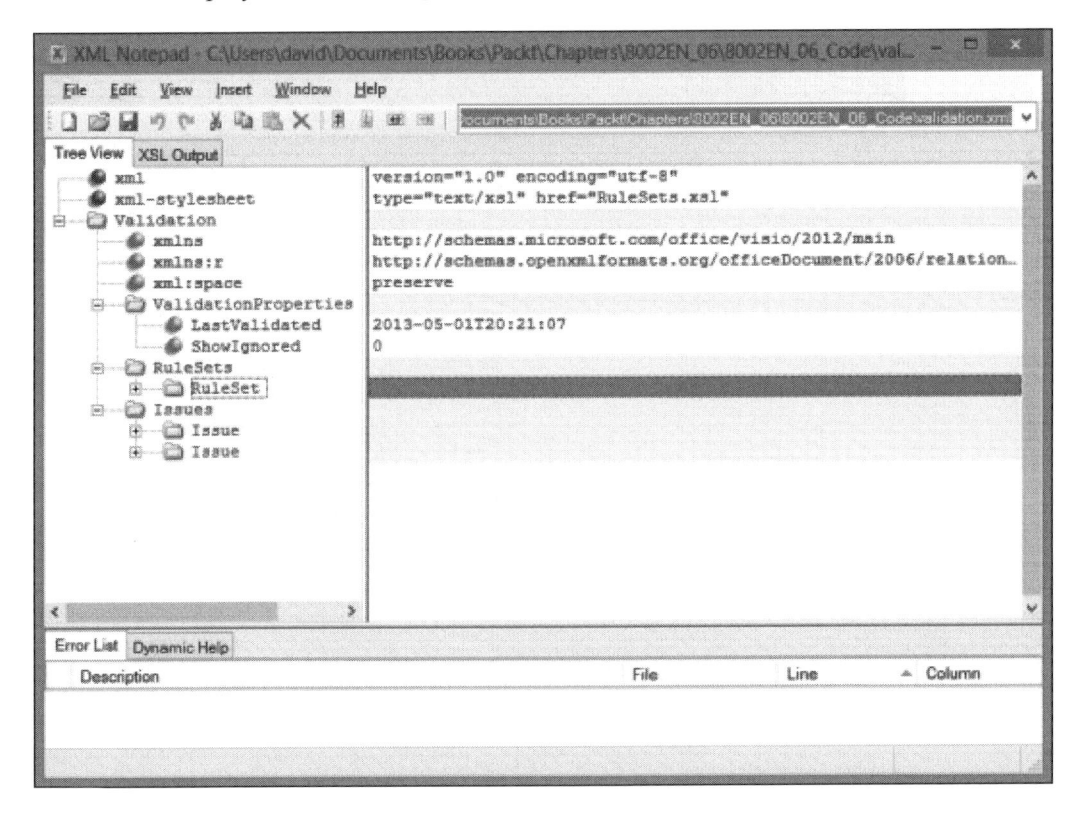

You can then enter the full path to the `RuleSets.xslt` file on the **XSL Output** tab in XML Notepad and press **Transform**. The **Visio Rules Tools RuleSets Report** will then be displayed.

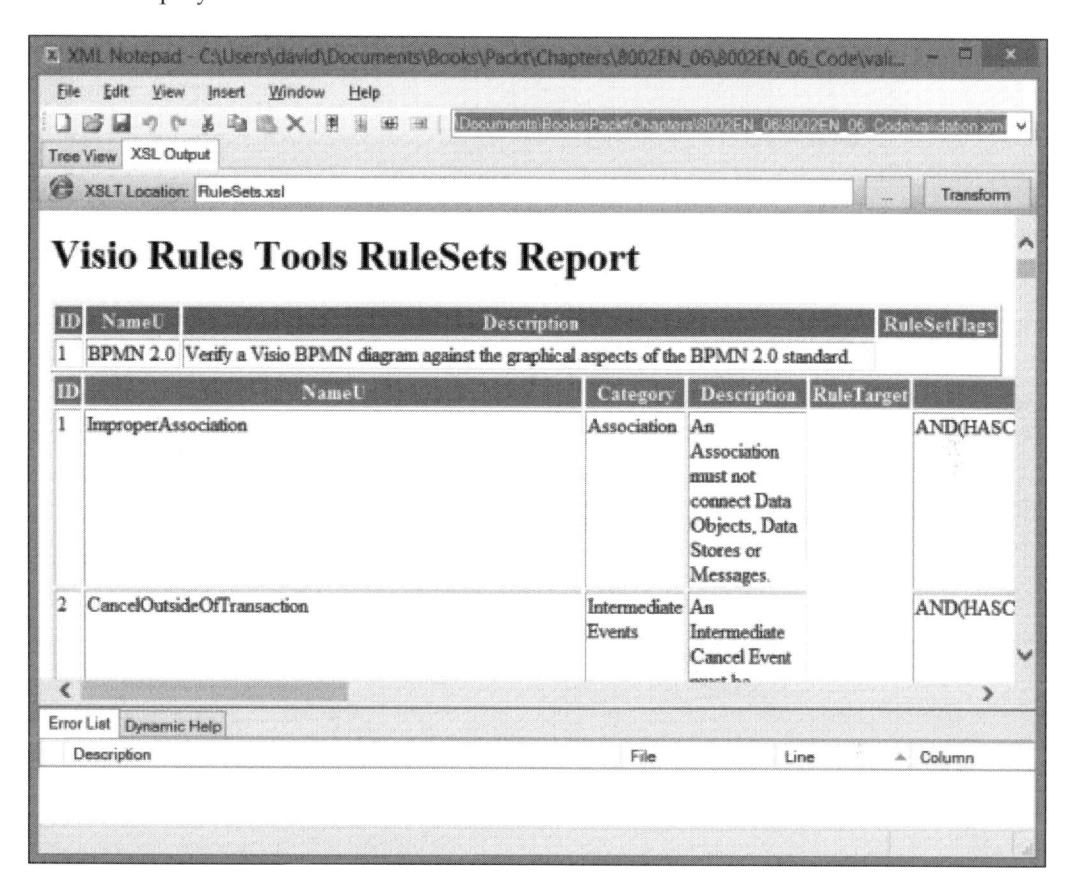

> Alternatively add the following line as line 2 in any XML file that contains rulesets (edit the `href` path accordingly):
>
> `<?xml-stylesheet type="text/xsl" href="RuleSets.xslt"?>`
>
> Open in your web browser to display the report!

Summary

In this chapter we have extended the **Rules Tools** add-in to provide the capability to export and import rulesets to and from an XML file. We have transformed the ruleset XML into an HTML report and we annotated pages with current issues. We now have a complete UI tool to create and test new rules.

In the next chapter, we are going to go deep into the validation functions and learn how to create test and filter expressions.

7
Creating Validation Rules

In the last chapter, we finished creating a tool to allow us to manipulate rules in Microsoft Visio 2013 Professional in the following ways:

- Review rules
- Edit rules
- Create rules
- Test rules
- Import rules
- Export rules

In this chapter, we will use this tool to create rules for structured diagramming. We will look at the common ShapeSheet functions that will be useful for rules, and the new validation functions.

We will also go through different scenarios for creating rules, especially with regard to the Filter and Test Expressions.

> You can also refer to an article that I wrote on MSDN to discover more information about validation rules: http://msdn.microsoft.com/en-us/library/ff847470(v=office.14).aspx.

Overview of the document validation process

The user can initiate the validation process by clicking on the **Check Diagram** button that is present on the **PROCESS** tab. This process will clear any existing issues for any changed pages in the document before looping through any rulesets. A changed page, sometimes referred to as *dirty*, is one that has shapes on it that have been altered in some way since the last validation. After validation, the process will re-mark as ignored any issues that were previously marked as ignored.

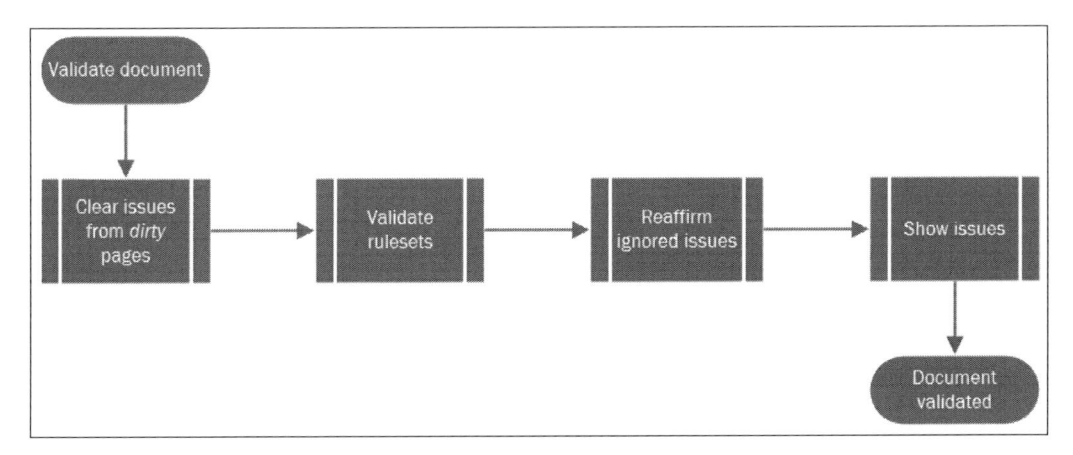

```
Validate document → Clear issues from dirty pages → Validate rulesets → Reaffirm ignored issues → Show issues → Document validated
```

Any custom validation rules for a ruleset should be executed in code whenever the relevant `RulesetValidated` event is fired. Visio does not automatically clear all issues in the document when the user selects the **Process** or the **Check Diagram** button. It only clears issues for pages that are *dirty*, that is, those that have had shape changes since the last time it was validated.

> If you are writing code to validate your ruleset, then you could just iterate through any existing issues to delete only those that are associated with your ruleset, because the `ValidationIssues.Clear()` method will remove all issues in the document.

After the rulesets are validated, Visio will check if the user has checked the **Show Ignored Issues** option. If **Show Ignored Issues** is ticked, issues for rules that have been marked as ignored will be displayed as grayed out in the **Issues** window.

Validating rulesets

The validation process will loop through all of the rulesets in the document, and will continue to process the ruleset if the `Enabled` property is `True`.

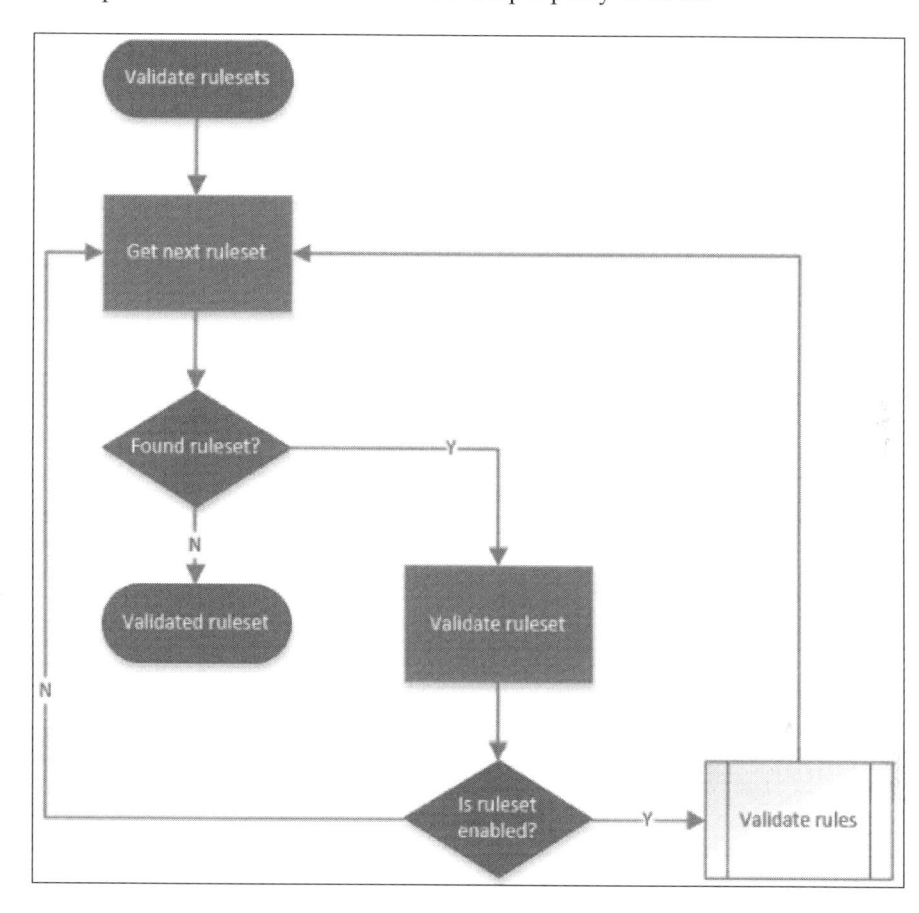

Validating rules

If the ruleset is enabled, then the process will loop through each of the rules in the ruleset.

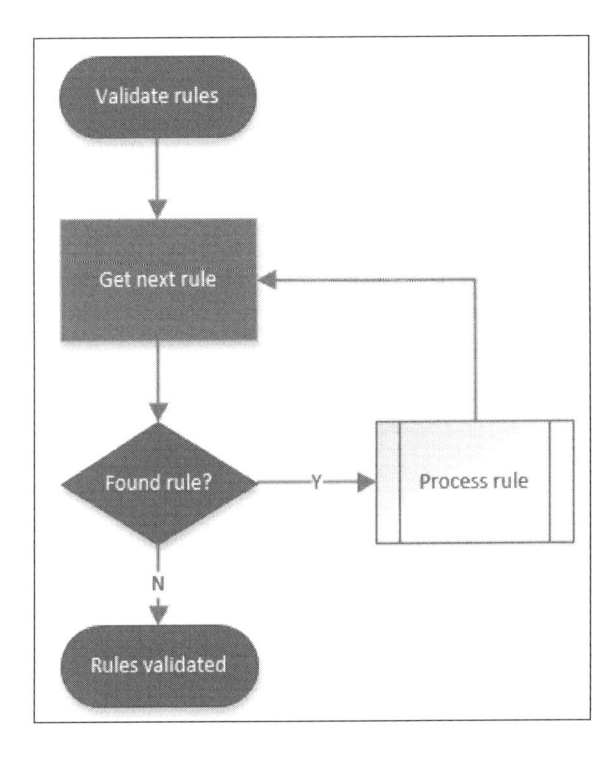

Processing a rule

Rules are processed even if they are marked as ignored, though the ignored marker will be preserved. The validation process will retrieve the target object, which can be a document, page, or shape (the default).

Chapter 7

Then, if the `FilterExpession` evaluates to `True`, the target will be passed through to `TestExpression`. Note that Visio will not pass the target through if there is an error in the syntax of `FilterExpression`.

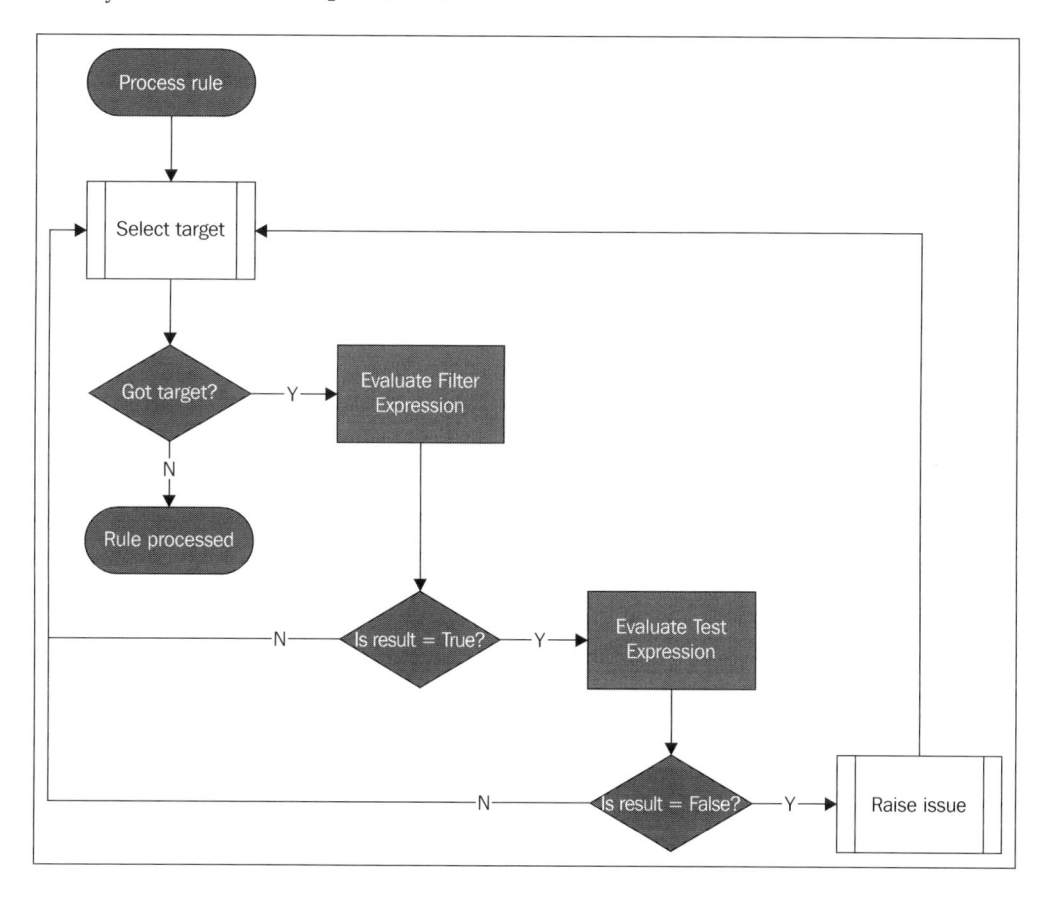

If `TestExpression` evaluates to `False`, or if there is a syntax error in the formula, then an issue is raised.

> To check that `FilterExpression` is syntactically correct, enter `True` in the `TestExpression` before validating, and then enter `False` in `FilterExpression` before validating again. If you do not get any issues on either pass, then there is something wrong with your syntax.
>
> Similarly, to check if your `TestExpression` is syntactically correct, you can alternately wrap your formula with `NOT (...)` to reverse its meaning.

[237]

Validation functions

The syntax for the `FilterExpression` and `TestExpression` formulae are the same as for the ShapeSheet formulae. However, Visio 2013 includes some extra validation functions such as the ShapeSheet functions, but these functions cannot be used in the ShapeSheet formulae, with the exception of those marked with an asterisk.

The following table is an extract from *The Diagram Validation API* blog:

http://blogs.msdn.com/visio/archive/2010/01/07/the-diagram-validation-api.aspx

It lists the special quasi-ShapeSheet functions that can be used in the `FilterExpression` and `TestExpression` formulae, and has been extended to include the new functions added in Visio 2013 (marked with *).

Function	Description
HasCategory(categoryName)*	Returns a Boolean indicating whether the shape has the specified category.
Is1D()*	Returns a Boolean indicating whether the shape is 1D or not.
Role()	Returns an integer indicating the shape role: {Element = 0, Connector = 1, Container = 2, Callout = 4}.
OnLayer(LayerName)	Returns a Boolean indicating whether the shape is a member of the specified layer. Returns a Boolean indicating whether a layer exists on the page if called on a Page.
ConnectedShapes(Direction)	Returns the set of shapes, matching the Direction criteria, connected to the shape.
GluedShapes(Direction)	Returns the set of shapes, matching the Direction criteria, glued to the shape.
ContainerMembers()	Returns the set of shapes that are members of the container or list shape.
ListMembers()	Returns the set of shapes that are members of the list shape.
Callouts()	Returns the set of shapes that are callouts on the shape.
ParentContainers()	Returns the set of containers that the shape belongs to.
ShapesOnPage()	Returns the set of top-level shapes on the page. If no page specifier precedes the function, the shape's containing page is assumed.

Function	Description
`AggCount(Set)`	Counts the number of shapes in a set.
`FilterSet(Set,FilterExpression)`	Returns the subset of shapes in a set that match an expression.
`OnBoundaryOf()`	Returns the set of containers such that the shape is on the boundary of these containers.

Useful ShapeSheet functions

This is a table of the ShapeSheet functions that are commonly used in the Filter Expression and Test Expression formulae:

Function	Description
`AND(logical expression1,logical expression2,...,logical expressionN)`	Returns TRUE (1) if all of the logical expressions supplied are true. If any of the logical expressions are false or 0, the AND function returns FALSE (0).
`OR(logicalexpression1,logicalexpression2,...,logicalexpressionN)`	Returns TRUE (1) if any of the logical expressions are true.
`NOT(logicalexpression)`	Returns TRUE (1) if `logicalexpression` is false. Otherwise, it returns FALSE (0).
`IF(logicalexpression,valueiftrue,valueiffalse)`	Returns `valueiftrue` if `logicalexpression` is true. Otherwise, it returns `valueiffalse`.
`INDEX(index,"list"[,[delimiter][,[errorvalue]]])`	Returns the substring at the zero-based location index in the list delimited-by-delimiter. Or, it returns -1 if not found.
`LOOKUP("key","list"[,"delimiter"])`	Returns a zero-based index that indicates the location of the substring key in a list, or returns -1 if the target string contains the delimiter.
`HASCATEGORY(category)`	Returns TRUE if the specified string is found in the shape's category list.
`IS1D()`	Returns TRUE if the shape is **1D (one-dimensional)**; returns FALSE if the shape is **2D (two-dimensional)**.
`IFERROR(primary expression, alternate expression)`	Returns the evaluated result of a primary expression, if it does not evaluate to an error. Otherwise, returns the evaluated result of an alternate expression.

Creating Validation Rules

Function	Description
CALLOUTCOUNT()	Returns the total number of callout shapes that are associated with the shape.
CALLOUTTARGETREF()!	Returns a sheet reference to the target shape of the callout shape.
CONTAINERCOUNT()	Returns the total number of containers that include the shape as a member (including nested relationships, that is, containers within containers).
CONTAINERSHEETREF(index [, category])	Returns a sheet reference to the specified container that contains the shape.
LISTMEMBERCOUNT()	Returns the number of member shapes in the list container shape.
LISTORDER()	Returns the 1-based position of the shape in the list.
LISTMEMBERCOUNT()	Returns a sheet reference to the list container shape that contains the shape.
<sheetref>!SHEETREF()	Returns a reference to the sheet (shape) that is specified in sheetref, or, if there is no sheetref qualifier, to the current sheet. You can use this function in other functions that take a sheet reference token.
SHAPETEXT (shapename!TheText,flag)	Retrieves the text from a shape.
MASTERNAME (langID_opt)	Returns a sheet's master name as a string, or the string, <no master> if the sheet doesn't have a master. The master name is in the form <master name>:<shape name>.
LEFT(text, [,num_chars_opt])	Returns the first character or characters in a text string, based on the number of characters you specify.
LEN (text)	Returns the number of characters in a text string.
STRSAME ("string1", "string2", ignoreCase)	Determines whether strings are the same. It returns TRUE if they are the same, and FALSE if they aren't. To compare multibyte strings or to do comparisons using case rules for a specific locale, use the STRSAMEEX function.

Function	Description
`FIND (find_text, within_text ,[start_num], [ignore_case])`	Finds one text string contained within another text string, and returns the starting position of the text string you are seeking relative to its position in the text string that contains it.

All the ShapeSheet functions are valid, but some are strongly discouraged because they cause an action to be performed rather than a value to be returned, and their impact cannot be predicted. The following list details the specific ShapeSheet functions that should not be used in the Filter Expression and Test Expression formulae:

- `CALLTHIS(...)`
- `DOOLEVERB(...)`
- `DEFAULTEVENT()`
- `DOCMD(...)`
- `GOTOPAGE(...)`
- `HELP(...)`
- `HYPERLINK(...)`
- `OPENFILE(...)`
- `OPENGROUPWIN()`
- `OPENSHEETWIN()`
- `OPENTEXTWIN()`
- `PLAYSOUND(...)`
- `RUNADDON(...)`
- `RUNADDONWARGS(...)`
- `RUNMACRO(...)`
- `SETF(...)`

Filter and Test Expressions

You should use the `FilterExpression` function to reduce the number of target shapes (or pages) to be tested. You can then use the `TestExpression` function to apply to this reduced set in order to obtain a Boolean result.

Creating Validation Rules

A good way to understand how to write these expressions is to review the ones already created by Microsoft for the flowcharts and **Business Process Modeling Notation (BPMN)** templates. You can use the **Rules Tools** add-in to review them interactively, or to create a report. For example, create a new Flowchart or Cross-Functional Flowchart diagram and review the 11 rules present in the document in the Flowchart ruleset:

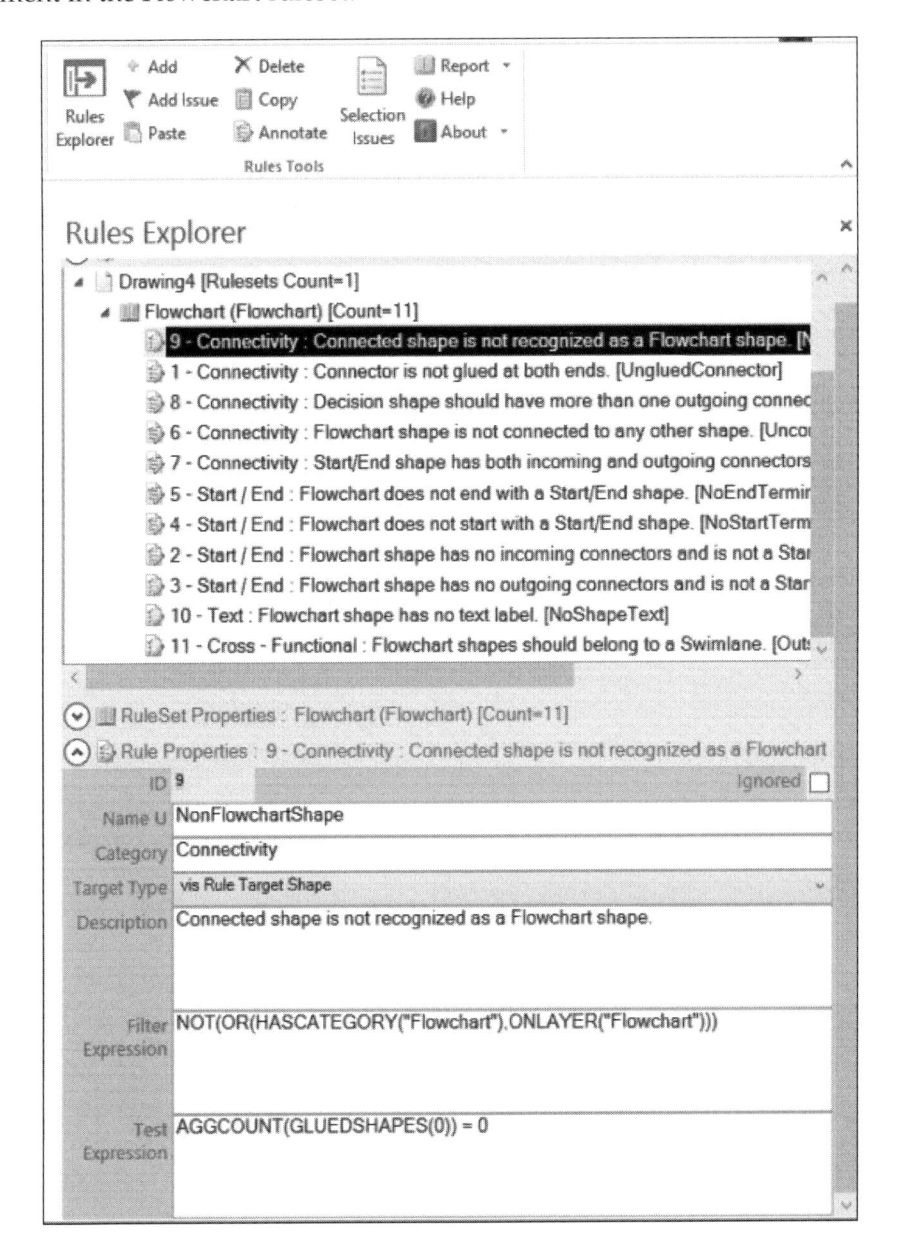

In fact, the same ruleset is applied to the Basic Flowchart and the Six Sigma diagrams too, so there are some rules that do not apply to all of them, such as the ones that involve swimlanes. These particular rules refer to containers, which do not exist unless the user manages to use a swimlane shape from the Cross-Functional Flowchart Shapes stencil.

So, in order to test a few expressions, untick the **Enabled** property of the Flowchart ruleset and you can add a new ruleset.

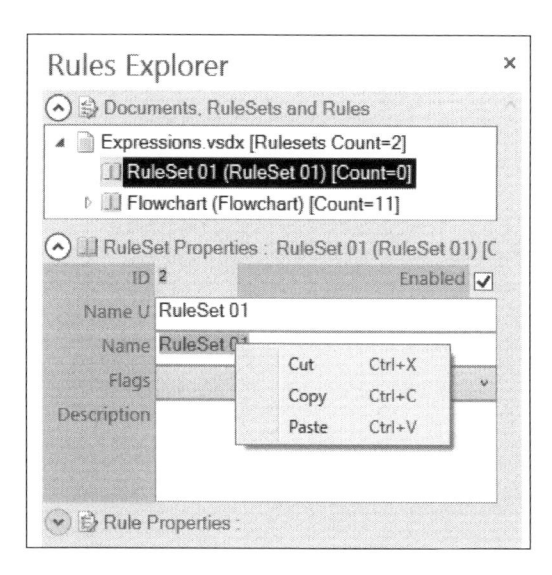

If you want to cut, copy, or paste text in the **Rules Explorer** window, then you can use the right-mouse menu rather than the accelerator keys (*Ctrl + X, Ctrl + C, Ctrl + V*).

Checking the type of shape

You can test whether a shape is 1D or not with the ISID() function, and you can test the type more specifically with the ROLE() function. For example, ROLE()=1 also returns True if the shape is a connector.

The ROLE() function matches against the following Visio.VisRoleSelectionTypes constant values:

- Default or element = 0 (this is not explicitly in the enum, but it is valid)
- visRoleSelConnector = 1
- visRoleSelContainer = 2
- visRoleSelCallout = 4

Creating Validation Rules

Let us create a test rule by selecting the **Add** button on the **Rules Tools** ribbon group. You can edit the **Category** and **Description**, if you like, but be sure to enter `ROLE()=0` in the Filter Expression, and `False` in the Test Expression, then select **Check Diagram**.

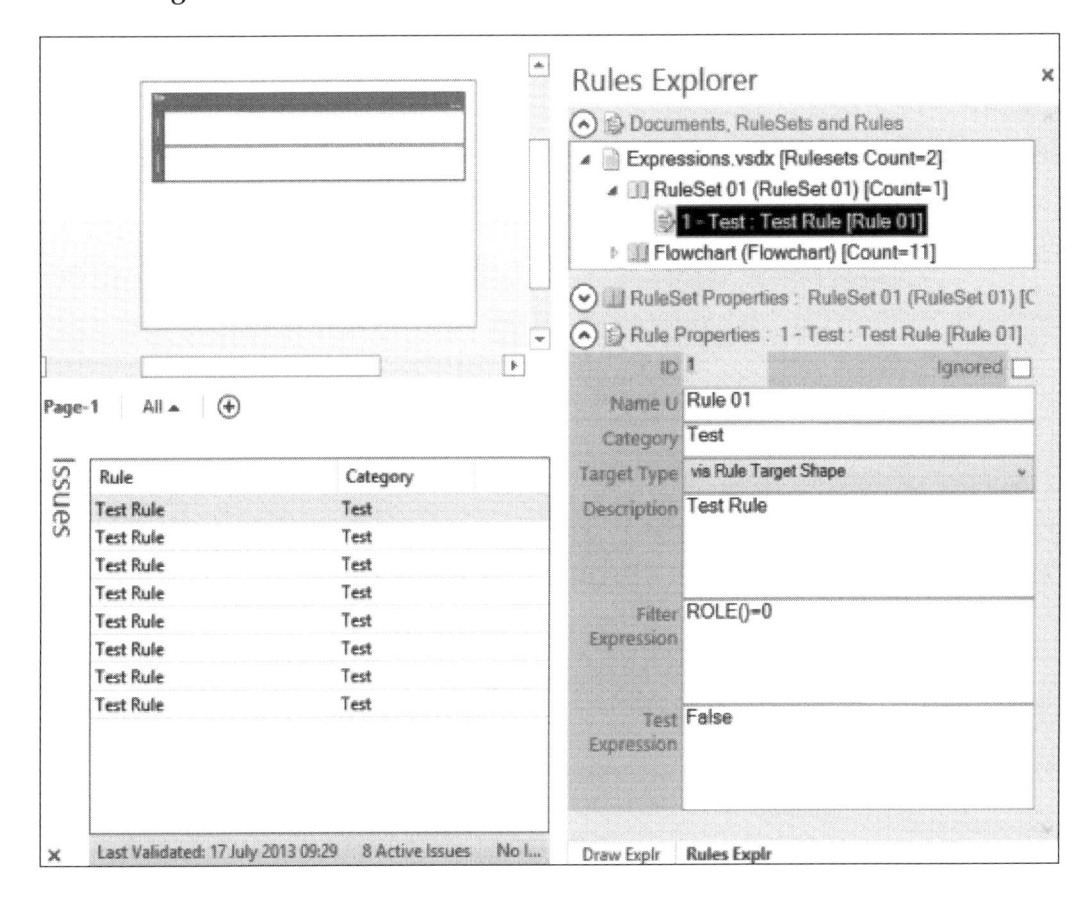

As you can see, there are **8 Active Issues**, so what is happening? Firstly, the Test Expression is obviously always going to return False, so there must be eight shapes being passed through to the Test Expression by the Filter Expression.

Chapter 7

The **Drawing Explorer** window reveals that there are six shapes in the shapes collection of the page, and four of these shapes have two subshapes. So, there are actually 14 shapes in total, but only eight of them are returned by ROLE()=0. By the way, if you were to change the Filter Expression to ROLE()=1 then there are no issues, because there are no connectors on the drawing page yet!

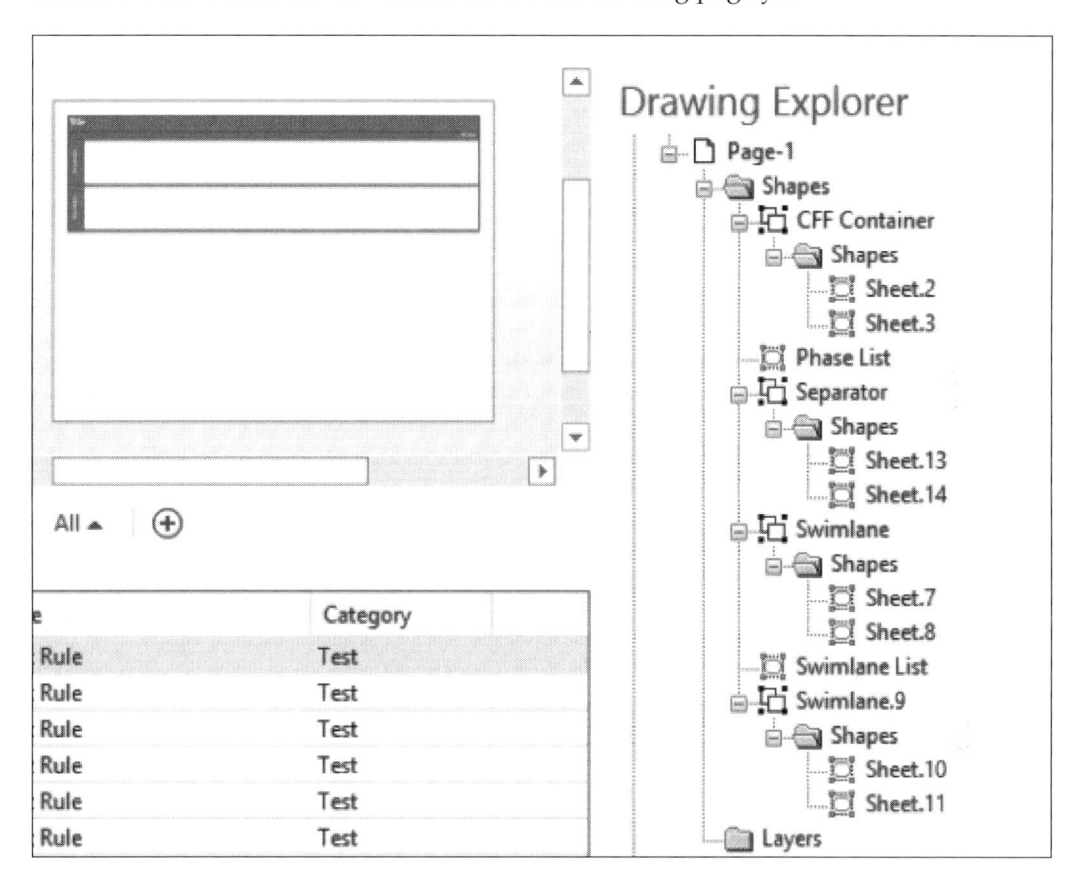

Creating Validation Rules

We can shed a bit more light on which shapes are raising issues by selecting the **Annotate** button on the **Rules Tools** ribbon group. You can double-click a row in the **Issues** window to select the shape or page that is causing that issue, but this does not give you an overview of the distribution of issues, nor does it display all of the issues for that shape.

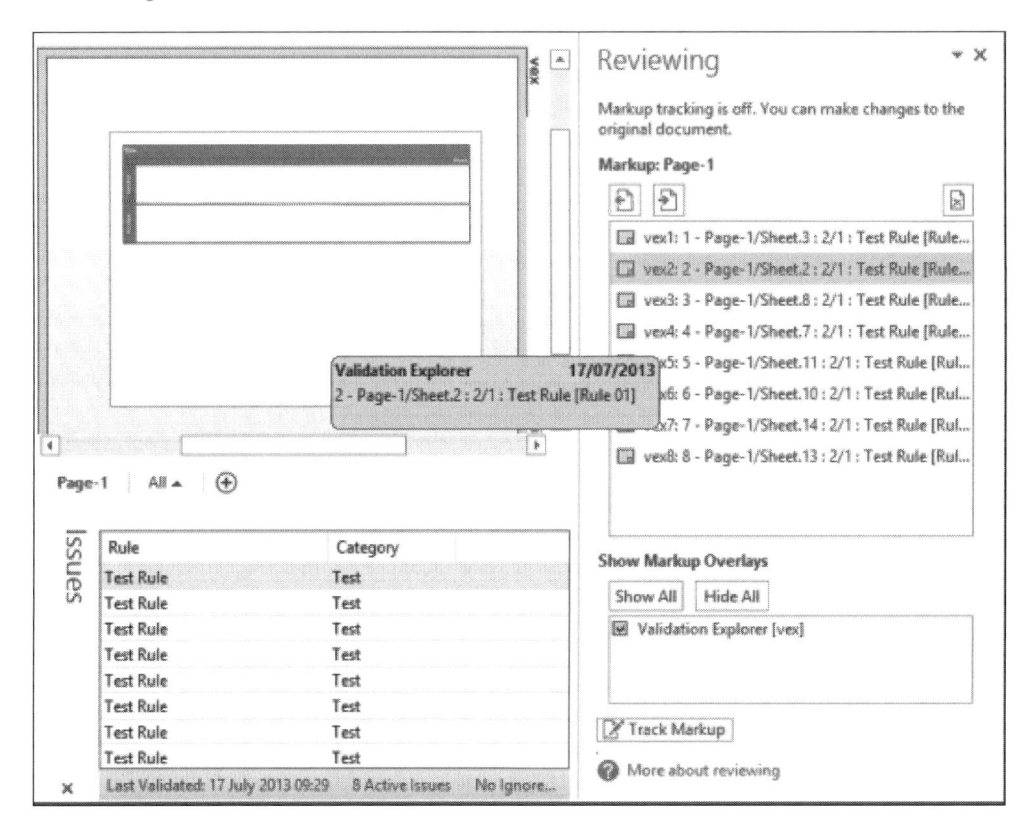

We can now see that the eight shapes raising issues are in fact all the subshapes! This is probably not desirable in this particular case, so a real rule will need to have a more refined Filter Expression.

Checking the category of shapes

Master shapes created for use in Visio 2013 may include the reserved user-defined cell, User.msvShapeCategories. This cell can contain the name of a single category, or multiple categories in a list separated by a semicolon. Therefore, you can use the HASCATEGORY(category) function on instances of these shapes. For example, the following formula will return True if the shape has the Flowchart category:

HASCATEGORY("Flowchart")

However, the shapes to test may be instances of masters that do not contain this cell; so, you may have to use an alternative approach. You could use the MASTERNAME(lang_id) function to get the name of the master, if any. You should use lang_id = 750 to specify the universal language. Often, though, users inadvertently create duplicate, or in fact multiple masters, through no fault of their own. In these cases, Visio automatically adds an .nn suffix to ensure uniqueness of name. Thus, you need to test that the first part of the name is a match by employing the STRSAME() and LEFT() functions too by using the formula:

STRSAME(LEFT(MASTERNAME(750),10),"Terminator",0)

Rather than counting the number of characters in the name, you could write:

STRSAME(LEFT(MASTERNAME(750),LEN("Terminator")),"Terminator",0)

> The MasterName() function actually returns both the name of the master and the shape in the master, with a colon separator. That is why you must use the LEFT() function.

If you look at the ShapeSheet of the outer shape labeled Title, and one of the swimlane shapes labeled Function, then you will see that they have User.msvStructureType="Container", but the User.msvShapeCategories are different:

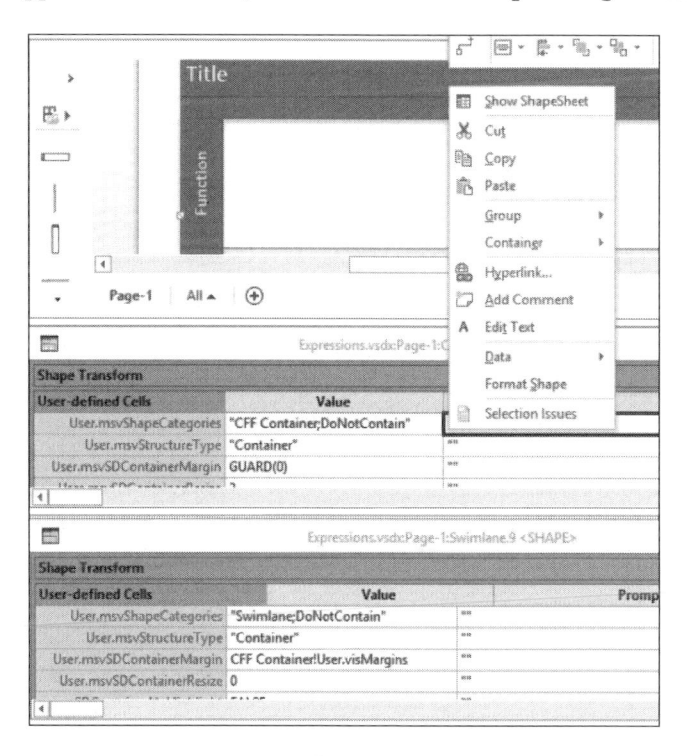

Creating Validation Rules

So, if you amend the Filter Expression to `AND(ROLE()=2,HASCATEGORY("Swimlane"))` then you will get two shapes raising issues.

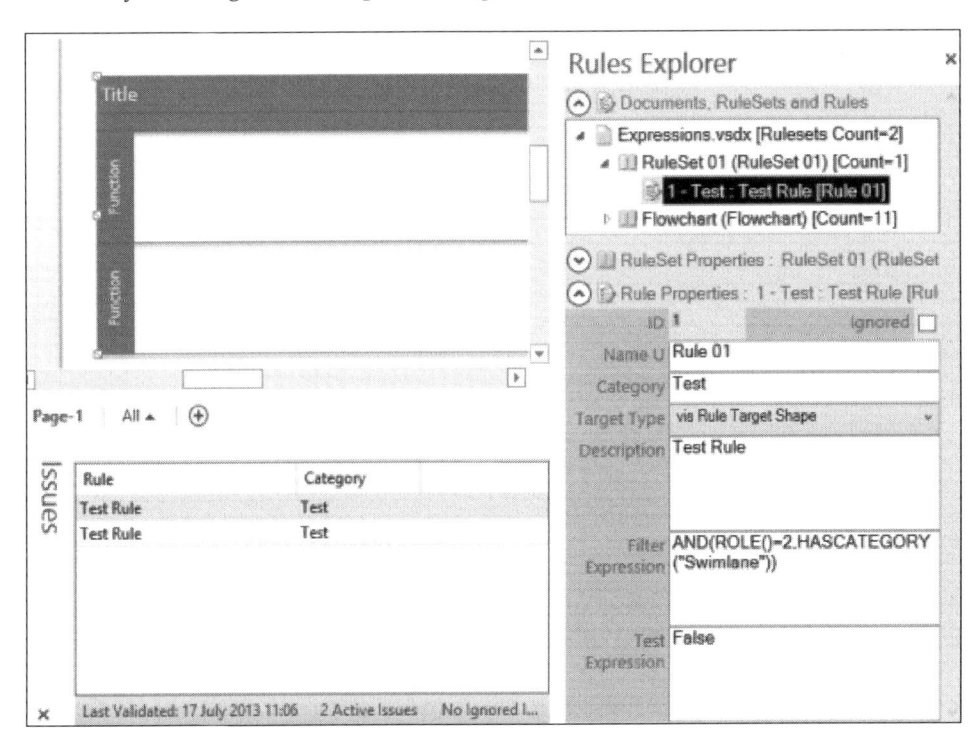

If you change the formula to `AND(ROLE()=2,HASCATEGORY("CFF Container"))` then you will get just one issue.

You will only get one issue if you were to change the Filter Expression formula to:

`STRSAME(LEFT(MASTERNAME(750),LEN("Phase List")),"Phase List",0)`

Checking the layer of a shape

Some shapes are assigned to a layer when they are dragged from a stencil. This can be because the master shape was pre-assigned to a layer, or because the user set an active layer when the shape instance was created. A user can also change the layer assignment interactively, and shapes can belong to either no layer at all, one layer, or multiple layers.

Knowing this, you should use the layer assignment of a shape with caution, but sometimes it may be the only way of distinguishing a shape:

`ONLAYER("Flowchart")`

So, if you were to amend our test rule accordingly, and then drag-and-drop a **Start/End** shape into the first swimlane, you will get one issue:

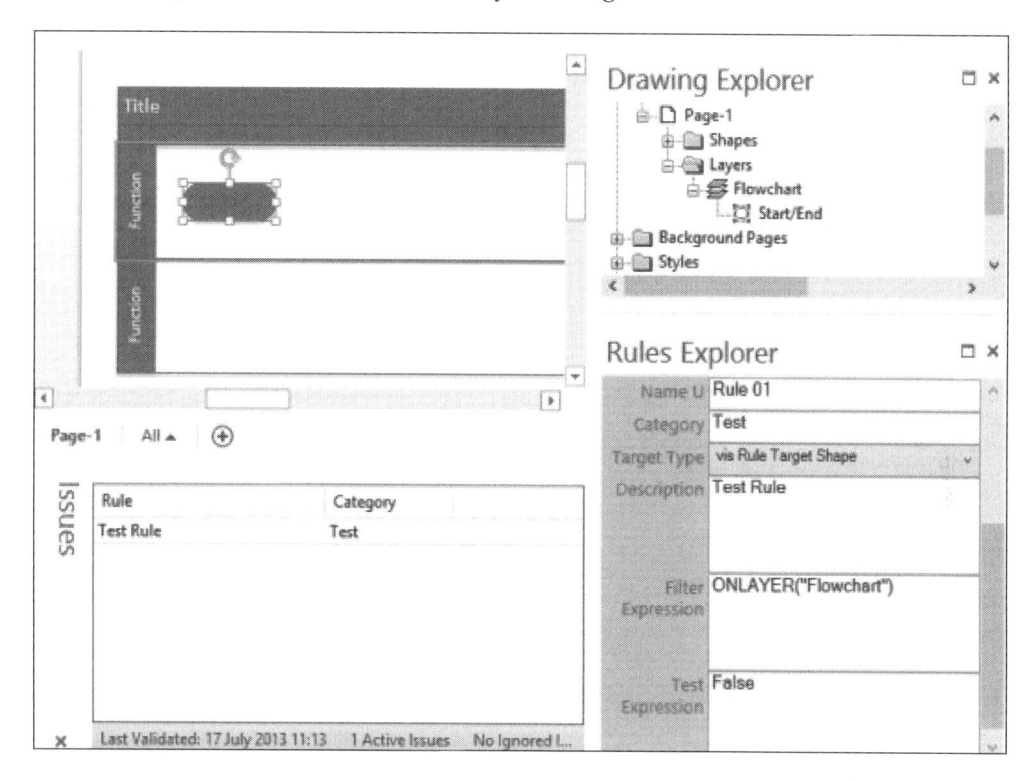

You can see in the **Drawing Explorer** window that the **Start/End** shape was pre-assigned to the **Flowchart** layer, and thus this layer was automatically created in the page when the master shape instance was dropped.

Checking if the page contains relevant shapes

Sometimes you may need to only continue testing the shapes on a page if that particular page contains specific shapes. In this case, you will need to get a collection of all of the shapes on the page using `SHAPESONPAGE()`, and then filter this set of shapes by matching their properties against an expression result, using `FILTERSET()`. This expression must be passed through as a string, thus any quotation marks must be re-affirmed by doubling them within the expression. Finally, a Boolean result must be returned by checking the count of matching shapes using `AGGCOUNT()`. For example, the following formula returns `True` if the page contains any swimlane shapes:

```
AGGCOUNT(FILTERSET(SHAPESONPAGE(),"HASCATEGORY(""Swimlane"")"))>0
```

Creating Validation Rules

So, using this formula in our test rule reveals 10 active issues:

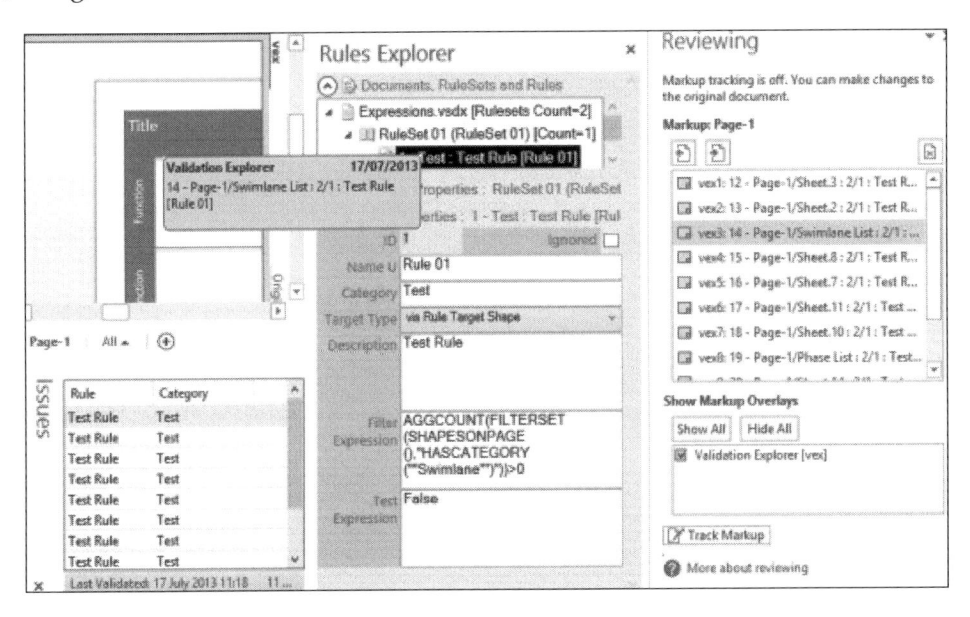

These issues are raised by all the shapes, except for the top-group shape of the container-type shapes.

If you change the **Target Type** to **vis Rule Target Page**, then you will only get one issue raised for the page:

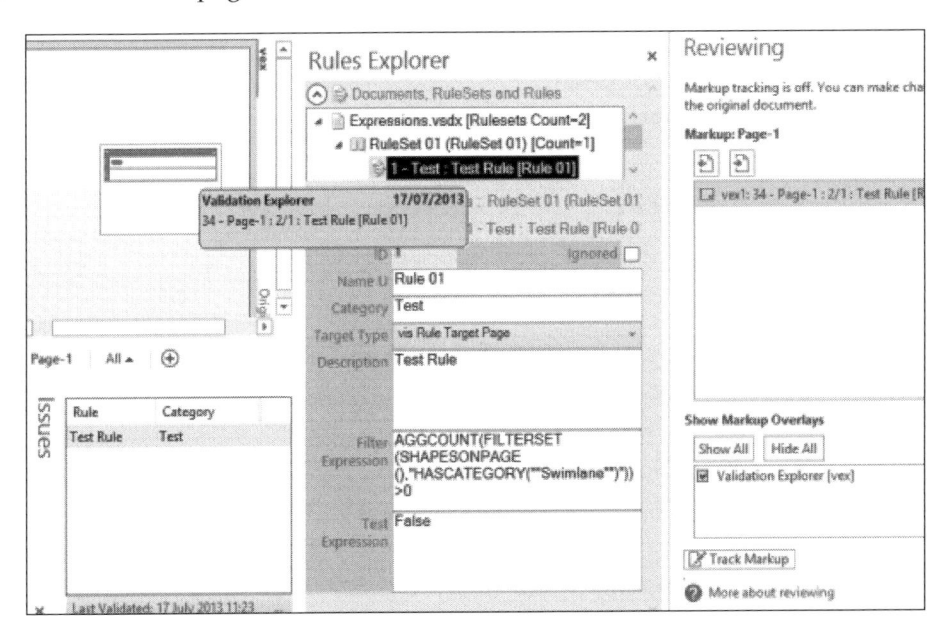

[250]

Of course, if you changed the **Target Type** to **vis Rule Target Document**, then there are no issues.

> The `ShapesOnPage()` function will cause Visio to check every shape on the page and will take more time if there are lot of shape on the page. Therefore, you should use this function sparingly.

Checking for specific cell values

You may want to test for particular values in a cell. Initially, you may want to check only the shapes that actually have that cell present. (Remember that some sections in the ShapeSheet are optional.) For example, all of the flowchart shapes contain at least seven **Shape Data** rows:

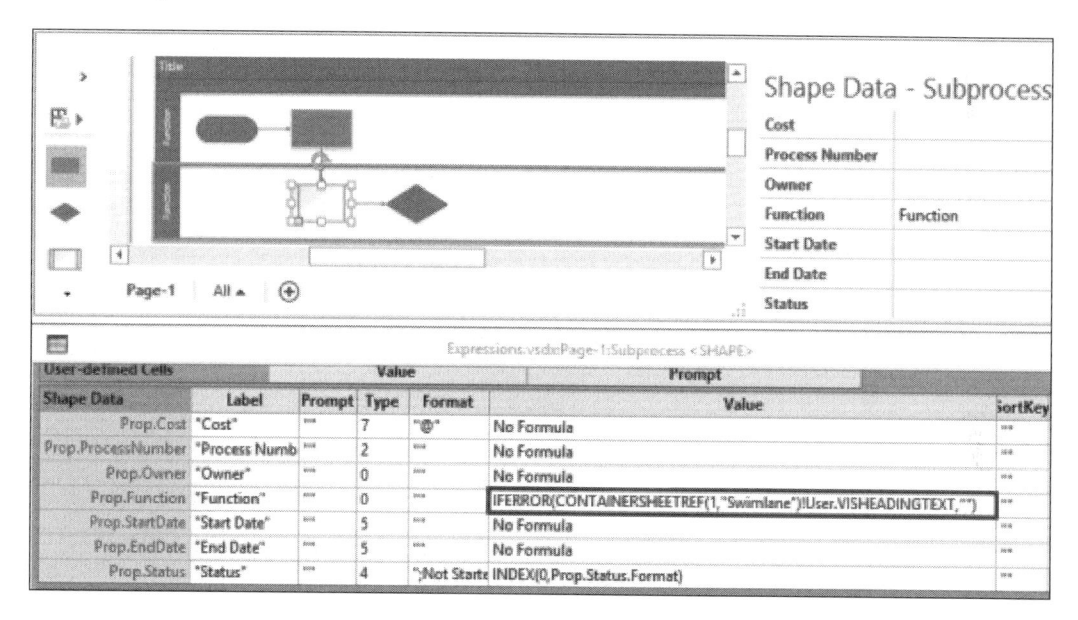

Creating Validation Rules

The connectors, swimlanes, and so on do not have these **Shape Data** rows. So, we can filter for the shapes that contain the **Prop.Owner** cell by entering the following **Filter Expression**:

```
NOT(ISERROR(Prop.Owner))
```

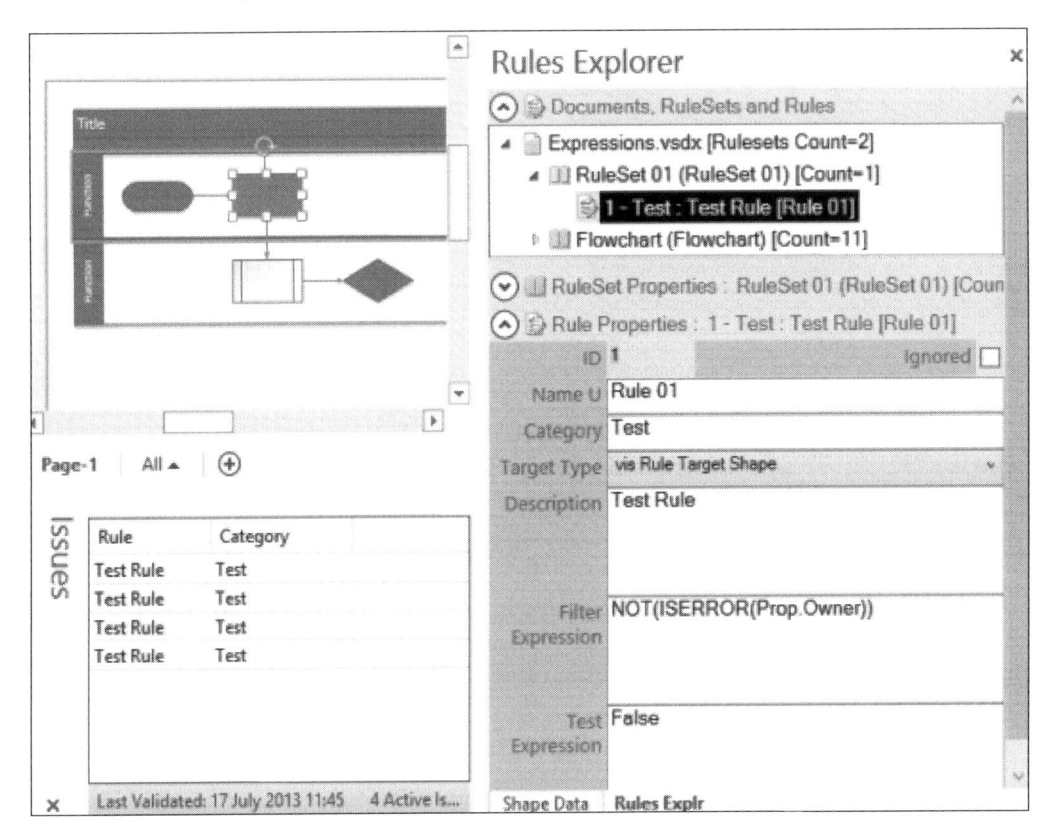

This formula works because the formula will return `True` if the **Prop.Owner** cell exists, because it will not return an error when requesting its value. This reveals that there are four such shapes on this page.

Now that you have established which shapes contain the **Shape Data** cell, you can test for actual values. However, you must exercise a little caution. You may have thought that an empty value in a **Shape Data** row is always the same, but it is not. This is the similar to the `null` versus `empty string` values in databases. In Visio, a master shape instance will have default **Shape Data** values inherited from the master, and in the case of the flowchart shapes, there is no formula in any of the **Shape Data** rows. As you can see, they do not display any values in the **Shape Data** window, except for the **Function** row. In fact, the **Function** row is updated by Visio automatically because it references the swimlane header text that it lies within.

Chapter 7

If a user enters some text in the **Owner** row, then decides to delete it, the underlying row has an `empty string` value, not a `null` value. So, if you want to ensure a value has been entered in a **Shape Data** row, then you need to check for the existence of a value using the `LOCALFORMULAEXISTS()` function. You also need to check that it is not an empty string, using the `STRSAME()` function. Consequently, the following formula will test if **Prop.Owner** contains a value:

`AND(LOCALFORMULAEXISTS(Prop.Owner),NOT(STRSAME(Prop.Owner,"")))`

If this is entered as the **Test Expression**, and one of the flowchart shapes had a **Prop. Owner** value entered and then deleted, and another flowchart shape has a value, then only three of the four shapes will raise an issue.

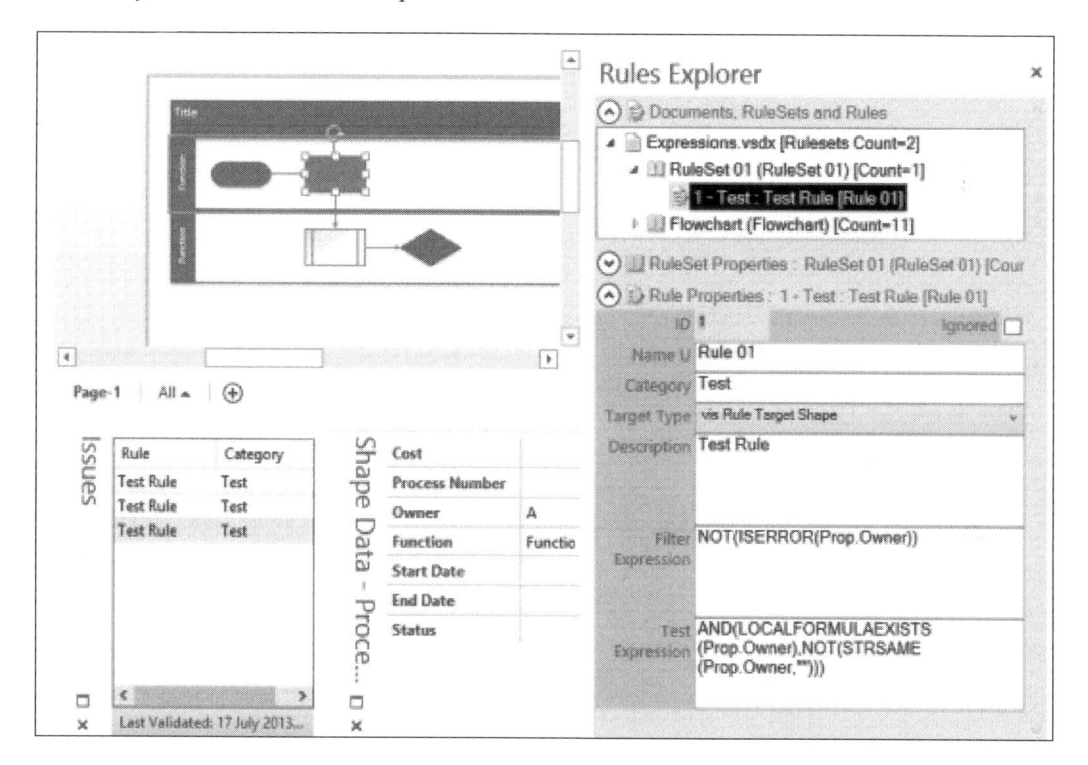

Of course, this will work for a text value too, instead of the empty string.

If you want to check for numerical values, such as the **Prop.Cost Shape Data** row, then you will need to amend the **Test Expression**. If you want to find all shapes that have not had any user input, then the following will suffice:

`LOCALFORMULAEXISTS(Prop.Cost)`

[253]

Creating Validation Rules

This is because numeric fields will reset to 0 if the user deletes an entry, as it can never be an empty string.

Of course, you could test that the user has entered a value greater than zero with the following **Test Expression**:

`AND(LOCALFORMULAEXISTS(Prop.Cost),Prop.Cost>0)`

Interestingly, dates do return back to no formula if the user deletes an entry. So, the following Test Expression is sufficient to check that an entry has been made:

`LOCALFORMULAEXISTS(Prop.StartDate)`

If you want to raise an issue for all shapes that do not have a **Prop.StartDate** value after today, then you could use the Test Expression:

`Prop.StartDate>Now()`

If your user can select values from a list, either fixed or variable, then you can use the `INDEX()` function with the `STRSAME()` function to test whether the value is matched. For example, the **Flowchart** shapes have a **Prop.Status** list, therefore, you could test whether the value is equal to the fifth value using the following Test Expression (note that the array is zero-based):

`STRSAME(Prop.Status,INDEX(4,Prop.Status.Format))`

Testing the value at a particular index position in the list is preferable to using actual values, because it will still work if the text has been localized.

Not all data is stored in the Shape Data rows. You may need to test whether the **Actions** row is checked or not. For example, the **BPMN** shapes have multiple options on their right-mouse menus, and the **ImproperAssociation** rule has the **Filter Expression**:

`AND(HASCATEGORY("Connecting Object"),Actions.Association.Checked)`

Checking that connectors are connected

One common structured diagramming error is leaving connectors unconnected at one or both ends. In these flowchart diagrams, you can filter for connectors, using `ROLE()=1` or the new `IS!D()` function, then check that there is one glued shape at either end of it, using the `GLUEDSHAPES()` function.

So, the following formula in the **Test Expression** will return `False` if there is a connection missing:

`AND(AGGCOUNT(GLUEDSHAPES(4)) = 1, AGGCOUNT(GLUEDSHAPES(5)) = 1)`

The `GluedShapes(n)` function has the following `Visio.VisGluedShapesFlags` constant values:

- `visGluedShapesAll1D = 0`
- `visGluedShapesIncoming1D = 1`
- `visGluedShapesOutgoing1D = 2`
- `visGluedShapesAll2D = 3`
- `visGluedShapesIncoming2D = 4`
- `visGluedShapesOutgoing2D = 5`

Consequently, if we have an unconnected connector in our test diagram, then it will raise an issue.

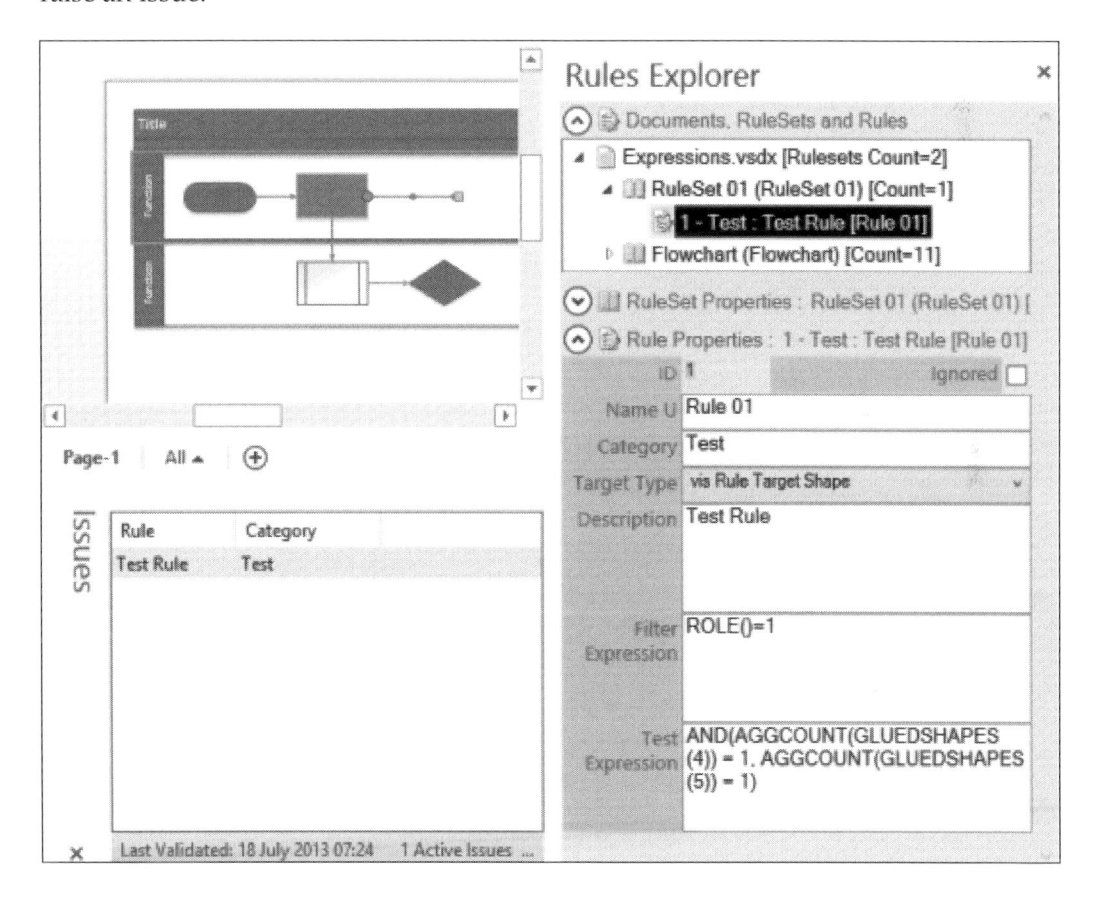

Creating Validation Rules

Checking that shapes have correct connections

A shape can be glued directly to other shapes, as is the case with connectors, or they can be connected via a connector to another shape.

You may want to ensure that certain shapes have incoming connections. For example, you could just filter for the **Decision** shapes by using the formula:

```
OR(HASCATEGORY("Decision"),STRSAME(LEFT(MASTERNAME(750),LEN("Decision")),"Decision"))
```

Then you can test that there is at least one incoming connection using the formula:

```
AGGCOUNT(GLUEDSHAPES(1)) > 0
```

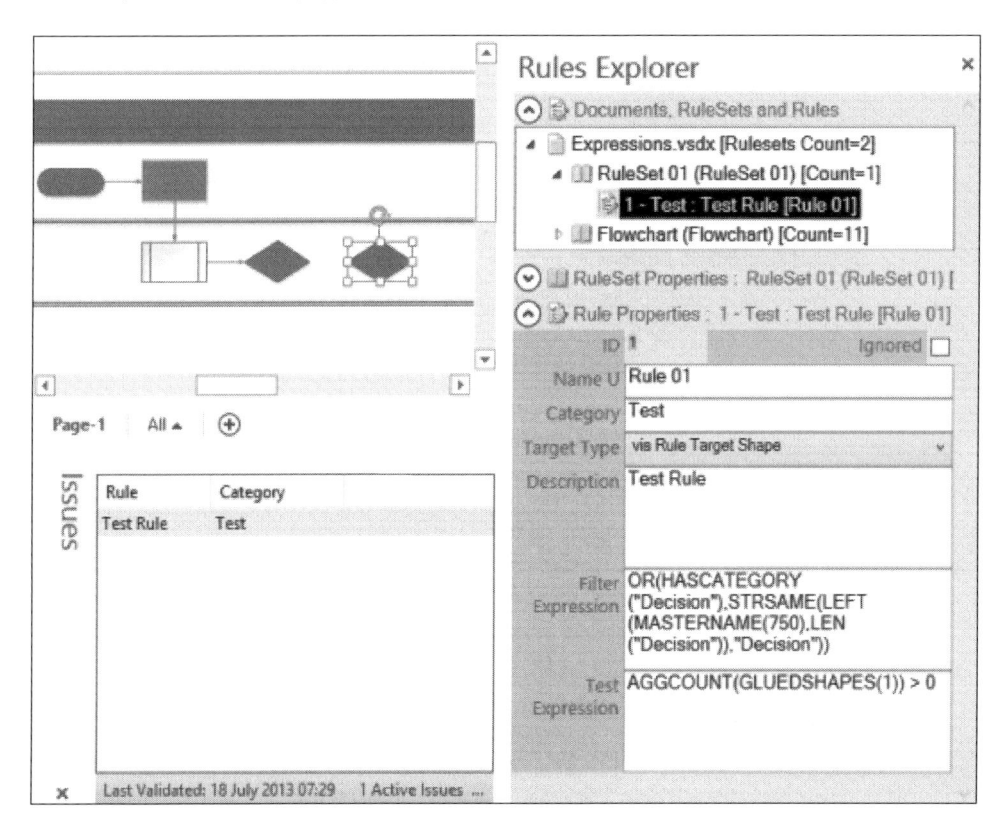

Similarly, you could ensure that each **Decision** shape has two outgoing connections using the Test Expression:

```
AGGCOUNT(GLUEDSHAPES(2)) = 2
```

[256]

Alternatively, you may want to try the following formula for the **Filter Expression** because it tests for all shapes on the **Flowchart** layer, except for the **Start/End** shapes:

`AND(ONLAYER("Flowchart"),NOT(STRSAME(LEFT(MASTERNAME(750),LEN("Start/End")),"Start/End")))`

The `ConnectedShapes()` function will return a collection of shapes at the other end of the glued connector.

`AGGCOUNT(CONNECTEDSHAPES(0)) > 0`

The `ConnectedShapes(n)` function has the following `Visio.VisConnectedShapesFlags` constant values:

- `visConnectedShapesAllNodes = 0`
- `visConnectedShapesIncomingNodes = 1`
- `visConnectedShapesOutgoingNodes = 2`

Checking whether shapes are outside containers

In a cross-functional flowchart diagram, you should ensure that all flowchart shapes are actually inside a swimlane. Visio 2013 has a cell in the **Shape Layout** section, called **Relationships**, that stores the values of related containers and lists.

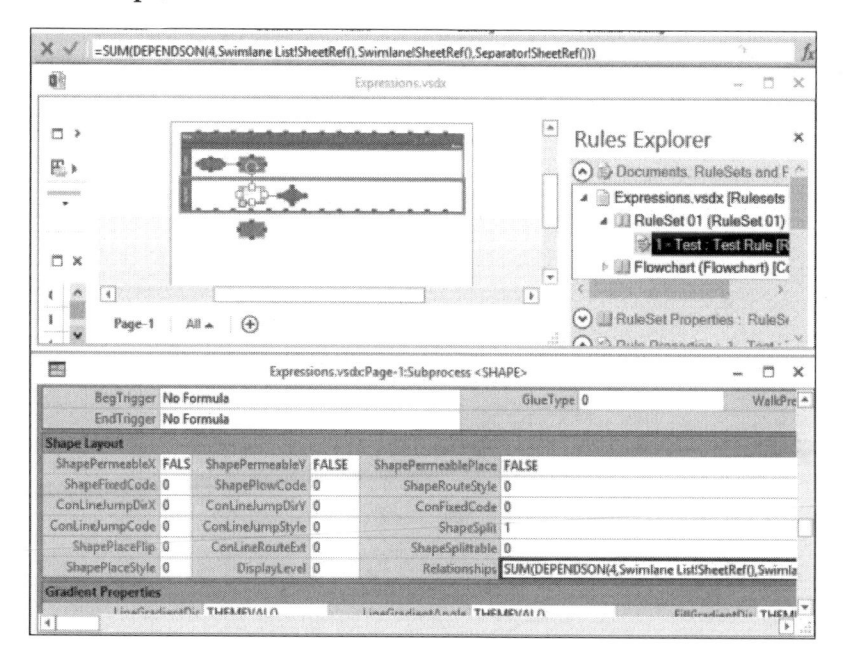

Creating Validation Rules

If you look at the **Relationships** cell for the **Process** shape below the swimlanes, then you will find that there is no formula in there.

You first need to check that the page has at least one swimlane on it. This can be done with the following **Filter Expression** formula:

```
AGGCOUNT(FILTERSET(SHAPESONPAGE(),"HASCATEGORY(""Swimlane"")"))>0
```

However, you do need to change the target type to the page for this filter to work efficiently, because you only want the rule to be validated once per page, not once per shape on the page.

Now, you need to test if there are any **Flowchart** shapes that are not within a swimlane. To do this, you need to use the `PARENTCONTAINERS()` function to get a collection of each shape's containers, then filter this set by the category **Swimlane**. So, this is a complete formula for the **Test Expression**:

```
AGGCOUNT(FILTERSET(SHAPESONPAGE(),"AND(OR(HASCATEGORY(""Flowchart""),
ONLAYER(""Flowchart"")),AGGCOUNT(FILTERSET(PARENTCONTAINERS(),""HASCA
TEGORY(""""Swimlane"""")""))=0)"))<1
```

You can use a similar formula for checking whether the shapes are on a boundary or not, by using:

```
ONBOUNDARYOF()
```

Checking whether a shape has text

In any flowchart diagram, you should ensure that all connector shapes exiting from a **Decision** shape are labeled, usually `Yes` or `No`, for example.

Firstly, you need to filter the connector shapes to those that are exiting a **Decision** shape. This can be done with the following **Filter Expression**:

```
AGGCOUNT(FILTERSET(GLUEDSHAPES(4),"OR(HASCATEGORY(""Decision""),STRSA
ME(LEFT(MASTERNAME(750),LEN(""Decision"")),""Decision""))"))=1
```

Next, you need to test whether the connector has any text or not with the following **Test Expression**:

```
NOT(STRSAME(SHAPETEXT(TheText), ""))
```

Then, when you run the rule, it will find any unlabeled connectors exiting a **Decision** shape.

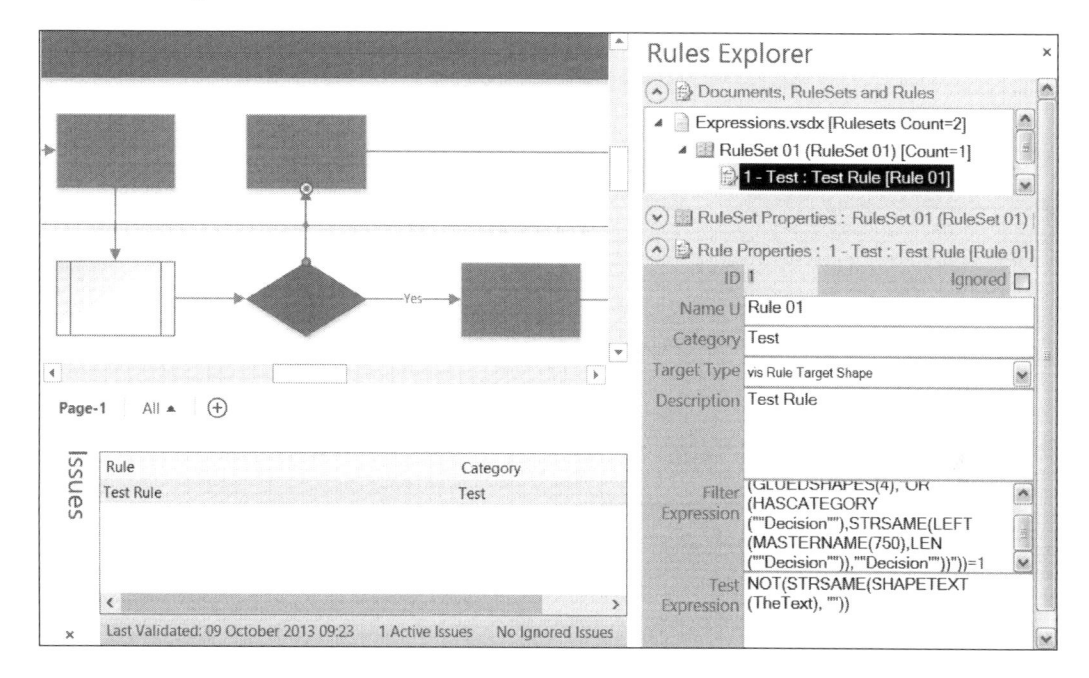

Custom validation rules in code

Previously, in *Chapter 4*, *Understanding the Validation API*, you learned that you can add custom validation rules in code. You would need to do this if the validation rule is too complex to phrase as the Filter and Test Expressions. For example, you might want to ensure that there are no cycles (paths that return to where they start from).

You could add code into a Visio add-in but I will demonstrate how you can put some custom code into the drawing document as VBA, because this will be in the document along with any ruleset that you may have written using the Filter and Test Expressions.

Creating Validation Rules

First, you need to listen for the `RuleSetValidated` event of the document, which can be added easily to the `ThisDocument` class in the VBA project. I have used the `getRule()` method from *Chapter 4, Understanding the Validation API* to ensure that there is a rule named `CheckCycle` present. If there is, then the `CheckCycle()` method is called.

```
Private Sub Document_RuleSetValidated( _
    ByVal ruleSet As IVValidationRuleSet)
Dim rule As Visio.ValidationRule
    'Check for custom validation
    Set rule = getRule(ruleSet, "CheckCycle")
    If Not rule Is Nothing Then
        CheckCycle rule
    End If
End Sub
```

The `CheckCycle()` method initially deletes any existing issues for the specified rule, then creates a new `CustomValidation` object before calling the `DoCycleValidation()` method.

```
Private Sub CheckCycle( _ ByVal rule As Visio.ValidationRule)
    ClearRuleIssues rule
Dim myCustomValidation As CustomValidation
    Set myCustomValidation = New CustomValidation
Dim valid As Boolean
    valid = myCustomValidation.DoCycleValidation(rule)
End Sub
```

The `ClearRuleIssues()` method steps backwards through the collection of `Validation.Issues` to delete any that are associated with the specified rule. Any other issues are left intact.

```
Private Sub ClearRuleIssues( _
    ByVal ruleToClear As Visio.ValidationRule)
Dim val As Visio.Validation
Dim issue As Visio.ValidationIssue
Dim rule As Visio.ValidationRule
Dim i As Integer
```

```
        Set val = Visio.ActiveDocument.Validation
        For i = val.Issues.count To 1 Step -1
            Set issue = val.Issues.Item(i)
            Set rule = issue.rule
            If rule Is ruleToClear Then
                issue.Delete
            End If
        Next
    End Sub
```

The `DoCycleValidation()` method loops through all of the page and, if the page is a foreground type, calls the `findCycle()` method.

```
    Public Function DoCycleValidation( _
        ByVal cycleRule As Visio.ValidationRule) _
        As Boolean

        'Declare variables
        Dim validationErrors As Boolean
        Dim issue As Visio.ValidationIssue
        Dim doc As Visio.Document
        Dim pag As Visio.Page

        'Use findCycle method to look for cycles"
        'Add issue if cycle is found on a page
        Set doc = cycleRule.Document
        For Each pag In doc.Pages
            If pag.Type = visTypeForeground Then
                validationErrors = _
                findCycle(pag, cycleRule)
            End If
        Next

    End Function
```

The `findCycle()` method is too long to list here (it's in the download) but it will add an issue for the first shape in any cycle found, along with an issue for each connector in the cycle.

Creating Validation Rules

Now that the code exists, it will be activated if a rule called `CheckCycle` is validated. The **Target Type** can be set to `visRuleTargetDocument`, and the **Filter Expression** can be `False` because it will not need to do any validation.

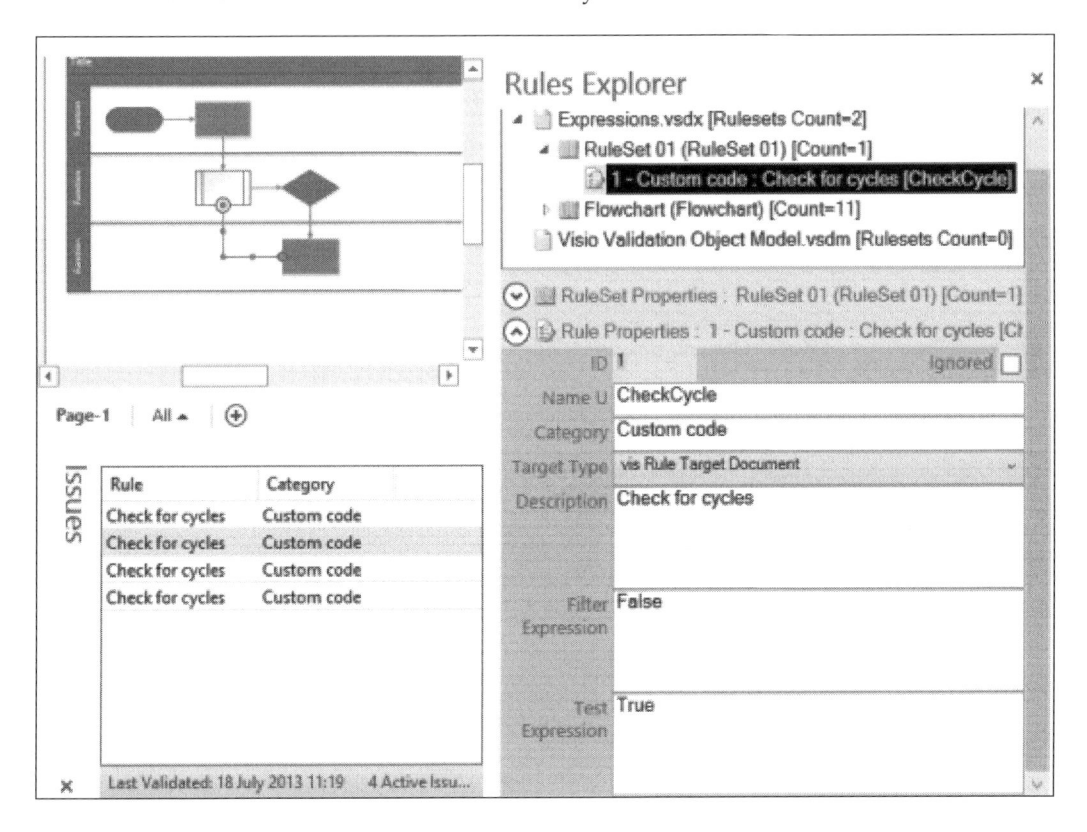

Of course, there could be many other validation rules in your custom code.

Summary

In this chapter we have learned how to use the target type to set the context for a rule. We then learned how to write a few Filter Expressions to reduce the shapes that need to be processed, and finally how to write Test Expressions that can raise issues. There are probably more expressions that could be written but we can work those out when we have specific requirements.

In the next chapter, we will learn how to publish custom templates with validation rules for deployment to other Visio 2013 Professional users.

8
Publishing Validation Rules and Diagrams

In the last chapter, we finished learning how to write validation rules for structured diagrams. In particular, we looked at the quasi-ShapeSheet formulae that are used to define Filter Expressions and Test Expressions. You should now know how to write validation rules for most implementations.

In this chapter, we will go through various methods for publishing Visio validation rules for others to use.

Overview of Visio categories and templates

The normal Visio user selects a Visio template from a category in the Backstage Getting Started view of the Visio user interface. If the user has both Metric and US Unit templates installed, then a choice of units will be offered.

Publishing Validation Rules and Diagrams

You can choose either of the two units. The following screenshot will help in elaborating the concept further:

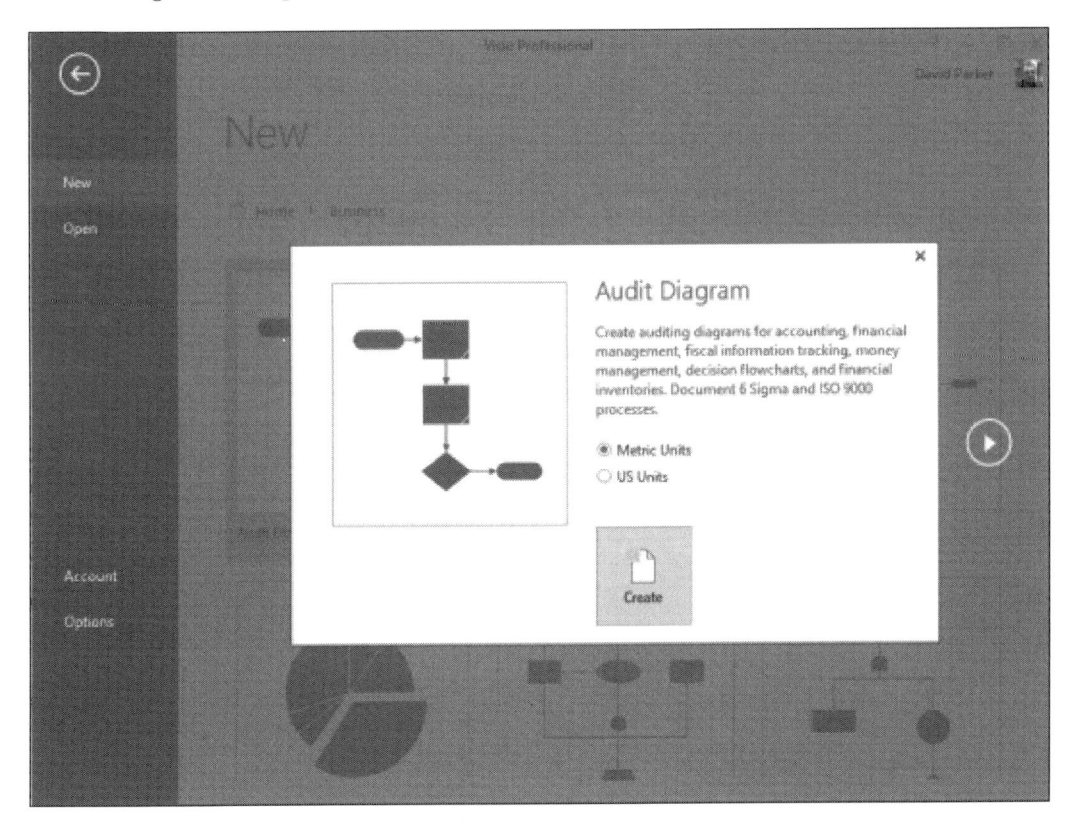

If you were to read the diagram template name, then you might think that there is a Visio template called `Audit Diagram (Metric).vstx`, in a folder named as `Business`, somewhere on your hard drive. However, that is not correct. In fact, there is a file called `AUDIT_M.VSTX` in `<Program Files>\Microsoft Office\Office15\Visio Content\1033`, although I have heard that some users may have a folder named `Microsoft Office 2013`. The `<Program Files>` folder is usually located at the location `C:\Program Files (x86)`, but this depends on whether you have installed the 32-bit or 64-bit Visio, and `1033` is the major language group ID. In my case, although UK English is `2047`, the major language is US English that is `1033`. Therefore, my Microsoft Office content is installed under the `1033` subfolder.

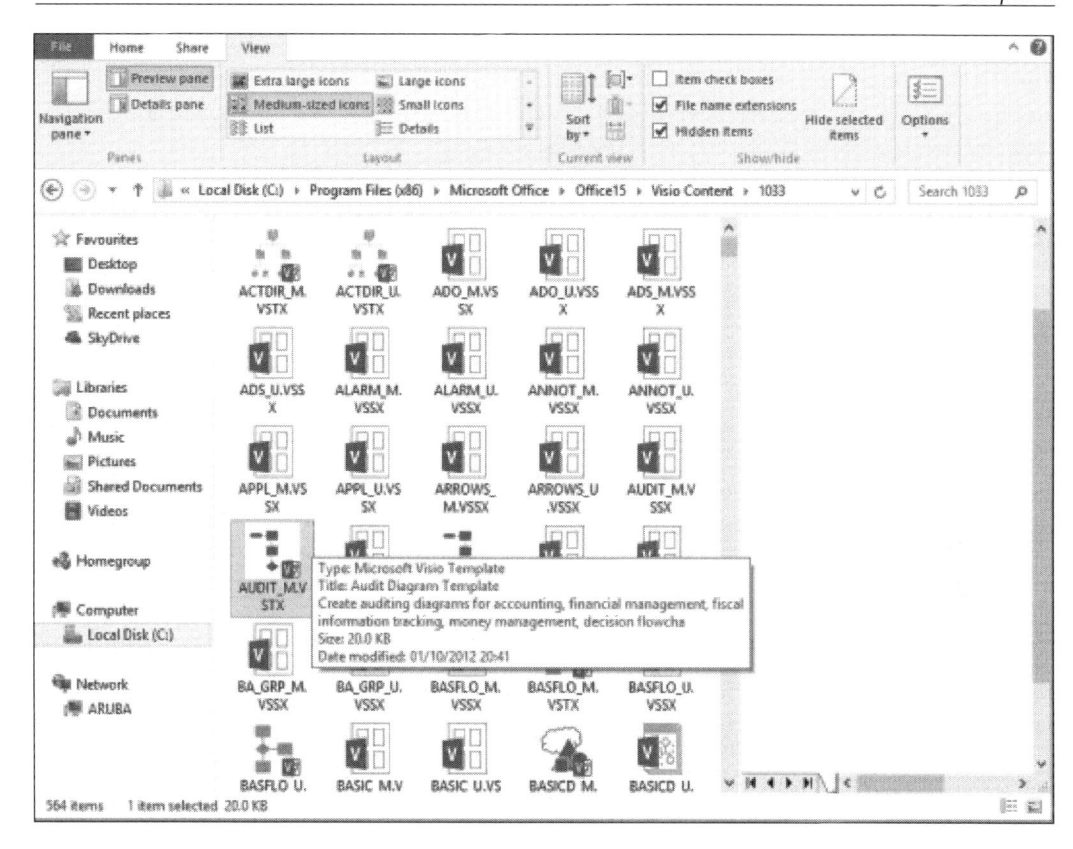

When Visio is installed, it has a files table in the installation file that contains the mapping of the terse name to the more verbose one, along with the long description. This mapping is then installed into the registry, and so the Visio interfaces then understand how to display the contents.

Some of this interpretation is hardcoded into Visio. For example, the built-in Visio templates and stencils all conform to the old **DOS 8.3** format, and the first part ends in **_M** or **_U**. This is how the Visio interface understands whether to display (**Metric**) or (**US Units**). It may be that the content is slightly different for each version, perhaps defaulting to *mm* rather than *inches*, or sized slightly different to fit on grid, for example, but the display in the Backstage view is controlled by the last two characters of the terse file name.

Publishing Validation Rules and Diagrams

You may notice that there is an option to create a Visio document from an existing one by selecting **New from existing** at the bottom of the Backstage view when **Template Categories** is selected. This will offer you the chance to browse for all types of Visio files, as listed in the following table:

Extension	Format	Description
*.vsdx	OPC	Visio drawing file
*.vsdm	OPC	Macro-enabled Visio drawing file
*.vsd	Binary	Visio 2003-2010 drawing file
*.vdx	XML	Visio 2003-2010 drawing file
*.vssx	OPC	Visio stencil file
*.vssm	OPC	Macro-enabled Visio stencil file
*.vss	Binary	Visio 2003-2010 stencil file
*.vsx	XML	Visio 2003-2010 stencil file
*.vstx	OPC	Visio template file
*.vstm	OPC	Macro-enabled Visio template file
*.vst	Binary	Visio template file
*.vtx	XML	Visio template file
*.vsw	Binary	Legacy Visio workspace file
*.vdw	Binary	Data-refreshable Visio 2010 drawing for use with Visio Services SharePoint 2010

However, if you want to present your users with a choice in one of the existing categories, or in a new one, then you need to create a template.

> Although most Visio 2003-2010 file types can be saved in binary or XML format, the latter is typically 7 to 10 times larger in disk size.

Creating a custom template

We will create a new template, and then go through several ways that we can make it available to others for use as a template. Firstly, create a new drawing from the **Audit Diagram** template, then go to **Process | Check Diagram | Import Rules From | Flowchart Rule Set**.

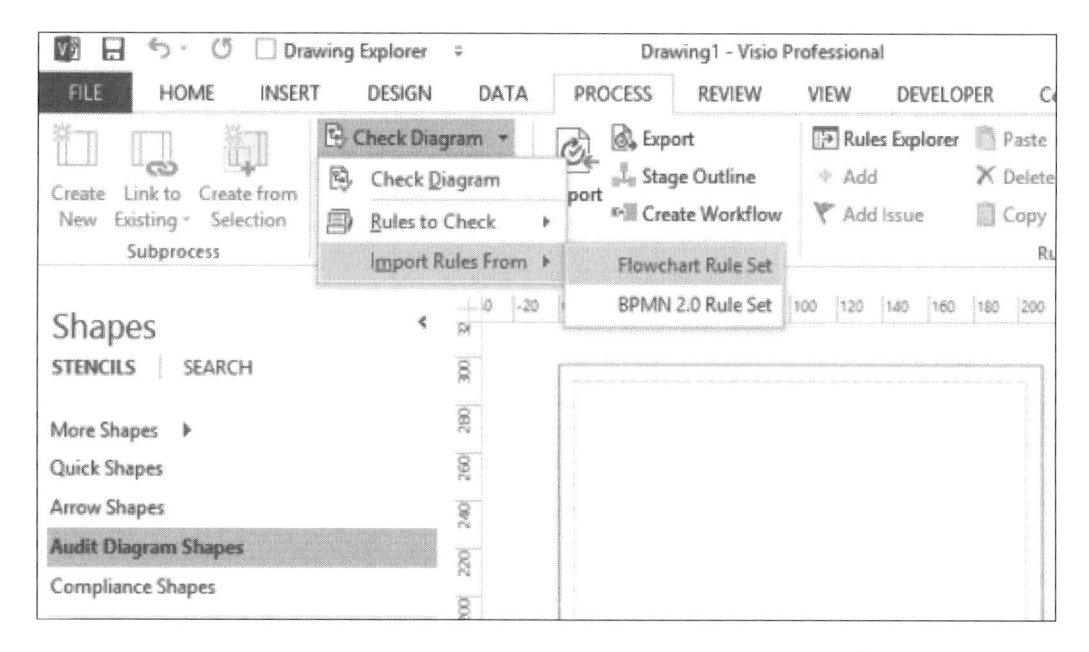

There are only two built-in ruleset in Visio, so we will use an import of the **Flowchart Rule Set** for this example. In fact, the procedure shown in this chapter is exactly the process that can be gone through in order to create Visio templates for companies who want customized versions of the ones supplied in Visio.

Adding embellishments

Most companies want to standardize the appearance of their Visio diagrams with, for example, company logos, borders, and titles. In this example, we are going to add a standard border and slightly modify it.

Select one of the **Borders and Titles** from the **Backgrounds** group on the **DESIGN** tab.

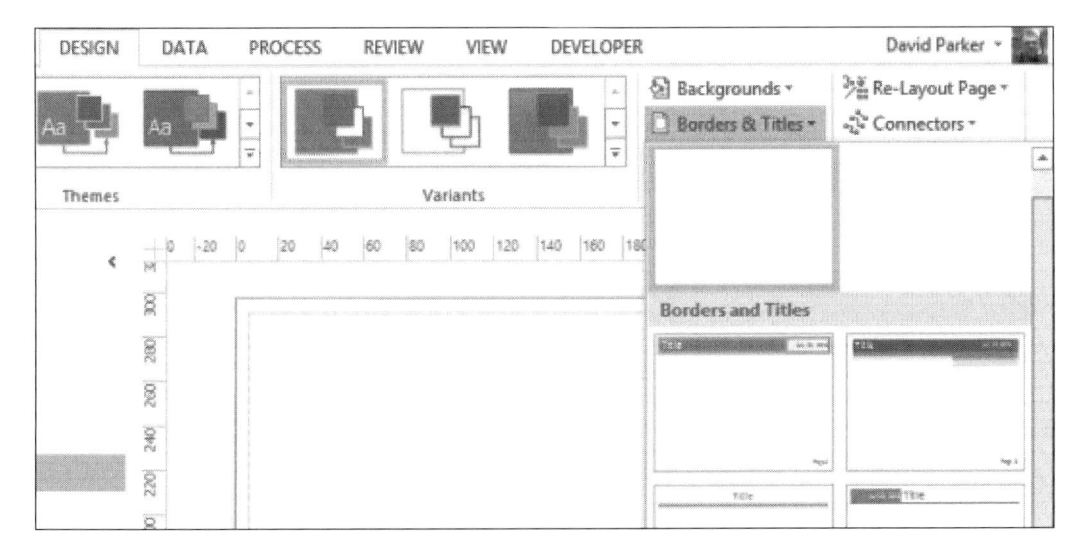

This action will automatically create a new background page, called **VBackground-1**. This will become the default background page for all new pages created in documents that are created from this template. In fact, you can add other backgrounds in a document, and you can have pages of different sizes. Visio is very flexible but you should consider whether you will be generally printing all pages in the document to the same printer, using the same printed paper size.

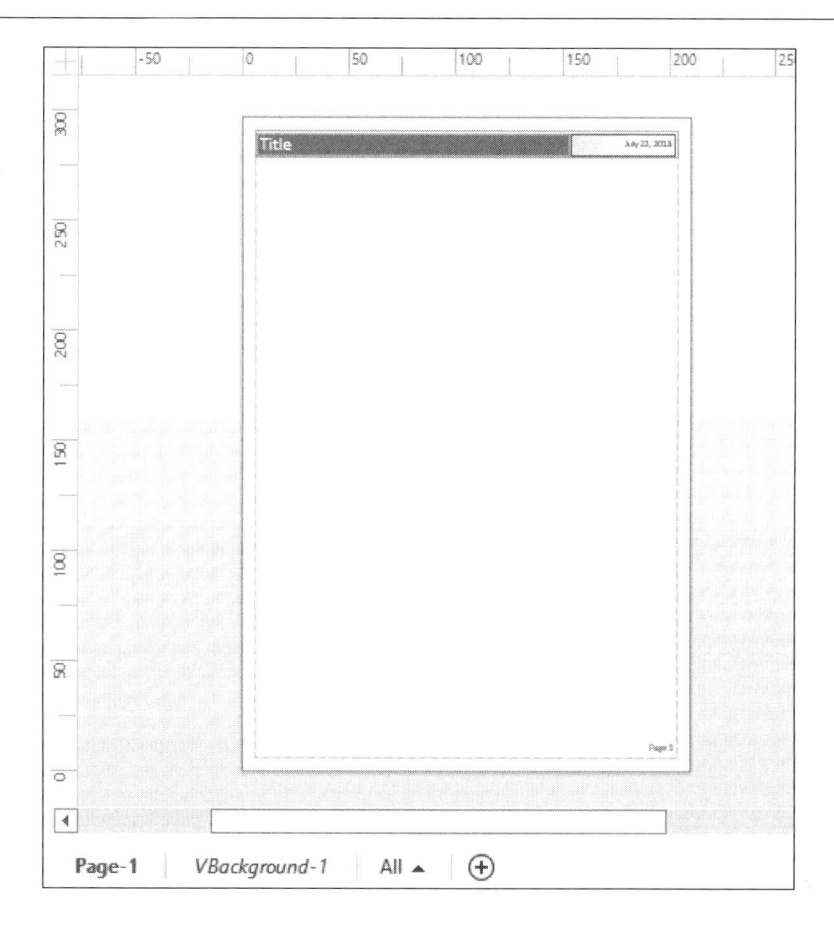

You can now select the **VBackground-1** tab, and you will then be able to edit the shapes on the background page.

Publishing Validation Rules and Diagrams

One of the coolest features in Visio is the ease with which you can create text that is automatically updated from a value in a cell. In this case, wouldn't it be nice if the page title automatically displayed the name of the page? Well, all you need to do is edit the text of the title box on the background page. In this case, it is in the top left of the background page. Usually you can just double-click on a shape to edit the text, but you can also just click to select it then press *F2* to go into text edit mode. You can then select **Field** from the **INSERT** tab. This action will open up the **Field** dialog where you can select a **Category** and **Field name**, or enter a custom formula. In this case, you need to select **Page Info** from **Category** and **Name** from **Field name**.

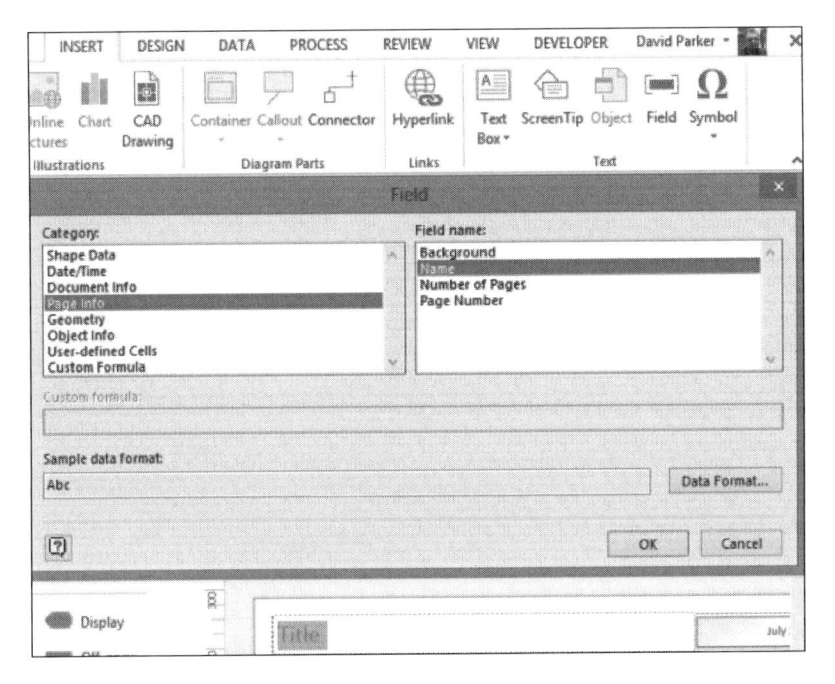

Actually, I will often add the **Document Info | Title** and **Document Info | Subject**, with a hyphen between them before the **Page Info | Name** field. Of course, you may want to create a rule that reminds users that they should fill in a **Title** and **Subject** for every document that they create.

[270]

Although we just specified that the title block displays the page name of the background page, Visio understands that you really want to display the page name of the foreground page. So when you click back onto **Page-1**, you will see that the text automatically displays **Page-1**:

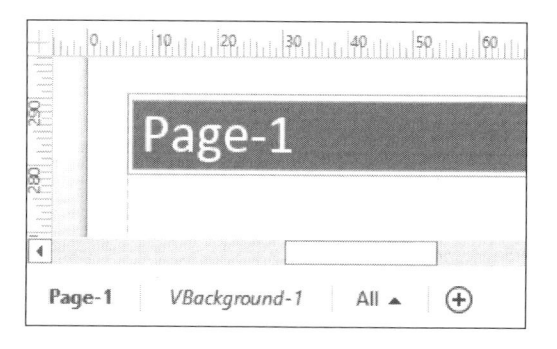

Clever isn't it? What is more, Visio will automatically change the size of the background page, if you change the size of the foreground page.

Adding the template description

You should now go into the Backstage view to edit the **Info** of the document. Once there, you can provide some information for future reference in the **Properties** panel:

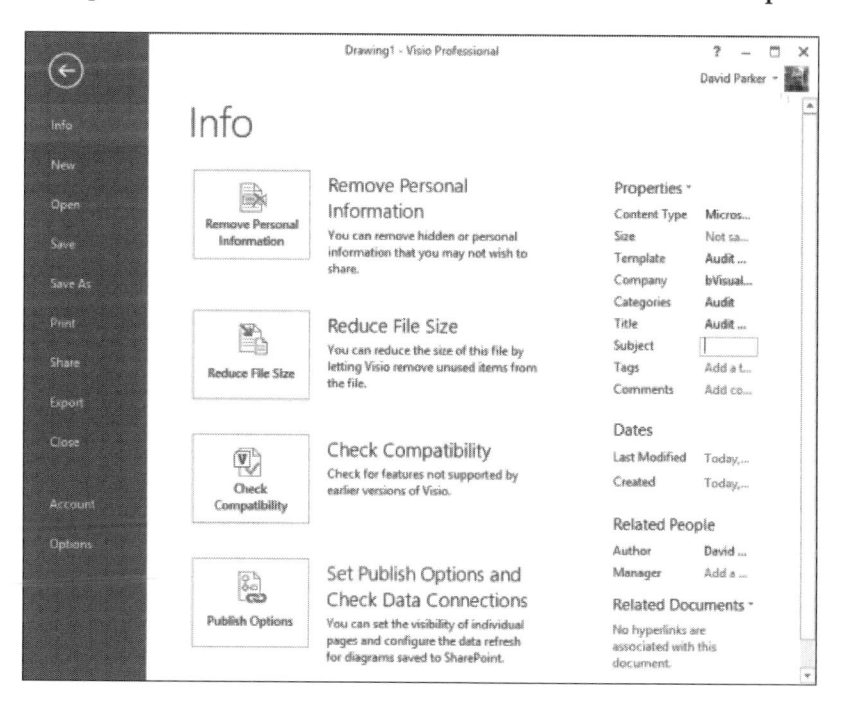

Publishing Validation Rules and Diagrams

You should fill in the **Comments** with a description that will help your users make the right choice of template, because this will be displayed in the Visio user interface later.

> You can also get to edit the document properties from the right-mouse menu on the document node in the **Drawing Explorer** window, which can be opened from the checkbox on the **DEVELOPER** tab. In this case, it will open the old **Properties** dialog.

The simplest method to provide a template

Now save this document as a Visio template (*.vstx) in the special folder `My Shapes` or, let's say, in a new folder called `My Templates`, with a subfolder called `Company Flowcharts`, inside the special folder, `Documents` (or `My Documents`) folder.

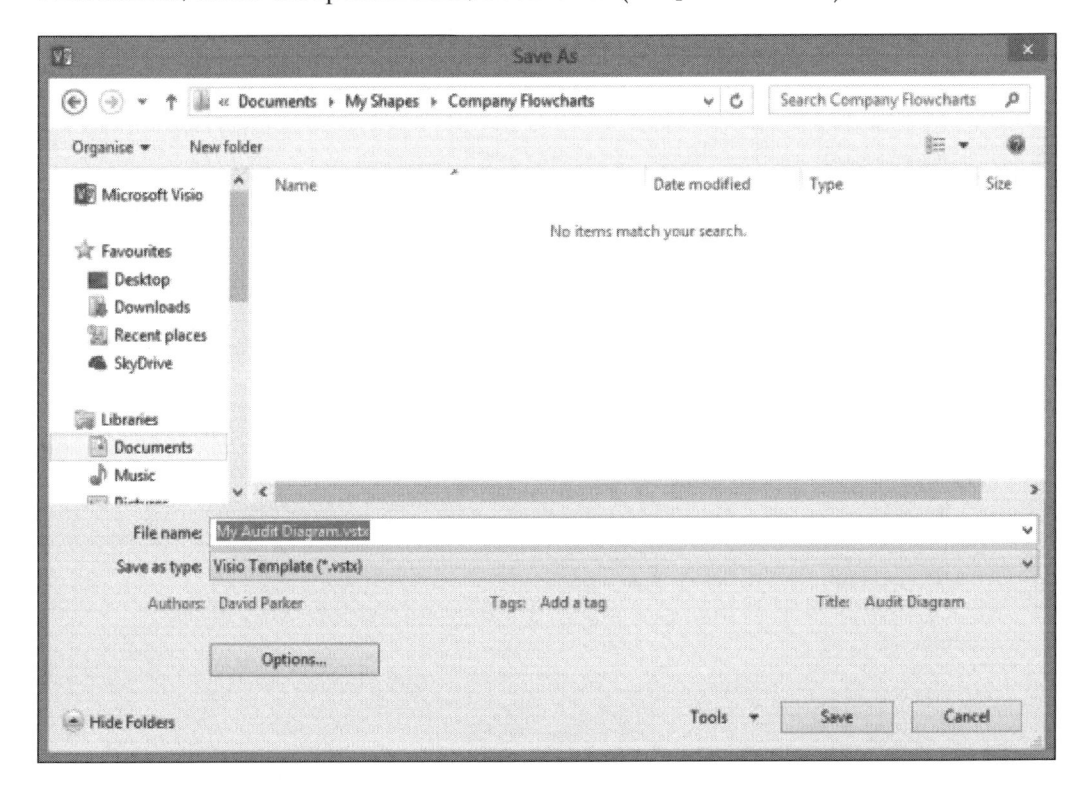

OK, so we now have a custom template. However, the Visio interface does not know where to find the templates, even though it is inside the special folder, Documents (or My Documents). There is a special folder called My Shapes in the Documents folder that is intended for Visio stencils, but it does not automatically display the contents for templates.

Editing the file paths for templates

Fortunately, we can tell Visio where to look for custom templates, and other custom files, from the **Visio Options** panel. Simply open the **File Locations** dialog from the **Advanced | General** section at the very bottom of the scrollable panel. You can then navigate to the My Shapes folder by clicking on the ellipsis button (**...**) to the right of the **Templates** textbox.

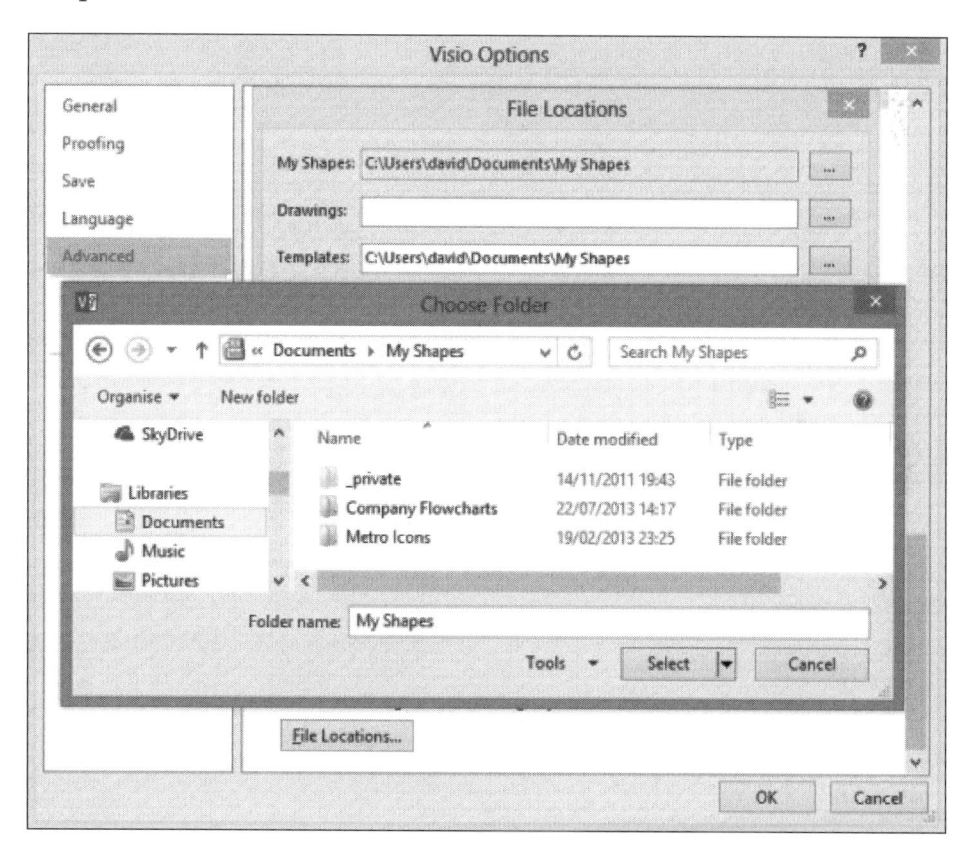

Publishing Validation Rules and Diagrams

You should select the `My Shapes` or the `My Templates` folder, not the `Company Flowcharts` subfolder, because **Company Flowcharts** will be used as the category name in the Visio interface.

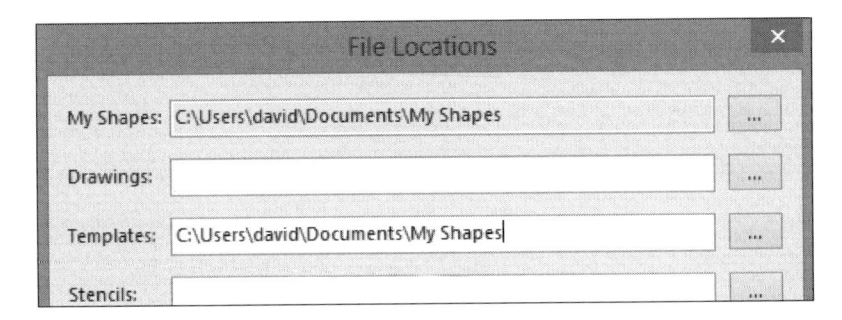

So now, when you want to select a template, you will find **My Audit Diagram** inside the `Company Flowcharts` folder:

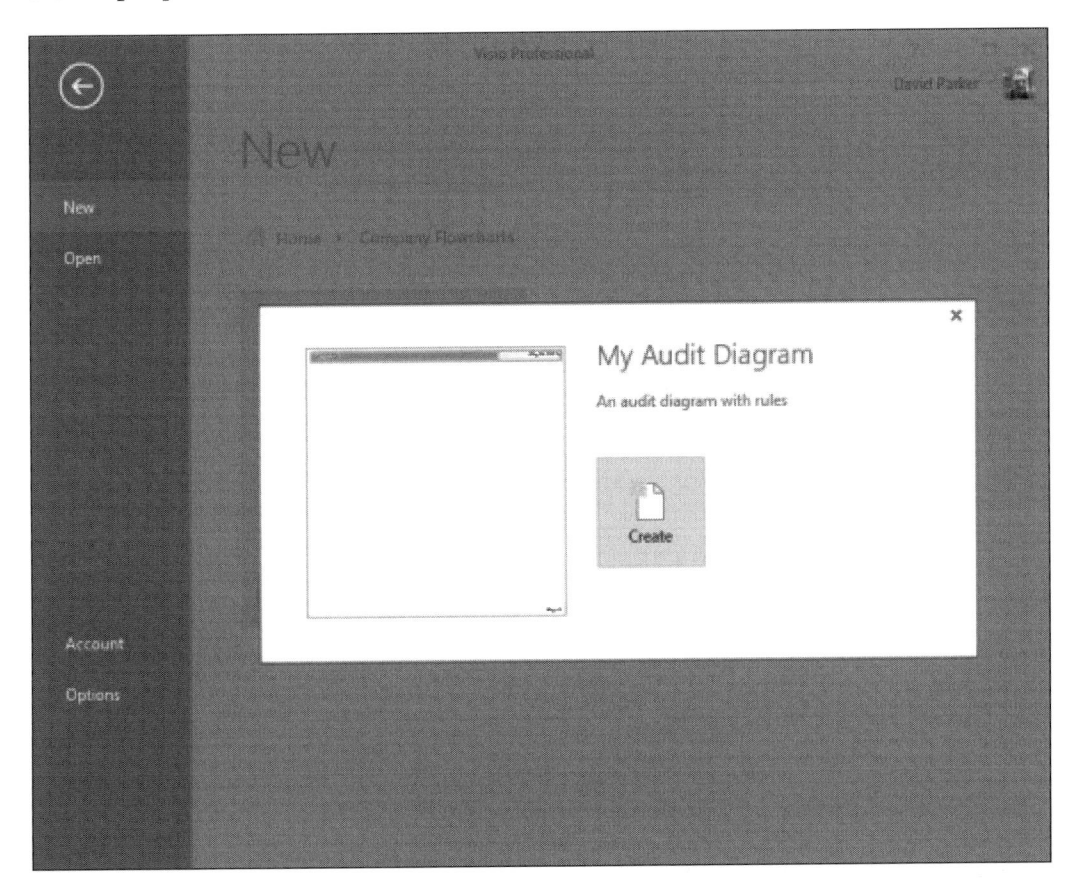

You should be aware that Visio will scan through every folder and subfolder, for every path listed in the **File Locations** dialog. This can be a very slow process if there are a lot of folders and files within them. Therefore, this method of deploying custom templates is not the recommended method but it is acceptable for certain situations, (for example, when no installations are permitted) provided it is done with care. You can imagine the effect that entering `C:` in just one of these locations could have, since Visio will attempt to read every folder and subfolder looking for suitable files. Visio will appear to stop responding, if you are lucky.

> You may have noticed that you can specify a path called **Start-Up** in the **File Locations** dialog. If you set a path here, Visio will attempt to run every executable file it finds! Imagine doing that from `C:`! Believe me this has happened on more than one occasion. The only remedy is to shut down as quickly as possible, restart the computer, then edit the following registry key to remove this path before starting Visio again.
>
> `Computer\HKEY_CURRENT_USER\Software\Microsoft\Office\15.0\Visio\Application\StartUpPath`

Setting the file paths for templates

Visio 2013 has introduced another way of setting the file path for templates with the **Default personal templates location** option in the **File | Options | Save dialog**.

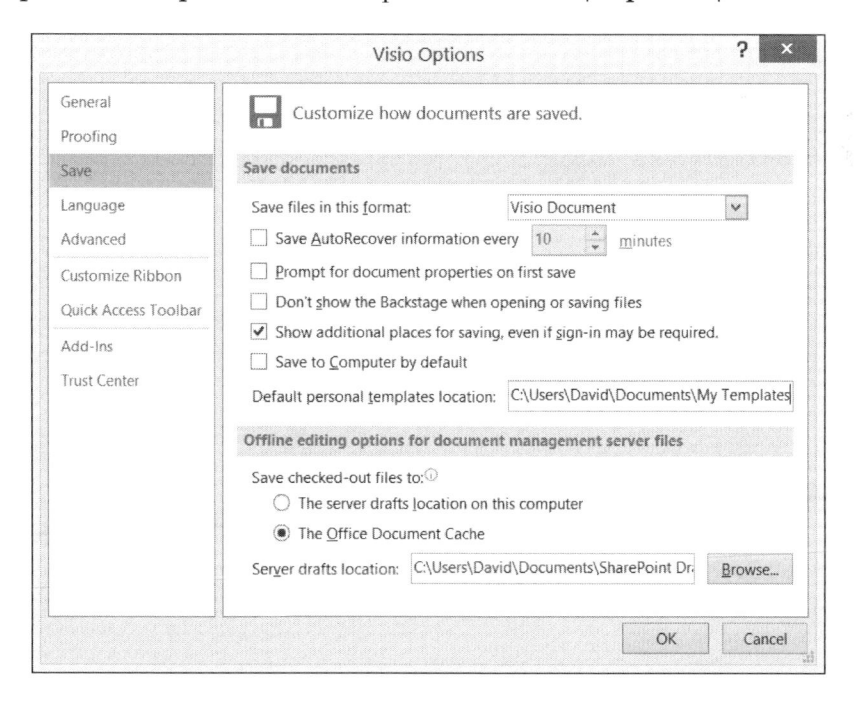

Publishing Validation Rules and Diagrams

This will introduce a new **PERSONAL** collection in the Backstage view when you want to select a new diagram type. As before, any subfolder will be treated as a category in the Backstage view.

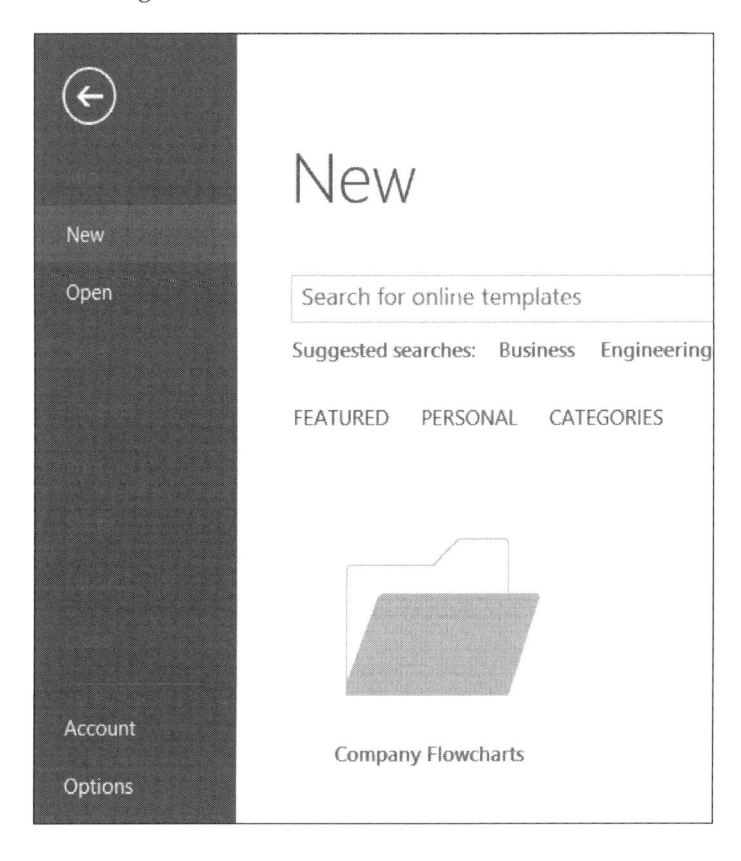

Creating a template preview image

You will have noticed that our new template looks pretty boring in the Backstage view. The default preview image in Visio is generated automatically from the first foreground page in a document. Therefore, you can create a new preview image for the template by mocking-up a new drawing, created from the template, with a suitable arrangement of shapes on it. You will then be able to copy the image from the drawing to the template using one line of VBA code.

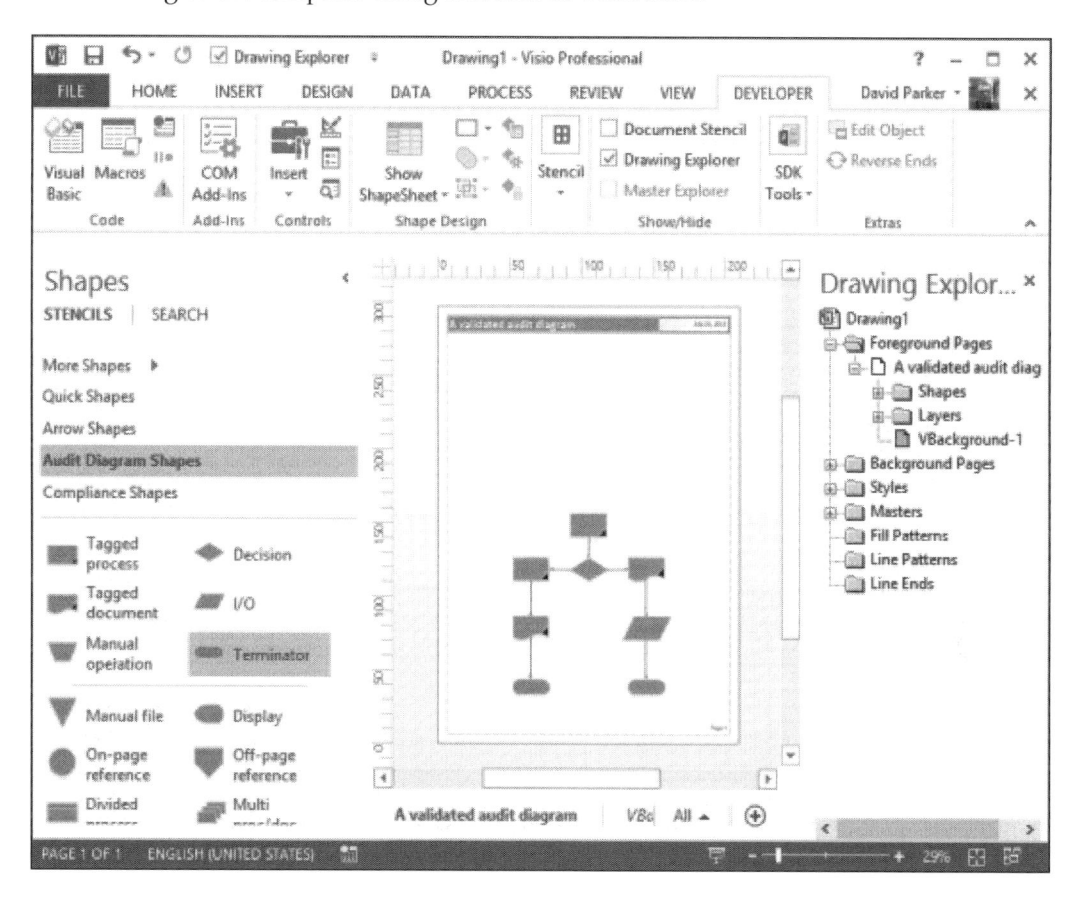

Publishing Validation Rules and Diagrams

Now, open the **Page Setup** dialog from the right-mouse menu, on the foreground page node of the **Drawing Explorer** window or from the **Size | More Page Sizes** option on the **DESIGN** tab. Select **Custom Size** on the **Page Size** tab, and edit the height to be the same as the width.

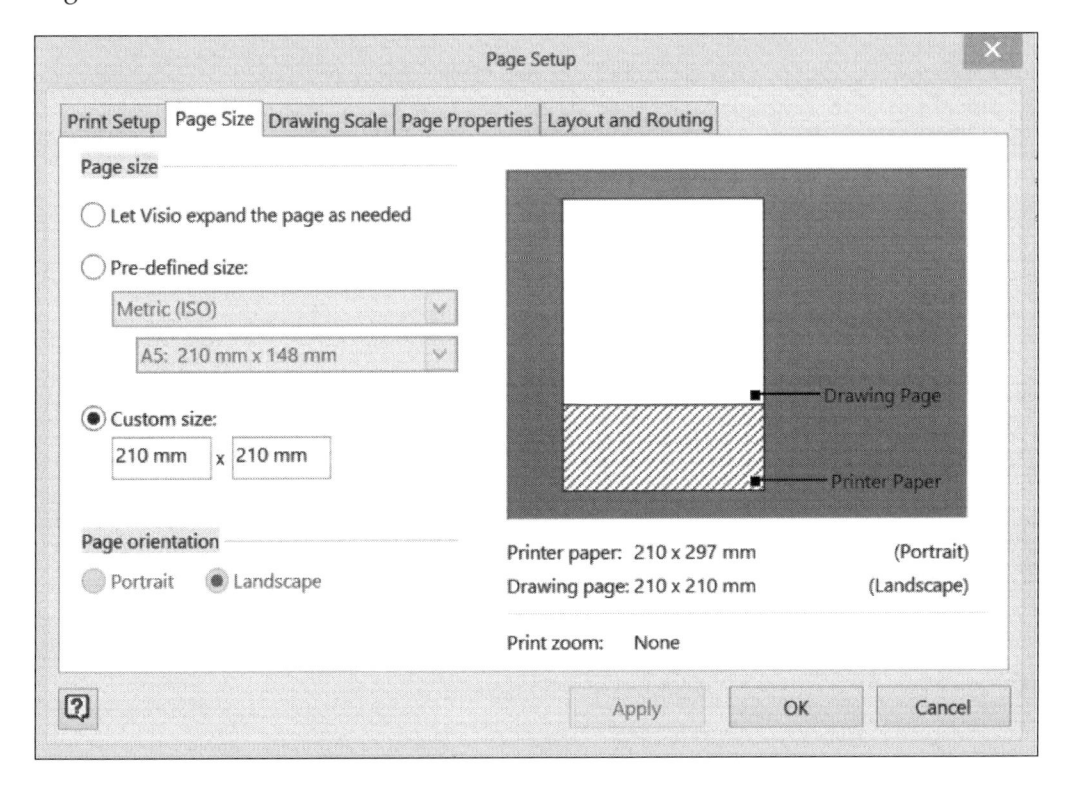

You are doing this because the preview image of the template in the Backstage view is square.

Open the **DocumentSheet** by selecting **Show ShapeSheet** from the right-mouse menu of the document node, on the **Drawing Explorer** window.

Then edit the **PreviewQuality** to be `1-visDocPreviewQualityDetailed`. This will ensure that the size specified in the **ThumbnailDetailMaxSize** registry key value is used.

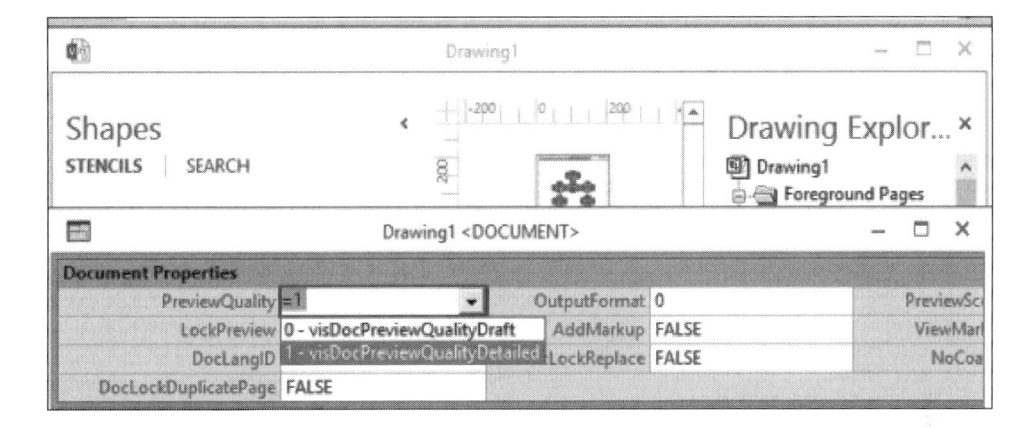

Close the ShapeSheet and then save the document as, say, `A validated audit diagram.vsdx`.

Next, you need to open the original `My Audit Diagram.vstx` document by using the **File** | **Open** menu; then select **Open** or **Open Original** from the options on the **Open** button.

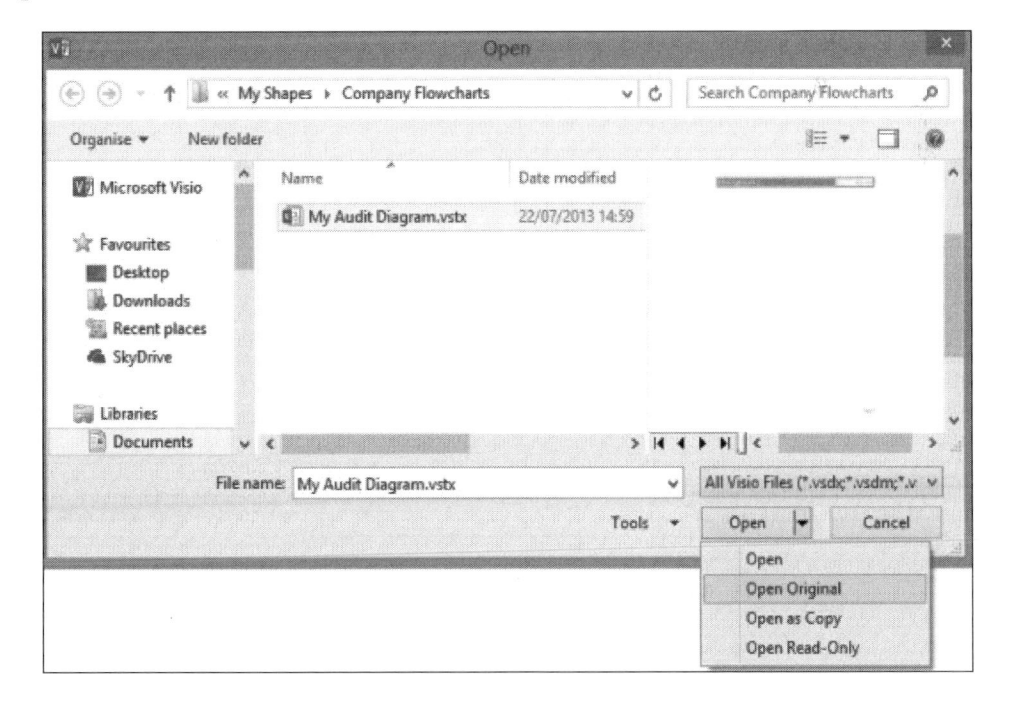

Publishing Validation Rules and Diagrams

So, you now have two documents open. This is necessary because you are going to copy the preview image from one to the other! You can verify the names of the files that you have open from the menu on the **Switch Windows** button on the **VIEW** tab.

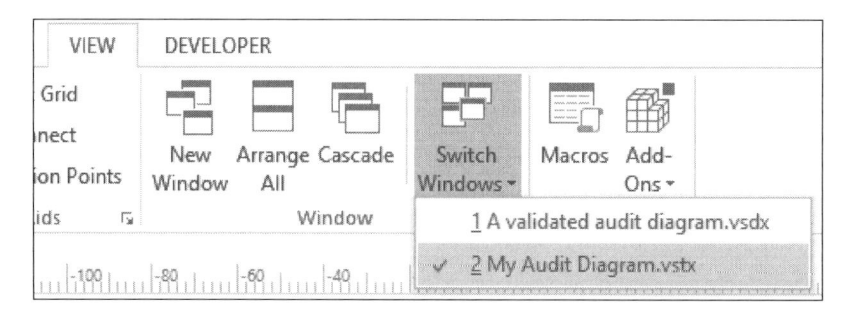

Simply go into the VBA environment (*Alt+F11* normally takes you straight there). You do not want to add any VBA code into the documents, because you just need to type one line into the **Immediate** window (*Ctrl+G*):

```
Visio.Documents("My Audit Diagram.vstx").CopyPreviewPicture Visio.Documents("A validated audit diagram.vsdx")
```

You have now copied the preview image from `A validated audit diagram.vsd` to `My Audit Diagram.vst`, but the template will lose the preview unless you edit the **LockPreview** value to `True` in the ShapeSheet of the `My Audit Diagram.vst` document:

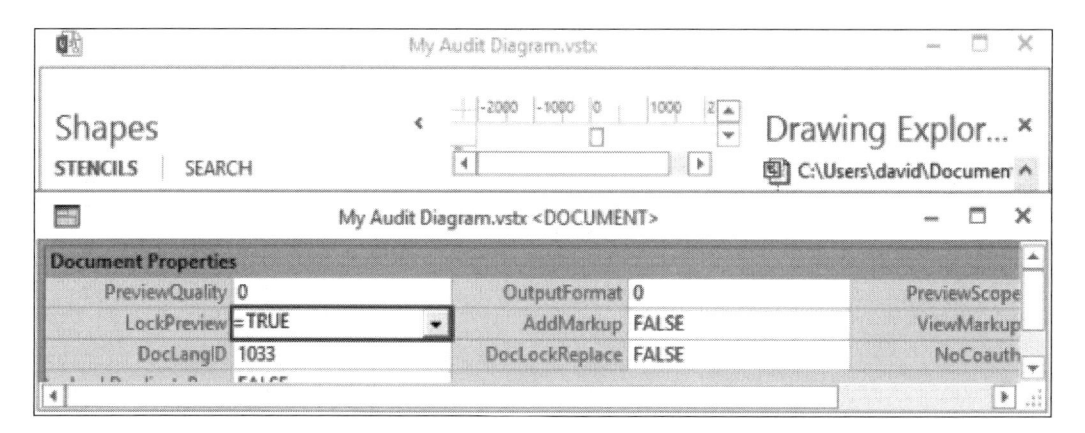

Now you can close the ShapeSheet and save the template; this time you will see that there is a preview image.

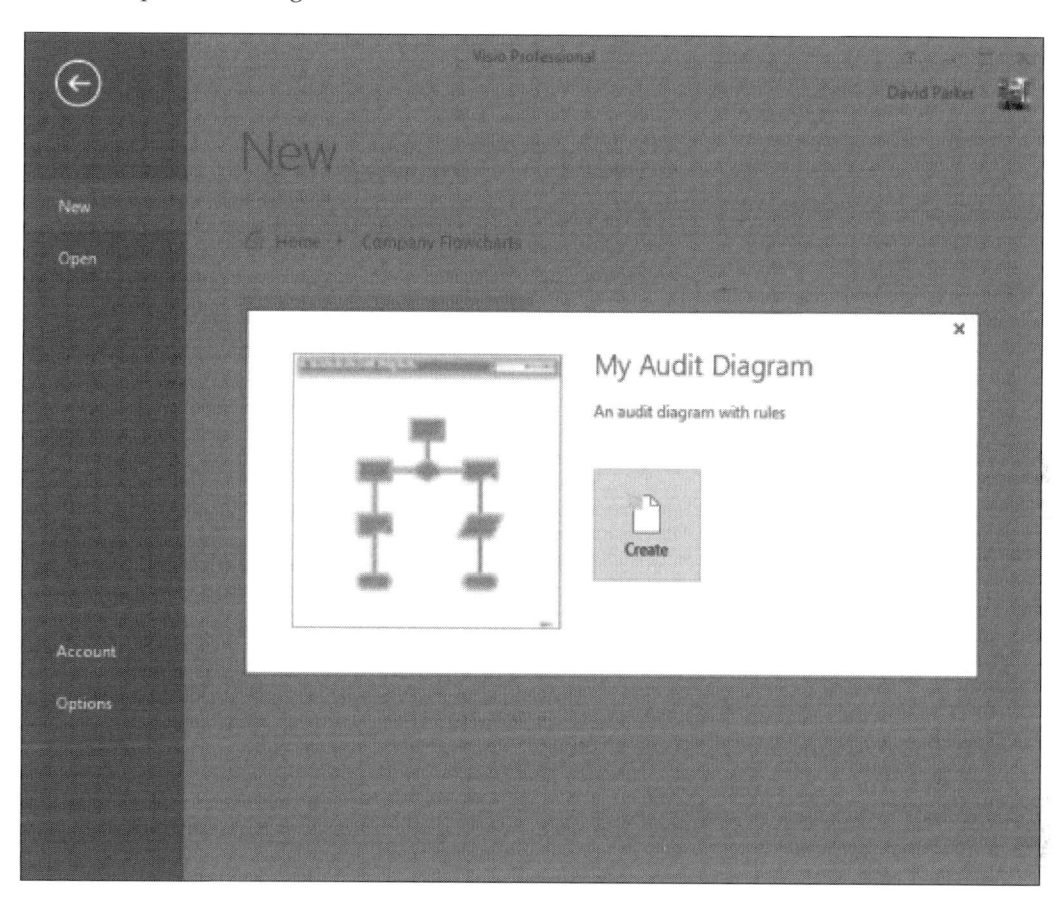

Remember that you will need to change the **LockPreview** back to 0 (`False`) if you ever want to update the image.

Alternatively, you could save this following VBA code in the `ThisDocument` class of the `A validated audit diagram.vsdm` file so that you can recopy the preview image at a later date. This method will assume that you also have the target template open.

```
Public Sub CopyPreview()
Dim docTarget As Visio.Document
Dim doc As Visio.Document
If Visio.Documents.Count < 2 Then
    Exit Sub
Else
    'Get the first writable drawing that is open
```

Publishing Validation Rules and Diagrams

```
        For Each doc In Visio.Application.Documents
            If doc.Type = visTypeTemplate _
                And doc.ReadOnly = False _
                And Not doc Is ThisDocument Then
                Set docTarget = doc
                Exit For
            End If
        Next
        If docTarget Is Nothing Then
            Exit Sub
        End If
    End If

    If MsgBox("Do you want to copy the preview image from " & _
        ThisDocument.Name & " to " & docTarget.Name & "?", _
        vbYesNo) = vbYes Then
        docTarget.DocumentSheet.Cells("LockPreview").FormulaU = 0
        docTarget.CopyPreviewPicture ThisDocument
        docTarget.DocumentSheet.Cells("LockPreview").FormulaU = 1
    End If

End Sub
```

Enhancing the quality of the preview image

You may be slightly disappointed with the quality of this image compared to the standard Visio ones. It is certainly less crisp but there is a way that you can fix this. Visio is rendering to a fixed size by default.

> This method requires a registry hack, so only attempt this if you are confident.

First, you need to tell Visio to store all of its settings that it is holding in memory into the registry so that you can edit them. This is done by ticking the **Put all settings in Windows registry** box in the **Visio Options** dialog, under the **Advanced | General** group:

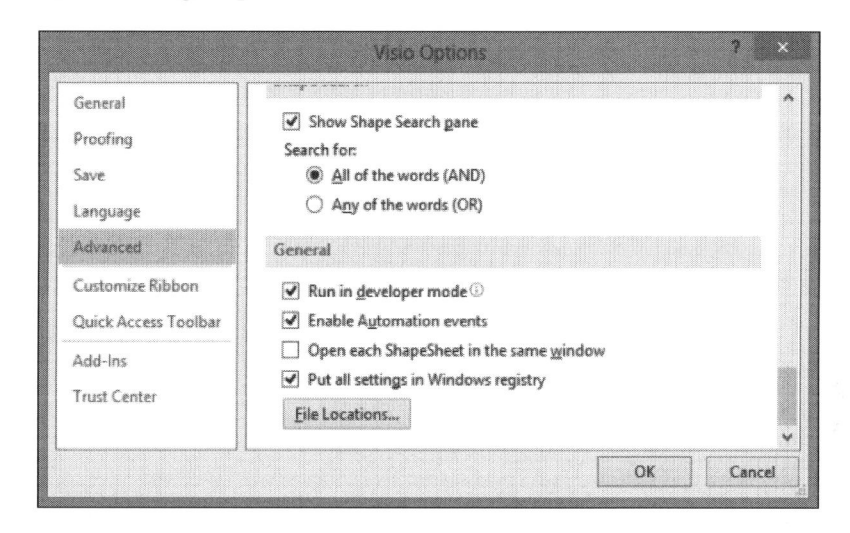

Then close Visio, and start the **Registry Editor** (type `regedit` at the **Start** command\screen). Navigate down to the following node:

Computer\HKEY_CURRENT_USER\Software\Microsoft\Office\15.0\Visio\Application

Then edit one of the two Thumbnail values as follows:

```
ThumbnailDetailMaxSize = 5000000
```

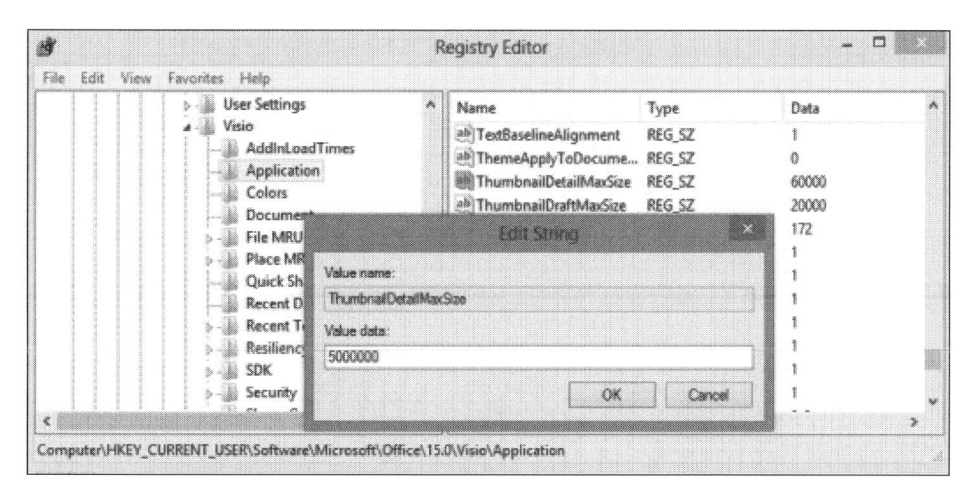

Publishing Validation Rules and Diagrams

Now, open `A Validated Audit Diagram.vsdm` that you previously created, and resave the document in order to update its preview image. You may then want to change the **LockPreview** value of this document to `True` by using the ShapeSheet as described earlier, in case you want to use it again.

Open the `My Audit Diagram.vstx` document and copy the preview image across, using the VBA line as mentioned earlier.

The VBA code will automatically unlock and then lock the preview image.

Now, you will see that the preview picture of the document is much crisper and clearer.

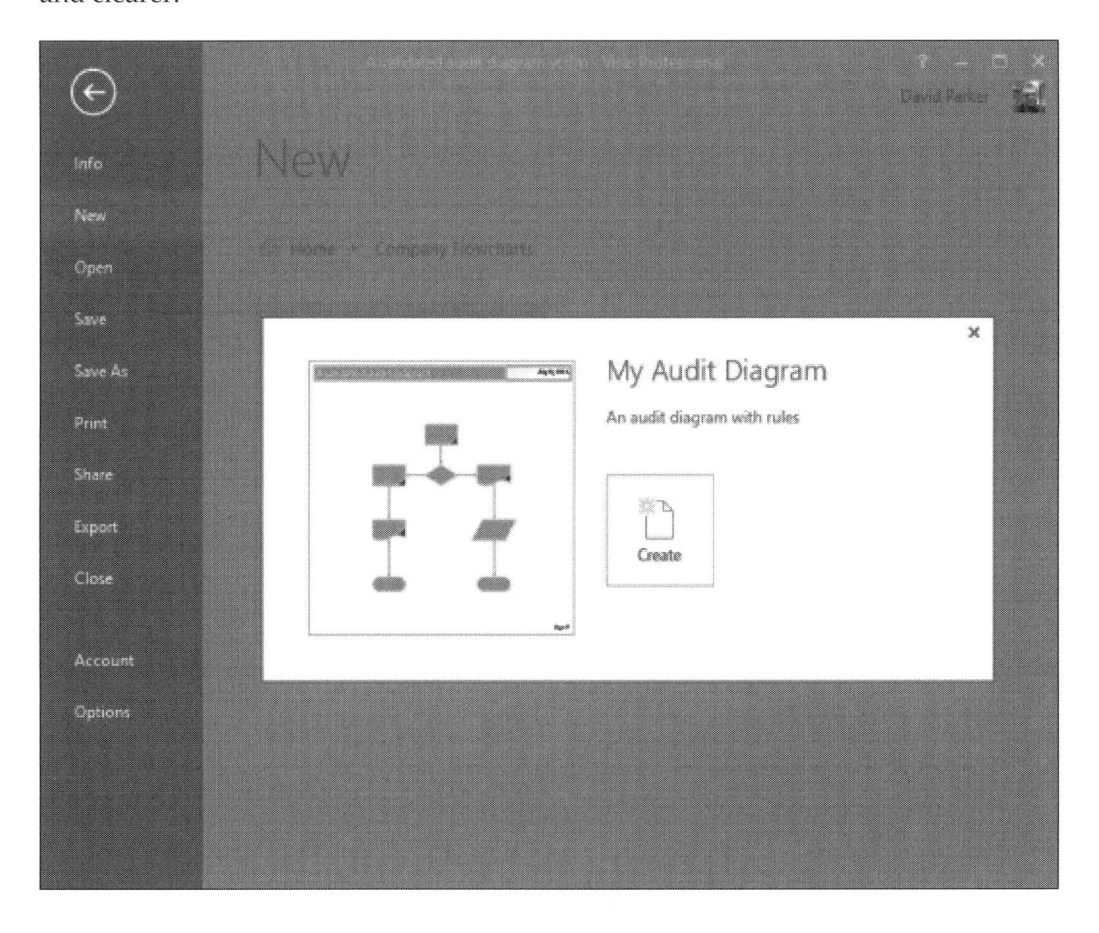

Finally, you could edit the registry values back to their defaults; otherwise, Visio will need to work harder, and your file sizes will be increased:

```
ThumbnailDetailMaxSize = 60000
```

The best method for publishing templates

Now you know how to publish a template and category using a simple method, you will now learn how to provide a setup package that can be distributed and installed. For this, you will need an application, such as Visual Studio, that can create an installation package (*.msi) file. Visual Studio had a **Setup and Deployment** project type prior to the 2012 edition, and you could use this and the **Visio Solution Publishing Tool** from the Microsoft Visio **SDK (Software Development Kit)**. However, Microsoft deprecated the **Setup and Deployment** project type, and encouraged most developers to use the **WiX Toolset** from http://wixtoolset.org/. This provides the ability to build Windows installation packages from the XML source code. Fortunately, an experienced Visio developer and blogger, *Nikolay Belyh*, has provided a WiX Setup Project for Visio, http://unmanagedvisio.com/products/visio-wix-installer-project-template/; this provides an extension to the WiX Toolset just for Visio projects. So, install them both.

> You can choose to enable the optional InstallShield Limited Edition in Visual Studio 2012, which will provide you with the ability to create an .msi file, but you will need to add a PublishComponent table by hand before using the Visio Solution Publishing Tool that is available in the Visio SDK.

Creating a setup project

In Visual Studio, create a new **Installed | Templates | WiX Toolset | WiX Setup Project** for Visio, called, say, MyAuditTemplateVisioSetup:

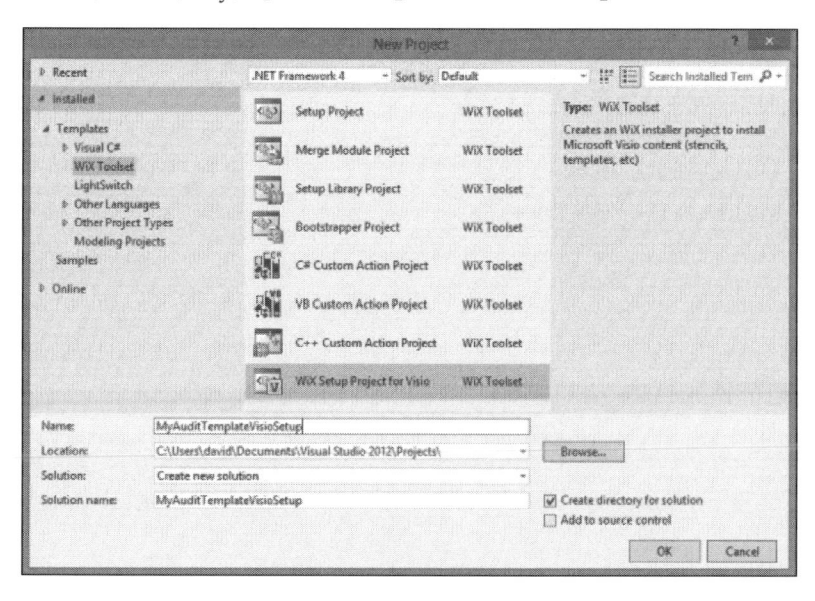

Publishing Validation Rules and Diagrams

In Visio, save the `My Audit Diagram.vstx` file as `AuditR_M.vstx` then, in Visual Studio, add the file to the `MyAuditTemplateVisioSetup` project. I removed the dummy `Stencil_1_M.vss` and the `Template_1_M.vst` from the project.

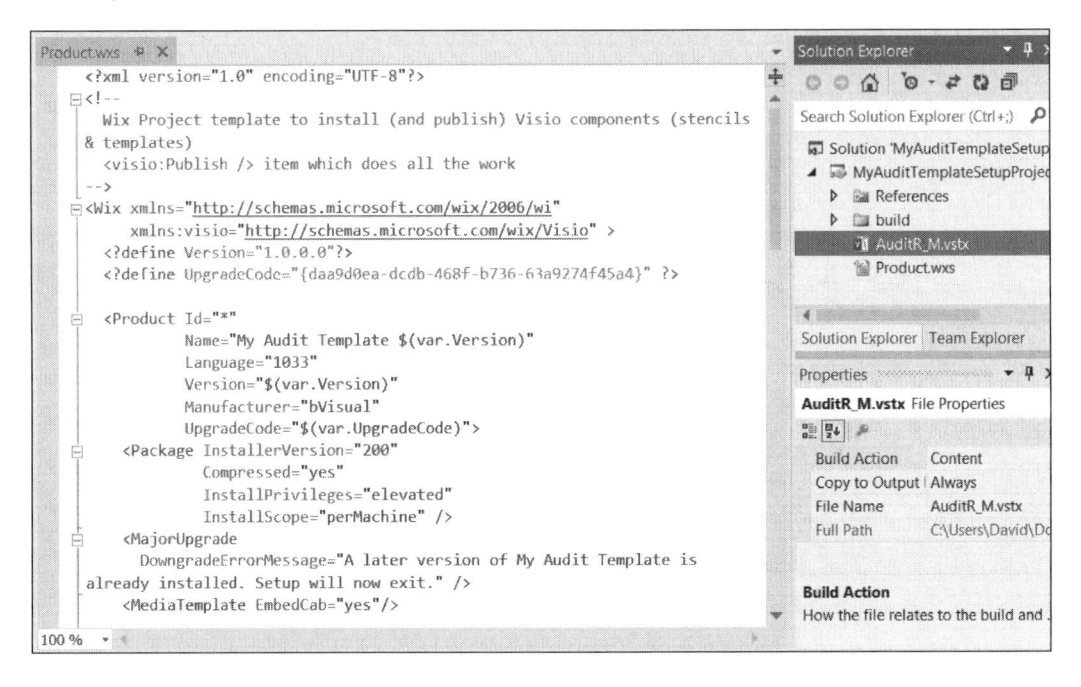

```xml
<?xml version="1.0" encoding="UTF-8"?>
<!--
    Wix Project template to install (and publish) Visio components (stencils
    & templates)
    <visio:Publish /> item which does all the work
-->
<Wix xmlns="http://schemas.microsoft.com/wix/2006/wi"
     xmlns:visio="http://schemas.microsoft.com/wix/Visio" >
  <?define Version="1.0.0.0"?>
  <?define UpgradeCode="{daa9d0ea-dcdb-468f-b736-63a9274f45a4}" ?>

  <Product Id="*"
           Name="My Audit Template $(var.Version)"
           Language="1033"
           Version="$(var.Version)"
           Manufacturer="bVisual"
           UpgradeCode="$(var.UpgradeCode)">
    <Package InstallerVersion="200"
             Compressed="yes"
             InstallPrivileges="elevated"
             InstallScope="perMachine" />
    <MajorUpgrade
       DowngradeErrorMessage="A later version of My Audit Template is already installed. Setup will now exit." />
    <MediaTemplate EmbedCab="yes"/>
```

Note that I also updated the Product.Name, Manufacturer, and so on, to suit my requirements shown as follows:

```xml
<Product Id="*"
         Name="My Audit Template with Rules $(var.Version)"
         Language="1033"
         Version="$(var.Version)"
         Manufacturer="bVisual"
         UpgradeCode="$(var.UpgradeCode)">
  <Package InstallerVersion="200"
           Compressed="yes"
           InstallPrivileges="elevated"
```

```
            InstallScope="perMachine" />
    <MajorUpgrade
       DowngradeErrorMessage="A later version of My Audit Template with
 Rules is already installed. Setup will now exit." />
    <MediaTemplate EmbedCab="yes"/>

    <Directory Id="TARGETDIR" Name="SourceDir">
      <Directory Id="ProgramFilesFolder">
        <Directory Id="ManufacturerFolder"
                   Name="bVisual">
          <Directory Id="INSTALLDIR"
                     Name="Company Flowcharts"
                     FileSource="." >
            <Component>
              <File Name="AuditR_M.vstx">
                <visio:PublishTemplate
                  MenuPath="Company Flowcharts\My Audit Diagram" />
              </File>
            </Component>
          </Directory>
        </Directory>
      </Directory>
    </Directory>

    <Feature Id="ProductFeature"
             Title="All Items" Display="expand" >
      <Feature Id="TemplatesFeature"
               Title="Install templates"  >
        <ComponentRef Id="AuditR_M.vstx" />
      </Feature>
    </Feature>
    <UIRef Id="WixUI_FeatureTree" />
  </Product>
```

You can then build the release of this package; you should find that two files are created, namely `MyAudtTemplateSetup.msi` and `MyAudtTemplateSetup.wixpdb`, in the `<Projects>\MyAudtTemplateSetup\MyAudtTemplateSetup\bin\Release` folder.

Publishing Validation Rules and Diagrams

Running the installation

Double-click on the `MyAuditTemplateVisioSetup.msi` file in the `Release` folder of the project, or select **Install** from the right-mouse menu on it. The Welcome dialog should appear as shown in the following screenshot:

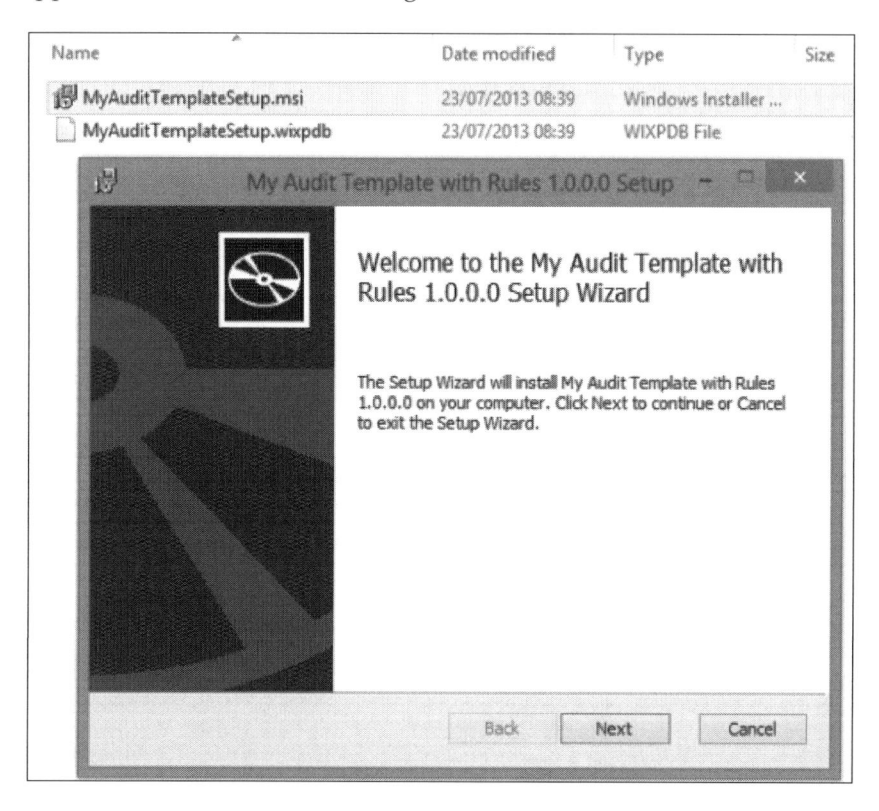

You can then click on **Next** on the **End-User License Agreement** after ticking the acceptance checkbox, then **Next** on the **Custom Setup** screen, and then **Install**. Once installed, you will finally see the completed screen.

The `AuditR_M.vstx` file will be installed into the `<ProgramFilesFolder>\bVisual\Company Flowcharts` folder.

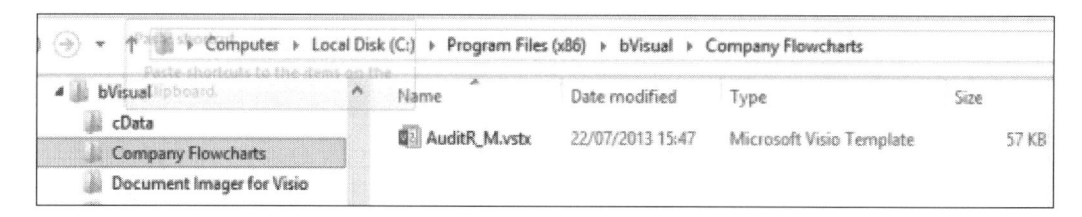

However, there will be a new category in **CATEGORIES**, though it will be a simple folder image. Unfortunately, Visio does not provide the ability to enhance this.

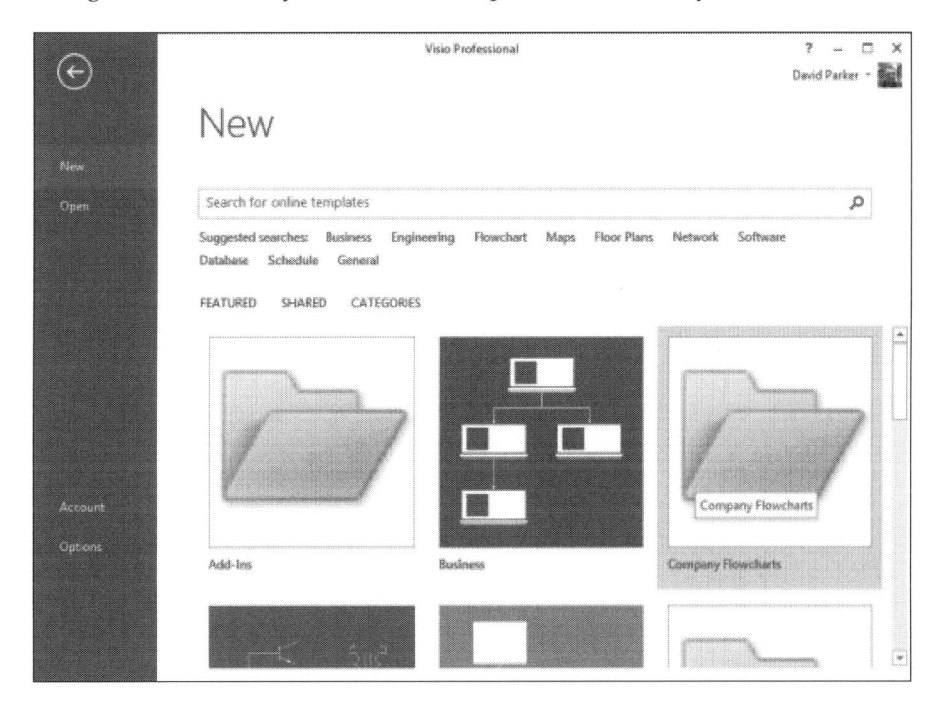

You will find the verbosely named template inside the category.

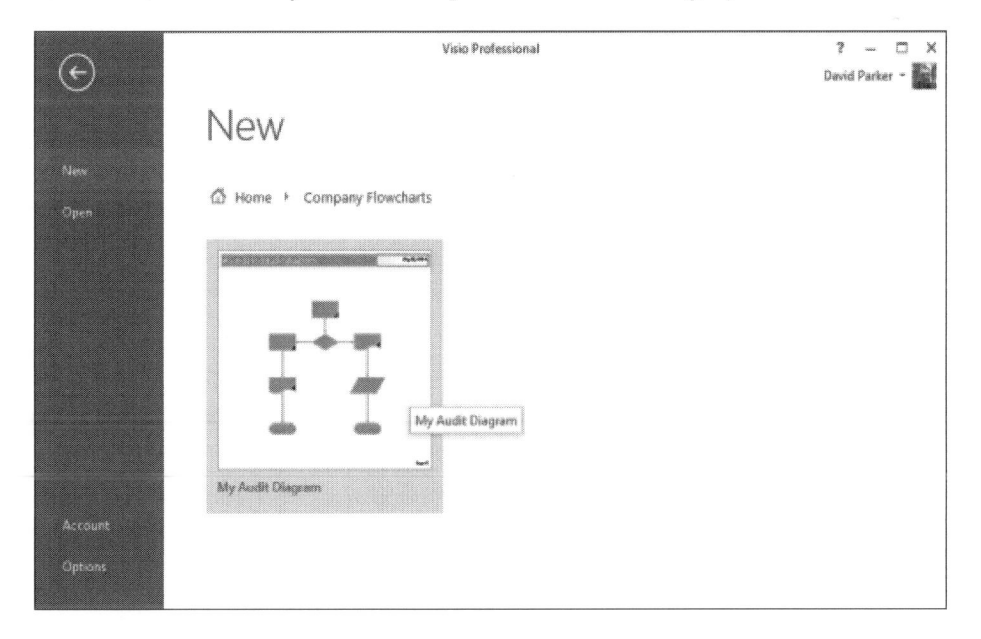

Publishing Validation Rules and Diagrams

Note that I have removed the file path changes that I made earlier in this chapter.

Of course, you do not need to create a new category. For example, you could have just put the existing Flowchart in the WiX XML:

```
MenuPath="Flowchart\My Audit Diagram" />
```

This will cause your template to appear in the existing category:

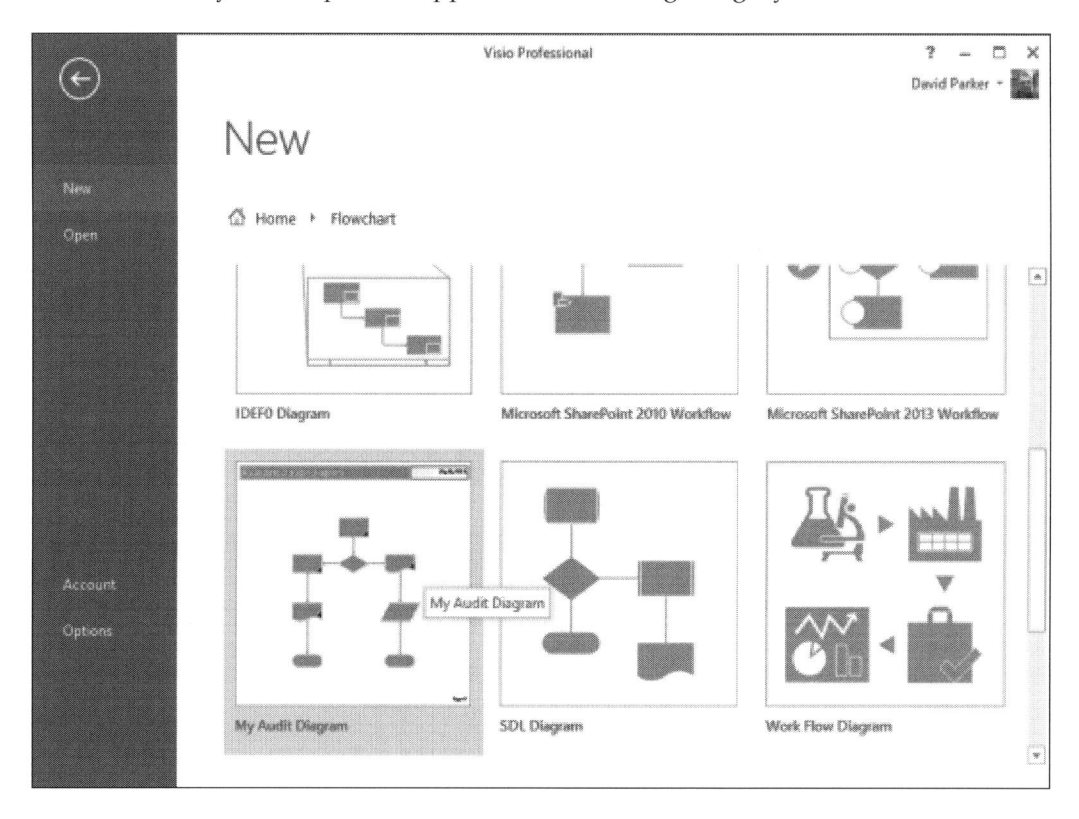

Of course, you do not have to have a separate installation package for each of your new templates, or even for multiple-language versions, because you can have multiple templates installed in one `.msi` file.

Also, the template could contain modified versions of standard Visio shapes, or even some extra ones on new stencils too. In this case there will be stencils to be deployed to the installation folder too; each stencil will require name and description enhancements entered in the WiX XML file.

And finally, if your rules are too complicated to be defined purely with the Filter and Test Expressions, then this method of installing custom templates could also contain custom validation code.

Uninstalling and Repairing

Once the template and\or stencils are installed, there may come a time when they need to be uninstalled. This can be done by running the installation `.msi` file again, or by selecting the program from the **Control Panel | Programs and Features** dialog:

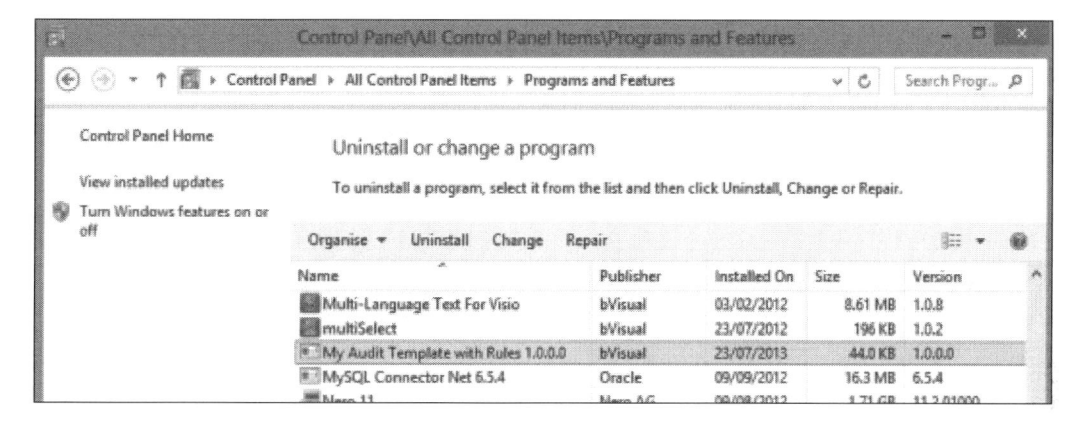

Summary

In this chapter we have learned two different ways of deploying custom Visio templates that contain validation rules. The first simple method does not require any extra tools besides Visio, but is more difficult to control. The second is more complex and requires additional skills and applications, but is more suitable for large-scale deployment and centralized control.

In the next and final chapter, we will walk through the creation and deployment of a new ruleset for **Data Flow Model Diagrams**. We will convert some plain English rules into ones that Visio can understand, in order to ensure that well-constructed diagrams are created.

9
A Worked Example for Data Flow Model Diagrams – Part 1

In the preceding chapters, we have learned about the Visio object model, the new Validation API, how to write validation rules, and how to publish these rules for others to use.

In this chapter, we are going to present a complete cycle for writing validation rules for the **Data Flow Model Diagram** methodology. I chose this template because there used to be an add-on associated with it in Visio; this add-on is unfortunately no longer provided, and there are no rules for it either.

Since we are going to produce a new template, we can then take the opportunity to enhance the master shapes too. This will provide some extra functionality, such as identifiers for each process, which could be used to detail the diagrams, and to make them suitable for export into other applications. I know that some of these enhancements are usually done by a ShapeSheet developer rather than a rules developer, but I have included fairly detailed steps because they give valuable insight into Visio shape behavior.

So, in this chapter, we will go through the following steps:

- Examining the existing template
- Making any shape enhancements we may want

What are Data Flow Diagrams?

The normal Visio user selects a Visio template from a category in the Backstage **Getting Started** view of the Visio user interface.

A quick search on the web reveals that **Data Flow Diagrams** (**DFDs**) are a graphical representation of the flow of data into, around, and out of a system:

`http://www.agilemodeling.com/artifacts/dataFlowDiagram.htm`

Throughout the seventies, various academics developed methodologies for modeling data flows. The one by **Gane and Sarson** is utilized in the **Data Flow Model Diagrams** template in Visio. This methodology has the following four elements:

- Squares representing external entities, which are the source or destination of the data. These are the places that provide the organization with data, or have data sent to them by the organization (for example, customers, partners, or government bodies).
- Rounded rectangles representing processes, which take data as input, perform an action with the data, and then produce an output.
- Arrows representing the data flows, which can be either electronic data or physical items. The arrows should be labeled with the name of the data that moves through it.
- Open-ended rectangles representing data stores, including electronic stores such as databases or XML files, and physical stores such as filing cabinets or stacks of paper. They can be manual, digital, or temporary.

With a dataflow diagram, developers can map how a system will operate, what the system will accomplish, and how the system will be implemented. It's important to have a clear idea of where and how data is processed in a system, to avoid double-handling and bottlenecks. A DFD also helps management organize, and prioritize data handling procedures and staffing requirements.

A DFD lets a system analyst study how existing systems work, locate possible areas prone to failure, track faulty procedures, and reorganize components to achieve better efficiency or effectiveness.

There are a number of rules that are commonly followed when creating DFDs:

1. All processes must have at least one data flow in and one data flow out.
2. All processes should modify the incoming data, producing new forms of outgoing data.
3. Each data store must be involved with at least one data flow.
4. Each external entity must be involved with at least one data flow.
5. A data flow must be attached to at least one process.
6. Data flows cannot go directly from one external entity to another external entity: such flows need to go through at least one process.

There are also a couple of conventions that could be considered:

1. Do not allow a single page of a data flow diagram to get too complex—it should have no more than ten components. If it has more than this, combine some components into a single, self-contained unit and create a new DFD for that unit.
2. Each component should be labeled with a suitable description.
3. Each data flow should be labeled describing the data flowing through it.
4. Each component and subcomponent should be numbered in a top-down manner.

Finally, there are two other connectivity rules that could be added:

1. A data flow must be connected to two data components.
2. A flow must not cycle back to itself.

Examining the standard template

You can find the standard **Data Flow Model Diagram** template in the Software and Databases category:

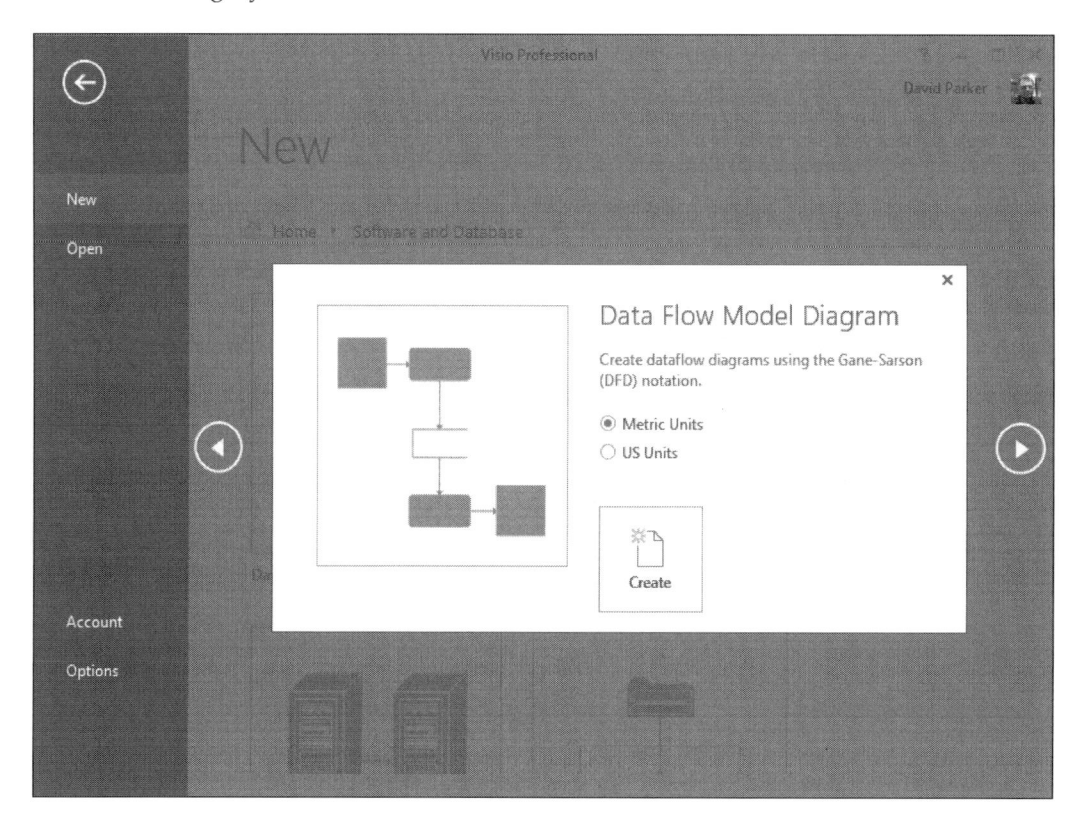

If you create a new document from this template, you will see that there are just four masters on the **Gane-Sarson** stencil, and there are no rules associated with it at all.

If you then drag-and-drop just one example of each shape onto the page, you will see that the graphics are not complicated either:

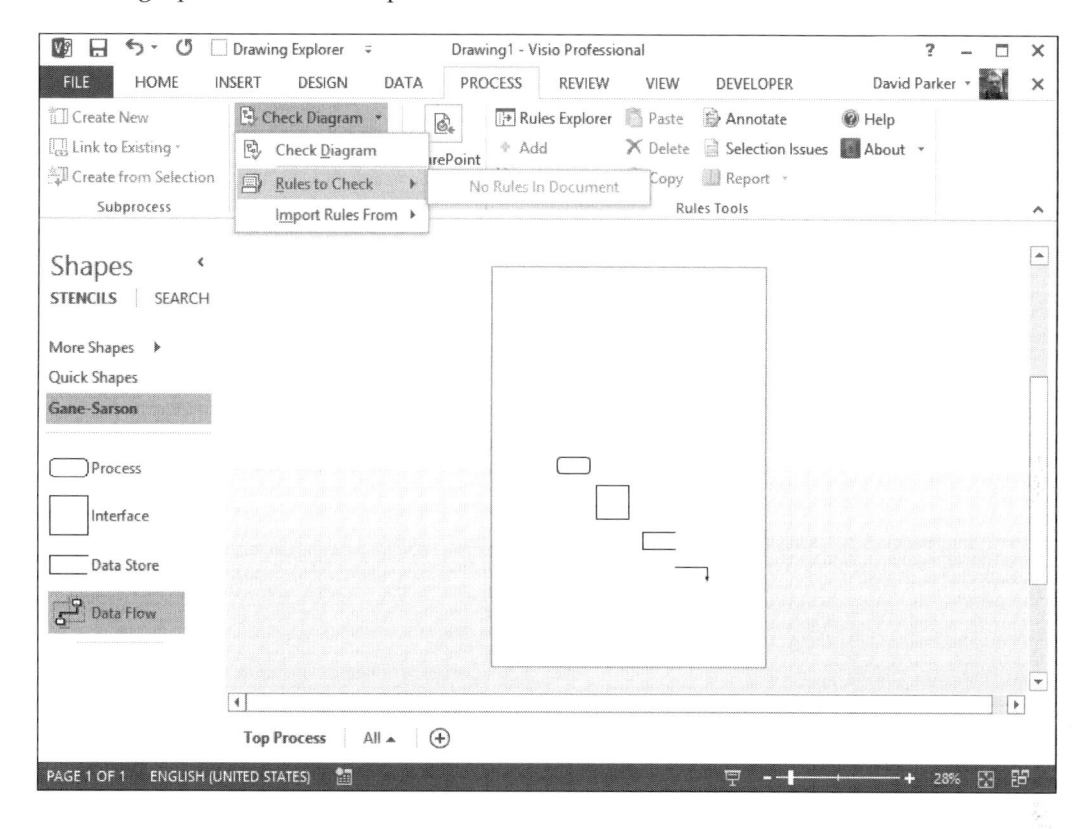

You now need to review the current shapes; one way to do this is to create a quick report in Visio. I started by reviewing the ShapeSheet of each of the shapes, and saw that each of them contains a few **User-defined Cells** that point to their role within UML diagrams. For example, the User.UMLShapeType cell contains a numerical value that specifies the type of UML shape and the User.visDescription cell contains a text description of this type.

A Worked Example for Data Flow Model Diagrams – Part 1

So, you can create a new report that lists all of the shapes on the current page using the **Shape Reports** button in the **Reports** group on the **REVIEW** tab. Then you can click on the **Advanced** button to open a dialog to set a filter. In this case, you can check for the existence of the `UMLShapeType` cell by selecting the `Value = TRUE` for the `Condition = exists`, before clicking on **Add**.

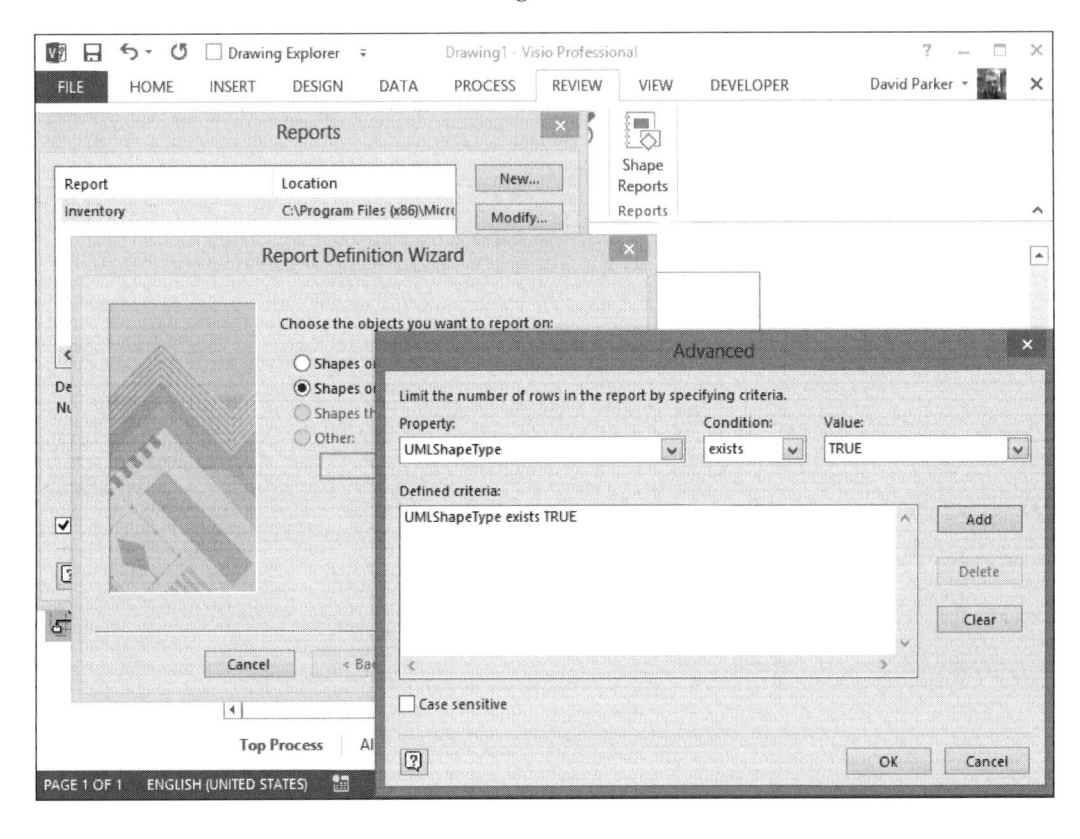

You can then proceed to select the properties that you want to display as columns in the report on the next panel. You should select `<MasterName>`, `UMLShapeType` and `visDescription`. You will need to tick the **Show all properties** option in order to see the last two, because user-defined cells are not displayed by default:

Chapter 9

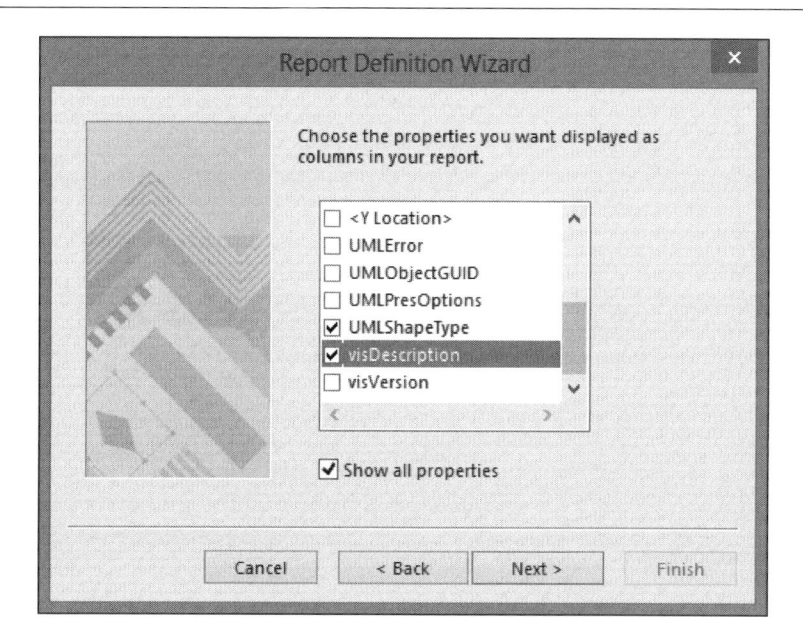

You can then proceed to save the report definition as, say **DFD Shapes**, and then run it as an Excel report format. You should get a report that looks like this:

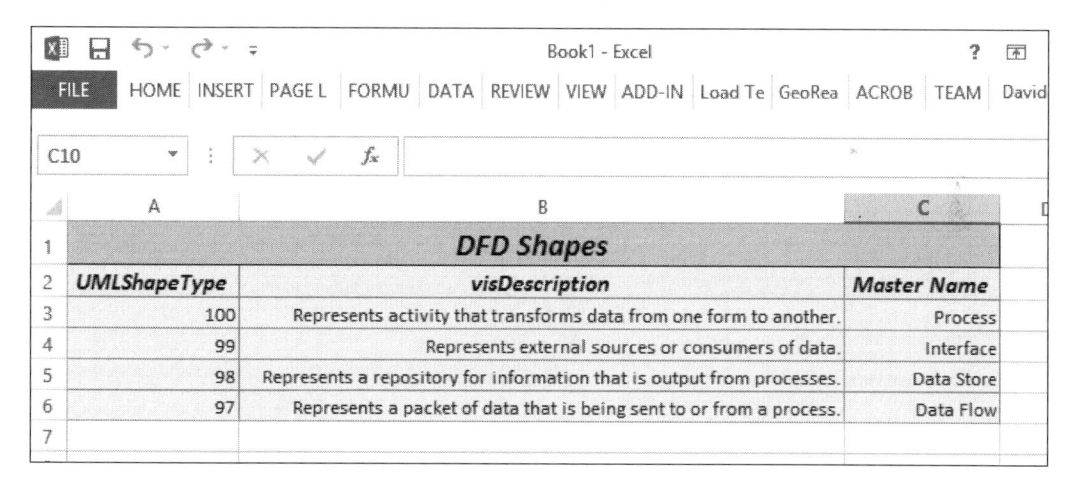

I changed the precision of the number format to 0, so that the **UMLShapeType** values did not have any decimal point.

Enhancing the masters

Before you start to enhance the masters in the document (not the original **Gane-Sarson** stencil), please open the **Master Properties** dialog for each of the four masters and tick the **Match master by name on drop** option. This will ensure that the enhanced masters will be used in this document, rather than the original masters, even if the user drags-and-drops from the original stencil. These enhanced masters will provide functionality that, in my humble opinion, should have been present in the Microsoft built-in masters. Since the built-in stencils and masters should not be edited, my approach is to provide enhanced masters in the custom template, and make the user employ the enhanced masters automatically, whenever they select a similarly named master from the built-in stencils.

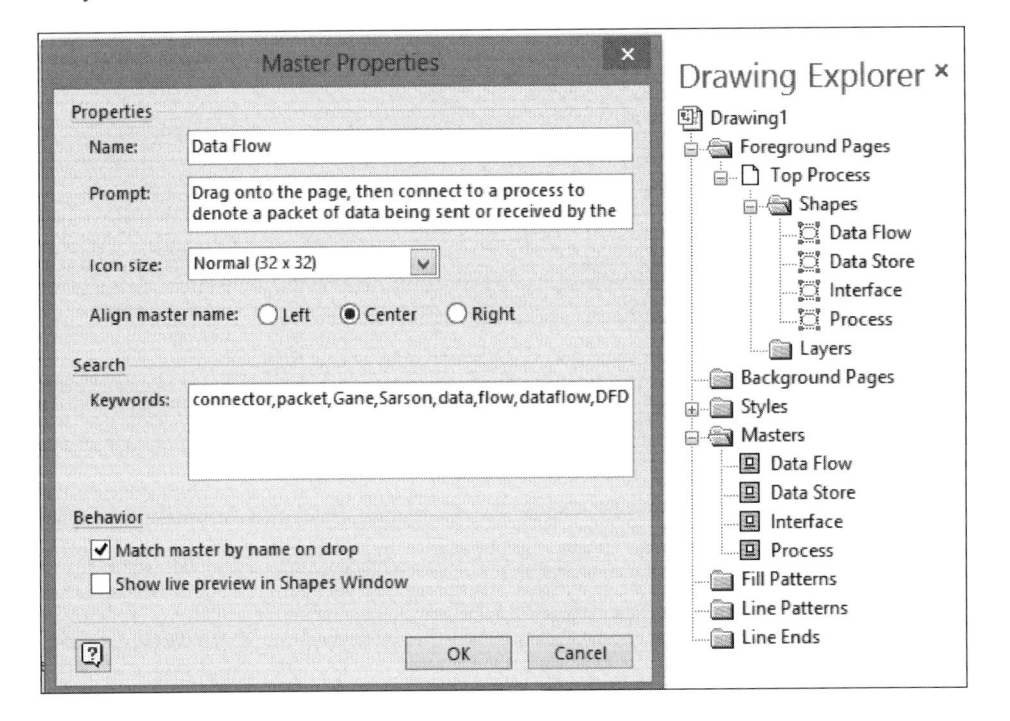

You can now edit each master in turn.

> You can access the masters in the document by using the **Drawing Explorer** window, which can be opened from the **Show/Hide** group on the **DEVELOPER** tab, or by ticking the **More Shapes \ Show Document Stencil** option in the **Shapes** window.

Editing the Data Flow master

The **Data Flow** master is used to connect the **Process**, **Interface**, and **Data Store** shapes. The user should enter some text on each **Data Flow** to name the data that is flowing along it. This description implies that the direction of flow is important, and that each data flow should be labeled appropriately. We can also enable some of the features in Visio, such as **connector splitting**, that were not available when the **Data Flow** master was first developed. This will improve the user experience because other shapes will be able to be dropped on top of a **Data Flow** shape and automatically insert themselves into the flow, rather than forcing the **Data Flow** shape to re-route around it.

The **Data Flow** shape looks like a simple connector with an arrow head denoting the flow direction:

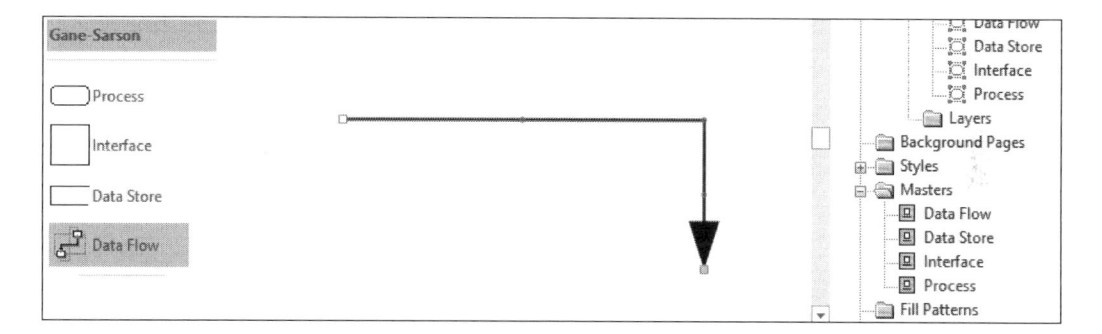

Now open the master shape by selecting **Edit Master Shape** on the right-mouse menu of the **Data Flow** node, in the **Masters** branch of the **Drawing Explorer** window.

Then ensure that the **Master Explorer** window is open, and select the shape.

A Worked Example for Data Flow Model Diagrams – Part 1

These shapes were created for an earlier version of Visio, before Microsoft added the ability for the 2D shapes to automatically split the 1D connectors when they are dropped on them. It would be useful to add this capability to the **Data Flow** shape by modifying its behavior. Click on the **Behavior** button in the **Shape Design** group of the **DEVELOPER** tab. Tick the **Connector can be split by shapes** option.

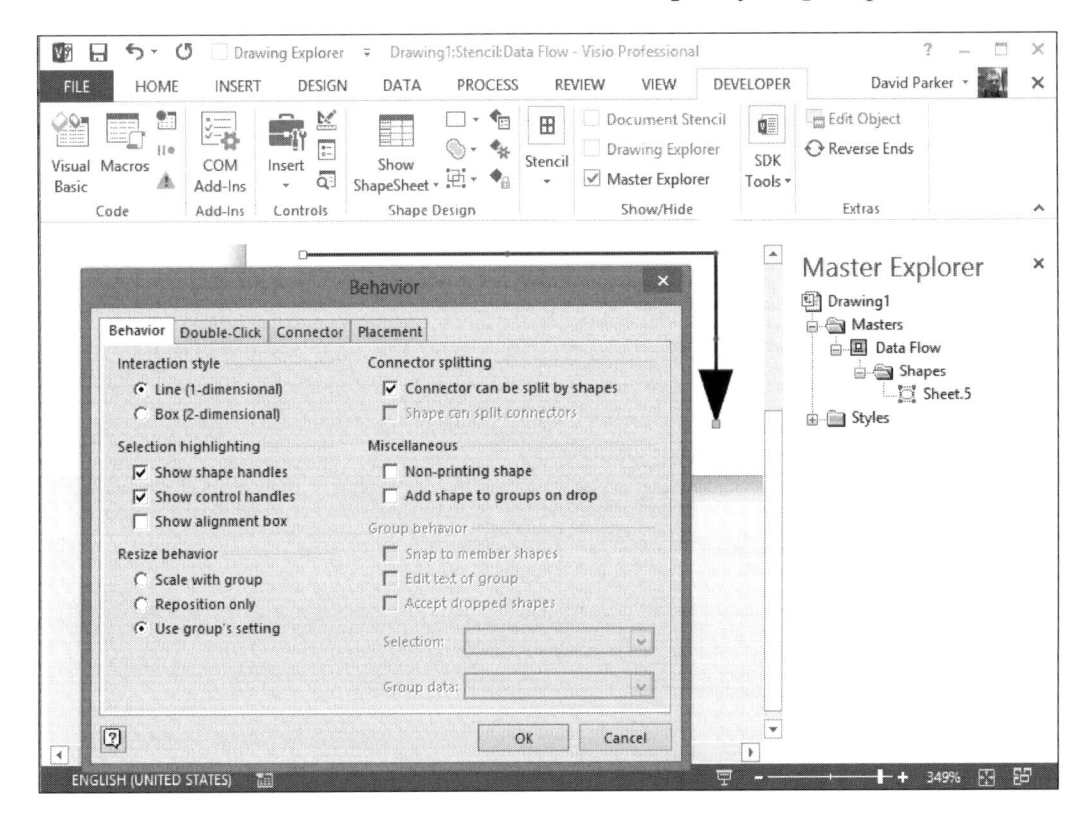

You can now click on the **OK** button of the dialog and close the master edit window.

Preparing for AutoConnect

You will want to ensure that the user does indeed use the **Data Flow** shape to connect the DFD shapes together. Therefore, we need to understand how a user can make connections.

The easiest method is to use the **AutoConnect** feature. This displays blue triangles around an existing shape as you hover over it. These triangles can be used to connect to an existing adjacent shape or even to drop a new shape by using the **Quick Shapes** selector.

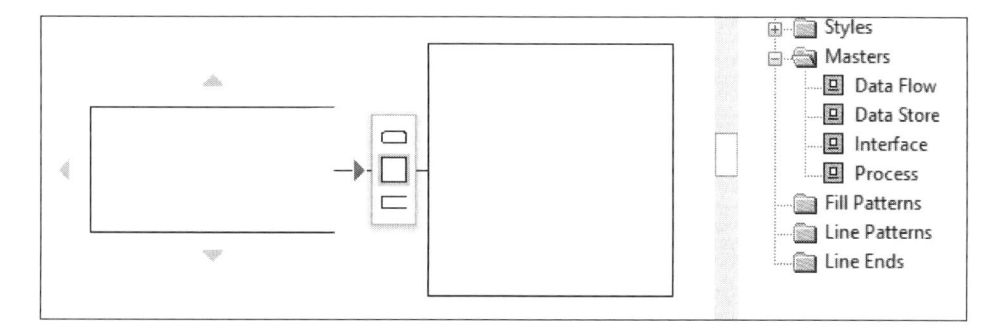

However, there is an unfortunate consequence of using this feature, as it will automatically create and use a new master called **Dynamic connector**.

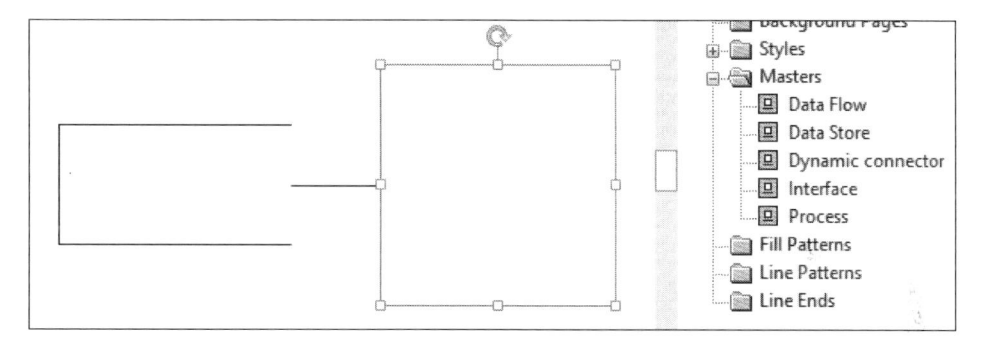

The **Dynamic connector** master is a rare hardcoded master in Visio, and it is also used by the **Connector Tool** in the **Tools** group on the **HOME** tab, unless you have preselected an alternative connector master on the active stencil.

Therefore, we need to anticipate how Visio works, and avoid having the wrong connector between our shapes. To do this, we will change the `NameU` of the **Data Flow** connector.

A Worked Example for Data Flow Model Diagrams – Part 1

So, first ensure that there is no **Dynamic connector** master present in the document (*CTRL + Z* to Undo the previous action), and then open the **Immediate** window in the VB Editor (*ALT + F11*).

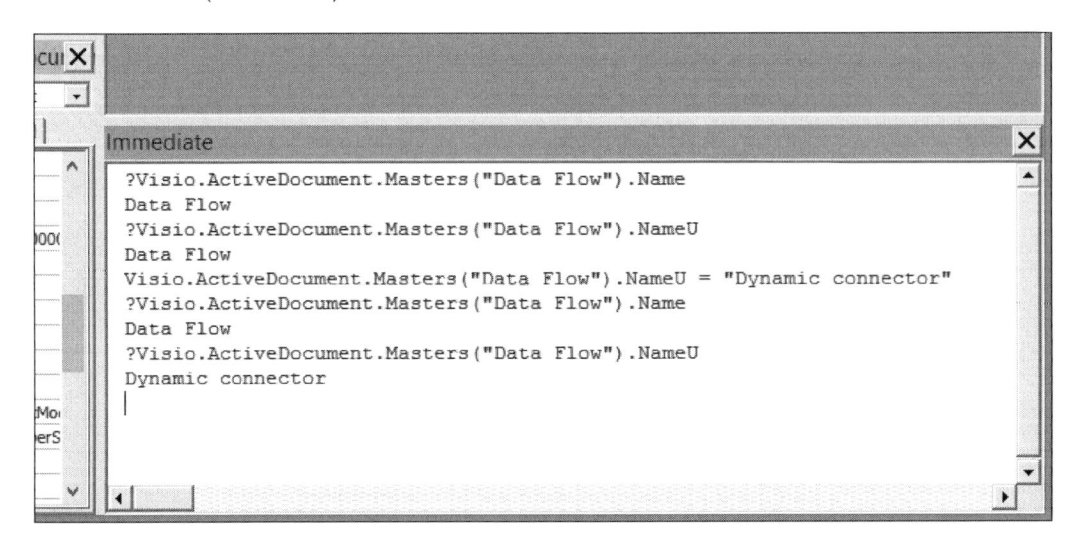

```
?Visio.ActiveDocument.Masters("Data Flow").Name
Data Flow
?Visio.ActiveDocument.Masters("Data Flow").NameU
Data Flow
Visio.ActiveDocument.Masters("Data Flow").NameU = "Dynamic connector"
?Visio.ActiveDocument.Masters("Data Flow").Name
Data Flow
?Visio.ActiveDocument.Masters("Data Flow").NameU
Dynamic connector
```

Initially, if you type `?Visio.ActiveDocument.Masters("Data Flow").Name` or `?Visio.ActiveDocument.Masters("Data Flow").NameU` in the **Immediate** window, then you will get the words **Data Flow** on the response line.

If you then type `Visio.ActiveDocument.Masters("Data Flow").NameU = "Dynamic connector"` into the window, and repeat the first two lines, you will find that `NameU` is now **Dynamic connector**.

Now, when you use the **Quick Shapes**, **AutoConnect**, or the **Connector Tool**, you should find that the **Data Flow** master is used in all cases!

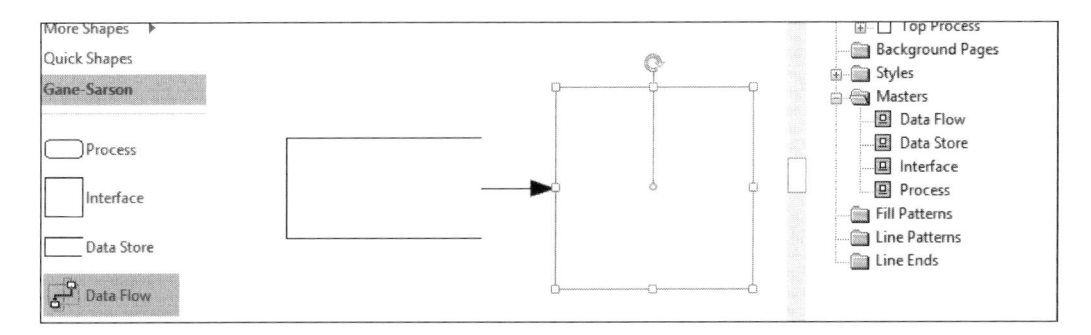

Editing the Data Store master

The **Data Store** master looks like an open-ended rectangle but we would like it to include an optionally displayed square that will display the **ID** of the store. Therefore, we will need to add Shape Data, and some extra graphics that will contain the ID text. The display of these extra items will be toggled according to a Shape Data row that we will put into the page.

Select **Edit Master Shape** from the right mouse menu on the **Data Store** master in the **Document Explorer** window, and you will see that the shape is a very simple three-sided rectangle:

Adding Shape Data

While looking at examples of DFDs on the web, it is clear that there is an alternate appearance for the Data Store shape that has a square containing an identifier to the left of the shape. Therefore, we can take the opportunity to add this option to the shape.

Since we need to have two distinct text areas in the shape, it will need to be a group shape. Therefore, select the shape in the **Master Edit** window and then select **Convert to Group** from the **Group** dropdown in the **Arrange** group of the **HOME** tab. It is important to convert to a group rather than just grouping the shape, because converting will maintain the user-defined cells at the top-level shape. You should notice a subtle change in the icon of the **Sheet.5** shape in the **Master Explorer** window after you have converted it to a group.

In order to provide the user with the option to display the ID boxes on the shape, I am suggesting that you should add a **Boolean Shape Data** row to the page.

A Worked Example for Data Flow Model Diagrams – Part 1

So, on the **VIEW** tab. open the **Shape Data** window from the **Task Panes** dropdown in the **Show** group. Alternatively, you can tick the **Shape Data Window** option on the **Show/Hide** group on the **DATA** tab. Then select the page by clicking on the gray area around the shape.

You will see that there is no shape data in the **Shape Data** window; thus, open the **Define Shape Data** dialog from the right-mouse menu on the header caption of this window.

You need to enter the following text into the boxes on the **Define Shape Data** dialog:

- **Label**: Display DFD IDs
- **Name**: DisplayID
- **Type**: Boolean
- **Value**: True
- **Prompt**: Select True to display the IDs in the DFD shapes

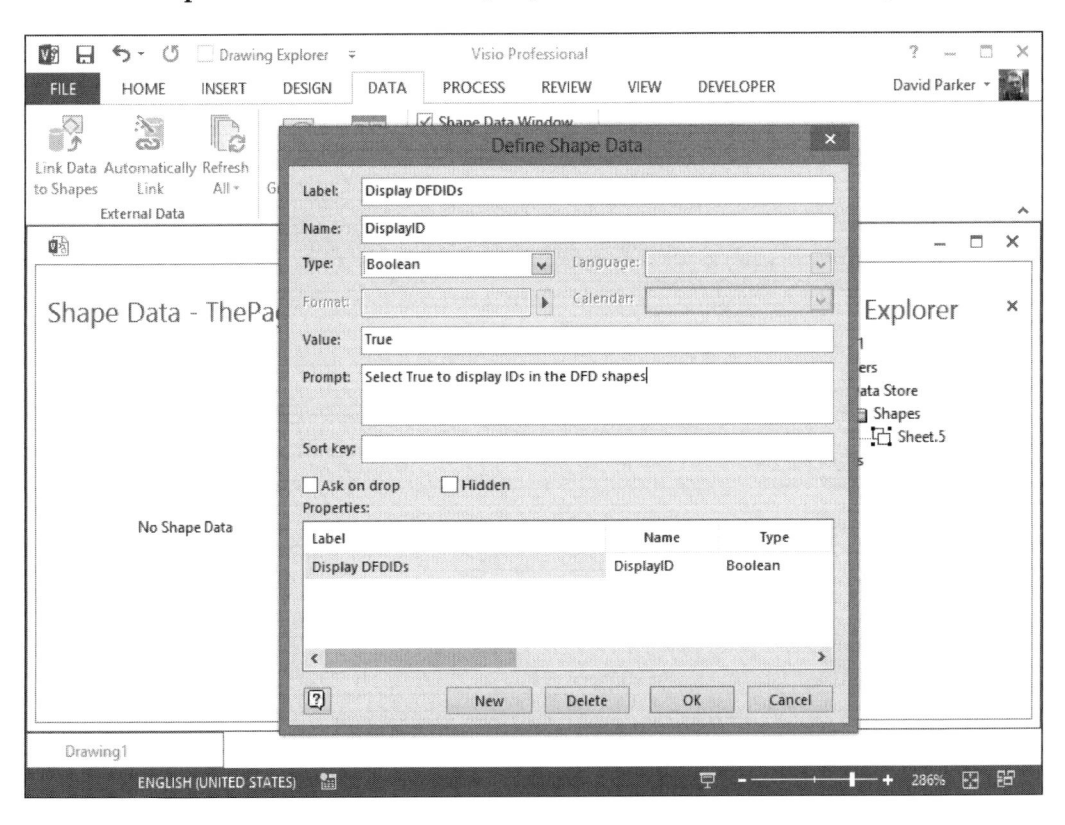

> If you do not see the **Name** text box in the **Define Shape Data** dialog, then you have not ticked **Run** in developer mode on the **File** | **Options** | **Advanced** panel.

Click on **OK** to save this Shape Data in the page of the master. Now, you need to add a new **Shape Data** row called **ID** to the shape itself by selecting it and then opening the **Define Shape Data** as before. You will need to add a Shape Data row named **ID** to the shape (called **Sheet.5**) shown as follows:

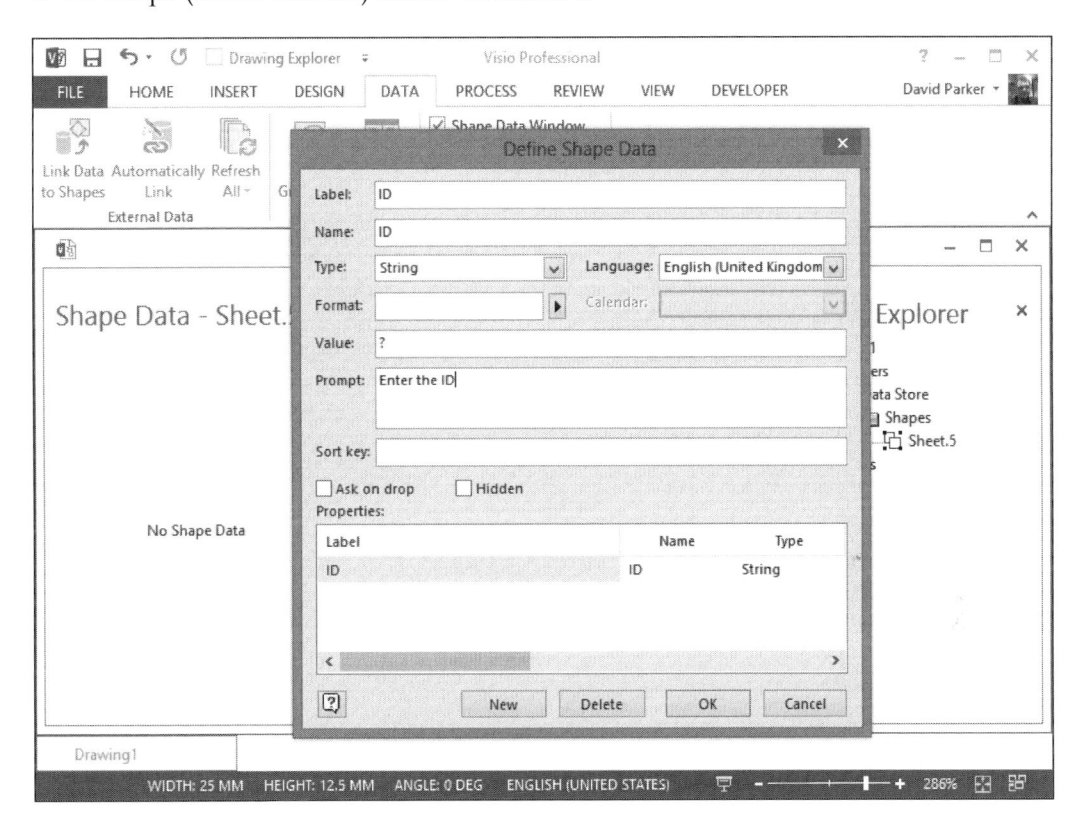

Enter a question mark for the **Value**, just for testing purposes.

Creating Shape Data using the **Define Shape Data** dialog actually adds rows to the Shape Data section in the ShapeSheet. You can only enter text, not formulae, into these ShapeSheet cells using the **Define Shape Data** dialog, so you will need to open the ShapeSheet of the shape.

You should edit the formula in the **Invisible** cell of the **Prop.ID** shape data row as:

`=NOT(ThePage!Prop.DisplayID)`

This will ensure that the **Prop.ID** shape data row is only visible if the value of the **Prop.DisplayID** shape data row is `True` for the page.

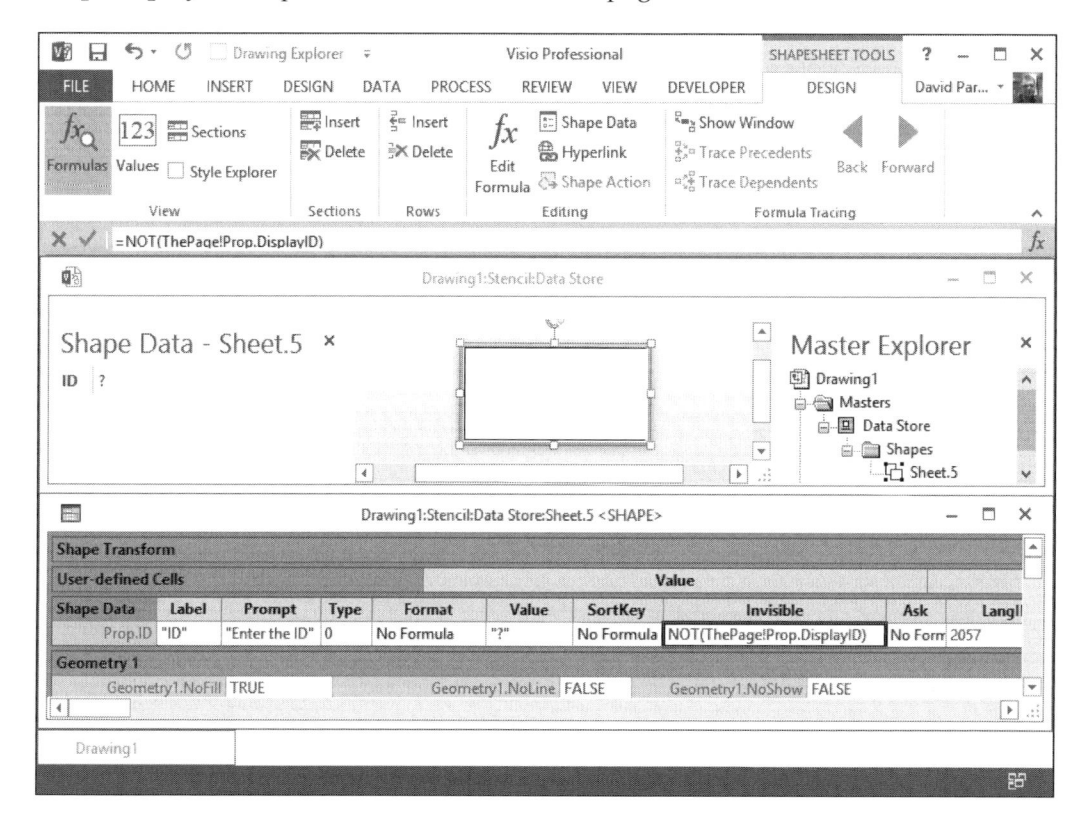

Enhancing the graphics

You now need to add a square into this master, so go to **Group | Open Group** from the right-mouse menu on the master shape. Now roughly draw a square using the **Rectangle** button on the **Tools** group of the **HOME** tab. You could change the **Line Weight** to ½ `pt` at this stage, using the right-mouse menu item **Format | Line**.

Displaying the ID value

Navigate to **Insert | Field** to add `Custom Formula =Sheet.5!Prop.ID`. This will ensure that the text inside the rectangle always displays the value of the **Prop.ID** shape data row, in the top level of the group:

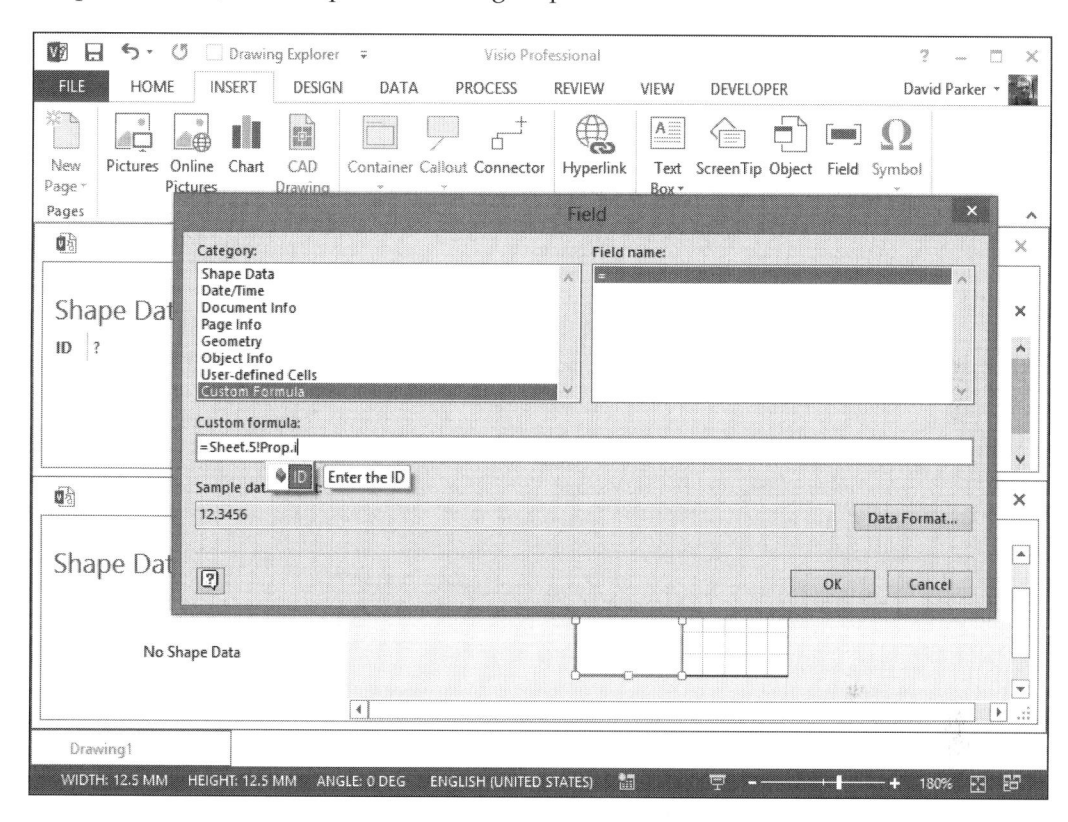

There are several formulae that you now need to edit in the ShapeSheet of the rectangle shape, to ensure that it is always the right size and location, and to control the visibility of the lines and text.

In the **Shape Transform** section of the ShapeSheet, enter the formula `=Sheet.5!Height*1` in the **Width** and **Height** cells, and then enter the formula `=Sheet.5!Height*0.5` in the **PinX** and **PinY** cells. This will ensure that this subshape is a square aligned to the left edge of the main shape.

A Worked Example for Data Flow Model Diagrams – Part 1

In the **Geometry1.NoShow** and **Miscellaneous.HideText** cells, enter the formula `=NOT(ThePage!Prop.DisplayID)`.

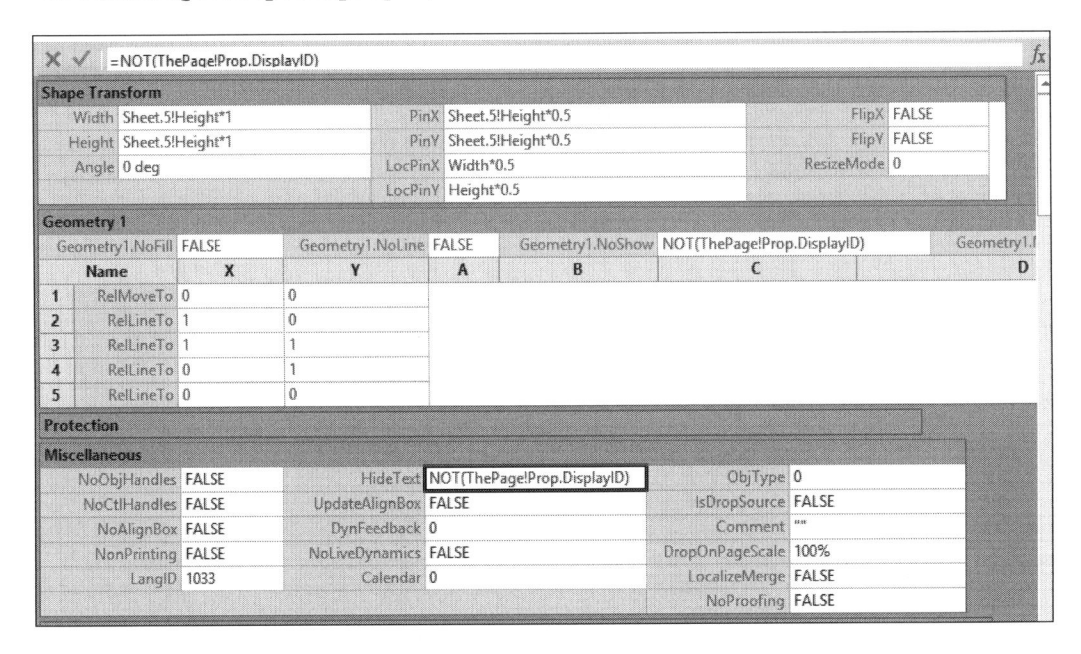

You can now close the ShapeSheet and group edit window, in order to return to the main **Data Store** shape.

Improving the group shape

Use the **Size & Position** window, that can be opened from the **View | Task Panes** menu or by clicking on the **Height**, **Width**, or **Angle** display in the status bar, to enlarge the shape width to 35 mm.

> You can open the **Page Setup** dialog from the right-mouse menu of the **Data Store** node in the **Master Explorer** window in order to change the page size to match the shape size, if you want.

Enter some temporary text into the shape, and then use the **Text Block** tool, on the **Home** | **Tools** group, to roughly resize the text block by selecting and moving one of the corners or midpoints of its edges.

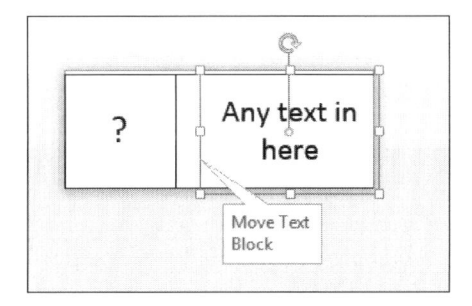

This last action will cause a new section, **Text Transform**, to be created in the ShapeSheet of this shape.

Navigate to this section and edit the **TxtWidth** cell formula to:

=GUARD(Width-IF(ThePage!Prop.DisplayID,Height*1,0))

Then edit the **TxtPinX** formula to:

=GUARD(TxtWidth*0.5+IF(ThePage!Prop.DisplayID,Height*1,0))

Close the ShapeSheet and click on the **Behavior** button on the **Shape Design** group on the **DEVELOPER** tab. In the **Group behavior** section, untick the **Snap to member shapes** option, then change the **Selection** to **Group only**. Also tick the **Shape can split connectors** option.

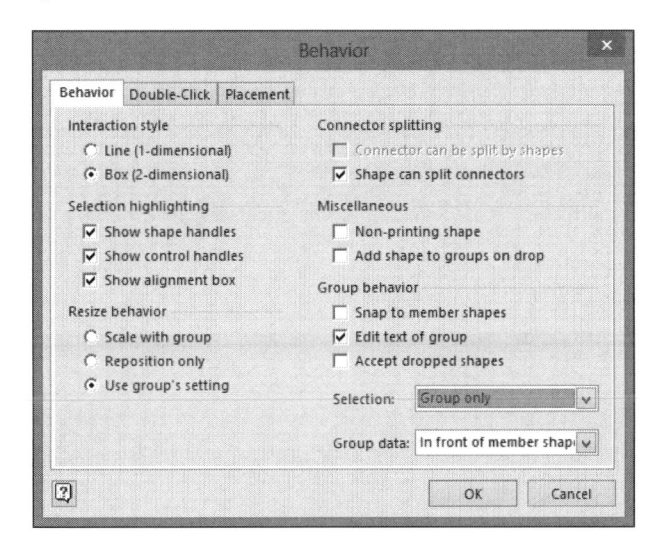

[311]

You can now delete the temporary text in the main shape, and the question mark in the **Prop.ID** shape data row using the **Shape Data** window. Close and save the **Data Flow** master.

Editing the Interface master

The **Interface** shape is used to represent external entities that are the source or destination of data. The only change required is to tick the **Shape can split connectors** option on the **Behavior** dialog, as for the **Data Store** master, so that the shape can automatically split the **Data Flow** connector when dropped on it. Optionally, you can convert the shape to a group, too, since any future use of Data Graphics will do this automatically.

Editing the Process master

The **Process** shape takes data as input and then transforms it in some way, before sending it as output.

The **Process** master looks like a rounded rectangle, but we would like it to include an optionally displayed header area that will display the **ID** of the process, and an optional footer area that will display **Category**. Therefore, we will need to add Shape Data and some extra graphics that will contain the **ID** and **Category** text. The display of these extra items will be toggled according to a Shape Data row that we will put into the page.

Adding Shape Data

Edit the **Process** master shape, and add a **Prop.DisplayID** shape data row to the page, just as you did for the **Data Store** shape. Convert the shape to a group and add a **Prop.ID** shape data row, also as you did to the **Data Store** shape. However, you should also add a new **Shape Data** row, called Category, with a String data type.

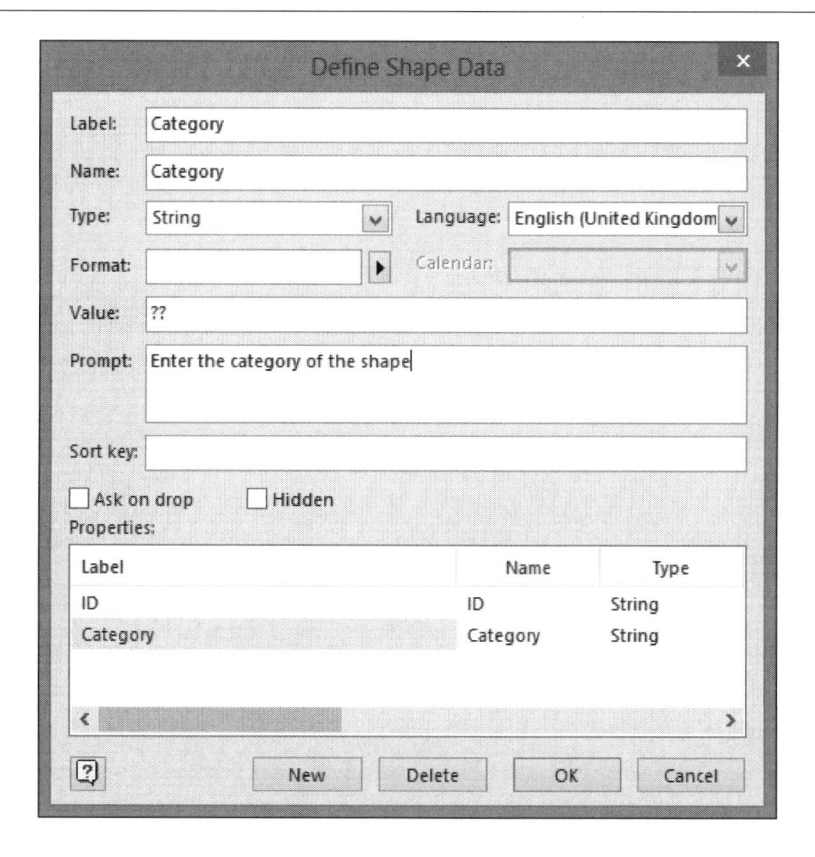

As before with the Data Store master, you should add the page Shape Data row; now open the ShapeSheet and edit the **Invisible** cell of these two shape data rows and enter the formula:

```
=NOT(ThePage!Prop.DisplayID)
```

Enhancing the graphics

Now you need to have the **ID** optionally displayed at the top of the shape, and the **Category** optionally displayed at the bottom of the shape. In the earlier **Data Store** shape, you added a new rectangle into the group shape, and you were able to see this rectangle and the text inside it. This worked because the group shape did not have any fill pattern. However, the **Process** shape is a solid shape, and therefore you need to remove the fill pattern. To do this, open the ShapeSheet of the Process shape, scroll to the **Geometry1** section, and change the **Geometry1.NoFill** formula to True.

A Worked Example for Data Flow Model Diagrams – Part 1

Having removed the fill from the group shape, you now need to add a new shape inside the group that can have a fill pattern. So, as with the Data Store shape, open the group, draw a rough rectangle, then show the ShapeSheet of this rectangle.

You should now edit the formula of Width =Sheet.5!Width*1, Height =Sheet.5!Height*1, PinX =Sheet.5!Width*0.5, and PinY =Sheet.5!Height*0.5. Then edit Geometry1.NoLine = True, and Rounding = Sheet.5!Rounding in the **Line Format** section.

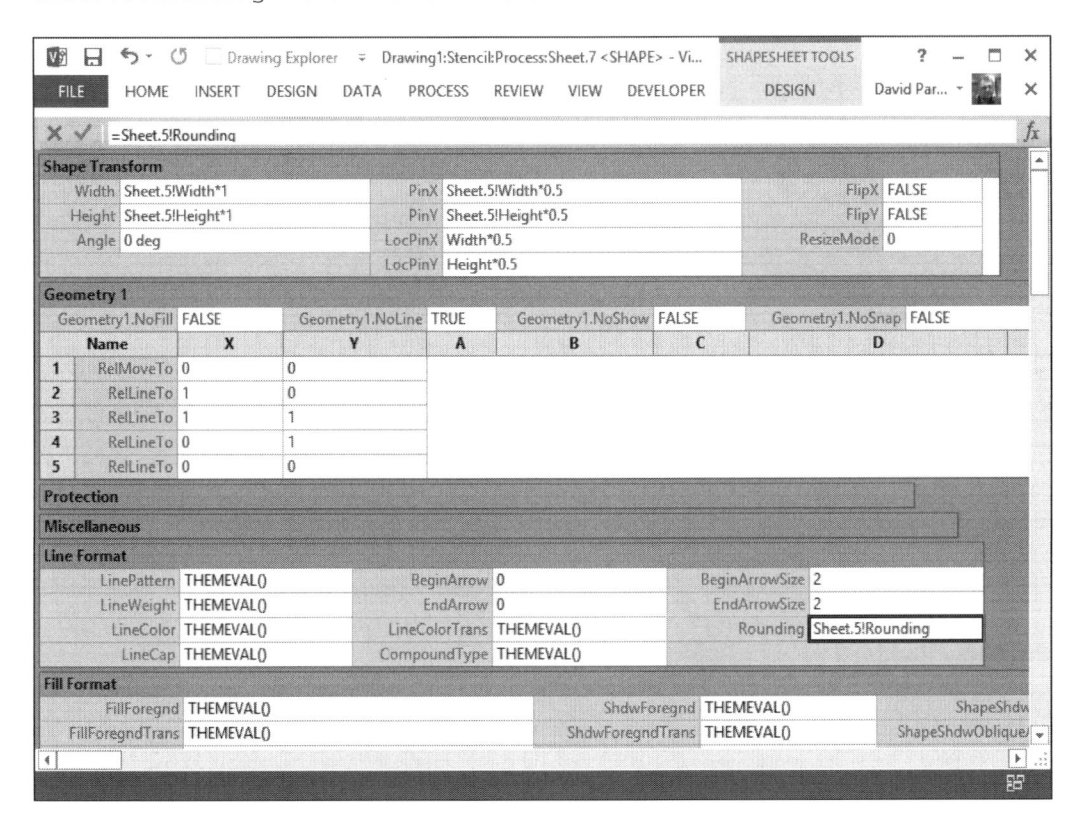

Displaying the ID value

Now you need to optionally display the **Prop.ID** value above a line at the top of the shape, so draw a line inside the group, creating another shape like the rectangle, then insert the =Sheet.5!Prop.ID formula using the **Insert | Field** action, just as for the **Data Store** shape. Then open the ShapeSheet and scroll down to the **Text Block Format** section to edit the **TextBkgnd** as 0, **VerticalAlign** as 2, and both **TopMargin** and **BottomMargin** as 0 pt.

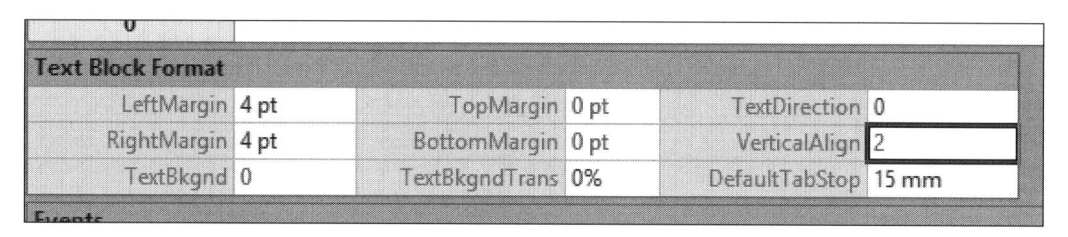

Text Block Format					
LeftMargin	4 pt	TopMargin	0 pt	TextDirection	0
RightMargin	4 pt	BottomMargin	0 pt	VerticalAlign	2
TextBkgnd	0	TextBkgndTrans	0%	DefaultTabStop	15 mm

Then scroll back up to the **1-D Endpoints** section to edit the **BeginY** and **EndY** formula `=Sheet.5!Height*1-TEXTHEIGHT(TheText,750)`, and the **BeginX** as `0`; and **EndX** as `Sheet.5!Width*1`:

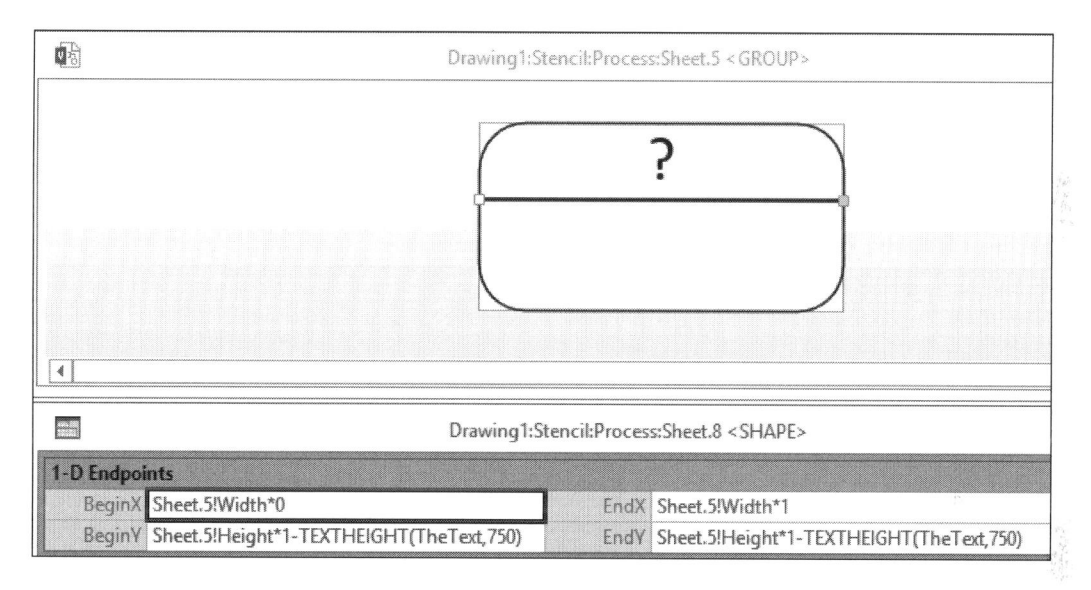

1-D Endpoints			
BeginX	Sheet.5!Width*0	EndX	Sheet.5!Width*1
BeginY	Sheet.5!Height*1-TEXTHEIGHT(TheText,750)	EndY	Sheet.5!Height*1-TEXTHEIGHT(TheText,750)

Lastly, you need to set the visibility of the line and text, as earlier, by inserting the formula `=NOT(ThePage!Prop.DisplayID)` into the **Geometry1.NoShow** cell and the **HideText** cell in the **Miscellaneous** section.

Displaying the Category value

Close the ShapeSheet, and then duplicate the line (*Ctrl* + *D*).

Open the ShapeSheet of this new line and scroll down to the **Text Block Format** section to change the **VerticalAlign** value to `0`.

Scroll up to the **Text Fields** section and change the **Value** cell to `=Sheet.5!Prop.Category`.

[315]

A Worked Example for Data Flow Model Diagrams – Part 1

Then scroll back up to the **1-D Endpoints** section to edit the **BeginY** and **EndY** formula `=TEXTHEIGHT(TheText,750)` and the `BeginX=0`, and **EndX**=`Sheet.5!Width*0`.

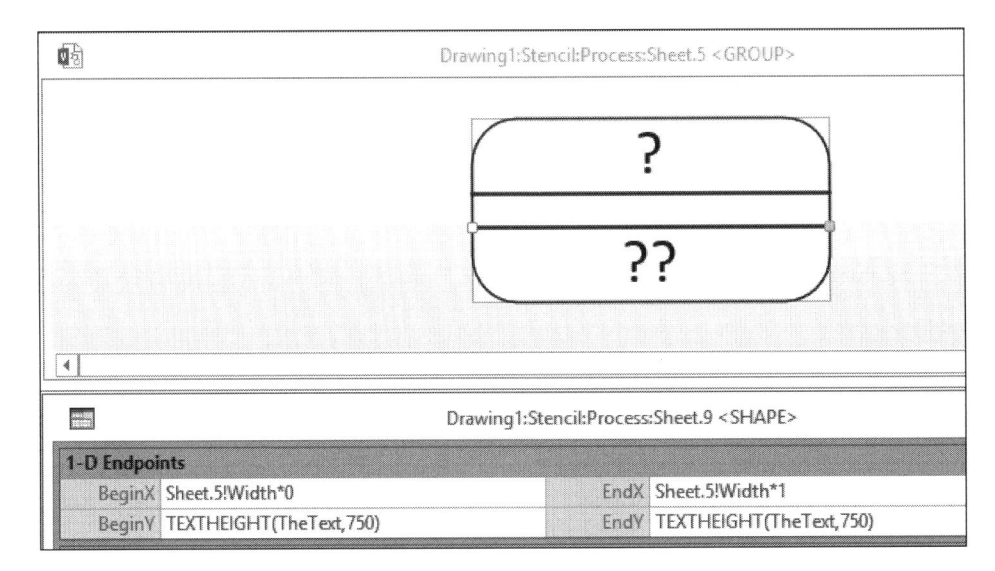

BeginX	Sheet.5!Width*0	EndX	Sheet.5!Width*1
BeginY	TEXTHEIGHT(TheText,750)	EndY	TEXTHEIGHT(TheText,750)

You can now close the ShapeSheet and the group window.

Improving the group shape

Use the **Size & Position** window to enlarge the shape to 35 mm wide, and 20 mm high.

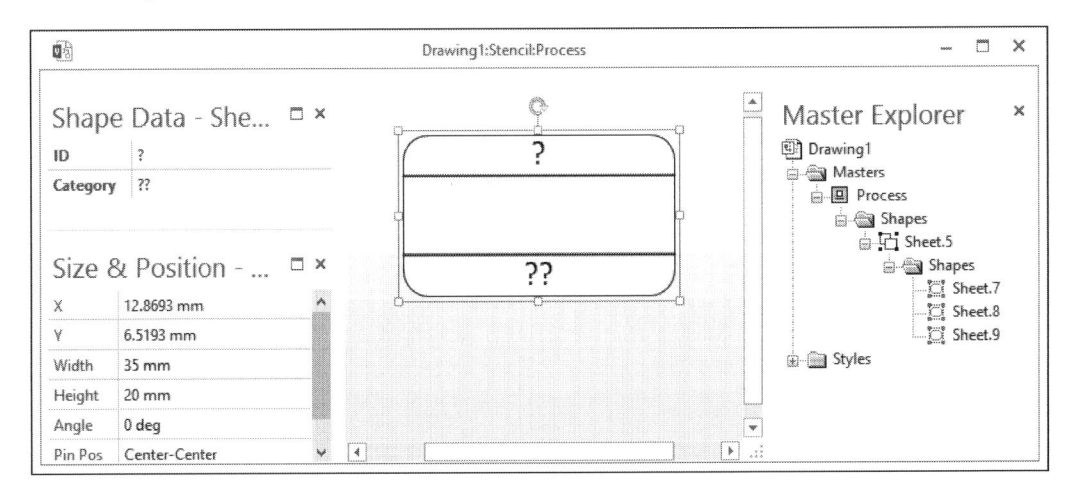

Again, click on the **Behavior** button on the **Shape Design** group on the **DEVELOPER** tab. In the **Group behavior** section, untick the **Snap to member shapes** option and then change the **Selection** to **Group only**. Also tick the **Shape can split connectors** option.

You can now delete the question mark(s) in the **Prop.ID** and **Prop.Category** shape data row using the **Shape Data** window; then close and save the **Process** master.

Setting the Subprocess master

Visio 2013 Professional edition has the ability to create a subprocess from a selection of shapes. Similar to the **AutoConnect** feature discussed earlier, an unnecessary master can be accidentally created by its use.

For example, if you select a few shapes on a document, the **Create from Selection** button is enabled in the **Subprocess** group on the **PROCESS** tab.

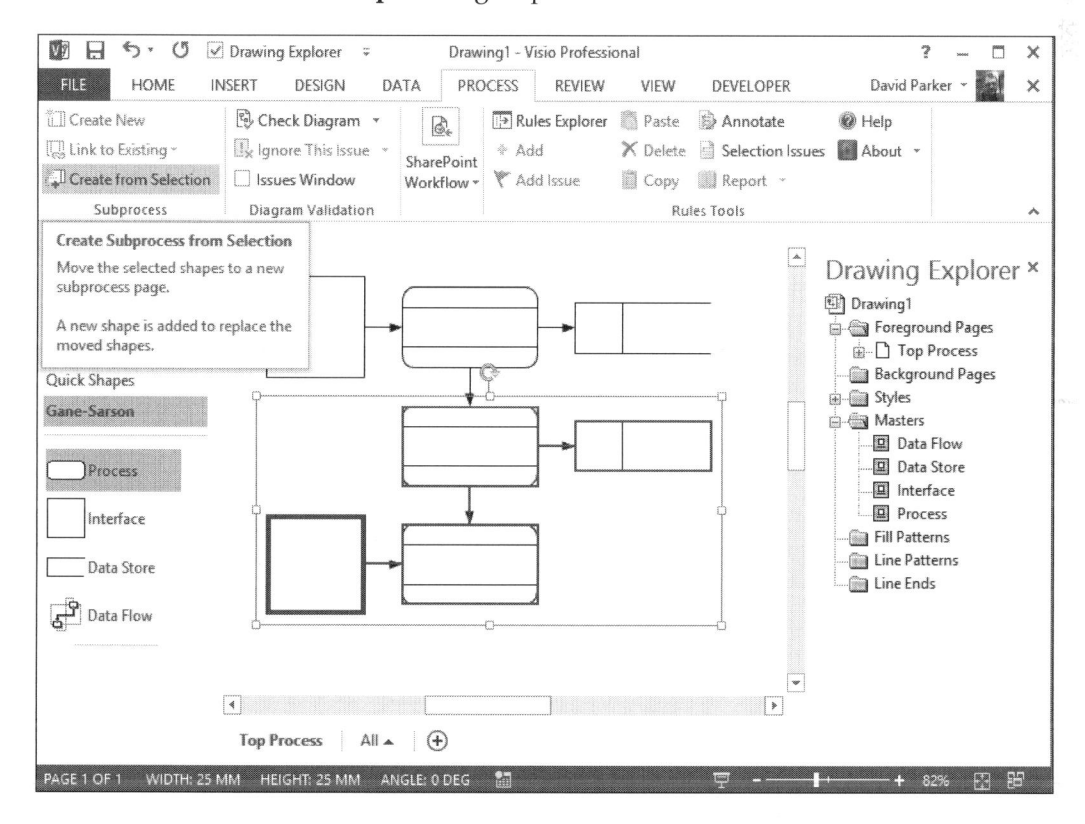

A Worked Example for Data Flow Model Diagrams – Part 1

Clicking on this button will move the selected shapes to a new page and replace them with a subprocess shape in their place, with a hyperlink to the new page.

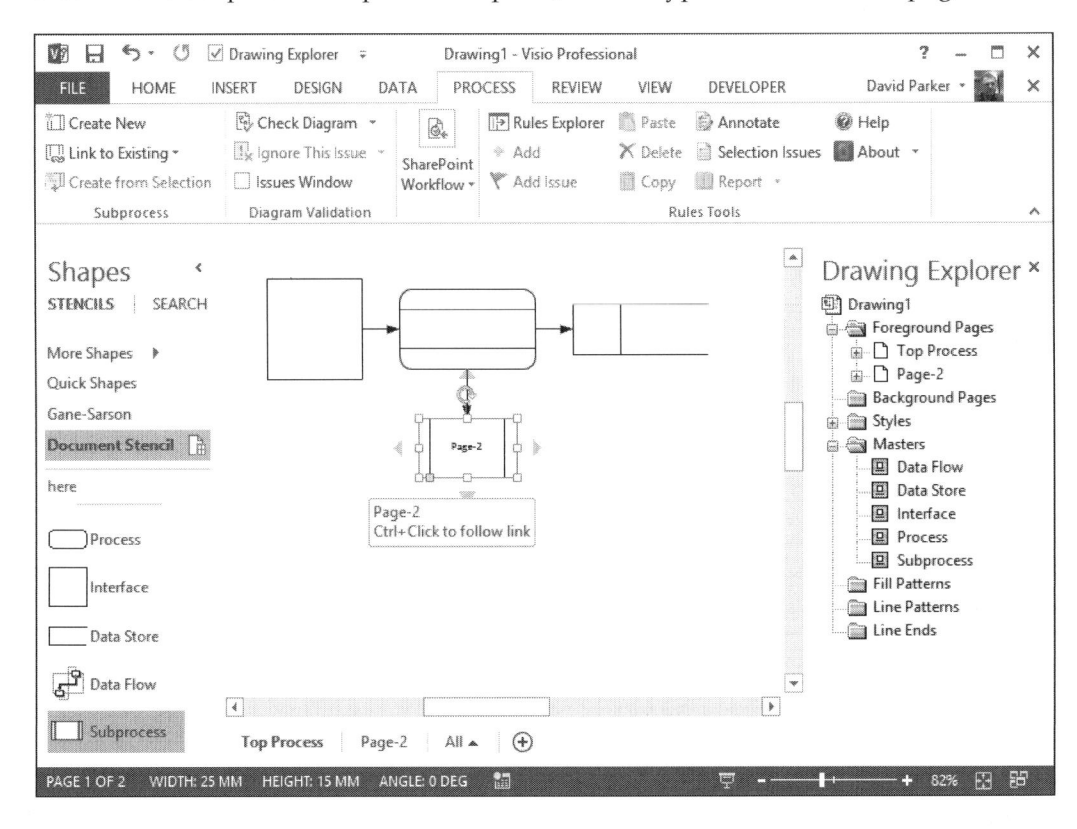

By default, a standard subprocess shape is used. We can change the default as follows:

Open the ShapeSheet from the right-mouse menu of the document node in the **Drawing Explorer** window. Create a new user-defined row and name it `msvSubprocessMaster`, then enter the formula `"Process"`.

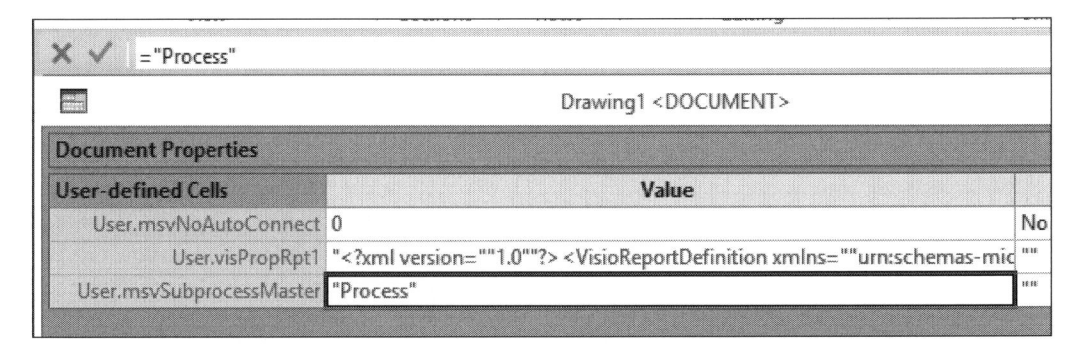

Now, when you use the **Subprocess** actions, you will find that your modified **Process** master is used.

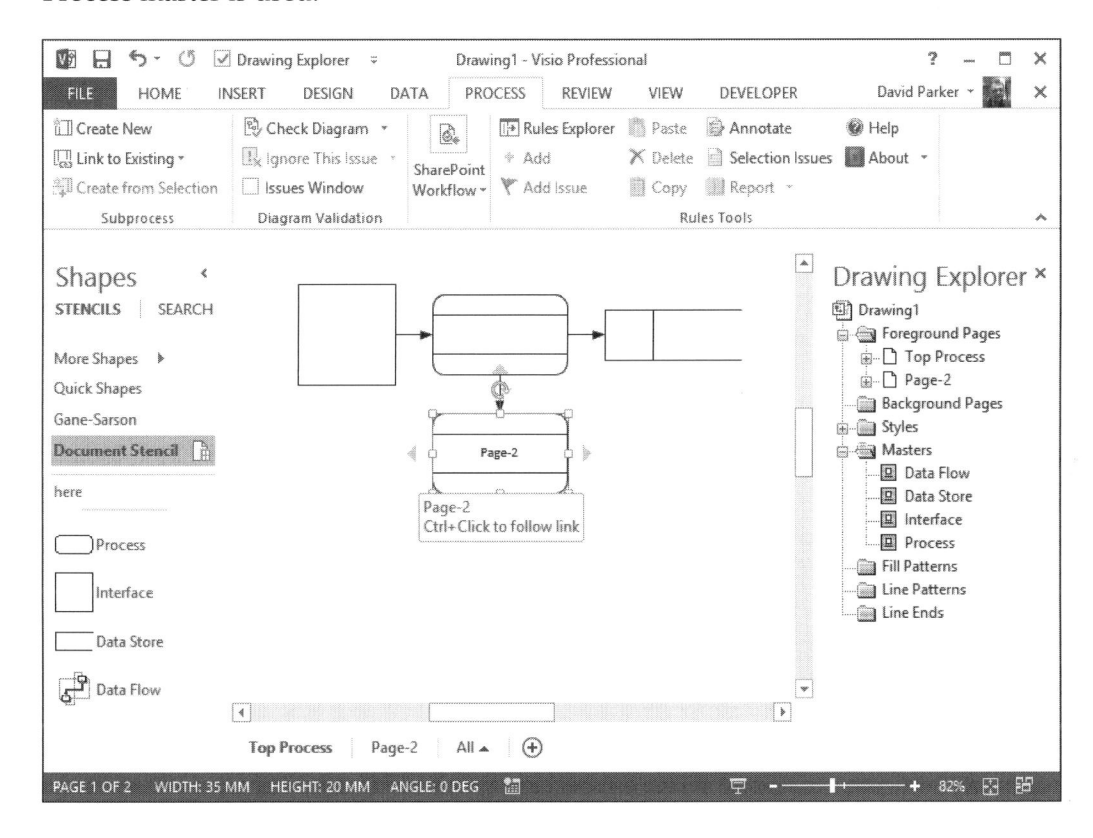

Now save your document!

Enhancing the page

Since you have increased the size of a couple of the master shapes, you should now check the layout options for the page. You can take the opportunity to tweak the default spacing of shapes and connectors, as well as allowing shapes to split the connectors.

A Worked Example for Data Flow Model Diagrams – Part 1

So, select **Page Setup** from the right-mouse menu of the page node in the **Drawing Explorer** window. Tick the **Enable connector splitting** on the **Layout and Routing** tab.

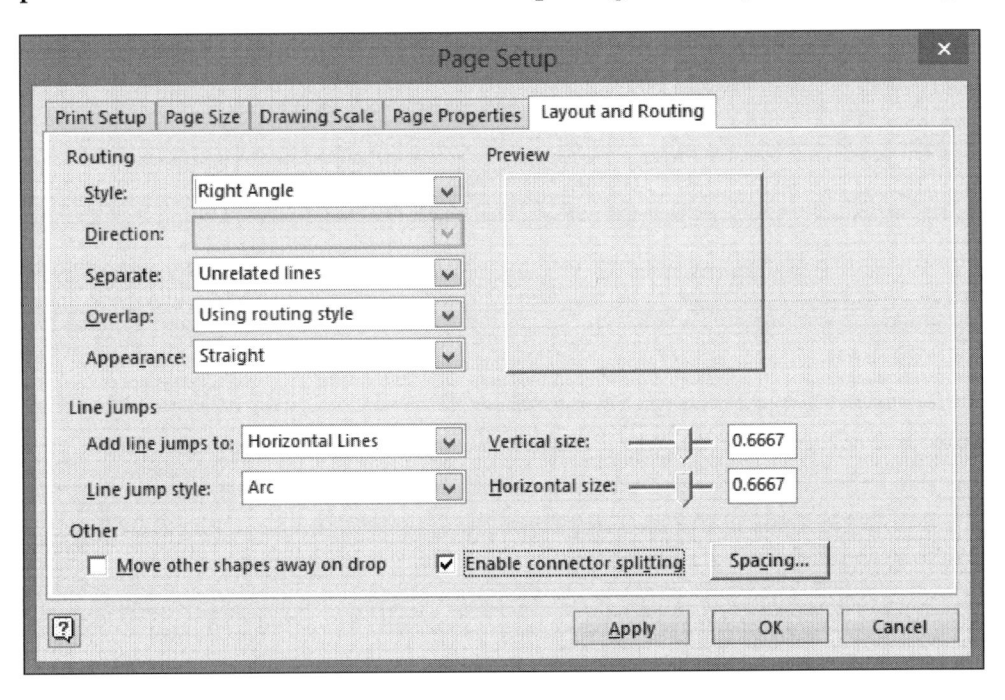

Select the **Spacing** button to open the **Layout and Routing Spacing** dialog. You should enter suitable values for each of the settings. Of course, mine are shown in millimeters, but you could enter yours in inches (7.5 mm = 0.29 in, 15 mm = 0.59 in, 20 mm = 0.79 in, 25 mm = 0.98 in).

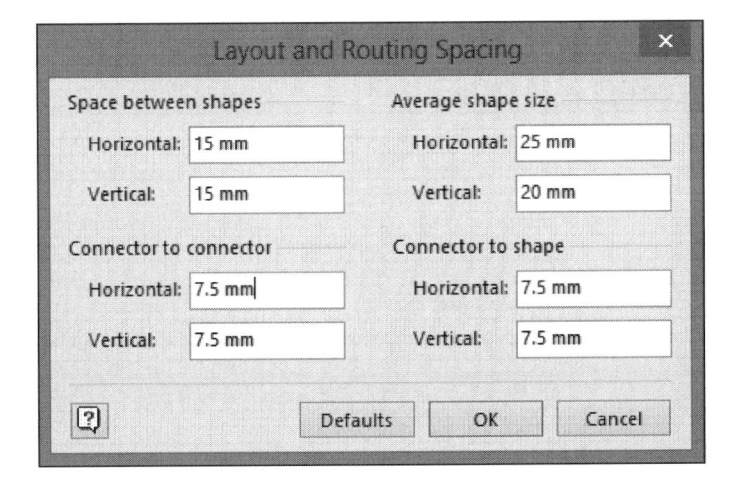

Click on **OK** to close both dialogs.

You have ensured that the Data Flow connector can be split by a suitable 2D shape, and that the three 2D shapes are splitters. You should also check that **Enable connector splitting** is ticked in the **Editing options** on the **File | Options | Advanced** panel.

Now when a user drops a DFD shape over an existing connector shape, it will automatically split and reconnect to the added shape.

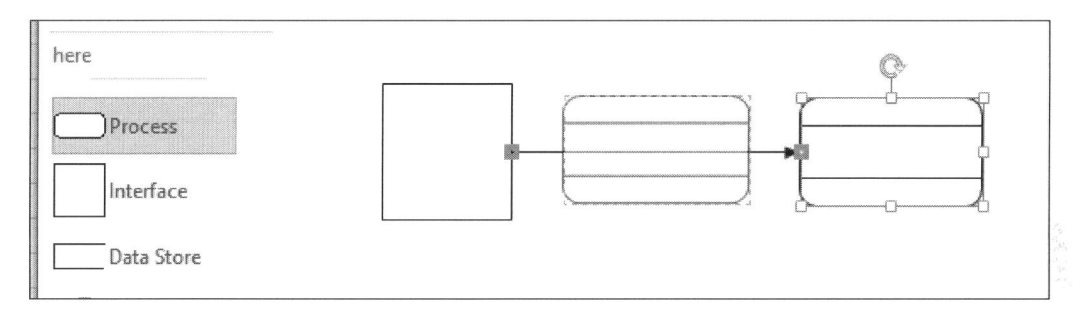

Summary

In this chapter, we have examined an existing template in order to make any changes that we need to make to the shape and page for our rules to work. We have enhanced the graphics and shape data to suit our requirements, and to improve the user experience. This involved adding Shape Data and user-defined cells to the page and masters; it also involved enabling some behaviors that were introduced to Visio after the original masters were developed.

We now have customized shapes that are ready to have rules applied to them. Thus, in the next chapter, we will analyze and write the ruleset that will satisfy all of the rules that we identified for Data Flow Diagrams at the start of this chapter.

10
A Worked Example for Data Flow Model Diagrams – Part 2

In the previous chapter, we listed the potential rules for the **Gane and Sarson** data flow diagrams, then we enhanced the masters in the Microsoft supplied **Data Flow Model Diagram** template. We also created a report to list the four DFD shapes, showing their unique values in the User.UMLShapeType cell.

In this chapter, we will go through each of the 12 rules in detail, and write a rule to enable us to validate the diagram for each one.

Writing the ruleset

In *Chapter 4, Understanding the Validation API* you learned how to write VBA code to add a ruleset and rules; although you could repeat this throughout the rest of this chapter, I prefer to use the user interface that we developed in *Chapter 6, Reviewing Validation Rules and Issues* and *Chapter 7, Creating Validation Rules*. Therefore, you will need to install the **Rules Tools** add-in, or run the **Validation Explorer** solution from Visual Studio 2012, in order to write the rules easily. However, I have included VBA methods to add (or update) the ruleset and rules; these can be written into the VBA project of any Visio document but should be run when the document that you want to add the rules to is active.

Open the **Rules Explorer** window from the **Rules Tools** group on the PROCESS tab.

A Worked Example for Data Flow Model Diagrams – Part 2

With your document node selected in the **Rules Explorer** window, click on the **Add** button then enter the **Name**, **NameU**, and **Description** of this new ruleset.

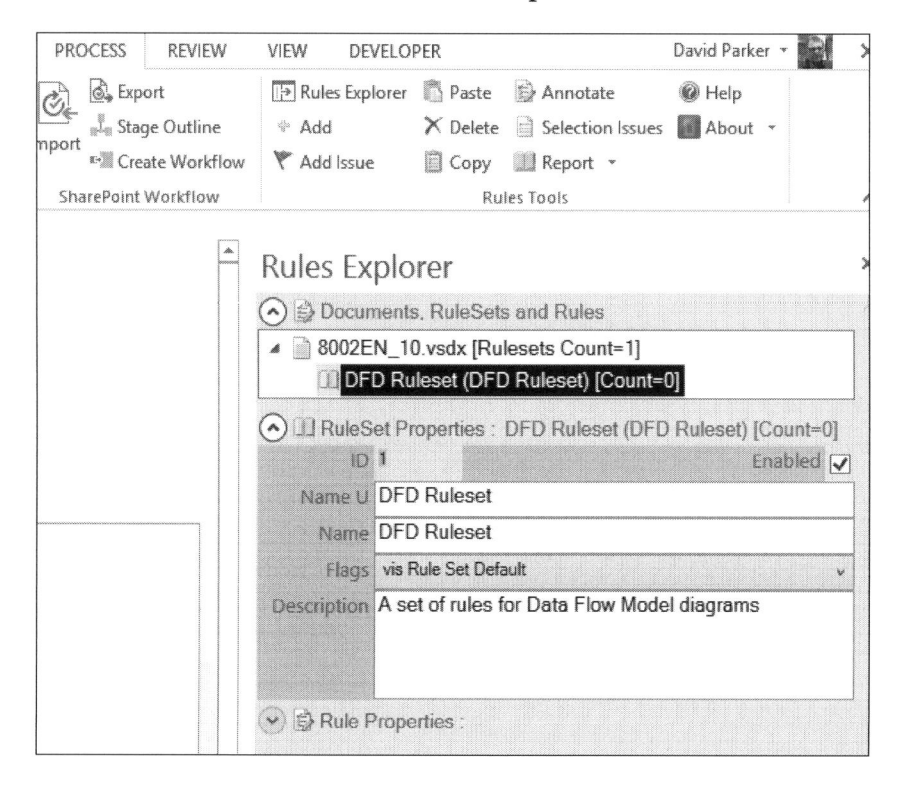

You can now add each of the new rules, by translating the previous descriptions into validation formulae.

The equivalent VBA code is listed as follows, adapted from the code in *Chapter 4, Understanding the Validation API* (and requires the `getRuleSet()` method from there):

```
Public Sub AddOrUpdateRuleSet()
Dim ruleSet As Visio.ValidationRuleSet
Dim ruleSetNameU As String
Dim doc As Visio.Document
    Set doc = Visio.ActiveDocument
    ruleSetNameU = "DFD Ruleset"
    'Check if the rule set exists already
    Set ruleSet = getRuleSet(doc, ruleSetNameU)
    If ruleSet Is Nothing Then
        'Create the new rule set
        Set ruleSet = doc.Validation.RuleSets.Add(ruleSetNameU)
    End If
```

```
    ruleSet.Name = "DFD Ruleset"
    ruleSet.Description = _
        "A set of rules for Data Flow Model diagrams"
    ruleSet.Enabled = True
    ruleSet.RuleSetFlags = visRuleSetDefault

    'Uncomment a method below as required
    'AddOrUpdateRule1 ruleSet
    'AddOrUpdateRule2 ruleSet
    'AddOrUpdateRule3 ruleSet
    'AddOrUpdateRule4 ruleSet
    'AddOrUpdateRule5 ruleSet

    'AddOrUpdateRule7 ruleSet
    'AddOrUpdateRule8 ruleSet
    'AddOrUpdateRule9 ruleSet
    'AddOrUpdateRule10 ruleSet

    'AddOrUpdateRule11 ruleSet
    'AddOrUpdateRule12 ruleSet
End Sub
```

Rule 1 – all processes must have at least one data flow in and one data flow out

A **Process** shape, `User.UMLShapeType=100`, must have the count of both the incoming and outgoing glued **Data Flow** connectors, `User.UMLShapeType=97`, greater than zero shown as follows:

- **Name U**: `ProcessInOut`
- **Category**: `Connectivity`
- **Target Type**: `vis Rule Target Shape`
- **Description**: `All processes must have at least one data flow in and one data flow out`
- **Filter Expression**: `User.UMLShapeType =100`
- **Test Expression**: `AND(AGGCOUNT(FILTERSET(GLUEDSHAPES(1),"User.UMLShapeType=97"))>0,AGGCOUNT(FILTERSET(GLUEDSHAPES(2),"User.UMLShapeType=97"))>0)`

A Worked Example for Data Flow Model Diagrams – Part 2

> The parameter for the `GluedShapes()` method has the values of the constant `Visio.VisGluedShapesFlags.visGluedShapesIncoming1D` (1) and `Visio.VisGluedShapesFlags.visGluedShapesOutgoing1D` (2).

You can test this rule by having a Process shape without any Data Flow connections; with only one Data Flow connection; or, as shown, with more than one Data Flow connection in the same direction:

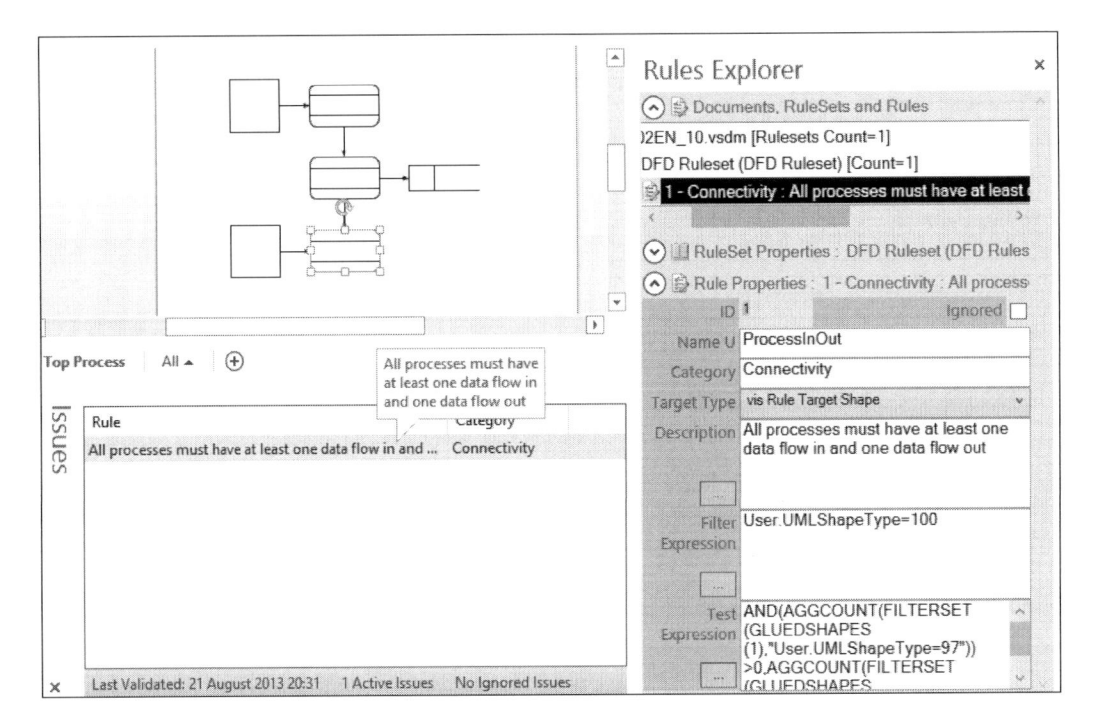

The equivalent VBA code is listed as follows, adapted from the code in *Chapter 4, Understanding the Validation API* (and requires the `getRule()` method from there):

```
Public Sub AddOrUpdateRule1( _
ByVal ruleSet As Visio.ValidationRuleSet)
Dim rule As Visio.ValidationRule
Dim ruleNameU As String
    ruleNameU = "ProcessInOut"
    Set rule = getRule(ruleSet, ruleNameU)
    If rule Is Nothing Then
        Set rule = ruleSet.Rules.Add(ruleNameU)
    End If
    rule.Category = "Connectivity"
```

```
        rule.Description = _
            "All processes must have at least one data flow in and one
data flow out"
        rule.TargetType = visRuleTargetShape
        rule.FilterExpression = _
            "User.UMLShapeType=100"
        rule.TestExpression = _
            "AND(AGGCOUNT(FILTERSET(GLUEDSHAPES(1),""User.UMLShapeType=97"
")) >0,AGGCOUNT(FILTERSET(GLUEDSHAPES(2),""User.UMLShapeType=97""))>0)"
End Sub
```

Rule 2 – all processes should modify the incoming data, producing new forms of the outgoing data

In other words, a Process shape must take input from a DFD component, and also send output to a DFD component.

A **Process** shape, `User.UMLShapeType=100`, must have the count of both the incoming and outgoing connected DFD components, `User.UMLShapeType=98` or `User.UMLShapeType=99` or `User.UMLShapeType=100`, greater than zero shown as follows:

- **Name U**: `ProcessToDFD`
- **Category**: `Connectivity`
- **Target Type**: `vis Rule Target Shape`
- **Description**: `A Process shape must take input from a DFD component, and also send output to a DFD component`
- **Filter Expression**: `User.UMLShapeType=100`
- **Test Expression**: `AND(AGGCOUNT(FILTERSET(CONNECTEDSHAPES(1 ),"OR(User.UMLShapeType=98,User.UMLShapeType=99,User.UM LShapeType=100)"))>0,AGGCOUNT(FILTERSET(CONNECTEDSHAPES (2),"OR(User.UMLShapeType=98,User.UMLShapeType=99,User. UMLShapeType=100)"))>0)`

> The parameter for the `ConnectedShapes()` method has the values of the constant `Visio.VisConnectedShapesFlags. visConnectedShapesIncomingNodes (1)` and `Visio.VisConnectedShapesFlags. visConnectedShapesOutgoingNodes (2)`.

A Worked Example for Data Flow Model Diagrams – Part 2

You can test this rule by having a Process shape connected with the Data Flow connectors to non-DFD shapes:

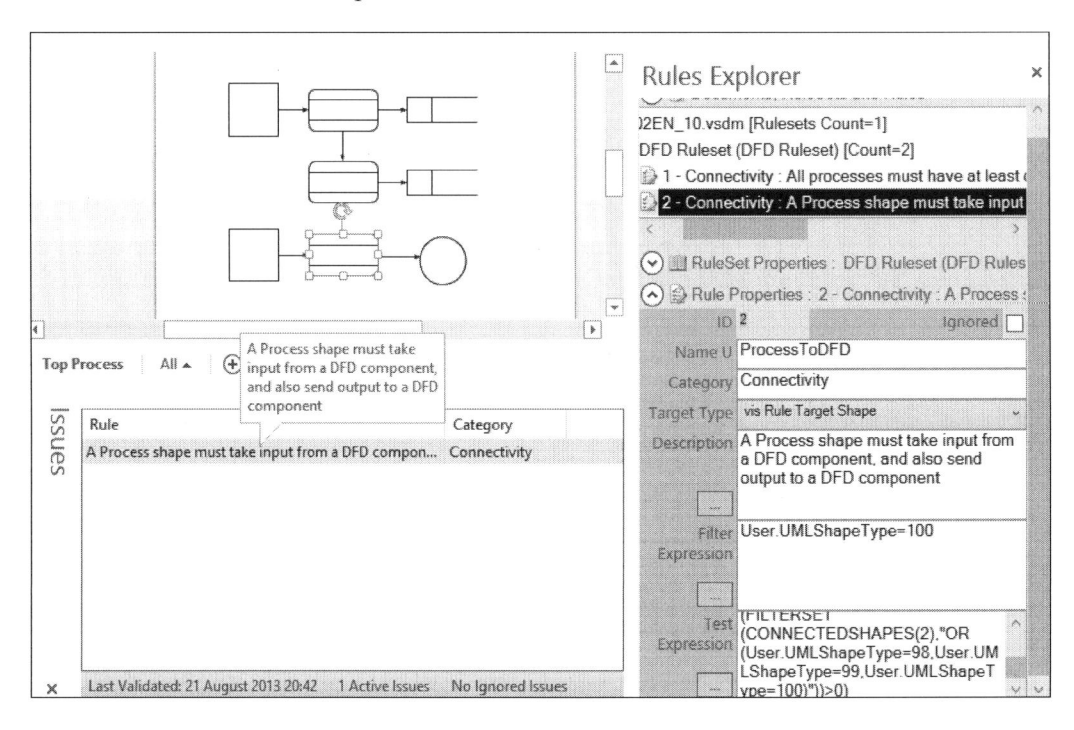

The equivalent VBA code is listed as follows:

```
Public Sub AddOrUpdateRule2( _
ByVal ruleSet As Visio.ValidationRuleSet)
Dim rule As Visio.ValidationRule
Dim ruleNameU As String
    ruleNameU = "ProcessToDFD"
    Set rule = getRule(ruleSet, ruleNameU)
    If rule Is Nothing Then
        Set rule = ruleSet.Rules.Add(ruleNameU)
    End If
    rule.Category = "Connectivity"
    rule.Description = _
```

```
        "A Process shape must take input from a DFD component, and
            also send output to a DFD component"
    rule.TargetType = visRuleTargetShape
    rule.FilterExpression = _
        "User.UMLShapeType=100"
    rule.TestExpression = _
        "AND(AGGCOUNT(FILTERSET(CONNECTEDSHAPES(1),""OR(User.
UMLShapeType=98,User.UMLShapeType=99,User.UMLShapeType=100)""))>0,A
GGCOUNT(FILTERSET(CONNECTEDSHAPES(2),""OR(User.UMLShapeType=98,User.
UMLShapeType=99,User.UMLShapeType=100)""))>0)"
End Sub
```

Rule 3 – each data store must be involved with at least one data flow

In other words, a data store must be connected to at least one data flow.

A **Data Store** shape, `User.UMLShapeType=98`, must have the count of glued **Data Flow** connectors, `User.UMLShapeType=97`, greater than zero shown as follows:

- **Name U**: `DataStoreHasDataFlow`
- **Category**: `Connectivity`
- **Target Type**: `vis Rule Target Shape`
- **Description**: `A data store must be connected to at least one data flow`
- **Filter Expression**: `User.UMLShapeType =98`
- **Test Expression**: `AGGCOUNT(FILTERSET(GLUEDSHAPES(0),"User.UMLShapeType=97"))`

> The parameter for the `GluedShapes()` method is the value of the constant `Visio.VisGluedShapesFlags.visGluedShapesAll1D`.

A Worked Example for Data Flow Model Diagrams – Part 2

You can test this rule by having a Data Store shape without any glued Data Flow connectors.

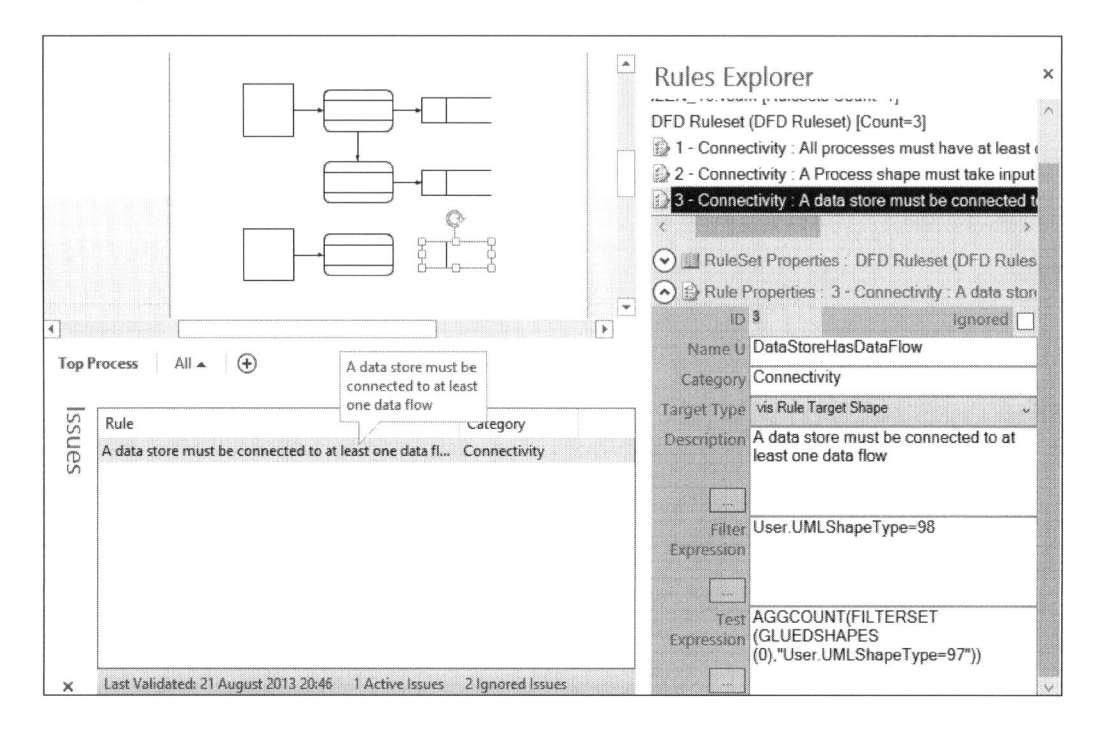

The equivalent VBA code is listed as follows:

```
Public Sub AddOrUpdateRule3( _
ByVal ruleSet As Visio.ValidationRuleSet)
Dim rule As Visio.ValidationRule
Dim ruleNameU As String
    ruleNameU = "DataStoreHasDataFlow"
    Set rule = getRule(ruleSet, ruleNameU)
    If rule Is Nothing Then
        Set rule = ruleSet.Rules.Add(ruleNameU)
    End If
    rule.Category = "Connectivity"
    rule.Description = _
        "Each data store must be involved with at least one data flow"
    rule.TargetType = visRuleTargetShape
    rule.FilterExpression = _
        "User.UMLShapeType=98"
    rule.TestExpression = _
        "AGGCOUNT(FILTERSET(GLUEDSHAPES(0),""User.UMLShapeType=97""))"
End Sub
```

[330]

Rule 4 – each external entity must be involved with at least one data flow

In other words, an interface must be connected to at least one data flow.

An **Interface** shape, `User.UMLShapeType=99`, must have the count of glued **Data Flow** connectors, `User.UMLShapeType=97`, greater than zero shown as follows:

- **Name U**: `InterfaceHasDataFlow`
- **Category**: `Connectivity`
- **Target Type**: `vis Rule Target Shape`
- **Description**: `An interface must be connected to at least one data flow`
- **Filter Expression**: `User.UMLShapeType=99`
- **Test Expression**: `AGGCOUNT(FILTERSET(GLUEDSHAPES(0),"User.UMLShapeType=97"))`

> The parameter for the `GluedShapes()` method is the value of the constant `Visio.VisGluedShapesFlags.visGluedShapesAll1D (0)`.

You can test this rule by having a Data Store shape without any glued Data Flow connectors.

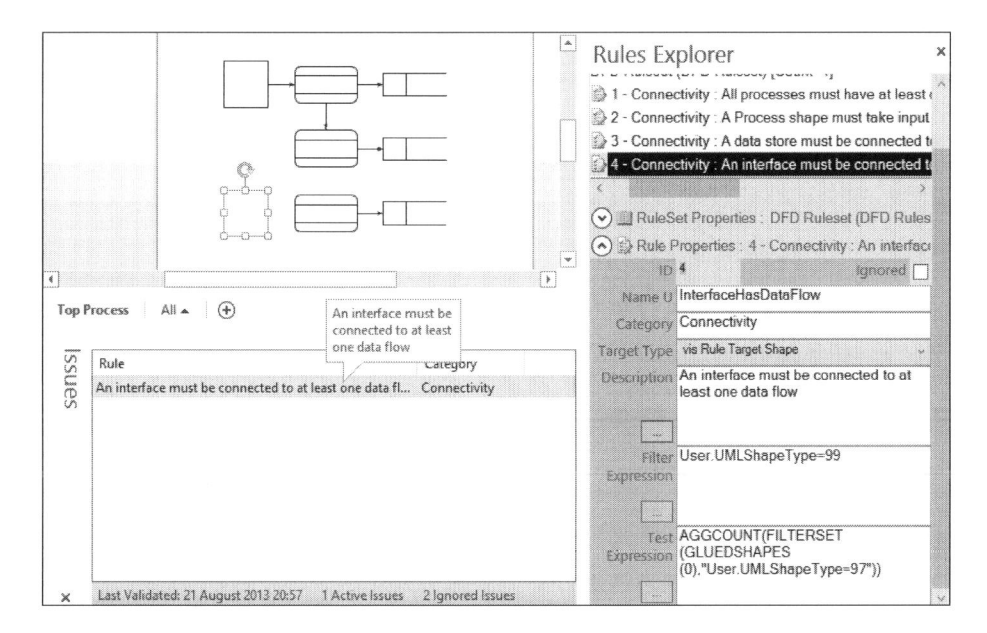

[331]

The equivalent VBA code is listed as follows:

```vba
Public Sub AddOrUpdateRule4( _
  ByVal ruleSet As Visio.ValidationRuleSet)
Dim rule As Visio.ValidationRule
Dim ruleNameU As String
    ruleNameU = "InterfaceHasDataFlow"
    Set rule = getRule(ruleSet, ruleNameU)
    If rule Is Nothing Then
        Set rule = ruleSet.Rules.Add(ruleNameU)
    End If
    rule.Category = "Connectivity"
    rule.Description = _
        " An interface must be connected to at least one data flow"
    rule.TargetType = visRuleTargetShape
    rule.FilterExpression = _
        "User.UMLShapeType=99"
    rule.TestExpression = _
        "AGGCOUNT(FILTERSET(GLUEDSHAPES(0),""User.UMLShapeType=97""))"
End Sub
```

Rule 5 – a data flow must be attached to at least one process

A **Data Flow** connector, `User.UMLShapeType=97`, must have the count of glued **Process** shapes, `User.UMLShapeType=100`, greater than zero shown as follows:

- **Name U**: `DataFlowToProcess`
- **Category**: `Connectivity`
- **Target Type**: `vis Rule Target Shape`
- **Description**: `A data flow must be attached to at least one process`
- **Filter Expression**: `User.UMLShapeType=97`
- **Test Expression**: `AGGCOUNT(FILTERSET(GLUEDSHAPES(3),"User.UMLShapeType=100"))`

> The parameter for the `GluedShapes()` method is the value of the constant `Visio.VisGluedShapesFlags.visGluedShapesAll2D (3)`.

You can test this rule by having a **Data Flow** connector glued between two non-Process shapes.

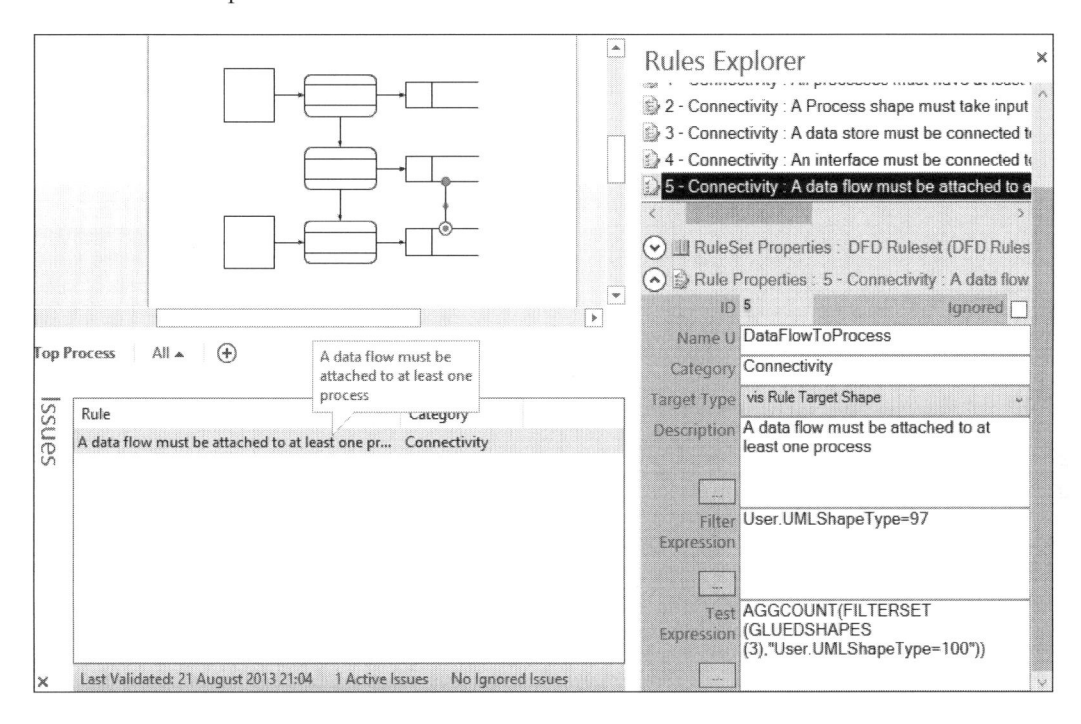

The equivalent VBA code is listed as follows, adapted from the code in *Chapter 4, Understanding the Validation API* (and requires the `getRule()` method from there):

```
Public Sub AddOrUpdateRule5( _
  ByVal ruleSet As Visio.ValidationRuleSet)
Dim rule As Visio.ValidationRule
Dim ruleNameU As String
    ruleNameU = "DataFlowToProcess"
    Set rule = getRule(ruleSet, ruleNameU)
    If rule Is Nothing Then
        Set rule = ruleSet.Rules.Add(ruleNameU)
    End If
    rule.Category = "Connectivity"
    rule.Description = _
        "A data flow must be attached to at least one process"
    rule.TargetType = visRuleTargetShape
    rule.FilterExpression = _
        "User.UMLShapeType=97"
    rule.TestExpression = _
        "AGGCOUNT(FILTERSET(GLUEDSHAPES(3),""User.
UMLShapeType=100""))"
End Sub
```

Rule 6 – data flows cannot go directly from one external entity to another external entity

Such flows need to go through at least one process.

This rule is already captured by the previous rule, since all the **Data Flow** connectors must be connected to at least one **Process** shape.

Rule 7 – do not allow a single page of a DFD to get too complex

It should have no more than 10 components. If it has more than 10 components, combine some components into a single self-contained unit and create a new DFD for that unit.

If there is a **Data Flow** connector, `User.UMLShapeType=97`, on the page, then the total count of DFD component shapes, `User.UMLShapeType=98` or `User.UMLShapeType=99` or `User.UMLShapeType=100`, should be less than 11. The parameters are as follows:

- **Name U**: `TooComplex`
- **Category**: `Count`
- **Target Type**: vis `Rule Target Page`
- **Description**: `This page is too complex. Combine some components into a single self-contained unit, and use a new page for this unit`
- **Filter Expression**: `AGGCOUNT(FILTERSET(SHAPESONPAGE(),"User.UMLShapeType=97"))>0`
- **Test Expression**: `AGGCOUNT(FILTERSET(SHAPESONPAGE()," OR(User.UMLShapeType=98,User.UMLShapeType=99,User.UMLShapeType=100)"))<11`

You can test this rule by having more than ten DFD component shapes on a page, with at least one Data Flow connector shape on it.

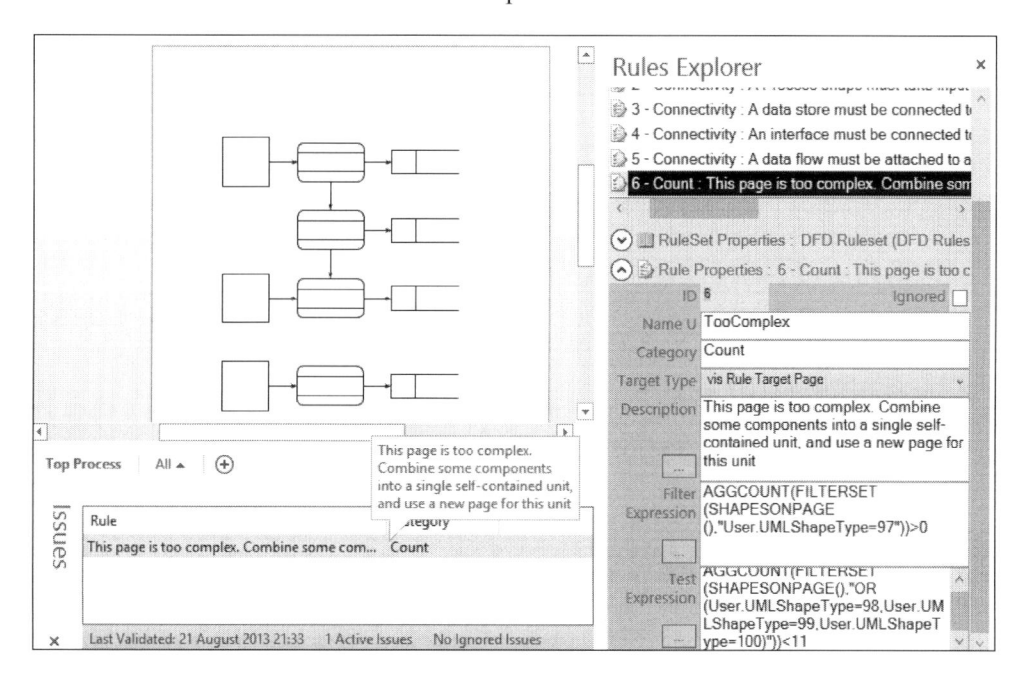

The equivalent VBA code is listed as follows:

```
Public Sub AddOrUpdateRule7( _
   ByVal ruleSet As Visio.ValidationRuleSet)
Dim rule As Visio.ValidationRule
Dim ruleNameU As String
    ruleNameU = "TooComplex"
    Set rule = getRule(ruleSet, ruleNameU)
    If rule Is Nothing Then
        Set rule = ruleSet.Rules.Add(ruleNameU)
    End If
    rule.Category = "Count"
    rule.Description = _
        "This page is too complex. Combine some components into a single self-contained unit, and use a new page for this unit"
    rule.TargetType = visRuleTargetPage
    rule.FilterExpression = _
        "AGGCOUNT(FILTERSET(SHAPESONPAGE(),""User.UMLShapeType=97""))>0"
    rule.TestExpression = _
        "AGGCOUNT(FILTERSET(SHAPESONPAGE(),""OR(User.UMLShapeType=98,User.UMLShapeType=99,User.UMLShapeType=100)""))<11"
End Sub
```

Rule 8 – each component should be labeled

Each DFD component shape, `User.UMLShapeType=98` or `User.UMLShapeType=99` or `User.UMLShapeType=100`, should have some text in it shown as follows:

- **Name U**: `NoComponentLabel`
- **Category**: `Text`
- **Target Type**: `vis Rule Target Shape`
- **Description**: `Each component should be labeled`
- **Filter Expression**: `OR(User.UMLShapeType=98,User.UMLShapeType=99,User.UMLShapeType=100)`
- **Test Expression**: `NOT(STRSAME(SHAPETEXT(TheText),""))`

You can test this rule by omitting to add any text to a DFD component shape.

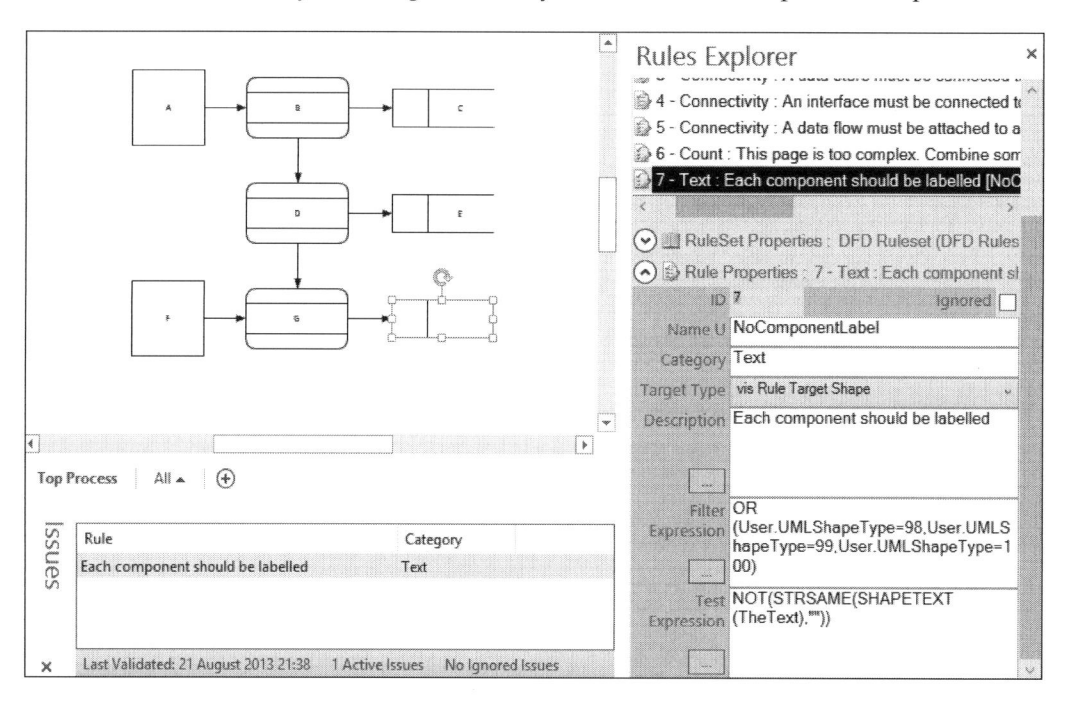

The equivalent VBA code is listed as follows:

```vba
Public Sub AddOrUpdateRule8( _
  ByVal ruleSet As Visio.ValidationRuleSet)
Dim rule As Visio.ValidationRule
Dim ruleNameU As String
    ruleNameU = "NoComponentLabel"
    Set rule = getRule(ruleSet, ruleNameU)
    If rule Is Nothing Then
        Set rule = ruleSet.Rules.Add(ruleNameU)
    End If
    rule.Category = "Text"
    rule.Description = _
        "Each component should be labeled"
    rule.TargetType = visRuleTargetShape
    rule.FilterExpression = _
        "OR(User.UMLShapeType=98,User.UMLShapeType=99,User.UMLShapeType=100)"
    rule.TestExpression = _
        "NOT(STRSAME(SHAPETEXT(TheText),""""))"
End Sub
```

Rule 9 – each data flow should be labeled describing the data that flows through it

Each **Data Flow** connector shape, `User.UMLShapeType=97`, should have some text in it shown as follows:

- **Name U**: `NoDataFlowLabel`
- **Category**: `Text`
- **Target Type**: `vis Rule Target Shape`
- **Description**: `Each data flow should be labeled with the data that flows through it`
- **Filter Expression**: `User.UMLShapeType=97`
- **Test Expression**: `NOT(STRSAME(SHAPETEXT(TheText),""))`

A Worked Example for Data Flow Model Diagrams – Part 2

You can test this rule by omitting to add any text to a DFD component shape.

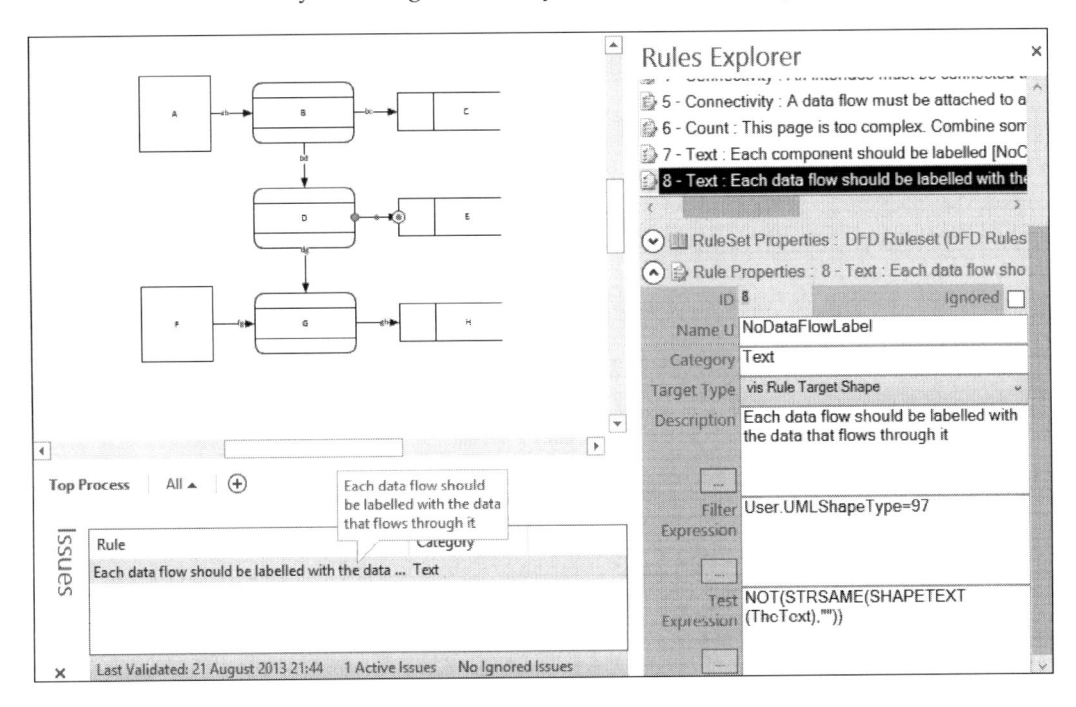

The equivalent VBA code is listed as follows:

```
Public Sub AddOrUpdateRule9( _
  ByVal ruleSet As Visio.ValidationRuleSet)
Dim rule As Visio.ValidationRule
Dim ruleNameU As String
    ruleNameU = "NoDataFlowLabel"
    Set rule = getRule(ruleSet, ruleNameU)
    If rule Is Nothing Then
        Set rule = ruleSet.Rules.Add(ruleNameU)
    End If
    rule.Category = "Text"
    rule.Description = _
        "Each data flow should be labeled with the data that flows through it"
    rule.TargetType = visRuleTargetShape
    rule.FilterExpression = _
        "User.UMLShapeType=97"
    rule.TestExpression = _
        "NOT(STRSAME(SHAPETEXT(TheText),""""))"
End Sub
```

Rule 10 – each component and subcomponent should be numbered

This rule starts with an example. For example, a top level DFD has components 1, 2, 3, 4, and 5. The subcomponent DFD of component 3 would have components 3.1, 3.2, 3.3, and 3.4; and the sub-subcomponent DFD of component 3.2 would have components 3.2.1, 3.2.2, and 3.2.3. This enables a developer to plan in a top-down manner: starting with representing large concepts, and then repeatedly breaking these objects into their components.

Each **Process** or **Data Store** shape, `User.UMLShapeType=98` or `User.UMLShapeType=100`, should have a **Prop.ID** value if the page has a **Prop.DisplayID** value of **TRUE** shown as follows:

- **Name U**: `NoID`
- **Category**: `Text`
- **Target Type**: `vis Rule Target Shape`
- **Description**: `Each component and subcomponent should be numbered`
- **Filter Expression**: `AND(OR(User.UMLShapeType=98,User.UMLShapeType=100),Prop.ID.Invisible=False)`
- **Test Expression**: `NOT(STRSAME(Prop.ID,""))`

You can test this rule by omitting to add an **ID** value to any Process or Data Store shape, when the page has the **Display IDs** value set to TRUE.

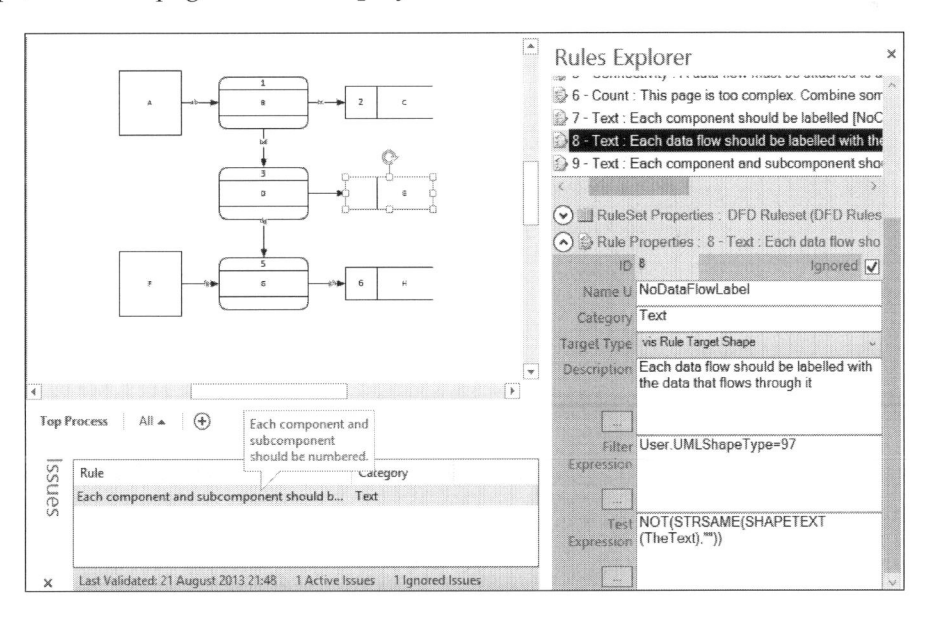

A Worked Example for Data Flow Model Diagrams – Part 2

So, if you change the page **Display IDs Shape Data** to FALSE, and then rerun **Check Diagram**, the page will pass validation because the **Prop.ID** Shape Data are invisible.

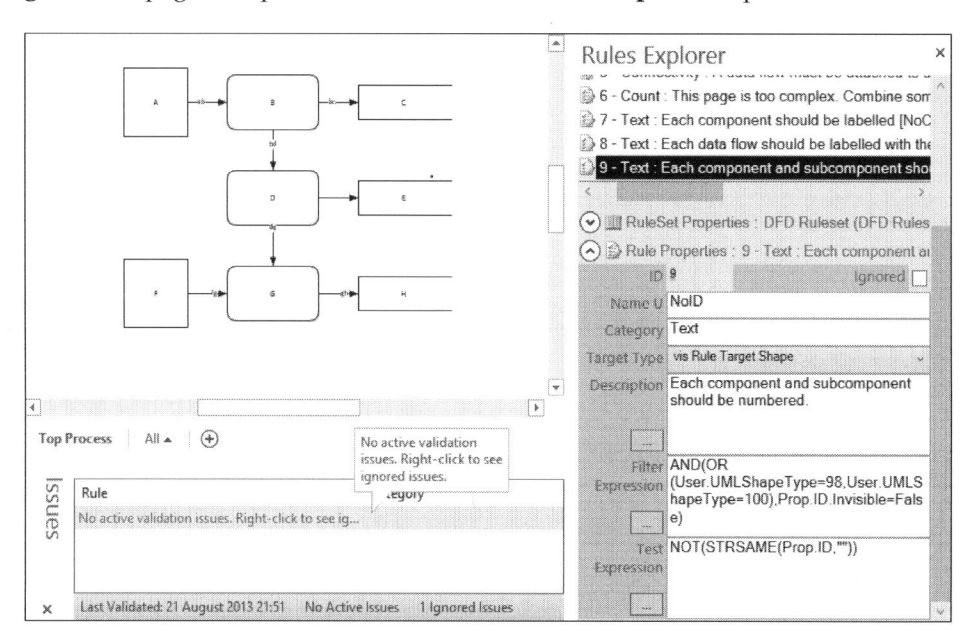

> In our case, the **Prop.ID** value defaults to an empty string (""), but some developers may leave the default value without a formula. In this case it would be necessary to amend the Test Expression to cater for both options:
>
> OR(STRSAME(Prop.ID,"") and LOCALFORMULAEXISTS(Prop.ID))

The equivalent VBA code is listed as follows:

```
Public Sub AddOrUpdateRule10( _
ByVal ruleSet As Visio.ValidationRuleSet)
Dim rule As Visio.ValidationRule
Dim ruleNameU As String
    ruleNameU = "NoID"
    Set rule = getRule(ruleSet, ruleNameU)
    If rule Is Nothing Then
```

```
            Set rule = ruleSet.Rules.Add(ruleNameU)
    End If
    rule.Category = "Text"
    rule.Description = _
        "Each component and subcomponent should be numbered. E.g. a
top level DFD has components 1 2 3. The subcomponent DFD of component
3 would have components 3.1, 3.2 and 3.3; and the sub-subcomponent DFD
of component 3.2 would have components 3.2.1 and 3.2.2"
    rule.TargetType = visRuleTargetShape
    rule.FilterExpression = _
        "AND(OR(User.UMLShapeType=98,User.UMLShapeType=100),Prop.
ID.Invisible=False)"
    rule.TestExpression = _
        "NOT(STRSAME(Prop.ID,""""))"
End Sub
```

Rule 11 – a data flow must be connected between two components

The previous rule, **A data flow must be attached to at least one process**, does not check that both ends are connected to a data component, therefore an extra rule is required to check for this.

Each DFD component shape, `User.UMLShapeType=98` or `User.UMLShapeType=99` or `User.UMLShapeType=100`, should have some text in it shown as follows:

- **Name U**: `DataFlowEnds`
- **Category**: `Connectivity`
- **Target Type**: `vis Rule Target Shape`
- **Description**: `A data flow must be attached to two data components`
- **Filter Expression**: `User.UMLShapeType=97`
- **Test Expression**: `AGGCOUNT(FILTERSET(GLUEDSHAPES(3),"OR(User.UMLShapeType=98,User.UMLShapeType=99,User.UMLShapeType=100)"))>1`

A Worked Example for Data Flow Model Diagrams – Part 2

You can test this rule by omitting to add any text to a DFD component shape.

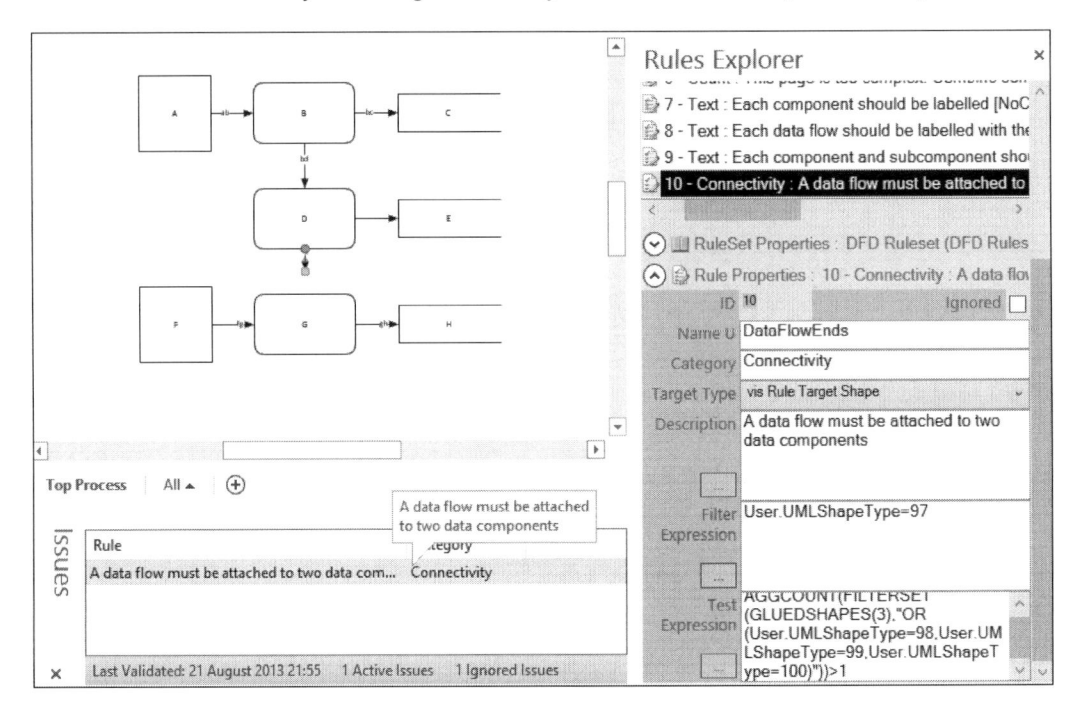

The equivalent VBA code is listed as follows:

```
Public Sub AddOrUpdateRule11( _
ByVal ruleSet As Visio.ValidationRuleSet)
Dim rule As Visio.ValidationRule
Dim ruleNameU As String
    ruleNameU = " DataFlowEnds"
    Set rule = getRule(ruleSet, ruleNameU)
    If rule Is Nothing Then
        Set rule = ruleSet.Rules.Add(ruleNameU)
    End If
    rule.Category = "Connectivity"
    rule.Description = _
        "A data flow must be attached to two data components"
    rule.TargetType = visRuleTargetShape
    rule.FilterExpression = _
        " User.UMLShapeType=97"
    rule.TestExpression = _
        "AGGCOUNT(FILTERSET(GLUEDSHAPES(3),""OR(User.
UMLShapeType=98,User.UMLShapeType=99,User.UMLShapeType=100)"")))>1"
End Sub
```

Rule 12 – a flow must not cycle back to itself

This rule is a variation of the one in *Chapter 7, Creating Validation Rules*, so the VBA code needs to be inserted into the template document has all of the rules in it.

A DFD component shape must not cycle back to itself by following the flow direction through other DFD components, shown as follows:

- **Name U**: `CheckCycle`
- **Category**: `Connectivity`
- **Target Type**: `vis Rule Target Page`
- **Description**: `A flow must not cycle back to itself`
- **Filter Expression**: `False`
- **Test Expression**: `True`

You can test this rule by creating a connecting DFD component together in a cycle.

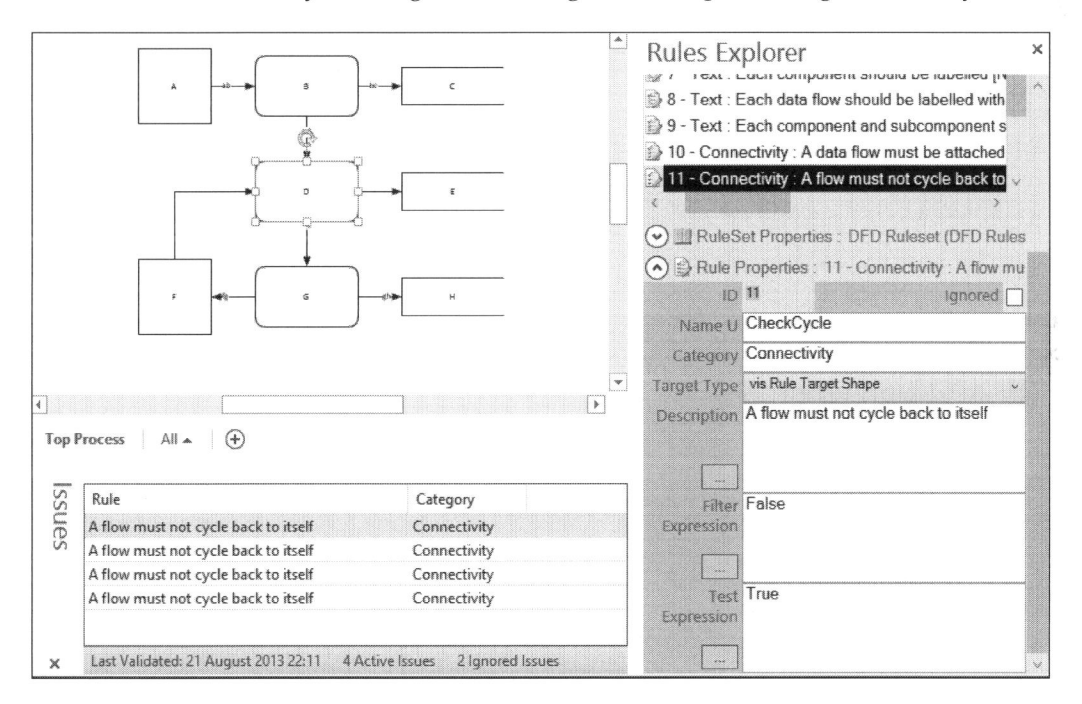

The `ThisDocument` class needs to include the `Document_RuleSetValidated()` event, `CheckCycle()`, `getRule()`, and `ClearRuleIssues()` methods as described in *Chapter 7, Creating Validation Rules*. Also, you must add a **Reference** to the **Microsoft Scripting Runtime**, as before.

A Worked Example for Data Flow Model Diagrams – Part 2

The `CustomValidation` class needs to copied, but the `InitializeValues()` method needs to be modified because the data components are not on the Flowchart layer. Instead, the code checks for the value in the `User.UMLShapeType` cell, if it exists.

```
Private Sub initializeValues(ByVal visPage As Visio.Page)
    Dim shps As Visio.Shapes
    Set shps = visPage.Shapes
    Dim shapeID As Integer

    Set flowchartShapes = New Collection
    Set hshTable = New Dictionary
    cycleFound = False
    Dim shp As Visio.Shape
    Dim i As Integer
    For Each shp In shps
        If shp.CellExistsU("User.UMLShapeType", _
            Visio.visExistsAnywhere) Then
            Select Case shp.Cells("User.UMLShapeType").ResultIU
                Case 97
                    shapeID = shp.ID
                Case 98, 99, 100
                    shapeID = shp.ID
                    flowchartShapes.Add shapeID
                    hshTable.Add shapeID, shapeStatus.[New]
            End Select
        End If
    Next
End Sub
```

The equivalent VBA code is listed as follows:

```
Public Sub AddOrUpdateRule12( _
   ByVal ruleSet As Visio.ValidationRuleSet)
Dim rule As Visio.ValidationRule
Dim ruleNameU As String
    ruleNameU = "CheckCycle"
    Set rule = getRule(ruleSet, ruleNameU)
    If rule Is Nothing Then
        Set rule = ruleSet.Rules.Add(ruleNameU)
    End If
    rule.Category = "Connectivity"
    rule.Description = _
        " A flow must not cycle back to itself"
    rule.TargetType = visRuleTargetPage
    rule.FilterExpression = _
```

```
            "False"
    rule.TestExpression = _
            "True"
End Sub
```

Summary

In this chapter, we have created validation rules to match all of the Data Flow model diagram rules that we wanted. We have used the **Rules Tools** add-in to write and test each rule, and provided equivalent VBA code to create each rule. We found that all but one of these validation rules could be written fully using the Filter and Test Expressions, while one had to be written with the custom code.

In the next chapter, we will prepare the template for publication, so that it can be deployed easily for use by others.

11
A Worked Example for Data Flow Model Diagrams – Part 3

In the previous two chapters, we enhanced the masters and wrote the rules for **Gane and Sarson** data flow diagrams, based on the Microsoft supplied **Data Flow Model Diagram** template.

In this chapter, we will prepare a new custom template and create an installation package for it.

Completing the template

Now that you have modified the masters, written the validation rules, and enhanced the first page, you need to give the finishing touches to the template before creating an installation file.

Follow the instructions in *Chapter 8, Publishing Validation Rules and Diagrams*, to add a title block, select a theme, and insert the page name field into the title shape in the background page. Then save your document as a template to `DFMD_M.vstm`, if it is metric units, or `DFMD_U.vstm`, if it is US units.

Test your template by creating a new document from it, and then resize the first page to a square.

A Worked Example for Data Flow Model Diagrams – Part 3

> If you hold down the *Ctrl* key and move your mouse cursor to the top of the page, then you will see that the cursor changes to a vertical two-way arrow. You can then click and drag the top edge of the page downwards, while still holding down the *Ctrl* key, until the page looks square.

Then arrange some of the DFD shapes on the page, as this page will be used as the preview image on your new template. Follow the instructions in *Chapter 8, Publishing Validation Rules and Diagrams*, for enhancing the quality of the preview image, before saving it as a new document, say as `8002EN_11_Image.vsdx`. You can then copy the preview picture, as in *Chapter 8, Publishing Validation Rules and Diagrams*, with the `CopyPreview()` method or by the following command in the VBA **Immediate Window**:

```
Visio.Documents("DFMD_M.vstm").CopyPreviewPicture
Visio.Documents("8002EN_11_Image.vsdx")
```

Of course, you need to ensure that the **LockPreview** cell in the document ShapeSheet of your new template is changed to TRUE before saving your template again if you do not use the `CopyPreview()` method.

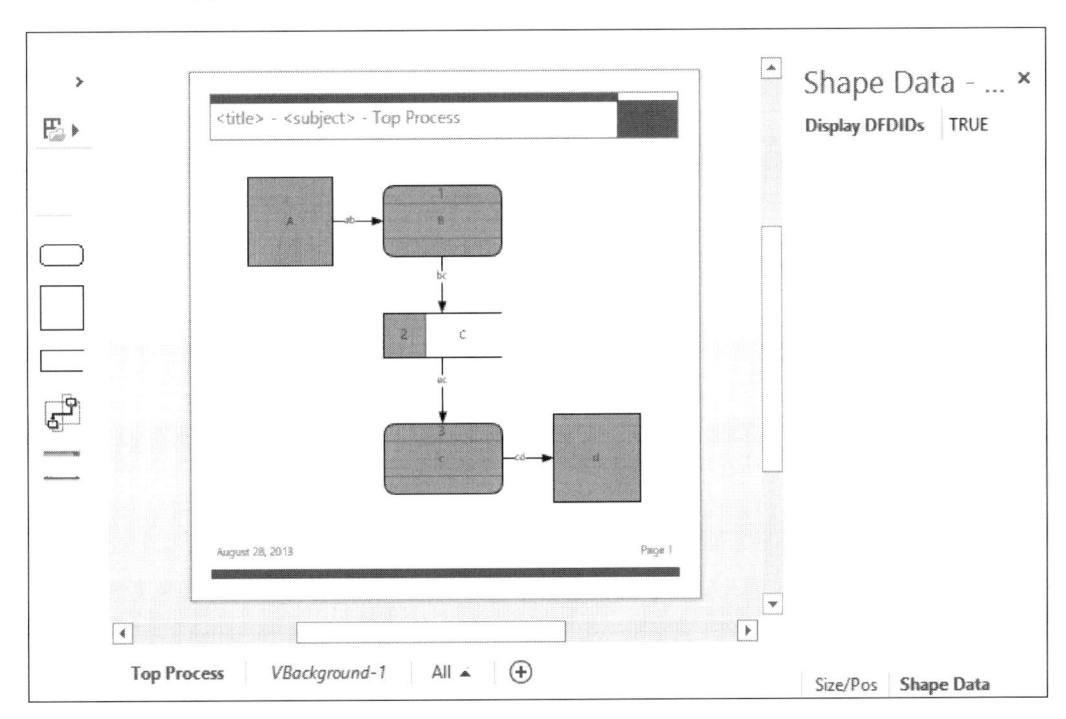

Chapter 11

I chose a color scheme that is compatible with the category that I intend the template to be part of.

You should edit the document properties using the **File | Info | Properties** panel. For example, I added **<title>** into the **Title** field, **<subject>** into the **Subject** field, and **This is a Data Flow Model Diagram template with validation rules** into the **Comments** field.

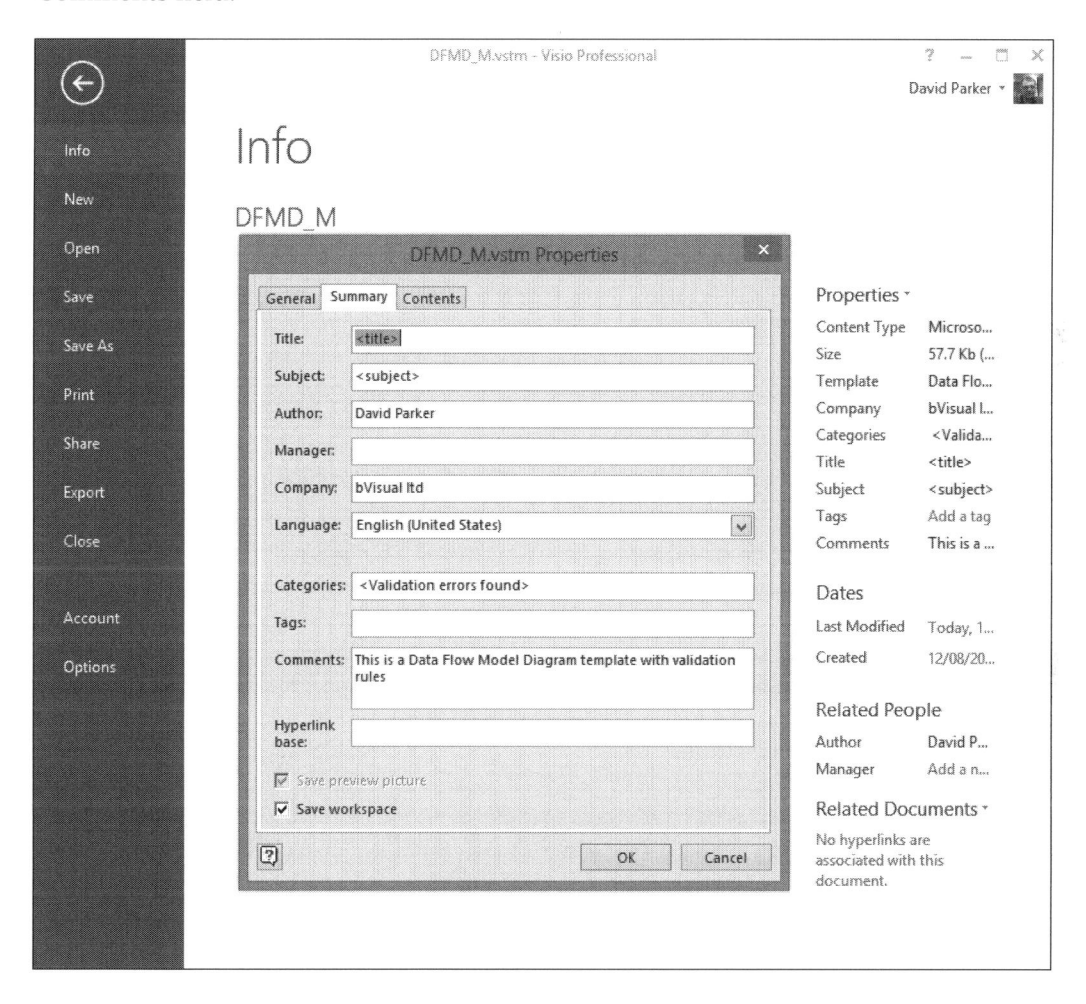

A Worked Example for Data Flow Model Diagrams – Part 3

Finally, ensure that you close **Document Stencil** in your template before saving it. You should still have the Gane-Sarson stencil docked when you save the workspace, but you do not need to include this in your installer because your target users should already have this installed. The user will drag-and-drop shapes off this stencil but your modified ones in the document stencil will be dropped instead.

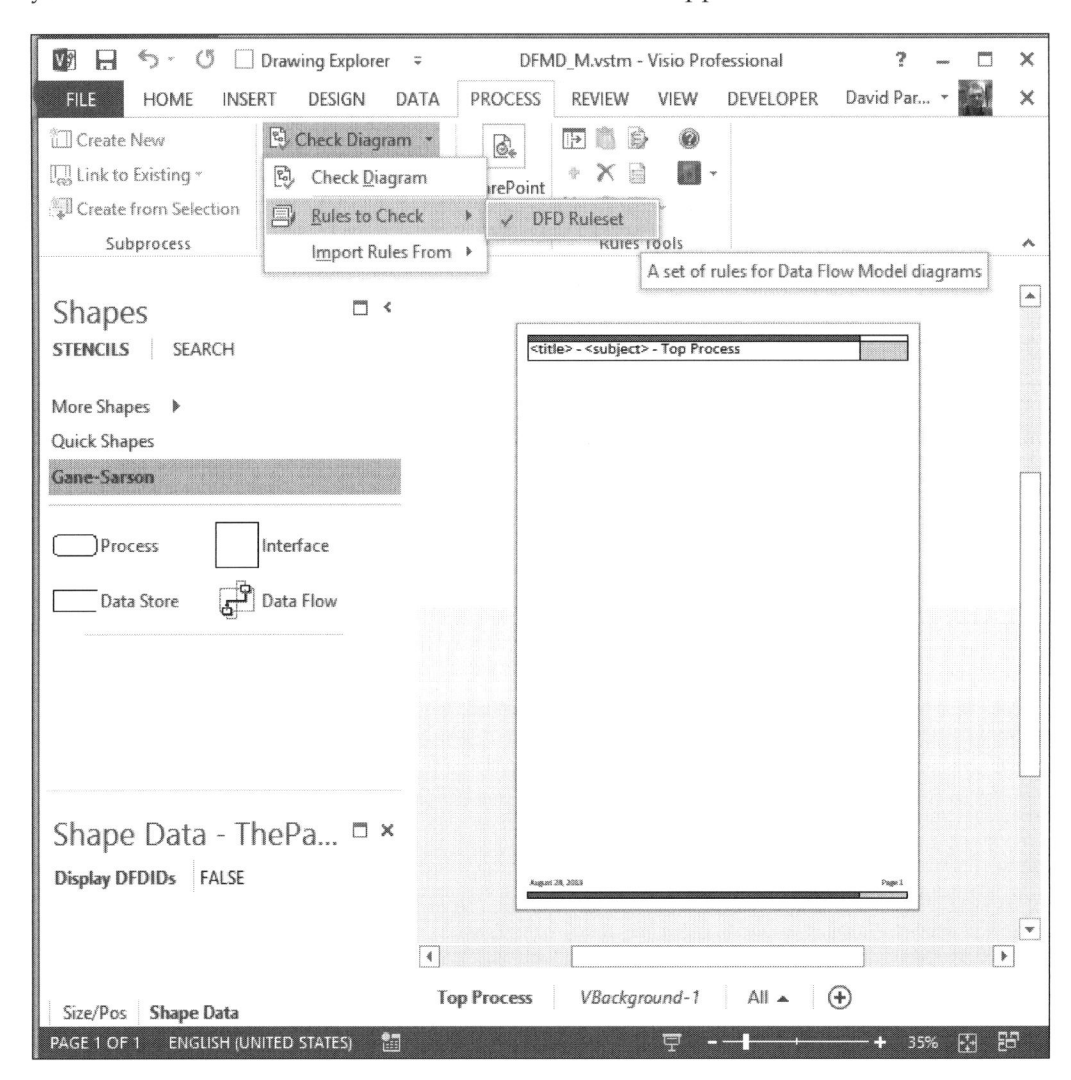

Notice that I set the **Display DFDIDs** Shape Data row to FALSE, and that there is a ruleset called **DFD Ruleset** in the document. I did this because a user will probably want to sketch out a DFD initially, and can progress to a more complete one later.

Do not be tempted to tick **Remove unused master shapes** on the **Remove Hidden Information** dialog, because you need to keep your custom masters in this template:

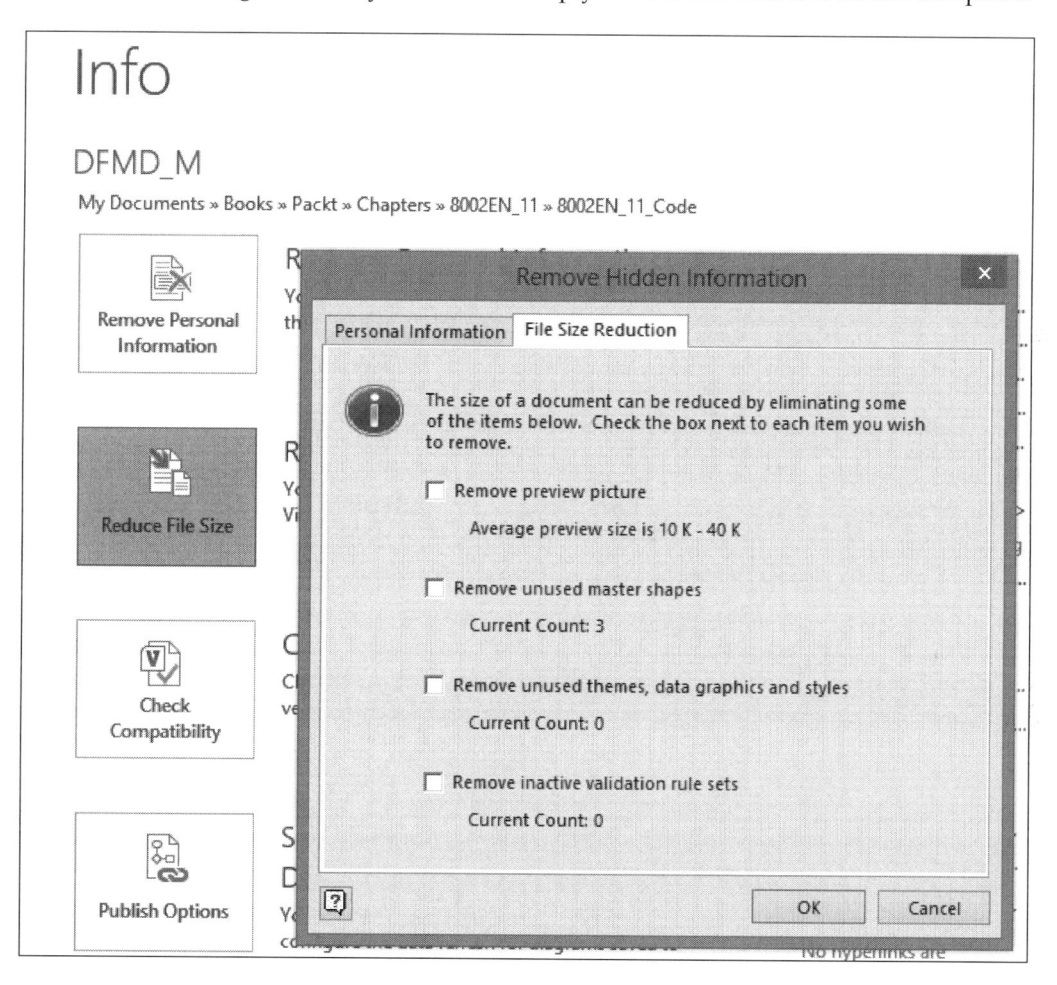

A Worked Example for Data Flow Model Diagrams – Part 3

Reviewing the template

If you look at the template in **File Explorer** in Windows 8 with the right **View** settings, then you should see the preview image of the template; however, the file detail preview panel displays the first page using the built-in Visio document previewer:

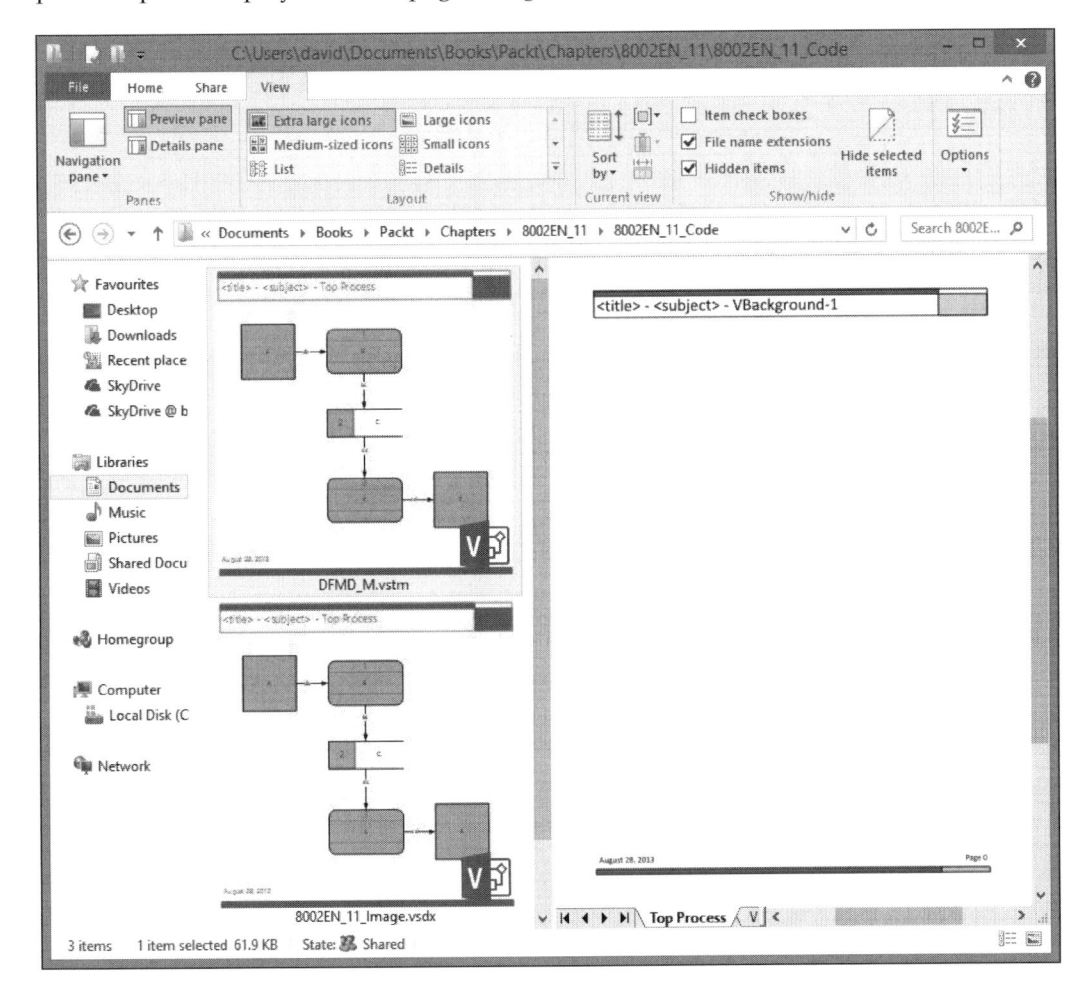

This Visio document previewer (Microsoft Visio Viewer) is the same one used by Outlook, and is also available as a free download from www.Microsoft.com. It is, in fact, a useful ActiveX control that can be used by developers (see my own **visViewer** at http://bvisual.net/Products/visViewer.aspx, for example).

[352]

> The preceding screenshot actually reveals a bug in the current Visio Viewer control, because the background page name is being displayed in the header rather than the active page name. If it is important that you display the page name automatically in this control; then you will need to put the text on the foreground page instead of the background page.

Creating the installer

In Visual Studio 2012, create a new **Installed | Templates | WiX Toolset | WiX Setup Project for Visio**, called, say, `DataFlowModelDiagramTemplate`.

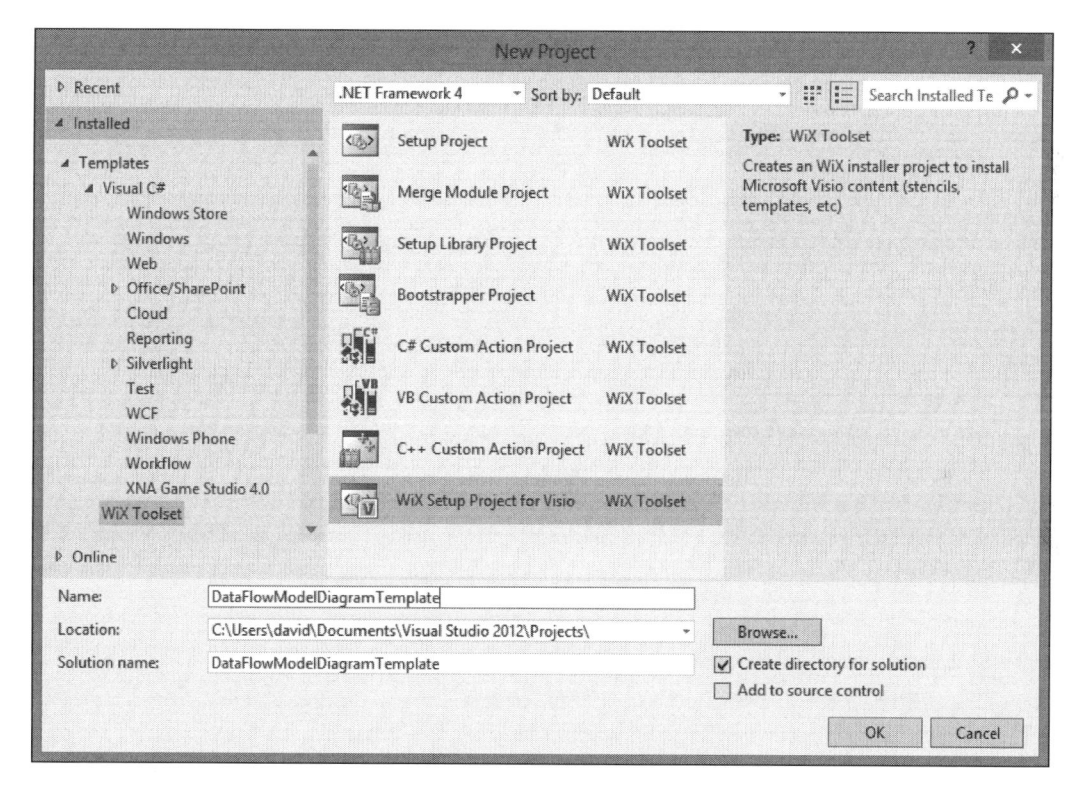

A Worked Example for Data Flow Model Diagrams – Part 3

Add your new template to the **Application Folder**. Then follow the instructions in *Chapter 8, Publishing Validation Rules and Diagrams*, for enhancing the properties of the deployment package.

Note that I also updated the Product.Name, Manufacturer, and so on to suit my requirements as shown in the following code snippet:

```xml
<?xml version="1.0" encoding="UTF-8"?>

<!--
  Wix Project template to install (and publish) Visio components (stencils & templates)
  <visio:Publish /> item which does all the work
-->

<Wix xmlns="http://schemas.microsoft.com/wix/2006/wi"
     xmlns:visio="http://schemas.microsoft.com/wix/Visio" >

  <?define Version="1.0.0.0"?>
  <?define UpgradeCode="{be8174da-cce0-4c71-bca1-86bba58b1cb0}" ?>

  <Product Id="*" Name="DataFlowModelDiagramTemplate $(var.Version)"
           Language="1033" Version="$(var.Version)"
           Manufacturer="bVisual" UpgradeCode="$(var.UpgradeCode)">
    <Package InstallerVersion="200" Compressed="yes"
             InstallPrivileges="elevated" InstallScope="perMachine" />

    <MajorUpgrade DowngradeErrorMessage=
            "A later version of Data Flow Model Diagram Template is already installed. Setup will now exit." />
    <MediaTemplate EmbedCab="yes"/>

    <Directory Id="TARGETDIR" Name="SourceDir">
      <Directory Id="ProgramFilesFolder">
        <Directory Id="ManufacturerFolder"
          Name="bVisual">

          <Directory Id="INSTALLDIR"
                Name="Data Flow Model Diagram" FileSource="." >

            <Component>
```

```xml
            <File Name="DFMD_M.vstm">
              <visio:PublishTemplate
                 MenuPath="Software and Database\Data Flow Model Diagram" />
            </File>
          </Component>

        </Directory>
      </Directory>
    </Directory>
  </Directory>

  <Feature Id="ProductFeature"
         Title="All Items" Display="expand" >

    <Feature Id="TemplatesFeature"
           Title="Install templates"  >
      <ComponentRef Id="DFMD_M.vstm" />
    </Feature>

  </Feature>

  <UIRef Id="WixUI_FeatureTree" />

  </Product>
</Wix>
```

I have set the menu attribute property to place the template into the existing **Software and Database** category, and I gave it the verbose name: **Data Flow Model Diagram with Rules**.

> The name should not be the same as an existing template name in the same category, because it will fail to appear in the Visio user interface.

A Worked Example for Data Flow Model Diagrams – Part 3

I added the **DFMD_M.vstm** file to the setup project.

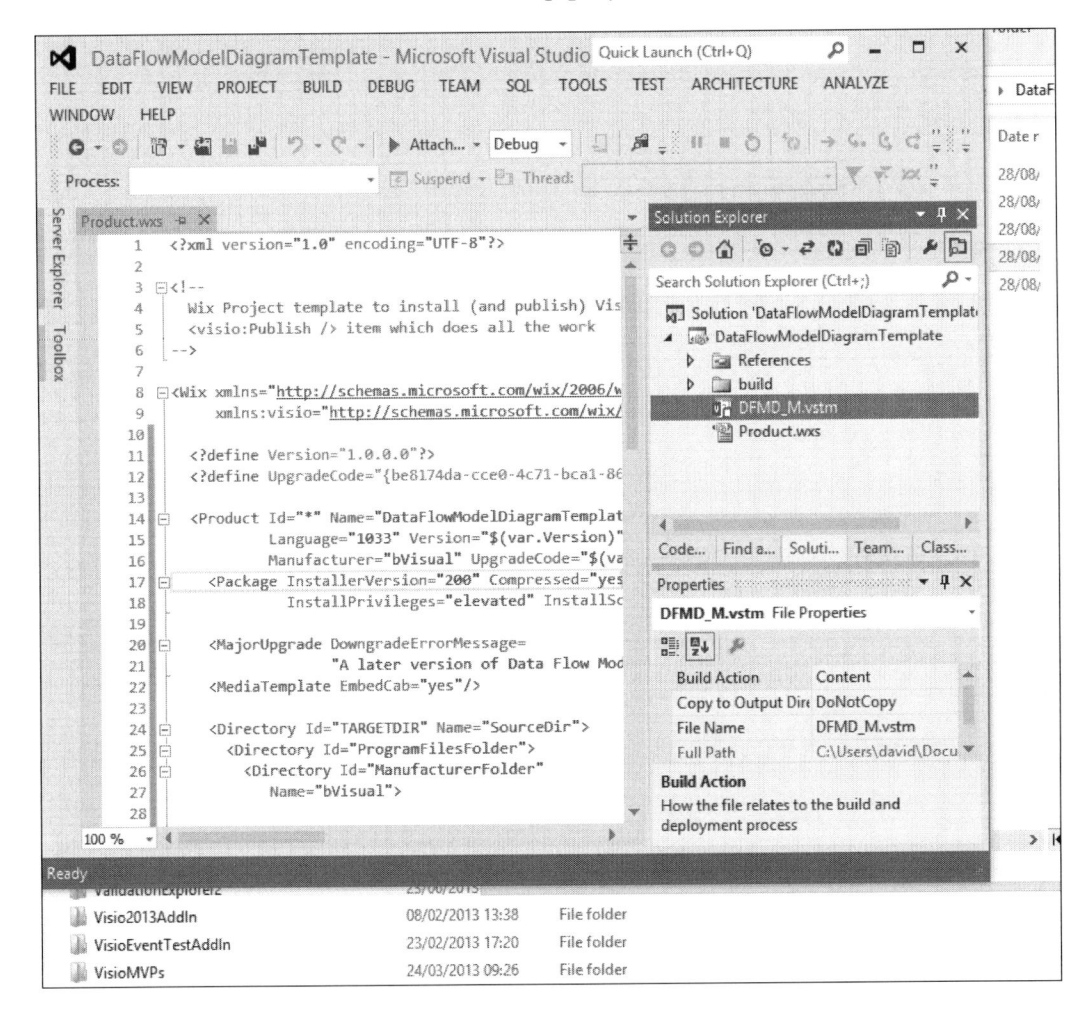

You can then build the release of this package, and you should find that two files are created, namely `DataFlowModelDiagramTemplateSetup.msi` and `DataFlowModelDiagramTemplateSetup.wixpdb`, in the `<Projects>\DataFlowModelDiagramTemplateSetup\DataFlowModelDiagramTemplateSetup\bin\Release` folder.

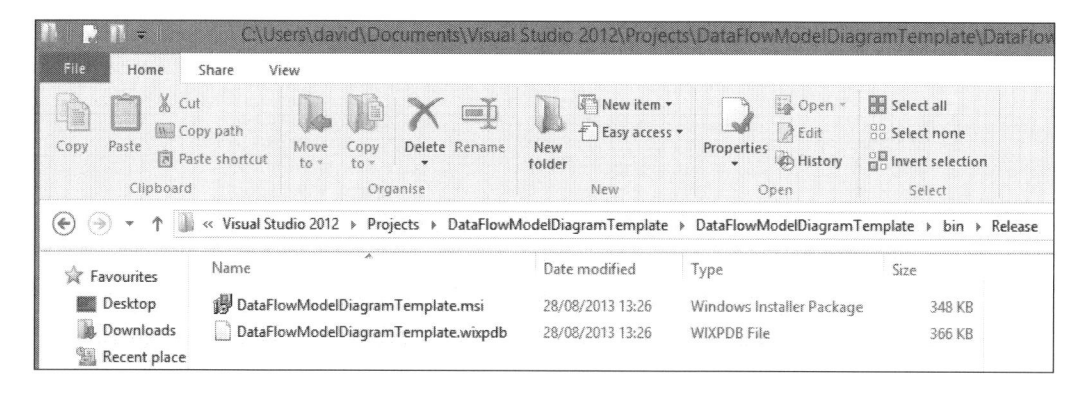

Testing the Installer

The `msi` file can then be double-clicked; alternatively, select it and then click on **Install** on the right mouse menu.

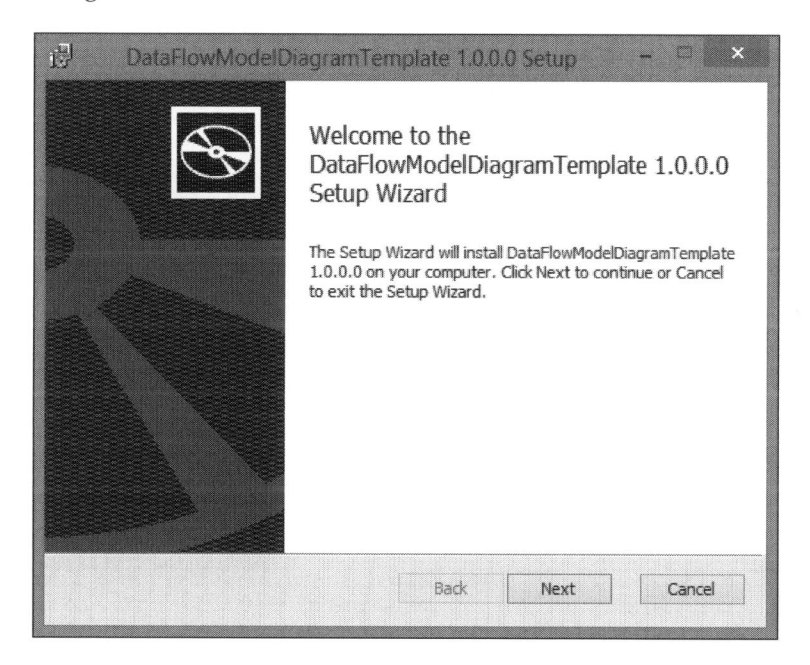

A Worked Example for Data Flow Model Diagrams – Part 3

When the installation is complete, the template can be found in all its glory in the existing **Software and Database** category.

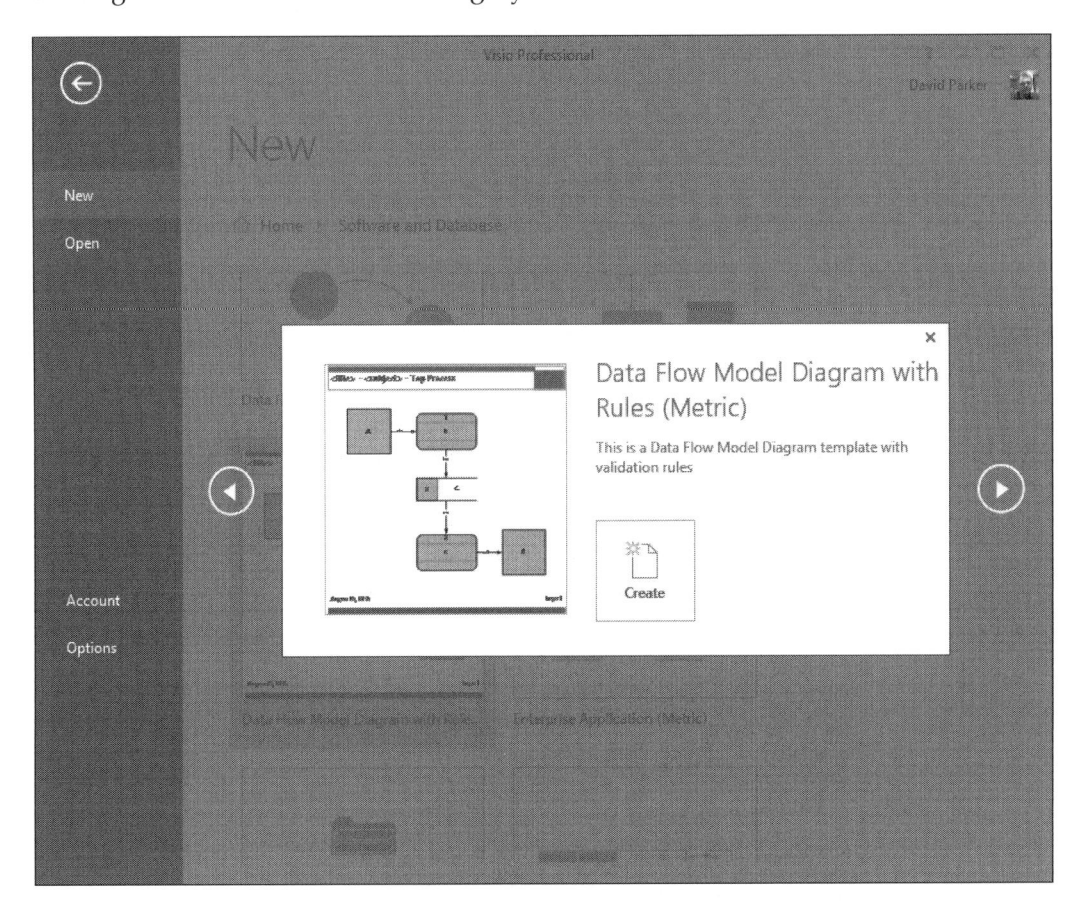

Note that the template's Comments property is displayed in the interface.

This particular template contains macros, so you will probably get a warning whenever a new drawing is created from it.

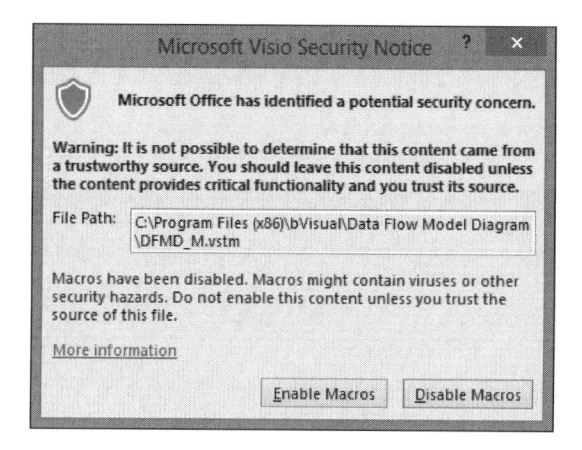

Using a digital certificate

Your company may not allow you to enable VBA macros from untrusted publishers because you might have a more strict policy in force. The Visio **Trust Center** provides the option to disable all macros except those from trusted publishers.

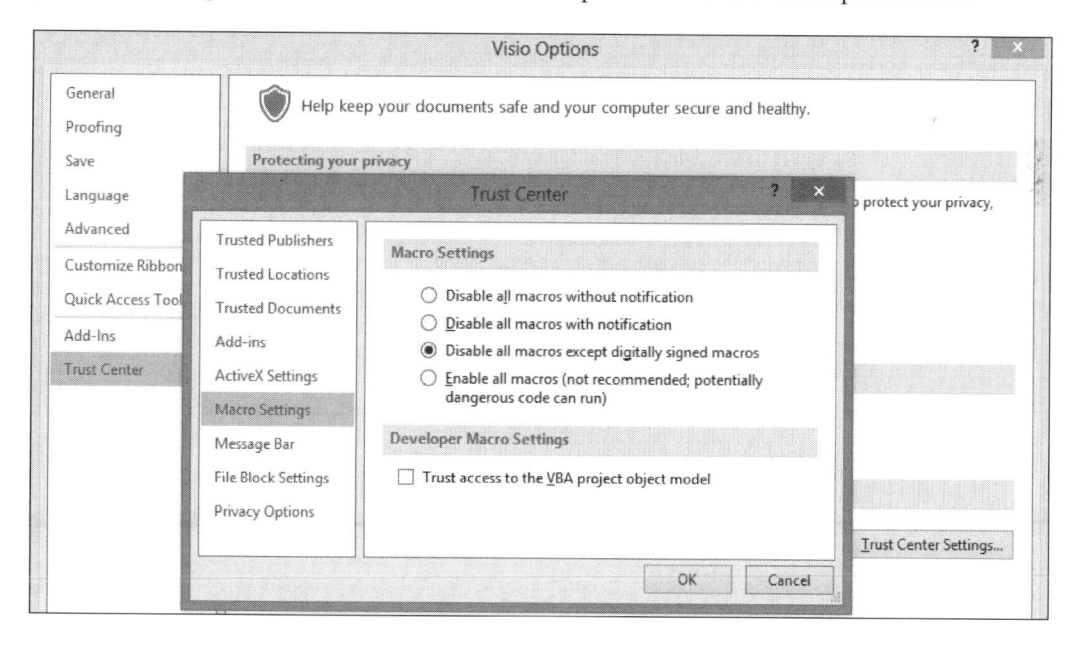

A Worked Example for Data Flow Model Diagrams – Part 3

If this is the case, then you can invest in a digital signature that you can apply to your VBA project.

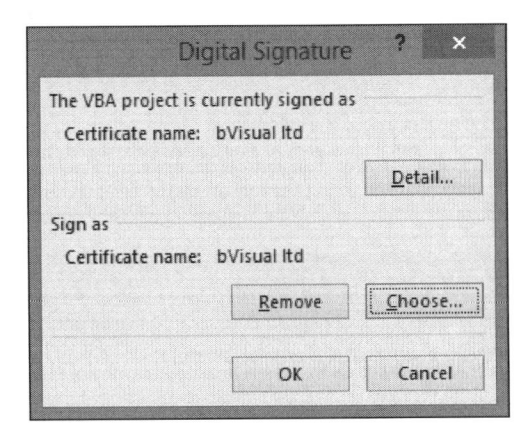

This can be done by navigating to **Tools | Digital Signature** in the **Microsoft Visual Basic for Applications editor**.

> There is also an option to hide the VBA code from prying eyes under **Tools | <project> Properties | Protection | Lock project from viewing**. If you use this option, then do not forget the password.

If you do apply a digital certificate, and the publisher has not yet been trusted, then you will be prompted again; however, this time the message is different and you have the option to **Trust all from publisher**.

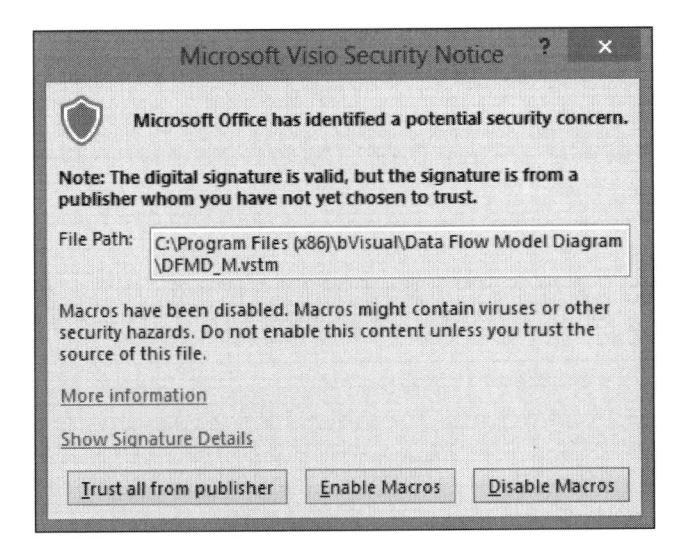

If you do trust the publisher, then you will see it listed in the **Trust Center** as a **Trusted Publisher**.

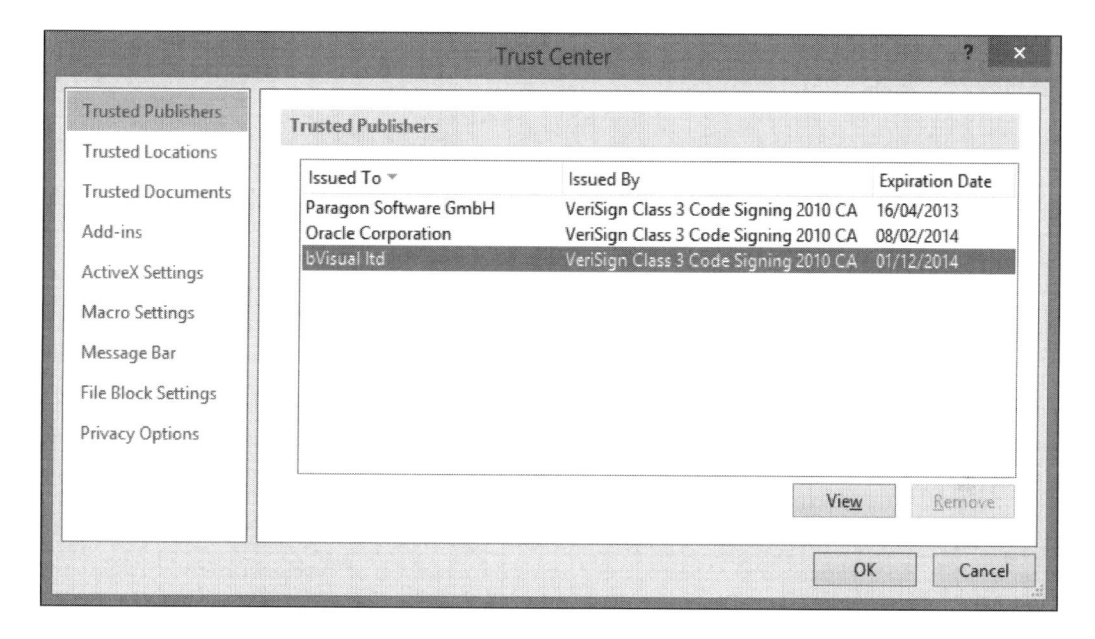

There will not be any prompts to enable macros from **bVisual ltd**.

Thoughts about code in templates

I do not normally leave my VBA code in Visio templates, because that would cause a copy of the code to be in every document created from the template. If you need to make changes to the code, then you would need to apply these changes to all of the Visio documents that contain the code.

A better solution for VBA is to put as much of the code as possible into a stencil that is normally docked with the workspace. This is a good solution if you can be sure that the user has access to the stencil, and that VBA is allowed to run.

The best solution is to have an add-in installed on the user's PC; I would normally do this with Visual Studio, just as with the **RulesTools** add-in that is available from the companion web site for this book.

For the purposes of this book, I have just used VBA within the document because it ensures that all rules are available without any other dependencies.

Summary

We have now completed an example template that contains a custom ruleset, and published it for others to use. In most cases, the ruleset will be saved in the template without the need for any extra code; however, for more advanced needs, we have also looked at VBA macros, with optional digital certificates, that could be included to extend the ruleset.

In the next chapter, we will consider the use of Visio documents with rulesets in Office365. We will also look at an alternative method of providing users with a custom Visio template, straight from Office365, rather than installing into their desktop.

12
Integrating Validated Diagrams with SharePoint 2013 and Office365

In the previous chapters, we have learned how to create validation rules in Visio, and how to deploy custom Visio templates to other Visio users.

In this chapter, we will look at some of the advantages of utilizing Visio with SharePoint with respect to validated diagrams, and how to provide a custom template via SharePoint.

Using SharePoint and Visio together

Microsoft SharePoint is available on the premises or in the cloud, principally via an Office365 subscription. Similarly, Visio is available as a desktop installation or via **Click-To-Run** from an Office365 Plus subscription. The **Click-To-Run** edition of Visio 2013 Professional, officially called Visio Professional for Office365, is exactly the same as Visio 2013 Professional but it can be accessed from the cloud on a number of Windows devices.

SharePoint not only provides a first-class document store with versioning and check-in / check-out capabilities, but it is increasingly becoming the hub of all digital activities in organizations with its workflow, data co-ordination, and dashboarding capabilities.

Visio Services on SharePoint 2013 enables Visio documents to be more deeply integrated than was possible with SharePoint 2010. For example, Visio diagrams can not only be viewed in web pages accessible in all modern browsers in all modern devices, but the data-linked shapes in these diagrams can also be automatically refreshed from their data source, without the user needing Visio installed locally. Visio 2013 diagrams are displayed in a special SharePoint web part, called the **Visio Web Access control**, which not only provides the ability to pan and zoom and to select individual pages from a drop-down list, but also allows the shape data and hyperlinks to be viewed and followed. Page and shape comments are not only viewable, but can be added via the browser, even without a Visio client.

Visio 2010 had to save the documents into a special web-drawing format (*.vdw) in SharePoint, if you wanted them to render in the **Visio Web Access** (**VWA**). This Visio document was in fact the binary (*.vsd) version of the Visio file formats, with an extra layer of **Silverlight** layered over the top. It is this Silverlight layer that contains the refreshable linked data and associated data graphics only. Any changes to this Silverlight layer are quickly applied to the underlying Visio document whenever it is opened in the Visio client application. You can still choose to save in this format from Visio 2013, but this only restricts the browser-based viewing. Visio 2013 documents do not need to be saved into a special format in SharePoint, and the Silverlight restriction is removed because the graphics are rendered in high-quality png on-the-fly.

You can, of course, fully edit a diagram in Visio, which is the graphics, the data within them, and any associated comments, as shown in the following screenshot:

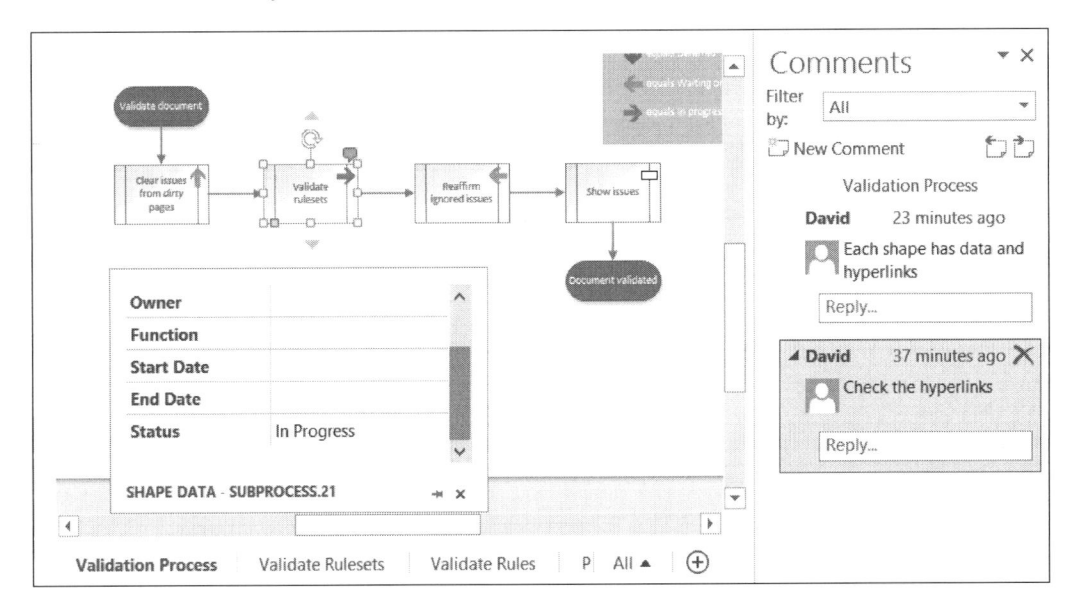

The same diagram can be viewed directly in SharePoint and the comments can be edited, if you are an authenticated user, as shown in the next screenshot:

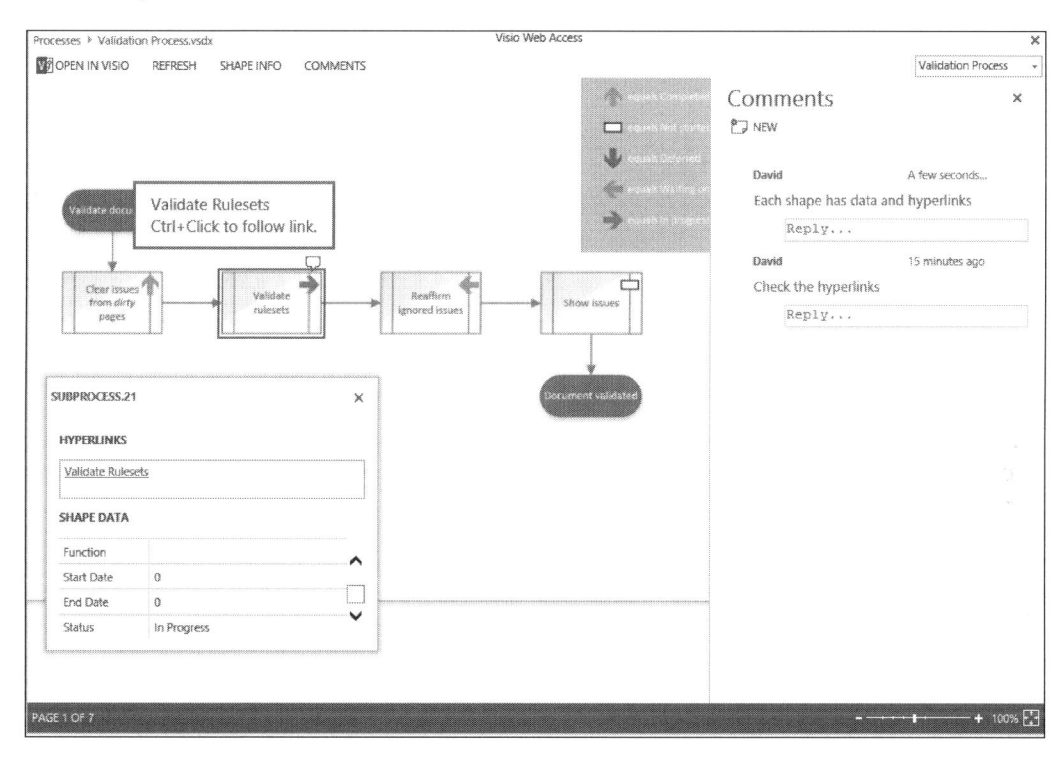

The Visio web part can just be one of many web parts on a web page hosted in SharePoint, and connections can be established between web parts so that, for example, different pages are displayed, specific shapes are highlighted, or lists are filtered by a selected shape. In addition, there is a **JavaScript Object Model** available, so that more fluid and compelling web pages can be developed. The skills and techniques for building these Visio-based dashboards would require another book to be able to fully describe them, so this chapter focuses only on validation integration.

> Visit the official Visio blog at `http://blogs.office.com/b/visio` for more information about Visio Services and Visio as a dashboard.

Visio documents can be stored in any document library in SharePoint, but there is also a special type of document library called the **Visio Process Repository** that has some built-in enhancements for use by validation diagram types.

Understanding a Visio Process Repository

A Visio Process Repository is an enhanced document library that has some default settings applied and automatically updates the validation status and swimlane headers (if any) into specific columns in the SharePoint list. This provides the ability to quickly view, for example, which processes involve a particular department, or which ones are not yet validated and approved.

The versioning settings, which are an optional setting for all SharePoint document libraries, are preset for the Visio Process Repository, in order to require content approval for submitted items and to require documents to be checked out before they can be edited.

> You will need to allow documents to be edited without checking out if you want SharePoint users to be able to edit comments using the SharePoint Visio Web Access control.

The following cross-functional flowchart in the `Visio Process Repository.vstx` document describes the different statuses that a validated diagram can go through:

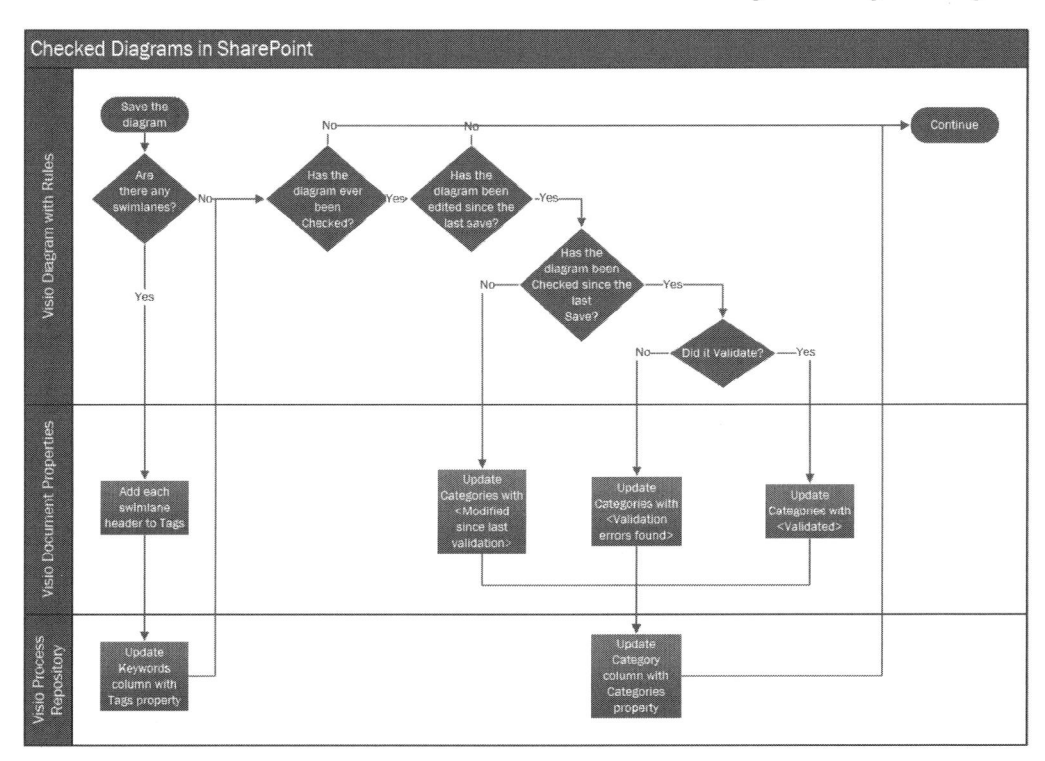

Initially, when a diagram is drawn, there is no validation status until the **Check Diagram** action is performed for the first time. Then the validation status can either be `<Validated>` or `<Validation errors found>`. If the diagram is saved to SharePoint then the validation status is automatically inserted into the **Category** column. If the diagram is then edited, and saved before the **Check Diagram** action is performed again, then the validation status becomes `<Modified since last validation>`. Notice the values in the **Category** column in the following screenshot:

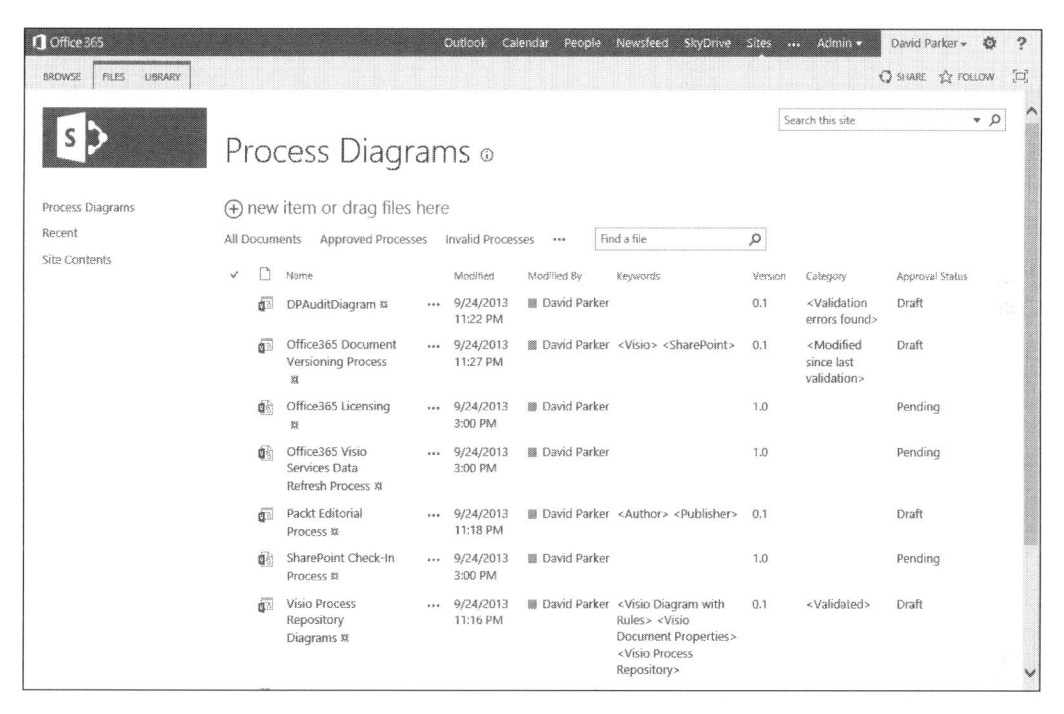

Similarly, any header text that is found in swimlane shapes is automatically inserted into the **Keywords** column in SharePoint.

Approving and rejecting Process Diagrams

The **Process Diagrams** library also has a built-in approval/rejection feature, and provides **Approved Processes** and **Invalid Processes** views.

You can edit the **Approval Status** of a document by selecting **View Properties** from the submenu of a row in the library.

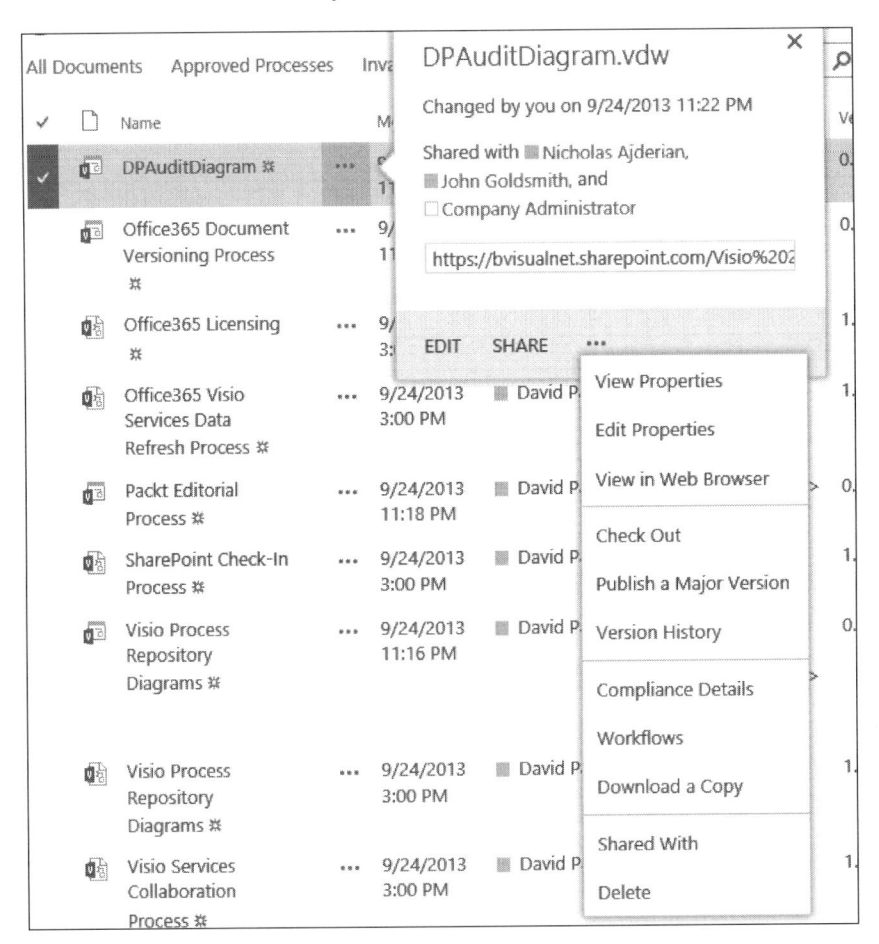

This link will open a new page from where you can **Approve/Reject** a document from the button in the **Actions** group, as shown in the following screenshot:

Chapter 12

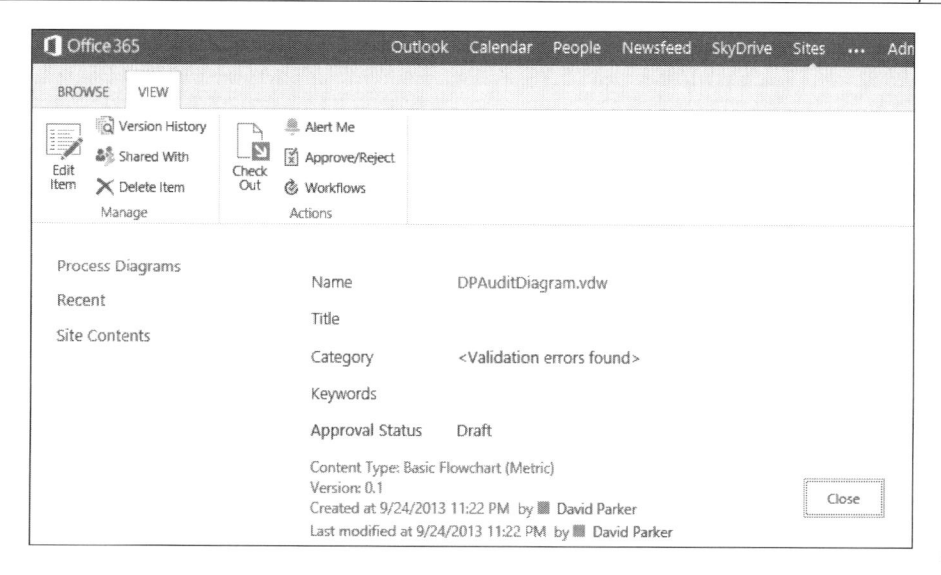

[screenshot of SharePoint document properties panel showing DPAuditDiagram.vdw]

As you can see, you also have access to normal SharePoint **Version History**, **Workflows**, **Shared With**, **Check Out**, and **Alert Me**.

Creating a Visio Process Repository

Firstly, you need to have the correct level of subscription in Office365 to create a **Visio Process Repository**. This is a site template, so one way of creating a subsite is to open the **Site Contents** page from your SharePoint site, as in the following screenshot:

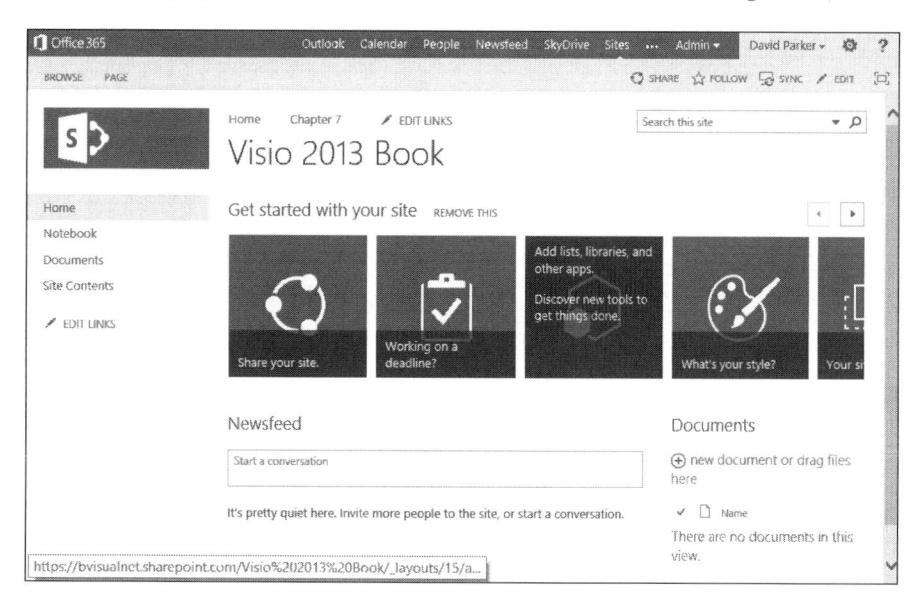

[screenshot of SharePoint Visio 2013 Book site home page]

Then you can select to add a **new subsite**, by selecting the command at the bottom of the page (easy to miss if you don't scroll down) shown as follows:

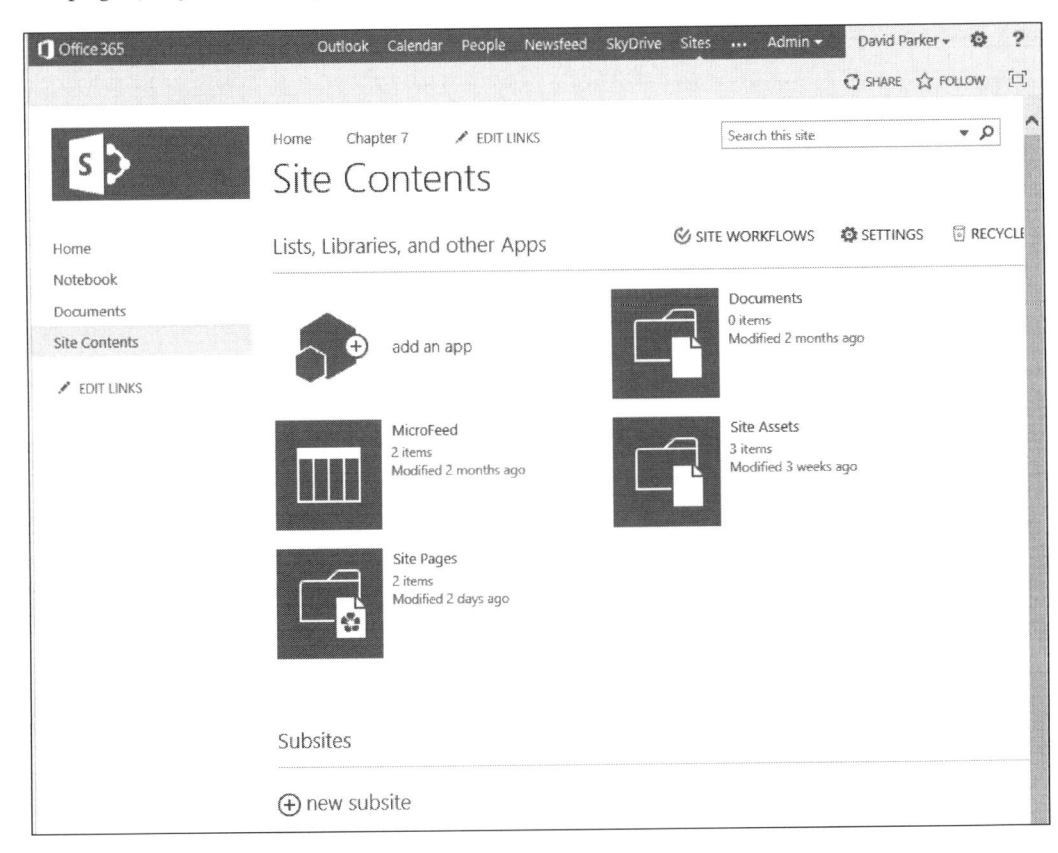

When you click to add a new subsite, you get presented with a list of different site templates. You will find **Visio Process Repository** under the **Enterprise** tab under the **Select a template** label, as shown in the following screenshot:

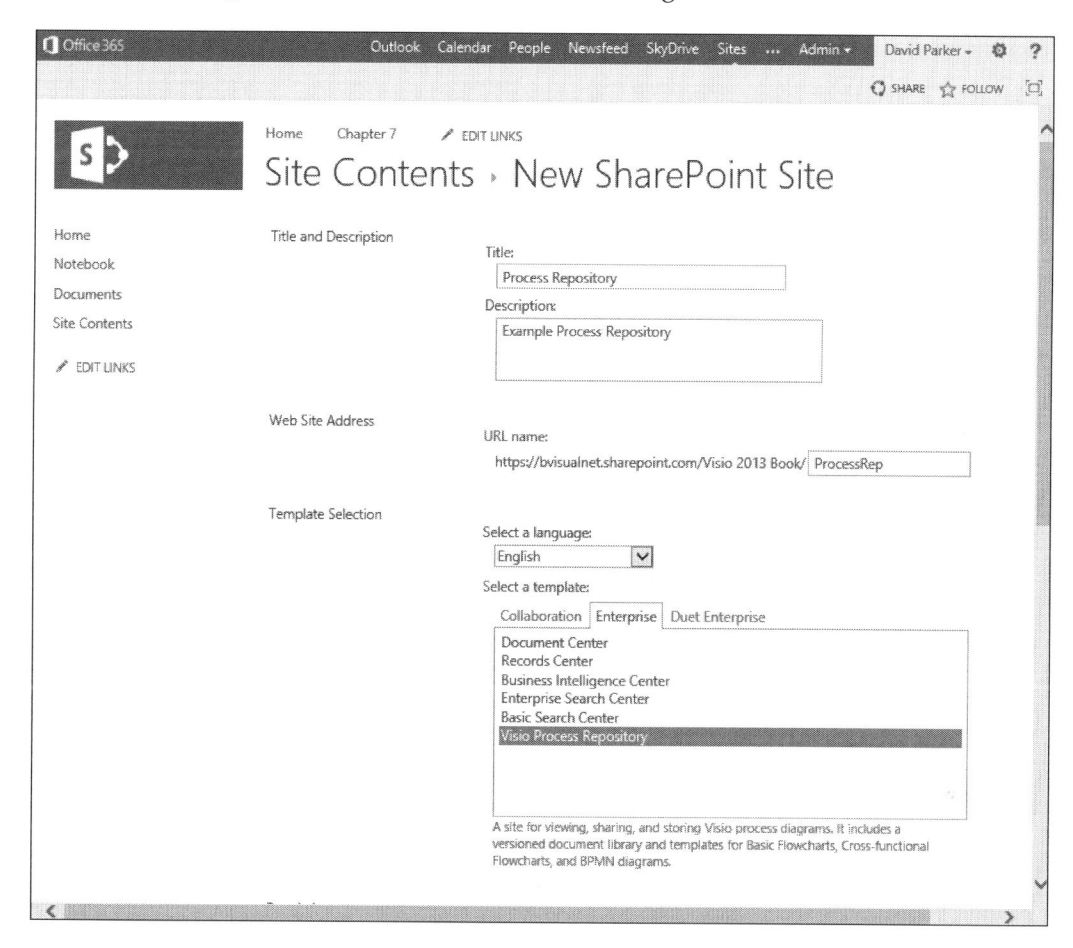

Integrating Validated Diagrams with SharePoint 2013 and Office365

Once you have created a Visio Process Repository, you will find that there is a **Process Diagrams** library that is already created for you. You can add more of these special libraries if you want to, by adding a **Process Diagram Library** app to the site contents. The next screenshot shows the new subsite before any process diagrams have been added to it:

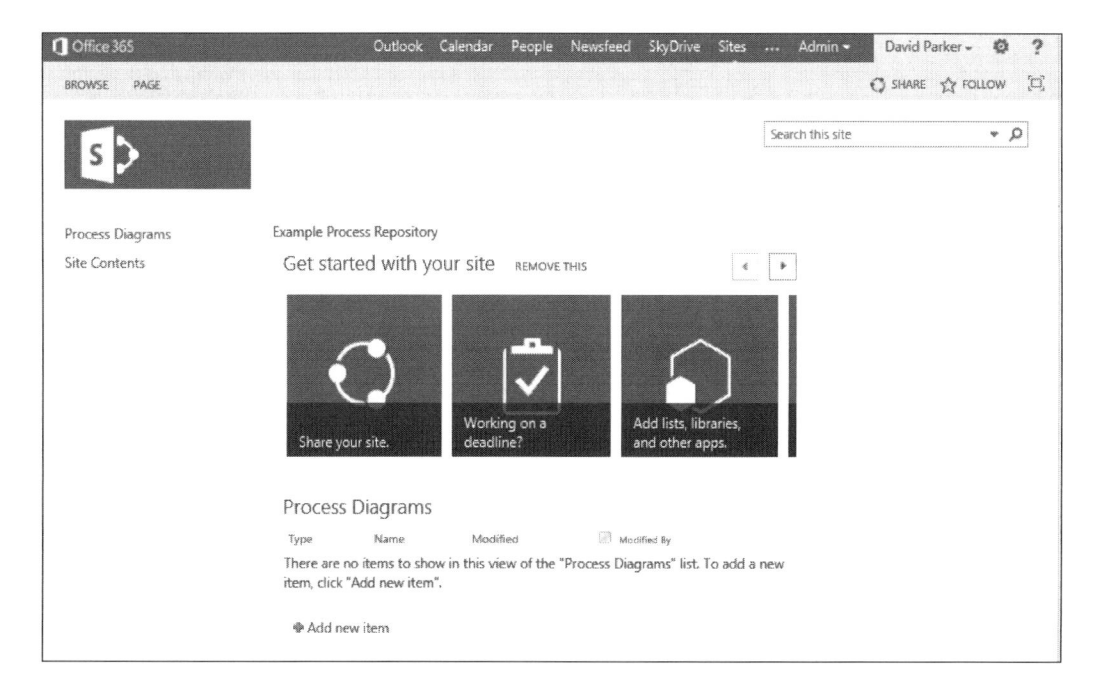

If you click on the **Process Diagrams** header, the document library list looks slightly different from the front page list because it displays some extra columns and views that have been provided especially for Visio diagrams with validation capabilities. For example, notice the **Keywords**, **Approval Status**, and **Category** columns in the following screenshot:

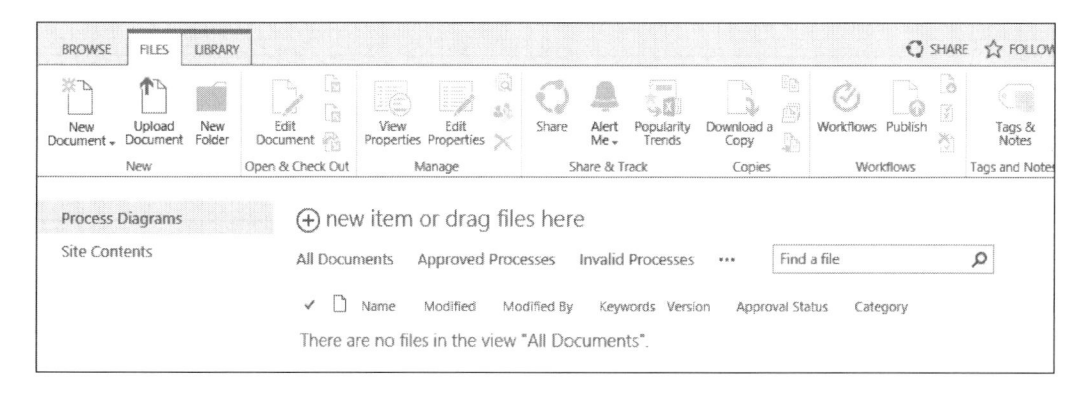

Chapter 12

If you select the **New Document** drop-down button, then you will see the existing Visio templates with validation rules. You may not have such a long list as this if you do not have both Metric and US Units installed.

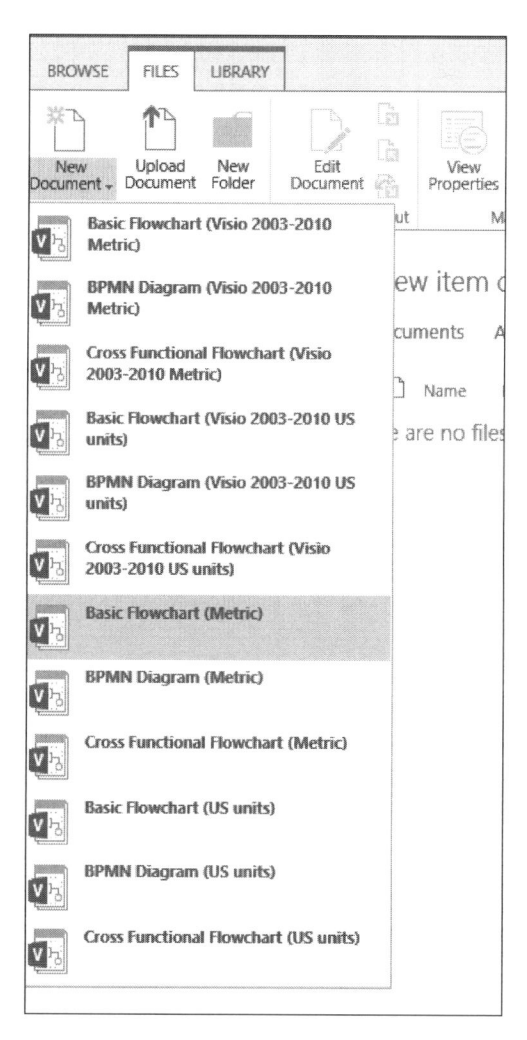

You can edit the visibility of these templates on this menu, as is shown later in this chapter, so I would hide the first six (for Visio 2003-2010) if all my users have Visio 2013.

> Visio 2010 Professional and Premium documents can be saved as Visio Web Drawings (*.vdw) for displaying in the Visio Web Access SharePoint web part.

Adding a Visio template to SharePoint

We published custom Visio templates in the previous chapters but we have an alternative method of making Visio templates available using SharePoint. We uploaded the `AuditR_M.vstx` Visio template that we created in *Chapter 8, Publishing Validation Rules and Diagrams*, in to an asset library in SharePoint.

Although we have used the SharePoint web pages in the following actions, you could use SharePoint Designer 2013, which is a free download from Microsoft, to change many of the same settings, but in a slightly different way.

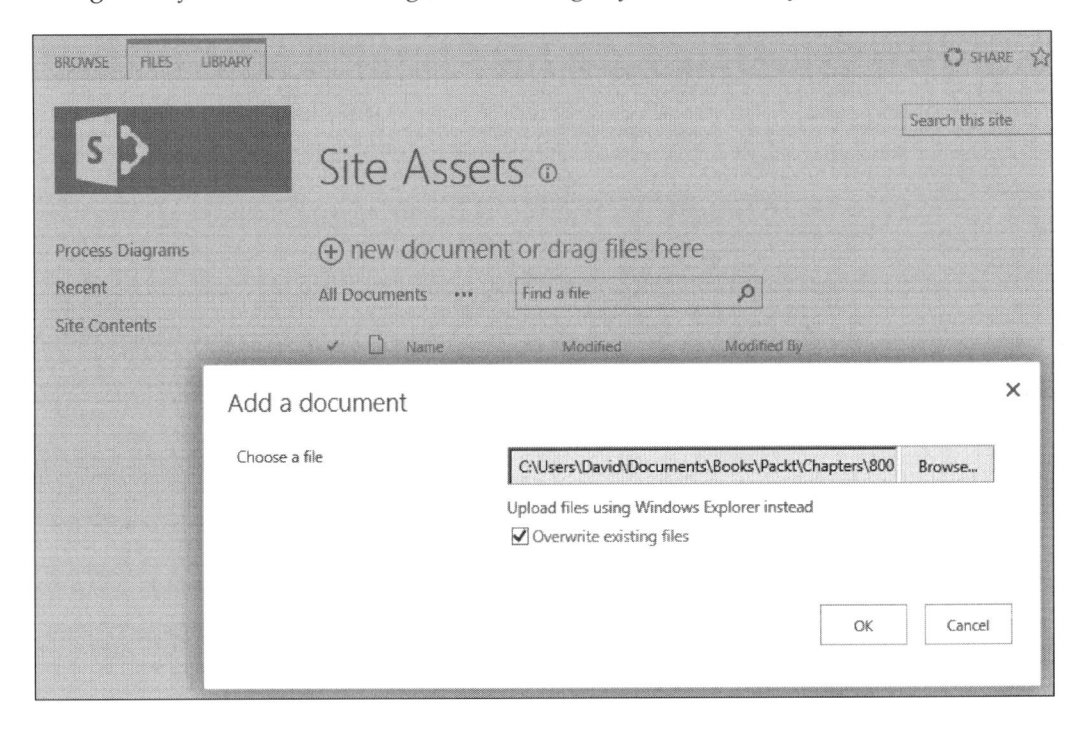

Adding a template as a Site Content Type

After uploading the template, you can edit the **Name** and **Description**, set the **Parent Content Type**, and put it in the **Document Content Types** group. This is necessary for the template to be available to all of your subsites.

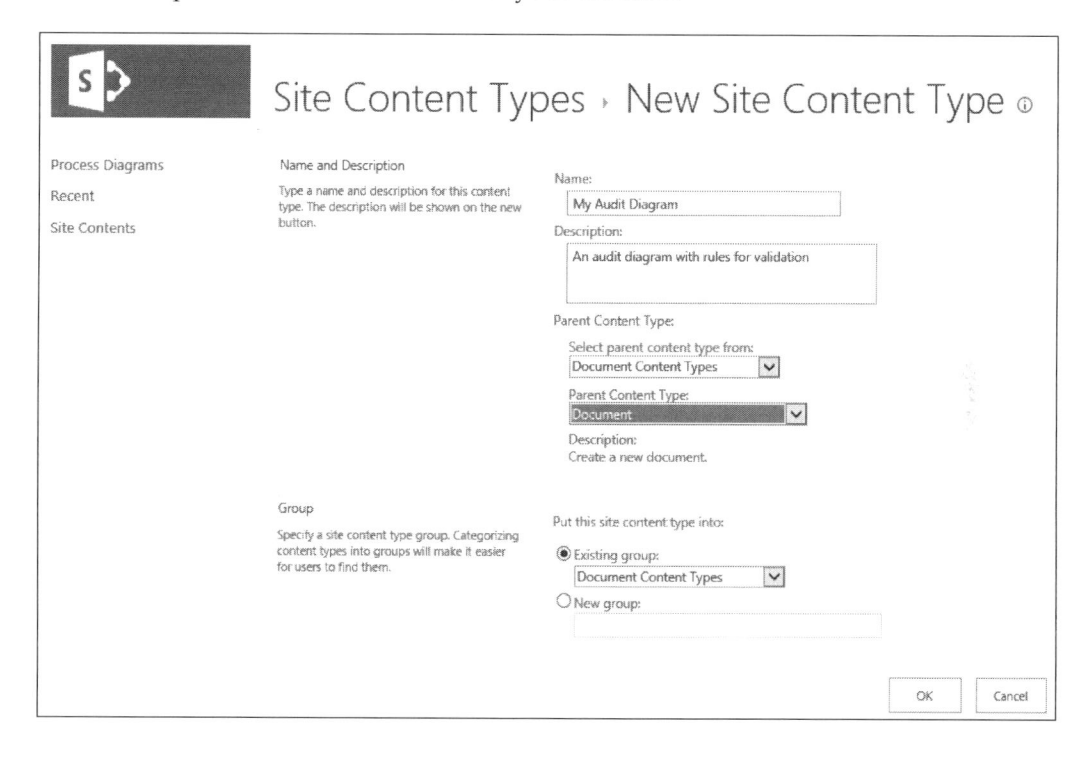

Integrating Validated Diagrams with SharePoint 2013 and Office365

You will then need to enter the URL of the document template that you have just added.

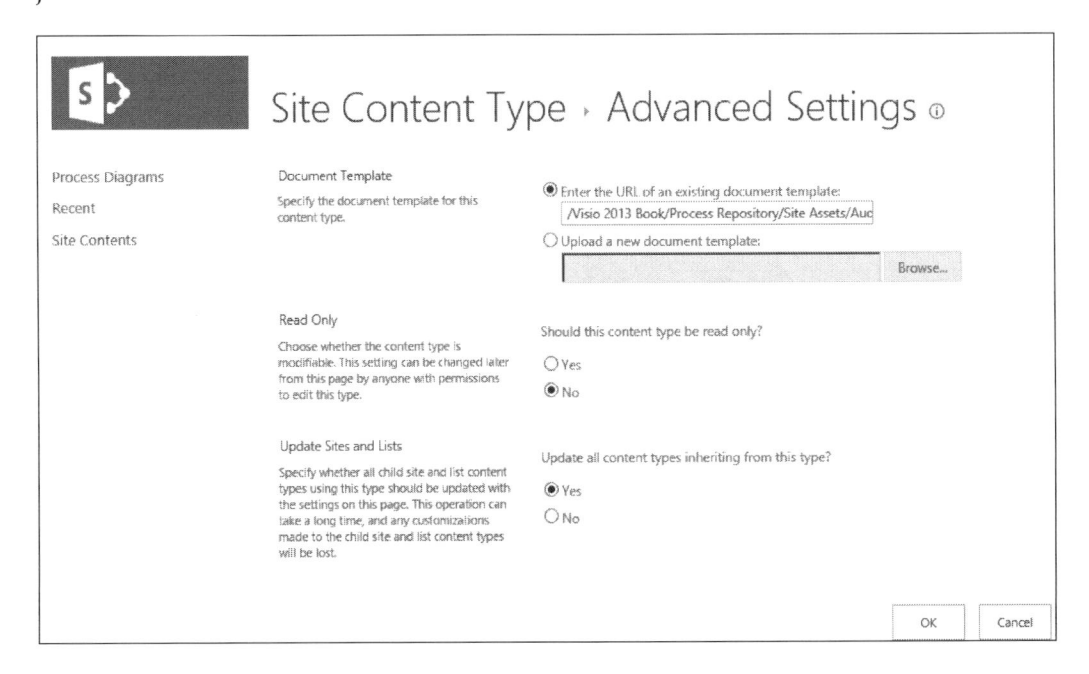

Adding a List and Library Content Type

Now that a new Site Content Type has been defined, it needs to be added as a Content Type to the Lists and Libraries that you want. In this case, you need to edit the **Settings** of the **Process Diagrams** library. As shown in the following screenshot, all of the available Visio templates are visible on the new button:

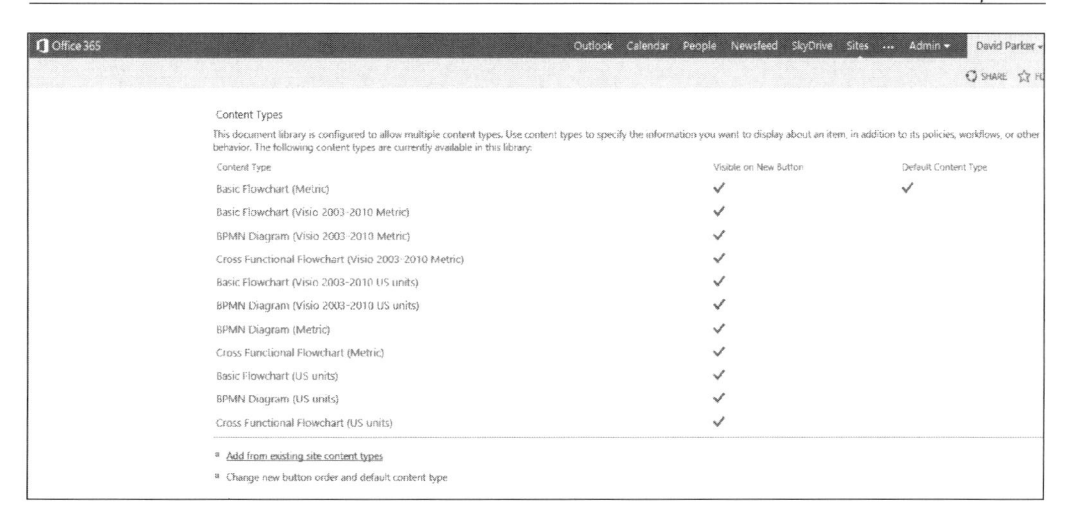

Simply select the desired **Available Site Content Types** and then click on the **Add >** button, as shown in the following screenshot:

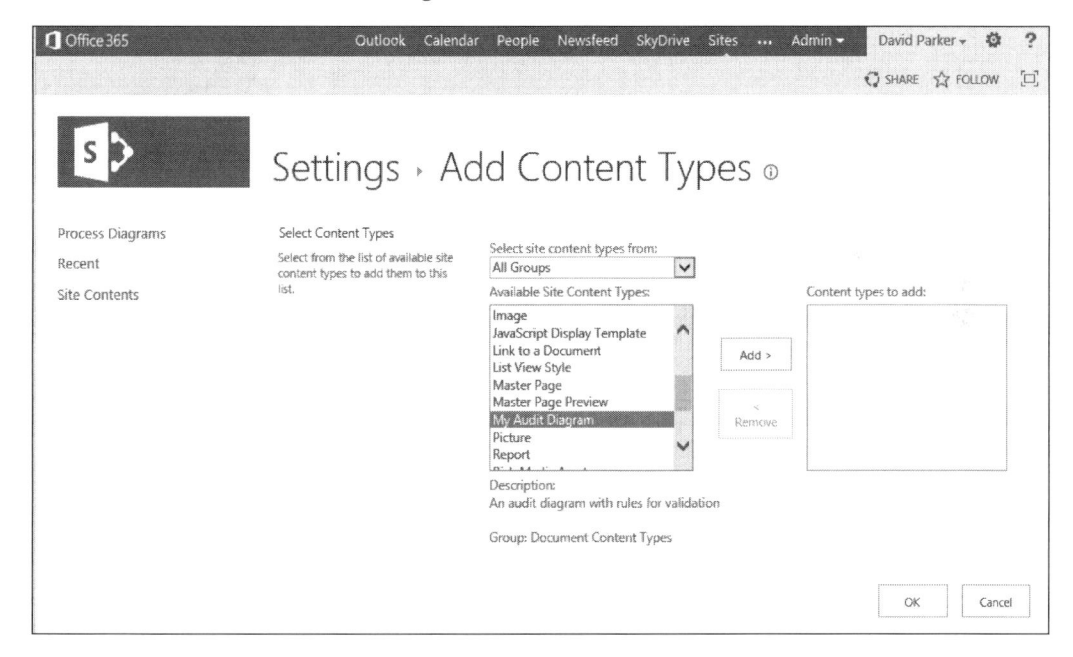

Integrating Validated Diagrams with SharePoint 2013 and Office365

We also selected the **Change New Button Order** page to make the pre-Visio 2013 templates invisible, and we could change the order of the drop-down menu items too:

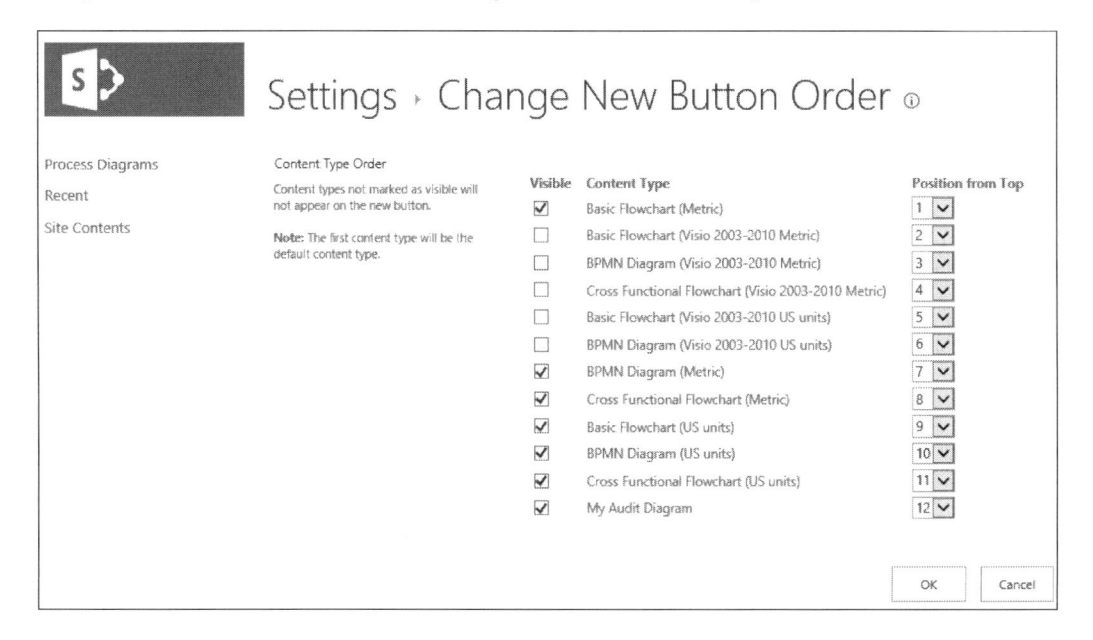

You can publish Visio templates that include custom stencils in the same way, as long as the stencils are in the same SharePoint folder as the Visio template. Visio will then open these stencils along with the new Visio drawing.

Creating a diagram from the custom template

Once this has been done, you will find that the custom template is now available for use from the **New Document** drop-down list in SharePoint as shown in the following screenshot:

Chapter 12

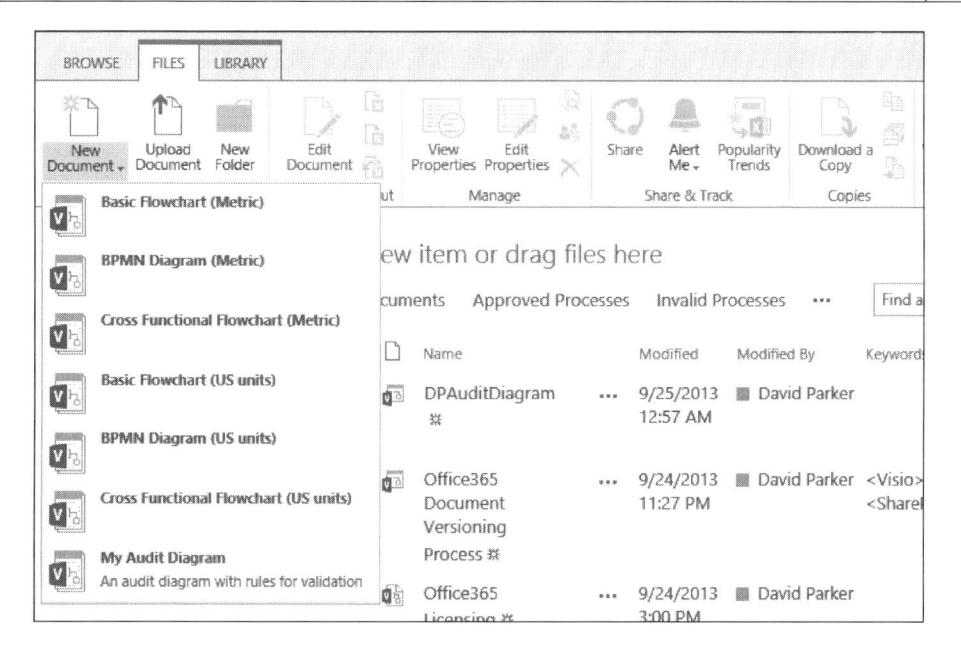

From here, your users can create rule-based diagrams without the necessity to install any custom Visio content on their own Windows PC.

Summary

In this chapter, you have learned about the Visio Process Repository in SharePoint 2013 through Office365. You have also learned how to add a custom Visio template to SharePoint so that your users can create Visio diagrams that follow your company's guidelines and for compliance.

Visio diagrams are a first-class consumer of data, especially using its linking-shapes-to-data feature, but this book has demonstrated how it can be an excellent generator of validated data too. A visual data tool makes comprehension of complex information far easier, and thus reduces the risk of mistakes arising from misunderstandings. The ability to define rules to validate diagrams of all types with Visio Professional ensures that consistency is applied and a specified structure is followed. The optional integration with SharePoint 2013 increases the auditability and reach of Visio documents, and can provide reviewing across any modern browser on any modern device.

Index

Symbols

1D (one-dimensional) 239
2D (two-dimensional) 239
=CONTAINERSHEETREF(index[, category]) function 103
<sheetref>!SHEETREF() function 240

A

ABS(number) function 112
Actions row 254
AddAvise method 156
Add button 244, 324, 377
AddCopy(RuleSet as ValidationRuleSet[, NameU]) method 127
AddIssue([][]) method 133
Add(NameU as String) method 127
AddRuleIssue() method 189
AddRule() method 187, 188
AddRuleSet() method 188
Advanced button 298
Advanced | General group 283
Advanced | General section 273
Advanced group 36
AGGCOUNT() function 249
AggCount(Set) function 239
AND function 239
AND(logical expression1,logical expression2,logical expressionN) function 239
Annotate button 204, 208-210, 246
Annotation section 208
Application.ConvertResult method 70

Application.Documents collection 44
application events
 listening for 155, 156
Application object
 about 33
 ActiveDocument object, reviewing 39
 ActivePage object, reviewing 39
 Addons collection, reviewing 39, 40
 COMAddIns collection, reviewing 41
 CurrentEdition property, reviewing 42
 DataFeaturesEnabled property, reviewing 42
 Documents collection, reviewing 43, 44
 examining 38
 TypelibMinorVersion property, reviewing 44
 Version property, reviewing 44
Application.Window_SelectionChanged() event 194
AssociatedObject property 60
attached Callout shape
 checking 105, 106
Audit Diagram template 267
AutoConnect feature 303, 317

B

Backgrounds group 268
BaseViewModel class
 creating 159
Basic Flowchart diagram 14
Basic Flowchart template 8, 14
Behavior button 302, 311, 317
Behavior dialog 312

Boolean Shape Data row 305
Boolean type
  using 113
Borders and Titles option 268
BPA 10
BPM 10
BPMN Attributes 17
BPMN Basic Shapes stencil diagram 18
BPMN Diagram
  about 8, 15-18
  URL 15
BPMN Diagram template 15, 242
Business category 8, 14
Business Process Analysis. *See* BPA
Business Process Modeling. *See* BPM
Business Process Modeling Notation
    Diagram. *See* BPMN Diagram
Business Rule Modeling 12

C

CALLOUTCOUNT() function 105, 240
callout management 13
Callouts() function 238
CALLOUTTARGETREF() function 106
CALLOUTTARGETREF()! function 240
Category column 367
CEILING(number[, opt_multiple])
    function 112
Cell object
  cells, iterating through 71, 72
  Column property, reviewing 70
  Error property, reviewing 70
  examining 69
  Formula property, reviewing 70
  FormulaU property, reviewing 70
  LocalName property, reviewing 70
  Name property, reviewing 70
  Result property, reviewing 70
  Units property, reviewing 70
cells
  about 88, 89
  iterating through 71, 72
CellsExists() property 69
CellsExistsU() property 69

cells properties
  reading 89-92
Cells() property 69
CellsSRC() method 33, 69
CellsSRC() property 69, 71
CellsU() property 69
Change New Button Order page 378
CheckAllPagesArePortrait() method 148
CheckCycle() method 260, 343
Check Diagram action 367
Check Diagram button 21, 234
Clear() method 137
ClearRuleIssues() method 260, 343
ClickOnce 152
code custom validation
  adding 261, 262
CollectionViewSource_Filter() method 200
Column property
  reviewing 70
COM add-ins 35
CommandBars API 168
Comments field 349
Comments property
  reviewing 58-60
Company Flowcharts 274
ConnectedShapes(Direction) function 238
ConnectedShapes() function 257
ConnectedShapes() method 65, 79, 327
Connectivity API
  about 13
  delving, into 73
  features 73
  process flow steps, listing 79-81
  Shape.CalloutsAssociated property 78
  Shape.ConnectedShapes method 74, 75
  Shape.GluedShapes method 76, 77
  Shape.MemberOfContainers property 77
connectors connection
  checking 254
Connects collection
  reviewing 53-55, 65
CONTAINERCOUNT() function 240
container management 12
CONTAINERMEMBERCOUNT()
    function 103

[382]

ContainerMembers() function 238
ContainerProperties object 77
Container shape
   checking 103
CONTAINERSHEETREF(index[, category])
   function 240
Containing MasterID property 66
ContainingMaster property 66
ContainingPageID property 66
ContainingPage property 66
ContainingShapeID property 66
ContainingShape property 66
Control Panel | Program and Features
   dialog 291
CopyPreview() method 348
Create from Selection button 317
Cross-Functional Flowchart diagram 14
Cross-Functional Flowchart template 8, 14
Currency type
   using 118
CurrentEdition property 33
current selection
   issues, diaplaying for 196-201
current user settings
   saving 210
Customize the Ribbon feature 206
Custom Properties 70
custom rules
   written in code, validating 126
Custom Setup screen 288
custom template
   creating 267
   diagram, creating from 378, 379
CustomValidation class 344
CustomValidation object 260
Custom validation rules
   adding, in code 259, 260
CY function 118

D

Data Flow connector 303, 312, 332-334
Data Flow connector shape 337
Data Flow Diagrams. *See* DFDs

Data Flow master
   AutoConnect, preparing for 302-304
   editing 301, 302
Data Flow Model Diagram methodology
   about 293
   elements 294
Data Flow Model Diagrams template
   about 294, 347
   Data Flow master, editing 301-304
   Data Store master, editing 305-312
   examining 296-299
   Interface master, editing 312
   masters, enhancing 300, 301
   page, enhancing 319-321
   Process master, editing 312-317
   Subprocess master, setting 317-319
DataFlowModelDiagramTemplate. *See*
   installer
Data Flow node 301
Data Graphics 96
Data Graphics features 42
data layer 154
Data Linking
   used, for creating, hyperlinks 65
Data Linking features 33, 42, 46
Data Store master
   editing 305
   graphics, enhancing 308
   group shape, improving 310-312
   ID value, displaying 309, 310
   Shape Data, adding 305-307
Data Store node 310
Data Store shape 312-314, 329, 339
Data tab 306
Date type
   using 115, 116
DAY(datetime[, opt_lcid]) function 116
DAYOFYEAR(datetime[, opt_lcid])
   function 116
DebugPrintValidation macro
   used, for Validation object detail
      displaying 125
Decision shapes 256, 258

[383]

Default personal templates location option 275
Define Shape Data dialog 306, 307
DEPENDSON() function 95
Description property 131
Design tab 268, 278
detail panels
  linking 179
  rule properties, editing 180-182
  ruleset properties, editing 179, 180
  special key strokes, handling 182-184
Developer ShapeSheet Reference 95
DFDs
  about 294
  creating, connectivity rules 295
  creating, conventions 295
  creating, rules 295
diagram
  creating, from custom template 378, 379
Diagram Validation group 20, 123, 193
Dictionary object 80
digital certificate
  template code thoughts 361
  using 359-361
Direction criteria 238
Display IDs value 339
DoCmd() method 215
Document Content Types group 375
Document Explorer window 305
Document object
  about 126
  Advanced Properties objects, reviewing 45, 46
  DataRecordsets collection, reviewing 46, 47
  DocumentSheet object, reviewing 47
  examining 44
  FullName property, reviewing 47
  ID property, reviewing 47
  Index property, reviewing 47
  Masters collection, reviewing 48
  Name property, reviewing 47
  Pages collection, reviewing 48
  ReadOnly property, reviewing 49
  Type property, reviewing 49
  Validation object, reviewing 49
Document_RuleSetValidated event 148
Document_RuleSetValidated() method 343
documents collection
  viewing 159-161
document validation process
  overview 234
  rule, processing 236, 237
  rulesets, validating 235
  rules, validating 236
DoCycleValidation() method 260, 261
DOS 8.3 format 265
Drawing Explorer panel 208
Drawing Explorer window
  about 36, 37, 245, 278, 318
  Masters collection 37
  Pages collection 37
  Shapes collection 37
Duration type
  using 117
Dynamic connector master 303, 304
Dynamic Connector shape 54

E

embellishments
  adding 268-271
  method used, for providing template 272-276
  template description, adding 271, 272
  template preview image, creating 277-284
  templates, publishing 285-291
Enabled property 235, 243
enhanced process flow templates
  Flowchart templates 14
  reviewing 14
Enterprise tab 371
EnumerateRuleSets macro
  used, for rulesets list displaying 128
EnumerateWindows() macro 140
EnumerateWindows() method 143
Error property
  reviewing 70
Explorer actions
  Add button, creating 186-188

adding 184, 186
    Add Issue button, creating 188, 189
    Copy button, creating 191, 192
    Delete button, creating 192
    Paste button, creating 190
Export button 19
ExportDocument() method 217
Export RuleSets button 205

F

Field dialog 270
File | Info | Properties panel 349
File Locations dialog 273, 275
File | Open menu 279
File | Options | Advanced panel 321
file paths
    editing, for templates 273-275
    setting, for templates 275, 276
Filter Expression formula 258
FilterExpression function 237, 238, 241
FilterExpression property 134, 136
Filter Expressions. *See* Test Expressions
FILTERSET() function 249
FilterSet(Set,FilterExpression) function 239
findCycle() method 261
FIND (find_text, within_text ,[start_num],
       [ignore_case]) function 241
Fixed List type
    using 111
flags parameter 126
Flags property 180
FLOOR(number[, opt_multiple])
       function 112
Flowchart category 8, 246
Flowchart layer 249, 257
Flowchart templates
    Basic Flowchart template 14
    Cross-Functional Flowchart template 14
    Six Sigma template 14
FormExplorer class 175
Formula property
    reviewing 70
FormulaU property
    reviewing 70

FromConnects collection
    reviewing 65
Function row 252
functions 95-97

G

Gane and Sarson data flow
       diagrams 323, 347
Gane-Sarson stencil 296
Geometry1.NoShow cell 315
Geometry1 section 313
getIssue() method 145, 147
getNextConnected() method 79
GetResourceImage() method 173
getRule() method 146, 260, 326, 333, 343
getRuleSet() method 146, 324
getRuleSetXSL() method 230
Getting Started view 294
getXDocument() method 226
glued Data Flow connectors 325, 329, 331
glued Process shapes 332
GluedShapes(Direction) function 238
GLUEDSHAPES() function 254
GluedShapes() method 65, 326, 329, 331, 332
GluedShapes(n) function 255
GotFocus event 184
Group behavior section 311, 317
Group dropdown 305
GUARD() function 105
GUID 47
Guide 66

H

HASCATEGORY(category)
       function 97, 239, 246
HasCategory(categoryName) function 238
HasTempRule property 192
HideText cell 315
Home tab 303, 305, 308
HOUR(datetime[, opt_lcid]) fucntion 116
Hyperlinks collection
    reviewing 65
hyperlinks section 118, 119

[385]

I

id attribute 172
idMso attribute 172
ID property
   reviewing 52, 55
IFERROR(primary expression, alternate expression) function 239
IF(logicalexpression,valueiftrue,valueiffalse) function 239
Ignored flag 133
Ignored Issues option 234
Immediate window 127, 142, 280, 304
Import button 19
Import RuleSets button 205
ImproperAssociation rule 254
include options 217
INDEX() function 254
INDEX(index, "list" [,[delimiter] [,[errorvalue]]]) function 239
IndexInStencil property
   reviewing 52
Index property
   reviewing 52, 55
InitializeValues() method 344
Ink 66
Insert | Field action 314
Insert tab 270
installer
   creating 353-356
   testing 357, 358
IntelliSense 41, 89
Interface master
   editing 312
Interface shape 331
Internal Units. *See* IU
INT(number) function 112
INTUP(number) function 112
Invisible cell 313
IS1D() function 239, 243
IsCallout property
   reviewing 65
IsDataGraphicCallout property
   reviewing 65
IS!D() function 254

IsExpanded property 153
IsSelected property 153, 195
issue
   adding, in code 146-148
   clearing, code used 145
   diaplaying, for current selection 196-201
   in code, retrieving 145
   in Issues window, retrieving 140-143
   rule, displaying for 193-195
issue mark-up page
   comments, adding 214, 215
   displaying 210-215
   hiding 215
Issues window 20, 124, 126, 156, 234
Issues window visibility
   toggling 143, 144
ItemTemplate attribute 176
IU 70

J

JavaScript Object Model 365

L

Label object 69
LayerCount property
   reviewing 66
Layer Membership 120, 121
Layer Properties dialog 56
Layers collection
   reviewing 55-58
Layout and Routing Spacing dialog 320
Layout and Routing tab 320
LEFT() function 247
LEFT(text, [,num_chars_opt]) function 240
LEN (text) function 240
Library Content Type
   Visio template, adding as 376-378
Line Format section 314
Link to Existing button 9
List Content Type
   Visio template, adding as 376-378
list management 13
LISTMEMBERCOUNT() function 105, 240
ListMembers() function 238

LISTORDER() function 240
List shape
  checking 104, 105
ListSheetRef() function 104
LOCALFORMULAEXISTS() function 253
LocalName property 70
LockPreview cell 348
LockPreview value 280, 284
LOOKUP("key","list"[,"delimiter"])
    function 239
LOOKUP() function 111
LOWER() function 109

M

main function 77, 78
Master Edit window 305
Master Explorer window 50, 301, 305, 310
MasterName() function 247
MASTERNAME(lang_id) function 247
MASTERNAME (langID_opt) function 240
Master object
  BaseID property, reviewing 51
  examining 50, 51
  Hidden property, reviewing 52
  ID property, reviewing 52
  IndexInStencil property, reviewing 52
  Index property, reviewing 52
  Name property, reviewing 52
  NameU property, reviewing 52
  PageSheet object, reviewing 52
  reviewing 66
  Type property, reviewing 52
Master Properties dialog 300
Masters 35
Master shape 18
MatchByName property 50
Microsoft Process Management Product
    Stack 10
Microsoft Scripting Runtime library 98, 343
Microsoft SharePoint 2013 Workflow
  about 19
  working 19
Microsoft SharePoint 2013 Workflow
    template 15, 138

Microsoft SharePoint Designer 19
Microsoft Visio 15.0 Type Library 31, 32
Microsoft Visio SDK (Software
    Development Kit)
  about 285
  URL, for downloading 93
MINUTE (datetime[, opt_lcid]) function 116
Miscellaneous section 315
Model View View Model (MVVM) 153
MODULUS(number, divisor) function 112
MONTH(datetime[, opt_lcid]) function 116
My Audit Diagram 274

N

Name property 70
New Document drop-down list 373, 378
new process flow templates
  BPMN Diagram 15-18
  Microsoft SharePoint 2013 Workflow 15, 19
  reviewing 15
NOT function 119
NOT(logicalexpression) function 239
NOW() function 95
Number type
  using 112, 113

O

OMG specification 17
OnAction event 204
OnBoundaryOf() function 239
OneD property
  reviewing 66
OnKeystrokeMessageForAddon event 182
OnLayer(LayerName) function 238
OnPropertyChanged() method 188
OpenAnnotateIssues() method 204
Open button 279
OpenSelectionIssues() method 198
Organization Chart solution 28
OR(logicalexpression1,logicalexpression2,...,
    logiclexpressionN) function 239
Owner row 253

P

page
  enhancing 319-321
Page column 139
Page.CreateSelection() method 80
PageID element 25
Page Info | Name field 270
Page object
  Comments property, reviewing 58-60
  Connects collection, reviewing 53-55
  examining 53
  ID property, reviewing 55
  Index property, reviewing 55
  Layers collection, reviewing 55-58
  PageSheet object, reviewing 58
  ShapeComments property, reviewing 58-60
  Shapes collection, reviewing 61, 62
  Type property, reviewing 62
Page Setup dialog 278, 310
PageSheet object
  reviewing 58
ParentContainers() function 238, 258
Parent object
  reviewing 66
Parent property 66
particular shape issues
  listing 144
PERSONAL collection 276
Pivot Diagram solution 28
Process button 234
Process Diagram Library app 372
process diagrams
  validating 20-25
  Visio Document structure, analyzing 21-25
Process Diagrams library 368, 372, 376
process flow
  steps, listing 79-81
process management features, Visio
  exploring 8-10
Process Management stack 7
Process master
  Category value, displaying 315, 316
  editing 312
  graphics, enhancing 313, 314
  group shape, improving 316, 317
  ID value, displaying 314, 315
  Shape Data, adding 312, 313
Process shape 110, 258, 325, 334
Professional edition 33
programming language
  selecting, to use with Visio 35, 36
Project | ValidationExplorer2 Properties menu option 210
Prop.Cost Shape Data row 253
Prop.DisplayID value 339
Properties button 46
Properties dialog 272
Properties panel 271
Prop.ID value 340
Prop.Owner cell 252
Prop.Owner value 253
Prop.StartDate value 254
Prop.Status list 254
Put all settings in Window registry box 283

Q

quality
  enhancing, of template preview image 282-284
quasi-ShapeSheet functions
  AggCount(Set) 239
  Callouts() 238
  ConnectedShapes(Direction) 238
  ContainerMembers() 238
  FilterSet(Set,FilterExpression) 239
  GluedShapes(Direction) 238
  HasCategory(categoryName) 238
  Is1D() 238
  ListMembers() 238
  OnBoundaryOf() 239
  OnLayer(LayerName) 238
  ParentContainers() 238
  Role() 238
  ShapesOnPage() 238
Quick Shapes selector 303

R

Rectangle button 308
Registry Editor 283
Relationships cell 258
relevant shape
  availability on page, checking 249, 250
Remove Hidden Information dialog 351
ReportDocument() method 226
ResourceKey property 176
Result properties
  .Result("m") property 70
  .ResultIU property 70
  .ResultStr() property 70
  reviewing 70
Reviewer section 209
Reviewing pane 209, 215
Ribbon class 172, 185, 204
Role() function 238, 243
RootShape object
  reviewing 66
ROUND(number,numberofdigit) function 112
RowCount method 67
RowName object 69
Row object
  examining 67
rows 88, 89
Rule.Delete() method 134
Rule Properties expander 180
Rule Properties panel 181
rules
  displaying, for selected issue 193-195
  functioning 136, 137
  processing 236, 237
  updating 134, 135
  validating 236
ruleset
  adding, to ValidationRuleSets collection 129, 130
  deleting 130
  exporting, to XML 216-223
  importing, from XML 223, 226
  updating 129, 130
  validating 235

  writing 323-344
RuleSetFlags value 128
RuleSet parameter 126
RuleSet Properties panel 179
ruleset reports
  creating 226-231
  XSL stylesheet, fetching 228-231
rulesets, exporting to XML
  VEIssue XElement method, fetching 222
  VERuleSet XElement method, fetching 221
  XDocument object, fetching 219-221
RuleSets Report button 205
RuleSetValidated event 126, 143, 234, 260
RuleSetValidated(RuleSet as ValidationRuleSet) event 138
Rules Explorer window
  about 151, 204, 205, 243, 323
  creating 174, 175
  detail panels, linking 179-184
  Explorer actions, adding 184-193
  self-describing tree views 176-179
Rules to Check dropdown 128
RulesTools add-in 208, 242, 323, 361
Rules Tools group 203
Rules Tools ribbon group 244, 246

S

Save As Web feature 25
Save As Web html pages control 26
Save As Web option 26
SaveFile dialog 217
Scalable Vector Graphics (SVG) 25
SECOND(datetime[, opt_lcid]) fucntion 116
Section.Index property 67
Section object
  about 67
  examining 67
Section Row Column 33
sections
  about 88, 89, 97
  hyperlinks section 118, 119
  Shape Data section 107-109
  User-defined Cells section 97
Select a template label 371

selectedVEDocument.
　　SetSelectedIssue(issue) method 194
SelectedVERule object 192
SelectedVERule property 186
SelectedVERuleSet property 186
SelectionChanged event 142, 156
Selection Issues button 168, 196
self-describing tree views
　about 176
　Informative tool tips, creating 177-179
Settings tab 210
Setup and Deployment project type 285
setup project
　creating 285-287
　installation, running 288-290
　repairing 291
　uninstalling 291
shape
　outside container, checking 257, 258
　structure type, using 102
　text availability, checking 258
Shape.CalloutsAssociated property 78
Shape can split connectors
　　option 311, 312, 317
shape category
　checking 246-248
　using 98-102
shape.Characters.Text property 64
ShapeComments property
　reviewing 58, 60
Shape.ConnectedShapes method
　about 74
　arguments, CategoryFilter 74
　arguments, Flags 74
　using 74, 75
shape connections
　checking 256, 257
Shape Data 18
Shape Data cell 252
Shape Data row 251-253
Shape Data section
　about 107-109
　Boolean type, using 113
　Currency type, using 118
　Date type, using 115, 116

Duration type, using 117
Fixed List type, using 111
Number type, using 112, 113
String type, using 109, 110
Variable List type, using 114
Shape Data window 252, 306, 312, 317
Shape Design group 302, 311, 317
Shape.GluedShapes method
　about 76
　arguments, CategoryFilter 77
　arguments, Flags 77
　arguments, OtherConnectedShape 77
　using 77
ShapeID element 25
shape layer
　checking 248, 249
Shape Layout section 257
shape.Master
　reviewing 66
shape.MasterShape object
　reviewing 66
Shape.MemberOfContainers property 77
Shape object
　Characters property, reviewing 64
　Connects collection, reviewing 65
　examining 62-64
　FromConnects collection, reviewing 65
　Hyperlinks collection, reviewing 65
　ID property, reviewing 65
　Index property, reviewing 65
　IsCallout property, reviewing 65
　IsDataGraphicCallout property,
　　reviewing 65
　LayerCount property, reviewing 66
　Master object, reviewing 66
　MasterShape object, reviewing 66
　NameID property, reviewing 65
　Name property, reviewing 65
　NameU property, reviewing 65
　OneD property, reviewing 66
　Parent object, reviewing 66
　RootShape object, reviewing 66
　Text property, reviewing 64
　Type property, reviewing 66
Shape Reports button 298

Shapes collection
　reviewing 61, 62
ShapeSheet
　about 85
　cells 88, 89
　cells properties, reading 89-92
　functions 95-97
　Layer Membership 120, 121
　rows 88, 89
　searching 85-87
　sections 88, 89
ShapeSheet functionality 31, 133
ShapeSheet functions
　AND(logical expression1,logical
　　　expression2,...,logical expressionN)
　　　239
　avoiding 241
　CALLOUTCOUNT() 240
　CALLOUTTARGETREF()! 240
　CONTAINERCOUNT() 240
　CONTAINERSHEETREF(index[, category])
　　　240
　FIND (find_text, within_text ,[start_num],
　　　[ignore_case]) 241
　HASCATEGORY(category) 239
　IFERROR(primary expression, alternate
　　　expression) 239
　IF(logicalexpression,valueiftrue,valueiffal
　　　se) 239
　INDEX(index, "list" [,[delimiter]
　　　[,[errorvalue]]]) function 239
　IS1D() 239
　LEFT(text, [,num_chars_opt]) 240
　LEN (text) 240
　LISTMEMBERCOUNT() 240
　LISTORDER() 240
　LOOKUP("key","list"[,"delimiter"])
　　　function 239
　MASTERNAME (langID_opt) 240
　NOT(logicalexpression) 239
　OR(logicalexpression1,logicalexpression2,
　　　...,logicalexpressionN) 239
　SHAPETEXT (shapename!TheText,flag)
　　　240

<sheetref>!SHEETREF() 240
STRSAME (240
ShapeSheet settings
　printing out 93, 94
ShapesOnPage() function 238, 249, 251
Shapes window 301
ShapeText() function 106
shape.Text property 64
SHAPETEXT(shapename!TheText[,flag])
　　　function 136, 240
Shape Transform section 309
shape type
　checking 243-246
shape.Type property 66
SharePoint
　using, with Visio 363-365
　Visio template, adding to 374-378
sheetref qualifier 240
Show all properties option 298
Show/Hide group 36
ShowIgnoredIssues property 124
SIGN(number[, opt_fuzz]) function 112
Silverlight 364
Site Contents page 369
Site Content Type
　Visio template, adding as 375, 376
Six Sigma Diagram template 15
Six Sigma template 8, 14
Size | More Page Sizes option 278
Size & Position window 310, 316
Snap to member shapes option 311, 317
Software and Database category 355, 358
Software and Database\Database Model
　　　Diagram solution 28
Software and Database\Data Flow Model
　　　Diagram solution 28
Software and Database\UML Model
　　　Diagram solution 27
Spacing button 320
specific cell values
　checking 251-254
SRC 92
Start command\screen 283
Start/End shape 249, 257

StartListening() method 143
String type
  using 109, 110
STRSAME("srting1","string2"[,ignoreCase])
    function 136, 240
STRSAMEEX function 240
STRSAME() function 247, 253, 254
structured diagram 12
structured diagramming foundations
  callout management 13
  Connectivity API 13
  container management 12
  list management 13
  reviewing 12, 13
  Validation API 13
structure type
  Callout 102
  Container 102
  List 102
Subject field 349
subprocess 9
Subprocess group 317
Subprocess master
  setting 317-319
Swimlane category 258
Swimlane shape 14, 109
Switch Windows button 280
System.XMl.Linq.XDocument object 218

T

targetPage object 145
TargetPage parameter 133
TargetShape parameter 133
TargetType="{x:Type TreeViewItem}"
    attribute 195
TargetType property 134
Task Panes dropdown 306
Task shape 17
template
  completing 347-351
  file paths, editing for 273-275
  file paths, setting for 275, 276
  providing, method 272-276
  publishing, method 285-291
  reviewing 352
  setup project, creating 285-287
  setup project installation, running 288-290
  setup project, repairing 291
  setup project, uninstalling 291
Template Categories 266
template description
  adding 271, 272
template preview image
  creating 277-284
  quality, enhancing 282-284
Templates textbox 273
TestExpression function 237
TestExpression property 134, 136
Test Expressions
  about 241
  code custom validation, adding 261, 262
  connectors connection, checking 254
  custom validation rules in code,
    adding 259, 260
  relevant shapes availability,
    checking 249-251
  shape category, checking 246-248
  shape layer, checking 248, 249
  shapes availability outside container,
    checking 257, 258
  shape's correct connections,
    checking 256, 257
  shapes label, checking 258
  shape type, checking 243-246
  specific cell values, checking 251-254
  writing 242, 243
Text Block Format section 314, 315
Text Block tool 311
TextBox_GotFocus() event handler 184
Text Fields section 315
ThisAddin class 204
  about 151
  application events, listening for 155, 156
  enhancing 154-156
  Visio Professional edition, checking 156
ThisAddIn_Shutdown() event 156
ThisAddin_Startup() event 154, 155
ThisAddin.VisioEvents_Connect()
    method 182

ThisDocument class 126, 142, 260, 281, 343
ThumbnailDetailMaxSize registry key 279
Title field 349
tool architecture 152-154
Transform button 231
TreeViewMain element 175
TreeViewMain_SelectedItemChanged()
       event 186
TxtPinX formula 311
TxtWidth cell formula 311
Type property
   reviewing 62

U

UI layer 154
UIObject API 168
UniqueID property 47, 52
Units property
   reviewing 70
Universal Name property
       (NameU property) 40
UPPER() function 109
UserControlExplorer.xaml.cs class 184
User-defined Cells section
   about 97
   attached Callout shape, checking 105, 106
   Container shape, checking 103
   List shape, checking 104, 105
   shape category, using 98-102
   shape structure type, defining 102
User.UMLShapeType cell 344

V

Validate() method
   using 126
Validation API 8, 13, 49, 123
Validation Explorer solution 323
Validation Explorer tree view 192, 193
validation functions
   about 238
   ShapeSheet functions 238
ValidationIssues.Clear() method 234
ValidationIssues collection
   existing issue, retrieving in code 145

issue, adding in code 146-148
issues, clearing with code 145
Issues window visibility, toggling 143, 144
particular shape issues, listing 144
selected issue, retrieving 140-143
viewing 166-168
working with 137-139
Validation object
   custom rules, validating 126, 127
   overview 123-125
   Validate() method, using 126
ValidationRule.AddIssue() method 127, 147
Validation Rules 127
ValidationRules.AddRule(NameU as string)
       method 131
ValidationRules collection
   rule, adding to 134-136
   rule, functioning 136, 137
   rule, updating 134-136
   viewing 164-166
   working with 131-134
ValidationRuleSets collection
   ruleset, adding to 129, 130
   ruleset, deleting 130
   ruleset, updating 129, 130
   viewing 163
   working with 127, 128
Validation.Validate([][]) method 137
Variable List type
   using 114
VBA 35
VBackground-1 page 268
VEApplication class 166
VEApplication.CopyRule() method 192
VEApplication.CopyRuleSet() method 192
VEApplication.PasteRule() method 190
VEApplication.SetSelectedIssue()
       method 194
Vector Markup Language (VML) 25
VEDocument class 189, 204, 210, 219, 223
VEDocument object 194
VEIssue object 222
VEIssue XElement method
   fetching 222, 223
VERule class 164

VERule object 182, 190
VERules class 165
VERules.DeleteRule() method 192
VERuleSet class 163
VERuleSet object 164, 165, 221
VERuleSets class 163
VERuleSets.DeleteRuleSet() method 193
VERuleSet XElement method
  fetching 221
VERules.PasteRule() method 190
ViewModel class
  BaseViewModel class, creating 159
  creating 157, 158
  documents collection, viewing 159-161
  ValidationIssues collection,
    viewing 166-168
  ValidationRules collection, viewing 164-166
  ValidationRuleSets collection, viewing 163
view model layer 154
View tab 280
View | Task Panes menu 310
Visible property 55
Visio
  abilities 32, 33
  programming language, using with 35, 36
  ShapeSheet 85
  using, with SharePoint 363-365
  visual data, publishing from 25, 26
Visio 2010
  ease-of-use features 10
Visio 2013
  Click-To-Run edition 363
  process management features 8-10
Visio 2013 editions
  about 27
  features, diagram 27
Visio 2013 process management
  capabilities, reviewing 10-12
  features 8-10
Visio 2013 process management capabilities
  Visio BPM Maturity Model 11, 12
VisioApplication_MessageForAddon()
    event 182
Visio BPM Maturity Model 11, 12

Visio categories
  about 263
  templates, selecting 263-266
Visio diagrams
  annotating, with issues 206-209
Visio diagrams, annotating with issues
  current user settings, saving 210
  issue mark-up page, displaying 210-215
  issue mark-up page, hiding 215
Visio document
  classifying 33-35
  Visio stencil 35
  Visio template 35
Visio Document object 123
VisioEvents_Connect() method 155, 166
VisioEvents_Disconnect() method 156, 166
Visio file types
  list 266
Visio Fluent UI
  modifying 168-173
Visio object model
  abilities 32, 33
  about 38
  Application object, examining 38-44
  Cell object, examining 69-72
  Document object, examining 44-49
  Master object, examining 50-52
  Page object, examining 53-62
  Row object, examining 67-69
  Section object, examining 67
  Shape object, examining 62-66
Visio Options dialog 36, 283
Visio Options panel 273
Visio Process Repository
  about 365-367
  creating 369-373
  Process Diagrams, approving 368, 369
  Process Diagrams, rejecting 368, 369
  using 25
Visio Professional edition
  checking for 156
Visio ribbon
  extensions 203-205
Visio.Selection object 80

Visio Solution Publishing Tool 285
Visio template
   adding, as Library Content Type 376-378
   adding, as List Content Type 376-378
   adding, as Site Content Type 375, 376
   adding, to SharePoint 374
   selecting, from category 263-266
Visio Trust Center 359
Visio Type Library 31
Visio Type Library objects 157
Visio.ValidationRule object 182
Visio Viewer ActiveX control 26
Visio Viewer control 25
Visio Viewer option 26
Visio.VisPageTypes.visTypeMarkup page type 207
Visio.VisRoleSelectionTypes constant values 243
Visio.VisRuleSetFlags enumerator 180
Visio Web Access control. *See* VWA
Visio Web Drawing 34
Visio Workflow Interchange (*.vwi) file 19
VisRuleTargets enumerator 133
Visual Basic for Applications. *See* VBA
visual data
   publishing, from Visio 25, 26
Visualization 12
Visual Studio Tools for Office template. *See* VSTO template
visViewer
   URL 352
VSTO template 41
VWA 34, 364

W

WEEKDAY (datetime[, opt_lcid]) function 116
WindowIssues class 197
Windows Presentation Foundation. *See* WPF
WithEvents object 143
WiX Toolset
   URL 285
WPF 32, 152
Write Chapter Sub-process page 73, 74

X

XDocument object
   fetching 219-221
XElement object 219
XML
   rulesets, exporting to 216-222
   rulesets, importing from 223, 226
XML Notepad 230
XNamespace object 219
XSL Output tab 231
XSL stylesheet
   fetching 228-231

Y

YEAR(datetime[, opt_lcid]) fucntion 116

[PACKT] enterprise
PUBLISHING
professional expertise distilled

Thank you for buying
Microsoft Visio 2013 Business Process Diagramming and Validation

About Packt Publishing

Packt, pronounced 'packed', published its first book "Mastering phpMyAdmin for Effective MySQL Management" in April 2004 and subsequently continued to specialize in publishing highly focused books on specific technologies and solutions.

Our books and publications share the experiences of your fellow IT professionals in adapting and customizing today's systems, applications, and frameworks. Our solution based books give you the knowledge and power to customize the software and technologies you're using to get the job done. Packt books are more specific and less general than the IT books you have seen in the past. Our unique business model allows us to bring you more focused information, giving you more of what you need to know, and less of what you don't.

Packt is a modern, yet unique publishing company, which focuses on producing quality, cutting-edge books for communities of developers, administrators, and newbies alike. For more information, please visit our website: www.packtpub.com.

About Packt Enterprise

In 2010, Packt launched two new brands, Packt Enterprise and Packt Open Source, in order to continue its focus on specialization. This book is part of the Packt Enterprise brand, home to books published on enterprise software – software created by major vendors, including (but not limited to) IBM, Microsoft and Oracle, often for use in other corporations. Its titles will offer information relevant to a range of users of this software, including administrators, developers, architects, and end users.

Writing for Packt

We welcome all inquiries from people who are interested in authoring. Book proposals should be sent to author@packtpub.com. If your book idea is still at an early stage and you would like to discuss it first before writing a formal book proposal, contact us; one of our commissioning editors will get in touch with you.

We're not just looking for published authors; if you have strong technical skills but no writing experience, our experienced editors can help you develop a writing career, or simply get some additional reward for your expertise.

Python Data Visualization Cookbook

ISBN: 978-1-78216-336-7 Paperback: 254 pages

Over 60 recipes that will enable you to learn how to create attractive visualizations using Python's most popular libraries

1. Learn how to set up an optimal Python environment for data visualization
2. Understand the topics such as importing data for visualization and formatting data for visualization
3. Understand the underlying data and how to use the right visualizations

Social Data Visualization with HTML5 and JavaScript

ISBN: 978-1-78216-654-2 Paperback: 104 pages

Leverage the power of HTML5 and JavaScript to build compelling visualizations of social data from Twitter, Facebook, and more

1. Learn how to use JavaScript to create compelling visualizations of social data
2. Use the d3 library to create impressive SVGs
3. Master OAuth and how to authenticate with social media sites

Please check **www.PacktPub.com** for information on our titles

Learning IPython for Interactive Computing and Data Visualization

ISBN: 978-1-78216-993-2   Paperback: 138 pages

Learn IPython for interactive Python programming, high-performance numerical computing, and data visualization

1. A practical step-by-step tutorial which will help you to replace the Python console with the powerful IPython command-line interface
2. Use the IPython notebook to modernize the way you interact with Python
3. Perform highly efficient computations with NumPy and Pandas
4. Optimize your code using parallel computing and Cython

Tableau Data Visualization Cookbook

ISBN: 978-1-84968-978-6   Paperback: 172 pages

Over 70 recipes for creating visual stories with your data using Tableau

1. Quickly create impressive and effective graphics which would usually take hours in other tools
2. Lots of illustrations to keep you on track
3. Includes examples that apply to a general audience

Please check **www.PacktPub.com** for information on our titles

Made in the USA
San Bernardino, CA
06 August 2014